EARLY ISRAEL

SUPPLEMENTS

TO

VETUS TESTAMENTUM

EDITED BY
THE BOARD OF THE QUARTERLY

J. A. EMERTON - W. L. HOLLADAY - A. LEMAIRE
R. E. MURPHY - E. NIELSEN - R. SMEND
J. A. SOGGIN - M. WEINFELD

VOLUME XXXVII

LEIDEN
E. J. BRILL
1985

EARLY ISRAEL

*Anthropological and Historical Studies on the Israelite Society
Before the Monarchy*

BY

NIELS PETER LEMCHE

LEIDEN
E. J. BRILL
1985

For
Elsebeth

The edition of this book has been supported by the Danish Council of Research in the Humanities. The author wishes to express his deepest gratitude for this substantial support.

ISBN 90 04 07853 3

PRINTED IN DENMARK BY FR. BAGGES KGL. HOFBOGTRYKKERI

TABLE OF CONTENS

FOREWORD

This work represent the fruits of af series of studies which I have published within the last twelve to thirteen years dealing with such matters as the »Hebrew-ḫabiru« issue, social conditions in Israel, and the study of the history of Israel. My work has now been additionally supplemented by the publication of my history of Israel, *Det gamle Israel* (»Ancient Israel«), which appeared in 1984, but which was written after the completion of the manuscript of the present work. The maniscript of this dissertation was finished in November of 1982, for which reason literature which has appeared since that date has not been included. This by no means signifies that I will not deal with such contributions at a later date. It would be quite impossible merely to mention such recent works by name, since such a list would encompass several hundred titels, which would necessarily have to be distributed throughout the present work.

Many individuals have influenced my thinking about ancient Israel, both in the course of my undergraduate training and, later, during my graduate education in Copenhagen. The list would include Svend Holm-Nielsen, John Strange, Arne Munk, Heike Friis, and many others whom it would be impossible to name here. The work itself was written after I acceded to a lectureship at the University of Århus in 1978; accordingly, it also bears the imprint of the fresh insights provided by my new circle of colleagues. In particular I should like to thank Benedikt Otzen, Knud Jeppesen, Hans Gottlieb, Bent Mogensen, and Kirsten Nielsen for many helpful and useful discussions.

I should also like to address special thanks to my friend, colleague, and translator, Frederick Harris Cryer, who has lived with my book for more than a year and had the thankless task of wrestling with its often difficult Danish idiom. No one who is familiar with the Danish text of this work will be able to avoid acknowledging how the English translation of it also contributes to the »translation« of my ideas.

Yet another friend to whom thanks should be directed on the conclusion of this work is my theacher, judge, and publisher, Eduard Nielsen, who hopefully does not feel today that he has helped to plant a »cockoo in the nest« of his OT colleagues. Although I have in the course of time gone my own way on many issues, the entire approach of this work would have been unthinkable without the thorough training in the OT discipline which I received at the hands of Eduard Nielsen, or without the attitude to scholarly research which has always been implicit in his teaching and counseling.

Finally, I should like to save my warmest thanks for my wife, Elsebeth, who has had much to bear with during the production of this manuscript. I think that anyone who is at present engaged in the composition of a dissertation or the production of af scholarly tratment at a comparable level would be inclined to acknowledge that such works in reality belong to an age when one's spouse both could and would remain at home in order to care for the embroiled scholar. In our day, such luxury is a rarity indeed. Nevertheless, the patience with which my wife has borne my moods and fancies while at the same time managing to meet the demands of both a job and her home can only inspire in me the deepest admiration. This work is thus rightly dedicated to her.

Århus August 1985
Niels Peter Lemche

ABBREVIATIONS

ANET³ Pritchard, J.B. (ed.): Ancient near Eastern Texts Relating to the Old Testament. *3. ed. Princeton 1969*

CAH³ Edwards, I.E.S., Gadd, C.J. og Hammond, N.G.L. (eds.):Cambridge Ancient History Vol.I–II. *3. ed. Cambridge 1970–1975*

EA Knudtzon, J.A.: Die El-Amarna Tafeln. *Vorderasiatische Bibliothek 2,1–2. Leipzig 1915*

EAEHL Avi-Yonah, M. and Stern, E. (eds.): Encyclopedia of Archaeological Excavations in the Holy Land I–IV. *London and Jerusalem*

GEL Liddell. H.G. og Scott R.: A Greek-English Lexicon. *9. ed. Repr. 1961. Oxford.*

KAI Donner, H. og Rölling, W.: Kanaanäische und aramäische Inschriften mit einem beitrag von O. Rössler I–II. *Wiesbaden 1962–1964*

KTU Dietrich, M., Loretz, O. og Sanmartin, S.: Die keilalphabetischen Texte aus Ugarit. *Alter Orient und Altes Testament 24. Neukirchen*

LD Lewis, C.T. og Short, C.: A latin Dictionary. *Repr. Oxford 1962*

OLD Oxford Latin Dictonary. *Oxford 1968ff.*

PRU Virroleaud, C.: Le palais royales d'Ugarit II. Textes en cunéiformes alphabétiques des archives est, ouest et centrales. *Mission de Ras Shamra T. VII. Paris 1957*

PRW Pauly-Wissowa Realencyclopädie der classischen Altertumswissenschaft. Stuttgart.

RŠ Ras Šamra *(udgravningsnummer)*

INTRODUCTION

Habent sua fata libelli, "books have their own fate". The process which has resulted in this monograph may be well described by this quotation, which is often attributed to Horace. This treatment, which was written in the period between March, 1979, and August, 1982, was originally conceived as an independent contribution to the discussion of the origins of Israel. Already in the planning stage it was not the writer's intention to follow the conventional pathways, but instead to attempt to include anthropological materials which had not previously been considered. It seems that for all too many years scholars have been content to utilize ethnographic information dating from the time of the First World War, or shortly thereafter. This entailed that they adopted a number of conventions concerning the understanding of traditional Near Eastern societies which provided the basis for the interpretation of a variety of social and cultural phenomena which are mentioned in the Old Testament.

However, the years since the Second World War have witnessed an explosive growth in the anthropological interest in the Near East. The result of this process is an extensive literature which quite dwarfs all earlier studies. Nevertheless, this anthropological research has been virtually ignored by Old Testament scholarship for a considerable period of time. Thus scholars have not properly appreciated that the anthropological description of the Near East is much more solidly founded than was previously the case.

This anthropological material began to be significant for our purposes when in particular American scholars began to call attention to it. This applies especially to G.E.Mendenhall and his disciples, and later to N.K.Gottwald and others. These scholars have employed their knowledge of anthropology to present a wholly different hypothesis as to the origins of Israel. This hypothesis largely ignores the Old Testament's own conception of an Israelite immigration; moreover, these scholars have seriously criticized the immigration hypotheses of earlier scholars, and in particular that which is associated with the name of A.Alt.

Nevertheless, it is clear that this new understanding of the origins of Israel contains problematical assumptions which result in particular in an idiosyncratic use of the OT sources. On this point G.E.Mendenhall continues a tradition peculiar to American scholarship, and which was permanently established by W.F.Albright; thus he ignores the critical analyses of the texts which

European scholars in particular have produced during the last century of study. For this reason, in spite of the emergence of a number of new treatments of Israel's earliest time there are ample grounds for reviewing this subject. However, I had scarcely begun to commit my own evaluation of this period to paper when the monumental monograph of N.K.Gottwald, *The Tribes of Yahweh*, appeared[1]. Already my first reading of this work convinced me that Mendenhall's revolution-hypothesis had now been supported in a *scholarly* manner. On the other hand, it was also clear to me that some of the weaknesses of Mendenhall's approach had survived in Gottwald's work and, further, that Gottwald's use of anthropological materials left something to be desired. Thus Gottwald's monograph had by no means rendered my project for a reconsideration of this theme redundant.

Nevertheless, the appearance of *The Tribes of Yahweh* entailed a revision of my original plans. The consequence of this was in practice that I was forced to take account of Gottwald's theses from subject to subject. This has to a certain extent determined the organization of this treatment, as will be apparent below. The necessity of following Gottwald closely means, naturally, that Gottwald's work is the immediate object of my criticism. As we shall see, it has not been difficult to uncover methodological weaknesses in Gottwald's monograph. One of these weaknesses is the shakey logic in various sections of his work. In particular I would mention the countless occasions in which the author merely postulates something *ex cathedra*. There are also some deficiencies in Gottwald's discussion of OT traditions, in that he postulates for them a *Sitz im Leben* which is more than doubtful and otherwise ignores the present scholarly discussion of the dating of the sources of the Pentateuch. Finally, it is also apparent that Gottwald's use of anthropological sources is not without its problems.

All of these issues will be discussed in what follows, but my most important intention is to offer an alternative to what both Mendenhall and Gottwald understand by *"current anthropological theory"*. For this reason my discussion of modern anthropological contributions to our understanding of the Near East occupies what many may take to be a disproportionate amount of space. But my decision to dedicate entire chapters to anthropology is not without precedent, since a model for this procedure has been provided by R.R.Wilson's study of the Biblical genealogies[2]. The anthropological materials relevant to this study are today so comprehensive and various that any serious consideration of them will necessarily also entail an investigation of them. This is all the more essential when we realize that these materials are not well known out-

---

[1] Gottwald 1979A. The work appeared towards the end of 1979 and reached me just before Christmas of the same year.

[2] Wilson 1977. Of Wilson's appoximately 200 pages, more than 25% are devoted to an anthropological survey, while less than 40% are concerned with ancient Near Eastern genealogies; only around 35% have to do with the OT genealogies.

side of professional anthropological circles and that to date they have not been evaluated in synthetic form by anthropologists.

A number of difficulties present themselves immediately to anyone who intends to make use of anthropological sources. One of these has to do with the extraordinary compass of the subject in question, as it is a discipline which is much more extensive than the traditional Biblical and Oriental disciplines. This fact means that it is in itself very difficult to get much perspective on the subject as such. Another difficulty is that so widely-ranging a discipline is, naturally enough, no less differentiated than is, for example, the study of the OT. In brief, there are quite a number of approaches within the confines of anthropology, and each has its own idea of the uses of anthropology. Thus, in having chosen to examine the relevant anthropological materials my intention is to introduce a body of sources of which others will subsequently be able to make use. Scholars will hopefully be able to decide for themselves which methods are the most reliable when they attempt to project information on the traditional societies of the Near East back onto the Near East in antiquity.

Of course, it would be both naive and erroneous simply to identify modern or relatively modern social conditions in the Near East with the circumstances which prevailed in the past. I certainly do not propose to do this, as should be apparent in part two, below. On the other hand, at the end of the day I am forced to admit that there is surprising continuity between many aspects of these societies then and now, as far as such things as forms of social organization, the forces of social control, the location of ethnic groups within larger contexts, the structure of complex societies, and so forth are concerned. This implies that it *is* permissible to offer a number of conclusions by analogy, conclusions which, however, must in each case observe the distinctive conditions prevailing then and now. This procedure is no different from that employed by scholars in the past and which in our discipline has entailed the consideration of Arabic sources and earlier ethnographical descriptions of, in particular, the Arabic Bedouin societies.

The literature on this subject is enormous and complex. I do not believe that I have presented more than a limited segment of it, but I have especially concentrated on the inclusion of ethnographic field reports. In my consideration of the scholarly literature on the OT I have consciously concentrated on the products of American and European scholarship. This means that I have also consciously neglected recent Israeli research, including many not unimportant studies. In saying that my choice in this matter is conscious I merely wish to indicate that I have no desire to comment on the dogmatic presuppositions which have provided the basis for entirely too many works by Israeli scholars. By "dogmatic presuppositions" I refer to the distinct conviction of these scholars that the Biblical account of the earliest history of Israel is on the whole to be taken on faith. Thus the Biblical view is presumed without discussion to be the presupposition for evaluating individual phenomena. It is hoped that my own understanding will emerge below with all the clarity one could desire.

PART I

THE REVOLUTION HYPOTHESIS: ITS FORMULATION AND PRESUPPOSITIONS

Chapter 1

REVOLUTION AS ALTERNATIVE

§ 1

G.E. Mendenhall: The "Hebrew" Conquest of Palestine

The study of the earliest history of Israel has been dominated for over sixty years by the opposition between two schools or paths of research. One of these, sometimes called the "Baltimore School", has argued that the description in the Pentateuch and in the Book of Joshua of Israel's past largely agrees with the historical facts. This school has been strongly supported by American archeologists in its claim that the results of archeological excavations in Palestine and the rest of the Near East generally substantiate the OT's own impression of the course of history[1].

Unlike the representatives of the Baltimore School, its counterpart, the so-called "Alt-Noth-School", has never acknowledged that its membership agrees to such an extent that it would be correct to regard them as comprising a single scholarly *"school"*. The most eminent of this group of scholars are Albrecht Alt and Martin Noth, whose names have come to stand for this entire scholarly direction. It is characteristic of this group that they do not feel that the OT account of Israel's past is as sacrosanct as their opponents suppose. These scholars differ with those of the Baltimore School on the interpretation of the excavations in Palestine, and they have attempted to fit their conceptions of ethnology and sociology to the special character of the ancient Near East. As a result they have claimed that what is described in the OT as a collective Israelite invasion of Palestine was in reality a gradual infiltration of nomads who originated outside of the country but who in the course of time became

---

[1] The most important scholar among this group was W.F. Albright, who died in 1971. Throughout a long lifetime he published and directed the periodical entitled Bulletin of the American Schools of Oriental Research, which was the most vocal instrument of this group of scholars. Albright himself discussed the question of Israel's origins in numerous works, of which the best-known are Albright 1946, 1949, and 1957. The "authoritative" version of Israel's history, as seen by the "Baltimore School", is that of Bright (1960; 3rd.ed.1981).

settled in Palestine[2]. The second thesis generally asserted by this group asserts that within a short span of time these newly-arrived immigrants were consolidated into a tribal league, which has been termed an ἀμφικτυονία on the analogy provided by a Greek model[3]. They maintain that the traditions dealing with the Israelite patriarchs, Israel's sojourn in Egypt and her time of wandering in the desert were collected and formulated within amphictyonic circles. They further claim that the idea of the collective Israelite campaign into the land of Canaan under the leadership of Joshua is to be understood against the background of the forging of an Israelite national identity in the period of the Judges[4].

In spite of the obvious disagreements between these two scholarly approaches as to the historical course of events, one ought nevertheless to note that both are based on the same presupposition, namely, that Israel immigrated into Palestine, even if they interpret such immigration differently. I shall comment on this feature at length below. Here it will be sufficient merely to emphasize that the proponents of both approaches embraced the same basic point of view, and that for many years the discussion was not enlivened by new material or new arguments. Thus, at the beginning of the 1960's the academic discussion had fossilized. At that time it was apparent that if the discussion of Israel's origins was to go any farther, it would be necessary to emphasize some new aspects of the problem.

However, when these new views did in fact emerge they appeared in such a form that a number of years passed before they had acquired sufficient respectability for scholars to begin to take them seriously. In 1962 G.E.Mendenhall published an unpretentious little article in which he on the one hand presented in popular form a critique aimed at the very foundation of the then-accepted scholarly positions, while on the other he made an attempt to prepare the way for a completely new understanding of Israel's origins[5]. Mendenhall introduces his article with a general revolt against the previously accepted presuppositions for an understanding of Israel's beginnings. He summarizes these presuppositions in two main hypotheses which together make up what he terms "the ideal model": first, the idea that nomadic tribes always and invariably tend to settle down, and, second, the notion of the repeated irruptions of

---

[2] The classical account of this sequence of events is Alt 1925B, followed by Alt 1930 and 1939. The authoritative version of Israel's history as seen by this group of scholars is that of Noth (1950A).

[3] In spite of a number of anticipations, it must be emphasized that the honor of having developed this thesis belongs to Noth, 1930. For a survey of the history of research in this area, see Lemche 1972 and Bächli 1977.

[4] Alt 1936:183f.; Noth 1953A:11f. Both Alt and Noth regarded the sanctuary in Gilgal as the place of origin or "crystallization" of the traditions contained in the pre-Deuteronomistic nucleus in Jos 2-9.

[5] Mendenhall 1962.

barbarian hordes into civilized societies[6]. Mendenhall points out that scholars had tended to take these views for granted since the 19th century and that their analogical basis was provided by Islamic and Roman (that is, European) history. These presuppositions had led scholars to compose the following picture of Israel's emergence onto the historical scene: Israel's twelve tribes had come into Palestine from an area outside of it; Israel's tribes originally consisted of nomads or semi-nomads who settled down on the territory they had conquered; and, finally, inter-tribal solidarity among the Israelite tribes was ethnic in nature and ultimately was based upon the difference between Israelite and Canaanite[7]. According to Mendenhall, these basic postulates have by no means the same weight, since the first and third of them are rooted in the OT, whereas the second, that is, the question of Israelite nomadic origins, is merely an academic construction[8].

Thus Mendenhall dedicates the first section of his little treatment to an investigation of the activity of nomads in the Near East[9]. Here he primarily asserts that this sociological phenomenon has ordinarily been wrongly interpreted. According to Mendenhall the nomad is not an individual who wanders about with no relation to others than the members of his tribe, who share the same existence as himself. Rather, the nomad is ultimately closely related to the farmer, whose life is circumscribed by the fellowship of the village. In short, in actual fact it is the case that it is impossible to distinguish sharply between farmer and nomad in the Near East. Indeed, they often belong to the same tribe, which is thus partially settled and partially on the move. Moreover, such wandering is not the maverick movement of a free man; it is the periodically recurring removal of the nomad's herds of sheep and goats from one pasture to another. As Mendenhall says, this is *transhumance*, that is, the annual following of established routes to established grazing sites as the climate dictates. Here there will be food for the nomad's animals, for example, on the steppes in the winter and in the mountains in the summer[10].

---

[6] Mendenhall 1962:100. Cf. also Mendenhall 1976B, where one finds a much more sophisticated account of this problem.

[7] Mendenhall 1962:101f.

[8] Mendenhall 1962:101f. Cf. 1976B:140, where Alt's immigration model is dismissed as impossible.

[9] Mendenhall 1962:102f.

[10] Strictly speaking, this use of the technical term "transhumance" is incorrect. "Transhumance" is actually associated with migrations in connection with mountain pasturage, as it has been practiced in the French, Spanish, and Italian regions of the Mediterranean area in recent times. Cf. Rathjens 1969:21f. In the spring the peasants have their flocks led up into the mountain pastures by professional herdsmen, while the owners themselves remain in the valleys and cultivate their fields. Thus "transhumance" is not synonymous with nomadism, in which both the animals and their owners are in motion. On the other hand, "transhumance" has been used with some reason by American ethnologists in connection with vertically-migrating nomads (mountain nomads), since these scholars have concentrated on the fact that the animals in question *must* be moved. Cf.e.g. Salzman 1967:117. On "transhumance" in general and its

Mendenhall subsequently addresses himself to the question of whether there exists a connection between the concepts of "tribe" and "nomad" such that we should be compelled to suppose that the former presupposes the latter, that is, that a tribal society will necessarily originally have been nomadic before it became settled. On Mendenhall's view this classical postulate is completely wrong. In the first place, he points out, the nomads of small cattle who are often called semi-nomads were originally farmers who have been forced to travel with their animals because of lack of arable land. In the second place a tribal organization is nòt reserved for persons or political systems of a nomadic nature or origin. In this connection Mendenhall mentions that in antiquity such cities as Athens and Byblos were divided into tribal areas (one wonders, incidentally, why he failed to mention Rome). Indeed, even in such great modern cities as Baghdad most of the inhabitants reckon themselves to belong to one tribe or another. On the other hand, as the writer further points out, in modern Syria there are both villages which are tribal and those which are not, as well as some containing both tribally organized dwellers and some who are not so affiliated. He maintains that in reality tribal organization is the norm for all societies which have not actually been urbanized, although this does not entail that such non-urban societies were formed by a population which had once been nomadic[11].

In connection with Mendenhall's account it should be stressed that the classical subdivision of human development into three phases is entirely incorrect (it is classical in the sense that it was the Greek philosopher, Dikaiarchos, who first proposed this theory long before the birth of Christ)[12]. As is well known, this thesis maintains that man originally lived at the hunter-gatherer stage. After the domestication of animals this phase developed into a nomadic stage, and the last phase of the process was the agricultural stage, which arose when the nomad settled down to cultivate the earth instead of eternally wandering about in search of pasture for his animals. There is a consensus on this subject among modern anthropologists: historically speaking, agriculture preceded the domestication of animals, which is to say that settled agricultural societies existed before nomads did. Thus nomadism is a declension from the agricultural stage, and sociologists speak of a cul de sac in this connection[13].

Mention should also be made here of Mendenhall's definition of the con-

---

various meanings, see Hoffmeister 1961. It should be noted in this connection that Mendenhall nowhere makes clear what he understands "transhumance" to mean (his remarks on the subject in 1962:102 are unclear). Cf. also Gottwald 1979A:444ff.

[11] Mendenhall 1962:103f.

[12] On this see Herzog 1963:23. Dikaiarchos was a Peripatetic philosopher (ca.300BC). His theory concerning the history of culture was contained in the now lost work Βίος Ἑλλάδος, in which he apparently succeeded in reconciling the classical Greek view of human history as a decline from an original golden age into poorer circumstances with the concept of man's continued progress. On this see PWR V:547f.

[13] See below, Part II, Ch.1.

cept of *tribe*[14]: a tribe is to be regarded as a type of society which is more extensive than the immediate surroundings of the individual, that is, usually, the village. Moreover, it is this wider society which the individual village has reason to believe will come to its assistance in the event of hostile attack by forces superiour to those available to a single village[15]. Urbanization entails a break with the tribal system, since urbanization brings with it the neutralization of the feelings of internal solidarity of the tribe. In the context of antique Near Eastern culture this means that the real social dividing-line was not that separating nomad from village or farmer, but that separating the farmer from the city and its central administration. Thus the conclusion to be drawn from this part of Mendenhall's article must be that it is unrealistic to suppose that nomads could have played any significant role in Israel's origins. Similarly, in calling the Israelites nomads, this by no means implies that their origins lay outside of Palestine, in the "desert".

This conclusion leads Mendenhall to place even greater emphasis on another sociological phenomenon which characterized the second millenium BCE, namely the Hebrews[16]. In Mendenhall's opinion the words "Hebrew" and *ḫabiru* refer to one and the same sociological phenomenon. He maintains that they refer to those who had reacted against the city societies, that is, those who rejected the dominance of the city-states over the local societies. The phenomenon included also those who abandoned the authority and laws of a given central power structure, since this will primarily have defended the interests of the cities: "For if the early Israelites were called 'Hebrews', they could be termed so only from the point of view of some existing, legitimate political society from which they had withdrawn"[17]. As the writer also points out, this statement is to be seen together with the fact that in statistical terms in Palestine during the Late Bronze Age and at the transition to the Iron Age there are no signs of any important invasion of new dwellers in Palestine, nor is there any indication of a radical ejection or genocide of an existing population. Thus Mendenhall concludes that the Israelite conquest of Palestine was "a peasant's revolt against the network of interlocking Canaanite city states"[18].

In so saying, Mendenhall arrives at his own view of the historical course of events in question: "The Hebrew conquest of Palestine took place because a religious movement and motivation created a solidarity among a large group of pre-existent social units, which was able to challenge and defeat the dysfunctional complex of cities dominating the whole of Palestine and Syria at the end of the Bronze age"[19]. The writer feels that it is possible to determine the

---

[14] Mendenhall 1962:103-105.
[15] Mendenhall 1962:104
[16] Mendenhall 1962:105-107.
[17] Mendenhall 1962:106.
[18] Mendenhall 1962:107.
[19] Mendenhall 1962:107.

cause of this revolt against the authority of the cities with great precision: it was started by the group of enslaved workers, who under the leadership of Moses, had fled from Egypt and who had established a relationship with a deity, Yahweh, in the desert. This marked the creation of a form of religion or a religious society which extended beyond the internal solidarity of the individual tribes. Thus this solidarity applied to the whole of the religious society, that is, Israel, rather than the individual tribe. In the nature of things, this "new" religion was forced to turn against the old system of power, which was "Canaanite", and so from the very beginning Yahwism rejected everything Canaanite[20]. Since Yahweh had bound the individual social groups to himself with bands of solidarity, here, too, from the very beginning it was the *covenant* that was the natural and central expression of the relationship between God and man[21]. The movement was revolutionary in accordance with its anti-Canaanite nature.

It would not be unfair to say that in his description of the origin of Israel Mendenhall is in reality not very far from the account of Israel's conquest of Canaan advocated by the representatives of the Baltimore School. However, according to Mendenhall the conquest was not brought about by the arrival of a new people; it is to be regarded as a development which took place within Palestine. But since Israel was mainly autochthonous, that is, deriving from the same origins as the rest of the population of Palestine, it was not to begin with a particularistic society, a closed political system; it was open to new membership. It was first after a historical development which included the many "national catastrophes" that Israelite society found its basis in a biological continuity that was based on endogamy and on strong hostility towards any foreigners who attempted to enter into the society[22].

It would be inaccurate to claim that Mendenhall's little article caused any notable fuss; in fact, for a number of years it was literally ignored. A number of reasons contributed to this fact. The first of these was that the form of Mendenhall's article, couched as it was in popular language, with no references to sources or any scholarly array of concepts, did not aid the reception of its thesis. Then there are the completely obvious weaknesses inherent in Mendenhall's "conquest hypothesis", which virtually blind one with their glare. To this should be added the fact that Mendenhall's criticism of the previous scholarly work on the origins of Israel introduced a series of new and not previously discussed aspects which would have required considerable openness of his opponents even to understand, since on a number of points they diverged radically from what were then the established positions of the debate. I shall

---

[20] Mendenhall:107ff.113ff.

[21] Mendenhall 1962:108f.

[22] Mendenhall 1962:118: Mendenhall goes to some lengths to emphasize that the reason for this was that in the earliest period Israel was a *religious society* rather than a political one, and that the type of religion around which this society was centered had nothing to do with any particularistic *tribal religion*.

return to these points below; here it will suffice to mention that these conjoined to lead other scholars completely to overlook the fact that in reality Mendenhall's critique was very important, and, as we shall see, that it may lead us to a new understanding of the origins of Israel.

A contributing factor to the rustication of Mendenhall's conquest hypothesis was the treatment his theories received in M.Weippert's thorough and highly-respected review of the academic discussion of the Israelite conquest[23]. Weippert appears to cite Mendenhall carefully, and his rejection of Mendenhall looks as if it rests upon assured facts. Nevertheless, if one looks more closely at the matter one discovers that Weippert has distorted several of Mendenhall's views. In consequence, Weippert does not concern himself seriously with the points which are central to Mendenhall's attack on the previously-existing scholarly debate. Moreover, he also fails to see the real problems inherent in Mendenhall's reconstruction. It is to be supposed that this oversight or distortion of the argument by Weippert is related to his acceptance of the account of Israel's immigration deriving from A.Alt's studies.

In actual fact Weippert only attacks Mendenhall on two points. First, he criticizes Mendenhall's treatment of the problem of ḫabiru/Hebrew, which led to one of the most worthwhile chapters in Weippert's book, that dealing with the ḫabiru-movements during the second millenium[24]. Second, he attacks Mendenhall's understanding of the nomads of antiquity, but prior to doing so he quotes Mendenhall's views inexactly. Weippert claims that Mendenhall (rightly, according to Weippert) distinguishes between two types of nomads, on one hand the herdsmen who lived in a system of transhumance in close association with sedentary societies, on the other the real nomads who lived outside of this association in freedom, and whom we know from the Near Eastern sources by the designation *sutu*[25].

Now, there are signs of this sort of distinction in Mendenhall's article, but these are restricted to a footnote of the sort that may be termed "preventive" notes, in which one protects oneself against possible surprises, possibly in the event of the publication of new material[26]. In reality Mendenhall says that if there were any independent nomadic groups at all which had no association with the established societies, it might be those which were described by the term *sutu*. However, he adds that such groups played no important role in the history of the ancient Orient at all, since there were very few of them. Thus the sutu-nomads may not be used as a paradigm to explain the Israelite invasion of Palestine. Parenthetically it may be remarked that close analysis of the sources dealing with the *sutu* (which are very difficult, as only a very limited

---

[23] Weippert 1967:59-66.
[24] Weippert 1967:66-102.
[25] Weippert 1967:60. It is possible that Weippert did not realize that Mendenhall uses *transhumance* in a wider sense; see n.10 above.
[26] Mendenhall 1962:103.

material is available) may show that they actually did not comprise a group which was sociologically distinct from other nomadic groups, the "herdsmen", to use Weippert's terminology[27].

Weippert further claims that Mendenhall cites Alt incorrectly in maintaining that Alt and Noth had held that the Israelite tribes existed prior to the conquest, which could be taken to indicate that Israel was originally a nomadic society, or perhaps more than one[28]. Mendenhall does not actually say that Alt and Noth felt this to be the case; indeed, he points out that one may not conclude on the basis of the description in the OT of Israel as a tribal society that she therefore had a nomadic past[29]. But since Weippert has thus summarily "demonstrated" that Mendenhall had misunderstood Alt and Noth, he in reality avoids a closer discussion of Mendenhall's very important section on the concept of "tribe". He simply ignores it. Unfortunately, this means that Weippert has completely ignored the burden of Mendenhall's argumentation. This observation emerges very clearly from Weippert's chapter on nomads in antiquity for, although it is well informed it is entirely traditional[30]. Weippert plainly does not realize that Mendenhall's attack on the traditional understanding of Israel's immigration, whether this be conceived as a relatively peaceful infiltration over a long period of time or as the headlong attack of barbarian hordes on the Canaanite borders, is based on new sociological models. Moreover, he does not realize that these models have been accepted by a number of anthropologists in place of the paradigm Alt, Noth, Albright, and others used as the basis of their studies of the origins of Israel[31].

A third reason for Weippert's misunderstanding of Mendenhall's views is probably that he supposes that Mendenhall had the German peasants' revolt in Luther's day in the back of his mind when he composed his "immigration hypothesis". In actual fact it is far from clear that in 1962 Mendenhall's knowledge of the history of the German Reformation was so thorough that the peasants' revolt had anything at all to do with his conception of the hypothesis in question[32].

---

[27] J.T. Luke, one of Mendenhall's pupils, has attempted to demonstrate that even in the Mari archives the term *sutu* refers to pastoral nomads like the Hanaeans and the Benjaminites (I prefer to retain this translation of DUMU.MEŠ-*jami-nu* in the Marian archives; cf. Lemche 1972:107n); see Luke 1965:105-138. The *sutu* nomads have been most recently treated by M.Heltzer (1981), although, curiously enough, Heltzer completely avoids use of anthropological literature. On the other hand, we should note that in the 25 years which have elapsed since Kupper (1957) the materials concerning the *sutu* have doubled (Heltzer 1981:V).

[28] Weippert 1967:61n.

[29] Mendenhall 1962:104: "There is no justification whatever for the idea that a tribal organization must be an indication of an originally nomadic background."

[30] Weippert 1967:102-123. The same characterization also applies to Weippert 1974 (a review of Giveon 1971). Of course, this does not necessarily mean that Mendenhall's understanding of nomadism is correct.

[31] See below, Part II, Ch.1.

[32] Weippert 1967:62f. However, Weippert is forced to admit that Mendenhall does not actually refer to the peasant revolt (Weippert 1967:63n).

Yet another factor is the circumstance that when Mendenhall discusses the original Israelite Yahwistic religion, Weippert maintains that this can only be understood against the background of Mendenhall's earlier theses concerning the Sinai Covenant and its relation to the Hittite vassal treaties dating from the end of the second millemium[33]. Weippert notes that since this relation – at least in the form adumbrated by Mendelhall in his articles published in 1954 – cannot be demonstrated, he is justified in ignoring this aspect of Mendenhall's immigration hypothesis[34]. Now, it is obvious that the idea of a connection between the Hittite treaties and the Sinai Covenant was important to Mendenhall, and he in fact calls attention to this in his article on the Hebrew conquest. Indeed, Mendenhall claims that there are connecting lines between Israelite covenantal theology and the Canaanite world – which shows, incidentally, that the revolution postulated by Mendenhall failed to sever all connections with Canaanite cultutal tradition[35] – but, at least in the sense advocated by' Mendenhall, the covenant between Yahweh and Israel is an independent quantity. It is unimportant whether or not there are formal parallels to the international treaties of the second millenium, since, on Mendenhall's view, the covenant between Yahweh and Israel is something wholly new.

Thus Weippert's criticism of Mendenhall's attempt to renew the discussion of Israel's origins misses the mark. Weippert does have some relevant objections to other aspects of the immigration hypothesis, as formulated by Mendenhall. Indeed, his work contains some elements of a constructive criticism of one of Mendenhall's more important presuppositions, namely his understanding of the problem of the ḫabiru. Nevertheless, Weippert ultimately fails to discuss the background of Mendenhall's criticism of the previous understanding of the Israelites as seminomads who either invaded or infiltrated into Palestine.

This evaluation of Weippert's treatment also applies to his section on the nomads in antiquity which, as mentioned above, is traditional, since Weippert fails to understand Mendenhall's intentions. The positive conclusion which may be drawn from these observations on the encounter between Mendenhall and his first critic, Weippert, is that even if one recognizes the cogency of Mendenhall's criticism of earlier scholars, one is not thereby also compelled to accept the correctness of his hypothesis concerning the immigration or conquest.

In his review of Weippert's book Mendenhall repeatedly correctly challenges Weippert's criticisms[36]. His first observation corresponds to my point,

---

[33] Weippert 1967:63n.
[34] Ibid.; cf.Mendenhall 1954A; 1954B.
[35] Mendenhall 1962:110.
[36] Mendenhall 1969.

that Weippert's discussion of the problem of the nomads does not enter into a dialogue with Mendenhall, and in fact is addressed elsewhere. The second point concerns the ḫabiru-problem and deserves to be quoted directly, since Mendenhall strikes at the heart of the matter:" ...it is completely irrelevant to ask whether or not the early Israelites were 'apiru ...the question is, why were they called 'apiru at all – and by whom?'"[37].

Furthermore, Mendenhall's last remark in his review provides a clearer idea than his article on the Hebrew conquest does as to his "sociological" understanding of Israel's origins: "Ancient Israel was, then, the first of those few movements in world history which resulted in the formation of a large social group on the basis of a religious and ethical 'ideology'"[38]. This is essentially the main theme of the most extensive treatment of the problem in question by Mendenhall to date[39]. Unfortunately, the work referred to is one of the strangest studies to have made an appearance in the field of OT research in recent times, and, to speak plainly, it would not be worthwhile to review it here. This is in part because of formal aspects of the book's argumentation (that is, if the work can be said to contain any argumentation at all), since most of the views it proposes are presented as postulates. Indeed, it is only occasionally that Mendenhall can be bothered to offer a scholarly explanation as to how he has arrived at one or another of his dicta.

To put it as simply as possible, in *The Tenth Generation* Mendenhall reveals that his intentions, both in his articles on the Sinai Covenant and the Near Eastern treaties in 1954 and in his article on the Hebrew conquest of Palestine, were two. The first of these was to *prove that the OT account of the Mosaic tradition is historically reliable*; the second was to *prove* that the Sinai event really constituted Israel as a society which differed radically from those previously known. Israel was a *theocracy*, the members of which were bound solely by the covenant between Israel and Yahweh, which is to say by the ethical demands which the covenant levied on the individual Israelite.

In his 1973 work Mendenhall does not attempt to conceal the fact that the most important presupposition for his hypotheses is not the conclusions of contemporary anthropology, but his own analyses of the Sinai Covenant and its presumed relations to the vassal treaties from the end of the second millenium[40]. It is entirely symptomatic of Mendenhall's style of argumentation that he nowhere refers to the extensive scholarly discussion which the publication of his theses on the Sinai Covenant provoked. Only very rarely does he refer to D.J.McCarthy's important contribution to this discussion[41]. Moreover, it is precisely in these rare references that Mendenhall displays his

---

[37] Mendenhall 1969:434.
[38] Mendenhall 1969:435.
[39] Mendenhall 1973.
[40] Cf. Mendenhall 1954A; 1954B.
[41] McCarthy 1963; cf. Mendenhall 1973:14n; 25n.

contempt for the opinions of other scholars, since he claims McCarthy's support for his own hypotheses, while in reality McCarthy was very critical of the way Mendenhall had presented his ideas[42].

Therefore there are only two sections of Mendenhall's book which are worthy of inclusion in the present discussion; these are the chapters dealing with the *ḫabiru* and with "tribe and state in antiquity"[43]. Neither of these chapters says anything fundamentally new in relation to the original article on the Hebrew conquest of Palestine; they do, however, develop some points made in that article. As for the rest of Mendenhall's work, it is purely speculative, occasionally subtle, and most often ruthlessly inconsiderate of the most elementary principles of humanistic research[44].

In this connection one last point deserves mention. Few scholars have claimed the authority of the results of modern sociological, and especially anthropological, research as Mendenhall has. This is true already of *The Hebrew Conquest*, but the tendency is pronounced in *The Tenth Generation*. In the former case one simply had to accept that the form and the publication in which Mendenhall's theories appeared prevented the use of a normal footnote apparatus. However, *The Tenth Generation* leads one to suspect seriously the depth of Mendenhall's reading within the twin disciplines of sociology and anthropology. In actual fact, Mendenhall utilizes only a single work, written by E.R.Service; on the other hand, he cites it frequently[45]. We shall return to this point later on, because Service is, of course, only one of many anthropologists, and it would be untrue to say that his theories have been generally accepted by any means by his colleagues[46].

---

[42] Note Mendenhall's remark (1973:25n): "....It has often been observed that the entire book of Deuteronomy has precisely the structure of the Late Bronze Age covenant form (see especially McCarthy, Treaty and Covenant)." McCarthy does not say this in his study of Deuteronomy (1963:109-140). In fact, McCarthy is actually much more reticent about the matter (cf. McCarthy 1963:141): "As is coming more and more to be realized, the characteristic features of Dt are deeply rooted in Israel's past, and this is true in the case of the covenant form as in others." McCarthy also argues that while the main part of Deuteronomy is a conscious literary product written in the style of a vassal treaty, this is done under the influence of elements deriving from the Assyro-Babylonian tradition, rather than the Hittite tradition of the second millennium (this applies especially to Deut 28). The closest parallels McCarthy is able to adduce derive from the 8th-7th centuries. On this point see also McCarthy's survey of research (1966:45ff, esp. 1966:50): "*Es besteht kein Zweifel, dass das Buch Dt eine Beziehung zur l i t e r a r i s c h e n Form der Verträge erkennen lässt.*" (emphasis mine).

[43] Cf. Mendenhall 1973: 122-141; 174-197.

[44] The worst example of this is probably his chapter on the "Sea Peoples" in Palestine (1973:141-173), in which it is claimed, among other things, that both the Hivvites and the Midianites must have been of Anatolian origin. His argument to this effect is a completely arbitrary use of fictive etymologies.

[45] Service 1971 (originally appeared in 1962). It can hardly be coincidental that Service was employed at the same university as Mendenhall when *The Hebrew Conquest* was published.

[46] See below, pp. 209ff. For "library-technical" reasons. yet another work from Mendenhall's hand (1976C), in which he summarizes his hypotheses, reached me too late to be able to figure in this presentation of his revolution model. However, the article in question does not say any-

§ 2

N.K.Gottwald: "Liberated" Israel

As should be evident from the preceding section, even if the ideas concerning Israel's origins presented by Mendenhall are provocative, it is extremely doubtful whether the means their author has chosen to propound them serve his purposes. Moreover, history has long since demonstrated that it is impossible to engage Mendenhall in a serious discussion of his theses[47]. However, Mendenhall is not alone in manning the trenches, since his ideas have been adopted by other scholars, mainly Americans, among whom N.K.Gottwald is, *sans pareille*, the one who has most impressively presented his ideas[48]. Moreover, Gottwald has succeeded to a vastly greater degree than Mendenhall in meeting the demands of an academically serious discussion. Gottwald published only a few years ago a sizeable monograph which had been long awaited; it contains his attempt to reconstruct the history and social structure of Israel in pre-monarchical times[49].

By way of introduction it would, however, be useful to examine an earlier study by Gottwald in which he discusses the question of methodology[50]. As his point of departure Gottwald asserts that the traditional view of the origin of Israel is quite simply founded on an inadequate knowledge of the results of sociological and anthropological research[51]. This applies to a scholar like

---

thing with respect to Mendenhall 1962 and 1973 (of which it is virtually a résumé). In other words, here too we find the emphases on the special character of Mosaic Yahwism, the covenant, the twelve-tribe league, the dichotomy between town and country, and so forth. However, Mendenhall's article is nevertheless notable because, being a résumé, it may be used as an introduction to and point of departure for a discussion of Mendenhall's ideas (although not at this point).

[47] Mendenhall demonstrates this with all desirable clarity in his response to the objections raised to his hypotheses which were voiced by A.J. Hauser and T.L. Thompson in the *Journal for the Study of the Old Testament*, 7, 1978 (= Mendenhall 1978). To quote Hauser's rejoinder, Mendenhall's response is as much an *argumentum ad hominem* as it is to the point. This style is also characteristic of the "take it or leave it" attitude which mars his *The Tenth Generation*.

[48] Already older "established" American scholars such as Albright and Bright were *moving* towards an acceptance of Mendenhall's revolution hypothesis (cf. Albright 1963:32-33). This step was definitive by the time the 3rd edition of Brights history of Israel was published (1981:107-143.144.182); Bright is here mainly reliant on Mendenhall 1962 and 1973.

[49] Gottwald 1979A. Gottwald announced his intention to publish his work as early as 1974.

[50] Gottwald 1975. Cf. also 1979B.

[51] It should be mentioned that anthropologists would not necessarily agree with Gottwald's characterization of OT scholarship. Cf. e.g., the evaluation of M.F.C. Bourdillon: "The long tradition of scholarship on the history and culture of ancient Israel makes it possible to look in historical depth at changes which occurred in Israelite society; and the present article uses this scholarship ...." (1977:124). Bourdillon attempts to compare Israelite prophecy with corresponding phenomena from Central Africa. P.C. Salzman, another well-known anthropologist whose specialty is Near Eastern nomadism, is not reluctant to utilize Bourdillon's understanding of Israelite prophecy, even though it is based on "traditional" OT scholarship, in his analysis of the relationship between ideology and change in Near Eastern tribal societies in recent times (Salzman 1978A:618f.).

M.Noth, whose sociological efforts are rendered nugatory by his exaggerated emphasis on the significance of the amphictyony as the collectivizing factor in ancient Israel[52]. Noth is frontally accused of having overstressed a single social segment because of his amphictyony hypothesis, namely the cultic institutions, and this emphasis was made at the expense of the collective social structure. Similarly, like most OT scholars in his day Noth assumed that Israel's forefathers were semi-nomads[53].

Gottwald's criticisms are more explicitly formulated when he attempts to demonstrate the "domain assumptions" which had governed previous research. The first of these domain assumptions is well known in all historical research: the exaggerated tendency to explain large-scale socio-political changes (the nature of which is of secondary importance) by presumed changes in the ethnic basis of a given population. As Gottwald says, scholars have been prone to assume that a given population in a given geographical area has been replaced by another and ethnically foreign group[54].

The second domain assumption is specifically concerned with Near Eastern conditions, since scholars have traditionally been all too inclined to regard the Syro-Arabian desert as the actual homeland of the Semites. It was from this region, it has been held, that the various Semitic "migrations" originated which swept over the borders of the adjacent civilized territories, while in the intervals between the great migrations small nomadic or semi-nomadic (pastoral) groups infiltrated these territories. We shall return to this question below, as it is in reality the cardinal issue in the entire discussion in recent times of Israel's origins. Moreover, it is so significant a question that Gottwald himself apparently saw the necessity to dilate on it already in a separate edition of the section dealing with the Israelites and nomadism in his major work on pre-monarchical Israel[55].

The third domain assumption singled out by Gottwald is a general criticism, but it nevertheless is also explicitly the most significant point as far as the traditional understanding of Israel's origins and history is concerned. This is the tendency to isolate a single phenomenon within the socio-political

---

[52] Gottwald 1975:89f. It would be appropriate to inquire as to whether it is Noth in particular who is singled out here, and not also Alt, who was certainly the most important single representative of this understanding of Israel's origins among this now deceased generation of OT scholars. Does this have to do with a certain lack of understanding on the part of Gottwald for the nuance and variety of the views of German scholars, as for example, in the case of Noth, the view that the amphictyony was created by the Israelite tribes in Palestine after the immigration? In Gottwald 1979B:73, Noth is no longer alone; indeed, he has been followed by Mendenhall, who has since remained a firm adherent of the twelve-tribe hypothesis. Cf. Mendenhall 1976B: 141.

[53] The third objection to Noth in Gottwald's work (1975:90) is less important in this connection. He maintains that Noth has misunderstood the nature of the Greek amphictyony. See also Lemche 1972:39ff. and 1977.

[54] Gottwald 1975:91.

[55] Gottwald 1974, which is largely identical with Gottwald 1979A: 435-463.

system of a nation, in order subsequently to project this phenomenon back-wards and uncritically to allow it to become either the only, or at least the dominant, factor active in the birth of the nation. In the case of Israel, when this society is examined in the light of the OT, the religio-symbolic and cultic dimensions seem to be the most characteristic (Gottwald's term is "idiosyn-cratic") in the nation. Thus, Gottwald claims, scholars have been far too prone to postulate that these very factors were dominant during the birth of the nation[56].

All three of these domain assumptions have retained their currency within OT scholarship, but Gottwald maintains that they have been surpassed and superannuated by developments within the various disciplines which OT scholars have usually employed to support their views. According to Gottwald himself these ancillary disciplines are prehistory, ethnography, cultural anthropology, the sociology of religion, and orientalia, understood as the study of the antique cultures of the Orient, exclusive of Israel[57]. As a result of these developments, whether one likes it or not one has no alternative to esta-blishing a different set of domain assumptions if one intends to present a coherent and logical picture of the history of Israel's origins up to the esta-blishment of the Monarchy[58].

The first of these new domain assumptions asserts the necessity to under-stand that ordinarily the cause of socio-political changes in a given society (in-cluding fundamental changes in the structure of the society) is *"inner societal pressure and conflict"*. It is possible that in a given situation there are many mutually independent causes which influence events in a particular direction. Nevertheless, Gottwald emphasizes that only rarely, and even then only when *"specific evidence"* so indicates, is it correct to explain changes in a society as the

---

[56] Gottwald 1975:91.

[57] I have chosen to reproduce here the terminology utilized by Gottwald. However, I am well aware that many other designations are also used for these subjects. This also applies to the term "anthropology", which has very little in common with the theological usage of this term. In theology, "anthropology" means "the study of the view of man" rather than "the study of man". Thus J. Nicolaisen emphasizes that Anglo-Saxon usage of the term "anthropology" really encompasses two different disciplines, each of which has its specific term in Continental usage. These terms are *ethnography* (ethnology) and anthropology (1965:7f.). J.W. Rogerson has expres-sed this problem quite trenchantly: "The German word Ethnologie conveys more of what is primarily meant in English by "anthropology" and the nearest French equivalent is probably sociologie" (1978:9). If one declines to be confused by the many different terms and instead rea-lizes that the entire spectrum of definitions may be subsumed under the heading of "cultural science" (*allgemeine Kultutwissenschaft:* also called "the anthropological sciences"), then the various terms will have no practical significance for the results which emerge from cultural-scientific research.

[58] Both Gottwald and Mendenhall seem to be convinced that the introduction of the monarchy signified the end of a lengthy socio-political evolution within Palestine; they also hold that this evolution was also a return to conditions which once obtained before the "Hebrew revolution". I shall later return to the question as to whether this view is not based on an antiqua-ted and false *domain assumption*. This is the claim that in the period of the Judges Israelite society will necessarily have differed signally from the other sociological groupings in Palestine and her environs during the Early Iron Age, both in socio-political and religio-political respects.

result of the replacement of one population by another, irregardless of whether this is thought to take place by peaceful or warlike means[59]. As presuppositions for changes in the structural organization of a society Gottwald mentions such factors as technical innovations, social conflicts, and a variety of political and religious orientations. He further maintains that in general it will not be one of such presuppositions which is the sole cause of changes in the social structure; rather, several, or even all such factors will conjoin to this result.

The second domain assumption is a negation of the now-antiquated domain assumption which supposed the Semite place of origin to be the desert. As a contributory factor to social change, the desert has played – even today – only a subordinate role. In this connection, semi-nomadism is virtually insignificant, as this category of nomads does not constitute an independent and foreign element in relation to civilized society. Rather, they represent a specialized single element in Near Eastern political and cultural systems, and this sociological group forms part of the culture to which it is subordinate[60].

Gottwald's third domain assumption entails the rejection of the third now-antiquated tendency to isolate a single aspect of the cultural pattern, which, in the case of Israel, has usually been religion. This tendency is to be replaced by a conscious consideration of all the aspects of the culture of a given society without regard to their nature or the emphasis which has been laid upon them in the sources. Indeed, some such cultural factors need not even be mentioned in the sources. They may be demonstrated and isolated in the course of an analysis of the entire cultural pattern of the society in question, seen in the light of the laws for cultural development which the anthropological sciences have established in recent times[61].

Then how are the origins of Israel to be understood when seen via this new set of domain assumptions? Gottwald replies extensively to this question in his monograph published in 1979, *The Tribes of Yahweh*, subtitled *A Sociology of the Religion of Liberated Israel*. In most important respects, Gottwald's views coincide with those of Mendenhall: Israel was the result of an evolution within Canaanite society itself. On matters of detail, however, there are considerable differences.

As a guide to his analysis of Israel's origins Gottwald adumbrates four central points. The first of these is the necessity to determine the composition and relative value of the sources for attempting a reconstruction of pre-monarchical Israel. Next, the sources are to be subjected to a sociological analysis which leads to the third step, an evaluation of earlier attempts to employ sociological methods in the analysis of ancient Israel. Finally, the goal of such

---

[59] Gottwald 1975:92f.
[60] Gottwald 1975:93.
[61] Gottwald 1975:93.

treatment is to arrive at a new model for describing pre-monarchical Israel; this is to be presented as a structural-functionalistic model which is the basis of a historical-cultural-materialistic model[62].

Gottwald is so helpful as to mention the results of his analyses prior to his presentation of them. He regards Israel as an eclectic conglomerate of many groups, as a phenomenon which did not occur as the result of the entry of new populations into the Palestinian sphere. Rather, it was the result of an internal social evolution of Canaanite society. In reality, as Gottwald claims, Israel was the product of a conscious revolt against the Canaanite hierarchical-feudal social system[63]. This revolt was a "retribalization", a return to a primitive and egalitarian social system. The unitary ideology of this revolt was the Yahwistic religion, which entailed a radical distinction between that which was proper to the Canaanite social and religious system and that which was entirely foreign to it. Thus the task of a sociology of Israelite religion is held to be to achieve an adequate description of the ways in which Israelite religion was decisively different from the other religions of the ancient Near East. Only an awareness of the connections between religion and the cultural-materialistic social system will enable us to determine the origins of the specifically Israelite religion[64].

In his analysis of the sources Gottwald follows the approach of M.Noth as closely as possible and adheres to Noth's results as far as he is able[65]. In reality, however, Gottwald goes even farther, in that he de facto accepts Noth's basic sociological model of pre-monarchical Israel, even though he correctly acknowledges that the designation employed by Noth, *amphictyony*, is unfortunate and entails unintended associations[66]. But if one retains Noth's fundamental concept, namely, that Israel must be understood as a *religious* league as early as the period of the Judges, and furthermore, if one also refrains from

---

[62] Gottwald 1979A:XXII.

[63] It should be noted that after he wrote *The Tribes of Yahweh*, Gottwald has revised his opinion of Canaanite society, which he no longer regards as "feudal" (cf. Gottwald 1976). He is surely right in this, to the extent that a social organization corresponding to the European feudal system of the Middle Ages was unknown in the Orient. In Europe the feudal system was practically a privilege system which defined the rights of the various estates with respect to one another (the sovereign included). It may be suggested that the system in the Orient was *despotic* in the sense that there was no system of clear rules as to the rights of the élite with respect to the lower class. Nor were there institutionalized instances which protected the subject classes from the abuses of the wealthy. On this point see Abrahamian 1975. On the other hand, the relationship in Palestine and Syria between the king and a powerful subordinate or between king and king during the Late Bronze Age would be best described as "feudal" because it encompassed the rights and duties of both parties. Cf. on this point Liverani 1967. In Liverani's opinion, the Egyptian was *despotic* (even though he calls it "bureaucratic"). One should also note that in Liverani's account the "feudal" system only included the highest layers of society and not the man on the street.

[64] Gottwald 1979A:XXIII.

[65] Gottwald 1979A:61-125.

[66] Gottwald 1979A:343-386.

associating the number twelve with the existence of such a league[67], Noth's model of Israel in the period of the Judges is essentially defensible. Thus Gottwald is also in a position to retain this religious league as the locus in which the traditions concerning Israel's most ancient period were formulated. In other words, these traditions were the centralized edition produced by the league of the numerous individual recollections preserved by the various subdivisions of the league[68]. This procedure enables one to retain the main lines of OT historical tradition with respect to pre-monarchical Israel as in principle useful for attempting a reconstruction of at least parts of the past of the league, that is, Israel. By the same token, these traditions may be used, or so Gottwald maintains, to describe the attitude of the league towards the other political groups in Palestine in the Late Bronze and Early Iron ages. This means that they apply to the hierarchical-feudal social system, whether this refers to the Egyptian conquerors, the local petits rois, or to the newly-arrived heirs to the Egyptian imperial tradition, the Philistines. Finally, such a sociological analysis of the sources will reveal the nature of pre-monarchical Israelite society, and it will illustrate the fundamental ideological themes which dominated society in the period in question. In this fashion we would arrive at the key to the question as to which social and cultural currents led to the emergence of Israel.

This argumentation is plainly circular, and if Gottwald's matrix for pre-monarchical Israel is to be defended it will be necessary to interrupt the chain of arguments at some point in order to isolate at least one element. If it can be shown that Gottwald has described this single element correctly from a methodological point of view, that is, that he has substantiated his postulates, whether these have to do with his literary analysis, his definition of specifically Israelite religion, or his description of the political organization, it will then be possible to determine whether his circular argumentation is closed. This will in turn indicate whether Gottwald's model of pre-monarchical Israel is a meaningful alternative to other understandings of the origins of Israel. It is accordingly a primary goal of this treatment to attempt to provide a control of Gottwald's "analysis" of pre-monarchical Israel on at least one of the three points mentioned above: literature, religion, or politics. I have found it convenient to concentrate on Gottwald's (and Mendenhall's) use of the OT and on their account of the socio-political relations. In order to do so, however, it will first be necessary to present Gottwald's matrix against the background provided by the theses of Mendenhall described above.

In Gottwald's opinion, the relations characterizing Israel's origins were far more complex than Mendenhall's original hypothesis of a peasant revolt

---

[67] The "twelve-scheme" cannot derive from a period earlier than the monarchy; cf. Gottwald 1979A:358-375.

[68] Gottwald 1979A:72-82, where the starting point is Noth: *"Das Wichtigste in dieser Hinsicht scheint mir im vorliegenden Falle das Problem zu sein, wie es zu der Einheit 'Israel' und zu dem israelitischen Gemeinbewusstsein gekommen ist..."* (1948:279). See also Gottwald 1979A:77f. and 81f.

would lead us to expect. Israel was namely not the result of a single spontaneous and decisive revolution. Instead, it is a question of a lengthy revolutionary evolution, in the course of which the rebellious and dissatisfied part of the
Canaanite population eventually developed into a social order which was not
hierarchically and feudally structured. Rather, it comprised a decentralized
and egalitarian system which was essentially opposed to the nation-state. This
revolutionary movement had arisen long before the introduction of the
Yahwistic religion, as is indicated by the fact that this alternative social system
had attained a certain degree of integration as the non-national league known
as Isra-El[69]. In reality, it was a movement which may be said to have *retriba-
lized* large segments of the Canaanite population of Palestine. The Israelite
league itself was a conglomerate of farmers and herdsmen who had organized
themselves, apparently consciously, into an egalitarian system of "extended
families"[70] which provided equal rights of access to the basic economic
resources. In political and social terms the establishment of Israel constituted
a breach with the traditional relationship between the city and rural popul-
tions in the Canaanite world. This development entailed a change in the
power structures of the country in favor of the populations in the villages.

The second phase in the evolution of Israel was characterized by the arrival
of the Moses-group from Egypt. This group imported the Yahwistic religion
with it, and its representatives thus became the nucleus of the future Yahwistic
Israel. It could be said that the egalitarian society, Israel, found at this time a
religion appropriate to it, as it was clearly opposed to the local Canaanite religious culture, just like the league itself. This means that even if Israel perpetuated Canaanite traditions in many ways touching on matters of custom and
usage, it nevertheless represented a new type of society characterized by a previously unknown variety of religion. This was *monoyahwism*, which may be
described by the pregnant formula, "one people-one God"[71].

In this connection it is not unimportant to note that Mendenhall and Gottwald differ on the question of the relationship between religion and politics[72].
In Mendenhall's opinion, the newly-emerged Israel is to be seen as a theocracy
in which the very concept of socio-political power was rejected in favor of the
rule of Yahweh. As far as I can see, Gottwald regards this as an example of the
third of the now-antiquated domain assumptions, according to which a single
social element is isolated and assigned significance at the expense of other
elements of equal or greater importance. Thus Gottwald emphasizes the
nature of Mendenhall's error. Being spellbound by the Near Eastern vassal

---

[69] Gottwald 1979A:493-497.

[70] Gottwald avoids using the term "clan" as a social unit in ancient Israel, since he denies
that Israel – like so many other traditional societies – was organized with the *exogamous clan* as
the most important element in the infrastructure of the society (1979A:301-315). However, see
below, pp. 231ff.

[71] Gottwald 1979A:647.

[72] Gottwald 1979A:599ff.

treaties, Mendenhall assumed that they provided a model of the religion on which the new society, Israel, relied. However, the understanding of Israel's relationship to Yahweh as a treaty obligation was secondary and could scarcely have arisen before the first millenium, or so Gottwald claims on the basis of D.J.McCarthy's fundamental discussion of covenant versus treaty[73]. In pre-monarchical Israel, Yahwistic religion was not based on the formalized sort of treaty which we find in the Deuteronomistic literature. Rather, it was based on a union of what Gottwald calls the Sinai themes: the theophany, the Covenant, and the Law[74]. On this view, "covenant" merely signified that there existed an ordered or reciprocal relationship between the deity and his people[75]. Furthermore, Yahwistic Israel by no means rejected political power. Instead, Israel's emergence signified that a particular power system, the hierarchical-feudal of Canaan, was replaced by yet another, the egalitarian system of Israel. This is reflected in the fact that at no point in her history did Israel disdain to exploit power, even if the Israelites officially assigned all political authority to Yahweh.

Gottwald agrees with Mendenhall that the Israelite tribes are not to be seen as original social units which historically preceded the formation of the tribal league of Israel. But he stresses that Israel's tribes arose as the result of a cons-cious process of retribalization which received additional stimulus from the pressure which the Canaanite state system exerted upon the Israelite tribal groups. This means that on Gottwald's view the concept of "tribe" is neces-sarily to be divorced from any notion of an *a priori* connection to a previous nomadic stage[76]. Gottwald expresses much more clearly than does Menden-hall, but nevertheless on the same wavelength, a rejection of the idea that the Israelite revolution led to an instantaneous conquest of the Canaanite world. Rather, it resulted in a "withdrawal" of large parts of the earlier population of the Canaanite states. This withdrawal was made possible by a number of tech-nical innovations which made possible the inhabitation of previously unpopu-lated areas of Palestine. Moreover, these innovations also made it possible to cultivate land in areas which had previously been inaccessible[77].

There is therefore no doubt that Gottwald's understanding of the origins of

---

[73] Gottwald 1979A:911.

[74] Gottwald 1979A:93.

[75] Gottwald 1979A:95.

[76] Cf. Gottwald 1979A:293-337. Just as Mendenhall seems to have a favorite anthropologist (F.R. Service), Gottwald also seems to be especially interested in the approach of a single figure, namely M.H. Fried, and in particular that of Fried 1967. On this see Gottwald 1979A:323-327. Unlike Mendenhall, however, Gottwald is aware of this weakness. Thus he mentions that by no means all of Fried's colleagues would agree with Fried's view of the process which leads to the formation of a tribe. He also points out that Fried's model of social development requires some modification if it is to be useful for reconstructing early Israel.

[77] Gottwald lists three elements which may have made it possible for an Israelite tribal society to emerge in the Palestinian mountainous areas around 1200: the introduction of iron tools; the new technique of lining cisterns; and the new method of cultivation, which entailed terrassing the mountain slopes in order to control the use of the available rainfall.

Israel is based on a considerable knowledge of that part of recent American anthropological research which has studied the relationship between ecological conditions and socio-political development. Two problems accordingly remain to be investigated. The first is whether Gottwald's application of this anthropological knowledge to the study of Israel in the most ancient period is adequate. The second is whether he is in reality completely *au courant* with the studies of primitive, or, better, traditional societies which the cultural sciences have undertaken. I shall return to both of these issues later. On the latter point there is some question as to whether Gottwald's use of a single circle of anthropologists is not too narrow, and requires to be compared with other results of research, which would entail a revision of his theses concerning Israel's most ancient period. As for the first point, the question is whether Gottwald's evaluation and use of the OT sources is other than a mere postulate.

A second phase in the examination of Gottwald's ideas is an investigation to determine whether he always adheres to the domain assumptions he has himself promulgated. Already here it would be appropriate to mention that in the case of his third domain assumption (namely, that one may not isolate late cultural features of a given society and project them back in time in order to elevate them to the status of dominant presuppositions for the birth of the nation), which he accuses Mendenhall of violating, Gottwald himself seems to trespass more than once.

One might also pose the by no means irrelevant question as to whether the religion of ancient Israel was a so "idiosyncratic and mutational" monotheism as Gottwald supposes. After all, it is possible that large sections of the Israelite population did not regard Yahwism as in any sense in fundamental opposition to Canaanite worship. In other words, did religion play any significant part at all in the "Israelite revolt" against the Canaanite dominance during the Early Iron age? In this connection yet another question is quite germane: namely, was the original Israelite population anti-Canaanite at all, so that it virtually instinctively reacted against Canaanite influence, including Canaanite religion? This question has many facets, of which the most important is as follows: was there an Israelite "revolution" at all? Or would it be more correct to speak of an evolution of the political and social pattern of Palestine which only resulted in the appearance of the Israelite state after many centuries? It was this state which the OT, and this means primarily the Deuteronomists and their contemporaries, insists existed from the very beginning. Furthermore, did this evolution in any sense cease with the introduction of the Israelite Monarchy?

To tackle these issues it will be necessary to examine more closely Gottwald's methods and conclusions and to examine the relationship between these and the evidence which may be derived from the OT by analysis. I do not refer to a naive acceptance of the historicity of the witness of the OT. However, European research into Israel's most ancient history has developed very thorough analyses of the OT texts. Of course, it is well known that these very analyses, and indeed their very relevance has been questioned by much recent scholarship, especially in America and Israel. To put the question simply: which scholarly traditions do Mendenhall and Gottwald belong to? Also, what part do the textual sources play for Gottwald, that is, how does he evaluate the results of literary and traditio-historical analysis in relation to his socio-religious argumentation? The issue is whether in his analyses he assigns first priority to the OT sources rather than to arguments deriving from his use of the methods of ancillary disciplines. Alternatively, do the OT materials in reality merely serve as supplements or illustrations of a sociologically-oriented argumentation?

Gottwald himself has hardly presented a completely satisfactory answer to the questions posed above. He comes closest to doing so in an article published in the same year as *The Tribes of Yahweh*, but which was clearly written later than this work[78]. In this article, Gottwald describes what he regards as the difference between historical and sociological methodology: historical method employs literary criticism, form criticism, tradition history, "rhetorical criticism", redaction history, history, history of religions, and Biblical theology, while sociological method is associated with anthropology, sociology, "political science", and economics[79]. However, I think it very likely that most contemporary historians would admit that they, too, make use of the disciplines which Gottwald reserves for the sociological approach to the study of ancient Israel.

Gottwald describes more closely his sociological method in the same article; this consists of the comparison of *entire social systems*, rather than just selected portions of societies. This means that Israelite society is to be analyzed in conjunction with a comparison with other entire comparable systems[80]. Gottwald himself admits the difficulties attendant on this procedure, since, as is well known, we have only a fragmentary knowledge of Israelite society. For this reason Gottwald maintains that we are reduced to proposing a "heuristic" model of the entire Israelite system, in order subsequently to test this model on the basis of the sources, be they written or archeological[81].

By way of conclusion, it is to be emphasized that, like Mendenhall, Gottwald, too, has arrived at his revolution hypothesis on the basis of an understanding of the beginnings of Israel that is wholly traditional[82]. The tendency of his earlier review of Israel's earliest history was characterized by a slight slant towards Alt's understanding of the immigration, in which the general idea was to retain as much of the OT's own self-understanding as possible (although he verged on surrendering the actual concept of a Conquest)[83]. It appears that in 1959 Gottwald assumed the existence of two amphictyonies, a northern "Shechem amphictyony" and a southern

---

[78] Gottwald 1979B.
[79] Gottwald 1979B:69.
[80] Gottwald 1979B:71.
[81] Gottwald 1979B:72. He speaks elsewhere of a "theoretical" model (1979B:73).
[82] Gottwald 1959, esp. pp.160-165.
[83] Cf. Gottwald 1959:162.

"Hebron amphictyony", where the 'former was presumed to have existed from 1500 to 1350 while the latter spanned the period from 1200 to 1100. In this connection, Gottwald's description of the significance of the Moses group is interesting. This people was held to have immigrated around 1230 under the leadership of Joshua, and to have associated itself with the amphictyonic center in Shechem, with the result that elements of the Canaanite (Shechemite) cult began to gain influence on the Yahwistic religion[84]. However, the point of departure for Gottwald's description of the period of the Judges is "the drive of Mosaic Yahwism", a concept which is based upon Albright's account of the religious evolution in this period[85]. Notwithstanding this viewpoint, one also discovers in this description of the period of the Judges the germ of Gottwald's later account in *The Tribes of Yahweh*, since he considers the nomadic culture of the Hebrews and their Yahwistic religion to be in opposition to Canaanite culture and religion, and yet, when he inquires as to what forces could conjoin to unite Israelites and Canaanites, he answers that it was the need to make common cause against external enemies[86]. This stimulus will have come from the Philistines, and its result was the emergence of the Monarchy.

§ 3

The Reception

As mentioned above, the form Mendenhall chose to present his ideas in did not aid the understanding of his intentions. To a certain extent, this is also true of Gottwald, in the sense that he allows himself to be lumped together, or is simply lumped together by others with Mendenhall, in spite of the obvious differences between these two scholars, both with respect to their views and their "scientific foundation". In consequence, the discussion of their respective hypotheses has primarily taken place within American OT circles, while European scholarship has only rarely found it worthwhile to deal with this debate, and in general has followed Weippert's rejection of these conceptions of the origins of Israel[87].

However, two exceptions to this deserve to be mentioned. The first of these was the Czechoslovakian OT scholar, J.Dus, who in 1971 published an article the conclusion of which is an account of Israel's origins which is reminiscent of Mendenhall's on a number of issues, while he differs from him on other[88]. According to Dus, Israel was never in Egypt at all, not even as a minimal "Mosesschar" (which never existed). There was no Exodus; nor did Israel encounter her God on Mt.Sinai, and in fact Moses is not even to be regarded as a historical figure[89]. The historical founder of the religion was Joshua, who united the "Palestinian Hebrews" in their struggle against Canaanite oppression and established Israel as a league of twelve tribes at the diet of Shechem[90]. The Palestinian Hebrews had earlier subsisted as small-cattle nomads outside of

---

[84] Gottwald 1959:164.

[85] Gottwald 1959:165-179; see also Albright: "Israel possessed an unusually powerful centripetal force in the Mosaic tradition" (1963:37).

[86] Cf. Gottwald 1959:166.

[87] Weippert 1967:59ff.

[88] Dus 1971.

[89] Dus reduces Moses to an eponymic figure for the priests serving at the bull sanctuary in Dan (1971:30).

[90] Jos 24 and Exod 19-24 are doublets, according to Dus.

Palestine, but they had been encouraged by the Canaanite *petits rois* – and, possibly, by the Egyptians – to settle in Palestine, where they were accorded land for cultivation. Which is to say, the Israelite immigration was peaceful from its inception. Matters changed, however, after a considerable period of time. The peaceful, centuries-old symbiosis between the Hebrews and the Canaanites gave way to hostilities because of Canaanite oppression. It was at this point that Joshua entered the scene like a *deus ex machina* and unified the previously divided Hebrews. Joshua himself had previously fled to Midian, where he had encountered Yahweh. Subsequently, using the Yahwistic religion as his ideological foundation, Joshua succeeded after his return to Palestine in unifying all of the Palestinian Hebrews in an anti-Canaanite liberation movement. This tradition is held to have been distorted in the OT, since the events have been moved from Palestine to outside of the country (with the exception of the narratives about the struggles with the Canaanites and the subsequent diet in Shechem). This transformation of the scenario took place already in the period of the Judges, "some generations after Joshua's death".

I will not deal with Dus' account here; it has correctly been ignored by scholarship, not least because it raises many more problems than it solves. Moreover, Dus' treatment of the OT tradition reminds one by its arbitrariness of the methods which were current before Alt and Noth introduced a degree of system into the study of the earliest history of Israel. Superficially, Dus' account might seem to be a synthesis between Alt's and Mendenhall's accounts of the origins of Israel. Nevertheless, it is indefensible because of a fatal misinterpretation. Dus namely identifies the Hebrews with small-cattle nomads, which is a completely antiquated attitude towards the Hebrew-problem[91]. Yet another striking weakness is the fact that Dus nowhere offers a reasonable explanation of why the tradition located the Israelite revolt in Egypt, if it in reality had taken place in Palestine. Nor does he explain why Joshua, the hypothetical hero of the revolt, was replaced by a previously virtually unknown local hero, Moses. Finally, it should be noted that, like Mendenhall, Dus simply presupposes the existence of an Israelite amphictyony without more ado.

The second exception is the Italian Assyriologist, M.Liverani, who has expressed himself positively on Mendenhall's basic idea that Israel had arisen because of an internal Palestinian development. Liverani's article appeared in the same year when Weippert published his monograph on the Israelite immigration[92]. Liverani's acceptance of this basic idea is to be seen against the background of his own sketch of an "internal" solution to the problem which he had published two years previously[93]. Now, on the one hand, there are significant differences between Mendenhall's and Liverani's approaches to the problem, while on the other Liverani's contribution is entirely free of the wild speculation which mars Dus' article. Liverani does not focus on the ideological-religious side of the matter. This emphasis is decisive for Mendenhall; it is not, however, for Liverani, not because Liverani is not interested in such matters (as a long series of contributions from his hand which have appeared over the past fifteen years indicates), but because he does not feel that we have sources in the OT which bear on this issue, that is, as far as religious and ideological phenomena around 1200 are concerned[94]. Liverani's own reconstruction is based on the *ḫabiru* phenomenon, which he sees as having exerted a dominant influence in the Middle East during the last part of the Late Bronze age, and as having been produced by turbulent social conditions[95]. The *ḫabiru* were refugees, on Liverani's view. When the concord established between Rameses II and Ḫattušiliš III (1284) ruled out the possibility of crossing the borders into other states, the *ḫabiru* were relegated to nomadic status[96]. Thus

---

[91] See Lemche 1979A; 1980.

[92] Liverani 1967:95. Cf. also Liverani 1976:148 and 154.

[93] Liverani 1965B.

[94] Cf. Liverani 1976:154n, and esp. Liverani 1980, where he points out that the OT does not contain sources about Israel's origins, but only about the views concerning them which were formed at much later periods in Israel's history, and which were probably formulated during the exilic and post-exilic periods (1980:21 – even though one must not overlook Liverani's reservation about being cited in favor of one or the other solution, 1980:31).

[95] 1965B:316f. Cf. also Liverani 1965A, which has to do with the efficient political exploitation of this situation by the kings of Amurru, Abdi-Aširta and his son, Aziru.

[96] Liverani 1965B:332ff.

this movement, in which people participated who had originally been settled, entailed the growth of nomadism in the region, and after the fall of the Egyptian and Hittite empires such nomadic groups returned to a sedentary life form under a new political structure. In Israel's case this took the form of an autonomous tribal league (in company with Mendenhall, Gottwald, and Dus, Liverani has had difficulty in detaching himself from Noth's old hypothesis about the Israelite tribal league, even if he, like Gottwald, refuses to call this an amphictyony)[97].

I shall not address myself to Liverani's contribution to the discussion here. His article was largely ignored, no doubt because of the language barrier, since, like the main part of the works of this important scholar, it was published in Italian[98]. In the conclusion of this treatment I shall offer a sketch of the evolution in Palestine during the second half of the second millenium which in many respects resembles that provided by Liverani's almost twenty-year-old "forgotten" article.

If one were to sample the main lines of the European discussion in order to determine whether the concept of a Hebrew revolt was well or poorly received in the 1970's, it would be appropriate to examine the "histories of Israel" which emerged in the German language area. Such an examination reveals that European scholars were practically untouched by Mendenhall's ideas. The quality of their reception ranges from G.Fohrer's contribution[99], which simply ignores these ideas, to S.Herrmann's mere statement that these "modern ideas" have been rejected by Weippert[100], and, finally, to lukewarm acceptance by A.H.J.Gunneweg. Gunneweg notes that something of the American position can be used to supplement the earlier immigration theories, so that this event may be described as more complex than, e.g., Alt and Noth had imagined[101]. One does not discover in Gunneweg's work any theoretical evaluation of Mendenhall's hypotheses, but this is understandable, since he only knew them in their original form from 1962.

The late French scholar, R.De Vaux, had a completely negative impression of Mendenhall's ideas. However, unlike many of his German colleagues he did exemplify his criticism of them on a number of points which, taken together, were intended to show that Mendenhall's position was untenable[102]. De Vaux asserts above all that this position contradicts the Israelites' own understan-

---

[97] Cf. Liverani 1965B:335.

[98] Although it no doubt has politico-cultural reasons, this situation has nevertheless prevented most OT scholars (and others) from making acquaintance with the very significant research centered around the Institute for the Near East at the University of Rome. This applies especially to Liverani's studies of the Amarna period and the Amarna correspondence, which anyone interested in the earliest history of Israel would find fascinating. Some of Liverani's works have recently been translated into English (Liverani 1979), but far from all of them; moreover, his most important works are still untranslated (e.g. Liverani 1965B, 1967, and 1974, the last-named of which is an intriguing study in which the model of the "suffering servant" is applied to Rib-Addu's correspondence).

[99] Fohrer 1977.

[100] Hermann 1973:129n. Cf. also Thiel 1976:152n (who does not even mention Mendenhall by name). Especially W. Thiel's studies of Israel's earliest history are revealing in this connection, since we find in them virtually all of the usual conventions (Thiel 1976, 1980A, 1980B).

[101] Gunneweg 1972:37 and 39.

[102] De Vaux 1971B:452-454.

ding of their past: that on the one hand they were foreigners to the land of Canaan, while on the other they had previously been nomads. But he also maintains that Mendenhall's views on both nomadism and the concept of "tribe" are fallacious as far as the Semitic world is concerned. This means, if we take De Vaux seriously, that a criticism of the positions of other scholars on the basis of Mendenhall's analysis of the concept of "tribe" is a vain undertaking. The third difficulty is that, on the one hand, Mendenhall entirely too optimistically identifies the Israelites with the Hebrews, while on the other he has misinterpreted the role of the *ḫabiru's* in the Amarna period[103]. The only one of Mendenhall's points which De Vaux feels inclined to retain is the concept of the "Moses group" as the one which imported the Yahwistic religion into Palestine. However, this point was not originally proposed by Mendenhall (although the context in which he places it *is* original).

It is only recently, and even then only in connection with studies in which the emphasis is laid elsewhere, that a few German scholars have concerned themselves somewhat more seriously with the problem complexes which Mendenhall and Gottwald claim require to be dealt with. Two studies may be mentioned for our purposes. The first of these is by B.Zuber, who, however, confines himself to a review of some aspects of the modern discussion on the relationship between nomads and sedentary populations in the Middle East. The other is by F. Crüsemann who, in connection with a work dealing with Israelite attitudes towards the Monarchy in the early days of the united Monarchy, discusses the structure of Israelite society during the period of the Judges without, however, discussing the problems connected with Israel's origins[104].

To return to the reception of the revolution hypothesis launched by Mendenhall and Gottwald, one first discovers a sophisticated response to it in a work published in 1977[105]. However, the attitude towards these theories is by no means univocal. There are significant differences between W.G.Dever's description of the archeological information about Palestine in the second millenium[106] and the understanding of the Israelite immigration tendered by J.M.Miller, and this in spite of the fact that he follows the same evaluation of the archeological picture that Gottwald endorses[107].

Miller's is only a preliminary critique, but he nevertheless does point to a number of difficulties which must first be clarified before Mendenhall's hypo-

---

[103] In this connection it is to be noted that in his later years De Vaux's understanding of *ḫabiru* diverged considerably from that espoused by modern research, in that he was inclined to regard the *ḫabiru* as an ethnic group. Cf. De Vaux 1968 and 1971B:106-112; 205-208. See also my remarks on this (Lemche 1980:175f.).

[104] Zuber 1976:99-138; Crüsemann 1978:194-222.

[105] Hayes and Miller 1977.

[106] Dever 1977.

[107] Miller 1977A.

thesis can be taken seriously. On the theoretical level he hails the fact that from now on it should no longer be possible to overestimate the role played by nomadism in the emergence of Israel. Scholars may not without more ado simply assume that Israel was a society which was created by nomads who had immigrated into the civilized society. However, as he says, the difficulties with Mendenhall's hypothesis are obvious. He limits himself to mentioning three important factors which require closer examination:

First is the question as to whether Mendenhall does not oversimplify the relationships among 'apiru, Hebrews, and Israelites, so that he for practical purposes treats them as synonyms.

The second is whether the concept of a "peasants' revolt" is not a modern invention which has been superimposed upon the Biblical materials without concern for their special character. Miller also asks whether the idea of a peasants' revolt is in any sense more convincing than the idea of intrusive nomads.

The third question concerns the relationship between Mendenhall's peasants' revolt model and the Biblical materials, which state that Israel came into Palestine from somewhere else. In other words, what are we to make of the fundamental Israelite self-understanding, that the people were not autochthonous?

Miller's reconstruction of the course of the immigration shows that he has not come much farther than Alt, in spite of his insight into the modern discussion of nomadism. In reality, he still feels that Israel came into being thanks to the intrusion of nomadic groups. He admits that the situation was extremely complex, and holds that the formation of the tribes first took place in Palestine; nevertheless, what actually happened was a movement from outside into the civilized land[108].

The most differentiated critique until the present was expressed in a dialogue published in the *Journal for the Study of the Old Testament* in 1978. Here first Mendenhall's and then Gottwald's theories are dismissed in contributions by A.J.Hauser and T.L.Thompson, respectively; rejoinders from both Mendenhall and Gottwald are published in the same issue[109]. Hauser's arguments are formulated in ten points for which he requires to be satisfied, if the revolution hypothesis is to survive as a serious theory, although Hauser himself feels that, taken together, his arguments practically destroy the theory. These points are as follows[110]:

---

[108] Miller 1977A:279ff.

[109] Hauser 1978A,B,C. Also Thompson 1978A. Mendenhall's reply, as well as its form, which rules out the very possibility of dialogue with him, has been mentioned above, but Gottwald's response is important and substantive.

[110] Hauser 1978A:13-14. Unfortunately, Hauser's criticisms are solely directed against Mendenhall, because Gottwald, who in scientific terms is far more interesting was still "hiding" his promised account of the revolution hypothesis.

The first is an attack on Mendenhall's "cyclical" view of history, as expressed in his book, *The Tenth Generation:* the claim that revolutionary and social tumult occurs in a given civilization with a surprising regularity, namely every tenth generation. It is childsplay for Hauser to demolish this "theory", which can scarcely be dignified with the term "philosophy of history", since it is rather historical mysticism[111]. Nor does Gottwald in his reply to Hauser attempt to defend this superfluous element in Mendenhall's revolution hypothesis[112].

Second, according to Hauser Mendenhall places far too much emphasis on material presuppositions as determinants of human history, so that he does not allow sufficient room to the complexity of Israel's history and religion. In the subsequent discussion it is probably on this point that Hauser himself is most seriously criticized by both Thompson and Gottwald[113]. Thompsom explicitly reprimands Hauser for his lack of respect for the importance of socio-economic factors as guides to the study of ancient Israel's history. Moreover, somewhat ironically, he simultaneously also accuses both Mendenhall and Gottwald for not taking sociology sufficiently seriously (i.e., because of their mixing together of sociology and religion). Hauser in fact gives way on this point, and states that while one may not dismiss socio-economic factors, neither may one make uncontrolled use of them, which is to say, without reference to other aspects of the culture in question[114].

Third, Hauser claims that Mendenhall's understanding of the content of Israelite religion is so narrow that it is reduced to a question of ethics. This indicates that Mendenhall fails to realize that there may have been other aspects of ancient Israelite religion which contributed to the formation of the Israelite social system. Gottwald mainly agrees with Hauser on this issue[115]. He says that Mendenhall confuses several elements in focusing to such an extent on the ethical aspect of the religion. Moreover, he interprets this ethical aspect onesidedly, as if it was solely concerned with the fair apportionment of material goods between individuals. Furthermore, he then associates this principle of equality with Yahweh's claim to be lord of all such material necessities[116]. Finally, Gottwald claims, Mendenhall has confused the relationship

---

[111] Cf. Mendenhall 1973:215-226; reiterated in Mendenhall 1976A.

[112] Gottwald 1978:37f.

[113] Thompson 1978A:20f.; Gottwald 1978:38f.

[114] Hauser 1978B:35.

[115] Gottwald 1978:39f.

[116] Cf. Mendenhall 1973:1-31. In this connection Hauser's suggestion that Mendenhall's original for this view of early Israel was not recent sociological research in this area, but ideas borrowed from the Social Gospel Movement (1978A:7ff.). Mendenhall reacts sharply to this suggestion (1978:29). The fact that Hauser is nevertheless on to something here can be seen from another of Mendenhall's works (1975), in which he claims that his sociological insights into the history of the emergence of Israel "is not only revolutionary so far as biblical studies and theology are concerned, it is potentially of crucial importance to the survival of modern civilization and its dense population." Of course, the question as to whether OT studies are to be used to

between a sociological theory, the task of which is to explain the character of a society, and the self-understanding expressed by the society under study[117].

The fourth point is somewhat related to the second criticism of Mendenhall. Mendenhall's method for studying the history of Israel leads him, according to Hauser (in a subsequent remark he addresses the same criticism, though more hesitantly, to Gottwald)[118], to underrate the Biblical traditions so that he interprets them in the light of modern views without consideration of their own witness. He points out that the Biblical traditions are, in the last analysis, the only *substantial* mass of source material available which deals with Israel's origin in Palestine[119]. Both Thompson and Gottwald contest this point with Hauser; Thompson does so on the basis of archeological arguments[120], while Gottwald does so on the basis of the Biblical materials, which leads us to his reply to Hauser's fifth point:

The Biblical sources do not mention with so much as a single word anything which might be taken to substantiate the notion of a "peasants' revolt". Gottwald attempts to defend against this charge by referring to several texts, such as Num 21:27b-30; Josh 12:9-24; 24; and Num 25[121]. In so doing, however, he is on the verge of putting his own neck in the noose, as Hauser indeed points out, since none of these passages can qualify as *prima facie* evidence capable of "proving" or of establishing the probability that a "peasants' revolt" had once taken place. It is only when one has decided on the correctness of this hypothesis that the texts in question can be interpreted in such a way as to support the hypothesis[122]. Anyone who doubts the validity of this argument should take the trouble to read Mendenhall's analysis of the episode at Ba'al-Peor in Num 25[123].

Hauser comes more explicitly to grips with specific details in Mendenhall's hypotheses in the following points:

"save the world" lies beyond the purposes of this treatment and will not be mentioned further; Mendenhall's words should be allowed to speak for themselves.

[117] Gottwald 1978:39. On the other hand Gottwald emphasizes precisely the methodological necessity to distinguish between the investigation of the origins of a society from that society's self-understanding (cf. Gottwald 1978:51n). This distinction becomes crucial when we consider the Biblical materials, since in the last instance they reflect the views of a much later Israelite society of its own origin and history.

[118] Hauser 1978C:47f.

[119] Hauser 1978A:10.

[120] Thompson 1978A:20f.

[121] Gottwald 1978:41.

[122] See Hauser 1978C:49n. The list in Jos 12,9-24 is significant in this respect. It is conceivable that it contains an ancient list of Canaanite kings; however, see Fritz 1969. V. Fritz denies that the list derives from the Late Bronze Age, since it includes localities which did not exist then (such as Arad). He therefore maintains that it is a town list from the time of Solomon which was secondarily reworked into a kinglist. Note also that the framework of the list is young, that is, probably Deuteronomistic (cf. Noth 1953A:71f.; repeated by Soggin 1970:109f.). This means that it was first when the framework was put in that the list came to be a sequence of conquered *kings*.

[123] Mendenhall 1973:105-121.

Since the conjectural peasants' revolt is supposed to have been directed against the Canaanite city-states, Hauser finds it strange that the areas where the Israelites in fact settled actually lay outside of such areas. Here Gottwald is forced to modify his and Mendenhall's revolution hypotheses, even though he attempts to explain this point away with the claim that if a revolution takes place in a Canaanite city-state, there is no guarantee that it will succeed. Thus many of them will no doubt have been suppressed by the Canaanite over-lords[124]. On this point it is clear that Gottwald practically presents us with an *argumentum e silentio:* since we have no information as to peasant revolts against the Canaanite city-states in the plains, such revolts will no doubt have taken place, but they were unsuccessful.

Gottwald's next remark, however, represents an important change with respect to Mendenhall's revolution model. While Mendenhall had conceived of the revolution as a once-and-for-all event, Gottwald is well aware that this view is untenable. Thus he maintains instead that the revolution was a lengthy process involving numerous reverses of fortune. It was finally completed when David assumed power and subdued the Canaanites definitively, but by the same token it was also the very heart of the revolutionary impulse in the Israelite movement, while this persisted. The reason the Israelites established themselves in the border territories of the Canaanite city-states was the collision between the disorganized revolutionaries and the solidly entrenched forces of order. For this reason peasants' revolts have a tendency to spread out away from the center in a state undergoing revolution[125]. In reality Gottwald is in close agreement with Hauser on this point, for which reason he also accepts Hauser's next critical objection:

That the Book of Judges and especially Jdg 1 demonstrates that the Israelite conquest of Palestine was a lengthy process which was carried out by the various tribes individually; this in turn leads to the next objection[126]:

That Mendenhall overestimates the degree of Israelite unity evident during the emergence of Israel and the beginnings of her history, an objection with which Gottwald is in full accord. At the same time Gottwald holds that this lack of cohesion on the part of the Israelites was nothing extraordinary; rather, it is the rule in the formation of confederations. In such processes unity is the result of a historical process of considerable duration[127].

Hauser's ninth point is that with respect to the divisions among the Israe-

---

[124] Gottwald 1978:42f.

[125] Gottwald 1978:44.

[126] Gottwald 1978:44. Note especially Gottwald's commentary on Jdg 1, and particularly the use of the verb ישב in this chapter. Gottwald suggests that it means "rule" or "dominate" instead of the more usual "dwell" or "reside". He refers to studies of ישב by F.M. Cross and D.N. Freedman (1955), and by W.G.E. Watson (1970); cf. Gottwald 1978:42f., and Gottwald 1979A:512ff. However, it would be correct to emphasize, as Hauser does, that this understanding of ישב is a result of exegetical necessity in connection with Gottwald's understanding of Jdg 1.

[127] Gottwald 1978:44f.

lites the Canaanite states were more than strong enough to resist the Israelite pressure. The burden of this objection is that Mendenhall has underestimated the strength of the Canaanite city-states. Here, too, Gottwald's reply signifies a modification of the revolution hypothesis, since he is once again forced to claim that Israel became the dominant political factor in Palestine, though only as the first phase of a lengthy evolution.

Finally, Hauser feels that Mendenhall has misunderstood the *ḫabiru* problem, in that he claims that the meaning of the phenomenon for the emergence of Israel had to do with a massive "withdrawal" of the peasantry in favor of an existence as *ḫabiru*. Hauser mentions the Amarna Letters in this connection and claims that they do not substantiate this view of Mendenhall's. The view does not even apply to the problems between Rib-Addu and the kings of Amurru, since Rib-Addu's "peasants" do not abandon their lord in favor of a life as *ḫabiru*, but to serve another king[128]. Although Gottwald modifies Mendenhall's understanding of the *ḫabiru*[129], there is some question as to whether Hauser really has grasped the essence of the *ḫabiru* problem. Hauser has, among other things, misunderstood the basis of the contention between Rib-Addu and the kings of Amurru, since these kings did not rule over a city-state like Rib-Addu's but over a larger geographical territory. Moreover, their appeal to Rib-Addu's subjects presumably contained a promise of social improvement. Nor does Hauser consider that in actual fact one became a *ḫabiru* from the moment one abandoned his hometown and sought refuge in another state, or in "no-man's land"[130]. Hauser has also failed to see that, rightly or wrongly, Mendenhall supposes that the designation "*ḫabiru*" was applied to people who were not *ḫabiru* in any technical sense, but who were simply regarded as rebels[131].

Thompson's criticisms of the revolution hypothesis supplement Hauser's ten objections on a number of points. Thompson's first two objections address themselves directly to the heart of Mendenhall's and Gottwald's positions: namely, the role of the nomads. Thompson asserts that Mendenhall and Gottwald have incorrectly made use of the materials from Mari to shed light on the situation in Palestine. The ecological presuppositions for nomadism in Mari were almost unimaginably different from those in Palestine, so the respective types of nomadism will also have differed. Mari was characterized by the dualism between the wide open steppes and the level cultivated land down by the Euphrates. Palestine, on the other hand, is a completely different landscape containing mountains and valleys, with steppes only on the borders of the territory.

---

[128] On this point see Hauser 1978A:12f.

[129] Gottwald 1978:46.

[130] Note also J. Bottéro's definition of *ḫabiru* as "refugee" (1954:194).

[131] More correctly, he limits the use of the term in the Amarna letters to apply to kings and their subjects when they were in revolt against the Egyptian overlordship.

This also applies to the question of "transhumance pastoralism". Thompson says outright that Mendenhall's and Gottwald's understanding of this concept, and especially of conditions in Palestine, is so deficient that there is no reason to believe their claim that nomadism was not active in the emergence of Israel. Although Gottwald does not acknowledge the justice of Thompson's criticism of his own and Mendenhall's use of the materials from Mari, he nevertheless once again modifies his revolution hypothesis. Gottwald now feels that the hypothesis cannot rule out the arrival in Palestine of other groups, such as for example, pastoral nomads from Syria or other areas[132].

The last element in Thompson's criticism has to do with Gottwald's and Mendenhall's understanding of the social conditions in the Canaanite states in Palestine. Unlike the Syrian states in Palestine there were many, often quite small, units, in which in reality individual towns were little more than fortified villages. The economic basis of such states was clearly agriculture. Two other conditions are essential to an understanding of the social process in Palestine during the Late Bronze age. Unlike what archeology has shown to be the case in the Middle Bronze age, in the Late Bronze age period in Palestine there existed no more a great number of unfortified dwelling places outside of the urban centers. This seems to imply that the contradiction between city and village which Mendenhall and Gottwald presuppose did not exist in Palestine during the Late Bronze age. In short, the hypothetical social polarization is a phantom. If we go on into the Early Iron age there is clear evidence of the Israelites' presence outside of the traditional Canaanite city-states. Such evidence takes the form of a number of (usually) unfortified settlements in marginal areas like the Shephelah, the central-Palestinian mountain regions, and so forth. The very organization of these small societies, as well as the considerable technological feat necessary to establish agriculture in such areas, indicates that in those days such societies must have been dominated by a centralized power center capable of maintaining the peace[133].

Gottwald has little difficulty in dismissing this aspect of Thompson's criticism[134]. While he is willing to surrender the idea of a polarization between city and village, he replaces it with the notion of a polarization between a have-not proletariat in the cities and the owners of the great estates, or capitalists, if you will. According to this scenario, it is no longer a case of peasants who rebel against their feudal lords, but of possessionless farm laborers, who revolt against their employers. Against Thompson's point concerning the new settlements Gottwald merely remarks that they by no means contradict the revolution hypothesis, but support it, since it was in precisely such areas one would

---

[132] Gottwald 1978:48.
[133] Thompson 1978A:24ff. Thompson was in a position to be able to refer to his own survey of settlement conditions in Palestine during the Late Bronze Age (1979). With respect to new settlements in the Early Iron Age, see below, pp. 401ff.
[134] Gottwald 1978:49f.

expect the creation of new settlements as a result of the rebellions against the
Canaanite states in the plains.

It is regrettable that the debate cited above took place prior to the publication of Gottwald's *The Tribes of Yahweh*. The publication of this work would lead
us to expect that more extensive discussion will arise, but up to this point very
little in this direction has seen the light of day. Moreover, the little that has been
published (up to mid-1982) has been predominantly positive towards Gottwald's account[135]. Here I shall confine myself to a brief discussion of G.R.
Brandfon's "mild" criticism[136]. Brandfon singles out four basic points in
Gottwald's discussion for closer study. His first has to do with "the revolt
model". On this issue Brandfon is basically in agreement with Gottwald, but
nevertheless asks the justifiable question, why? The question seems to hang
somewhat in the air, since Gottwald never answers it satisfactorily, which in
turn has to do with Gottwald's unsatisfactory description of the Canaanite
societies and their evolution during the close of the Late Bronze age[137]. The
problem is not, however, that Brandfon is in the right (although he is at least
in theory), but that up to this point we do not have sufficient sources to inform
us as to the social development of *Palestinian* society during the Late Bronze
age. I have attempted elsewhere to describe the background for the emergence
of the *ḫabiru* groups in this period; but I am forced to admit that as far as Palestine is concerned during the period between Amarna and the formation of
the Israelite state we are for the most part reduced to guesses because of the
lack of *written* sources[138].

Brandfon's second point has to do with the Israelite tribal league. Brandfon
acknowledges the relevance of Gottwald's criticism of Noth's amphictyony hypothesis and praises him for replacing it with a more"complex" model. Here
Brandfon mentions that Gottwald thinks to have shifted from a historical evaluation of his sources to a sociological one. But in this connection Brandfon
asks whether we have criteria which would allow us to differentiate between a
source which is appropriate to sociological analysis and one which is suitable
for historical analysis[139]. The question arises because Gottwald owes us an
explanation as to how he arrives at his sociological solutions. As we shall see
below, this is a central issue in the criticism of Gottwald's use of the OT sources. Gottwald never replies to this fundamentally important question, and one
is tempted to suppose that this is because he has chosen his sociological model
prior to undertaking his sociological analysis of the sources[140].

---

[135] Cf.e.g. Christensen 1980.

[136] Brandfon 1981.

[137] Brandfon 1981:104-105.

[138] Cf. Lemche 1979A:3ff. The same applies to Liverani's corresponding reconstruction of
the flowering of the *ḫabiru* phenomenon towards the end of the Late Bronze Age (1965B).

[139] Brandfon 1981:105-106.

[140] See especially Part II, Chapter 3, below, which contains a detailed criticism of Gottwald's

Brandfon's fourth basic point has to do with the alledged opposition between town society and village society. Here Brandfon has no objection to
Gottwald's understanding of village and city as "antimorphemes", but he does
request some substantiation of this point in the form of archeological evidence
on the development of Palestinian village culture in the Early Iron age. We
shall return to this point later, since Gottwald's understanding of the relationship between city and country can hardly be correct *as far as the Near East is concerned*[141].

Finally, Brandfon finds Gottwald's "materialistic" sociology of religion a
refreshing alternative to the usual "idealistic" approaches to the study of
Israel's religion[142]. However, Brandfon very pertinently asks whether Gottwald is not in reality encumbered by idealistic presuppositions similar to those
of the scholars he criticizes[143]. Here one should recall Hauser's criticism of
Mendenhall and Gottwald for seeking their point of departure in the American "social Gospel" movement. In the next chapter we shall deal with yet
another issue, namely the extent of Mendenhall's and presumably also of
Gottwald's dependence on the "idealistic" attitude towards the study of the
history of Israel's religion of which Albright was the great exponent.

Brandfon's four points are extremely relevant in this context, and in what
follows an attempt will be made to explore the detailed criticisms of the revolution hypothesis more thoroughly. In particular, the logical weakness e.g. in
Gottwald's *The Tribes of Yahweh* will hopefully be made evident. Here it is sufficient to emphasize that the discussion of the revolution hypotheses of Mendenhall and Gottwald up to the present has shown that they are indefensible in
matters of detail. Furthermore, Gottwald in particular has realized, or at least
now publicly states, that the revolution possibly did not have the character
originally attributed to it by Mendenhall.

Nevertheless, the criticisms of these hypotheses have not succeeded in
demolishing these suggestions for a new understanding of Israel's origins, no
matter how many weaknesses in matters of detail they have revealed. To put
it more bluntly, one might say that there are two sets of problems which
require to be dealt with more thoroughly than has been the case so far. First,
it will be essential to examine the process which the OT describes as one of
immigration and conquest, but which many scholars regard as one of slow
infiltration of foreign elements into Palestine, to determine whether it may not
better be described as the result of internal Palestinian developments. If this

---

account of the egalitarian society. In this connection it would be appropriate to ask whether the
extensive use of "heuristic" models does not simply invite such a procedure. Are they not really
mere Procrustes' beds which require that the object of study be cut down in order to fit, rather
than fruitful starting points for detailed analyses?

[141] See Part II, Chapter 2.
[142] Brandfon 1981:103.
[143] Brandfon 1981:108-109.

investigation should demonstrate that such an internal evolution is conceivable or provides a more probable explanation than the previous immigration model does, then the next step in this investigation will be an analysis of the various stages in this process. Thus we should be in a position to determine whether the process may be correctly described as a revolution, or whether it would be better to speak of a gradual evolution.

I mentioned above that there are some unclear points in Gottwald's account, such as his understanding of the pre-monarchical Israel and his reasons for holdning that the process which led to the Israel of the OT (i.e., the picture of Israel in the OT) was completed by the introduction of the Monarchy into Israel. Similarly, Gottwald, Mendenhall, and their critics simply assume that Yahwism was the sole or at least a dominant factor in Israel from the very moment this society first appeared on the historical scene. In the opinion of this writer, none of these points has been corroborated to such a degree that we are justified in regarding them as *a priori* truths. As mentioned above, these assumptions seem to be the result of the third *domain assumption* which Gottwald himself has rejected, namely the tendency to isolate specific features of a given society at the expense of others.

However, before it will be possible to examine the revolution hypothesis in detail, it will be necessary first to consider the state of scholarly research out of which the revolution hypothesis arose. In other words, we shall now turn to the older understandings of the origins of Israel to establish a foundation which will enable us to evaluate the revolution hypotheses of Mendenhall and Gottwald.

Chapter 2

IMMIGRATION OR CONQUEST

§ 1

A.Alt and M.Noth: the Immigration of Israelite Semi-Nomads into Palestine

The objections of both Mendenhall and Gottwald to the concept of an Israelite "immigration" as proposed by earlier scholarship was founded on the charge that such scholarship either ignored or was not sufficiently informed about sociology and anthropology. Against this, the critics of both Mendenhall and Gottwald have attempted to demonstrate that not only is their criticism wide of the mark, it also makes use of an oversimplified understanding of the views of scholars like Alt and Noth concerning the immigration. They are furthermore accused of oversimplifying the significance of nomadism in the Orient in ancient (and perhaps also in modern) times. Thus T.L.Thompson claims that the polemics of Mendenhall and Gottwald are not actually aimed at Alt and Noth, as they affect rather positions embraced by such earlier scholars as C.Steuernagel[1].

Thus there is reason once again to subject the accused, that is, Alt and Noth, to closer scrutiny in order to determine what they actually wrote about these questions, even if a thorough examination of this subject already exists[2]. It would naturally also be a good idea to let the accused themselves take the floor in their own defense. The rationale for this is that even if such a review will not contribute to a new understanding of the problems connected with the immigration, it will at least serve to clarify the extent of correspondence between the views of Alt and Noth on the immigration and the apparently antiquated domain assumptions which Mendenhall and Gottwald maintain have misled them.

Mendenhall emphasizes two elements he finds to be present in the *"ideal model"* of Alt and Noth. First, they assume that nomadic tribes continually long to settle down; and, second, they presuppose the invasion of the civilized country by barbaric hordes. In connection with Israel this means that the twelve tribes entered Palestine from without, that is, that they were originally

---

[1] Thompson 1978A:21 (with reference to Steuernagel 1901). However, it should not be forgotten that Alt did not "invent" the semi-nomads. The notion of the Israelites as small-cattle nomads had been expressed many years before Alt's immigration studies appeared, as, for example, by Wellhausen 1894:39 (in contradistinction to the Midianite camel nomads).

[2] Weippert 1967:14-51.

nomads or semi-nomads, and that the solidarity between the Israelite tribes was based on ethnic considerations.

For his part, Gottwald mentions as causes of the antiquated domain assumptions in question that earlier scholarship simply did not know enough about sociology and anthropology. Thus earlier researchers were captivated by three antiquated domain assumptions: first, that sociopolitical changes are caused by the entrance of foreign elements; second, that the Semites were originally nomads who dwelled in the desert; and third, that scholars were prone to emphasize a single cultural characteristic at the expense of others which were perhaps equally important to the society.

With respect to the first general accusation, namely that Alt and Noth were not sufficiently familiar with the results of sociology and anthropology, it should be stressed that this objection is not very cogently formulated. The problem is rather that the positions within the two disciplines mentioned to which Alt and Noth adhered have largely been abandoned today. One might alternatively maintain that the critics of Alt and Noth are dependent upon different branches of the disciplines in question.

To begin with sociology, both Noth and Alt acknowledged their indebtedness to the great German sociologist M.Weber, even if they ordinarily only indirectly made use of his conclusions. Without going into detail, it is at least obvious that the accusations against the German research that took place between the two world wars for lacking sociological insight was only possible because of ignorance of the critics. The critics were not abreast of the general situatibn of the cultural sciences in Germany; they were unaware of the extensive influence on these disciplines exerted by the works of Weber, on the one hand, and by the so-called *"Kulturkreis"* theory, which dominated German-language ethnography in this period, on the other. The critics themselves were academically rooted in Anglo-Saxon, and in particular, American sociological and anthropological research, and were in fact isolated from the German tradition. Weber does not seem to have become important for American social anthropology until after the Second World War. During the period in question American anthropology was dependent upon a research tradition within these disciplines which was rooted in the earlier French sociological thought, in particular as represented by E.Durkheim.

Weber himself had contributed significantly to the study of Israelite society[3]. However, as of this date no one has undertaken a thorough analysis of Weber's studies of Israelite history and society and attempted to relate them to the rest of his sociological research. Nor has anyone as yet satisfactorily accounted for Weber's significance for OT research. As far as I am aware only a pair of short studies by J.A.Holstein and D.L.Petersen[4] have addressed themselves to this subject. One of the points made in Holstein's article is that in general those OT scholars who

---

[3] Weber 1921.
[4] Holstein 1975; Petersen 1979.

have claimed the authority of Weber in support of their own positions have scarcely interpreted him correctly, and that on decisive issues they have simply misunderstood his intentions. This applies, for example, to the question of the "charismatic leader". Petersen mainly provides us with a lengthy account of Weber's understanding of ancient Israel, but he unfortunately fails to evaluate Weber's significance for OT scholars since Weber. It should be parenthetically mentioned that, as presented by Petersen, Weber is virtually to be acclaimed as the father of the revolution hypothesis[5]. The previous lack of interest in Max Weber which was characteristic of the English-speaking world is characterized by the fact that very little of his written production was translated before the Second World War[6]. Among American OT scholars, on this question as well as on so many others, Albright was not like the rest, even if it is doubtful that he knew other works by Weber than his investigation of Israel[7].

In this period German ethnology was completely dominated by the adherents of the *"Kulturkreis"* theories. With the exception of individual figures like F.Graebner and W.Schmidt, these theories led scholars into irresponsible speculations which discredited German scholarship elsewhere. *"Kulturkreis"* theories basically maintain that cultural and material products are only "invented" once, and at a single site *(monogenesis)*, after which they pass by diffusion into other cultures. In practice this approach virtually became a German philosophy of history. German scholarship derived extremely wide-ranging consequences from these theories, and in their most grotesque form they developed into racialism pure and simple[8]. However, none of this prevented the German and Austrian scholarship of the day from producing superb ethnographic works, some of which are still of value with respect to the study of the Near East. I refer in particular to works by A.Musil, M.Von Oppenheim, and G.Dalman[9]. In recent years the studies of Musil have awakened renewed interest since they contain a remarkable literary documentation of the self-understanding of the bedouin[10]. Finally, it is imperative that we not forget that the diffusionistic theories contain considerable elements of truth. Practically no culture can be regarded as an isolated quantity; all are interrelated by a network of political, economic, and social factors[11].

All this implies that Alt and Noth are being criticized for not knowing developments within the field of social anthropology which first gained recognition *after* the appearance of their works dealing with Israel's origins. Or, to be more accurate, such works only began to be important for German-language sociology or ethnology at a much later date. In reality this means that such criticisms are wide of their mark. Alt and Noth were both well informed on the sociology and anthropology of their day; thus it would be unfair to criticize them for ignorance of developments they would have been unable to predict. However, this does not entail that the criticisms of Alt and Noth, as such, are

[5] Cf. also Petersen 1979:140-141 on the similarities between Weber and Gottwald.

[6] Note that Weber is not mentioned with as much as a single word by Lowie 1937 (cf. the treatment of Durkheim in the same volume, 1937:156ff.).

[7] Cf. Albright 1957:95, and compare Holstein 1975:176ff.

[8] On this point see Heine-Geldern 1964, as well as the judicious account and criticism by Lowie 1937:177ff. Among recent Scandinavian contributions see that of Nicolaisen 1963A:130ff.

[9] Musil 1907; 1928; Oppenheim 1939; Dalman 1928.

[10] For a new evaluation of this part of Musil's studies, see Meeker 1979.

[11] See Trigger 1978:144ff.and 216ff. Note also the rather positive evaluation of diffusionism by Nicolaisen 1976:225f., to the extent that it is used as a controlled working tool. Also archeologists sometimes react against an exaggerated antidiffusionism (which was itself a healthy reaction against the speculations of the earlier diffusionists; cf. Adams 1968, and Adams, Van Gerven and Levy 1978); thus, for example, Muhly 1980:30.

unwarranted, since they claim that recent developments within the social sciences necessitate a revision of Alt's and Noth's hypotheses. In other words, it is possible that their conclusions deserve to be annulled, not because they were unreasonable in the context in which they once arose, but because, like most scientific theories, they have been overtaken by later developments within the same scientific disciplines.

The same point also applies to the specifically anthropological or ethnological part of Gottwald's and Mendenhall's criticism of Noth and Alt. Once again it is the case that they operated on the basis of views which were acceptable according to the social anthropology of their time. This applies especially to the relationship between nomads and sedentary dwellers in the Orient, and to the question as to the localization of nomadism within the anthropological developmental scheme. On these issues there are differences of nuance with respect to Alt's and Noth's reading in the field of ethnology. One only occasionally discovers a footnote referring to ethnographic studies in Noth's works, while such references are by no means unusual in those of Alt[12]. Probably one of the reasons for Noth's failure in this respect is that he relied on Alt's authority as the main witness to the account he presented in his *Geschichte Israels* of the immigration of the tribes[13]. Thus if one consults other works by Noth, it appears that he was just as well versed in such matters as his teacher, Alt[14].

Thus Gottwald's criticisms of Alt and Noth miss their target. They are either based on an insufficient knowledge of Noth's work as a whole, or else Gottwald disregards the fact mentioned above, that all scientific theories go out of date sooner or later, and that this fact must be considered in one's evaluation of earlier scholars.

I shall return later on to the question of Mendenhall's and Gottwald's knowledge of modern anthropological research. This problem is, however, irrelevant for our present purposes. What is relevant here is an investigation of the views of Alt and Noth concerning the Israelite immigration with respect to the then-current state of anthropology in the German-language tradition during the period 1920-1940[15].

Before proceeding with this examination, however, it must be emphasized that while scholars ordinarily refer to the "school" of Alt and Noth, and while it is undeniable that they were mainly on the same wavelength, these scholars nevertheless did differ with respect to details. By the same token, of the two figures it was mainly Alt who systematically unfolded his theories concerning the process of immigration. Thus it would be reasonable to concentrate in this

---

[12] See the relevant notes in Alt 1939:141ff.
[13] See Noth 1950A:67n.
[14] Thus Noth 1962B:41-44.
[15] I have no intention of ignoring the extent to which they were limited by the horizon of their times. On this point, see Sasson 1981:8ff. Sasson's criticism of them is, however, unduly

investigation mainly on Alt's description of this process. Noth will only be mentioned where he disagrees with Alt or has something additional to say. One might add that where Alt emphasizes the historical analysis of the process of the immigration, Noth's significance resides in his analyses of the literary witnesses to this process. In this respect Noth achieved more than Alt did by way of clarifying the traditio-historical problems connected with the OT traditions concerning the formation of the Israelite state in Palestine. In practice this entailed that while Noth relied heavily on Alt's historical interpretation, Alt himself, especially in his later works, was able to utilize Noth's literary analyses.

The first question which presents itself is that of historical method. Alt himself defined his method as a *"territorialgeschichtliche Fragestellung"*[16]. This choice of method reveals the extent and nature of Alt's orientation with respect to other disciplines than the narrow field of OT scholarship, since in his own time precisely this approach was current in historical research in general[17]. This method requires one to describe the topographical relations of a particular area, that is, the potential for settlement inherent in a given territory. One is further constrained to analyze the information concerning conditions of settlement which is contained in the available historical sources. If one seeks to understand the Israelite immigration correctly, one is obliged to take into account both the topographical (ecological) situation in Palestine and the written (and archeological) evidence relevant to Palestine in the periods both prior to and subsequent to the Israelite immigration. This method is essential, since the only written sources dealing with the Israelite immigration process derive from a period much later than the events such sources attempt to depict[18]. By comparing information about settlement conditions in Palestine both before and after the Israelites' arrival it should be possible to demonstrate the meaning of this immigration for the pattern of settlement in Palestine. Furthermore, retrospectively, it should be possible to say something about the character of the immigration in question.

I shall not devote space here to an account of the source materials employed by Alt. Alt's account has been overtaken by new finds which have changed numerous details. This is, for example, true of Alt's reconstruction of the

---

severe, since how could they possibly have avoided this traditional pitfall, when we consider that *all* historical research is limited by the knowledge available?

[16] Alt 1925B:90.

[17] Alt himself referred to a study of the immigration of Germanic tribes into the Roman provinces (Alt 1925B:90n).

[18] In his two studies of the immigration (1925B; 1939), Alt only rarely mentions archeological problems. This is not because he lacked interest in archeology, but because of the extremely unsatisfactory situation of the excavations in his day. Indeed, Alt states directly that the solution of the archeological problems must be the work of others, once the situation had improved (Alt 1925B:92).

developmental history of the Palestinian city-states during the second millenium, as recorded in his first article on the immigration, which was already
dated by the time his second article had appeared because of the publication
of the Egyptian *execration texts*[19]. Also, the publication of new documents and
of new information, especially archeological, has not slowed since Alt's day.

There are two sizeable collections of written sources relevant to settlement
conditions in Palestine during two periods: the Amarna period, in the first half
of the fourteenth century, and the period of the Judges, in the twelfth to the
eleventh centuries. The documents relevant to the first period are the Amarna
archives, while the OT sources bear on the period of the Judges[20]. The
Amarna letters indicate that during the fourteenth century Palestine was divisible into two zones. One of these was the densely populated plains which were
politically fragmented by a large number of small city-states. The other was
the mountainous regions which were only sparsely populated, and which were
in general beyond the reach of the law and order of the country[21].

Moving down to the period of the Judges, it is apparent that Palestinian
settlement conditions have changed. At this time it is still the case that there
is a noticeable difference between the patterns of settlement on the plains and
in the mountains. However, where large sections of the mountainous regions
were virtually unpopulated in the Amarna period, in the period of the Judges
the same territories contain a league of sedentary tribes named Israel. On the
other hand, settlement conditions in the plains were largely the same in the
period of the Judges and in the Amarna period, even though one significant
alteration of the political picture had come about as a result of the immigration
of the Sea Peoples, that is, the Philistines.

The result of this territorial-historical investigation is clear: during the
period between Amarna and the period of the Judges, about which we have no
information, areas which were once unpopulated have been taken over by
settlers who have established some form of political existence for themselves in
the mountainous regions of Palestine. This was the first conclusion Alt derived
from his written sources. His second conclusion is equally important, namely
that societies in the plains continued their political existence into the period of

---

[19] The first lot were published by K. Sethe a year after Alt's first investigation of the immigration had appeared (Sethe 1926). Ironically enough, a new series was published the year after
Alt's second article on the immigration appeared (Posener 1940). All of these materials have
been studied by Helck 1971:44-67. Alt carried out his own analysis of these materials as early as
1941 (Alt 1941). The latest thorough survey is that of Thompson 1974:98-117.

[20] There are also a few sizeable Egyptian sources, especially the topographical lists which list
the towns and cities which had been "conquered" during the various Pharaohs' Asiatic campaigns. The most important of these is the list of Thutmose III (cf. Simons 1937; Helck 1971:
256ff.; Noth 1971B).

[21] Alt's analysis is actually much more thorough; cf Alt 1925B: 100ff., and see Weippert
1967:23f.

the Judges. The societies of these city-states do not seem to have been influenced by the political developments in the mountain regions, and changes in their status seem to have taken place during the late phase of the period of the Judges and towards the beginning of the history of the Israelite monarchy[22].

Alt's most significant point with respect to an understanding of the Israelite immigration was that the OT picture of a collected and pre-planned Israelite assault upon the land of Canaan which swept away the previous inhabitants with fire and sword lacks all basis in history. In the places where the Israelites established themselves after their immigration there were originally no, or at any rate very few, Canaanites to liquidate. This demonstrates that the OT account of the Israelite Conquest is a fiction. Moreover, this tradition is not unambiguous in the OT itself. To the contrary, it is essential to describe the immigration in a different fashion than that present in the Book of Joshua. It was in this context that Alt attempted to utilize the understanding of nomads and their relationship to civilization that was dominant in his own time[23].

The first and most important presupposition for an analysis of the immigration was a clarification as to the type of nomad of which it was possible to speak. Like Noth at a later time, Alt was fully aware that such nomads could not possibly have been camel nomads, the historical bedouin, since such groups first make their appearance in the sources at an epoch which was long after the latest conceivable date for an Israelite immigration. Thus he concluded that the nomads in question must have been semi-nomads whose most important domestic animal was not the camel, which was first domesticated quite late, but goats and sheep. It was characteristic for these nomads both in past and present that their lifestyle was cyclical. They are not the "free sons of the desert"; rather, they live in an alternating system which entails passage from winter pasturage in the steppes in the marginal regions of Palestine, towards the east and south, to the mountainous regions in the summer.

Alt regarded the Israelite settlement as the result of this annual trek from the steppes into the mountainous territories of Palestine and back again. In the course of time some of the wandering nomadic tribes began to "hang around" within the borders of Palestine and eventually made the transition to another way of life, one which was characterized by primitive agriculture in areas where no one had previously been willing to settle. Subsequently more and more tribal groups followed these pioneers, so that all members of the tribes at last were permanent residents of Palestine[24]. Thus the first phase, which Alt

---

[22] Alt 1925B:100ff.

[23] Alt 1939:141ff.

[24] Alt 1939:151f.

imagined to have taken place over a long period of time, was ended[25]. According to Alt, this was the real period of the *Landnahm.*

This phase was speedily succeeded by that which Alt termed the *Landesausbau*[26], which he held was necessitated by the need to make room for the rapidly growing Israelite population. The previous phase had been characterized by peaceful relations with the indigenous population of the country, which was the natural result of the fact that the Israelites otherwise only occasionally penetrated into previously populated areas, and when they did they established themselves in the marginal regions of the Canaanite states, often in close harmony with them. The new phase, however, was to the contrary characterized by increasing friction between the Israelite tribes and the Canaanites. The competition for land soon led to a regular conflict which was determined by the growing Israelite pressure upon the territories of the Canaanite states.

Once again, this was held to have been a lengthy process, about which we receive some information in the Book of Judges, where Ch.1, in contradistinction to the Book of Joshua, reveals the nature of the relationship between the Israelites and the Canaanites at the beginning. The process came to an end only just prior to the establishment of the monarchy[27].

Alt and Noth were generally in agreement on all these points. There nevertheless remains one point on which Noth apparently went further than did Alt, namely the question as to whether the Israelites who immigrated did so on a tribal basis. Alt seems to have assumed that entire tribes did not settle down all at once, and that it was instead individual clans which decided to remain in Palestine during the winter, more or less independently of each other. He did, however, feel that the Israelite tribes had existed prior to the immigration[28]. Against this, Noth held that the clans which ultimately developed into the Israelite tribes only developed their tribal affiliations after arriving in Palestine. His argumentation for this thesis was not based on any special ethnological knowledge which he did not share with Alt; rather, his view was based upon his analysis of the tribal names. Noth observed that several of the tribes were not named after individuals, that is, after mythical ancestors, but after localities in Palestine. He held this to be unquestionably the case with the tri-

---

[25] In Alt's opinion the immigration may have started as early as the close of the 14th century and ended at the beginning of the period of the Judges (1939:153ff.). Apparently, Noth did not completely agree with this. He appears to have regarded both dates as the extremes of the spectrum, but he personally felt that the immigration itself could not have taken more than a couple of decades (1950A:79). He never explained why it could not have taken longer; moreover, his view does not seem to be essential to his version of the immigration hypothesis.

[26] Alt 1939:137f.

[27] Alt 1939:157.

[28] Alt 1939:141ff.

bes of Judah and Ephraim, and perhaps also Naphtali[29]. But if the tribes were named after Palestinian localities, they must have been established on Palestinian soil. Furthermore, if this was true of three of the Israelite tribes, then it will also have been true of the others[30]. Naturally, both Alt and Noth fully agreed on the later history of the tribes, that is, that not long after they had established themselves in Palestine they joined together in a tribal league (amphictyony).

Up to this point the discussion has only had to do with conditions in West-Jordanian Israel. Alt was generally silent as to the Israelite settlement of the Transjordanian area, and in fact he limited his inquiries to conditions west of the Jordan. On this issue one must turn to Noth in order to find a close description of the process of Israelite settlement[31]. Noth was concerned to a much greater degree than Alt to attempt the settlement of the individual Israelite tribes, whereas Alt was content to work out the broader implications. However, it would be appropriate to ask whether Noth's analysis of the history of the individual tribes did not in reality approach the methods and conclusions achieved by scholars prior to Alt, since, with a very few exceptions, Alt's territorial-historical method can hardly be used to develop more than one description of the general conditions.

However this may be, even if both scholars believed that the Israelites were originally semi-nomads who had trekked into Palestine from the desert to the south and east, Noth was forced by his analyses of the settlement in East Jordan to claim that with a single exception (Gad) the region east of the Jordan was not colonized by the Israelite tribes as part of their crossing of the desert into Palestine. He held instead that this was accomplished by the tribes which had already settled in the area west of the Jordan and who then crossed the Jordan during their *Landesausbau*-phase in an effort to acquire more tribal territory eastwards.

The task remaining to Alt and Noth was to explain the connection between their understanding of the Israelite immigration and the picture preserved by OT tradition of a united Israelite conquest of the land of Canaan. Thus one may emphasize the fact that one of the results of their analyses of the OT immigration tradition was that it forced their contemporaries to revise their conceptions of the immigration. Two main points govern this discussion: first, the demonstration by Alt and Noth that in reality the OT does not contain any tradition about the immigration of all the Israelite tribes. Rather, the tradition

---

[29] It is of lesser importance that, in company with Alt, he felt that the tribe of Ephraim was a secondary fraction formed from the originally larger Joseph tribe (or *"Sippenverband"*) (1950A: 60).

[30] Noth 1950A:71. On this question see also Thiel 1976, who advocates a "both/and" solution.

[31] Noth 1950A:61ff. His basis for this was a number of detailed studies from his own hand (cf. Noth 1941; 1944; 1946; 1953C; 1959).

has a limited perspective, at least in its oldest form. Second, it must be stressed that Jos 1-11, the main source describing Israel's immigration, is nevertheless not the only source on this subject, since the introduction to the Book of Judges must be acknowledged to be an independent source.

Any attempt to regard the Book of Joshua as a "historical account" of the immigration of the Israelite tribes is put to shame by closer analysis of this part of the OT. Already Alt was able to show that the main part of the events described in the first part of the Book of Joshua is only concerned with the tribe of Benjamin. As he maintained, the narratives in Jos 1ff. may at best be regarded as a description of the conquest by this tribe of geographically limited area in central Palestine[32]. Joshua, the hero of the immigration, originally had nothing to do with this cycle of narratives; rather, he was added to it at a later date and described as the leader of the conquest by a collector[33]. Nor are the conquest narratives in the first half of the Book of Joshua genuine historical accounts. Even without consideration of the available archeological data, and even if at least in their earlier works Alt and Noth could not have known that such data seems practically to confirm their theses, their "form-critical" description of the main body of these narratives entailed that they must be seen as etiological legends, which renders their value as historical sources dubious at best[34].

Noth went even further in this direction with his work on the entire Deuteronomistic tradition which both demonstrated its extent as well as its importance for the establishment of the OT understanding of history[35]. Nevertheless, he continued to accept an early date for the collection of the etiological narratives in Jos 1ff., which he believed to have taken place in Gilgal[36]. In Noth's opinion the Benjaminite traditions were also made pan-Israelite at an early date, perhaps as early as the period of the Judges or the time of Saul, when the sanctuary at Gilgal played a very important role. Since this sanctuary continued to serve as a place of pilgrimage well into the period of the

---

[32] Alt 1936:178f.

[33] Noth 1953A:12; see also Noth 1950A:72 and Alt 1936:186f. In brief, the problem is that the oldest form of the Conquest Narrative in Jos 2-9 was only concerned with Benjaminite territory, whereas there is no doubt that Joshua himself was an Ephraimite; see the notice in Jos 24,30. Alt himself noted the difficulties implicit in the theory which scholars before him had advocated, according to which Benjamine was originally part of the greater Rachel tribe, so that it was only after the settlement in Palestine that it became separated from the Joseph tribes (Ephraim and Manasseh). The consequence of this view was simply that Jos 2-9 was the Conquest Narrative of the Rachel tribes. This is impossible, as the geographical horizon of Jos 2-9 is clearly limited to Benjaminite territory alone. Moreover, the description equally clearly "puts the brakes on" when it arrives at the extremeties of this region, as is the case with Ai (Alt 1936:187).

[34] See Alt 1936:182. This definition was derived from Gressmann 1913:127ff.

[35] Noth 1943; see esp. 1943:40ff., and, of course, more thoroughly in Noth 1953A.

[36] Cf. Noth 1953A:11f.

monarchy, Noth proposed that the collector of the pre-Deuteronomistic conquest narratives in the Book of Joshua must be dated to around 900[37]. With the exception of the Benjaminite legends, the rest of the accounts in this part of the Book of Joshua, which pretent to account for the conquest of the rest of Palestine, are best characterized as a desperate attempt to compensate for the fact that the main collection is only concerned with Benjaminite territory. Thus they are presumably secondary to this larger collection; moreover, they realize only poorly the intentions of the collector, since they contain some regrettable lacunae[38].

Noth further maintained that the second part of the Book of Joshua, that is, the catalogue of the tribal borders in Jos 13ff., which might be considered to be a source for Israel's most ancient period, is no homogeneous collection of sources[39]. Both Alt and Noth claimed that the main section of these materials was old, and that it derived from the period prior to the introduction of the monarchy[40]. This list is especially remarkable in that it is by no means complete[41]. On the other hand, the special section dealing with the tribal territory of Judah was to be regarded as very late, and both scholars held that it could scarcely be earlier than the time of Josiah[42]. Thus Noth was surely right to point out that even though the section on the tribal borders could at the earliest have been assembled during the reign of Josiah (but probably later), it was not even a part of the first Deuteronomistic Book of Joshua, but an addition (albeit a Deuteronomistic one) to it[43].

The first chapter of the Book of Judges cannot have formed an integral part of the Deuteronomistic Historical Work, as this was delimited by Noth. This chapter reveals that the understanding of the Israelite immigration promulgated by the Book of Joshua is a fiction. Jdg 1 does not so much affect the *Landnahm*-phase as that of the Landesausbau. However, this chapter also shows that even in the latter period the Israelite tribes failed to function as a collective body. Jdg 1 depicts the individual tribes as acting independently in a histori-

---

[37] Noth 1953A:13. This collector was accordingly the one who added Joshua to the series of narratives. However, Noth also felt that the Benjaminite legends had become pan-Israelite even earlier (1953A:13).

[38] The conquest of both the southern and the northern part of Palestine is described in the summary sections Jos 10,28-43 and 11,1-15. It is quite striking that what were perhaps the most important central parts of Israel, that is, the tribal er territories of Ephraim and Manasseh (the later Samaria), are not even mentioned in the older versions of the Conquest Narrative. Jos 8,30-35 is a secondary notice of Deuteronomistic provenance (Noth 1953A:51). On this see Alt 1936:178f.

[39] Both Alt and Noth performed exhaustive studies of the catalogue of tribal boundaries (Alt 1925A; 1927; cf. Noth 1935). Furthere on this matter below, pp. 285ff.

[40] Cf. Alt 1927:201, and Noth 1953A:14.

[41] Cf. Alt 1927:194. In addition to Levi, there is no information as to the tribal territories of Simeon, Dan, and, seemingly, Issachar.

[42] Cf. Alt 1925A:276ff. Thus also Noth 1953A:14.

[43] Noth 1953A:15. On the Deuteronomistic character of the framework materials in Jos 13ff., see Noth 1943:186.

cally faithful manner. Thus there is no doubt that large parts of Jdg 1 are very old and thus reflect a historical tradition which has not yet been influenced by the systematizing tendencies of the Deuteronomistic historical vision. This also emerges from the fact that Jdg 1 directly contradicts the conception in Jos 1-12 that the conquest took place in one fell swoop, since it informs us that the Israelites were unable to establish themselves in one place or another because the Canaanites who dwelled there were too strong[44].

There is no reason to enlarge on this point, but it should by now be obvious that if Alt's and Noth's analysis of the immigration traditions is mostly correct, then we have no further obligations to the understanding of Israel's earliest history which is preserved by the OT tradition. The most interesting problem in this connection is not so much what these sources have to say about the immigration, but why they have the form they now possess. More precisely, it is more important to discover the time when the concept of a pan-Israelite prehistory arose than it is to determine what this tradition is trying to say. In fact, this conclusion shows that this tradition tells us more about the society that formed it than it tells us about that society's early history.

The same observation is true is we go even farther back into the history of Israel than to the period of Israelite immigration, that is, if we follow Noth's analyses of the Pentateuchal traditions[45]. Noth himself took this step in his *Geschichte Israels*, when he located his description of this phase of Israel's pre-history in his section dealing with Israel in the period of the Judges[46]. He did so on the theory that Israel in the period of the Judges was a more definable quantity, since he in this connection relied upon his amphictyony hypothesis. It should be equally obvious that if the amphictyony hypothesis is taken away, then there is no longer any rationale for describing the prehistory of Israel on the basis of the Israelite "national society" of the period of the Judges. Thus, *without further discussion one would be obliged to point to some other period in Israelite history as the "Sitz im Leben" of the establishment of the tradition about the earliest period.*

By way of recapitulation: the question I posed at the beginning of this chapter was concerned with how Alt and Noth measure up against the criticisms of them tendered by Mendenhall and Gottwald. It has been shown that it would be incorrect to criticize them for *ignorance* of some auxiliary scientific disciplines. In fact, the criticisms in question were based upon a lack of understanding of the status of these disciplines in Germany in the time of Alt and Noth, that is, in the period when they formulated the greater part of their hypotheses concerning Israel's early history. This part of the criticisms is accordingly unfair to the accused.

On the other hand, it is difficult to agree with Thompson's assertion that the

---

[44] Jdg 1,19.21.27-35.
[45] Noth 1948.
[46] Noth 1950A:105-130.

views on nomadism proposed by Alt and Noth differed essentially from the views of other early scholars and so were not affected by a criticism deriving from a contemporary understanding of this sociological phenomenon. Nevertheless, if one seizes on certain isolated elements in the account of nomadism offered by Alt and Noth coupled with their claim as to its significance in connection with the emergence of Israel, it is obvious that they made use of certain basic ideas which are now thought to be doubtful.

This remark applies above all to the view (shared by both scholars) that in the course of time the Semitic nomads came out of the desert as foreigners and entered into the civilized land. Here the basic notion is that the Israelites were *foreigners* with respect to the culture into which they entered. On the other hand, it is uncertain whether Alt and Noth also thought that the Israelites more or less grew up out of the sand in the Syro-Arabian desert, or whether they were speaking of a sociological formation which existed in the marginal areas of the civilized territory, that is, between the desert proper and the civilized land (by which I mean a territory capable of cultivation). Probability favors the first alternative, since it was the view current in the days of Alt and Noth, and this is indirectly confirmed by the fact that they do not discuss the matter, which means that they must have accepted the then-prevalent understanding of nomadism[47].

The next issue which is immediately open to criticism is the understanding of the concept of "tribe" to which both Alt and Noth adhered, and on this issue in particular Mendenhall's early attack in *The Hebrew Conquest* was exceptionally well formulated. This criticism remains true even though, as mentioned above, there are differences between Alt and Noth with respect to the question of the origins of the Israelite tribes. In all important respects, as far as the concept of "tribe" is concerned, they do not seem to have gone any farther than those who preceded them It is also doubtful whether their insights were especially penetrating on the subject of the social process which produced the Israelite tribes and bound them together. Moreover, it is questionable whether they understood what sort of internal development these tribes must have experienced from the time of their immigration until the establishment of the Israelite monarchy, as this development appears like a fly frozen in amber in Noth's amphictyonic model.

On the other hand, it is doubtful whether one can find support in the pronouncements of Noth and Alt for Mendenhall's criticism of them according to which they are supposed to have argued on behalf of Israel's "nomadic" past on the grounds that Israel was a tribal society in the period of the Judges. Here, too, we have to do with a critical intuition which could well be true, although the matter was of no consequence to Alt and Noth, especially since

---

[47] See further below, pp. 90-95 on the significance of this view for the study of social conditions in ancient Israel.

Mendenhall's concept of an evolution within Canaanite society simply never occurred to them. It is more likely that on this issue we have to do with force of circumstance. Both Noth and Alt and all the other OT scholars of their day simply *knew* that Israel came into Palestine from without. In a similar fashion, they also *knew* that Israel was a tribal society which had originated outside of Palestine. This does not entail that they felt some law of nature existed which decreed that all tribal societies have their origins in nomadism. Had they done so, they might just as well have claimed that all tribal societies are foreign to the territory they presently inhabit, which is patently nonsense.

Finally, the last basic idea which governed the views of Noth and Alt (in his later works) concerning ancient Israel, was the concept of the Israelite amphictyony, which they understood as a religious society which already contained most of the elements present in Israelite religion and historical thought at a later date. Here it would be reasonable to recall Gottwald's third domain assumption, that is, that we have to do with a one-sided emphasis on a single aspect of later Israelite culture, namely, the religious factor, which Alt and Noth elevated to the status of a dominant feature already in pre-national Israel. There are immediate and serious consequences for Alt, Noth, and the entire group of scholars who adopted the amphictyony hypothesis if it should prove to be untenable. In this event, the question remaining to be answered is whether it is reasonable to assign the unquestionably idiosyncratic features of late Israelite-Jewish culture back to the period of the Judges. Any period at all in Israel's later history (including the Exile) may be understood as the time when Israel became a unique case in the history of religions. These considerations become even more significant should we follow Alt's and Noth's analysis of the OT traditions concerning the origin of Israel, since this analysis shows that the idiosyncratic features in question can scarcely have played any major part (that is, if they had any importance at all, or were even known) prior to the Israelite immigration into Palestine. Finally, should we conclude that this conception of an immigration is untenable, it will then become obvious that the most pressing task for OT research in future will be to demonstrate the most likely time for the emergence of Israel as a phenomenon unique in the history of religions.

§ 2

W.F.Albright: The Israelite Conquest of Palestine

Any preoccupation with the approach favored by W.F.Albright must primarily concern itself with an introduction to the ideas developed by the leader of the Baltimore school, that is, Albright himself, concerning the origin of Israel.

Admittedly, Albright himself never wrote a history of Israel (if we ignore his popular introduction to L.Finkelstein: *The Jews. Their History, Culture and Religion)*[48]. However, for more than forty years he dealt with the question of Israel's origin in innumerable publications; he was no less concerned with problems concerning the peculiar character of Israelite religion and the historicity of OT tradition. Accounts of these matters by disciples of Albright may be said to contain more concise efforts at historical reconstruction in a traditional sense, but these are far less complicated and lack to a high degree Albright's own broad and visionary perspective[49]. In fact, his disciples' works only rarely constitute more than a simplified reiteration of the main lines of the understanding of the origins of Israel and Israelite religion which we encounter in Albright's own work[50].

Already Weippert's history of research contains an account of the so-called "archeological" explanation of the Baltimore school of the origins of Israel. However, although Weippert's account is reasonably precise, it is limited in its approach to Albright's ideas and does not clarify the basic concepts which governed Albright's scholarly procedure[51]. One way of approaching the problem represented by Albright is nevertheless demonstrated in T.L.Thompson's work on the Abraham tradition, since, whatever else one may feel about Thompson's work, it remains his achievement to have been able to present Albright's basic ideas and to have reviewed them in detail[52].

As anyone who has ever studied Albright's works is well aware, the main difficulty in dealing with them is their enormously broad scope. Both argumentation and documentation relative to Albright's various assertions, which are part of the mosaic of reasons forming the basis of his hypotheses about ancient Israel, are literally derived from the entire ancient Near East. It is not least in arguments having to do with the history of religions that Albright leads us far afield. Here Egyptian, Mesopotamian, Hittite, West Semitic (Canaanite and Ugaritic) and sometimes even early Greek sources are utilized, usually at one and the same time and as elements in the same chain of argumentation; furthermore, Albright generally has his own personal position as to the contents of the individual sources[53]. Albright employs the same method in his

---

[48] The work used here is the revised special edition (Albright 1963).

[49] Compare the account in Bright 1960, which is not far distant from Albright's; nor are there any signs of independence of Albright's views with respect to the use of non-Israelite materials. See also Wright 1957.

[50] This applies to Bright 1960. In Bright 1981 one detects a great deal more uncertainty about what may be affirmed regarding the earliest history of Israel.

[51] Weippert 1967:51-59.

[52] Thompson 1974.

[53] This type of argumentation is omnipresent in Albright's works. My assertion is clearly illustrated in several sections of Albright 1957 (1957:243-249), as in his last major work (Albright 1968:101-122). One could also go as far back as the first of his more survey-like works, namely Albright 1932A:48ff., in which the patriarchal narratives of Genesis are compared without more ado with the Iliad and the Nibelungenlied.

historical-materialistic evaluations, among which it would be appropriate to emphasize his study of the *ḫabiru* problem[54]. On the other hand, he does not seem to have been much interested in socio-anthropological questions; thus he virtually never cites anthropological treatments by his American contemporaries or others. Moreover, this is a curious fact when we note that he displays knowledge of some of the leading ethnographers of his day, such as the Polish-born English scholar, B.Malinowski[55].

Thus we should expect that Albright would be a far more suitable target than Alt and Noth for a criticism for not paying attention to the methods of anthropology and sociology, such as that contained in the works of Mendenhall and Gottwald. However, this is hardly the case. One finds no fundamental criticism of Albright or of his disciples in works by these scholars. There must be some natural explanation for the lack of such an explicit criticism as was the case with the two German scholars mentioned above, but what is it?

In other words, our task for the present is to attempt to examine the basic ideas used by Albright and his disciples as their point of departure for their studies of the history of ancient Israel. Moreover, we shall attempt to demonstrate the relationship obtaining between these basic ideas and the concepts which are fundamental to the accounts of Israel's origins tendered by Mendenhall and Gottwald. Thompson's analysis of Albright's understanding of the patriarchal traditions has revealed that this undertaking is not as simple as one might suppose, since he has shown that Albright is difficult to grasp on a number of points. Thompson succeeded without great effort in demonstrating that there are a number of phases in Albright's understanding of the social location of the patriarchs. The question is whether in all matters Albright diverged from his basic ideas, or whether there were conditions and ideas which he retained and allowed himself to be led by throughout his scientific career.

At least one of Albright's established features was his conviction that in one way or another the Israelites had been represented in Palestine by newly-arrived immigrants since 2000[56]. This means that Albright generally attempted to retain the OT view of the era of the patriarchs as an epoch which preceded Israel's actual emergence and settlement in Palestine, which he took to be an

---

[54] Albright dealt with the *ḫabiru* problem countless times, of which only the most important will be mentioned here: Albright 1961B; 1968; 64-79; 1975:110ff. These three works represent his most developed views on the Hebrews as caravaneers.

[55] Cf. Albright 1957:6, in which Malinowski is mentioned together with A.R. Radcliffe-Brown in a passage in which Albright rejects functionalistic anthropology as irrelevant to the study of the ancient Near Eastern cultures. The section in question is called, rather significantly, I think, *"Toward an Organismic Philosophy of History"* (1957:5-8).

[56] See Albright 1932A:140ff. Already at this time Albright emphasized that Gen 14, which he dated to the 19th century (a date he withdrew later because of his shifting views on the chronology of the second millennium) was one of the main arguments for this. More extensive argumentation for this date is to be found in Albright 1957:236-243; 1961B and 1968:56-64.

event which followed on the sojourn in Egypt. Albright's argumentation for this is well known, and it has been subjected to devastating criticism by Thompson[57]. For our purposes, what is of interest is not the fact that Albright retained an early date for the Biblical patriarchs, and that in order to do so he made use of arguments covering the entire ancient Near East, as well as the OT, but that he was inconsistent in his sociological description of the patriarchs.

Early works by Albright conform to the classical pattern, according to which the patriarchs were nomads or, to use Albright's own term, "donkey-nomads", who had immigrated into Palestine from northern Mesopotamia (the region around Ḥaran) towards the beginning of the second millenium[58]. Albright's reason for assuming that they were donkey-nomads was primarily that it would have been impossible for the patriarchs to employ the camel, since it had not been domesticated in this period[59]. However, he also associated the term with the word *"Hebrew"* in Gen 14,13, where it serves to describe Abraham. It is a consistent feature of all of Albright's works on the patriarchs that he does not detach the OT designation "Hebrews" from the term *ḥabiru*, which in the ancient Near East either designates an ethnic group or else is a sociological term. On the basis of the spelling in Ugaritic and Egyptian, Albright claimed the correct Akkadian reading to be *ḥapiru*. From this, however, he concluded that there must have been a sound change in Hebrew; thus where the original root will have been עפר, it came to be written עבר (which is to say that we have to do with the not unknown exchange of -b- for -p- in the Semitic languages). עפר has the well-known meaning "dust", "earth", which means that when Abraham is termed "the Hebrew" in Gen 14,13, the idea is "the dusty one". Albright felt that the reason for this resided in the fact that Abraham was a nomad, since nomads wander entire days on the dusty steppes and pathways of the Orient[60].

Albright continued to assert this etymological interpretation until the end of his life; he did, however, change the sociological contents of his explanation in significant ways in later treatments in which he seemed to be on the verge of abandoning the notion of Israel's nomadic prehistory. He never offered any

---

[57] Thompson 1974.

[58] Albright 1932A:130ff; cf. p. 131, where the patriarchs are to be compared with the more recent *'arab*, "semi-nomad", and not with the *bedu*, or "pure nomad". Elsewhere Albright is much more cautious with respect to the use of modern parallels from the Middle East (1946: 100f.). On the question of "donkey nomads", see Albright 1946:97 and 1949:206f.

[59] As emphasized by Albright (1932A:96; 1949:206; and 1961B:38). In his later works Albright made use of R. Walz' articles on the taming of camels (Walz 1951;1954).

[60] Albright 1932A:44. At this point Albright still insisted on the reading *khabiru*. His change of opinion was mainly the result of the spelling *'-p-r* in the Ugaritic texts, to which Albright made reference in connection with his own studies of the Egyptian form (in Albright 1934:42; see also 1957:240 and n.54, plus 1968:65f. and 1975:111).

extensive explanation for his change of opinion, but merely stated that recent studies of the patriarchs had made such revision necessary[61]. It is accordingly only by supposition that we may conclude that Albright had realized that his original understanding of the patriarchs was unreasonable, in that it would not be incorrect to maintain that his was a somewhat peculiar conception of nomadism. Among nomads the only role played by the ass has been its function as pack animal. Later, after its domestication the camel either served as a supplement to the ass, sheep, and goats, or it more or less replaced them, since the camel is capable of doing double duty as both pack animal and food animal. As I have mentioned, there is no way of knowing whether such considerations were at the root of Albright's thinking, or whether he gradually realized that anthropological research had made questionable the understanding of nomadism which was dominant in Albright's early days, and which he himself had espoused.

Albright appears to have camouflaged his change of attitude, since he claimed that it was the result of new information about the phenomenon of the ḫabiru in the ancient Near East. Thus Abraham and the other patriarchs were not so much to be considered nomads as caravaneers. Their treks from Ur to Ḫaran and from Ḫaran to Canaan reflected, according to Albright, the trade routes which ran from southern Mesopotamia down the fertile crescent into Palestine and Syria[62]. However, this view of the patriarchs is hardly more than a variant of Albright's earlier view. Albright acknowledged that the ḫabiru were not nomads, and thus he simply evolved another explanation of the ḫabiru which still enabled him to maintain, first, that the patriarchs were foreigners who had recently arrived in Palestine at the beginning of the second millenium, and second, that the patriarchal traditions of Genesis inform us about social conditions in the beginning of the second millenium. Thus in Albright's

---

[61] Albright 1961B:36ff. The point of departure here was a number of surveys undertaken by N. Glueck in the Negeb during the 1950's. They were held to reveal the presence of a large number of seasonal settlements dating from MB I (Albright's terminology) which could be taken to provide evidence of the extensive caravan trade in this period. Albright proceeded from this assumption to a general discussion of the caravan trade in the early part of the second millennium. In this discussion Albright associated Abraham with these trade conditions as if the period in question were the only one which could conceivably have had this trade structure (he was aided in this assumption by Gordon 1958; cf. also Gordon 1963). Gen 14,13 made it possible to bridge the gap between Abraham and ʿapiru, since "these caravaneers (i.e., from the 19th century) are known *today as the ʿApiru*, later *ʿAbiráya*, Hebrew *ʿibri*" This allows Albright to conclude that "the writer has collected a mass of evidence...for the equation ʿApiru ='donkeyman, donkey driver, caravaneer'". Elsewhere one finds a different argument on this point; Albright maintains that SA.GAZ were nomads, but not pure nomads, since the women in the SA.GAZ groups produced textiles - indeed, quite an odd conclusion (1968:68). Albright was also able to speak of the "Hebrew tribes" (1968:71), but in this connection it would be appropriate to ask what Albright can possibly have meant by "tribe". Yet another work provides with a wholly different argument: he distinguishes sharply between ʿapiru and *sutu*: "*both were donkey nomads, but the ʿApiru were less nomadic than the sutu*"(1975:111). What can he have meant by this?

[62] Albright 1961B:44f.; cf. also 1963:6ff.and 1968:57ff.

opinion he had succeeded in explaining the scattered references to the *ḫabiru* we find in the entire ancient Near East and in showing that Genesis presents us with historically reliable information.

It is not my intention to criticize here the justifiability of Albright's changed understanding of the patriarchs. However, it should be noted in passing that Albright's view entails both a extremely optimistic evaluation of the value and reliability of the Biblical sources, coupled with an idiosyncratic understanding of the problem of the *ḫabiru*.

Moreover, Albright attempted to find other arguments intended to show the correctness of his claim that our information about the patriarchs derives from a period which was not far removed in time from the era of the patriarchs themselves. This explains why it is difficult merely to isolate a single element of Albright's argumentation, as Weippert does. Everything Albright had to say about the conquest was indissolubly connected to his numerous studies on the literary forms of the OT as well as the history of religions and history, proper, of Israel and the rest of the ancient Near East. His main argument for the great age of the historical traditions was based on *oral tradition*. A number of individual studies of both poetic and prose passages in the Pentateuch led Albright to conclude and to attempt to show that the Pentateuchal traditions were originally formulated in poetry, rather than prose. Poetic or epic form, as Albright claimed, is characteristic oral tradition (for mnemonic reasons). Thus, having demonstrated that the Pentateuchal traditions were originally formulated in epic form, Albright concluded that the original form of these traditions was oral. In this connection he made reference to the large epic works of the ancient Near East, as well as to the Homeric poems; all were lumped together in this category, and an oral background was asserted for them. Above all, Albright concluded, the Homeric poems and the modern confirmations of the reliability of their account of Mycenaean Greece provide us with yet another witness to ability of oral tradition to reproduce historical traditions accurately, in spite of the fact that we should otherwise expect the process of oral transmission to create possibilities for error because of the lack of controls on the materials thus transmitted[63].

In reality, this sort of argumentation is difficult to deal with, even though Albright's disciples have perpetuated his concern with "the earliest Hebrew epic"[64]. What is required is a foundation for the following two hypotheses:

---

[63] On Albright and the epic literature: a general treatment is to be found in Albright 1957: 64-76. On the situation in the OT see Albright 1968:1-46. Albright's contribution was not limited to an attempt to demonstrate that the prose tradition in the patriarchal narratives and similar materials was derived from originally epic narratives. With the aid of comparative studies in Israelite and Oriental, specifically Ugaritic, poetry he attempted to show that a number of the poetic passages which are preserved in the OT in late contexts actually derive from pre-monarchical Israel (cf. Albright 1944; 1950A; 1950B).

[64] See Cross and Freedman 1948, 1955, and, more thoroughly, Cross 1973.

first, that the patriarchal traditions were originally orally transmitted in poetic form, despite the fact that they are now preserved in prose, and, second, that this same oral tradition is just as or even more reliable than written transmission, since we cannot possibly determine whether this is the case. In spite of the fact that these are ideas which are not far removed from the ambit of, for example, Scandinavian traditio-historical research, as it was above all promulgated by I.Engnell, the notion of the reliability of the oral tradition has by no means won general acceptance[65].

Yet another matter of decisive importance for Albright was the credibility of the Mosaic tradition in the OT[66]. The most important implication of Albright's analyses of the history of early Israelite tradition was that this tradition could be taken to be extremely reliable, not just as the instrument of textual transmission, whether oral or written, but also in the sense that the historical traditions thus transmitted were also to be trusted. This means that there is a high degree of correspondence between OT historical tradition and "reality"; the Biblical witness is an invaluable source about the prehistory of the Israelite nation.

Applied to the traditions about Moses and the advent of Yahwistic religion in Israel, this entailed two conclusions for Albright. The first was that Moses was a historical personage, and that the OT biography of him was extremely accurate and credible. The second was that the tradition concerning the revelation at Sinai was to be understood as an expression of the historical experiences garnered by the Israelites after their flight from Egypt[67]. In this connection it was of paramount importance to Albright to demonstrate that Israel or some fraction of what was later to become Israel in fact had resided for a number of years in Egypt as described in Genesis and Exodus[68]. Albright himself connected this sojourn with the Hyksos conquest of Egypt around the middle of the second millenium, but he also emphasized that there was a considerable transit of people from Palestine to Egypt in the form of nomads seeking refuge from famine throughout the entire period of the Middle Kingdom[69].

---

[65] For a brief account of the oral tradition, see below, pp. 381ff.

[66] See Albright 1957:254-257 and 257-272. This is Albright's central account, but note also the constancy of his understanding of the Mosaic tradition by comparing the account in Albright 1932A:151-169 with that in Albright 1968:143ff.

[67] Once again, Albright 1957:254ff. In his later works Albright was influenced by Mendenhall's ideas about the origin of the Israelite covenant tradition in the vassal-treaty system of the Late Bronze Age; see therefore Albright 1968:145f.

[68] Albright 1957:254ff.; 1963:10ff.; 1968:133ff.

[69] On the Hebrews and the Hyksos: thus Albright 1968:133; however, even in this, his last major work, Albright offers no real argument for this position. He mentioned that his work on the Hyksos was not concluded, and that he would publish his analysis in due course. As far as I am aware, this never occurred. A special problem in this connection is Albright's inclusion of the photo-Sinaitic inscriptions from especially Serabî t el-Ḥâdem, concerning which he published several provisional interpretations, the latest of which appeared in 1966. There is also argumentation concerning the Hyksos in Albright 1957:241ff.; cf. already Albright 1932A:143f.

The events which transpired during Israel's sojourn in Egypt were decisive for the Mosaic tradition, with its powerful emphasis on Yahweh as the only god, for it was in precisely this period, that is, in the 14th century, that Egypt herself experienced a monotheistic religious reform[70]. Although we need not therefore conclude that this led Israel to adopt the worship of Aton under the auspices of Amenophis IV, the very fact that this sort of religion appeared at this time shows that the period was conducive to the reception of monotheistic religious initiatives.

The forefathers of the Israelites, that is, the patriarchs, were polytheists, as Alt demonstrated in his work, *Der Gott der Väter*, according to which the individual patriarchs had their own more or less private divinities which were subsequently worshipped by their descendants as their own[71]. After the work of Moses, Israel was a monotheistic society in which Yahweh was the sole and exclusive God of the society[72].

As this section shows, Albright made use of both traditio-historical arguments and arguments based on the history of religions. However, there are few signs of a sociological or anthropological approach, which is explained by the fact that Israel was for Albright and his disciples a unique society in her time. They also regarded Israelite religion to be unique.

The Sinai tradition, which Albright regarded as historical, is supported by mentions of the presence of foreigners in Egypt during the 18th Dynasty, by archeological evidence from the Sinai peninsula, and by information in the OT concerning the Exodus, the journey to Mt.Sinai, and the conquest of Palestine. Thus in Albright's case argumentation on behalf of the historicity of the Mosaic tradition required one to take seriously the traditions in the OT dealing with the Israelite immigration: they are faithful witnesses to events which took place in Palestine towards the end of the 13th century.

The OT narratives about the Israelites' corvée labor in Egypt and their subsequent flight from Egypt were accomodated by Albright to other historical information, thus dating them to the time of Rameses II[73]. In conse-

---

[70] The most important treatment of this subject by Albright is Albright 1957:218ff. At this point there is no reason to concern ourselves more extensively with whether or not Albright's account of the reformation of Amenophis IV is satisfactory. For further information see Aldred 1975, and on the religion of Aton, see Assmann 1973.

[71] Alt 1929. Albright's use of this is to be found, among other places, in Albright 1932A:130; 1957:247f.; 1968:146.

[72] This is the leading motif of Albright 1968, but the question was also important in his earlier works, such as Albright 1946:110-119.

[73] Albright and the chronology are a problem in their own right. Thus we shall not be concerned with these matters here. The reason for Albrights changing views as to the accession date of Rameses II (i.e., 1304 or 1290) is Rowton 1960, who in turn bases his study on analyses published earlier in Rowton 1959. On this basis Albright calculated from an accession date in 1304 to an Exodus which must have taken place in 1297, cf. Albright 1968:138. However, in spite of the fact that W.C. Hayes has accepted the 1304 date (1970:192), it must be acknowledged that the problem of Rameses II's accession to the throne has not yet been solved satisfactorily. Note

quence of this, Albright dated the Exodus to the first part of the reign of Rameses II, and he affirmed the correctness of the course of the flight as depicted
in Exodus. Now and then one discovers a tacit admission in Albright's writings
that the event itself is not mentioned with a single word in the Egyptian sources. This means that Albright was forced to admit that there is no *external evidence* confirming the Israelite Exodus from Egypt during the reign of Rameses
II[74]. In this connection we should note that Albright's position was that
everything was to be accepted until the opposite had been demonstrated.
Accordingly, the lack of Egyptian confirmation cannot prove that the Biblical
account is a-historical. Albright's student, J.Bright, adds further that the histo-
recal Exodus was of so little consequence that Pharasoh had no reason to mention it[75].

The same attitude also furnished the basis for Albright's analysis of the Israelite immigration: what is not demonstrably wrong is necessarily true. In
other words, in Albright's opinion the last century of archeological excavation
in Palestine has demonstrated the credibility of the OT tradition about the
Israelite immigration. However, there are problems in connection with the
individual traditions about the Israelites' activities under the leadership of
Joshua when they returned to Palestine towards the close of the 13th century.
Albright had addressed himself to these difficulties on a number of occasions;
they have arisen because there are a number of disagreements between the
archeological facts and the Biblical story of the conquest as recorded in the
Book of Joshua. Therefore Albright attempted consistently to interpret the
results of excavations in such a way that it is at least possible to retain the concept of the immigration/conquest. Thus, for example, when *Tell es-Sultan*, the
ancient Jericho, demonstrably contains no sign of occupation in precisely this
period, Albright argues that such evidence has been "washed away" by erosion[76]. Similarly, when we discover that Ai, the present *et-Tell*, proves not to
have been inhabited for a millenium when Joshua arrived, Albright argues
that the account in Jos 8 simply has nothing to do with Ai, but with the neighboring Bethel *(Beitin)*, where the excavators have found a destruction layer

---

the criticisms of Rowton's arguments as well as argumentation for a date in 1290 in Hornung
1964:50ff. Thus there is no compelling reason to adhere to Albright's reconstructed date for the
Israelite Exodus (1297/1283).

[74] Cf. also Bright 1960:111: "Of the Exodus itself we have no extra-biblical evidence. But the
Bible's own witness is itself so impressive as to leave little doubt that some such remarkable deli-
verance took place." Bright's attitude towards the Exodus is unchanged in Bright 1981 (indeed,
the quotation has been preserved in 1981:122).

[75] Bright 1960:112 (1981:122).

[76] This explanation recurs frequently in Albright's works, in spite of the fact that Jericho
must be regarded as one of the best excavated tells in Palestine. See thus Albright 1949:109: "The
problem of Jericho has become more obscure since Miss Kenyon's work, which showed that the
Late Bronze level was almost completely denuded by wind and rain during the long abandonment after the conquest." See also below, p. 390 n.

which seems to derive from this period. There has been an exchange of names between Bethel and Ai, so that the conquest of Bethel has now been transferred to Ai[77].

In fact, in general, according to Albright and his disciples, Palestinian archeology reveals numerous layers of destruction which must date from the Israelite conquest of the places in question[78]. They also maintain that we are confronted with a new material culture, as evidenced by a new type of pottery, a new sort of house, plus a materially poorer culture in those regions which were rebuilt after the destruction[79]. According to Albright the last was the result of the fact that in this period Israelite society did not tolerate slavery; all Israelites were free men who might not be compelled to do corvée labor. Thus it was not possible for a collective leadership, whose authority in Israel's earliest period was limited, to re-establish the labor system of the Late Bronze Age, in which state slaves and conscripted local residents were made to construct palaces and fortifications[80].

Nevertheless, Albright did not regard the Israelite conquest as total, as at least one of his students claimed[81]. On the one hand, the Canaanites were not eliminated according to plan, apart from isolated occasions in the beginning of the conquest phase, while on the other hand Israel did not achieve complete control of the country, as the OT claims. Rather, as her later history shows, Israel only reached the ascendancy over the rest of the land of Canaan after laborious wars with the remaining Canaanites over a long period of time.

One area is not mentioned in the conquest traditions: this is the central Palestinian massif, the territories of Ephraim and Manasseh. Albright ignores the problematical aspects of the OT silence about this region and instead stresses that already prior to Joshua's arrival a group of pre-Israelite tribes who were kin to those who had gone down to Egypt dwelled in the region[82]. When their relatives returned, all that remained was for the long-separate groups to be reunited, and for those of Israelite descent, but resident in Palestine, to abandon their own gods and to embrace the Yahwistic religion of the returnees. Having surmounted these difficulties, Israel was in a position to continue as an amphictyony (Albright accepted Noth's hypothesis as the best explanation of the victory of Israel and the Yahwistic religion in the period of the Judges)[83].

---

[77] See Albright 1939; also repeated by Bright 1960:119 (1981:131), and by Wright 1957:80f. Se also below, pp. 398f.

[78] Albright 1939:11ff.; repeated in, for example, Bright 1960: 118ff. Bright is now much more hesitant about this issue (1981:130ff.).

[79] Cf. Albright 1949:119f.

[80] Albright 1949:119.

[81] See his commentary (1963:30ff.).

[82] Albright 1957:277; 1963:32f.

[83] See Albright 1957:281; 1963:36ff., and compare with the thorough-going description of the amphictyony in Bright 1960:142-151. In Bright 1981:144f. the tone has changed; here the

In evaluating Albright's description of Israel's origin, it is of course possible to separate out his ideas about the conquest and confine onself to a study of his archeologically-inspired interpretation. However, this is only one aspect of a critical examination of Albright's understanding of ancient Israel. Yet another step would consist of an evaluation of the way he conceives the transmission of the OT text to have taken place. A third approach would require an evaluation of the anthropological and sociological views Albright espoused. On the other hand, it would simply be wrong to isolate Albright's religio-historical arguments on behalf of the Mosaic tradition, which, as we have seen, were at the root of his account of Moses and the Yahwistic faith, and then to criticize his views on these matters in isolation from his reconstruction of Israel's history. It should be obvious that even if Albright's description of the immigration is inadequate in view of the present status of Palestinian archeology, this does not necessarily entail that his ideas concerning Israel prior to the conquest are incorrect.

On the other hand, there is no question but that there is a real disparity between the results of excavation and the evidence of the OT. It is accordingly necessary to stress that this fact must have consequences for our evaluation of the OT as a historical source, which means that we have arguments which oppose Albright's understanding of these sources. This distrust must also have consequences for our evaluation of the conditions prior to the immigration. Quite impressive arguments would be required in order to convince us that precisely these early traditions are especially reliable, when the younger traditions in the Book of Joshua are marred by serious errors. This in turn means that we should be sceptical of the attempts of Albright and his disciples to avoid a holistic traditio-historical analysis of the OT tradition about ancient Israel. Such an analysis should not merely be concerned with the relationship between the poetic and prose materials of the Pentateuch; it should also attempt to evaluate the significance of the fact that this tradition will in any case first have received its final form at a late date. Finally, and this is the third control to which it is possible to subject Albright's hypothesis, it will be necessary to examine the various sociological types or arguments proposed by him in order to determine whether they are relevant. Naturally, this will apply especially to Albright's understanding of the problem of the *ḥabiru*, which was decisive for his understanding of the patriarchs; but it will also apply to his views on Israel and Egypt in the Late Bronze Age.

Ultimately, there remains the question of the relationship between Albright on the one hand and Mendenhall and Gottwald on the other. Have Mendenhall and Gottwald been influenced so much by Albright that certain of the lat-

---

author directly states that we should avoid use of the term "amphictyony" (1981:163). Nor is there any longer reference to a tightly-organized league of twelve tribes, but to a much looser organization.

ter's basic ideas play a vital role in the theory of the "Hebrew conquest of Palestine"? Here it should be noted in advance that the probability is greater that Albright has influenced Mendenhall than that he has influenced Gottwald, since Mendenhall seems to have belonged to the circle surrounding Albright, as is implied by the fact and nature of his contribution to the Albright Festschrift in 1961[84]. The contribution in question is interesting, in that it appeared as late as the year before Mendenhall's article on *"The Hebrew Conquest"* was published, and yet he still did not make use of the arguments based on sociology and anthropology which characterize the 1962 article. This fact reveals, much as one might expect from a reading of *"The Hebrew Conquest"*, that Mendenhall's original point of departure was the same as Albright's. The basic elements in *"The Hebrew Conquest"* are all present in the article in the Albright Festschrift; like Albright, Mendenhall accepts the great historical worth of the patriarchal traditions, on the assumption that their historicity is supported by an overwhelming mass of external evidence[85]. Mendenhall's article associates the patriarchs with events thought to have taken place in Palestine and the rest of the ancient Near East around 2000. Interestingly, in spite of the fact that in his later works Mendenhall makes a case for not including mass migrations in one's argumentation, there are certain details in *"The Hebrew Conquest"* which show that he nevertheless does so himself when dealing with the OT patriarchs[86]. This suspicion is confirmed by perusal of the article from the preceding year, since we find here considerable agreement with respect to the patriarchs between Mendenhall and Albright, indeed, to such an extent that Mendenhall's account must be described as a variant of Albright's. Mendenhall goes his own way with respect to the *ḥabiru* question, which, however, is not mentioned in the article in the Albright Festschrift, while the patriarchs are directly stated to be semi-nomads[87].

If we go on to the period after the emergence of Israel towards the conclusion of the 13th century, it seems as if the more or less shared view of Mendenhall and Albright on Israel's prehistory from 2000 down to 1300 also entails that they agree closely in their evaluation of early Israel. This applies also to the consolidation of Israelite society as a "period of the Judges", since their

---

[84] Cf. Mendenhall 1961.

[85] Mendenhall 1961:38ff.

[86] Mendenhall 1962:117f. Mendenhall reckons here with a sizeable immigration in the period around 2300-2000 (the Amorite wave), just as Albright does. However, we are then forced to ask what has become of his sociological argumentation, when he practically arbitrarily explains conditions in Palestine at the beginning of the second millennium by the assumption of the intrusion of foreign groups, but denies that this can have been the case in the 13th century? Is it more important for him to retain the Biblical tradition than to adhere to a sound and consistent method?

[87] Mendenhall 1961:39f. Mendenhall compares his pre-Israelites with the *sutu*, but he declines to identify these two terms. As a result, in his 1961 article Mendenhall understands the nomads completely traditionally as new-arrived population groups in Palestine around 2000, with no sign of the claim of "sociology" which resounds in Mendenhall 1962.

understanding of the patriarchs allows them to assume the existence of "pre-Israelite" elements which had been left behind in Palestine when other large groups had gone down to Egypt in connection with the Hyksos movement. This view is most clearly expressed in Mendenhall's article in connection with the covenantal ceremony in Shechem (Jos 24), where only slight differences separate him from Albright; moreover, these are once again details relating to Mendenhall's special understanding of the *ḥabiru* problem[88]. Finally, both scholars accept that the amphictyony hypothesis is the best explanatory model for pre-monarchical Israel. Both utilize this model as "Sitz im Leben" for the establishment of and ultimate cementation of specifically Israelite tradition, and both regard the amphictyony as the most important reason Israel survived as a society distinct from that of the Canaanites[89]. The only major difference between these two scholars resides in their respective evaluations of the *ḥabiru* problem, which, as mentioned, Mendenhall does not regard as an Israelite phenomenon, even though the *ḥabiru* played a decisive role in connection with the creation of Israel in the period of the Judges.The *ḥabiru* were not necessarily of pre-Israelite origin, according to Mendenhall, although Albright seems to have thought the reverse to be the case[90].

Both scholars agree as to the value of the OT tradition. Mendenhall has never formulated any objections to Albright's idea of an originally epic tradition which was later converted to prose, and he accordingly also accepts Albright's "positive" attitude towards the historical source value of these traditions. This agreement continues on into *"The Hebrew Conquest"*, but it is explicitly mentioned in the Festschrift article[91]. In consequence, Mendenhall displays exactly the same confidence in the great age of the Mosaic traditions as Albright, and as a result, like Albright Mendenhall allows this tradition to be the catalyst for pre-monarchical Israel. Thus both Albright and Mendenhall also agree on the view that Israelite tradition was fundamentally different from Canaanite tradition. Moreover, both agree on the peculiar nature of Israelite religion in pre-monarchical times[92]. Thus we are forced to conclude

---

[88] Cf. Mendenhall 1962:107ff.; Albright 1962:37. Albright here admits his debt to Mendenhall's analysis of the covenant tradition (cf. also Albright 1968:145, and Mendenhall 1954A,B); see also Bright 1960:123 and 127 (1981:143).

[89] On Albright, see n.83 above; Mendenhall 1961:42ff.

[90] See p. 5 with respect to Mendenhall's understanding of the *ḥabiru*, and above in this section for Albright's views.

[91] Cf. Mendenhall 1961:38f.

[92] Some doubts are expressed in Mendenhall 1962:110: "The best illustration of the continuity of Canaanite and indeed international patterns of thought is to be found in the covenant itself....". Farther down on the same page we read "Early Israelite tradition everywhere presupposes Canaanite culture as a contrast, *or as the origin of* certain features" (emphasis mine). In reality Mendenhall, Albright (plus disciples), and, for that matter, also Gottwald completely agreed about "the extremely low level of Canaanite religion, which inherited a relatively very primitive mythology and had adopted some of the most demoralizing cultic practices then existing in the Near East". All three scholars feel that this was the most important factor for the early

that Mendenhall's understanding of an Israelite seizure of power in Palestine is largely a variant of Albright's view. This is immediately apparent in Mendenhall's formulation of his hypothesis, as he avoids serious consideration of the archeological evidence. Furthermore, it is indirectly evident in his revision of his own earlier views, when he borrows new arguments from the social anthropologists. However, the result is the same for both scholars, since both are confident that Israel was a unique society possessing a unique and individualistic religion which was innocent of all influence from the sinful Canaanite "religion of violence" and which existed in sharp opposition to it[93].

Precisely the same characterization may be said to apply to Gottwald. However, Gottwald is far more free of the influence of Albright and his disciples and their reconstruction of history than is Mendenhall. However, Gottwald does share the main emphases, namely the accuracy of the Mosaic tradition and the Israelite tribal league during the period of the Judges as the locus which preserved this tradition. Unlike Mendenhall, Gottwald realizes that Albright's use of the archeological sources is now untenable, and that the conceptions of Albright and his disciples about the history of Israelite traditions are entirely too precarious and lack scientific confirmation[94].

Thus Gottwald utilizes M.Noth's analyses of the Pentateuchal traditions, while in reality he rejects Noth's analyses of the Book of Joshua. As a result, Noth's analyses of the Pentateuch are the basis of Gottwald's reconstruction of the Mosaic tradition, but he draws completely different conclusions than Noth does. He understands Noth's localization of these traditions to the amphictyony as a decisive argument in favor of their historical reliability. Noth, however, felt that this Sitz im Leben showed instead that the Pentateuchal sources were of only limited value for the reconstruction of Israelite prehistory.

Unlike Albright and Mendenhall, Gottwald does not feel impelled to accept that the entire Pentateuchal tradition is authentic. Instead, he attempts to provide some criteria to assist in showing which portions derive from the centralized cult of the tribal league, and which are independent of it, that is, have been developed in isolation from it.

It should be clear that in Gottwald's work we encounter a far more sophi-

---

Israelite condemnation of everything Canaanite. The quotation is from Albright 1961A:338. On the same page we are also treated to the following characterization of Canaanite mythology: "The brutality of Canaanite mythology...passes belief....". This basic attitude towards Canaanite culture regularly features in Albright's accounts of Israelite religion versus Canaanite religion. Thus it is hardly strange that in reality Albright never managed to arrive at any real understanding of the Canaanite world.

[93] This has been most extensively treated in Albright 1946:95ff, and especially 1968:133ff. Cf. Mendenhall 1962:107ff. This view is the basis of Mendenhall 1973. Bright's latest description of Israel's prehistory is a perfect illustration of how easy it is to reconcile the views of Albright and Mendenhall (and Gottwald). See Bright 1981.

[94] Cf. Gottwald 1979A:192-203 on the archeological evidence. I shall return to the question of Gottwald and the formation of the Israelite tradition below, pp. 294ff.

sticated picture of the historical beginnings of ancient Israel than any we might hope to find from the hands of Albright and Mendenhall. Mendenhall's position may be attacked from a number of sides, since his account of the earliest period is open to the same objections as those which apply to Albright's historical reconstruction. Moreover, in the later period he is vulnerable for the special use he makes of anthropological arguments. One might also point out that if the issues on which Mendenhall and Albright agree should prove to be fallacious, then Mendenhall's own reconstruction can scarcely be maintained. On the other hand, Gottwald's work must be evaluated separately from that of the other two scholars in spite of the fact that his results resemble those of Albright and Mendenhall. He may only be evaluated with respect to the merits and demerits of his position on the basis of a direct study of his own examinations of the history of Israel.

Excursus:
The Study of Israelite History from J.Wellhausen to A.Alt

It would by no means be superfluous to inquire as to the reasons why Alt's account of the Israelite immigration came to dominate European research for more than a lifetime. The answer is to be found in the studies of Israel's earliest history which were conducted in the previous epoch. If we confine our focus to the period between the publication of Wellhausen's *Prolegomena* and Alt's first article on the immigration (less than 50 years in all), and if we then briefly examine the most important treatments of Israel's origins, two characteristic features are immediately apparent[95]. In the first place we find very detailed attempts to reconstruct the immigration into Palestine in which the texts are pushed to the utmost in order to derive a maximum of information[96]. In the second place these analyses are strangely lacking in theoretical considerations, which is to say that they are tenuous and lack any form of control. Only one major treatment within this period can be termed an exception to this description, and it was not carried out by an OT scholar, but by the virtually universal historian of antiquity, E.Meyer. In his monograph on the Israelites and their neighbors Meyer gave voice to sometimes sharp and occasionally sarcastic differences of opinion with his contemporaries, although he himself was no more fortunate in solving the problems and formulating a fertile alternative to the shots in the dark of his colleagues[97].

However, my characterization of the scholarship of this period as non-theoretical is only partially just. It is true that much of this scholarship may best be described as speculation, but one's main impression is that scholars had difficulty in casting off the spell of the Biblical narrative, or, to be more precise, towards the end of this period they were attempting to retain as much of the OT tradition as possible. Thus on the one hand scholars attempted to harmonize the various

---

[95] This brief description of the attitude towards Israel's origin prior to Alt is mainly based on the following studies: Wellhausen 1878; 1894; Stade 1887; Guthe 1904; Steuernagel 1901; Meyer 1906; 1931; Böhl 1911; Kittel 1932; 1925; Gressmann 1913; Sellin 1924, and, as the only work not in the German language, Burney 1921.

[96] Cf. on this point Guthe and Steuernagel, who constructed entire systems designed to wrench information about the history of the tribes from the patriarchal narratives (see particularly Guthe 1904:4-6).

[97] See Meyer 1906:50. Meyer clearly acknowledged the fact that the source value of the OT for the period before the introduction of the monarchy is extremely limited. He regarded the genealogical materials as the most important information. Nevertheless, Meyer did not refrain from presenting a very detailed description of the course of the immigration.

divergent OT traditions, while on the other they saw themselves as compelled to establish some sort of connection between the Biblical sources and the extra-Biblical materials which were accumulating very rapidly at this time[98].

The harmonizing tendency came to expression in practice particularly in the efforts to force the various external sources to fit in with the OT account of Israel's earliest history. Thus, efforts in this direction increasingly concentrated on "saving" the patriarchs as the historical forerunners of the later Israel. On the basis of extremely ambiguous sources both within the OT (such as Gen 14) and without it, scholars tried to establish a connection between the patriarchs and the *ḫabiru*, and then, once again on the basis of the OT; they attempted to prove links relating the *ḫabiru*, the patriarchs, and the Aramaeans, in order to retain the conception in Genesis of the so-called patriarchal age[99]. However, in order to retain this period, it was soon discovered that it was necessary to abandon other parts of the OT tradition. Thus, for example, scholars were prepared to admit that the account of the conquest in the Book of Joshua was not a historical picture, and instead of following Joshua the conquest was divided up into a number of phases which as a rule followed the division between Lea and Rachel tribes[100].

Accordingly, accounts of the immigration in the latter part of the period in question saw it as taking place around 1500. This made it possible to maintain a connection with the *ḫbiru*, and so to claim that the Israelite immigration was reflected in the references to the *ḫabiru* in the Amarna Letters[101]. However, it also became evident in the course of this period that if one intended to insist on the historicity of the sojourn in Egypt[102] it must necessarily have occurred later than the Amarna Period, since the OT tradition refers to conditions which may be dated to the 19th Dynasty at the earliest (Pithom and Rameses), which means during the reign of Rameses II. This in itself produced problems, since it was discovered that Merneptah, the successor of Rameses II, mentions the presence of an "Israel" in Palestine[103]. But if Rameses II was the pharaoh who so oppressed Israel that the Israelites were forced to flee, and if they first did so during the reign of his successor, then there was precious little room for a period of wandering in the desert[104]. Strangely enough only a very few scholars in this period attempted the

---

[98] Clear examples of the helplessness in question are Sellin 1924 and Burney 1921; both works contain a mixture of retellings of the Biblical text plus completely free speculations; among the latter, Sellin's repeated "murders" of OT figures (such as Moses and Jeruba'al) are amusing today (Sellin 1924: 77f. and 110). The uncertainty is obvious when we, for example, compare Burney 1921 with Steuernagel 1901. Burney rejects the Biblical chronology, only in order subsequently to retell long passages in the OT, whereas Steuernagel preferred to retain the chronology in order to have a free hand with the textual tradition.

[99] At the time there was no precise understanding of the *ḫabiru* problem (cf. Lemche 1980: 163ff.), since this concept was interpreted on the basis of the references to "Hebrews" in the OT in passages which designate Israelites. In other words, scholars regarded *ḫabiru* as an ethnic term, and because of the then-dominant understanding of early Israel, they were regarded as nomads (thus, for example, Böhl 1911; Kittel 1932:281ff.).

[100] Thus Wellhausen 1894:14f.; Guthe 1904:56ff., who identified the *ḫabiru* with the Leah tribes (cf. also Kittel 1932:291ff.); Steuernagel 1901:123-125. Sellin offered a novelty, in that he regarded the division into Rachel and Leah tribes as a secondary systematization of individual tribes with respect to the main tribe, namely Israel (1924:33ff.). He nevertheless retained the distinction between an early and a late immigration. Stade, too, went his own way; almost like Alt later, he conceived of the immigration as a process of infiltration, not of nomads, but of peasants from the region east of the Jordan who intruded into Palestine (1887:134f.).

[101] On the first wave of immigration around 1500, see Steuernagel 1901:123f.; Gressmann 1913:399; Sellin 1924:23ff. Guthe dated the first wave of immigration to shortly after 1400 (1904: 56ff.), while Kittel dated it to between 1570 and 1550 (1932:291ff.).

[102] Scepticism is expressed by Sellin (1924:54) and, above all, by Meyer (1906:229), who regarded the Joseph Novella as a literary work with no historical contents, but one which was written in order to "remove" Israel from Palestine in order to "make room for" the narratives of the Exodus and the desert wandering.

[103] Decisive for the dating of the concluding wave of immigration was the discovery of Mernephtah's "Israel stela", the text of which was published by W. Spiegelberg (1896).

[104] Thus Kittel 1932:364ff.

solution proposed later by Albright to unify these contradiction between the date of Israel's slavery in Egypt and her entrance into Palestine. Albright simply exploited the very long reign of Rameses II so as to locate the Exodus in the early part of it, after which he counted forwards 40 years and dated the immigration to the latter part of Rameses II's reign[105].

To return to the traditions concerning Israel's wandering in the desert, it appears that scholars felt themselves to be without clear guidelines. Admittedly, attempts were made to develop principles for utilizing these legends in the service of history, but it proved possible only on a few issues to retain individual elements of the legends and still arrive at an academic *consensus*[106]. I am referring to the attempt to retain the references to the names of both persons and places in the Moses traditions. The determination to retain these features characterizes such scholars from the later part of the period as Sellin, Kittel, and Gressmann. However, in reality these efforts go no farther than to state that Moses once lived and played some part during the period of the desert wandering in connection with the introduction of the Yahwistic religion, and that Kadesh and Sinai were not simply invented locations. It proved impossible to agree as to whether Kadesh and Sinai were in reality two names for the same place; it was not possible to localize them, nor could anyone agree whether Yahweh had revealed himself in one place or the other, or both.

The same was the case with the rest of the traditions dealing with the desert period. There was not even a suspicion of agreement as to Moses' role, origin, and relations to the Israelites in Egypt, the Midianites, the oasis of Kadesh, and so forth. About all it was possible to agree on was that Moses must have played a not-inconsiderable part in things. Nor was there any agreement as to the location or interpretation of other events which took place during the period in the desert, such as the miracle at the Sea of Reeds, the route of Israel's wandering, or the sojourn in the area East of the Jordan. Altogether the impression one gets from these early accounts of Israel's earliest history is that they are founded on an eclectic, not to say arbitrary, evaluation, and that no one was in a position to develop a method which might eliminate the accidental associations which were rooted in the psyches of individual scholars.

As mentioned above, only E.Meyer stood out against his contemporaries as far as method is concerned, and he solved the problem by refusing to acknowledge the OT sources as primary sources, even if this should prove to entail the surrender of large parts of the Biblical tradition. Few scholars have been apostatized as Meyer was in his own day because of this attitude, and it is possible that as far as the historical worth of the OT traditional materials is concerned Meyer's radical scepticism actually provoked the production of the more conservative accounts of Israel's earliest history which saw the light in the last decades before Alt's innovative treatment of the immigration.

These remarks on the study on Israel's earliest history from 1878 until 1925 reveal the reason Alt's articles on the subject mark a turning-point in the discussion: not so much because of his conclusions, which were first brought into sharp focus in his second article on the immigration in 1939, but because of his method. Alt chose namely to evaluate the source value of the legends in question as second or even third-rate sources for the history of Israel's earliest times. Instead, as we have seen, he made use of an approach which was free of the earlier arbitrary exploitation of the legendary materials. This means that he primarily made use of such information as actually could be extracted from the texts, and which had to do with cultural, social, political, and historical and topographical conditions in Palestine. Moreover, this sort of information was found both in and outside of the OT. Furthermore, Alt was the first to attempt to make use of ethnographic information (in this connection the extent to which such information may have been antiquated is quite irrelevant), and he incorporated such information in his description of the Israelite immigration. It is precisely because Alt employed such methods and avoided the exaggerated confidence in arguments derived from an arbitrary selection from among the elements of various legends that his studies appeared to be methodologically sound. It seemed as if an *objective* criterium was about to be produced by means of which it would be possible to evaluate the OT traditions about Israel's origins.

---

[105] Thus also Gressmann 1913:404.

[106] Gressmann offers the most thorough description of the methods to be used in order to dissect historical information out of legendary materials (1913:345-392).

Noth continued in Alt's footsteps, since he presented a model which brought order into the often chaotic ideas about the period of the Judges which we meet in the works of earlier scholars. I am referring to the amphictyony hypothesis; its perhaps most immediate effect was probably psychological. Once Noth (and, for that matter, also Alt) had demonstrated that in the period of the Judges we are faced with a tangible cultic and political reality in Palestine, namely Israel, it became possible to locate the OT tradition, or to argue for its localization within the context of the amphictyony. Thus, in the opinion of very many students of the OT, numerous aspects of the OT's own self-understanding had been preserved. It was now possible to claim that in spite of the complicated picture of the immigration phase which arose after the surrender of the idea of a collective conquest, the Israelite idea of national unity was very ancient and preceded the introduction of the monarchy. The role of Yahwism as the center of pre-monarchical Israel was thus also maintained, whether or not one agreed with Noth's scepticism with respect to the traditions bearing on the advent of Yahwism in Israel. This in its turn entailed that it was now possible to ignore Meyer's lack of confidence in the source value of the traditions, while on the other hand it became equally possible to ignore Wellhausen's equally radical claim that the religious unity of which the OT speaks first arose at a late point in Israelite history. The organ by means of which Israelite tradition had been canonized had been revealed, and, of no less importance, this organ had been dated prior to the much-apostatized period of the monarchy[107].

---

[107] This survey of the history of research from Wellhausen to Alt leads one's thoughts to T.S. Kuhn's description of the situation of a discipline before a useful paradigm is derived (Kuhn 1962). On the other hand, "normal science" was no longer in possession of a single paradigm, but of two of them, which strongly competed with each other. The question is now whether the presentation of the "revolution model" confronts us with a scientific *revolution* (Kuhn's terminology), that is, with a legitimate formulation of a new paradigm. In the opinion of this author, this can hardly be the case.

Chapter 3

ISRAEL IN THE PERIOD OF THE JUDGES

§ 1

C.H.J. de Geus: Social Structure in the Period of the Judges

We have several times touched on the question of the development of social structure in Israel prior to the introduction of the monarchy. The opinions of virtually all older scholars concerning social development in Palestine subsequent to the immigration were dominated by the theory that Israel emerged after nomadic groups had immigrated into the civilized land, whereupon the Israelites abandoned their old way of life and settled down. The transition to another way of life entailed the assumption of other forms of life, which in turn led to the accelerating Canaanization of the Israelite populace.

This view, which also served to explain the Canaanite features in Israelite religion, has remained largely unchanged throughout this century. I have no intention of presenting here a history of research illustrating this point. Such a history would be quite monotonous, since new aspects only rarely entered into the discussion, for the reason that Israel's supposed nomadic past remained the dominant view. But this also means that the representatives of the various scholarly approaches had similar views as to Israel's social development in many respects. In fact, at most the differences among such scholars may be described as matters of nuance; most were (and remain) agreed as to the significance of the Israelite immigration and the settlement of the Israelite nomads in Palestine, no matter which approach or "school" they favored. In general, scholars were concerned to concentrate on the definition of the type of nomadism it was appropriate to refer to in connection with the discussion of Israelite culture before the immigration.

Alt was fully aware of the various possibilities, although he did not possess the data now available as to the relationship between the two types of nomadism, in that he reckoned the migrating Israelites to the group of small-cattle nomads. However, this did not deter other scholars from describing ancient Israel on the basis of conditions among camel-nomads in modern times; an example of such an effort is S. Nyström's *Beduinentum und Jahwismus*[1]. Nyström admitted that the Israelites were semi-nomads rather than

---

[1] Nyström 1946.

nomads proper at the time of their immigration; however, he claimed that this was a result of the fact that at this time they were already on their way to settling down, that is, they were in transition from nomad to small-cattle nomad, a process which was accompanied by the adoption of the special characteristics of the latter group[2]. Thus remnants of this originally bedouin existence are discernible throughout the rest of the history, culture, and religion of Israel, although such remnants were continually reworked in Israelite tradition. This is the original aspect of Nyström's work, since for him this revised Israelite tradition was namely Yahwism, which he did not feel had taken its origins in the life style of the desert; rather, it was Yahwism which functioned as a censor with respect to the survival of bedouin culture which were present among the Israelites.

As Nyström depicted bedouin existence, this social type is characterized, on the one hand, by a hospitality which knows no bounds, and where any attempt to prevent the display of such hospitality constitutes an insult which can only result in feuds with lethal consequences to one or the other party. On the other hand, he maintained, the bedouin was what we should regard as a virtually asocial individual in that he was completely dominated by his concepts of honor and refused to acknowledge any authority above himself, whether god or man (although Nyström did hold that bedouin nevertheless have an abiding respect for demons). Furthermore, on Nyström's view, the bedouin was no respecter of property, whether his own or others', and he was always engaged in the pursuit of spoil by means of razzias, that is, plundering expeditions. He had no interest in legal norms if such conflicted with the above-mentioned concepts of honor, and the characteristic bedouin form of justice on this asocial plane, the Sitz im Leben of which was desert culture, was the vendetta[3].

With respect to Israelite society before the introduction of the monarchy this signifies that a number of social phenomena and customs once originated in the supposed nomadic past. On this point there is no great difference between the views of such scholars as J.Pedersen, S.Nyström, R.de Vaux, and others; indeed, even in more recent decades works have been dedicated to this theme, and the same views have been aired; an example would be that of M.S. Seale[4].

In the opinion of these scholars the following features may be understood as survivals of the nomadic ideals in Israel after the settlement: hospitality, of which the best-known examples, however, concern the patriarchs, but are also mentioned elsewhere[5]; blood-revenge[6]; Israelite tribal structure, including its

---

[2] Nyström 1946:77.
[3] Nyström 1946:5-23.
[4] In addition to Nyström, this survey also covers Pedersen 1958: 10-72, De Vaux 1961:13-33, and Seale 1974 (with the very significant title, *The Desert Bible*).
[5] See Nyström 1946:24-31; De Vaux 1961:25f.
[6] Nyström 1946:31-40; De Vaux 1961:26-28; Pedersen 1958:294ff.

subdivision into families, clans, and tribes[7], and with the marital relationships this tribal structure entailed [8]; the special emphasis upon preferred
types of marriages (marriages with the daughter of one's paternal uncle), as
well as the institution of levirate marriage[9].The wars of ancient Israel are
held to have been conducted in bedouin fashion; it is often maintained that an
indication of this is the special war shout which characterizes each of the
warring parties, as well as their respective war palladia (the Ark is ordinarily
mentioned in this connexion as the Israelite war palladium). Nyström, however, felt that the razzia was a thing of the past already quite early in Israel's
history[10].

It is furthermore claimed that her past inhibited Israel from forming hierarchical structures above the level of the family and clan, since as late as the
period of the Judges the Israelite tribes still retained their social organization
from the period prior to their immigration. This means that the Israelites did
not recognize any higher authority, and the tribal leader, or sheik, if you will,
was not a chieftain, but a *princeps inter pares*[11].

There is nothing unfamiliar in any of the above statements; rather, the
entire litany has entered part and parcel into the vocabulary of most OT scholars, and it has been virtually unconsciously transmitted from work to work.
However, the following question poses itself: if we abandon the concept of
Israel's nomadic past, will this require us to regard as entirely wrong the
earlier accounts of primitive or "traditional" elements in Israelite culture?
Alternatively, is it possible that despite the views of a scholar like de Vaux (or
Pedersen, Nyström, etc.) these elements are not survivals of nomadic culture,
but belong instead to a social system which had not yet completed its evolution
into a socially stratified state, that is, irrespective of whether the members of
such a system were nomads? I shall not attempt to answer these questions
here, but it should be clear that as far as the matter of Israel's social structure
during the period of the Judges is concerned a hypothetical nomadic past is
entirely irrelevant if it can first be shown that the so-called"nomadic" survivals
in Israelite culture do not derive from a nomadic way of life but are instead
typical of tribal societies. It is for this reason that, no matter how unsophisti-
catedly Mendenhall has presented his views the last twenty years or so, his criticisms are nevertheless of great importance on precisely this issue. This
implies that the study of Israelite social structure may turn out to be of only
secondary importance for the study of Israel's origins, but it remains of crucial

---

[7] Nyström 1946:40-50; De Vaux 1961:17ff. and 21ff., and Pedersen 1958:23-34. However, it
should be noted that Pedersen warned against identifying the Arab tribes with the Israelite ones
because of the differences in their respective socioeconomic conditions (1958:24f.).

[8] Nyström 1946:55-61; Pedersen 1958:45-61; cf. also on this point Chamberlayne 1963.

[9] Nyström 1946:57; De Vaux 1961:63ff.; Pedersen 1958:57ff.

[10] Nyström 1946:51.

[11] Nyström 1946:43ff.; De Vaux 1961:22f.

importance to clear the discussion of arguments which result from OT scholars' ignorance of primitive (traditional) culture.

An excellent point of departure for the future discussion of this issue is offered by C.H.J. de Geus' monograph, *The Tribes of Israel*[12]. I do not mean that de Geus has no predecessors, such as Mendenhall himself, or Gottwald (i.e., in some of their earlier writings on the subject), and an unpublished dissertation by S.Schwertner which contains one of the first extensive analyses of nomadic life in the Near East by an OT scholar should also be mentioned here (it has unfortunately been virtually unacknowledged)[13]. As the title and conclusions of his work indicate, de Geus' main goal is not so much to present a sociological analysis of ancient Israel as to criticize Noth's amphictyony hypothesis, and it might accordingly be supposed that his monograph should be dealt with elsewhere. Nevertheless, his work requires our attention. Admittedly, as far as the classical bones of contention between proponents and opponents of the amphictyony hypothesis are concerned de Geus' contribution is banal, and he does not add new aspects to this debate. He does dedicate considerable space in his treatment to the questions concerning Joseph's house and the original status of the tribe of Levi in connection with an analysis of the OT 12-tribe system. Indeed, he arrives at conclusions which are of importance for the amphictyony hypothesis, such as, for example, that the designation "house of Joseph" represents a secondary grouping within Israel which, in agreement with theories previously argued by E.Täubler, can scarcely be traced farther back than to the beginnings of the monarchy[14]. Further, de Geus' analysis of the traditions concerning the tribe of Levi place him among the growing group of scholars who do not feel able to demonstrate that this tribe ever enjoyed "secular" status[15]. But the real thrust of de Geus' book primarily resides in his thorough-going analysis of the social structure of Israel in the pre-national period[16].

De Geus' point of departure is the question of the primacy of the nomadic way of life with respect to sedentary agriculture. In this connection he investigates recent anthropological studies whose results point to the need for a fundamental revision of the old basic presupposition which decreed that nomadism was an evolutionary stage midway between hunter-gatherer culture and sedentary agriculture. In the first place, as he points out, it has so far proved impossible to demonstrate that nomads even existed as far back as the neolithic period, even though it has also proved equally impossible to demonstrate the contrary[17] This entails that we must abandon the old notion that the

---

[12] De Geus 1976.
[13] Schwertner 1966:38-51.
[14] De Geus 1976:70-96. Cf. Täubler 1958:176ff.
[15] De Geus 1976:97-108.
[16] De Geus 1976:120-192.
[17] De Geus 1976:125 and n.19.

Semites were originally nomads who emerged from the Syro-Arabian desert and invaded the civilized land in successive waves. De Geus says that this is a necessary conclusion, since the bedouin type, that is, the camel nomad, was a very late development. Thus in his opinion we must seek another entry point for the Semites into the Middle East, perhaps in the northwest[18].

De Geus' second point is the question of a closer distinction between the nomadic way of life and sedentary culture, with a view to identifying features in the latter which have previously been described as manifestations of nomadic lifestyle. De Geus is referring to *transhumance*, which he maintains is not identical with nomadism. Rather, transhumance is a form of behavior associated with agriculture, and de Geus even goes so far as to describe the behavior of groups mentioned in the Mari letters which have been ordinarily taken to be nomads as providing examples of this sort of transhumance[19].

This leads the author to his third important point, namely the question of the connection between Semitic tribes and the nomadic way of life. Here he utilizes his demonstration of the secondary character of nomadism in the evolutionary scheme of things in order to maintain that it is incorrect to claim that tribal organization is necessarily associated with non-sedentary culture and that when we find evidence of such organization in a sedentary society, it consists of survivals from an earlier nomadic stage. Just as it is often asserted today that nomadism is a sociological *cul de sac*, tribal organization cannot be proclaimed an intermediate evolutionary stage en route to the formation of the nation state. As de Geus points out, the basic error scholars have committed in this respect is that they have assumed that when a horde develops into a tribal society this represents a step on the way to the politically integrated form known as the state. This has also been held to apply to Israel. It may be said that the picture painted by above all Alt and his disciples showed a gradual immigration into Palestine of groups of Israelites who in time became consolidated as individual tribes, then as a system of tribes, and finally as a state. De Geus asserts that just as nomadism is a blind alley, so too is the tribal system, since "tribe" as a concept is not a political entity; rather, at this stage the center of political power is to be found elsewhere. Thus when we examine the faint beginnings of a state, we most often encounter special political factors in which some groups participate which are not rooted in tribal organization, while in some cases individuals are motivated by reasons which have nothing to do

[18] De Geus 1976:125.

[19] On the question of *transhumance* see de Geus 1976:127 (but see also above, p. 3, n.10. On conditions in Mari: de Geus 1976:173ff. It should be mentioned here that de Geus' knowledge of the literature on the Mari nomads seems to be somewhat limited, even when we consider that he only presents us with a "selective" bibliography mentioning among others Kupper 1957; 1959; plus Klengel's lesser contributions on this subject (Klengel 1959; 1962; 1966). However, he does not mention and apparently is not familiar with the not unimportant attempt of J.T. Lukes to criticize Kupper (Luke 1965); nor has he seen Klengel's unpublished dissertation (Klengel 1958A; cf. Klengel 1958B).

with tribal politics. The best known examples of this in the OT are the actions of Jephthah and, of course, David[20].

In the central section of his monograph de Geus substantiates these observations by a thorough analysis of the various aspects of Israelite tribal structure. Here he points out that it would be an error to take such late descriptions of the Israelite understanding of the tribe as that provided by, for example, Josh 7,16-19, as adequate descriptions of tribal organization in the pre-national period[21]. If one examines the various facets of the structure in question, de Geus maintains, we find the smallest organizational unit to be the "father's house", בית אב, which de Geus renders as "the extended family", a unit which may contain as many as four generations, and whose most characteristic feature is its marital regulations, which reveal that the group is exogamous.

Ranged above this basic unit is the collectivity of father's houses which are united by marriage, which is to say that in the OT sources we encounter as a rule the *endogamous clan* although there are exceptions. In the period of the Judges the clan was the most important political group in which the real power in society was concentrated. The significance of the clan is above all evident in the pattern of settlement. In the Israel of the period of the Judges, which was primarily sedentary, we usually find that a clan made up the population of a small town. In some cases we discover that there were several clans in the same town; the Hebrew term for this important sociological unit is מֹשׁפחה[22].

But what role did the tribe play in Israelite society? De Geus emphasizes that the tribe was primarily a geographical concept, since those dwelling in a given geographical area understood themselves, possibly for ethnic reasons but more probably because of historical factors, as a tribe[23]. The motive for describing such unity as the result of blood relations was that in the Semitic world ties of solidarity were usually (and still are) expressed as familial ties in the form of fictive genealogies[24]. Therefore the function of the tribe in Israelite society was not so much political as a means of enabling the individual Israelite in a given region to define his relationships to other Israelites in other parts of the country. According to de Geus this means that the significance of the tribe resided in the fact that it constituted a branch of the entirety of Israel, and that the tribe had no significance in isolation from this greater unit[25].

The limited political influence of the tribe is also to be seen in the fact that it does not appear to have had any political leadership structure; nor is it possible to point to a title descriptive of such an office. This also applies to נשיא

---

[20] De Geus 1976:131.
[21] De Geus 1976:133-150. For the rejection of Jos 7,16ff. see de Geus 1976:133.
[22] De Geus 1976:136.
[23] De Geus 1976:144.
[24] De Geus 1976:146.
[25] De Geus 1976:149f.

which was not a chieftain designation; rather, it always applied to the father's house, of which the figure in question was the leader (איש)[26].

In accordance with this analysis of the concept of tribe and its meaning in Israel one is forced to abandon Herodotus' definition of a people: blood ties, language, and religion. The borderlines between the various groups may easily contradict such criteria, and sufficient examples are available in the ethnographic literature to illustrate this point. It would be more appropriate to seek explanations for the emergence of the tribe as a sociological type among such concepts as *connubium* and *forum*[27]. De Geus' analysis of this form of organization in Bronze Age Palestine, and of the relationship between the Israelites and the Canaanites does not suggest that these groups had different origins, but rather that groups with different forms of social organization were to be found in Palestine[28].

When the analysis is brought to bear on the question of the origins of Israel, it suggests the emergence of an ethnic distinction between Israelites and Canaanites, but this distinction is not the product of different origins, but of different economics and social situations, by which the writer means the antinomy between town and country. In this context de Geus has good reason to emphasize the difficulties attendant upon the attempt archeologically to demonstrate that the immigration of a new Semitic population took place in Palestine in this period[29]. The fundamental alteration of this dualistic social structure in Palestine, with its town zones on the one hand and its independent rural zone, took place when iron was introduced as a result of the new possibilities inherent in this metal. It led to a violent expansion of the arable areas which it was possible to govern, and in the end it led to the emergence of the territorial state[30].

---

[26] De Geus 1976:157.

[27] De Geus 1976:163. *Connubium* refers to the marital rules which bind different groups together, or, more properly, it refers to the groups which are held together by the marital rules (de Geus 1976:146ff.). By *forum* de Geus understands the group which recognizes a group of norms in common as regulating the legal aspects of the existence of the group.

[28] De Geus 1976:166. The economic and social dividing-line, understood as the decisive factor in Palestine before the introduction of the monarchy is also of central importance to W. Dietrich (1979). However, Dietrich's intentions are marred by the fact that he simply assumes that there was an Israelite immigration which took place along the lines sketched out by Alt. On the other hand, he expresses some hope for mediation between Alt's view of the immigration and Mendenhall's revolution model, even though he has no suggestion as to how such a reconciliation is to come about (Dietrich 1979:11n). Nevertheless, Dietrich recognizes that the same dividing-line continued down into the period of the monarchy and at least at some points it became stronger, rather than weaker (1979: 32ff.). It seems to me that Dietrich has seen the matter more clearly than de Geus, who regards the advent of the Iron Age as the beginning of the end of the dichotomous social structure in the country. If the dichotomous model is correct at all, then there is no reason to assign to the technological changes which transpired in the Iron Age any part in the breaking of a barrier between town and country. See also below, pp. 428f.

[29] De Geus 1976:159 and 166ff.

[30] De Geus 1976:181. Cf. also de Geus 1983 (I should like to take the occasion here to thank de Geus for allowing me to see this article prior to its publication). On the significance of iron at this time, see below, pp. 428ff.

De Geus is nevertheless unwilling to abandon completely the OT claim that Israel originated outside of Palestine. He admits that the traditions concerning Israel's history just prior to the so-called "Settlement" contain no evidence sufficient to prove that the Israelites arrived in Palestine around 1200. This is mainly because the traditions about the sojourn in the desert do not contain any kind of accurate historical memory of a nomadic phase in Israel's past[31], but in spite of this de Geus claims that the Israelites were not autocthonous to Palestine. In this connection he asserts that this recollection is not so much attached to the traditions about a settlement around 1200, but to the patriarchal traditions[32]. These narratives, however, do not primarily seek aetiologically to explain why Israel came to dwell in the land of Canaan; rather, they are intended juridically to legitimate Israel's possession of the land. As de Geus says, this concept is not founded on mere fiction. The patriarchal traditions conceal historical realities[33].

In so saying de Geus is not insisting, like Albright and, as mentioned above, Mendenhall, on an earlier Israelite immigration which tradition has preserved in the patriarchal narratives. Rather, on the basis of a somewhat cursory analysis of the socio-economic conditions in Syro-Palestine in the Middle and Late Bronze Ages he argues that this period includes the milieu in which the patriarchal narratives had their Sitz im Leben[34]. In reality, however, de Geus does not clearly explain whether he considers the patriarchs to have been an autocthonous group or a group which entered the land from outside of Palestine, that is, not as an actual wave of immigration, but as a purely local displacement of population. But it was precisely the previously-mentioned antinomy between town and country zones which comprised the basic geographical structure during the main part of the second millenium, and it is this bipartite division of the region which is emphasized in the patriarchal narratives[35].

Now, it should be clear – and de Geus himself freely admits it – that the author has not settled the question of Israel's origins, and in fact this is only a secondary aspect of his work. Nevertheless, de Geus' treatment is open to criticism since he nowhere attempts seriously to test the OT traditional materials. As far as the patriarchs are concerned, this entails that his conception of the patriarchal age is primarily based upon external evidence. In this

---

[31] De Geus 1976:172. De Geus bases his account here on Fritz 1970.

[32] De Geus 1976:170f.

[33] De Geus 1976:170f.

[34] De Geus 1976:171-181. De Geus claims that the milieu of the patriarchs was the Amorite nomadic cultural sphere in Syro-Palestine during the Middle Bronze Age, which he has previously described more closely (de Geus 1971). To this end he follows K.M. Kenyon's definition of the term "Amorite" in contradistinction to the term "Canaanite": the Amorites were the nomadic population, while the Canaanites were the urban population (Kenyon 1966). On this point one should read the devastating criticisms of Liverani 1970; 1973C.

[35] De Geus 1976:176ff.

connection it is noteworthy that de Geus' cautious rejection of the connection between the patriarchal traditions and the milieu of the Iron Age which has been proposed by such scholars as Thompson ignores the many relevant objections which Thompson has de facto presented to such an early date for the patriarchs[36]. Thus it is obvious that de Geus' insufficient concern with the OT traditional materials leaves his presentation rather one-sided, with the result that in reality he has not achieved all that much by way of an answer to the question of the origins of Israel.

This criticism does not touch the main body of de Geus' work. Thus it does not contest his legitimate efforts to discover an alternative model for describing Israelite social structure in the period of the Judges. It could be said that the author does not achieve his goals with respect to historical matters because he has neglected the question of the nature of his sources. Nevertheless, he has provided other scholars with a viable point of departure. Finally, one must admit that concentration on the formation of the Israelite traditions and the many possible reconstructions which they make possible would have threatened to overflow the bounds of de Geus' work. An example of this tendency is surely Gottwald's colossal and in many respects amorphous monograph, *The Tribes of Yahweh* (another, it might be claimed, is the present study).

Because his own study was delayed for over five years, Gottwald was in a position to comment on de Geus' views[37]. On most questions of detail Gottwald agrees with de Geus, mainly because the latter in general lives up to the demands posed by Gottwald for an adequate historical and sociological analysis of ancient Israel[38], but also because both simply agree on a number of points. Gottwald's criticism of de Geus is based on the fact that the latter rejects Mendenhall's theories of a peasants' revolt without discussion. Gottwald further points out that de Geus' own comments on the question of Israelite origins are far from clear[39]. Gottwald correctly characterizes de Geus' work as a prolegomena to the production of "an indigenous ethnic model" of early Israel. In reality, de Geus' *The Tribes of Israel* has the same significance for the present work[40].

On the other hand, I should like to emphasize that as far as the consideration of the ethnographic material is concerned upon which both Gottwald and de Geus base their respective works I am far from convinced that the last word has been said. As I mentioned previously in my discussion of Gottwald's contribution, it is also true of de Geus' work that his selection of source materials for his sociological investigations is far from satisfactory. Admittedly, it would be quite unreasonable to require of these scholars (or of this writer,

---

[36] De Geus 1976:171n (against Thompson 1974).
[37] Gottwald 1979A:894-899.
[38] Cf. Gottwald 1975.
[39] Gottwald 1979A:896; cf. de Geus 1976:184.
[40] See Gottwald 1979A:895.

for that matter) that their studies of the anthropological literature be comprehensive. Nevertheless, their own work with the OT texts should have taught both figures to seek guidance in primary sources. By this I do not mean that they ought to have undertaken ethnographical fieldwork, which is naturally an indispensable prerequisite for a professional anthropologist, but which is out of the question for those who lack the necessary training. Moreover, such efforts would scarcely lead to rewarding results. By the same token, it is essential not to confine one's reading mainly to secondary sources which summarize the results of a number of ethnographic basic studies. Rather, one must go directly to the firsthand accounts in order to get an impression of the forces which are decisive for any society which is least theoretically on the same developmental level as premonarchical Israel. This would be like making use of archeological data without recourse to excavation reports. At the present time there is a relatively large number of monographs which describe individual nomadic groups, but neither of the scholars in question seems to be familiar with them.

I shall return to this observation later as a point of departure for a control and a necessary correction of Gottwald's and de Geus' evaluations of nomadism and its relations to sedentary culture. The reader will perhaps find such an examination longwinded and boring, but there is no question but that it is absolutely essential if we are to gain more accurate insight into the factors which may have been operative during Israel's emergence. For example, de Geus' cursory use of sources relevant to nomadism has resulted in an inadequate understanding of conditions in the state of Mari during the Middle Bronze Age. Further, he fails to describe with sufficient precision just what type of nomad might have been active in Palestine during the transition between the Bronze and Iron Ages. De Geus has not realized that it is not enough simply to describe nomads on the basis of criteria derived from their migratory patterns or the types of animals they employ. Nor does either Gottwald or de Geus inform us clearly as to the significance of topography for nomadic life. Unlike these two scholars, H. Klengel alone has attempted to depict the differences between the nomadic groups which wander the steppes and the so-called mountain nomads[41]. The topographical situtation in Palestine requires a serious consideration of this aspect in one's evaluation of ancient Israel. In this connection I would also like to stress that it is possible to describe more clearly than Gottwald and de Geus (but also Alt, Noth, etc.) have done those factors which determine whether a nomadic group settles down or fails to do so – even in localities which might seem open to the possibility of settlement.

De Geus' and Gottwald's contribution to the possibility of primitive social structure seems to be solidly anchored. However, here too it will be necessary to seek recourse to the ethnographic materials, since both scholars clearly

---

[41] See Klengel 1972:213-218.

differ as to their evaluation of the significance of the so-called egalitarian social system for the emergence of the state. Admittedly, it is possible that we shall not be able to arrive at any simple solution, but if this is the case the reason is to be sought in the complexity of the source materials, where by "source" I understand both the OT and the ethnographic materials. Should this indeed prove to be the case, we must conclude that it will not do to attempt to paper over the difficulties in an attempt to present what Gottwald has termed "a comprehensive model" of ancient Israel. It will then instead be necessary to work out a number of possible models for the reconstruction of the history of Israel during the second millenium and subsequently. The next step would be to use the OT and archeological sources to test our models in order to arrive at the most likely paradigm. In this connection one must emphasize that such efforts are entirely tentative and provisional.

CONCLUSION

Having discussed de Geus' contribution to the question of the character of Israelite society in the period of the Judges, we have returned to our original point of departure, namely whether it is possible to maintain that the OT description of Israel's past, according to which the Israelites were not autocthonous to Palestine but came instead from elsewhere in the Near East can withstand critical investigation. The corollary to this question is whether there is an alternative explanation of Israel's origins.

The sketch of the history of the discussion offered above indicates that we are confronted by two hypotheses which are mutually exclusive: immigration or revolution. At first glance it might seem as if the OT evidence unambiguously supports the notion of an Israelite immigration into Palestine. However, an examination of the various approaches to an Israelite immigration, as tendered by Alt and Noth on the one hand, and by Albright, on the other, shows that the OT sources which bear on the origins of Israel are by no means unambiguous.

The discussion described above which demonstrates the polarisation between the Alt-Noth group and the "Baltimore school" nevertheless reveals that some clarity has been achieved in relation to the in many ways chaotic efforts of earlier scholarship. It was first with the contributions of these two approaches that it became possible to claim that some consistency had entered into the discussion, for it was with their presentation that it became possible to speak of an either/or rather than, as seems often to have been the case with earlier scholarship, a both/and. It may be said that Alt's methodological rigor and stringency had a liberating effect, in that he detached the question of Israel's origins from the grip of literary criticism without ignoring the merits of the latter method. By the same token, the understanding of Israel's beginnings which was promulgated in Albright's countless works had a similarly liberating effect on those who rejected the scholarly discussion of the OT literature towards the end of the last and the beginning of the present century. Albright's use of external evidence gave his adherents the same self-assurance as that displayed by the followers of Alt and his method. Indeed, it was felt that the study of Israel's history had been rescued from the arbitrariness which many scholars felt characterized the so-called "higher criticism". The fact that Albright also embraced very conservative views will scarcely have made him unwelcome in the circles in question. Thus it is understandable that the discussion of Israel's origins quickly degenerated into a sort of trench warfare between the two approaches, and it is easy to understand why it was difficult to renew the discussion for so many years.

There were two reasons why it became necessary to attempt to work out new pathways in the discussion of Israel's prehistory. Both of the classical positions were undermined by developments within the disciplines upon which they relied. Albright and his disciples were seriously and frontally assaulted (frontally, in that no one who has studied the issues can fail to see the difficulties), since it has become ever more clear that Albright's theories about Israelite origins both before and after the supposed immigration in the 13th century are dependent upon an interpretation of the external evidence which is now extremely questionable. Here I am referring to the archeological evidence from Palestine, concerning which only Albright's great authority succeeded in repelling criticisms of his positions for a considerable period of time. It is to be seen that after Albright's death in 1971 even archeologists whose earlier work seems to have been influenced by him have turned sharply against his interpretations of the archeological finds in Palestine. This explains why the reaction against the earlier understanding of Israel's origins came from circles which were closely related to the Baltimore School, since it was precisely their credibility which had been challenged by the results of archeological excavation. In the post-war period these results have become so precise that it is no longer in any way possible to distort their evidence in the event that they contradict what are popularly called the OT accounts.

However, as I noted above, this breach with Albright's theories was not seriously carried out. Instead, as I have pointed out, this critique was carried out along the lines drawn by Albright himself. Thus major parts of the OT tradition were retained on the assumption that it was possible placidly to adhere to Albright's religio-historical interpretation of the significance of Moses, the role played by Yahwistic religion in ancient Israel, and so forth.

Thus it seems that instead of Albright it was the German scholars Alt and Noth who came under criticism, even though these figures and their followers do not seem to have been affected by the problems which the Baltimore School's use of archeological evidence entailed. To the contrary, it is noteworthy that especially Noth repeatedly warned that the American use of archeology was "fragwürdig" as far as method was concerned[1]. In Mendenhall's works this feature is especially murky, which is why it was Alt and Noth who were the objects of criticism in earlier research. As I have pointed out, this criticism of Alt and Noth was scarcely conducted fairly, in that they were accused, among other things, of ignorance of subjects of which they could not possibly have been informed unless they were clairvoyant. This criticism is accordingly to be dismissed and sent back to its place of origin. In this event one quickly discovers that the criticism in question applies much better to earlier American scholarship, since it appears that in their enthusiasm for pick and shovel work in Palestine American scholars have ignored virtually all other questions, such as the analysis of the literary sources and the inclusion of relevant ethnological information. Against this, the German scholars undertook analyses of the OT materials and developed them to a fair degree

---

[1] See Noth 1938; 1957; 1960A.

of sophistication, just as they also made reasonable use of extra-Biblical written sources. They also revealed themselves to be fully au courant with respect to archeological developments, and made use of such evidence in a responsible way. It is furthermore clear that these scholars were well versed in the *Kulturwissenschaft* of their day. It is hardly surprising that they followed European and specifically the continental (German) approaches, while they appear to have been ignorant of American methods. The reason for this seems to have lain in the general situation within ethnology and anthropology, since there seems to have been a mutual lack of understanding between the German and English language communities in this respect[2]. It is entirely intelligible that the German OT scholars who developed the model of slow Israelite infiltration into Palestine relied on their own ethnographic tradition. If anyone is to be criticized in this respect, it is the German ethnographers and not the OT scholars who based their efforts on the works of the former.

When all this has been said, our preliminary observations above revealed that at least since the Second World War social anthropology has developed so much that a revision of Alt's and Noth's immigration model is surely indicated. Gottwald mentions three areas, namely the theory of Israel's nomadic origins, her beginnings outside of Palestine, and the idea that violent historical changes are the result of factors from without. This criticism led to the development of a completely new theory about Israel's emergence, a theory which ignores the premises upon which Alt, among others, relied. Thus while virtually all previous researchers had maintained that Israel arose as the result of the immigration of nomadic tribes into the civilized land, it is now claimed that this occurred as the result of an internal Canaanite evolution. Where scholars once asserted that Israel came into being *outside of* Palestine (though Alt can hardly be included here), it has now been claimed that the Israelites were Canaanites who revolted because of social imbalances and established a completely new revolutionary society in competition with the Canaanite city states.

The reception of the revolution hypothesis has been mixed. In the beginning the theory was dismissed outright, but after Gottwald had published a series of studies culminating in *The Tribes of Yahweh*, reactions to this approach to the study of ancient Israel have been increasingly positive. It is for this reason that it is important to attempt to determine whether this, the present model for the understanding of Israel's origins, is based on a solid foundation. Alternatively, it is possible that we have to do with an entirely arbitrary use of external evidence which is fully in the tradition of the Baltimore School.

---

[2] See above, pp. 36-37.

PART II

THE PRESUPPOSITIONS OF
THE REVOLUTION HYPOTHESIS

INTRODUCTION

We have previously discussed the most recent studies of the beginnings of Israel; in this connection we noted that we have to do with a frontal collision between two hypotheses. The first of these claims that Israel came into being because foreign ethnic groups trekked into Palestine around 1200, became sedentary, and in the course of time took complete control of a country which was not actually theirs. The other hypothesis maintains that on the whole Israel was the result of a revolutionary movement aimed against the Canaanite political structures.

These two views would seem to be irreconcilable, although this has not prevented individual scholars from cautiously suggesting that we ought to attempt a solution which unites the more important features of the views of Mendenhall and Gottwald with the classical description of the Israelite immigration as promulgated by Alt[1]. Although there is no reason to believe that scholarship has to obey the dictates of the Hegelian view of history, it nevertheless appears that we are in the throes of a process in which thesis and antithesis become reconciled in a synthesis. It is conceivable that this will prove to be the correct conclusion. Before going so far, however, it will first be necessary to look more closely at the ideas which underly the respective theories of Israelite origins. In this fashion it will be possible to determine whether we are really confronted by a valid alternative, that is, that the evidence actually supports the conception of an Israel which immigrated into Palestine as well as the opposite conception of rebellious Israel. If this should prove to be the case, both hypotheses may be maintained independently of each other as independent explanatory models for the emergence of Israel towards the close of the second millenium. However, should we discover that there is insufficient evidence for one or the other of these two conceptions, then obviously any attempt to create a synthesis of their contents necessarily collapses. The theory about Israel's origins which survives such a test may accordingly be held to have been verified.

However, it is also conceivable that neither of the two hypotheses will prove to be viable. In this event it will be necessary to offer a third hypothesis which will better be able to explain the appearance of that rather peculiar society to which the OT is the main witness. My reason for mentioning this third alter-

---

[1] See above, p. 72, n.28 (on Dietrich 1979).

native is that significant objections have been voiced against Alt's conception of the Israelite immigration. As of yet it has not been made fully clear to what extent these objections are based upon the supplementary discipline which both Mendenhall and Gottwald claim as their own witness, that is, sociology, or, perhaps better, social anthropology. Both scholars have clearly embraced a particular approach which has won currency in certain American anthropological circles; it may be described under the rubric of *cultural evolutionism*. Within the framework of this approach, these scholars have taken as their own the models of socio-political development which have been presented by E.R. Service, M.D. Sahlin, and M.H. Fried. The approach itself is furthermore assumed to have universal applicability to all humanity.

This is not the appropriate place to deal with the merits and demerits of the school in question; the evolutionistic schemes of Service, Sahlin, and Fried will be dealt with later in this treatment[2]. For the present it will be sufficient to mention that countless social anthropologists would not hesitate to declare their opposition to this sort of evolutionary theorizing, which they regard as little more than disguised ideology, an inheritance from the uninhibited speculations of the 19th century concerning human development[3].

Any criticism of Mendenhall's and Gottwald's use of anthropological information must needs itself include a broader spectrum of anthropological studies than those utilized by these scholars. In what follows I shall especially emphasize the use of a long series of ethnographic field reports as well as analyses based upon such reports, and which neither Mendenhall nor Gottwald has utilized. Especially in recent decades these field reports have formed the basis for a far more sophisticated and wellfounded picture of traditional oriental societies than has previously been available. Among other materials I shall make use of studies emerging from the heart of the structural-functionalistic tradition; these are often dedicated to the minute description of small and carefully defined societies[4]. There are also comparative studies which concentrate on the study of a number of variable conditions in order to attempt

---

[2] See below pp. 209-216.

[3] Among others, Honigmann (1976:273-283) offers a survey of this approach. Opposition to this approach is indirectly expressed by the leading English structural-functionalist anthropologist I.M. Lewis, who has chosen to ignore *Cultural Evolutionism* in his well-received introduction to modern social anthropology (Lewis 1976). One also encounters similarly negative attitudes towards this American school among European anthropologists. In this connection I refer to the late Danish scholar J. Nicolaisen (who was, incidentally, a specialist on the North African nomads; cf. Nicolaisen 1963B). Nicolaisen points out, among other things, that Service's notion that contemporary primitive societies may be regarded as *'our contemporary ancestors"* is misleading, because most hunter and gatherer societies today are not Paleolithic, nor are there any Neolithic peasant societies (1976:223). The description of this approach as "disguised ideology" is borrowed from Hastrup and Ovesen 1980:182 ("Ideology disguished as scientific method").

[4] A general description of this anthropological school and its presuppositions is to be found in Lewis 1976:46-60; cf. also Honigmann 1976:232-246, on the founders of the school, A.R. Radcliffe-Brown (1881-1955) and B. Malinowski (1884-1942); see also Honigmann 1976:262-273 for later developments.

to isolate and describe processes which take place in a society[5]. I further make use of studies which operate with so-called "dynamic models" of the interaction among various sectors within the same geographical area. The approaches attempted are innumerable; in the last decade they have become characterized by the demand of anthropologists for greater precision through, above all, the utilization of relevant statistical materials and methods.

It is unavoidable that large segments of the discussion below will strike the reader as heavy going and perhaps irrelevant, and to a certain extent it may be admitted that it is not directly relevant for the study of an ancient Near Eastern society like Israel. However, it is this sort of evidence which in the last analysis must form the basis for the underpinnings – or the rejection – of generalizing theories about social and political conditions in the Near East.

The ethnographic description of the Near East is thus of considerable interest, in that such evolutionistic models as those of Service and others have been primarily constructed on the basis of data which was derived from other parts of the world, such as Africa south of the Sahara, America, Australia, Polynesia, and so forth. Only subsequently have the models derived from such studies been applied to past and present Oriental societies[6]. However, it is an open question as to whether theories based on the study of the above-mentioned societies are of any use at all for understanding the development of the Near East in historical and late pre-historical times. I shall return to this problem below in connection with a discussion of some of Gottwald's more important presuppositions for his account of Israel in pre-national times.

One might say that there are two difficulties connected with the inclusion of socio-anthropological materials in this work. The first of these has to do with the question of whether it is at all possible to propose a general culture-historical model capable of use as a pattern for describing the history of ancient Israel. The second question is related to the first, but has nothing to do with general models. Instead, we must ask whether we can point to a single example which can be taken in isolation and regarded as providing an analogy to Israel, so that Israel's development may be described as a parallel to the example in question. The history of research has been well supplied with attempts in the latter direction. Alt's immigration hypothesis represents an eclectic isolation of a sociological type, namely the small-cattle nomad. The original Israelites are accordingly depicted as if they belonged to this type. The tendency in earlier scholarship to focus upon the Arab bedouin is a similar sort of classification, as is Noth's use of the Greek amphictyony as the pattern of the Israelite tribal league. Yet another method scholars have attempted entails

---

[5] A variable condition or factor (or simply a "variable") should be distinguished from a "variant"; a "variant" is something different, heterogeneous. A "variable factor" is something which is capable of variation. Kingship as an institution is a variable factor; absolutism and constitutional monarchy are variants, like the dynastic monarchy and the elective monarchy.

[6] Cf.e.g. Service 1975; 1978.

concentration upon a single anthropological approach, which is then used as the basis for a description of Israel. Thus, for example, F.Crüsemann constructs his account of pre-national Israelite society on the basis of a study of segmentary social systems by C.Sigrist. In doing so, he ignores the possibility that there may have been criticism of Sigrist's account, or that such criticism is possible; he further fails to consider whether Sigrist's system is based on sources which are at all germane to a Near Eastern context[7].

One of the purposes of the following section is to present materials which are sufficiently rich to illustrate the fact that there are very many possible variations in spite of the fact that the variable factors may in reality be few in number. This account is not intended to lead to a model for the study of Israel, but to show that the ethnographic materials provide us with what might be termed a *databank*[8]. Thus, for example, it is possible that there are as many as seventeen different types of nomad. Accordingly, this would entail that if one assumed that the first Israelites were nomads, we would then have seventeen different analogies to these Israélites, all of which are entirely credible. Closer examination of our sources would then possibly reveal which analogy was the most compelling. Alternatively, it is possible that none of these analogies would prove suitable to describe the Israelites, which would lead us to conclude the existence of an eighteenth type. As a third possibility, it is conceivable that we should be forced to conclude that the OT sources do not permit us to determine the type to which the Israelites conformed, or perhaps that they appear to have been most closely related to types four, five, six, and eight, and that closer identification on the basis of our sources is impossible. Similar examples in all other areas are equally conceivable, as concerns kinship relations, marital praxis, political and economic conditions, and so forth. The results of such study might be thought to have limited value. However, a broad general knowledge of anthropology will limit the number of more or less arbitrary common sense explanations of those social conditions which may have served as the presuppositions for concrete historical events. Furthermore, such a use of social anthropology will emphasize that the study of Israel's history and social existence must necessarily be based on the actual sources, be these written and primarily preserved in the OT or the products of archeological excavation. Anthropological models may not be superimposed upon the sources of Israel's history; instead, the sources are to be brought into relation with them.

---

[7] Cf. Crüsemann 1978:201-208, whose study is based on Sigrist 1967.

[8] Cf. I.M. Lewis 1968:XV, and, in this connection (and on the same wavelength) Thompson 1978C:8.

CHAPTER I

NOMADS

§ 1

N.K. Gottwald's Description of Pastoral Nomadism

The most cogent arguments against the traditional view that the Israelites were originally nomads who immigrated into the civilized land and subjugated it have been presented by N.K. Gottwald. As mentioned above, his arguments are based on his knowledge of a series of modern treatments of the phenomenon of nomadism both within and outside of the Near East. Gottwald's starting point is not the question as to whether there actually were any nomads in the ancient Near East. Everyone who has studied the history of the region over the last 4000-5000 years is obliged to acknowledge that there were nomads practically everywhere in the Near East for as far back as our written sources extend. Thus one's starting point must be, as Gottwald says, "the forms, functions, locales, incidences, population size, and overall significance of pastoral nomadism in that time and place...."[1]. Gottwald does not dismiss the possibility that some Israelites may have lived as nomads, but he does challenge the significance usually attached to a nomadic population in connection with the formation of Israel.

The basic problem is the question of symbiosis. In other words, what was the relationship between agriculture and animal domestication in the Near East in ancient and modern times, and, secondarily, what was the relationship between nomads and the sedentary population in this area? Gottwald devotes little time to the question of the origins of nomadism; instead he simply presupposes that nomadic cultures are secondary cultural phenomena. As he sees it, nomadic culture arose later than agriculture, since the domestication of animals took place first after the transition to the cultivation of grain. He also holds that nomadism is a subspecialty of agricultural life and that it is dependent upon the breeding of cattle in conjunction with grain production in an agricultural community. Thus we must abandon the now antiquated evolutionistic conception of human development which assumes a progression from the hunter-gatherer stage to the nomadic one, and finally to the non-nomadic agricultural stage[2]. Gottwald admits that nomads have occasionally settled

---

[1] Gottwald 1979A:436.
[2] Gottwald 1979A:441. This discussion of this topic has at times been rather heated; see, for example, the survey of Vajda 1968: 55ff. The basic problem situation has been presented by Butzer 1971:541-565; the theme itself has been dealt with by Ürpmann 1979.

down and become agriculturalists, but he maintains that movement in the opposite direction is found with equal frequency[3]. This means that the productive preconditions for the emergence of nomadism are not present until the domestication of such animals as sheep, goats, and (later) camels has taken place. Thus nomads are descended from agriculturalists, and it is in this connection that Gottwald speaks of a *withdrawal* and a *retribalization* of some elements of the Near Eastern civilized societies within historical times[4].

However, even nomadic culture itself is not integral, that is, it is not based on stockbreeding alone. Although this is a traditional and popular understanding of nomadism, it is nonetheless quite fallacious, since no nomadic culture is able to make do without the produce of the agriculturalists[5]. Thus nomads are either forced to cultivate such produce themselves in conjunction with their stockraising or they must buy or steal it from the sedentary populace. Theft, however, that is, by means of the razzia, is an aberration in the relationship normally obtaining between nomads and the sedentary populace. Instead, razzias are far more often directed against other nomadic groups, rather than the dwellers in settlements. The purpose of the razzia is personal aggrandizement rather than to supplement the diet; thus livestock are ordinarily the main plunder. In addition to this is the fact that nomads are themselves often agriculturalists, over and above their other activities. In this connection there are countless variations ranging from situations in which the same people are involved in both types of food production to situations in which the individual types of production are distributed among different groups within the population. Even in the latter case it is possible to regard the society in question as a single ethnic group or tribe[6]. This implies that it is a gross oversimplification merely to distinguish between semi-nomads and nomads per se; there are innumerable types of nomads. Nor is there any clear boundary between these two categories of employment, as the spectrum between the nomad and the sedentary dweller is quite fluid[7].

---

[3] Gottwald 1979A:443.

[4] The words *"withdrawal"* and *"retribalization"* are keywords in the accounts of Gottwald and Mendenhall of revolutionary Israel. On Gottwald's understanding of this problem, see Gottwald 1979A:323-327.

[5] Gottwald 1979A:437-439. This association may be explained by dietary necessity, since it is necessary for nomads, who are stock-breeders, to supplement their intake of animal proteins with carbohydrates provided by vegetable products. See especially Ürpmann's reflections on this side of the problem in Ürpmann 1979:132; Ürpmann feels that the population explosion in the Near East during the Neolithic Age was brought about by the improvements in the diet caused by the introduction of stock-breeding into the already existing agricultural cultures.

[6] Gottwald 1979A:438.

[7] This is unquestionably a correct, but nevertheless frequently overlooked observation. Even professional ethnologists underestimate this fact in their typologies. See for example Hastrup and Ovesen 1980:161f., who distinguish between semi- and pure nomads. The semi-nomad is the *desert nomad* or *steppe nomad*. Thus they have overlooked the possibility of such nomads as the *mountain nomads*.

Similarly, in Gottwald's opinion scholars have concentrated too exclusively on so-called pastoral nomadism. In doing so they have overlooked the fact that there are several types of nomadism whose existence is not based on stock-breeding but on a variety of handicraft specialities or on trade. Even in the OT there is evidence of nomadic groups which are not pastoral and whose specialization is concentrated elsewhere, such as the Kenites or the Rechabites, who seem to have been itinerant smiths[8].

The role of the nomad in the history and life of the Near East has been far more modest than most treatments on Israel's prehistory would lead us to believe[9]. In actuality, only a fairly limited territory was available to the nomads in their migrations; prior to the domestication of the camel towards the close of the second millenium this territory was limited to the steppe regions between the civilized areas and the deserts. That is, they were confined to areas where the annual rainfall was between 100 mm and 250 mm[10]. Regions which exceed this annual average precipitation are susceptible to cultivation; regions under the lower limit may be described as uninhabitable deserts. The areas in the Near East falling within the extremes of 100 mm and 250 mm were and remain the preferred nomadic hearthlands. However, such areas as these are not the only parameters favorable to a nomadic way of life. This way of life is not only characterized by livestock breeding (which is practiced in common by both settled populations and by nomads), but also by seasonal migrations with the herds. In winter residence is on the steppes, while during the summers it is in the civilized regions. A variation on this theme is not based on *horizontal* movement, but by *vertical* migrations; thus in the summers residence is in moutainous regions, while in the winters it is in the valleys[11]. There were excellent possibilities for this type of nomadism, or *transhumance*, to use Gottwald's term, in the Levant in all of its historical periods, and there are indications of its practice also in the OT. Nevertheless, Gottwald claims that in Israel vertical transhumance was a monopoly of the crown. Thus during the monarchy it was the royal flocks of goats and sheep which were led up into the highlands in the summer, but on the basis of a pattern which was already established in pre-monarchical times[12]. But in spite of this observation, the author also maintains that nomadism was never a dominant phenomenon in the totality of the Near Eastern demographic spectrum.

The limited zones which were available to nomads can scarcely have provided a living for a population larger than at best 10% of the total population[13].

---

[8] Gottwald 1979A:440, who follows an understanding of the Rechabites originally presented by F.S. Frick (1971).

[9] Gottwald 1979A:443.

[10] Gottwald 1979A:444.

[11] Gottwald 1979A:444-448.

[12] Gottwald 1979A:446f.

[13] Gottwald 1979A:443.

These figures alone, as Gottwald emphasizes, should point to the need for caution if we intend to assign greater political significance to the nomads or to describe them as destroyers of existing cultures. In general we are forced to conclude that nomads were too few and impotent to have been able to play the role of conquerors which e.g., scholars have assigned them on the basis of the OT Conquest narratives[14].

If we transfer these observations to the study of the ancient history of Israel, especially those concerning the relationships ordinarily obtaining between nomads and sedentary groups in the Orient, Gottwald affirms that the result is a correct evaluation of the so-called nomadic traditions embedded in the patriarchal legends. Such study shows that these traditions are best understood against an agricultural background. Similarly, the narratives of the later desert wanderings en route to the land of Canaan following the Exodus from Egypt do not describe a nomadic migration, but a more extensive population displacement[15].

Gottwald's conclusions are not primarily aimed at the nomads, but at ancient Israel. He claims that the few nomads who were present in this Israel must have shared the understanding of the Canaanites (i.e., the Canaanite city-states) of their grainraising fellow countrymen. By the same token, even in its most ancient period, as described by the OT sources, the nomadic element was never more than *"a subsidiary sub-specialization"* of those Israelites who were sedentary agriculturalists. This entails that if Israel was a tribal society it was not as a result of her once having lived in a nomadically organized system of production[16].

§ 2

A Test of Gottwald's Description of Pastoral Nomadism

The point of departure for our discussion of the view of nomadism presented by Gottwald as an alternative to the classical model of nomads in Israel in ancient times is the question of the extension of the nomadic zones during the second millenium. According to Gottwald's theory, these areas will generally have had the same extension in the past as they have today. Of course, this is not necessarily the case. There may sometimes have been periods in the history of the Orient in which regions favorable to nomadism were far larger than today; thus their populations may also have been larger. Such factors will

---

[14] Gottwald 1979A:443.
[15] Gottwald 1979A:448-453.
[16] Gottwald 1979A:459-461.

naturally also have been determinative for the ratio between the settled and nomadic populations in the regions in question.

Another issue on which Gottwald may prove to be vulnerable is the matter of the relationship between livestock breeding and the cultivation of cereals, a question with both a diachronic and a synchronic aspect. The diachronic aspect has to do with the domestication of animals in the Near East; goats and sheep were domesticated about 5000-6000 years before the emergence of Israel irrespective of whether the latter event occurred before or after cultivation of cereals was introduced. This implies that by the time Israel appeared on the scene there had long been the possibility of nomadic life throughout the Near East. In this case the question of whether one production form is older than another has only peripheral interest; the decisive question is how the nomadic livestock breeders behaved with respect to the sedentary agriculturalists. This is the synchronic aspect of the matter; it means that a changed understanding of the origin of nomadism does not necessarily entail that the classical understanding of Israel as originally (semi-)nomadic is passé. It is entirely conceivable that once nomadism had established itself in the region its character was as OT scholars have traditionally described it.

The third problem which must be considered in an evaluation of the new pastoral-nomadic model of ancient Israel has to do with Gottwald's analysis of the phenomenon of "pastoral nomadism". Is his account an adequate and accurate summary of the discussion of this cultural phenomenon, or has he presented us with an oversimplification which lacks analytical value because of a limited knowledge of the literature about nomads?

It would be unfair to allow this critical remark to apply to Gottwald alone, especially since his reading within the field of social anthropology is quite extensive. My remark applies equally to all the others who have concerned themselves with the origins of Israel in recent years. Thus, for example, M.Weippert does not cite a single treatment about nomadism which is based upon field work in a nomadic society; moreover, he mentions only a single author who is not a member of the circle of O.T. scholars, Assyriologists, and historians of ancient history, namely W. Dostal[17]. C.H.J. de Geus mentions only studies by T. Ashkenazi, E. Marx, W. Dostal, and L. Stein[18], while B. Zuber mentions a certain amount of (in particular) early literature on the Palestinian nomads (including the Negev), but limits his list to this area[19]. Zuber is apparently an adherent of "ecological determinism", and thus asserts that a given set of ecological preconditions results in no less given social, political, and economic conditions. However, more detailed study of the history of the ancient Orient reveals that political conditions are also significant for social development. Zuber's delimitation of his anthropological material is accordingly too narrow[20]. The superficiality of the use by OT scholars of ethnographic materials is especially

---

[17] Namely Dostal 1958. Cf. Weippert 1967:108. There is no change with respect to this issue even in Weippert 1979; nor, for that matter, is there in Y.Yadin's contribution to the same work, in which Weippert's study is also published (Yadin 1979).

[18] Ashkenazi 1938; Marx 1967; Dostal 1967 and Stein 1967. See especially de Geus 1976: 127ff.

[19] Cf. Zuber 1976:99-138.

[20] It is almost embarrassing to note that as late as in studies from the 1970's scholars still focused exclusively on investigations of the Semitic-language-speaking nomads, as if there existed a special type of nomadism which only Semites practiced. This is an unfortunate reminder

evident in de Geus' and Zuber's use of the works of the well known Norwegian ethnologist, F. Barth; although they refer to short studies published by Barth, both fail to make use of his most important treatments dealing with Near Eastern societies[21]. Naturally, it would be unreasonable to require a scholar to read everything within a parallel discipline. Nevertheless, anyone who intends to discuss the role of nomadism in ancient Israel must include at the very least a couple of descriptions of nomadic societies by modern ethnographers. Such materials *supplement* our sources from the ancient world. Ancient Near Eastern sources only regard the nomads from the point of view of central authority, or from that of the sedentary urban cultures. We have no sources whatsoever as to how things looked from the nomads' point of view. Accordingly, ethnographic materials may be helpful in correcting this imbalance, although they cannot replace ancient sources, since modern data has been collected under conditions which differ in innumerable ways from conditions in the ancient world[22].

Of course, there is a question as to whether a series of individual investigations will be able to reveal such constantly recurring conditions that it would be legitimate to draw general conclusions. It is entirely possible that there are so many variations that such a universal model would be either meaningless or disingenuous. If it should prove the case that nomadic societies are so varied that it would be misleading to subsume them under a single paradigm our next task will then be to inquire as to the implications of this conclusion for the understanding of ancient Israel. By this I mean that it may nevertheless prove to be possible to maintain the conception of Israel as a society whose origins were in nomadic culture in spite of the fact that generalizing models apparently rule this possibility out of court. Such a decision could not be made on the basis of external evidence, that is, on a scientifically derived paradigm of nomadic societies, but only on the basis of written sources in and outside of the OT, plus the Palestinian archeological evidence applicable to the period in question.

We have accordingly far to go before we may conclude this chapter. My first intention is briefly to examine the understandings of nomadism to which Gottwald is opposed, after which I shall offer a sketch of the origin of this model. I shall subsequently correct the earlier understanding on the basis of more recent studies of nomadic societies and their relationships to other forms of culture. In the process we shall also determine whether Gottwald's understanding of nomadism is correct.

---

of how deeply-rooted the racial theories or earlier times in reality are (and for the scholars in question, this is surely quite unconscious).

[21] De Geus mentions only Barth 1954 (1976:138); Zuber refers only to Barth 1962 (which he even cites incorrectly; see Zuber, 1976:140). Barth's studies of the Jaf Kurds (Barth 1953), the Swat Pathans (Barth 1959), and his very important investigation of the nomads of southern Persia, the Basseri (Barth 1964A), are not mentioned at all.

[22] I should like to recommend that by way of introduction scholars make the acquaintance of at least a couple of the more recent surveys of anthropological research in the Near East. In this connection I should like to recommend Gulick 1976 and Binder 1976, as well as the on-going reports in the *Annual Review of Anthropology* (e.g. Fernea 1975; E. Cohen 1977, and N. and R. Dyson-Hudson 1980).

§ 3

The Popular Understanding of Nomadism
and its Influence on the Scholarly Discussion

Lo, the wretched Asiatic – it goes ill with the place where he is, afflicted with water, difficult from many trees, the ways thereof painful because of the mountains. He does not dwell in a single place, (but) his legs are made to go astray. He had been fighting (ever) since the time of Horus, (but) he does not conquer, nor yet can he be conquered. He does not announce a day in fighting, like a thief who... for a gang. ...He is (only) an Asiatic, one despised on his (own) coast. He may rob a single person, (but) he does not lead against a town of many citizens[23].

Countless ancient Near Eastern texts strike this tone in their descriptions of the nomads, that is, as seen from the viewpoint of the sedentary populations. There is no difference with respect to their understanding of the nomads between Egyptian and Mesopotamian texts. Furthermore, the same view of nomads and their home territories is likewise discernible in the OT[24]. The situation is the same outside of the Near East. Nomads are invariably characterized in terms which clearly reveal the disgust felt by members of sedentary, civilized cultures towards the primitive status of the nomads in question. Such sources also reveal the explicit horror aroused by the threat which the nomads pose[25].

If one undertook to evaluate the phenomenon on the basis of texts which derive from cultures which were in primary contact with nomads, one would be forced to conclude that there are no indications of any symbiosis between nomads and the sedentary populations. Instead, both seem to be sharply distinguishable cultural types. One rediscovers precisely the same basic attitude in the self-consciousness of nomads, combined with a general contempt towards all other cultures than their own. In the self-understanding of the nomad, however, those characteristics which others describe as his most repulsive aspects are correspondingly emphasized as his most admirable qualities, such as his bravery, boldness, and complete independence of all entanglements[26].

---

[23] From the "Instruction for King Meri-ka-re", cited after J.A. Wilson's translation in ANET³:416.

[24] See Jer 3,2. On the attitude towards the nomads by the Mesopotamian urban culture, see Klengel 1972:31-34 and Malbran-Labat 1980.

[25] Cf. L. Vajda, who covers Chinese sources and sources from late antiquity, as well as earlier European authors, such as Olaus Magnus, who compared the Laps with the Scythians (1968:20ff.)

[26] This observation has been made by virtually every author who has studied nomadic

This implies that the structure of Oriental society was firmly dualistic in this respect, in that the nomad was permanently entrenched on one side of the divide, while the city-dweller inhabited the other. Thus it is intelligible that both the pre-scientific and, later, the European scholarly traditions both contributed to a conventional picture of the nature of the nomad. L.Vajda describes this process as one in which scholars adopted an unscientific convention and then in later European tradition used it as the basis of their theory formation and typologizing, without, however, first having acquainted themselves with the actual situation. Once this understanding had been accepted by the scholarly world, it was passed on from generation to generation of Orientalists until by reason of its age alone it became canonized as the truth concerning the relationship between nomads and sedentary dwellers[27].

In addition to this basic view of the antinomy between the sedentary populace and the nomad, an equally conventional tripartite scheme was developed. Here scholars adopted and refined an understanding of the world which derived from antiquity and which had been fossilized in Muslim tradition, above all thanks to Ibn Khaldun's extensive concern with it in his *Muqaddima*[28].

There is no reason to examine the theories of the ancient world or the Middle Ages here, since it is sufficient to refer to Vajda's excellent account[29]. On the other hand, there is reason to examine Vajda's account of Ibn Khaldun's understanding of the development of humanity from the nomadic stage to that of urban culture. According to Vajda, Ibn Khaldun developed the Greek tripartite scheme in such a way that in Ibn Khaldun we virtually encounter a series of cultural stages. The first stage was that of the warlike bedouin, the next that of the peasant, while the last was that of highly developed city culture[30]. In reality, Ibn Khaldun seems to have spoken of five different phases: warlike nomadic, in which the bedouin tribes were united by their community feeling, or *'aṣabija*[31]. This stage was followed by the esta-

---

groups; this characterizes all of the nomads' relations to the sedentary agricultural cultures. An exception is Black-Michaud, who claims that no such animosity exists among the Lurs of western Iran (1976:32). Among Arab bedouins this self-understanding is linked with their genealogical ideology. This entails that even if these nomads should settle down, it takes generations before they have forgotten their nomadic origins – if they ever do so. This feature sometimes achieves grotesque proportions, as, for example, among the "weekend" nomads of Kuwait. The same is also true when external circumstances force traditionally sedentary peasants *(fellahin)* to take to a nomadic existence, for neither they nor their descendants become accepted as "real" bedouins by the established bedouin groups. On this point see Musil 1928:45.

[27] Vajda 1968:27. Vajda includes of ancient literature the Greek Deukalion traditions (Flood story), Homer's description of the Cyclopses, plus Plato, Dikaiarchos, M. Terentius Varro, and L. Lucretius Carus.

[28] The following translation has been used: Ibn Khaldun 1958, by F. Rosenthal. The relevant sections are Ibn Khaldun 1958: I: 247-310 and 313ff; 1958: II: 128ff., 235ff., and 279ff.

[29] Vajda 1968:35-50.

[30] Vajda 1968:47ff.

[31] On *'aṣabija* see R. Rosenthal's introduction to Ibn Khaldun 1958:I:lxxvii ff. The basic

blishment of sedentary agricultural societies in relatively arable areas. Here
the original natural state was exposed to a process of corruption because of the
more comfortable and luxurious circumstances, and it was in this process that
the feeling of community, 'aṣabija, disintegrated. In the next stage it became
necessary to defend the surplusses which had been acquired and their attendant higher standard of living against the inroads of those still ensconced in the
first phase. This process resulted in the establishment of urban communities,
which relegated 'aṣabija to a spectral status. In its first phase urban society was
strong, but the decrepitude of old age soon caught up with it, and this process
made such a society ripe for the last phase, namely the destruction of the society in question when groups of warring nomads arrived on the scene. This
fifth and last stage is identical with the first stage, so that the way becomes clear
for the repetition of the cycle with new actors[32].

This seems to be a reasonable interpretation of Ibn Khaldun, and it should
accordingly be a simple matter to demonstrate how this view of culture came
to dominate the scholarly understanding of the development of nomadic cultures towards permanent residence and the formation of territorial states, an
understanding which has also been significant for OT scholarship. The origin
of the conception of the Israelites as the "fresh" and as-yet-unspoiled desert
nomads who gradually became corrupt after the Settlement, and who lost
their feeling of community in the process, is evident. So too is the understanding of the subsequent formation of the Israelite state as the culmination of this
process. The same also applies to the description of Israel's degeneracy during
the period of the monarchy, which corresponds to the phase of old age in Ibn
Khaldun's work.

Vajda shows us how this scheme survived in European tradition, only to be
revived during the Enlightenment and in early Romanticism by Herder,
among others, who, as L. Perlitt has argued, was one of the models of J. Wellhausen[33]. When we consider the extraordinary knowledge of Arabic language and culture which was the common property of earlier OT scholars,
and in particular of Wellhausen, we should have no difficulty in identifying the
models for the scholarly reconstruction of Israel's prehistory.

However, matters are not quite as simple as we might suppose, especially if
we go directly to Ibn Khaldun's description of the relationship between
nomads and sedentary populations, since the tripartite scheme sketched out
by Vajda is by no means prominent[34]. It is true that Ibn Khaldun operates

---

elements are the 'aṣabat, "relatives"; thus 'aṣabija means "to make common cause with one's
relatives". However, Rosenthal emphasizes that in Ibn Khaldun's original use of the concept –
which was otherwise lowly esteemed in Islamic tradition – there was also an association of this
concept with 'iṣabah and 'uṣbah, "group" (in a wider sense).

[32] Vajda 1968:47.
[33] Cf. Perlitt 1965:178.
[34] It should be noted that Ibn Khaldun's knowledge of the bedouins and their way of life was
predominately literary. He can hardly be held to have had actual "ethnographic" knowledge of
them.

with a development from a bedouin phase to a phase of urban culture. However, there is reason to doubt whether he ever reckoned with a middle stage consisting of a sedentary peasantry. Rather, he seems in reality to have regarded the emergence of peasant culture as an alternative option available to the more powerless groups among the bedouins or in the civilized state, an option which entails the surrender of their independence[35]. In all likelihood, the transitional phase in Ibn Khaldun's work is the emergence of the "monarchy". Since Ibn Khaldun was well aware of the strictly hierarchical structure of Arabian bedouin societies, in which it is not individuals who are located within the hierarchy, but rather groups of individuals or entire tribes ('aṣil contra sleib groups), he asserted that it was the internal 'aṣabija feelings of the leading groups which encourage the individual group to consolidate its position into a monarchy[36]. Thus such development is not an automatic process leading to the founding and growth of the towns; rather, we have to do with a development associated with the monarchies. Similarly, it was not primarily the urban societies which were debilitated by "senility", but the individual royal dynasties[37]. Ibn Khaldun declared that individual dynasties collapsed because of the onset of senility[38]. Such senility has two possible consequences: one is that the urban society which had arisen around the dynasty in question disintegrates together with the dynasty. The other is that one dynasty is simply replaced by another, which in turn suffers the same process of aging[39]. It would accordingly be wise to be cautious when attempting to cite this Arabic Middle Age author as a proponent of a mechanical understanding of culture, as Vajda attempts to do.

Nevertheless, it is clear that in the European scholarly tradition the reservations mentioned above went undetected, with the result that the mechanical view of culture became so powerfully established that until quite recently only a handful of scholars made serious objections. Furthermore, since such protests were not launched on a scholarly basis, they were ignored by most scholars[40].

The difficulties in promulgating a different view of culture than the one depicted above are illustrated by the reactions to the view of the development of human civilization proposed by the ethnologist F. Hahn in 1891[41]. Briefly,

---

[35] Cf. Ibn Khaldun 1958:II:335f.

[36] Ibn Khaldun 1958:I:269-282 and 284-286.

[37] See Ibn Khaldun 1958:II:235ff. Also, 1958:I:313ff. and 339ff.

[38] Ibn Khaldun 1958:I:278ff. and 346ff.; II:286ff.

[39] Ibn Khaldun is not completely clear on this matter, but see Ibn Khaldun 1958:I:296-299 and 1958:I:300-302. The role of the (Arab) bedouins in this process of destruction is emphasized in Ibn Khaldun 1958:I:302-305.

[40] See Vajda 1968:50ff, who lists both adherents and opponents of the three-stage theory.

[41] Vajda 1968:55f. refers to E. Hahn, *Waren die Menschen der Urzeit zwischen der Jägerstufe und der Stufe des Ackerbaues Nomaden?* 1891, which has not been available to me, but see Hahn's major work (1896), especially 1896:132-139 (on *"die Hirten"*), as well as his *"Wirtschaftsgeographie"* (1896: 384-423).

Hahn operated with five cultural stages, starting with hunting and gathering followed by hoe-agriculture, which was in turn succeeded by the introduction of oxen into the agrarian domestic economy. This stage was followed by the use of the plow, and finally by the emergence of nomadic culture. As this short sketch shows, Hahn's concepts were not far removed from the views on the origins of nomadism which have since been proposed by such scholars as Gott-wald. On the other hand, it is also clear that Hahn had no scientifically assembled source materials available. Had he done so, he would have realized that the domestication of oxen occurred at a very late phase in the prehistoric development of man, subsequent to the domestication of sheep and goats[42].

As an example of the dominant views in the first part of this century I shall emphasize only the so-called Vienna School of ethnology[43]. The representatives of this school maintained that nomadic cultures had their origin in hunter-gatherer societies. At the same time it was held that the evolution from the hunter-gatherer stage to the nomadic stage was *monogenetic*, that is, it was a process which could only have taken place in a single region, namely central Asia, after which it spread outward like rings in the water[44]. The various members of the School disagreed on points of detail, but in general they were on the same wavelength and represented the mainstream of the then current understanding of prehistory.

Already on the basis of this brief sketch it is possible to determine the background of the conception of the Israelites as semi-nomads who had migrated into Palestine. Scholars adopted the tripartite scheme of historical development. According to this scheme it was reasonable to assume that like all other Semitic *peoples* the Israelites had passed through a phase of wandering prior to settling down. No one inquired as to whether this development from a hunter-gatherer stage to a nomadic stage and ultimately to an agricultural stage had been completed in the ancient Near East long before Israel made her appearance on the historical scene, or whether it was an evolution experienced by each agricultural society in the Near East individually and in its own time. Further, scholars retained the old notion that the nomadic stage and the agricultural stage were to be understood as two distinct types of societies. The idea of a dualism or *dichotomy* within Israelite society was a remote thought to these scholars. They found it far more natural to associate the two types of culture (nomadic and agricultural) with different ethnic units. Thus they saw the Israelites as nomads on the one hand and the Canaanites as peasants and city-dwellers on the other. In the process, the idealized self-understanding of the Arabic bedouins as the free sons of the desert was adopted, and this picture of the "noble savage" was superimposed upon the original Israelites.

[42] The dates of sheep and goats: before 7000; cf. Ürpmann 1979:110. Oxen appeared in the Middle East around the middle of the sixth millennium.
[43] Cf. Vajda 1968:60ff.
[44] See above, p. 37.

In short, it was a long series of romantic and stereotypical ideas about nomads and their way of life in relation to sedentary societies in the Near East that formed the basis for the description of ancient Israel in innumerable histories of Israel. Against this we have Gottwald's new 'pastoral model which contradicts these ideas on virtually every point. In what follows I shall attempt to mediate between Gottwald and earlier scholarship. By including a study of modern anthropological material I shall attempt to determine whether it is at all relevant to undertake to propose a model of pastoral nomadism as a basis for studying Israel's beginnings. In this connection I shall make reference to a small number of individual societies to provide a foundation for the subsequent attempt to decide whether such a model is feasible or not[45].

§ 4

Nomadic Ways of Life I: Examples of Nomadic Societies

In the following section I shall attempt briefly to characterize some selected examples of nomadically organized Near Eastern societies. My principle of selection is arbitrary in several respects, as is my restriction to Near Eastern materials. My subjects have been selected from among Arabic-speaking nomads in Saudi Arabia and the Negev, various Iranian nomadic groups, and from among the nomads of southeastern Turkey. The selection has been determined by the ethnographic situation, since it has been my intention to utilize materials which have emerged from the study of traditional Near Eastern societies in recent decades.

This procedure entails a number of disadvantages, of which the most obvious is that the material discussed only touches a single time on the area proximate to, or that inhabited by, the Israelites in antiquity. Yet another moment of uncertainty is furnished by the fact that the modern study of these nomadic societies was first seriously undertaken at a time when major and apparently permanent changes had affected them.

---

[45] It is insufficient to refer to, for example, Vajda's history of research into this area (1968: 71ff). As far as the 20th century is concerned, Vajda's section deals almost exclusively with German ethnographers; furthermore, since the beginning of the 1970's a long series of important studies have appeared which should be included in the discussion, if our discussion is to have any pretensions to relevance at all. On the other hand, such reports as the one by N.and R.Dyson-Hudson 1980 or the summaries by Marx 1973, 1977A, and 1978 are also inadequate, since they lack historical perspective. This means that they are either synchronically organized, or else there is only very little depth in the historical perspectives they present. Finally, some of them generalize at a much too simplistic level to permit them to be used as other than introductions to some of the problems.

There is therefore reason to ask why I have not instead preferred to make use of earlier treatments of nomadic groups in Palestine and its environs. To answer this question it is once again necessary to refer to the contemporary status of research in ethnography. It was first at a late date that the Near East began to be studied by professional ethnographers. Admittedly, there is a small number of studies from the time prior to the First World War, and a few from the period leading up to World War Two. However, some of these derive from more or less scientifically unqualified explorers, while others are of limited value because an inadequate methodology was the basis of their fieldwork. To mention a single example, no one would deny that A. Musil's well known studies of the Rwala bedouins and other North Arabian nomadic societies contain an invaluable trove of ethnographic materials. On the other hand, it is possible to criticize both the organization of Musil's fieldwork and the system according to which he collected his data. Very little precise information is presented, and much of it is found in a context which makes it difficult, if not impossible, to determine its accuracy[46].

The origin of the modern detailed studies of primitive or traditional societies is generally ascribed to the Polish-English social anthropologist, B. Malinowski. The procedure essential to such undertakings, that is, rules as to duration of fieldwork, the philological education of the ethnographer, and the objects of study which might be considered relevant were based on field studies undertaken by Malinowski in the Trobriand islands while he was technically an Australian internee during the First World War[47]. Scholars added a series of corresponding field studies during the period between the world wars, but their areas of concentration were generally outside of the Near East. This means, as far as the Near East is concerned, that in the period in question there are no studies even remotely approximating to the quality of, for example, E.E. Evans-Pritchard's classical discussion of the African Nuer[48]. It was first in the postwar era that some degree of reorientation took place and a number of professional ethnographers turned their attention to the societies of the Near East. The consequences of this new interest have been the production of a far more solidly founded ethnographic knowledge of the region than was previously available. Moreover, in recent years there has been serious

---

[46] Musil 1907, 1927, and 1928. Some of Musil's materials have recently been re-evaluated by M.E. Meeker (1979). Meeker's treatment stresses that it would be useful if a contemporary professional anthropologist would undertake to examine these old reports with a view to determining whether they do not contain materials which might be important for the current discussion of Near Eastern nomadism. Such a study might be able to add some historical perspective to the day-to-day character of contemporary studies. Such a reevaluation of Musil's studies of the Rwala bedouins is to be found in Lancaster's recent monograph on this Arab nomadic tribe (Lancaster 1981). Unfortunately, this treatment reached me at so late a date that I have been unable to make direct use of it here.

[47] On Malinowski, see above, p. 81; to which should be added Lewis 1976:52-55, and Hastrup and Ovesen 1980:47-48.

[48] Evans-Pritchard 1940A.

discussion of many of the pillars of earlier anthropological theory-formation, such as the theories of segmentaty societies, endogamy versus exogamy, and so forth[49].

Now, the materials in question are unevenly distributed throughout the Near East, since in the beginning scholars were not primarily interested in the Arabic-speaking areas of the region. They examined instead the eastern reaches, and especially Iran, and, to a lesser extent, Afghanistan and Baluchistan, the western part of Pakistan. Other studies were undertaken in North Africa where above all the Tuaregs were the focus of interest. Outsiders to the field may only speculate as to reasons for this range of emphases; a not unimportant factor will surely have been political, which is to say that during the reign of the last Shah Iran was probably more open to Western ethnographers than some of the Arab states were. Also, it is conceivable that scholars felt that there was more likelihood of finding societies in Iran which had been less contaminated by "Westernization" than was the case in the Arab world. Thus it was presumably thought possible to find rather more "unspoiled" traditional societies in Iran and Afghanistan. Thirdly, some of the Arab societies had been described previously and, although this could scarcely be held to have been satisfactory, the deficiencies in question will probably not have been striking at the time those new field studies were in the planning stage which have been published within the last ten or fifteen years as monographic field reports[50].

1:

al-Murrah (Rub' al-Khali)

Bearing all of the above considerations in mind, the first example is from Saudi Arabia; it describes a society of nomads which may be held to approximate in terms of life style as closely as possible to the conception of the "pure nomad"[51]. By the "pure nomad" I mean the nomad who lives entirely in

---

[49] See further below Ch.3, §§ 4 and 6.

[50] It should be added that the exclusion of other nomadic societies than the Near Eastern ones (especially the nomads of Central Asia and East Africa) is arbitrary, and is primarily the result of considerations of space. On the other hand, the Middle Eastern materials are perhaps more relevant in this connection, since in the Near East we invariably discover a complex connection between various types of production and marketing systems (although we must not ignore the fact that in most cases the latter quantity must be much more important today than was previously the case, especially because of the improved communications between local societies).

[51] Source: Cole 1975. Also, Cole 1973, which is specifically concerned with the incorporation of the al-Murrah into the Saudi Arabian society. Cole's work is based on a field study conducted between April 1968 and May 1970.

7

independence of other, non-nomadic societies. The home territory of this nomadic group, the *al-Murrah*, is the most desolate and infertile part of the Arabian desert, *Rub' al-Khali* ("The empty square"). As its name suggests, this is a section of the Arabian Peninsula where one would think it impossible for humans to exist, and indeed, this judgement is shared by the Arabs who dwell in the town and village societies around the periphery of the region[52]. Rain is a rarity and is randomly distributed. Nevertheless, around 15,000 bedouins live in the territory even though, as D.P. Cole's account illustrates, they themselves are well aware of the necessity to deal with their limited resources judiciously[53]. Naturally the most important domesticated animal of these nomads is the camel, and it is only recently that sheep and goats have been added to the animal stock in peripheral areas[54]. The inconstancy of the rainfall in the area rules out the establishment of a permanent tradition of migration, although in general the al-Murrah trek southwards through the Rub' al-Khali in the summers, while in the winters they migrate northwards to an oasis-region on the borders of their territory[55]. Migration is quite frequent, so that no portion of the society covers less than two thousand kilometers a year. This is to be understood in comparison with the fact that taken together the al-Murrah reign over a territory covering 600,000 km², that is, an area somewhat larger than France[56].

According to Cole the al-Murrah are to be understood as organized as a patrilinear segmentary lineage system[57]. The nucleus of the society is the individual household, which is described as "extended"; it contains on the average not fewer than seven members. The next stage on the hierarchical ladder is the lineage, which is composed of an average of fifty families, and is a descent group of five generations. Five or six lineages make up a clan structurally, and the tribe is composed of six or seven clans[58]. Marriage is endogamous, which means that in the first instance marriages are entered into within a single lineage, and thereafter within structurally higher levels. Mar-

---

[52] See W. Goldschmidt in Cole 1975:7.

[53] Cole 1975:35. This by no means applies to all nomadic societies; cf. Black-Michaud 1976:150ff., who carefully describes how in their remorseless search for profit the Luri nomads increase their stocks of animals, so that their territories are exposed to destructive over-grazing.

[54] Cole 1975:24,36,158.

[55] Cole 1975:39-53.

[56] Cole 1975:28.

[57] Cole 1975:82. At this point it would be inappropriate to determine the adequacy of the characterization of Near Eastern societies as segmentary lineage systems (see rather below, pp. 223ff.). By "patrilinear" is meant the fact that descent is reckoned along the father's line. We shall not be concerned with this aspect here, as all of the systems we encounter are patrilinear ones. Here I use the technical term "lineage", and I shall continue to use it to refer to actual descent groups, in close agreement with the usage common to Anglo-Saxon anthropology.This term has also been adopted by other language groups; it is not uncommon to meet it in German anthropological literature, and it has also figured in a recent Danish textbook on anthropology (Hastrup and Ovesen 1980).

[58] Cole 1975:82-104.

riages across tribal boundaries are practically unknown. The only exogamous unit is the household or family[59].

Every household is economically autonomous, which is to say that it has its own herd of animals[60]. Tribal territory, however, is common property, although the wells situated within the tribal territory belong to the individual lineages[61]. A group of households whose composition and number varies throughout the year make up a camping group. Each camp is ordinarily composed of families which are closely patrilineally related to one another[62]. These nomads meet to form large aggregates only in the winter-areas to the north which lie outside of the tribal territory, and where a number of other significant Saudi Arabian nomadic groups also have their winter quarters[63].

These nomads are not self-sufficient; they are obliged to purchase quite a number of products, including agricultural ones, in the town markets in the vicinity of the tribal territory. The nomads obtain the necessary currency for such purchases via service in the national guard or as day-laborers. In past times they secured economic advantages via levies of ḫūwa (protection money) from the oasis communities[64].

The political significance of the description of the al-Murrah as a segmentary lineage system could be held to be that the tribe consists of groups which are equally situated on the various structural levels, an assertion which corresponds to the fact that the ideology of the tribe is egalitarian. Cole, however, observes that the different degrees of affluence separating the individual lineages plays a significant role for the political decision making process of the tribe[65]. The tribe is governed by the superior sheik (paramount chief), but in practice he seems not to play any great role in tribal political affairs. However, the fact that there are all of three princely families within the tribe indicates

---

[59] On marital relationships, see Cole 1975:70-76. Cole mentions that the preferred type of marriage in the Near East is the marriage with one's parallel female cousin (i.e., connections with the father's brother's daughter, or bint al-ʿamm).

[60] Cole 1975:69.

[61] Cole 1975:86.

[62] Cole 1975:63f. There is no corporate economic cooperation in connection with the composition of the camp (1975:63).

[63] Cole 1975:48. A variety of client groups, gypsy tribes and specialists (i.e., artisans) meet here. The same region is dottet with sedentary agrarian societies (the oasis populations) and small towns (1975:49). It should be added that within the political hierarchy of the Arab nomads the al-Murrah belong to the ʿaṣil tribes (the "aristocratic" tribes), whereas the gypsy and artisan groups are reckoned to belong to the sulubba (non-aristocratic) ones.

[64] 1975:27. Ḫūwa actually means (brotherhood('s money))". The term is not used by Cole, but the phenomenon is well known at all locations where nomads were once in contact with sedentary agrarian societies; thus it will reappear regularly in what follows. On the general aspects of this "protection money", see Weullersse 1946:60ff. The fellahin were compelled to purchase peace with the bedouins by paying ḫūwa money. Also, weak nomadic tribes were sometimes obliged to make similar payments to the stronger nomads. On this, see Patai 1962:18f.; further Rosenfeld 1965:76f.; Peters 1965; and Musil 1928:59f.

[65] Cole 1975:103.

that there has been a tradition of monopoly of the exercise of power in the tribe. In past times the sheik sometimes served as war leader; today his most important function is to serve as mediator in matters pertaining to various members of the tribe and the national authorities[66].

In daily life the fact of tribal membership is of no great importance, since it is the individual lineages which make the necessary political and economic decisions, such as those concerning the routes and times of migration[67].

We have little information about the earlier history of the al-Murrah, but it seems that in earlier times they were rather more warlike than is now the case, much like other Arab bedouin tribes. Moreover, like other camel nomads, much of the impulse to attempt military adventures was channeled into razzias in which the main spoils were camels, while the main victims were other bedouin groups. As a military power the al-Murrah played a part in the early growth of power of the Saudi dynasty in the 19th century. Their association with reigns of authority is still manifested by the fact that al-Murrah bedouins are members of the national reserve guard, the leader of which is the sheik of the al-Murrah[68].

2:

Basseri (Fars in Iran)

The *Basseri* are a Persian-speaking nomadic society (pop. 16,000) whose home territory is in the dry steppes and in the mountains around the city of Shiraz in the province of Fars in Iran[69]. Their migratory area is almost fifteen hundred kilometers long and up to fifty kilometers in width along a line running from north to south. Climatic factors lead these nomads to ascend into the mountains in the northern part of the region in the summer period, while in the winter they dwell in the steppes in the southern area. Unlike the al-

---

[66] Cole 1975:95ff.

[67] Cole 1975:87. Cole emphasizes that the lineage was in earlier times the most important defensive unit (for example in the event of feuds in connection with water rights) and solidarity group (for example in the event blood revenge is to be exacted). He also mentions that the lineage is the only group at a higher level than that of the family which meets regularly, whereas the clans do not play any political, social, or economic role.

[68] Note that C.M. Doughty mentions a coalition in support of the Saud family in which the same tribes participated which according to Cole continue to meet at the winter campsites (Doughty 1888:II:424; cf. Cole 1975:48. On the role of the bedouins see also Rosenfeld 1965; Rosenfeld assigns them a decisive part in the formation of the state. Asad 1973 sees the matter differently and argues against the notion that the bedouins were a major military factor in the Middle East).

[69] Source: Barth 1964A. Barth's fieldwork took place between December 1957 and July 1958.

Murrah, the peregrinations of the Basseri are coordinated and generally include the entire populace. Moreover, their migration is compact in form, as the tribe is never spread out over an area of more than about eighty kilometers. It is also significant for an understanding of the migratory pattern of the Basseri that the territory through which they progress is interspersed with villages, and that there is at least one sizeable town, Shiraz, within easy reach[70]. The Basseri are keepers of camels, sheep, and goats.

The basic unity of the Basseri is the individual family, which possesses its own tent. F. Barth characterizes the Basseri family as "elementary"; its average membership is 5.7 individuals[71]. The family is economically autononous in the sense that each owns its own herd outright. By the same token, however, each family is part of a larger camping community the size of which varies with respect to the summer and winter campsites. The basic group is the camp. Its nucleus is stable from year to year, and its leader is the "headman". Herding the livestock is a communal task.

The next structural unit is the *oulad*, which is part of a *tire*; twelve *tires* comprise a tribe (*il*)[72]. These nomads' most important unit is the oulad, since this is the unit which controls the grazing rights and possesses as well a leader who is acknowledged by the chief of the tribe[73].

According to Barth, the economic structure of the Basseri is capitalistically oriented. Produce is developed for sale in the marketplaces, and the proceeds of such sales are used to acquire produce from the markets or from the various village communities in the area[74]. Barth maintains that the nomads generally do well at this sort of trade and seem to acquire a not unimpressive surplus at year's end. The profits, which are the personal property of the individual nomadic families, are reinvested. Among other things, a goodly part of such surplusses is reinvested in land[75]. This is not because the nomads see any advantage in a sedentary life, but is rather in the nature of a security precaution in the event that their livestock breeding should fail. However, individual nomads have in the course of time acquired sufficient parcels of land that their economy has been determined by such possession, so that sedentarization seems to be the natural result[76].

Not all nomads manage to do well out of their commerce with the agrarian communities. Indeed, some become impoverished by debts encountered in

---

[70] Barth 1964A:1. A map of the region in question, including the migratory routes is included, opposite p.1.

[71] Barth 1964A:12.

[72] Barth 1964A:50.

[73] Barth 1964A:54f. Barth has no use for either the lineage or the clan. However, according to his description, the *oulad* seems to be equivalent to a lineage, but it is uncertain whether a *tire* corresponds to a clan or a *maximal lineage*.

[74] Barth 1964A:101-111.

[75] On this point see especially Barth 1964B.

[76] Barth 1964A:104ff.

the process of purchasing agricultural produce, and which they are unable to pay off because of failures in stock breeding. As a result, nomads in such cir-cumstances are obliged to supplement their incomes by service as day-labo-rers, with the result that this group, too, is eventually forced to settle down[77].

Tribal political life is dominated by the presence of the supreme tribal chief-tain, known as the *khan*, who invariably descends from one of the princely families *(khavanim)*[78]. The khan is of decisive importance for the life of the tribe, which he governs in its various levels with the help of the leaders of the different subsections. These leaders are directly responsible to the khan, but they have no possibility to organize in opposition to him[79]. For his part, the khan is more than just a tribal leader, since he also functions at the national level as a mediator between the tribe and the state authorities. On the purely local level he arbitrates in conflicts between the nomads and the settled com-munities. He often dwells quite distantly from the members of his tribe and may even reside in Teheran for long periods of time, where he is one of the elite figures of the nation[80]. Barth has noted that this position has entailed that in modern times the attachment of the khan to his tribe has been weakened[81].

The Basseri belong to a coalition of nomads called the *Khamseh*. This unit is composed of five such groups, including both Persian and Arabic-speaking members. This coalition, which was originally formed back in the 19th cen-tury, is not a strong political organization capable of exercizing control of its membership. It is rather a superstructure, perhaps somewhat like a club to which the individual tribal leaders belong[82]. E. Abrahamian, an Iranian historian, adds that the Khamseh coalition was established by the Iranian central authority as a counterweight to the far more centralizing tribal coali-tion known as the *Qashqa'i*. The member tribes of the Qashqa'i are neighbors of those belonging to the Khamseh, and the purpose of the latter group was to establish a parallel organization which did not try to compete with the cental authority[83].

---

[77] Barth 1964A:108ff.
[78] Barth 1964A:71-90.
[79] Barth 1964A:74 and 81.
[80] Barth 1964A:74.
[81] Barth 1964A:97.
[82] Cf. Barth 1964A:86ff.
[83] Abrahamian 1975:152. Concerning the Qashqa'i reference should be made to Oberling 1974, which, however, is not an ethnographic study, but a historical survey of the history of this confederation. A short ethnographic description is to be found in Beck 1980.

3:

Baḥtiyari (Persia: Zagros)

The features of this society are much more complicated than is the case with the Basseri and the al-Murrah. At least according to the ethnographers who have described them, the two previously mentioned groups are relatively homogeneous bodies which generally pursue the same life style. The *Baḥtiyari*, however, represent an extremely heterogeneous sociological and political group. I should add that this account of the Baḥtiyari is based on a different sort of analysis than those covering the two previously-mentioned groups, since the main source utilized here, published by D. Ehmann, is more a geographical-historical or culture-geographical study of an entire region than an ethnographic field report[84]. Furthermore, the two ethnographers who have worked with the Baḥtiyari do not agree as to the social and economic circumstances of their subject[85].

The nomadic Baḥtivari migrate through a territory spanning from the plains of Khuzistan and the heights of the Zagros mountains, which exceed 2,700m. Thus their winter residence is situated in Khuzistan, while in the summers they dwell in the Zagros mountains[86]. The region is reasonably well supplied with pasturage and watering sites, and in other political circumstances it would be possible to maintain some type of agriculture with permanent settlements in the valleys and mountain pasturage elsewhere (transhumance)[87].

The Baḥtiyari keep both goats and sheep; in earlier times they invested in horsebreeding, but this is no longer a major employment[88]. The migratory routes follow the same pattern year after year, and the same routes are followed for passage in both directions[89]. The territory of the Baḥtiyari covers about 30,000 km², and the average population density is slightly more than 17 per km². The total population of the region is around half a million; of this figure the share made up of nomads, which is difficult to determine, is estimated by Ehmann to be between 200,000 and 250,000 individuals[90]. Although

---

[84] Ehmann 1975, whose work is based on field studies from 1972.

[85] Cf. Digard 1979. J.-P. Digard's ethnographic description of the Baḥtiyari (from 1969) has unfortunately not been available to me.

[86] See Ehmann 1975:16-34, which presents a number of detailed maps of the territory indicating the degree of exploitation.

[87] Cf. Ehmann 1975:34. Ehmann demonstrates that in this case the origin of the new type of nomadic exploitation of the district is more the result of social, political, and cultural factors than ecological ones. See also the short historical sketch below.

[88] Ehmann 1975:91ff.

[89] Both Ehmann and Digard use the term *"constricted oscillatory"* of this migrational pattern; the concept was invented by D.L. Johnson (1969:170-173). See also below.

[90] Ehmann 1975:15 for the extent of the territory, and 1975:80 for the population statistics.

Ehmann declines to operate with ideal types, he nevertheless distinguishes three main types of employment in the territory in question. He maintains that the population is composed of a settled population with no tribal structure, some larger groups at a stage of transition between nomadic existence and sedentary life which still retain their tribal structure, and a nomadic part of the population which is decidedly tribal[91]. Moreover, the population is ethnically heterogeneous, as it is a conglomerate of individuals of Persian, Arab, Armenian, and Mongolian descent[92].

The social structure of the Baḥtiyari is more complex than is that of the Basseri; both Ehmann and J.-P. Digard have described several different levels[93]. At the most elementary level we find, as usual, the individual family or household, whose average number of members is not significantly different from that of the Basseri, and whose ideology of kinship follows the usual pattern of such Near Eastern societies. Families work together in tenting groups, the size of which varies throughout the year. The next level of integration above the family is the *mal*. The *mal* is not precisely described by Ehmann, but seems to be a *minimal lineage*. Above the *mal* we find the *oulad*, which Ehmann describes as a "Grossfamilie", which in this connection probably means a lineage. The higher levels in sequence are the *tash, tirah, tayefe*, and finally the *il* (tribe). Ehmann lists ten such tribes, all of which are members of the baḥtiyar league. This body is itself divided into two sub-confederations of five tribes each[94]. There are official leaders at each level from the confederation to the *tayefe*. The supreme figures are entitled *khans*. The khans always belong to the princely families, and they have traditionally competed among themselves for the position of leader of the coalition[95].

In terms of economics, we once again encounter the pattern of the autonomous family which, however, cooperates with other families in caring for the herds. The greater part of the income of a nomad (70-80%) comes from animal husbandry, but he also supplements this source with income from secondary employments, among which a limited agriculture is also of some importance[96]. In past times the Baḥtiyari were "robbers before the Lord", but this source of income has vanished since the pacification of the tribe in this century[97].

---

[91] Ehmann 1975:78.
[92] Ehmann 1975:14.
[93] Cf. Ehmann 1975:56-65; Digard 1979:129.
[94] See the structual scheme in Ehmann 1975:60-62. Digard speaks of the family, the extended family (*oulad/tash*) which is decisive for the composition of the camp. Above the family is the *tire*, which is the largest regularly functioning solidarity group. The highest levels referred to by Digard are the *tajefe* and the *il*; however, since he estimates the *tajefe* to amount to 25,000 individuals and the *il* to 50,000, it is obvious that his *il* corresponds to Ehmann's confederation, and his *tajefe* corresponds to Ehmann's *il*.
[95] Ehmann 1975:63.
[96] Cf. Ehmann 1975:87-112 on the economic structure.
[97] Ehmann 1975:110.

The extensive trade between the nomads and other parts of the society, some of which is conducted by middlemen while the rest takes place directly in the markets, means that there is a large degree of symbiosis. Ehmann maintains that the nomads usually profit from such trade, and in company with Barth he claims that a considerable surplus remains which is reinvested in either animals or in landed property[98]. In this connection Ehmann discusses the question of the transition to sedentary ways of life. His point is that it is necessary to distinguish between the voluntary and spontaneous settlement of, for example, impoverished nomads, and the compulsory settlement imposed by the state upon the nomads. However, as he also notes, a renomadization of the settled population is also observable[99].

Scholars have been prone to interpret the earlier Baḥtiyari society as virtually a tribal state whose supreme figure was the all-dominating khan. Ehmann takes exception to this characterization and instead emphasizes the possibilities of the individual nomad families effectively to avoid the control of the khans[100]. Unfortunately, Ehmann does not offer much information as to equalities and inequalities within the Baḥtiyari populace in general. Digard, however, describes this society as non-egalitarian to a high degree, involving significant differences between the various parts of the society[101]. The causes of such inequality, which is not founded in tribal ideology – quite the contrary, in fact – will be discussed below.

As I have mentioned, Ehmann's study contains an important historical section. It contains significant information concerning the question of the relationship between the existing ecological and political conditions and the situation of the nomads[102]. The Baḥtiyari society of today is the result of an evolution which began back in the Middle Ages. If we go back even farther, we discover that while there were indeed nomads even then they were much fewer in number and more poorly organized than the later Baḥtiyari. Nor did they follow the characteristic migratory pattern of the latter. The main part of the population of the region was composed of sedentary peasants who were divided into tribes and politically organized in *"Gaufürstentümer"*[103]. This political system was destroyed by the Arab invasion, even though only small numbers of Arabs penetrated into the Zagros mountains. The economic structure was first transformed with the entrance of the Mongols onto the scene around 1200 and, as elsewhere in the Near East, this led to an extensive nomadization of the populace[104].

[98] Ehmann 1975:113-115.
[99] Ehmann 1975:124.
[100] Ehmann 1975:64.
[101] Digard 1979:130ff. .
[102] Ehmann 1975:34-77.
[103] Ehmann 1975:41.
[104] Ehmann 1975:4ff. Ehmann does not say that the Mongols created the nomadism in the Zagros mountains, as it already existed to a lesser extent. However, they created the "external conditions" which enable it to develop and thrive at the expense of other parts of the society.

4:

Yörük (southeastern Turkey)

Having covered the politically well organized baḥtiyari whose combined number exceeds half a million, we shall proceed to study one of, if not the, smallest nomadic societies in the Middle East to have caught the eye of an ethnographer, namely the Yörük of Turkey[105]. The Yörük territory is in southeastern Turkey along the coast of the Mediterranean and in the mountainous country immediately to the north. The Yörük are mountain nomads like the Basseri and the Baḥtiyari, which is to say that their winter residence is on the prairies to the south, near Antakije, while their summers are spent in the mountains 200 km to the north. The altitude difference between their summer and winter campsites is more than 2,500 m[106]. The nomadic part of the Yörük is extremely small, being scarcely 1,400 individuals. They differ in this respect from the examples mentioned previously; yet another difference consists in the fact that these nomads never own their own pasturage, but are forced to rent it from the sedentary populace. The domesticated animals they possess are sheep and a few camels, of which the latter are used as pack animals[107].

Once again in the Yörük we encounter the traditional social structure whose basic unit is the individual family (aile). Here, too, the family joins with other closely related families to form a campsite community of varying size[108]. D.C.Bates describes the highest structural levels of this society as consisting of the sülale (lineage), kabile (maximal lineage), and asiret (tribe). The relationships between the various levels are determined by kinship, although there is no traditionally established genealogical system embracing all members of the tribe. As described by Bates, a Yörük tribe is officially composed of twelve kabiles, although in reality there are others which also account themselves members[109]. A peculiarity of the social organization of the nomadic Yörük is that most families have relatives among the sedentary Yörük, a factor which is important for the process of sedentarization[110].

Since the nomadic Yörük are few in number and do not possess their own pasturage, they are compelled to live in pronounced symbiosis with the settled

---

[105] Source: Bates 1973; see also Bates' short studies in detail (Bates 1971 and 1972). His fieldwork was undertaken in 1968.
[106] A map of the territory which includes the migratory routes is to be found in Bates 1973: opposite p.6.
[107] Bates 1973:147-156.
[108] On the social structure, see Bates 1973:35-57, and on the composition of the camp see Bates 1973:121-125.
[109] Bates 1973:45.
[110] Bates 1973:25-27.

populace of the region. In conseqence of this, each individual family is obliged to rent pasturing rights everywhere in the course of their migrations[111]. Each household is economically autonomous to such a degree that cooperation between households is a rarity even within a campsite community. Each family produces and consumes on its own responsibility. The pattern of trade is correspondingly fragmentary; thus every individual family both buys and sells at the markets in the towns or villages along their route. This often takes place with the aid of middlemen who are attached individually to the various families[112].

Bates' description of the Yörük devotes considerable attention to an analysis of the production sector; this need not occupy our attention here, although it is worth noting that Bates maintains that in earlier times the nomadic Yörük were economically well off[113].

The political organization of the Yörük is ephemeral, since there is neither a supreme chief at the top nor official leaders farther down the ladder. Instead, there are only unofficial speakers representing individual groups. Thus Bates concludes that the Yörük are a society possessing an egalitarian ideology, a fact which is not contradicted by the further fact that there are economic differences between the various families[114]. The lack of political centralization has contributed to the fact that the Yörük have been able to maintain their nomadic existence up to the present, although they are seriously reduced in number. This observation emerges from the history of the Yörük. They are relative newcomers to their present territory, which was inhabited by Kurdish nomads until the close of the last century, when they were forcibly settled by the Young Turk government as part of its efforts to neutralize the political influence of the tribal societies. Thus it may be said that when the Yörük migrated into the Antakija area around 1900 they filled a vacuum created by the sedentarization of the Kurds[115].

The Yörük maintained their migratory pattern in their new surroundings for fifty years. After this period, however, they began to settle down, with the result that today the main part of the Yörük are either sedentary peasants or merchants. The process of settlement has been the same as in Barth's description of the Basseri, according to which both the richest and the most impoverished of the population settle down first. They do so, however, for quite different reasons, as the wealthy establish themselves as land-owning farmers, while the poor become day-laborers. Interestingly, the Yörük retain their tribal affiliation, whereas the Basseri sever this connection upon settlements[116].

---

[111] Bates 1973:125-130 and Bates 1972.
[112] Bates 1973:143-189.
[113] Bates 1973:198.
[114] On the leaders, the egalitarian ideology, and the economic differences, see Bates 1973: 133-141.
[115] Bates 1973:21; cf. Bates 1971:123ff.
[116] Cf. Bates 1973:23, 26f., and 35; cf. Barth 1964:108.

Those Yörük who have already settled down make the transition easier for nomadic members of the tribe. This has been particularly important in two villages in which the Yörük make up a significant portion of the population; here tribal organization has secured for them political advantages with respect to the non-tribal village inhabitants[117]. Bates, however, has noted at least one example in which the importance of tribal organization in this sort of village community has begun to lose ground, owing to the emergence of hierarchical party systems[118].

5:

The Bedouin of the Negev

The last example to be discussed here entails a return to the Arab bedouins. However, the bedouins in question live under entirely different circumstances that do the al-Murrah mentioned above. Our subjects are the bedouin of the Negev who have remained in Israel[119]. At the time these bedouins were studied by E. Marx, they were in all only 16,000 individuals, a figure which is to be compared with the fact that when the state of Israel was constituted in 1948 there were between 55,000 and 65,000 bedouin in the Negev[120]. The region to which these bedouin were relegated on the founding of the state is a "reservation" of limited size located in the eastern part of the Negev[121]. In geographical terms this region may be described as consisting of steppes and mountainous territory in which annual precipitation is very irregular. The migratory routes of these nomads lead them from their winter campsite east of Beersheba up along the eastern margin of the coastal plain to the area around Ramle and Lod or, in times of drought, even farther to the north[122]. They

---

[117] Bates 1973:191-222. On the village containing a significant proportion of Yörük, see Bates 1973:201ff. The data in Bates 1973 have been brought up to date in Bates 1980.

[118] Bates 1973:216.

[119] Source: Marx 1967. The main part of the fieldwork took place between October 1960 and December 1961. Marx has repeatedly turned to these bedouins in later treatments, and in the wake of the Six Day War in 1967 he was able to resume his studies of their southern relatives, the Sinai bedouins (cf. Marx 1977B; 1980). Here we shall focus on the data collected in Marx' main study from 1967. It should be added that it was composed in the style of the classical structural-functionalist tradition, so that its main emphasis is on a minute description of the social and political structure; thus there is much less detail as to the economic life of the society.

[120] Before 1948: Marx 1967:10 (divided into 55 tribes and 8 coalitions); after 1948: Marx 1967:3.

[121] There is a map of the territory in Marx 1967:6. According to this map, the bedouin reservation is not much over 1100 km², that is, only 1/10 of their previous territory (1967:14).

[122] Marx 1967:84f.

keep herds of goats, sheep, and camels; economically, however, agriculture is today of great importance for the prosperity of these peoples[123].

The social structure of these nomads will be familiar: the family is the basic unit; on the next organizational step upwards we find the camp. The camp may vary considerably with respect to its extent and composition, but kinship appears to be the leading principle of its organization. We find a number of levels above the family culminating in the tribe *(asirah)* and subtribe *(ruba')*, which in earlier times formed a tribal coalition[124].

In addition to this Marx stresses the existence of a solidarity group which he defines as a "co-liable group"[125]. This unit is an agnatically organized system the general composition and function of which corresponds to the *hamsa* of other Arab tribal societies. It is composed of the five individuals who are most closely related on the paternal side[126].

Because of the limited extension and political encapsulation of their territory, it is necessary for the bedouins in question to subdivide their economic activities in both a pastoral and an agricultural sector, a subdivision which remains in force in both the summer and winter residences[127]. As early as 1960 it was noted that the arable land within the territory was being exploited to such an extent that its resources would be depleted in a short space of time[128].

Since the formation of the state of Israel the political structure of the tribe has been determined by the needs of the state authorities to treat with particular leaders of the bedouin groups, which is to say that a considerable degree of centralization of power has taken place within the tribal society[129]. As a result, the solidarity group of the tribal leader is the natural center of the tribe, and the lineage of the leader is the most important political unit in the society around which the other units are orgainzed[130].

The social and political structure of the area is additionally complicated by the presence of two other portions of the Arab population, namely the "peasants" *(fellahin)* and "slaves" *('abd)*. The former are relative newcomers to the Negev, having arrived during the period of the British Mandate. Political circumstances have forced these "peasants" to accomodate themselves to an economic structure not essentially different from that of the bedouin. Nevertheless, a number of characteristics continue to enable us to distinguish be-

---

[123] Marx 1967:22f. and 52f. Marx also mentions the participation of the bedouins in Israeli economic life.

[124] Marx 1967:61-80.

[125] Marx 1967:63ff. and 124, as well as the last two chapters in the book (1967:177-242).

[126] Marx 1967:64. A *hamsa* may be defined as a solidarity group which is united in cases of blood revenge, and among which the victims of a bloodfeud are to be found.

[127] On the migrations, see Marx 1967:81-100.

[128] Marx 1967:19.

[129] Marx 1967:40ff.

[130] Marx 1967:66.

tween peasants and bedouin, such as, among other things, shorter migratory routes. The inferior position of the peasants is signalled by the fact that while it is permissible for the bedouin to marry women from among the peasant population, their own women are never given in marriage to the *fellahin*[131]. As for the *'abd*-group, while their way of life is not significantly different from that of the other two groups, they are nevertheless lowest in social status, as they are the descendants of earlier slaves[132].

As mentioned above, we have to do with a survival of earlier greatness, and in this connection Marx presents a sketch of the historical development in the Negev area within the last centuries[133]. The Negev did not become an isolated territory until 1948. Until that date the region functioned as a natural continuation of the Sinai Peninsula, a situation which was outwardly symbolized by the fact that the nomads of the Negev were kin to those in Sinai and reckoned Sinai as their place of origin. Moreover, these bedouins did not feel themselves hemmed in either to the east or the southeast, and they had ready commerce with their relatives east of the Arabah. The far larger bedouin population was organized in a considerable number of tribes and tribal coalitions. These were first pacified towards the end of the Osmannic period, although this process was not completed until the advent of the British Mandate. At this time the present commercial situation established itself because of decreasing demand for the bedouins' own products[134]. Furthermore, Marx maintains that until pacification was completed a bedouin tribe was practically a fighting unit, that is, a politcal formation encompassing all the population which could be assembled under the leadership of a single individual. However, this individual did not have the prerogatives with respect to his tribe with which the centralized state authority was later to endow him[135].

§ 5

Nomadic Ways of Life II: Pastoral Nomads

Already at this juncture it should be evident that it is a precarious undertaking

---

[131] On the *fellahin:* Marx 1967:95ff. Concerning the marital practices in question, see Marx 1967:66f. A considerable ideologically founded interest underlies the bedouins' insistence that they are bedouins, whether or not their economic situation differs fundamentally from other parts of the society. Genealogical recollection is the primary means of maintaining this premise (cf. Marx 1967:95ff., and 186ff.). A similar resistance to assimilation is evinced by the relationship of the *'asil* bedouins to the *sulubba* (cf. Musil 1928:45), as well as by the relationship of the bedouins of Cyrenaica to *marabtin* (client) groups (cf. Peters 1968:171).

[132] On this see Marx 1967:63.

[133] Marx 1967:7ff. and 31ff.

[134] Marx 1967:34.

[135] Marx 1967:63.

to attempt to characterize Near Eastern nomads according to a single description. Admittedly, these five societies have some features in common. For example, all of them have a social structure of apparently the same variety, and livestock raising is an important element in their economies. Furthermore, all are dependent on products not deriving from their pastoral way of life. But it is already at this point that differences emerge, since there is considerable variation in the ways individual nomadic societies organize their accumulation of agricultural products. Some purchase them, while others are self-sufficient. In the latter case some of the differences are the result of the varying significance of agriculture in the individual societies. In some of them agriculture is an activity in which the entire society participates, while in others a section of the society become specialists in the agricultural sector, while other members remain shepherds. There are also numerous variations among the nomadic societies with respect to political organization. Some are organized without strong and centralized apparatuses of power, like the Yörük, while others are governed by a supreme tribal leader or chieftain, as in the Basseri. A nomadic tribe may be a society unto itself, like the Baḫtiyari, or it may be part of a more comprehensive system, such as that the Yörük and Negev bedouins participate in. The possible variations are manifold; they are by no means confined to the differences separating our five examples. Other differences among such societies may be politically determined and relative to the degree of integration of the society in question into the appropriate Near Eastern state. Some nomadic groups have subsisted virtually as a state within the state, while others must be regarded as entirely encapsulated within the wider political system of the region in question.

A number of questions remain to be answered before it will be possible to determine whether some sort of "pastoral nomadic model" can usefully serve as a sort of lowest common denominator for the nomads of the Middle East. In the event that this should prove possible, it need not necessarily be a model which applies to all possible variants; but it must at least attempt to describe a "normal nomadic type" which must be held to figure everywhere the necessary conditions are present. In advance, however, it should be mentioned that there is no apriori reason why it should be possible to construct such a model (that is, in order subsequently to superimpose it upon the study of ancient Israel and claim it to be the background against which Israelite society is to be understood). The subjects which must be studied more closely are five in number. First it will be essential to examine the typology with reference to the recent discussion concerning it. This clarified typology may serve as an introduction to the other subjects, which in turn may be used as a control of the various models. Alternatively, it would be equally acceptable to deal with the other points first with a view to the subsequent discussion of ideal types. I prefer the latter course.

The other subjects to be discussed are those dealing with the social, econo-

mic, and political structures. To what extent do we have to do with unambiguous patterns which encompass all or most nomadic societies? In this connection it will be useful to examine the relationship between reality and ideology
in conjunction with these societies. This will enable us to study the bases of
equality and inequality in the society in question. Also, it will enable us later
to examine the questions of identity and self-understanding as an element in
the relationships between individual societies in the Orient. The question is:
are Oriental societies divided into sharply divided sectors? Can the relationship between nomad and peasant be described as a *dichotomy* which is characterized by an antagonism between two discrete forms of culture? Alternatively,
would it be more correct to characterize the relationship between sedentary
dwellers and nomads as *dimorphous*, that is, as characterized by a symbiosis of
two independent groups? A final possibility is that we have to do with a social,
political, and economic *continuum* in this part of the world[136].

One feature that all nomadic societies have in common is that the individual
family is the basic social unit. The family may be described as nuclear, extended, polygynous, and so forth, but the data themselves indicate that the
nuclear family is the foundation stone, since the average number of members
in a family is between five and eight individuals. The individual societies
present only insignificant variations[137]. Extended families are known in
which up to three generations live together; however, such families are relatively few in number. The composition of the family is dependent upon the
developmental pattern of each society (that is, its so-called "domestic cycle").
This pattern may vary between systems in which a family endeavors to stay
together as long as the male leader lives, after which they divide into a number
of new families, and systems in which the sons leave the family either on the
occasion of marriage or shortly afterwards[138]. The family does not continue
for generations. In the case of the Yörük Bates claims that the ideal is the preservation of the extended family; against this, however, is the fact that the
average age of such families is not above fifteen years[139].

The family is exogamous everywhere we encounter it. This means that

---

[136] The concept of a *dimorphous society* has played a central role in a number of recent studies
of the nomadic societies of the ancient Orient by M.B. Rowton (cf. Rowton 1973A; 1973B; 1974;
and 1976A; explored more thoroughly in Rowton 1976B; 1976C; 1977; and 1980. See also Gottwald 1979A:465-467). A further issue in connection with the pastoral nomads is the question of
immigration and settlement. This will not be dealt with here, but in the next section.

[137] The average among the Basseri is 5.7 persons (Barth 1964A:12); among the Yörük it
ranges between 6.7 for nuclear families and 13.4 for families which are both extended and polygynous (Bates 1973:171). However, families of the last-mentioned type make up only 6% of the
total number of families studied (7 out of 121) (Bates 1973:172). Other figures, such as those of
Black-Michaud, agree with these (1976:326). Further information in Ehmann 1975:83.

[138] Cf. Irons 1972, who compares the developmental pattern of the households of the Basseri
and the Yomut; these are superficially similar, but the differences in the family patterns are of
significance with respect to the transition to permanent settlement.

[139] Bates 1973:168.

marital contacts are established between families and never within them. All marital relations ought ideally to be established between agnates, but in actuality things are often otherwise, not least in the "princely families", when political considerations often motivate alliances outside of the paternal line[140].

The well-being of the family is connected with the domestic cycle. To understand this, it is important to recognize that the family is economically autonomous in virtually all nomadic societies, which is to say that each owns its own livestock. The reason why each family's well-being is dependent upon its developmental pattern is that ordinarily there is no strict rule of primogeniture to dictate that the oldest son must inherit a larger share than the others. Instead, all sons have equal rights of inheritance.

Now, there are some differences in the event that a son abandons the family tent after marriage instead of remaining resident in it. When this occurs the departing son receives his part of the communal property in toto, rather than as a part-share in advance of inheritance. When this transpires the youngest son usually remains with his father and thus becomes the heir proper. In the event that all sons continue to live with the family their inheritance is first apportioned after the death of the father and the dissolution of the family[141].

This domestic cycle entails that a newly established family has only a relatively few years in which it must prove whether it will develop in an economically sound manner, or whether its efforts will culminate in poverty. The family's communal property is divided when the sons depart from the collective. On the other hand, scholars frequently stress that nomads are generally fairly well situated with respect to other elements of the populations of the Near East, since their occupation offers the possibility of more sizable surplusses. This is held to be a by-product of the reproductive capability of the livestock, since over a span of years it should be possible for an average household to accumulate a considerable surplus[142]. This is surely correct, all other things being equal, but in recent years it has been pointed out that they seldom are. A number of factors such as drought, sickness among the livestock, political disturbance, and so forth continually persist in threatening the nomad[143].

---

[140] Anthropologists distinguish between *agnates*, that is, relatives on the paternal side, and *affinal* relations, on the maternal side.

[141] See conditions among the Yörük (Bates 1973:87-120). According to the ideal, the eldest son marries first and continues to dwell in the paternal tent until the death of his father. In actual practice, he departs from the tent when a younger brother marries, taking his part of the familial property with him, and so on. The departing son has no subsequent inheritance rights (1973: 105). This example is fairly typical and illustrates the importance of distinguishing between ideology and reality in these societies. In terms of sentiment the extended family is the ideal, but in practice this ideal is only seldom realized.

[142] Cf. Barth 1964B.

[143] On this issue note the analysis of Barth's "nomadic family budget" in Huntington 1972. Recent descriptions have emphasized the extent to which the possibilities for profit are limited by the factors mentioned; cf. Black-Michaud 1976:276ff., and especially Dahl and Hjort 1976, which contain a voluminous analysis of an extensive material concerning the nomads' stock-

This means that his is an uncertain means of earning his bread; on the one hand he has the prospect of economic advancement, while on the other he is constantly confronted with the possibility of speedy impoverishment. Nevertheless, nomads usually cling to their way of life as long as possible, since at least the hope of survival exists as long as the rudiments of a herd do so[144].

The economic independence of the family means that it is to be understood as a unit both with respect to production and consumption. Thus it is also responsible for its own fate and accordingly must bear the burden of its own mistakes. It is sometimes said that other portions of a lineage may occasionally contribute assistance to an impoverished close relative. However, it is simply not the case that the *economy* of a lineage is characterized by some kind of "all for one and one for all" mentality.

At the political level the family has no great significance. To put it another way, the level of political integration within a tribe which is officially recognized by the tribal leader or by the central authorities lies above the level of the family. However, the family is autonomous to the extent that it is free to decide for itself in matters such as settlement or change of camping community. This fact is reflected in another easily-observable situation, which is probably characteristic of every nomadically organized Near Eastern system, namely the fact that no family lives alone if it can possibly avoid it. Thus if one encounters an individual family which is migrating on its own it is entirely certain that it has only recently abandoned a larger unit, and if one encounters it again later it will then almost assuredly have joined forces with other families and entered into a camp[145]. The camp is the next step on the structural ladder; as a unit it has numerous possible variations. However, it must be emphasized that it is found in literally all nomadic societies, no matter which category to which they belong. A camp is made up of families which travel together through the annual cycle; however, its organization and the principles which govern such organization are various. Kinship (in the paternal line) plays a major role in many societies. Thus it will often be members of the same lineage

---

breeding, and which analyze the presuppositions for the growth of the respective types of animals. Dahl and Hjort also caution us not to entertain overly optimistic ideas as to the economic potential of the nomads.

[144] The Luri are apparently an exception to this; there do not seem to be strong ideological ties binding a Luri to the nomadic sector of society, in spite of the fact that by far the greater part of the Luri were nomads until only two generations ago, and despite the fact that most contemporary Luri have been nomads at least once in their lives (Black-Michaud 1976:13).

[145] This is a result of the fact that it is necessary for nomads to be as numerous as possible for reasons of self-defence; the counter-force to this tendency is the danger of overgrazing a given territory. At the same time, however, the autonomy of the individual family means that it is free to seek to form alliances where these are acceptable to both parties. See Barth 1964A:22 and especially Bates 1973:121ff. Once again we find a different attitude expressed by Black-Michaud, who maintains that among the Luri the acceptance of an individual family into a camp is contingent on the approval of the leader of the camp, which, or so he holds, is also true in the event that anyone desires to leave the camp (1976:335). A corresponding system exists among the Yomut (Irons 1975:46f.).

(but not necessarily a whole lineage) which associate with one another. Affinitive ties sometimes also play a part[146].

Ordinarily the individual camping community has certain rights with respect to migratory routes, grazing territories, and water for the livestock. These are jealously guarded, even though at this level there is seldom any question of official property rights[147]. The camp is usually a cooperative unit, which means that in addition to the common migration the members also share in caring for the animals and, where applicable, in tilling the soil[148]. The camp does not own property in common, since cash and livestock are the property of individual families, while grazing rights are normally owned at a higher level of the tribal organization. Camps have different political significance in different nomadic societies. In some societies the camp, like the family, has no significance as a group led by an officially acknowledged or recognized leader, while in others such leaders are indeed found.

The political status and other relationships of the camp vary widely within individual nomadic tribes; nor are these factors static. Here I shall mention only a few examples. Among the Basseri the camp has not traditionally enjoyed status as a political and administrative unit among organizations wider than the tribe itself. Each Basseri camp is individually bound to the supreme chieftain; its leader is appointed by him, and the authority of the leader derives solely from this direct connection between the camp leader and the chieftain. Mohammad Reza Shah replaced the chieftain by a military governor who subsequently became the instance to which the individual camp leaders were responsible[149]. Among the Yörük there is no political hierarchy at all, but only informal leaders on all levels[150]. To take an example from outside of the five groups discussed previously, there is the case of the Baggara, an Arab nomadic group from the Sudan.

---

[146] Materials concerning the camp and its composition have been published by, for example, Stein 1967:31ff, and Marx 1967: 81-100. In this connection both Sweet 1965A and W.W. Swiddler 1972 are also important. See further Johnson 1969:9ff.; Hütteroth 1959:64ff.; Ehmann 1975: 89ff.; Cunnison 1966:42ff., and, above all, Barth 1964A:25ff. These differences can also occur within the same *ethnos*, as we learn from materials from Baluchistan, which inform us that the camps of some tribes are based on lineages (Marri Baluch; cf. Pehrson 1966:86ff., who, however, asserts that the lineage basis in question is of ideal character, and Yarahmadzai; cf. Salzman 1971C:435), while other camps are not so organized (in the province of Makran in Pakistan; cf. Pastner and Pastner 1972; C. Pastner 1978:265f.).

[147] Cf. Johnson 1969: *passim*; Johnson emphasizes that these conditions are extremely flexible (see especially Johnson 1969:6f.). As for the Yörük and other nomads in the mountainous regions, it is the case that they can no longer be said to possess their own territories, since they are now obliged to purchase grazing rights (see above, p. 107.). This is, however, a modern development (which occurred in Turkey as a result of a land reform in 1906; cf. Hütteroth 1959: 45f.). The special circumstances of the Iranian Shahsevan are also the result of political measures. Among the Shahsevan pasturage is in private ownership and is an object or commerce (cf. Tapper 1979A; 1979B:48-54). A related system in which there are individual rights to pasturage is found among the Qashqa'i (Beck 1980:329).

[148] Cooperative camps have been mentioned in connection with the Basseri (Barth 1964A: 22), the Yomut (Irons 1975:46f.), the Shahsevan (Tapper 1979B:93ff.), the Brahui (Swiddler 1972:74), and the Baggara (Cunnison 1966:66ff.). Bates, however, mentions that this is not the case among the Yörük (see above, p. 107.).

[149] On this see Barth 1964A:26ff. and 96f. The final deposition of the tribal leader occurred after Barth's stay among the Basseri, in the 1960's (cf. Fazel 1973:136 and 139f.).

[150] Bates 1973:44.

On the local level the Baggara camp is run by the camp leader who, however, enjoys no official authority in the eyes of the national political authorities unless he is also the leader of a lineage or has some other function at a higher organizational level[151].

The next level in the hierarchical social structure which characterizes Near Eastern nomadic societies is the lineage, that is, the social formation which consists of a number of related families who reckon themselves descendants of the same tribal ancestor.

By way of introduction it should be mentioned that the ethnographic literature has not developed a standardized technical terminology to describe the levels between the family and the tribe. This is apparent already in the examples mentioned earlier, in which two ethnographers describe the same society, the Baḫtiyari, in different terms. To mention but a couple of other examples, Barth makes use of the following terms: "tribe", "maximal lineage", "family"[152]. I. Cunnison, however, prefers "tribe", "main section", "sections", "divisions", "subdivisions", etc.[153]. In conjunction with his study of the Negev bedouin Marx uses the terms "tribe", "sub-tribe", "co-liable group", "family", and so forth[154]. The usage of the societies in question offers no help at all, since it is usually quite confusing, and individual terms in a particular nomadic society may often comprehend a variety of social levels. To choose but a single example, according to Musil[155] among the Rwala bedouin the word *qabile* signifies "tribe", but it thus also competes with the terms *'asire*. Among the Šammar, qabile is used of tribal confederations, while *'asire* is reserved for the meaning "tribe". Among the Baggara, *qabile* designates the tribe, the "main section" and the "subsection"[156]. One could easily multiply examples, but these should suffice. It ought also to be added that the same lack of clarity is demonstrable in the language of non-Arab nomads, in the event that one attempts to translate their usage to the conceptual terms of modern anthropology.

While the camp sometimes but not always bears a name, the lineage almost always does so, and it retains its name for considerable lengths of time. The lineage is accordingly the first reasonably constant group we encounter in tribal structure. On the other hand, it is not unchangeable, but is sometimes the victim of divisions which may lead to the emergence of new lineages. In terms of genealogical structure, we have at this level to do with what seems to be a reasonably certain recollection of the ancestors which goes back at least a few generations. Appearances, however, are deceptive, as such genealogies are not immutable. All of them are susceptible to adjustment, and I shall subsequently have occasion to discuss the processes which provide the basis for the genealogical pattern[157]. At this juncture it will suffice to say that as far as a particular lineage's tradition about its descent is concerned, it may well contain historical recollections, some of which may in fact be of great antiquity. However, the actual form of every contemporary genealogy provides the ideo-

---

[151] Cunnison 1966:72.
[152] Barth 1964A:49ff.
[153] Cunnison 1966:8ff.
[154] Marx 1967:61ff.
[155] Musil 1928:47. Cf. Lancaster 1981:28, who also notes that *'asire* is usually used of larger units than is *kabile*.
[156] Cf. Stein 1967:142 and Cunnison 1966:8.
[157] See p. 229ff.

logical basis for the *contemporary appearance and composition of the lineage in question*. This means that genealogies change to keep pace with structural changes in the lineage.

It is essential to the individual nomad to be able to attach himself in some way to this lineage system, since his position in society is determined by his position in the system, and since in most cases the lineage enjoys both political and economic importance for the individual. Ordinarily rights of pasturage, water, and so forth belong to the various lineages of a nomadic group. Exceptions to this rule are found in societies in which the entire tribal territory is considered a common possession[158]. The lineage functions in a similar fashion as a solidarity group. This means that the lineage defends the rights of its membership, and it serves as the group which protects the individual member in the event of problems involving one or more members of a given lineage and members of other lineages within the same society. Ideally, lineage members are obliged to participate in feuds within the tribe such as, for example, those concerned with pasturage rights. In practice the lineage is also the unit which is drawn into service in connection with killings, that is, in which it is necessary to pay blood money in order to prevent feuding (subject to the condition that such payments are accepted by members of the society in question)[159]. The solidarity function is also expressed via the marital praxis of the lineage, since we usually discover that the lineage is an endogamous unit, that is, marital ties are usually formed within the circle of lineage members[160].

The unitary character of a lineage is also evident in other external areas than the aforementioned. It is to be understood as a relatively homogeneous group, which does not mean that there are no differences with respect to the economic status of the various members, but that the members of a lineage will often be socially located at the same level as their lineage. Thus if a lineage

---

[158] Some exceptions exist, such as the previously-mentioned al-Murrah and the nomads of Somalia, both of which groups live in regions in which rainfall is so sporadic that it would scarcely be possible to maintain a rigid division of grazing areas. Still, these societies normally have certain customary rights with respect to wells and watering sites (on the Somali nomads, see Lewis 1961:49). The Shahsevan offer another exceptional example in which individual families are in possession of the rights in question; cf. Tapper 1979A.

[159] In striking contrast with our often exaggerated fantasies about the savage thirst for revenge of the nomads, it is a fact that most, but not all, of these societies contains mechanisms intended to ward off the harmful repercussions of homicides, which can easily develop into bloodfeuds. These mechanisms were already described by Doughty, who noted the various tariffs applicable in cases in which the crime was committed by a tribal kinsman of the deceased or by a foreigner (Doughty 1888:I:475-476; cf. also Musil 1928:47). E.L. Peters describes the conditions among the bedouins of Cyrenaica, but he also mentions that it is impossible to arrive at a solution if the crime is committed by close relatives of the deceased; in such cases no redress is possible, so that one must simply live on with the murder unavenged (Peters 1967:264). Further on such systems of compensation, see Lewis 1976:325-333 (with examples drawn from the Somali nomads).

[160] I shall return to this issue subsequently; yet already at this point it should be emphasized that endogamous marital practice (or ideology) is characteristic of virtually all traditional Near Eastern societies.

has become impoverished because of loss of pasturage, such impoverishment affects all of its members at once. If a lineage has achieved an advantageous position, this also affects its subdivisions. If such societies contain any sort of leadership stratum at all, one usually notes that the tribal leader derives from a particular "princely lineage". On the other hand, the lineage need not necessarily have a common occupational pattern, as for example, in the case of a nomadic group which also practices agriculture to some extent. In such a case it would be conceivable for one lineage to undertake cultivation while another looked after the livestock. Even if examples of this sort of division of labor within a tribe are known, other examples indicate that commercial specialization usually takes place within the lineage, or even within the families which are components of it[161]. Finally, the lineage also functions as a unit in that it is as a rule governed by an officially acknowledged leader whose task is more concerned with the relationship of his lineage to other areas of the society or its surroundings than with the government of the lineage itself (that is, if the entire tribe is not ruled by a supreme chief who also regulates such matters).

The maximal lineage, clans, and subtribes are all above the level of the lineage. All of these are to be regarded as solidarity integration levels like the lineage, but they have decreasing importance in the order cited for the nomad's daily life. In the last analysis this is also true of the tribe, which in general can best be characterized as the maximal solidarity group, which means that it encompasses the greatest number of members who are prepared to defend the rights of the tribe. In actual fact it is often emphasized that it is quite rare for an entire tribe to function collectively. As I indicated previously, there is considerable uncertainty in the literature as to the definition of the concept of "tribe". This uncertainty is reflected by the fact that groups have been designated as "tribes" which have ranged in size from a few hundred individuals to hundreds of thousands. I shall return to the concept of tribe in a later chapter, because the disagreements are so fundamental in nature that it would be correct to inquire as to the usefulness of the term as an analytical tool[162].

At the tribal level one invariably encounters some sort of official leadership structure; this most often takes the form of a single officially designated leader. On the other hand, it is not difficult to find exceptions to this rule, such as, for example the Yörük (as described above). Yet another is the Luristani tribal society as described by J. Black-Michaud[163]. No official leadership stratum has existed among this people since the 1920's, when Reza Shah eliminated it physically.

It must additionally be noted that upon closer inspection we discover that

---

[161] Concerning lineages, it is sufficient to refer to a couple of selected descriptions of this level in Bates 1973:38-57, Lewis 1961:127-160, and Peters 1967: See also Ch.3, below.

[162] See below, p. 237ff.

[163] 1976; cf. already Black 1972.

the leadership function varies widely in different societies; there may be major differences between the authority exercized by leaders over the rank and file members of their tribes, or with respect to their economic foundation or role in the interplay between the state and the tribal society in question.

It is not unusual to see the Arab *sheik* described as a *primus inter pares*, where emphasis is often placed on the word *pares*, which is to say that it describes his function as in reality only a coordinator of equals, rather than as their superior[164]. One wonders, however, whether this is always the case, or whether it would not be more correct to place one's emphasis on the *primus*-aspect (corresponding, for example, to Augustus Caesar's use of this title). The title is in any case a well chosen one, in that it simultaneously points to the fact that the societies in question are characterized by an egalitarian ideology while also stressing the fact that this ideology does not mean that all are in reality equal with respect to political and economic potential. It is usually the case that the *sheik* among the Arab nomads, the *aga* or *khan* among those of Turkey or Iran, belongs to a leading family or lineage in the society in question. Moreover, this family or lineage will have monopolized the leadership position for up to quite lengthy periods of time, so that it would not be unreasonable to characterize it as dynastic.

On this issue I follow the evaluation of the position of the tribal leader which has been presented by L. Stein[165]. Among the Šammar the office of sheik is heritable within a single family, but the principle of primogeniture is not decisive. Instead, the most capable member of the sheik's family is selected. A portion of the Šammar migrated into the *Ğezira* of Iraq during the 17th century from their original tribal territory at Ğebel Šammar, in the northern part of central Arabia, *Šammar-Ğerba*[166]. It is the case where these nomads are concerned that throughout history a single family, the *Ğerba*, has completely dominated the selection of tribal leaders. In the past there were three such offices: the tribal leader or top sheik, who was the leader of a college of subordinate sheiks; the war leader *(aqid)*, and the judge *(qadi)*[167]. Among Iranian nomads the tribal leader occasionally achieved a position with broader powers than have usually been available to the traditional Arab tribal chieftain such as we find among the Baḫtiyari or the Qashqa'i[168].

Naturally, the position of tribal leaders covers a broad spectrum, and the means of selecting him may also vary considerably. However, in general we may say that they are persons who are reckoned to possess particular political significance and authority as leaders of the tribe in question by both tribal members and foreigners. It is also clear that in spite of the fact that the tribal leader often has to pay for his position in terms of sizable demands upon his hospitality, generosity, and so on, he nevertheless accedes to a position among those who are economically best situated in his society. To mention an extreme

---

[164] Cf. above, p. 99-100, and also B. Glatzer's description of the Durrani khans (1977:173-184).

[165] Stein 1967:130ff.

[166] Cf. Stein 1967:14ff.

[167] Stein 1967:135.

[168] On the Qashqa'i, see Oberling 1974; on the Baḫtiyari, Ehmann 1975:65-74.

case, E. Wirth describes the rank and file Arab bedouin as possessing an average herd of around 300 animals, whereas the sheiks usually possess as many as 3,000, a statistic which does not prevent some individual sheiks from owning from 20,000 to 50,000 sheep[169].

Against this, it would be unwise to overestimate the powers of a tribal leader with respect to his tribal kinsmen, since in most cases he does not control a power apparatus capable of executing his decisions against the wishes of the ordinary member of the tribe. The tribal leader ordinarily does not dispose over a body capable of subduing the other members of the tribe to his will, and in fact there is only a limited number of areas in which his will is ultimately decisive. The areas in which the leader of the tribe has no say include in the first rank matters pertaining to the individual families, especially their economic affairs. Further, he has no authority in matters involving several families within a lineage. By the same token, the tribal leader is also in principle powerless with respect to corresponding cases taking place higher up the social ladder, that is, at the level of the lineage or the tribal section, unless he is employed as an arbitrator between such fractions.

Having noted all this, we should also remark that the traditional picture of the powerful sheik as incarnated in such figures as *Nuri Ibn Sa'alan*, the supreme sheik of the Rwala[170], and *Auda Abu Tayi*, the *Howetat* leader[171], both of whom are described by T.E. Lawrence as apparently exercizing absolute power over their tribes, is far from wrong. The central concept in this apparently contradictory account is *prestige*. The kinsmen of the tribal leader regard him as the exceptional individual in the tribe, for which reason he is assigned special importance. As a result, the individual bedouin in reality has no chance to reject the decisions of his leader and still remain within the tribal fellowship. The sheik's prestige is associated with a number of factors of which only a few can be mentioned here; these are such qualities as wealth, warlike accomplishments, and eloquence. Therefore a leader who is not equal to the tasks confronting him will not be able to remain in power. If he is found to be inadequate, he can be deposed without more ado and replaced by another. In certain eventualities an entire family may be removed from power if it has supported a weak tribal leader chosen from its ranks too long. In this connection Barth mentions an instructive example which illustrates the truism that the leader position must be assigned to a significant personality. The supreme

---

[169] See Wirth 1969:98, as well as Barth 1953:40, who speaks of economic differences among the Kurdish nomads ranging from fifty to two thousand animals.

[170] Lawrence 1935:173f. Musil also refers to this tribal chieftain (1928:59) in his section of the position of the chieftain of the Rwala, which he describes with the words "chief" and even "prince". See also Oppenheim 1939:I:23f. Oppenheim uses the term "Fürsten" of the supreme sheiks; this corresponds to the title *emir* applied to them by the officials of the French mandate. Cf. Meeker's recent publication (Meeker 1979: *passim* on this "prince" of the Rwala (Meeker's term).

[171] Lawrence 1935:221ff. Cf. also Oppenheim 1939:II:293ff.

chieftain of the Basseri took control of another tribe back in the 1920's by simply intervening in the dispositions of the leader of the tribe in question, with the result that he ultimately directed the tribe himself. This was not a temporary situation, but one which ended with the complete deposition of the tribal leadership in question[172].

Although we might be tempted to think otherwise, the collision between the tribal society and the world at large need not necessarily result in the undermining of the leader's position. In fact, it would be more accurate to say that the reverse has generally been the case, as examples from the entire Middle East testify. Where this has not been the case, it has been because forces outside of the tribal society, that is, the nation states, have felt themselves to be so strongly or so directly involved in the development of the society that they have consciously striven to destroy the power of the leaders.

The Pahlevi dynasty of Iran furnishes us with an example of this latter process. During the rule of the first member of the dynasty a large number of tribal leaders were either deposed, liquidated, or abducted to Teheran as hostages. Following this the government itself assumed the direct leadership of the tribes with the aid of gendarmes and military governors[173]. In other cases, however, the central authority has either chosen to strengthen the position of the tribal leader, or else it unintentionally managed to do so. This was normally the case everywhere the power of the colonial government clashed with local societies, as manifold examples illustrate[174].

To return, then, to our question: is the tribal leader a *primus inter pares*? In the last-mentioned example this is scarcely the case in actual practice, but additionally the information provided by Wirth suggests that although an egalitarian ideology permeates these societies, in reality this is merely a curtain concealing a rather more harsh situation. The question is, then, how are we to reconcile such contradictory information, that is, the fact that in many nomadic societies their members ordinarily regard themselves as equals, while at the same time it is easy to demonstrate that the very same social systems also display very considerable differences in the social status of their members? It should be possible in advance to isolate a number of possible explanations. A

---

[172] Barth 1964A:85. The Arabic-speaking tribe of the Nafar have served as an "annexed tribe" of the Persian-speaking Basseri since the 1920's. However, at the time the khan of the Basseri won control of this tribe, it was about the same size as the Basseri.

[173] The procedure of the Iranian state has been described in several works: Oberling 1974: 149-167; Tapper 1979B:21ff.; Black-Michaud 1976:197ff.; Ehmann 1975:74ff.; Fazel 1973; and Salzman 1971B.

[174] Cf. on this point Salzman 1974; Glatzer 1977:187ff. An example would be the collision between the British and the Kalat khan institution (described by N. Swiddler 1972); cf. S. Pastner 1978:254ff. In the previous period this institution had developed into a "quasistate", but after the entry of the British onto the scene the stratified social structure became fixed. Another example is the meeting of the Tuaregs and the French colonial authorities; cf. Nicolaisen 1963B: 398. See also W. Caskel, who describes similar conditions in pre-Islamic Arab tribal societies (1962:144).

simple solution is to suggest that the characterization of a given society as egalitarian tells us much more about the attitudes of the ethnographer who studied it than about the society itself. This explanation is not easily dismissed, as Black-Michaud's criticisms of his earlier colleagues indicates[175]. Against this is the fact that as late as 1970 there were tribal societies in the Near East which were described as fiercely egalitarian. Thus, for example, B. Glatzer depicted the *Durrāni pashtun*[176].

Other, more constructive explanations are also possible; for example, one might point to ecological or political conditions as the reason for the growth of inequality in a tribal system, or one might claim that proto-stratification occurs as a result of the interaction of these two factors[177]. To return to the Durrāni nomads, Glatzer's description of the circumstances of their life reveals that they are not confronted by either natural or political obstacles to their independent development as nomads. This means that in their environment there are sufficient resources that the nomad has only himself to blame if he fails to make the best of his situation. Moreover, at least until 1970, no serious political effort had been made from the central authority to prevent these nomads from freely pursuing their way of life[178]. Therefore some anthropologists have maintained that egalitarian nomadic societies emerge in surroundings which do not not directly hinder the possibility of such development, that is, in areas in which a nomadic society would not be forced to compete with other sectors in order to utilize the local resources[179].

This model for explaining both equality and inequality would seem to be applicable to most of the cases. However, it nevertheless fails to explain why even hierarchically structured nomadic societies take their societies to be egalitarian when there is clearly no correspondence between ideology and reality.

To mention a pair of examples, the Arab *Kababish* of the northern Sudan were organized, according to T. Asad, in more or less loose associations of tribelike units. Admittedly, there was a supreme sheik over this league, but Asad describes his powers along the lines of the remarks above concerning prestige. The subsections and lineages of the tribe at the lower levels also possessed lesser leaders. When Kababish became part of the British Empire, one of the first actions of the colonial government was to acknowledge the chieftain as the actual tribal leader. In other words, the chieftain was singled out as the individual through whom the English direc-

---

[175] 1976:10-59, esp. pp.40ff; cf. Black 1972:614ff.

[176] Glatzer 1977, especially his conclusions on pp.203-206.

[177] See the discussion in *Pastoral Production and Society*: Salzman 1979; Asad 1979; Irons 1979; Burnham 1979; Bonte 1979; and De Planhol 1979.

[178] See Glatzer 1977:185ff.

[179] Cf. Glatzer 1977:191ff. See also De Planhol 1979, who distinguishes between unsaturated milieux which are secure, unsaturated milieux threatened by uncertain conditions, and saturated milieux (here "saturated" means that all of the available resources have been exploited, so that there is no surplus of land). However, see also Lefébure 1979B, who points out that two different saturated milieux, the Zagros mountains and the Atlas mountains, have witnessed the emergence of two different political systems in spite of ecological and demographic similarities.

ted the affairs of the tribe. The result of this remarkable situation was that the sheik usurped to himself and his family all effective power among the Kababish, since the tribesmen were at his mercy whenever they were forced to deal with the national authorities. This brought about the deposition of the leaders of the tribal subsections and the emergence of a princely lineage which speedily exploited its position in monopolizing both the political power and the economic surplus of the tribe. To follow Asad one might say that the tribe became a solidly united political unit in this fashion, a unit which had been more or less created by the colonial power. Within a short span of years the society became divided into two spheres: the rulers and the ruled. A stratified system had arisen. Members of the elite emphasize their right to govern in part by emphasizing that they are the rightful and necessary rulers, and in part by stressing that all of the Kababish act as one man. In other words, they refer to the existence of an egalitarian ideology which claims that all Kababish are to be regarded as equals who defend each other's interests, while at the same time they have monopolized all political authority in the tribe and have no trouble distinguishing between patron and client in the system. The individual Arab does not rebel against the system because on the one hand he still retains the illusion of freedom, while on the other he actually has no alternative[180].

Thus it is legitimate to inquire as to whether one can speak of a just government in such a society, that is, to ask whether the conception of the Kababish as full equals is not in reality used to manipulate the subjects (Asad's view). Alternatively, one might, with Black-Michaud describe the relationship between ruler and ruled as a tyrannical system[181].

Black-Michaud has himself undertaken a similar examination of the consequences of the intervention of an external authority in the workings of a previously autonomous local system; his example is from Luristan in Iran[182]. In Luristan a college of khans governed the individual tribes until Reza Shah subdued the Iranian tribes during the period between the world wars. However, as in the case of the Kababish the Luristanian leaders also enjoyed only limited powers with respect to the individual nomads. Unlike the efforts of the English colonial government, Reza Shah's policy was aimed directly at the leadership stratum, which he succeeded in eliminating. In their place he established district authorities to represent the central government; these were for the most part simply gendarmeries. Such a situation, or so one might have supposed, would have encouraged the traditional egalitarian ideology of the Luri, but this was far from the actual result. Instead, the next stage in the political development of the area was the compulsory settlement of the nomads without regard to the suffering this step entailed. The nomads were assigned territory within their previous migratory territory, but there was no question of an equitable distribution of the available land. Rather, the strongest lineages arrogated the best land and the largest territories to themselves by sheer force majeure. Thus the way was paved for the emergence of a society with social inequalities between rich and poor peasants. This development continued; a few years later some of the forcibly settled lineages were permitted a certain amount of nomadic activity. Once again the larger lineages made the best of this change since they were already in possession of greater economic resources in the form of land. Thus they were able economically to dominate other parts of the society, and also because they were in control of the tribal grazing areas thanks to their extensive land ownership. The result was a system in which the society of the Luri became divided into two main groups, the haves and the have-nots. Furthermore, in order to survive at all the latter were forced to bind themselves to the wealthy by means of client contracts. This system survived the temporary suspension of the national government during the Second World War, which suggests that the development had become irreversible in spite of the fact that there were no longer polical constraints to prevent the re-establishment of the earlier system. It may accordingly be said that the disappearance of the traditional leadership stratum among the Luri resulted in a stratified class society consisting of the free and the unfree; nevertheless, the egalitarian ideal that all Luri are equals remains the dominant ideology. Black-Michaud offers a functionalistic explanation for this situation; he claims that the consciousness of equality is an essential presupposition for being

---

[180] On this see Asad 1970 (where it is the main hypothesis in his description of the Kababish Arabs); 1973.

[181] See Black 1972:614: "not equality but tyranny is the *Leitmotif* of Luri social structure".

[182] Black-Michaud 1976.

able to enter into client-contractual relations, since it provides the client with the illusion that he remains free to choose his own path. In practice, however, this freedom is illusory, since the current occupational situation in Luristan offers only meager chances for survival to anyone who does not belong either to the by no means numerous leadership stratum or to the stratum of de facto tyrranized clients[183].

There are accordingly clear examples to prove the point that egalitarian socie-ties may well be stratified, or, more to the point, it must be recognized that there is no direct connection between egalitarian ideas and the actual political and social structure of a given system. To the contrary, the examples mentio-ned above show that an egalitarian ideology may very well contribute to the evolution of hierarchical forms of government and thus ease the transition to a differentiated economic system which contradicts the ideology. This is so because opposition to the emergence of social inequality is mediated by the idea that all are equal before the Lord. On the other hand, no one has as yet provided an explanation of how such an ideology can arise once a society has been divided into social classes or strata. It is possible that the retention of the egalitarian principle is a facet of the ethnic self-consciousness of a given tribal people. By "ethnic self-consciousness" I mean to signify ties of solidarity, understood as a superstructure which unifies a tribe, so that all members are prepared to join in the common defence in the event that external enemies are thought to threaten the existence of the society in question. Perhaps it is still necessary for a Kababish or a Luri to retain their social identification in the presence of a third party, or, to put it another way, perhaps the leadership stra-tum convinces the subject class that it is in their own interest for the society to continue to exist as an independent unit with respect to others.

This brings us to the most precarious topic as far as the pastoral nomads are concerned, namely their relationships to other social groups, and the relation-ship between the tribal society as a discrete (i.e., delimited and definable) unit and the rest of the society[184]. With respect to occupation the examples offered above suggested that there are considerable differences among the various nomadic societies with respect to the manner in which they secure a dietary supplement from the agricultural sector, which the tribes themselves do not control. There was only absolute agreement on one point, namely that in all five cases deriving from the Near East the tribes were dependent on a supply of vegetables. In this sense it is inappropriate to speak of "pure nomads" in connection with the Near East, since this description implies that pure no-mads are able to survive without such a dietary supplement. If one were to erect a typology on the basis of the five examples, one might conclude that at any rate the al-Murrah and the Basseri are pure nomads, in the sense that no part of their populations pursues a non-pastoral means of earning a living.

---

[183] Others have discovered similar features in other nomadic societies; cf. e.g. D.A. Brad-burd (1981).

[184] On the distinctions between "people", "tribe", and so forth see below, pp. 237-244.

Furthermore, the al-Murrah are to be described as bedouins, that is, camel nomads, and it is only recently that other types of animals have begun to play a part in marginal areas, where they are bred for sale in town markets. The Basseri are largely small-cattle nomads. Unlike the Basseri and the al-Murrah, the Baḥtiyari are to be classified as only partially nomadic, since we find within this population representatives of both the pastoral and agricultural sectors. The same is also true of the Yörük, among whom we encounter former nomads who now live as merchants in their part of Turkey[185]. Other rules apply to the bedouin of the Negev, among whom the same individuals serve both as shepherds and as peasants. They are at best to be classified as part-time nomads.

It is also possible to classify these peoples according to the migratory systems, since these may be roughly divided into two categories, namely those nomads who migrate *vertically* and those who migrate *horizontally*. To use a different terminology, one might say that they may be assigned to the categories of mountain and steppe nomads. The al-Murrah may, for example, be termed steppe nomads (even though it would probably be more correct to define them as desert nomads, properly so conceived), while the Basseri may be characterized as mountain nomads like the Yörük and the Baḥtiyari. Finally, the Negev bedouins may be assigned to the horizontally wandering steppe nomads, even if they do touch upon modest mountain reaches in their migrations.

As far as the relationships to the settled population are concerned, the examples cited above also reveal a number of variations. In the case of the al-Murrah their connection with the oasis farmers and town dwellers is a fact, even if this confrontation is concentrated within particular periods of the annual cycle. According to Barth the Basseri nomads also comprise a special social group in the province of Fars. Even though countless nomads of Basseri descent become sedentary in the course of time, no change in the status of the tribe occur, since nomadism and membership of the Basseri tribe are inseparable quantities. As far as the Baḥtiyari are concerned, Ehmann maintains that a Baḥtiyar belongs to the Baḥtiyari society merely by inhabiting its territory[186]. On the other hand, the Yörük are divided between a nomadic element and another of sedentary village dwellers who inhabit the entire range of the migratory area. At least within the period this people has been studied this bifurcation has not entailed that nomads who have settled down have abandoned their relationship to Yörük society. Finally, the bedoiun of the Negev diverge from the other patterns discussed by virtue of the feature that a population of *fellahin* dwell among them who generally have the same em-

---

[185] Bates 1973:26.
[186] Ehmann 1975:14ff.

ployment as the bedouin, but who nevertheless are not accepted as members in equal standing of the bedouin's organizations.

At this juncture, two questions virtually beg to be asked: first, is it possible to find a lowest-common-denominator-model which does not generalize at a level which would render it useless for the understanding of an individual society, but which is at the same time so flexible that most societies can be accomodated to it? Second, is the particolored spectrum of nomadic ways of life presented above only an expression of a modern and quite unique evolution? In other words, is the existence of a plethora of types characteristic of modern nomads alone, or may we assume that similar differences have also existed in earlier periods? The first question will be answered mainly synchronically; the second diachronically.

The answer to the first question is to be sought in the contemporary anthropological debate as to the possibility of compiling a catalog of nomadic systems based upon a limited number of *ideal types*, understood as heuristic tools for use in further analysis. To put it another way, this subject is identical with our point of departure for this chapter; is it meaningful to operate, as Gottwald does, with a "type" of pastoral nomad who lives in symbiosis with sedentary societies which themselves live in peace and have no significance for the social, economic, and political development of the area in question, which would permit us to dismiss the other types as irrelevant in this connection?

Before I attempt to discuss this on-going debate concerning the nomadic types, it will be necessary briefly to comment on the concept of *pastoral nomad*. Etymologically considered the phrase is a tautology, as already the combination of the two words indicates, as it consists of the Latin *pastor*, "shepherd", (and *pastoralis*, "that which is associated with shepherding")[187] and Greek **νομεύω**, "to wander about seeking pasturage" (cf. **νομεύς**, "shepherd")[188]. There is therefore some uncertainty as to the use of the term. Its etymology suggests that it has something to do with cattle-breeding. According to C. Rathjens, the Greek origin of the word implies the underlying concepts of **νέμος** and **νόμος**, where **νέμος** has the meaning "flock", "cattle-raising", while **νόμος** signifies "law", "rule". This is a somewhat imprecise translation[189]. In Greek **νέμος** is a rare parallel formation of **νομός** and is translated by "wooded pasture", "glade"[190]. **Νομός** itself has several meanings: "pasture", "habitation", "district", "province" (and is used in the latter sense of the Egyptian administrative districts, the so-called *nomes*)[191]. This is to be kept separate from **νόμος** "law", "rule", etc. All three words are actually derivations of the verb **νέμω**, which has two main senses: "to deal out", "dispense", "pay out" (as well as "to possess", on the one hand, and on the other – in connection with shepherd – "to pasture", "graze", but it is also used of the cattle who graze and of fire consuming something)[192]. **νομάς** and **νομάδες**, "pastoral tribes" (used by, among others, Herodotus)[193] is a special development of the word, as is the verb **νομεύω**, "put out to graze", "drive afield". However, **νόμος** is also used of "division", "distribu-

---

[187]   OLD 1306.
[188]   GEL 1178.
[189]   Rathjens 1969:20. A better attempt at an etymological solution is to be found in Vajda 1968:501-502.
[190]   GEL 1167.
[191]   GEL 1180.
[192]   GEL 1167.
[193]   GEL 1178.

tion", and in juridical language refers to "possessio". Roman authors adopted the term in the same sense, and which we now use in daily speech. The Romans used it especially of the Numideans, presumably as a pun (thus, for example, Vergil, whose "original" in this respect was Polybios)[194]. It is characteristic that the technical meaning of the word arose in cultures which were not in primary contact with the phenomenon, whereas ancient Near Eastern societies themselves lacked corresponding designations for nomads as a sociological type. In the OT one encounters circumlocutions such as in Gen 4:20 "those who dwell in tents and have cattle". In Akkadian in ancient times a geographical term was most often used for the Semitic nomads, namely *amurru* (MAR.TU).

It would be possible to examine quite a number of attempts at a classification of the sort mentioned above. I shall confine myself here to relatively few, but nevertheless distinct examples, of these. To mention one well-known earlier system, that of E.E. Bacon, it is noteworthy that the author distinguishes between three different types of nomads[195]. "The true" or "pure" nomads, that is, peoples who take their dwellings with them throughout the year, and who have no recourse to agriculture. Their migratory routes are irrelevant in this connection. Alongside these we find the "semi-nomads", who also have portable dwellings, and who cultivate small plots of land in their home territory. Finally there are the "semi-sedentary" nomads, by which Bacon refers to peoples who dwell in villages for part of the year and cultivate their fields, but who at other times keep to a pastoral way of life and dwell in tents. This means that Bacon does not primarily distinguish between mountain and steppe nomads, or between camel nomads and keepers of small-cattle; rather, her classification is dependent on the significance of agriculture for the society in question. Her system has been improved by K. Ferdinand, who acknowledges the importance of her basic principle, namely that of measuring nomads by the significance which agriculture enjoys in the society in question[196]. Ferdinand, however, points to a number of problems connected with Bacon's definition of semi-nomads, which he finds too rigid. Ferdinand suggests instead that we characterize the semi-nomad as a person for whom the agrarian sector is of equal importance to the pastoral sector. Against this the semi-sedentary type would be one for whom agriculture indisputably plays the greatest role. This means that Ferdinand rejects the type of dwelling as the decisive criterium and retains only the ratio between the agrarian and pastoral sectors.

The writer emphasizes that a classificatory system must be flexible, which itself poses problems for the demarcation of these three types: how does one draw the line so as to identify the pure nomad? Where is the dividing-line which identifies the semi-nomad, and at what point are we justified in saying that he is semi-sedentary? Is a pure nomad no longer pure when more than 33% of his time is devoted to cultivating crops? Or does "pure nomad" signify that 100% of his time is devoted to cattle-raising? Is the semi-nomad still semi-

---

[194] OLD 1185.
[195] Bacon 1954.
[196] Ferdinand 1969B:128f.

sedentary if his agriculture yields two thirds of his income, while he himself lives in a tent for most of the year, or while he still feels himself to be most attached to his existence as a herdsman?

Other attempts to derive various types have been based on the migratory patterns of the societies in question. Here it would be appropriate to mention the proposal of D.L. Johnson[197]. Johnson distinguishes between horizontal (i.e., steppe) nomads and vertical (i.e., mountain-) nomads. He subdivides the first type into two subsections: *pulsatory nomadism*, in which the routes out and back coincide, and *elliptical nomadism*, where the route back home differs from the route out. The second type is again subdivided into three categories: *constricted-oscillatory nomadism*, in which the migratory paths both out and back follow the same course (they also follow the same routes from year to year), *limited amplitude nomadism*, in which the migrations are of limited extent, and *complex nomadism*, in which the migratory pattern is so complex that it cannot be subsumed under a single rubric.

The second group proposed by Johnson may be compared with that of the German cultural geographer, W.-D. Hütteroth, who has attempted to distinguish between mountain nomadism and other types of cattle-raising in the mountainous regions of the Middle East[198]. Hütteroth mentions three forms, those of *transhumance*, *Alpwirtschaft*, and *Hirtennomadismus* (pastoral nomadism). The first two forms are associated with sedentary societies. Hütteroth's system is based on studies of the Kurdish mountain nomads of Turkey, but he himself points out that the type of nomadism in the region in question is strongly bound up with similar (but less extensive) vertical movements among the local populace of mountain peasants (the so-called *yayla*-peasants). Thus it may be maintained that it is really impossible to distinguish the mountain nomads from the yayla-peasants[199].

Similar classificatory efforts are to be found in the works of other German cultural geographers, such as F. Scholz, E. Grötzbach, and C. Jentsch, to name only a few of those who have concerned themselves with this topic in recent years[200]. However, it is still an open question as to whether these efforts

---

[197] Johnson 1969.

[198] Hütteroth 1959:37-42; 1973:148ff.

[199] See Ehmann 1975:13, as well as Hütteroth's description of the mountain nomads (1959: 42-47). E. Grötzbach regards the mountain nomads described by Hütteroth as semi-nomads (1973:104).

[200] Grötzbach distinguishes between nomads and sedendtary dwellers as fundamental types, but then subsequently subdivides into full nomads, semi-nomads, semi-settled, and fully settled. *Transhumance* overlaps all of these categories, as does *"Teilnomadismus"*. The semi-nomad is associated with a wandering existence which is combined with settled agriculture, whereas the semi-settled dweller is permanently attached to a single place, but wanders periodically (1973:101-107). C. Jentsch also retains the distinction between full and semi-nomads, although he also recognizes the existence of a number of intermediate forms. However, he regards the existence of such forms as an indication that a process is underway which leads from one of the main categories to the other (1973:14-20). F. Scholz smooths things out even more by utilizing a "nomadic typology" of no fewer than 8 different types (1972).

have touched on anything besides migratory patterns in Near Eastern societies which practice cattle-raising. In reality these typologies do not say very much about the peoples who make use of these migratory systems.

In spite of the difficulties involved, one also encounters scholars who maintain that the subdivision of nomads into types ought to be retained even though there is no question of sharply delimited forms, simply because the ability to isolate such ideal types possesses didactic value for the understanding of the nature of nomadism[201]. The difficulty with this suggestion, however, is whether our understanding is actually aided by such a procedure, or whether it is not instead inhibited by the use of ideal types which may encourage us to concentrate on isolated phenomena. This could prevent us from realizing that such phenomena might best be understood in a wider, which is to say, a regional, context. To mention but a single example, Ehmann says in connection with the Baḫtiyari that their society is divided into three occupational categories[202]. The difficulty with this notion, however, is whether there de facto exist three clearly discrete sectors within Baḫtiyari society, or whether the boundaries between them are fluid. If we turn our gaze to Luristan, which borders the territory of the Baḫtiyari, it is to be seen that Black-Michaud distinguishes between six categories of Luri within the same "ethnos", but he emphasizes that in this case we have to do with two clearly distinct classes, each of which is divisible into three strata[203]. As far as the territory of the Iranian Kerman (to whom I shall return later) is concerned, G. Stöber maintains that the nomads in this region cannot be subsumed under a single type, but that there is instead a continuum of forms. In other words, there are no clear boundary lines separating the various types of nomadism from one another, nor are there any such lines sharply demarcating between nomadism and agriculture[204].

This discussion accordingly indicates that if we are to seek a definition, then it must necessarily be sufficiently flexible to permit the existence of a continuum of forms, since it does not seem to be possible to define a particular culture as proper to the nomads alone. Thus it would be appropriate to point to the definition of nomadism which has been presented by, among others, N. Dyson-Hudson and P.C. Salzman. In Dyson-Hudson's view, nomadism is simply that region in which two special cultural forms overlap one another: on the one hand, cattle-raising, and on the other, spatial mobility[205]. In this connection it may be stressed that nomads have in common with many sedentary societies the raising of cattle, while their propensity to move about is a phenomenon they share with many other migratory groups who, however, do not

---

[201] See Stöber 1978:253f.; cf. also Ehmann 1975:10.

[202] Ehmann 1975:78.

[203] Black-Michaud 1976:239-275. It is characteristic of the *Luri* that the economically dominant group combines the nomadic way of life with the ownership of land.

[204] Stöber 1978:258.

[205] Dyson-Hudson 1972:23. See also Salzman 1967:116, who holds that nomadism is a combination of migration and stock-breeding (further, Spooner 1972:130).

transport domesticated animals with them, such as, for example, itinerant merchants and tinkers. Salzman has developed this conception with the addition of a concept which he describes as *multi-resource nomadism*. In this connection he divides the nomadic existence into a number of sectors, all of which contribute to the maintenance of that existence. These are such things as (naturally) cattle-breeding, agriculture, trade, hunting, and day-labor activity[206]. Most nomadic societies will in practice prove to be dependent upon at least two of these strategies. It is to be seen that this conception is so flexible that it may not be used as a solidly based model, but as a working tool which is capable of application to individual objects of study. In reality it also signifies that nomadism is not an occupation which is distinct from those pursued in the sedentary societies. Instead, it is to a great extent governed by the same interests as those of the sedentary societies, and the usefulness of this conception resides in the fact that it focuses our attention upon the interactions among the groups involved, rather than on the differences obtaining among them.

Such an understanding of Near Eastern nomadism would seem to support Gottwald's thesis that pastoral nomads cannot be understood as a threat with respect to sedentary peasant societies, since both nomads and peasants enjoy a symbiotic relationship to each other. However, one wonders if it is really as simple as all that. If such a symbiosis *were* the case, we would be forced to shake our heads in wonder at the innumerable historical testimonies to a clear opposition between the various sectors in the Near East. Why should the peasant feel insecure with respect to the nomad if both parties in reality are not wedded to contradictory interests, but are close friends who dwell in close proximity with one another, the only difference actually separating them being the fact that for part of the year the nomad dwells elsewhere, while the rest of the time both parties live in peaceful coexistence? This question reveals the limits of the attempts at classification, that is, that they tend to erase substantive differences among different social groups within a given Near Eastern region.

In the first place it must be emphasized that although we attempt to describe the relationship between the peasant and the nomad as a continuum, this does not signify that there are neither peasants nor nomads, but that – seen in the total context of the Orient – it is impossible to point to a sharp distinction between them as two different types of organizations. A local society may very well contain various sectors which diverge radically from each other. However, it is important to observe that the differences are not only related to the presence of discrete occupational groups, but are more probably to be seen as the result of competition between numerous groups for a limited supply of

---

[206] Salzman 1971C; 1972. Compare with other efforts in the same direction, such as that of O.H. Volk, who distinguishes between *Hirtennomadismus*, *Handelsnomadismus*, and *Ackerbaunomadismus* (1969). K. Ferdinand applies a similar classification to Afghan conditions (1969A).

resources. For example, there may be conflicts of interest between a nomadic group (irrespective of how the group in question has organized its way of life) and a village population, but the conflicts thus arising may be of the same nature as those which may occur between two different villages, or between two different nomadic tribes which encounter one another in the course of their annual migratory cycle. Such conflicts may involve herdsmen who have been hired to look after the herds of a village and nomads, or they may involve shepherds from two different villages, and so on. In the event of conflict between nomads and sedentary dwellers the national authority will be prone to take the part of the latter; in recent times this policy has had quite serious consequences for the well-being of the nomads on a number of occasions. This applies, for example, to the Yörük, who are obliged to pay imposts for grazing rights everywhere they attempt to camp[207].

In other words, the nomads have always drawn the short straw in encounters with the national authorities and their representatives in the modern Near East. This is presumably one of the reasons why scholars have gotten the impression that these nomads are peaceable and somewhat wretched figures. This picture has subsequently been projected backwards in history and has acquired paradigmatic character. This paradigm depicts a peaceful nomad who is generally at the mercy of others, and who wrests from a merciless Mother Nature the scant wherewithal of survival. This "nomadic type" has been understood as a small-cattle nomad, that is, a herder of sheep or goats. this type was then located in a niche between the camel nomads and the peasants, and he was thought to be unpleasantly squeezed between two such obvious oppositional quantities. Furthermore, it was thought possible to maintain that this impoverished sort of nomadic population never made up a majority in any region they inhabited, and that in fact they comprised a scanty few alongside of an impressive number of *fellahin*[208].

However, there is reason to believe that this description of the Near Eastern nomad is a caricature deriving from the quite special situation in which a number of modern migratory societies have found themselves. Also, scholars have transferred to this ideal type of the "small cattle nomad" qualities and characteristics which are applicable to the relationship between the aristocratic

---

[207] On the relationship of state, nomad, and peasant *versus* that of state and peasant, see Bates 1971.

[208] Cf. Patai 1962:16f. According to Patai's count the nomads make up about 10%-15% of the total, while 12%-14% dwell in the towns. J. Weullersse emphasized that during the Mandate the nomads in Syria and Iraq made up about 10% of the population; he also held that this percentage will have been higher earlier (1946:60f.). The most recent estimate as to the nomadic percentage of the population is in Ehmann 1975:2. According to Ehmann's account, the figures range between ½% in Israel and 25% in Yemen. With the exception of Israel, in the states within the Fertile Crescent the percentage ranges between 2% in Iraq and 5% in Jordan. However, we should recall that considerable settlement has taken place in the course of the 20th century; this tendency has certainly been strengthened since the Second World War.

Arab nomad and his client group. The camel bedouin have traditionally forced other segments of oriental societies, be they nomads, peasants, or towndwellers, into client relationships, and in this connection they have imposed imposts on them simply for allowing them to live in peace (the so-called "brotherhood monies", or *ḫuwa*, which were briefly described above). The al-Murrah may be regarded as an example of such an aristocratic tribe which once gathered significant income by this practice. By the same token, the camel bedouin have been described in a number of accounts as extraordinarily warlike, even though one ought not to disregard the fact that in most cases their desire for military adventure was usually directed against their peers (which is to say that aristocratic tribes victimized tribes of equal standing, as, for example, in reciprocal hostilities between the Rwala and the Šammar, in which the targets of such activities were invariably camels)[209]. Thus scholars arrived at the concept of an antinomy between two distinct types of nomads, the warlike camel bedouins and the peaceable small-cattle nomads, a view which has, as we have seen, become classical.

However, in introducing this distinction as a paradigm for the socio-economical organization of ancient Near Eastern society, scholars neglected to note that fully developed camel nomadism can scarcely have arisen before around the time of the birth of Christ at the earliest[210]. This implies that the special pattern which has been observable in the Arabic-speaking world in particular, and which consists of a distinction between aristocratic nomads on the one hand and groups of *sulubba* or *fellahin* on the other does not antedate the birth of Christ. This in turn signifies that the peaceful small-cattle nomad, considered as an ideal type, also failed to appear prior to the beginning of the Christian era. Thus, in order to get some idea of the way conditions in the Near East may have been prior to the bifurcation into patron and client tribes occurred, it would be worthwhile to investigate regions in which camel nomadism did not play any significant role. Such a procedure reveals a wholly different picture of the "peaceful" sheep and goat nomads from that which was constructed on the basis of studies carried out in the Arabic-speaking world in the decades subsequent to 1900. A common feature of the nomads of Baluchistan and Afghanistan is the fact that although their mobility was considerably less

---

[209] Meeker 1979 presents an interesting account of the bellicosity of the camel nomads; Meeker's account is mainly based on Musil's notes of the traditions of these societies. However, Meeker represents these bedouins as virtually prisoners of their own warlike ideology. L.E. Sweet attempted earlier to offer a functionalistic explanation of the razzias, namely to the effect that these plundering expeditions are almost a substitute for an exchange of gifts. Thus, instead of giving gifts to each other, the nomads' need for excitement was fulfilled by stealing each other's livestock (Sweet 1965B). Sources from the Osmann period reveal just how disruptive the bedouins' warlike activities were for other aspects of society, trade included; these sources speak of long periods in which not even the *ḥaǧǧ* caravans to Mecca could get through (cf. Sharon 1975:18ff.).

[210] See Dostal 1958; 1959.

than that of the camel-riding bedouin it was nevertheless sufficent to enable them to play a corresponding role with respect to the even less mobile populations with which they came in contact, that is, until the modern national authorities forced them to cease such practices[211].

Little knowledge of military tactics is required in order to understand the reasons for the superiority of such nomads. Military dominance is not synonymous with either quantitative or qualitative superiority on all fronts; rather, it consists in the potential to create a temporary, local superiority at the appropriate place and time[212]. Other types of nomads than just the bedouin are capable of realizing such a strategy in their encounters with other parts of society. Moreover, their mobility makes swift retreat possible in the event that this becomes necessary. Also, the segmentary organization of such nomadic populations has made it possible for them to mobilize larger groups of warriors than local peasant societies are able to assemble, since these may not be members of a solidarity group larger than a village. Thus W. Irons has argued for a hypothesis which although it applies to the Turkmenian Yomut, may also be applicable to corresponding societies. Irons maintains that for the Yomut nomadism is more a way of securing military advantages than a means of accomodation to natural conditions, since the migratory territory of the Yomut leaves open the possibility of settlement for the main part of the migrating tribal people[213]. Once again in the case of the Yomut we may observe that a determined effort on the part of the central authorities has been able to defeat such a tribal policy by countering it with military units which are even more mobile than those of their opponents. This task was made all the easier by the fact that the nomads have naturally been forced to take account of the fact that they are encumbered by their families and livestock in the event of retreat.

In the professional literature one occasionally encounters the assertion that certain ecological zones are specially suited to a nomadic existence, namely those regions which are not conducive to agriculture. However, nothing could be farther from the truth than the notion that a nomad prefers to dwell in a marginal territory, if he has the possibility to control more prosperous re-

---

[211] I shall confine myself here to referring to Black-Michaud's description of the Luri plaguing both peasant and town societies outside of Luristan (1976:195ff.). See also Ehmann's corresponding description of the Baḫtiyari (particularly his survey of the period 1846-1925 in Ehmann 1975:65-74).

[212] "The first principle of war is to concentrate superior force at the decisive point, that is, upon the field of battle." Formulated in this manner by G.F. Henderson in his biography of Stonewall Jackson (cited in Liddel Hart 1976:197). Throughout history, numerous campaigns have demonstrated the correctness of this maxim. Perhaps it would be most appropriate in this connection to point to the use made of mobile bedouin troups by T.E. Lawrence and Sherif Nasir against a stationary Turkish army during the First World War.

[213] Irons 1974. This is also the main hypothesis of Irons 1975, namely, that the nomadism of the Yomut was primarily the result of a politically conditioned choice of way of life. See Salzman, with a similar argument on the basis of an example from Baluchistan (1978D:131).

gions[214]. Also, an account such as that of Gottwald gives the impression that the far from numerous nomads are unable to remodel a (hypothetically) ancient peasant culture so that it conforms to their own socio-economic system. In practice, however, it turns out that nomads have done just this on more than a few occasion, where the regions in question were not dominated by the power of a central authority. To take but a single example, it would be appropriate to refer to Turkish history. In the 11th century the Osmann Turks migrated into Asia Minor and eventually seized control of this Byzantine province after the battle of Manzikert in 1071. Subsequent to the establishment of the Osmann Empire a partial, but nevertheless extensive destruction of the peasant societies in Anatolia in particular followed. The background for this destruction is to be sought in, among other things, the concern of the new Turkish ruling class to preserve their traditional way of life[215]. A corresponding development took place in the Near Eastern provinces of the Osmann Empire from the close of the 16th to the middle of the 19th centuries. During this period, Turkish sovereignty over the region in question was more nominal than real. Thus a power vacuum arose caused by the fact that the Turkish government only occasionally intervened in local conditions, which accordingly sometimes approached a state of anarchy. As a result, a number of agrarian societies degenerated and good arable land became pasturage for the nomads' livestock. At the same time, large parts of the settled peasant population abandoned their precarious hold on existence and instead sought the safety of migration.

We are in the fortunate situation that as far as Palestine is concerned these developments have been quite well illustrated thanks to the publication by Hütteroth of information from the Turkish national archives from the time around 1600. Hütteroth has compared this data with information from the first part of the 19th century; thus, he has been able clearly to demonstrate the extent of the degeneration of the permanent settlements in Palestine. Furthermore, the destruction of the Palestinian agricultural milieu can be documented from province to province. As far as Palestine as a whole is concerned, it is possible to show how the number of villages declined between the 16th and 19th centuries to between 2/5 and 1/3 of their original number[216]. Cor-

---

[214] It is sometimes claimed that nomadic cultures are *niche* cultures, in the sense that the nomads only fill up the niches in the local ecology which are left when the agrarian societies have seized all the territories suitable for their purposes. However, this is an extremely imprecise oversimplification. On this question, see Salzman 1971A, and in particular Bates 1971 and Irons 1971. See also Marx 1973, who emphasizes the necessity for nomads to possess pasturage in areas which could just as easily be utilized for cultivation; as a reserve resource for the driest periods of the year.

[215] The consequence of the Turkish conquest of Anatolia after the battle of Manzikert, as well as the death-thrust administered to an already mordant peasant culture has been described in detail by X. De Planhol (1958:85ff.). The further history through the Middle Ages has been similarly studied by De Planhol (1958:109-131).

[216] See Hütteroth 1970; 1975, and Hütteroth and Abdulfattah 1977. The special conditions

responding conditions seem to have applied elsewhere in the Near East during this period[217].

It was only during the last fifty years of the Osmann Empire that the government in Istanbul attempted to alter this state of affairs. However, these efforts by the Turks did not accomplish much before the Arabian provinces were lost during the First World War (this policy, however, has since been actively pursued by most of the existing Arabic-speaking nation-states). In Asia Minor, however, this intensification of political control, plus the clear tilt of the authorities in favor of the sedentary populations actually did change the social landscape. The nomads' freedom of action was significantly reduced, indeed, to such a degree that it became so difficult to lead a nomadic life that today the phenomenon has largely vanished from contemporary Turkey[218].

By way of summary, we may say that as it appears in the Near East nomadism is an indication of the fact that Oriental societies adjust their socio-economical organization in accordance with whatever political constellation happens to be in the ascendant. A strong and well organized state only occasionally provides nomads with the possibility of expansion at the expense of other elements in society. On the other hand, the reduction of the effectiveness of central authority seems to favor the expansion of nomadism. One must further note that the socio-economical organization accomodates itself to the prevailing ecological situation. This fact has led to the emergence of innumerable different cultural forms in the region, so that it would be reasonable to speak of the existence of a continuum rather than a sharply differentiated scale of types.

Furthermore, the last part of the discussion above has revealed that the theory of *multi-resource nomadism*, coupled with the notion of a continuum, can be a useful tool for the sociological analysis of existing societies. However, it proves to be extremely difficult to use in connection with a historical sketch such as that offered above, as our sources do not provide much relevant information. This observation is by no means less true in conjunction with the study of ancient societies. The problem may be posed as follows: on the one hand we know nomadism to be a multi-facetted phenomenon, a fact which it

---

which obtained towards the end of the 18th century, when the extortion of the peasant societies by the nomads was supplemented by heavy taxation on the part of the authorities has been sketched out in Am. Cohen 1973:324ff. The entire course of development has been broadly surveyed by M. Sharon(1975).

[217] On the conditions in Transordan, see Antoun 1972A:16ff., and Gubser 1973:12ff. In the case of Syria I shall mention only L.E.Sweet's data about conditions in the district of Aleppo. Sweet mentions that censuses of villages from the beginning of the Osmann period contain more than 3,000 names. 300 years later there were hardly 400 left (1960:43). These figures speak for themselves.

[218] These developments have been described in Hütteroth 1959:70ff. Cf. also Eberhard 1953:38ff. Bates' study of the Yörük shows how a once numerous nomadic population can be impoverished in both economic and political terms by the consciously antinomadic policies of a central government.

is essential to recall in the course of historical analysis. On the other hand, this knowledge is not of much use to us in conducting diachronical studies, unless some quite exceptional sources should happen to contain the sort of information pertinent to such study. To the contrary, the historical scholar is well aware that there are significant risks involved in operating with ideal types, even understood as heuristic models, since such a procedure may produce false results by, for example, describing the so-called non-warlike pastoral small-cattle nomad as the only relevant type in a discussion such as this one, which deals with the origins of Israel. I shall return to the question of nomads in antiquity in the final section of this chapter.

§ 6

From Nomadic to Sedentary Life

Questions similar to those mentioned above, also concerned with the character of our sources, arise when we attempt to get some perspective on the processes which cause some nomads to settle down, or those which lead some peasants to take up a nomadic way of life. Nomadic societies are usually a-historical, which means that with the exception of a few rather general features they do not recall historical events which are more than a few generations old. Moreover, such memories as are preserved tend to take the form of historical legends[219]. There is no major difference in this respect between nomadic and other societies (smaller than the nation-state) in the Near East. Nor does the village often have any clear understanding of the history of the society in question. Should one undertake to compare the sort of recollections it is possible to encounter with those preserved by other sources (i.e., sources whose origin lies outside of the village in question, such as national archives or tra-

---

[219] Only a very few ethnographic descriptions of the sort of nomads who are here the basis for my description of these societies are concerned with this tradition. References are indeed often made in quite vague terms to the existence of heroic accounts about earlier warlike achievements, before the modern states succeeded in pacifying the tribal societies. It would certainly be a shame if these oral traditions were allowed to be lost, in part because they just *might* contain important historical information, and in part because they are in any case an expression of the ideological self-understanding of the society in question. In recent years a new orientation has been noticeable; this entails placing more weight on the significance of the ideology for determining the pattern of actions of tribally organized individuals. However, the materials such studies could be based on are (as yet) very few. See for example M. Meeker's use of Musil's collections of Rwala traditions (Meeker 1979), and his criticisms of Barth's description of the Swat Pathans (Barth 1959; cf. Meeker 1980).

velogues), one soon discovers that such sources do not necessarily agree with one another.

This implies that a study of the process of sedentarization must be based on existing conditions, even though there is a possibility that this procedure would be misleading if we attempted to transfer the results it makes possible to other epochs in the history of the Orient. Unfortunately, we have no alternative, as is shown by earlier studies of the process of Israel's sedentarization, including Alt's account of Israel's immigration and the efforts of both Gottwald and Mendenhall to counter this theory. Now, it is true of Alt, Mendenhall, and Gottwald that they have attempted to isolate a single type of nomad, namely the small-cattle nomad or "pastoral herdsman" from the total spectrum of nomadic ways of life. They have then subsequently claimed in connection with this ideal type that it is associated with a characteristic pattern of settlement.

However, the previous discussion about nomadism shows that this sort of concentration on a single type of nomad does not pay due attention to the continuity of the concept of the nomad. It is unacceptable to single out a particular category, define it as pastoral nomadism on the basis of modern materials, and then retroject it into the past in order to claim that it was the only type possible in the Near East in antiquity. I accordingly submit that the only correct approach available to us on the basis of the source materials at hand is to examine the question of the pattern of settlement as a general complex of problems touching on all nomadic societies. Only then may we attempt to clarify the factors which are active in the process of sedentarization. In this fashion one will arrive at a conclusion applicable to all varieties of nomads. Such a course, however, will reveal a general pattern, but one which includes so many possible variations as to prohibit its use as a paradigm for an individual society. Instead, the individual society is to be studied in isolation from the paradigm.

The first issue on which this approach has significance has to do with the question of large-scale migration. If one were to take the descriptions of pastoral nomadism offered by Mendenhall and Gottwald at face value, one might be led to believe that nomads simply never abandon a particular territory and move to another, on the theory that nomadism and sedentarism are merely two different methods of production which are employed by one and the same population (understood as the sum of individuals who dwell in a single geographically delimited area in the Near East). Now, it is true that scholars have been entirely too prone to attempt to explain historical and social changes in a given society as the results of large-scale migrations [220]. On the other hand, it would be no less naive to imagine that such migrations have never taken

---

[220] See the fundamental discussion in Adams 1968, plus Adams, Van Gerven, and Levy 1978.

place. Indeed, the materials we possess describing the Near East during the last couple of centuries reveal that such a view would be wrong-headed, since not a few nomadic societies are clearly relatively new arrivals in their present situations. One could refer to the immigration of central-Asiatic nomads into Turkey and Persia during the Middle Ages, or to the Arabs in the Sudan[221], but one could with equal justice point to the equally well attested immigrations of such nomadic groups as the Šammar-Ǧerba into Ǧezira in Iraq, which took place in the 18th century[222]. The Šammar-Ǧerba are part of the Šammar tribe; they have their own migratory territory around Ǧebel Šammar which is named after them, in the northern part of the Arabian Peninsula. To speak more accurately, the Šammar-Ǧerba are that portion of the Šammar who were forced two or three hundred years ago, probably by drought, to abandon their traditional tribal area. Thus they extended their annual northward route on into Ǧezira in Iraq. Naturally, this process was not carried out in the course of a single season; a long period of time passed before the establishment of the Šammar in Ǧezira was an accomplished fact. This process was not peaceful, since in order to settle down in Ǧezira it was necessary to expel the already resident nomadic population by force of arms[223]. By the 19th century, however, the territory was completely in the hands of the Šammar, and has remained so ever since[224].

Other examples derive from 19th century Turkey. As mentioned above, the Yörük pushed their way into their present migratory area in the latter half of the last century, replacing in the process the Kurdish nomads who had been expelled by the Turkish central authorities[225]. This was a remarkable event, when we consider that the Yörük probably correspond more to the picture of the pastoral nomad advocated by Mendenhall and by Gottwald in particular as a paradigm of ancient Palestinian nomads than does any of the other nomadic societies which form the basis for this "type" of nomad. For their part, the Kurds traverse, or at least have traversed, territories once inhabited by the Armenians. Especially since the First World War and the Turkish massacres of the Armenian population the area has become inhabited by the Kurds and

---

[221] On the first-mentioned groups of Turkish nomads, see especially De Planhol 1958 and 1969. On the Iranian nomads there is a historical sketch in Ehmann 1975:34-77, and in Oberling 1974:27-34 and 35-45. With respect to the Arabs and the Sudan, reference should be made to Ḥasan 1967, and on the Baggara see especially Cunnison 1966:1. According to the historical-genealogical recollection of the Baggara, they are connected with the Ǧuheina, of Qaḥṭan descent (i.e., they are of south-Arabian descent). The exact date of their arrival in the Sudan is not known, but according to Cunnison it must have been many centuries ago. Cf. also Ḥasan 1967:154ff., who maintains that we must go back more than a thousand years to find the early Arabian invasion of the Sudan.

[222] See Stein 1967:13-23.

[223] Stein 1967:16f.

[224] Stein 1967:16f. See also 1967:23, where an unofficial reckoning arrives at a population of 300,000 persons (Stein himself finds this figure too high).

[225] Bates 1973:21, 197f., 225.

may thus be said to have made the transition from agricultural area to nomadic area in this very century[226]. Similarly, since the close of the 19th century
Afghanistan, too, has witnessed a nomadic renascence. In this case, however,
this development was the result of a conscious policy on the part of the government in Kabul, which desired to encourage the localization of nomads in the
northwestern part of the country in order to produce a buffer zone against
Russia[227]. Already at this juncture, the spectrum which ranges from an Arab
asil tribe of camel nomads to the Kurdish mountain nomads to the acephalous, egalitarian and pastoral *Yörük*, shows that the traditional view according to which Israel was founded by nomads who had immigrated into
Palestine around 1200 cannot be rejected on the basis of the history of modern
nomads. Of course, it is equally impossible to deny that there are many nomadic tribes which have remained within the same migratory territories for centuries or even for millenia, as is indicated by the studies of South Arabian
bedouin groups which W. Dostal has carried out[228]. Thus there is no distinct
pattern in the historical attachments of nomadic societies to their tribal territories which may be simply transferred to nomads in other periods as a tool for
understanding their histories.

My next point has to do with the immigration by nomads into areas previously foreign to them. It is possible to point to manifold examples where this
has occurred. However, the question is whether nomads necessarily tend to
settle down in such new territories. It is especially interesting to examine how
nomads behave in areas where the previous inhabitants were sedentary peasants. Our sources suggest that *immigration and settlement are two distinct processes
which are not to be confused at the theoretical level in one's description of the history of a
nomadic society.* None of the examples mentioned above from the Middle Ages
or more recent times provides us with an example in which a nomadic group
which migrates into a territory previously devoted to agriculture, and in which
such immigration is followed by the spontaneous settling down of significant
sections of the new arrivals. Rather, such nomads have always persisted in following their traditional way of life until other factors determined that settlement was to be their fate.

These considerations lead me to my third general remark concerning the

---

[226] See Hütteroth 1959:107ff. There were already enclaves of Kurdish peasants in the area
prior to the expulsion of the Armenians; cf. Hütteroth 1959:110. On the consequences of these
developments for the area, see Hütteroth 1959:142ff; further, Hütteroth 1961:39.

[227] On this issue see Glatzer 1977:14ff; cf. also Ferdinand 1969B:137f.

[228] Dostal 1967 including perhaps the al-Mahra (1967:34), who, according to the author
display a number of south-Semitic features. Furthermore, with respect to social structure and
marital regulations they also differ from the other tribes dealt with in Dostal's work. See also
Dostal 1967:84f. It is therefore difficult to agree with B. Spooner's description of nomadic societies as "fluid, marginal, transitional, and unstable" (1972:130). In the respects considered, the
nomadic societies of the Middle East are not significantly different from other political and social
groups in the region.

question of the Settlement. It is to be observed that if we encounter nomads in a given territory, and if the ecological conditions permit, then we also often discover a sedentary population, that is, peasants, who are kin to the nomads in question. However, in other cases there is no question but that the sedentary population are the descendants of an earlier population. Finally, we also discover situations in which this older element of the population has been allocated a role within the political organization of the new population influx. This may perhaps occur if local conditions encourage such a development as, for example, when such measures take place in response to pressures external to the territory in question. This sort of integration of the population of a sizeable territory is to be found at many sites in Iran; it is thus typical of the Baḥtiyar confederation and seems also to apply to the Qasqa'i federation. In some cases it can be difficult to determine whether a sedentary population was once originally nomadic, even if the population in question claims this to be the case and is able to list names and places of origin. This is true of several of the peasant societies in Palestine and Jordan which have been described by modern ethnologists[229]. It is also the case that there are numerous examples in which the sedentary portion of a predominantly nomadic tribe actually derives from nomadic forefathers. Such groups are usually reckoned to be members of the tribe even by the nomads themselves, a feature which seldom occurs unless there is some historical basis for the assertion of tribal affiliation[230].

The accounts of both Barth and Bates suggest that the process which has led to the sedentarization of elements of the Yörük and Basseri tribes is to be understood as the result of *individual*, rather than *communal*, factors. Thus in studying the question of sedentarization it is necessary to distinguish between a development which includes entire nomadic groups or tribes and a development which mainly concerns individuals or families. Individual settlement is characteristically spontaneous, which means that it is not caused by the intervention of forces external to the life of the nomad in question. Perhaps it would be better to say that authorities outside of the nomadic group have not carried out *pre-planned* measures intended to compel the nomadic family to change its way of life.

By way of contrast, communal settlement, in which an entire nomadic tribe abandons it previous way of life, is normally the result of intervention into the essential conditions for nomadic existence by national authorities. In this event we generally have to do with a premeditated strategy intended to transform the nomads in question into law-abiding peasants.

This prompts the question as to why we do not (at least in modern times)

---

[229] Thus Lutfiyya 1966:14 (on the area in question in general), and Lutfiyya 1966:36f. on the "historical" recollections of the inhabitants of Beitin (Bethel). See further Ab. Cohen 1965:7.
[230] Cf. Bates 1973:21-34, esp. pp.26f., and Hütteroth 1959:107ff.

find examples of the spontaneous communal settlement of sizeable groups of nomads. A number of scholars have attempted to answer this question, among them being B. Zuber. Zuber claims that sedentarization is not a form of social advancement for the nomad. Alternatively, as Weullersse puts it, it is not the victorious bedouin who settles down, but rather the defeated one[231]. I shall presently return to the deeper implications of these views, but before doing so it would first be appropriateto consider a matter touching on the relationship between the ecological and political presuppositions. It is noteworthy that there are only limited resources of arable land in the Near East, whereas no such limits apply to the potential for nomadically administered cattle-raising. Admittedly, scholars are prone to claim that regions within the Fertile Crescent with an annual precipitation ranging between 100 and 250 isohyetes provide the optimal conditions for small-cattle nomads (camel nomads are clearly exempted from these limits). However, as mentioned above, the 250 isohyetes are a limit which is contingent upon the political situation, that is, it is dependent upon the existence or non-existence of organized states which are able to preserve arable areas from dominance by nomads. Throughout the entire history of the Near East it has repeatedly occurred that the central authorities have lacked the determination equal to the task, so that nomads have been able to expand their grazing areas so as to include good farming country. When the states have been able to support the local peasant societies, the nomads have usually been kept out of such areas. I have mentioned examples from Palestine, among other places, and there is no reason to repeat them here.

My second observation concerning the relationship between ecological conditions and nomads has to do with the situation in which the national authorities are in a position to control the activities of the nomads. In this case conditions tend towards a natural equilibrium in the areas concerned, so that the nomads tend to remain within the areas which only they may exploit, while the peasants make use of the regions which may be cultivated. In this situation both regions are optimally exploited. A corresponding situation may also occur in areas in which so-called *enclosed nomadism* flourishes, among which we may reckon the greater part of Palestine. In this sort of territory determined central leadership provides parameters favorable to the establishment of equilibrium between the various ways of life in the region. Thus the optimal number of nomads will be able to maintain their position alongside of the other cultural forms. Where such a situation obtains we may expect spontaneous movements in the population in which individuals change their way of life in such a way that some nomads may become sedentary and vice versa. On the other hand, difficulties occur in the event that either the nomadic or the agrarian sector is exposed to *stress* via the expansion of the population base

---

[231] Zuber 1976:113; Weullersse 1946:65.

over the limit the territory is able to provide for, or if for ideological reasons a government expels the nomads from their natural ecological niche with, for example, the intention of cultivating the region by means of irrigation. This sort of situation will perhaps prove to be stable for a few years, but time has nevertheless revealed numerous catastrophic results of such projects, which have often collapsed after a couple of years of drought.

Zuber's claim that the transition from nomadic existence to sedentary life is not synonymous with advancement for the individuals involved may be supported by at least three arguments. The first of these is economic in orientation. As mentioned previously, the average nomad is not poor by definition, although he may have few material possessions. Rather, his economic status is invariably better than that of the fellahin. The second argument is related to the first. The nomad's great advantage over the peasant lies in his mobility, which entails that he is vastly more difficult for the central authorities to control than is the peasant. This in turn signifies that it is quite difficult for the central authorities to tax the nomad, and there can be no question of the extortionate taxes which have often been levied on the fellahin in the Near East. Finally, Barth has pointed to the health factor, which is dependent on climatic conditions in the Orient[232]. While the peasant is rooted to one place the whole year around and thus is exposed to climatic vicissitudes which often include extremes of temperature and extended drought, in his peregrinations the nomad always pursues that climate which best favors his activities. This point will not be developed more fully here, but Barth mentions that it appears to be the case in the Basseri territories that there is a much higher mortality rate among peasants than among nomads. Indeed, he claims that the nomadic Basseri have to reckon with a striking population surplus which is managed by the continuous settling down of small groups of Basseri. Correspondingly, Barth notes indications of such high mortality among the peasant population that there is actually room to accomodate the influx coming from the nomads without straining the agricultural resources[233].

But how does the selection of nomads who wish to settle down actually take

---

[232] Barth 1964A:113ff.; cf. Ferdinand 1969B:146.

[233] Barth 1964A:115. Barth reckons the rate of population growth among the nomadic Basseri to be such that the population will triple in 30 to 40 years. He further maintains that this growth rate is not a result of improved medical care among these bedouins in recent times, as at the time Barth undertook his field study of the Basseri modern medical services had scarcely touched this people. In short, since the Basseri's migratory area can hardly feed a larger group of nomads than the total which existed already around 1960 (ca. 16,000 individuals, to which should be added a number of members of small client tribes which are in a confederation with the Basseri (Barth 1964A:1)), this surplus population must be settled in the villages within the region. In recent times it has been possible for the villages to absorb this nomadic surplus because of the high mortality in these villages (however, contemporary medical services have now upset this situation, with the result that violent population pressure has arisen in the entire territory involved); cf. Barth 1964A:120f. See also Jettmar 1969:81, and compare with Ferdinand 1969B:146 (on Afghanistan).

place? This is clearly a matter of compelling reasons, since the advantages of this change of occupation seem to be modest indeed[234]. One could maintain that sedentarization occurs either because the nomad has become too "heavy" or because he has become too "light" to persist in his migratory activities. "Too heavy" signifies that the nomad has acquired so much wealth that it is difficult for him to administer it as a nomad, for which reason he chooses to settle down. This fate traditionally accrues to the leadership stratum, and one often discovers that this class is considerably less mobile than the rest of the population of the tribe.

Barth has presented a thorough description of the causes of the sedentarization of the wealthy nomad[235]. Among other things, he shows that the Basseri have proved unable to develop a system which is able to ensure the care of the often very large herds owned by the wealthier nomads. One of the reasons for this inability is a general disinclination to employ herdsmen of foreign, i.e., non-familial, origins. This means that the *per capita* profits decrease as the herd grows significantly above the natural average. Thus the nomad who has a sizeable stock of animals is motivated to invest some share of his wealth in other means of production, which in traditional terms means land, which he then rents out to local peasants. This process is cumulative, so at some point when the main part of the wealth of the succesful nomad has been invested in land he will elect to establish residence in his domains, and thus enters the ranks of the better situated farmers in the region. In Persia and in large parts of the Near East this development has not been inhibited by the presence of an hereditary aristocracy along European lines which is in possession of traditional family estates, and which can only be induced to sell of them in cases of extreme need. This has been so because there has ordinarily been sufficient land available to anyone who has the means to purchase it. A similar situation has been observed among the wealthier Yörük nomads, as among those of Afghanistan[236]. L.E. Sweet has demonstrated in connection with the village society of Tell Toqaan that the same phenomenon is present among the Arabic-speaking nomads of Syria[237].

On the other hand, to say that a nomad has become "too light" signifies that he has become too poor to be able to maintain a nomadic existence. Here we should recall that nomadic societies cultivate private capitalism. Thus the economic autonomy of the individual family may become a negative factor if the family founders, especially by the loss of its herd, which is the most important means of production available to the nomad. In such a case the impoverished family cannot simply assert that there exist ties of economic solidarity among the individual families within its lineage (or higher up), so that they would be obliged to advance them the means which would enable the family to remain within the nomadic group. This situation, too, would lead to settlement, but this would undeniably take place on terms far different from those applying to the wealthy nomad.

Thus the pathway of the poor nomad to settled life does not involve the purchase of land. Instead,

---

[234] See also Bates 1973:194-196.
[235] Barth 1964A:101ff.
[236] See Bates 1973:146f.; Ferdinand 1969B:145.
[237] Further on Tell Toqaan below, pp. 171-173.

a nomad who has lost his herd, or whose herd has diminished below the threshhold necessary to guarantee his continued survival, is forced to seek employment as a professional shepherd either in the service of a wealthy nomad or in that of a village society, since villages often have their own herds, in particular, of sheep. If this possibility is not present, the nomad's options will be confined to the wretched existence of a day-laborer. Once again reference should be made to Barth's description of the situation in Persia, which is characterized by only possessing two social classes, the haves and the have-nots. The wealthy nomad ends up in the first group, while the unfortunate lands in the latter. In Persias villages there is no middle class which corresponds to the ordinary nomad[238].

Other factors which might contribute to the impoverishment of the nomad would be irrelevant in this connection. One of these has to do with the taxation of the nomad, that is, both direct taxation by the state and indirect taxation in the form of imposts levied on the nomad as a *quid pro quo* for grazing rights in certain areas of the Near East. Another factor is the vastly reduced significance of the camel in modern times, a factor which has deprived the camel nomads the considerable side incomes they once earned in earlier times by participating in the caravan trade.

A third major reason for a family to abandon its nomadic existence is its lack of juridical and legal rights with respect to the sedentary dwellers. This situation is acute today; the uncertain existence of the nomad at times borders on complete deprivation of the benefits of legal protection. This is a feature of the policy towards the nomads which is often pursued by central authorities, since, as we have seen, in modern times the governments of most Near Eastern states have tended to favor the peasants at the expense of the nomads. This situation applies to juridical clashes between peasants and nomads as well.

All of the factors mentioned above have in modern times resulted in the fact that especially in the period since the Second World War nomadic cultures have severely declined across the entire belt stretching from West Africa to western India, where these cultures once prospered. Although the argumentation concerning the spontaneous settlement of individual families has been presented in such a way that it seems to form a connected whole, one ought in reality to analyze every case of settlement in isolation in order to determine what the decisive factors involved are.

The process of sedentarization often seems to be facilitated by the presence of an element of the tribe which has already settled down, since this precondition makes it easier for the nomad who chooses this option (for whatever reason) to accomodate himself to his new circumstances. With respect to this point we are restricted to modern illustrative examples of the phenomenon[239].

---

[238] Barth 1964A:109f.

[239] Once again the most thorough materials are presented in Barth 1964A:101f. and 113ff., and in Bates 1973:21ff. and 191ff. Cf. also N. Swiddler 1973 on the Brahui settlement, in which the transition from one economic strategy to the other has been facilitated by the fact that it has not entailed any change in the status of the people in question within the tribal society. See also R. Bulliet's description of the mass settlement of Arab nomads in two southern Iraqi towns during the 7th century AD. According to Bulliet, this process was made much easier by the fact

In the Basseri territory a very large portion of the sedentary population is descended from the Basseri, even though the familial and kinship relations of these elements to the nomadic Basseri may only be retained to a limited extent. The same pattern also holds for the Yörük district, although to a lesser extent. Bates' treatment of this question is illustrative, in that he emphasizes the advantages available to the nomad of Yörük descent who is on his way into agrarian life and who settles down in the vicinity of tribal relations. In this event the nomad enters into a social context in which he is immediately a fully acknowledged member of the peasant society; this would not be the case if the village population contained no or only a few Yörük elements. One of the main reasons for the differences involved is the tribal system, since it is characterized by considerable flexibility within the tribe, being as it is composed of segments (i.e., units which have the same structure, such as family, clan, and so forth). A society of this type structurally possesses the ability to form new segments identical to those preceding them. An individual segment is usually autonomous, even in its familial relations to other and similar segments. It tends to align itself politically so as to obtain maximum advantage for itself. This entails that in Near Eastern tribes one discovers a continually changing organization, since the alignments of a family towards its kin will only persist as long as this association corresponds to the needs of the family. The relationship between a given lineage and a subsection of a tribe are similarly circumscribed by the political conditions. If political conditions change, the subgroups have complete freedom to change their political and, in the next instance, their familial orientation towards other substrata within the tribe, or even to other tribes altogether. Correspondingly, any social entity at all within the spectrum running from the family to the tribe also has the possibility to absorb foreigners into its circle. As is often stressed in the anthropological literature, such assimilation often implies an acceptance with respect to rights and kinship ties which places the new members on an equal footing with older members of the unit. The official acknowledgement that such an alliance has been established is the composition of a genealogy which accomodates the newly-assimilated group into the genealogical system adhered to by the tribe in which acceptance takes place.

In many cases the presence of a heterogeneous population within one and the same tribe reflects the fact that such a process may have taken place earlier. In other cases the integration of new members into the tribe will not have been unproblematical. Examples of the latter type are primarily to be found among the Arab bedouins, who are clearly reticent about accepting new members into a tribe if the social background of those seeking acceptance does not correspond to that of the tribe in question. Investigation of the Arab aristocratic tribes reveals this quite clearly, as already noted by Musil, who points out that

---

that the bedouins were able to retain their social structure within the two town societies (Bulliet 1980).

non-"aristocratic" applicants are not accepted by the tribe; rather, they continue to be regarded as pariahs or as clients of the aristocratic tribe. Even among the Negev bedouins, who definitely have no claim to noble ancestry, it is noteworthy that applicants of peasant origin are not accepted on an equal footing with the bedouins. Instead, a stigma attaches to nomads of peasant origin which underlines the fact that they are reckoned to be less worthy than the bedouins. In the case of the Negev bedouins this difference in parentage is further reflected in the economic conditions, way of life, and particularly in the marital relations of both groups[240].

To turn to the matter of communal sedentarization, it is often seen that there is a direct connection between such settlement and the settlement of the tribal leaders. The tribal leaders and their group are often forced to change their way of life by an embarassment of riches which makes continued nomadic existence impractical. Like the wealthy nomad, a tribal leader will sooner or later be inclined to settle down on his (frequently) not inconsiderable lands and allow his herds of animals to be cared for either by male members of his own family or by professional shepherds.

For its part, the central authorities have a number of options with respect to their behavior towards the tribal leaders. The most obvious of these is to encourage their interest in settlement in the hopes that they will also convince other elements among the nomadic populace to abandon their migratory existence. A number of methods have been employed in recent times to this end, among them being donations of what are sometimes very large lots of state-owned land as well as appointments in the state administration. Thus the tribal leaders not only become the greatest seigneurs in their districts; they also become their administrative leaders. As W. Eberhard puts it, in the eyes of the state the tribal leader becomes the administrator of a district, while in the eyes of the members of the tribe he becomes the feudal lord of the territory[241]. There is no reason to expect that such a development will awaken the envy of ordinary members of the tribe with respect to their leader since, it should be recalled, his basis in the tribe is primarily definable in terms of *prestige*. In the eyes of the ordinary nomad the prestige of the leader becomes multiplied inconceivably by such intervention on the part of the central authorities, and the nomad sees no evil in this.

The next point on the program of the authorities will be the settlement of the rest of the leadership stratum. In this endeavor the authorities will be able to count on the cooperation of the tribal leader, and the procedure will be analogous to that used in dealing with him, although, of course, the gifts and honors showered upon the leaders in question will be less impressive. Once the

---

[240] On this issue see above, p. 109-110.

[241] Eberhard 1953:38f. The tribal leaders within the Turkish region actually understood the awards of state offices as extraordinary honors paid to them personally by their "big brother", the Sultan in Constantinople.

leadership stratum has been pacified in this manner by the central authorities, it will seldom be difficult to obtain control of the rest of the nomadic group, whether or not the group desires to continue its earlier existence, as was the case with Šammar-Ǧerba, or it chooses to settle down in greater numbers than previously. In the case of the Šammar-Ǧerba, the result has additionally been the impoverishment of the average nomad since the best pasturage has been accorded to the ruling group. Thus only the poorest reaches of Ǧezira are available to the remaining nomads. Stein adds additionally that this situation has now led to the degeneration of the social structure of this tribe, so that now there is a notable schism between the ordinary man and the leadership stratum[242].

Finally, once matters have advanced so far the central authorities may attempt to undermine the position of the leaders by reducing their prerogatives, so that in reality they lose their positions of power within their own groups[243]. A variant of this procedure has been practiced in Iran by recent governments (not least that of Reza Shah), which have simply attempted to destroy the leadership group physically[244].

There is little evidence to indicate that the same or similar procedures were employed by the central authorities against the nomads in earlier times. Moreover, even in connection with the procedures mentioned above it is the case that no two of the modern examples are identical. There is no mechanical execution of a typical procedure, and no actual paradigm underlying the methods mentioned above. To the contrary, these examples clearly show that nomads who undertake sedentarization are often recognizable by a hierarchical social organization which is rooted in unequal access to land, unequal access to the positions of leadership in a given district and, consequently, to the offices of the central administration. For this reason such sedentarized nomadic societies will also contain considerable socio-economic inequalities[245].

---

[242] Stein 1967:107. Stein mentions that in 1962 the supreme sheik owned over 40,000 hectares of land, and that, further, 250,000 hectares of the best land in the Šammar district were owned by a mere 52 individuals, while the vast majority of the Šammar-Ǧerba did not even own land.

[243] Such a policy was enforced by the Turkish central authorities with respect to the Kurds; cf. Hütteroth 1961:22f. Eberhard relates that this earlier leadership stratum nevertheless manages to get along today, since they have invested a considerable part of their substantial wealth in education, which has paved the way for their entry into the Turkish élite (1953:45f.).

[244] See, for example, Ehmann 1975:74ff., and Oberling 1974:149-167. However, Oberling calls attention to the fact that neither the bloody procedure of Reza Shah towards the tribal leaders nor his corresponding compulsory settlements were able to prevent the main part of the forcibly settled nomads from migrating again within a couple of months of his abdication (1974: 169; cf. also Barth 1964A:3). The same sort of return to nomadism and tribal life seems to be underway once more in the wake of the Iranian revolution of 1979; cf. Beck 1980:348f. In general it may be said that the forcible ensettlement of nomads has only been effective when sufficient means of compulsion have been available, and only as long as such means have been ready to hand. Note also the unsuccessful Turkish policies with respect to the Šammar as described in Stein 1967:100ff.

[245] Note De Planhol's categorical (overly so?) remarks on this issue (De Planhol 1972).

Excursus:

The Desert as the Semitic Place of Origin

One of the main arguments against the earlier theory concerning Israel's hypothetical nomadic origin took its point of departure in a criticism of the conception of the nomads' "desert" origin. If, however, the role of the nomads in the history of the Near East is to be discussed on the basis of modern parallels, it will be necessary to investigate the extent to which the cultural-geographical conditions of ancient and modern times have been taken into account. If it should prove the case that the ecological conditions of the ancient Near East differed significantly from those of the 20th century, then the study of the nomads in antiquity cannot merely consist in using the modern sociological conditions as a blueprint for ancient societies, on the assumption that the ecological conditions in both eras are identical, which would permit us to conclude that nomads behaved in the past as they do now.

One of Gottwald's presuppositions is the notion that nomads cannot have lived in isolation of civilization prior to the domestication of the camel. This means that the Syro-Arabian Desert must have been inaccessible until around 1000 (BC)[246]. Thus the Semites cannot have come from the desert, and the nomads in question must have been practitioners of the so-called "enclosed nomadism" which has been described by M.B. Rowton. However, this theory presupposes that the Syro-Arabian Desert was unsusceptible to human habitation until the camel had been domesticated, and it is this presupposition I shall deal with in the following. By way of introduction I shall set two earlier views up against each other (by E. Meyer and V.G. Childe, respectively):

"...die grosse Steppe und Wüste Arabiens mit dem vorgelagerten Kulturland in Syrien und am Tigris und Eufrat bildet dagegen den Bereich der semitischen Stämme". Thus Meyer expressed the classical understanding of the place of origin of the Semites[247]. At the same time, however, he also claimed that the topological conditions in the region did not change a whit through an historical period of 5000 years. Taking his point of departure in the ideas of his time concerning large-scale migrations, Meyer added that new and fresh waves of Semitic peoples, which he understood to be nomads, continually erupted from this desert and invaded the civilized lands successively[248]. Meyer did not attempt to go back before historical times, although he did touch on the possibility of conditions more conducive to human life in the arid zones during earlier periods[249]. Meyer reckoned Arabia to be the primeval home of the Semites, and in his description of the geographical situation in the Arabian Peninsula and the Syro-Arabian Desert in modern times he attempted to show that human existence was possible there, including a certain amount of agriculture and some cattle-raising in the most favored regions of the area.

Against this we have V.G. Childe's "oasis theory"[250]. According to Childe's hypothesis, an ongoing process of dehydration has characterized the Middle East and North Africa since the last Ice Age. During its first period, which scholars at the time thought was a rainy one, the Orient was (according to Childe) a "parkland" and a "savannah". He compared the ecological conditions with those of modern Rhodesia. At first a rich hunter-gatherer culture, followed by a nascent agricultural and cattle-raising one, had excellent possibilities for development in this vast area. However, later the increasing aridity entailed that the population, which Childe supposed to be as numerous as that in contemporary northern Europe, became compressed into a few localities. In Arabia and the Sahara this signified very dense concentrations of peoples around the oases in Mesopotamia, and the Nile Delta. These peoples were squeezed out of the arid territories so that they appropriated to themselves the previously uninhabitable alluvial valleys[251]. Thus in historical times the population pressure which continually threatened the civi-

---

[246] Cf. Gottwald 1979A:436.
[247] Meyer 1913:378.
[248] Meyer 1913:381.
[249] Meyer 1913:381.
[250] See Childe 1958 (originally appeared in 1928):14-30.
[251] Childe 1958:31ff., on Egypt, and pp.102ff., on Mesopotamia.

lized areas was a result of this continuing dehydration, which forced population surplusses to emmigrate from the Arabian Peninsula.

My challenge to these conceptions of the development of the Oriental cultures is based on an evaluation of the possibility of survival in the desert during the period in question. As far as the oasis theory is concerned, the decisive question is whether such oases were situated sufficiently closely to the more integral civilized lands of the Fertile Crescent as to be accessible from peripheral areas. It is in this connection that the recent discussion concerning the domestication of the camel has played an important part in rendering doubtful Childe's conception of Semitic origins. I have no intention of rehearsing this discussion, since its results are unambiguous. As the "ship of the desert" the camel was a late arrival in Oriental history (even though it is possible that the two-humped variety may have been domesticated several thousand years earlier in Central Asia)[252]. It was first around 1000 that the taming of the single-humped camel (dromedary) was an accomplished fact in the Near East, even if it is reasonable, with R. Bulliet, to claim that this domestication must have taken place over a considerable period of time[253]. Thus most of the the areas in Coele Arabia which have been considered to have been the primeval home of the Semites were inaccessible to man until around 1000, on the assumption that the ecological conditions of the time correspond to those obtaining at this time. At most there will have been a few favored marginal areas along the western coast of the Arabian Peninsula, plus a few oases which were sufficiently close to civilization to allow communication without the use of the camel as beast of burden.

Now, in recent years there has been considerable debate as to the ecological conditions in the Middle East in antiquity. K.W. Butzer was one of the pioneers of this field, and since the 1950's he has attempted to present a history of the Near Eastern climate in antiquity in an extensive series of articles[254]. Butzer's most important conclusion is his demonstration that during the period following the last Ice Age (Würm) climatic conditions in the Near East were neither characterized by gradual dehydration nor by static climatic conditions (so that, for example, life-conditions will have been identical between 8000 and 1000). Instead, as he points out, we must reckon with numerous shifting phases, so that a predominantly wet climate will have given way to a dry one, which in turn was succeeded by a wet one, and so on[255]. If we set Butzer's observations in relation to the historical developments in the Near East, it accordingly becomes possible to regard certain events as the results of climatic improvements and deteriorations. It we turn to Palestine in historical times, one coincidence is immediately striking. It is well known that the prosperous Early Bronze Age culture in Palestine collapsed sometime between 2500 and 2000, which in archeological terms is indicated by the fact that a well developed urban culture disappeared and was replaced by a transitional phase (Kenyon's Intermediate Bronze Age) at the end of the third millenium[256]. Ways of life were altered in such a way that the urban and

---

[252] See Henninger 1968:15-23, where one encounters an extremely detailed bibliography on the question of the domestication of the camel. Both Henninger and B. Brentjes (see, among other things, Brentjes 1960) maintain, like A. Pohl, that the domestication of the camel by the Semites actually goes much farther back, perhaps as far back as the 3rd or 4th millennium. However, arguments in favor of such a date are discounted by most historians. Of course, it is obvious that the camel existed in the Orient long before it was domesticated. However, in order to maintain that a given find indicates the presence of domesticated camels, skeletal remains would have to be present in such quantities and in particular age patterns so that we would then be in a position to state that the society in question had other uses for it than merely hunting it. On this point, see Dyson 1953:662.

[253] Cf. Bulliet 1975:37ff. Bulliet rules out the Arabian Desert as the original place where the camel was domesticated, since, as he rightly remarks, "the Arabian desert offers little chance of survival to anyone who does not already know how to live in it before he gets there and who has no one to teach him how" (1975:47). For the most recent remarks on the taming of the camel, see Zarins 1978.

[254] Butzer 1957; 1958; 1970; 1971; 1975; 1976; 1978.

[255] Butzer 1958:127f.

[256] Here reference should be made to Kenyon 1965:130ff. and 135ff. (1979:114ff., and 119ff.), as well as to Kenyon 1971, Prag 1974, and a number of articles by W.G. Dever and his disciples (Dever 1970; 1976A; 1977:82ff., plus, above all, Dever 1980, Richard 1980, Gerstenblith 1980,

agrarian society of the earlier Bronze Age was replaced by a nomadic pattern in the country, and in general it appears that in this period the country was without fortified cities[257]. If these developments are taken in conjunction with Butzer's remarks about climatic conditions, there is an impressive coincidence. Butzer had defined "the neolithic moist interval" to the period between 5000 and 2400; in 2400 this was succeeded by a much drier age which lasted until around 850[258]. Thus in the years preceding 2400 we must reckon with climatic conditions which were more favorable to agriculture in Palestine and the Near East than is the case in our time, while these conditions deteriorated in the subsequent period, so that conditions for life became, if possible, even more severe than they are now. Similar developments seem to be detectable elsewhere in the Orient, particularly in the Arabian Peninsula and Egypt. In fact, Butzer feels that this was one of the main reasons for the decline and fall of the Old Kingdom in Egypt[259].

The perennial problem of the Near East is the question of the water supply. The moist interval from 5000 to 2400 will no doubt have meant more water resources, which means a greater extension of the arable area. Furthermore, the steppes on the periphery of the uninhabitable desert will have been pushed even farther out. It is accordingly possible with the aid of surveys and excavations to demonstrate that in the third millenium there still existed agricultural communities, including towns, in areas which are dominated by the desert today[260].

Butzer's analysis has been generally substantiated by other investigations. However, the discussion in the collection of studies dealing with the history of the ecology of the Orient which has been published by W.C. Brice indicates that scholars in the field are by no means agreed in matters of detail[261]. Therefore, at present it would be the wisest course to exercize extreme caution if one intends to introduce climatological considerations in a historical reconstruction. However, it would be appropriate briefly to mention some thoughts concerning the possibility of more favorable climatic conditions in the Orient in the periods just prior to historical times which leading scholars have presented. For example, W. Nützel maintains that the period between 5000 and 3000 must have been relatively warm and moist; he also claims that it must have succeeded a cold and arid period, and that it was decidedly more moist than the periods which followed it[262]. H.H. Lamb, yet another climatologist, largely agrees with the conclusions of Butzer and Nützel. He operates with an optimal period of warmth and moisture spanning the period between 6000 and 3000, and with a dry period beginning around 3000 and ending at some point between 1000 and 500[263]. Lamb rules out the possibility of any regular yet gradual

---

and Kamp and Yoffee 1980).The last-mentioned scholars now prefer the designation EB IV for this period and reckon it to be a continuation of the local EB II-III culture.

[257] Only a single scholar in recent times has opposed this understanding of the *Intermediate Bronze Age*, namely Thompson 1974:144-171, and 1978C. Admittedly, Thompson regards the period in question as a serious period of crisis like many others, but he emphasizes that this was a development internal to Palestine, where the tendency was to establish small settlements and to practice more or less transhumant stock-breeding (cf. also Prag 1974:106f.). Dever, who has sharply criticized Thompson on a number of occasions (most recently Dever 1980:53 and 56), also emphasizes an internal development, but he characterizes the disappearance of the urban culture as a result of the nomadization of the country. However, since Dever operates with a concept of "semi-nomadization" I think the distinctions he tries to make are purely academic. There is little which actually separates Thompson's transhumant peasants from Dever's semi-nomads.

[258] On this see Butzer 1958:116f. and 128.

[259] Cf. on this point Butzer's description of the gradual drying out of Egypt (1976:26ff.). See also Bell 1971 and Butzer 1978:10f.

[260] Cf. Butzer 1958:117, and Liverani 1968:84f.

[261] Brice 1978, esp. his conclusions on pp.351-356. See also Crown 1972, who offers a somewhat different reconstruction of the climatological developments. Crown's most distinctive point is his argument for an extremely dry period from 4500 to 3500, which was followed by a wet period lasting until 2300 (on the last point Crown and Butzer agree, also as far as the consequences for the EB culture in Palestine are concerned).

[262] See Nützel 1975A; 1975B; 1976A; 1976B; 1980A; 1980B. See esp. Nützel 1976A:134.

[263] Lamb 1977:372f.

dehydration of the Near East; instead, he maintains that the periods in question were climatically irregular, characterized as they were by intervals of cold and warmth which were followed by periods of warmth and moisture, and so forth. He nevertheless claims that wet periods were progressively less and less moist[264].

In the opinion of Lamb and other climatologists the occurrence of a period of warmth and rain between 6000 and 3000 is associated with changes in the course of the climatic belts, since the wind zones (the trade wind and monsoon belts) appear to have moved northwards[265]. Lamb only touches on the consequences of this change for the deserts of the Middle East. There is, however, no reason to believe that these areas were less influenced by the climatic improvements after around 6000 than the Sahara was, and in this period the Sahara was virtually transformed into a savannah[266].

These climatologico-historical considerations suggest that it would be incorrect to imagine that the same ecological conditions prevailed in the Near East as those which obtain today. During the neolithic moist interval the border between desert and civilized land must have lain farther out in those regions which are desert today. It is even possible that such a border did not even exist until after 3000; that is, it is conceivable that the desert regions of the Near East may first have (re)appeared after this date.

For this reason it is not out of the question that the Arabian Peninsula could have been the "primeval home" of the Semites, or, more correctly, it is possible that in this period the Arabian Peninsula may have received a migrating population surplus from other areas in the Near East. On the other hand, it is entirely possible that the deteriorating climate subsequent to 3000 eventually entailed increased pressure on the civilized regions. In the case of the Arabian Peninsula we are only poorly informed as to its appearance in prehistoric times. However, recent excavations and surveys, especially those conducted in the region around the Persian Gulf and Saudi Arabia are already beginning to imply that we shall in future be forced to revise our impressions of the ecological status of the Peninsula in earliest antiquity[267].

On the other hand, it would be rash to claim that one can explain historical developments in the Middle East in the period subsequent to 3000 on the basis of the changes in the ecological picture alone. For one thing, these developments will scarcely have been uniform in all areas, and for another we are insufficiently informed as to details at present[268]. Nor should one overlook the fact that even brief, but dramatic changes in climatic conditions may often have had more extensive consequences than a gradual dehydration of the Near East since the last Ice Age. For example, in recent historical times we have been witnesses to the catastrophe which has affected the nomadic and agricultural societies in the western Sahara (the *Sahel* region)[269]. Similar events may have occured in certain periods in antiquity, even though we have no sources referring to such events.

To recapitulate: it is probable that the ecology of the Middle East has evolved in the course

---

[264] Lamb 1977:373.

[265] Lamb 1977:414. In other words, the entire Near East up to the southern part of Turkey was effected by this climatic improvement. However, one should also consult Brice's discussion of the extremely arid conditions in Anatolia during the same period (Brice 1978:87-147).

[266] See Lamb 1977:415.

[267] On this see Stevens 1978; Butzer 1978:10f., and Masry 1974.

[268] See Butzer 1978 . Butzer mentions a subdivision of the Middle East into three climatic zones in prehistorical times: the northern mountainous areas, the Levant plus Mesopotamia, and the *"desert belt"*, that is, Egypt and the Arabian Peninsula. He claims that the third of these was especially favorable in climatic terms at this time; note that Palestine and the Sinai Peninsula fall within this region. Others emphatically reject the possibility of climatic changes in Mesopotamia within the last 8,000 years; thus, for example, C.L. Redman (1978:18). However, this does not prevent Redman from personally hypothecating climatic changes as contributory factors in the Neolithic revolution during the period prior to 6000 (1978:112-116).

[269] On the Sahel drought and its consequences in general, see Swift 1977, and cf. Balland and Kieffer 1979 for an example from Afghanistan. The events in the Sahel region have been used by B. Brentjes as an analogical explanation of the great Semitic mass migrations (Brentjes 1979).

of time, antiquity included. Even if it may be difficult for us to describe individual changes, it would be methodologically unsound to formulate theories which presuppose an "immutable Orient". Conversely, it would be equally incorrect to postulate that, for example, the Israelite invasion of Palestine was the result of suddenly transformed climatic conditions which compelled nomads who once dwelled on the borders of Palestine to enter into the civilized land, since we are unable at present to demonstrate that the period in question was a period of drought. Here it would be wise to recall the admonitions of A.D. Crown, who has pointed out that although it is clear that ecological changes occurred in the region, it remains difficult to determine just which changes were the results of climatic factors and which were the results of human activity[270].

§ 7

Nomads in the Second Millenium BCE

In the preceding section three problems were selected as the objects of this study of Middle Eastern nomadism. These were the questions of the extent of the territories inhabited by nomads, the period of the emergence of nomadic cultures, and finally the ideal type of the pastoral nomad. The second point was dismissed without more ado, since nomads may well have existed for several thousand years when Israel made her appearance on the scene. The first question was the subject of the preceding excursus. Even though there are a number of indications that the ecology around 2000 differed somewhat from modern conditions, climatological historians have not been able to agree on matters of detail. Thus at present climate must be regarded as a variable factor which it would be improper to include in the discussion, although a time will probably come when we will have sufficient knowledge that it would be correct to introduce the possibly decisive condition of climate into the debate. In other words, it is now impermissible to utilize more or less conjectural climatic changes as some sort of *Deus ex machina* in our historical analyses. On the other hand, it would be equally incorrect to rule out in advance the possibility that ecological change was in fact brought about by altered climatic conditions in the period in question.

On closer examination the ideal type of the pastoral nomad proved to be a fiction, in that it is not a delimitable form of nomadism. So many factors are involved that it appears more correct to describe conditions in the Middle East as a continuum ranging from the quasi pure nomad ("quasi" in acknowledgement of the fact that it seems very likely that the full nomad does not exist in this part of the world) to the sedentary peasant. Thus it makes no sense to speak of a dichotomous culture or a dimorphous one, as does M.B. Rowton[271]. There is no sharp distinction between nomad and peasant; nor is it

---

[270] Such as timber felling. On the period after 2000 see Crown 1972:329.

[271] Cf. also Thompson 1978C:11. Like the present writer, Thompson speaks of a continuum.

reasonable to attempt to camouflage this lack by suggesting that a symbiosis between the two "distinct" sectors "conceals" the cleft between them. On the other hand, it would be likewise unreasonable to maintain that there are no differences, that is, to assert that the various line (or lines) of the continuum are invariably present in a given area. Areas which appear to be dichotomies because two populations compete for the same resources are entirely conceivable. However, such a situation need not necessarily pit a nomadic group on one side and a peasant society on the other, as the same sort of competition could apply to two peasant societies or to two nomadic ones. Elsewhere we might discover three (or more different types of occupation in the area in question; moreover, we can not exclude the possibility that some territories will only contain a single culture, as, for example, territories where only the nomad has the skills enabling him to utilize the natural potential available.

By the same token, I have warned against concentrating on one particular type of pastoral nomad as the only relevant one in connection with the study of the ancient Near East. This has been done by Mendenhall and Gottwald and, for that matter, also by Rowton, all of whom emphasize the peaceful nature of the pastoral nomad[272]. It was pointed out above that transhumant small-cattle nomads can in fact be just as bellicose as bedouins, and they may be just as difficult for state authorities to deal with. In the event that a particular state proved unequal to the task, the result was often that peasant communities disintegrated and substantial areas became nomadic. Of course, in matters of detail there are many differences among the examples mentioned, but in general the results have been the same whether the pressure upon the agrarian sector was imposed by small-cattle nomads or by camel bedouins.

In what follows I shall attempt to comment on some studies of sociological conditions in antiquity, particularly those of the second millenium, in order to determine whether we at present possess information sufficient to allow us to draw firm conclusions as to Israel's hypothetical nomadic origins.

I shall briefly touch on the methodological warnings which have been presented by A.S. Gilbert[273]. Gilbert attacks sharply the efforts of scholars to draw parallels between modern and prehistorical nomads. Gottwald has clearly felt the sting of Gilbert's contribution, as he is now inclined to give ground on several issues and seems to be abandoning parts of his own analysis of pastoral nomads[274]. Gilbert's main objection is that in modern times nomads have been subject to the compulsions which strong and centralized authorities have been able to exert upon them. As a result, they have not only been forced to accomodate themselves to the ecological conditions which prevail in their respective territories, they have also had to adjust to the political situation. This in turn has produced an integration and strengthening of tribal fellowship in

An alternative would be to define conditions as *polymorphous* in order to avoid the latent suggestion of polarity in the term *"dimorphous"*. It is interesting to note that Rowton's dimorphous "model" has been rejected by such a contemporary anthropologist as G. Stöber, who also emphasizes the continuity of the cultural forms present in the Near East (1978:274).

[272] See above, pp. 132ff.
[273] Gilbert 1975.
[274] Gottwald 1979A:891f.

modern times; in particular this development has led to the emergence of powerful tribal leaders. Against this, Gilbert maintains, since prehistorical nomads lived in periods when strong central governments simply did not exist, they had no use for political integration at a higher level than that of the family. V.H.Matthews has recently rejected Gilbert's arguments, but his attempt to do so produces its own difficulties[275]. Matthews maintains that the relevant analogies are to be sought among nomadic groups which have been depicted in studies based on fieldwork performed before the First World War. This suggestion ignores the fact that such ethnographic studies are vitiated by serious deficiencies and thus do not provide the modern analogies which Matthews requires for his own study of nomads in and around the city state of Mari, and to which Gilbert is so staunch an opponent.

Nevertheless, I find myself unable to agree with Gilbert's criticisms. In fact, his remarks might better be described as irrelevant to a discussion of nomads during the second millenium, since the nomads in question at that time were not prehistoric nomads who were free of the embraces of higher political instances. To the contrary, these nomads were absolutely subject to the influences of centralized states. Gilbert's objections retain some actuality nevertheless, since they advise against the use of a deductive procedure in which modern analogies becomes a Procrustes' bed for the understanding of the nomads in antiquity. However, they have no relevance to an inductive procedure in which modern "analogies" merely provide a frame of reference which contains information pertaining to mechanisms which may (or may not) be of significance in a nomadically organized economy.

As far as Palestine is concerned, in the second millenium it is possible to point to two periods in which the country seems to have experienced a development similar to that which took place during the overlordship of the Osman Empire. These are the time between the conclusion of the Early Bronze age and the Middle Bronze age, and the transitional phase between the Late Bronze age and the Early Iron age. In the first period the disintegration of urban culture might have had something to do with deteriorating ecological conditions, understood as the result of the earlier more rainy period. However, if one were sceptical of this sort of explanation, one might instead attempt to formulate a political one (they are not mutually exclusive types of explanation). The extensive abandonment of permanent settlements which took place in Palestine towards the close of the third millenium could well have been the result of the nomadization of the country, as mentioned previously[276]. The economic basis for the retention of the great urban societies will have been destroyed by the collapse of the Old Kingdom in Egypt. On the other hand, a rich urban culture flowered in Syria at precisely the same time as the urban cultures declined in Palestine[277], as is indicated by the excavations at Tell Mardiḫ (Ebla). Although it seems doubtful that Ebla politically controlled Palestine[278], we must nevertheless suppose that great city-states like Ebla played an important part in the maintenance of the caravan routes to Egypt,

---

[275] Matthews 1978:3f.

[276] Cf. e.g., Bright 1960:37 and 48f. Numerous others have been discussed in Thompson 1974:144-171.

[277] In spite of the destruction of Ebla by Naram Sin around 2250, the city continued to exist throughout the rest of the third millennium; cf. Matthiae 1980B:105-111.

[278] Cf. D.N. Freedman (1978:147ff.), who argues on the basis of the "presence" of Palestinian placenames in the Ebla texts. For a categorical rejection of this by the excavator, see Matthiae 1980A; 1980B:11. See also Archi 1979:562-564.

which was a presupposition for the flowering of the Palestinian towns. In any case, the disappearance of the Egyptian economic center must have been synonymous with a noticeable weakening of Palestinian urban culture because of the disruption of international trade. As a result, it could be claimed that this contributed to the acceleration of the process of nomadization of the previous sedentary population. In other words, this destruction of the country was not the result of the arrival of large numbers of immigrants (the Amorites), but it nevertheless changed the economic balance of the society at the expense of the sedentary portion of the population[279].

If we turn to the period between the close of the Late Bronze age and up to the Early Iron age it is at once apparent that we again discover a political situation in which the decline of the great powers has created a vacuum in the regions around Palestine. One would have expected the same or a similar process to have taken place some thousand years previously, and in the event it would have been reinforced by the so-called Israelite immigration. Thus our expectations are fully rewarded when we learn that a number of urban societies were destroyed in precisely this period. This need not be the result of the depredations of the Sea Peoples in the country, or of the conquests carried out by the Israelites or of natural disasters. Its cause could just as easily be that the altered economic balance of the country militated against the retention of large concentrations of the population in the form of cities and towns.

However, the fact that this destruction of the urban culture did not affect all of the towns in the country, coupled with the fact that it did not last long, ought to give us food for thought. Most of the urban societies were re-established within a relatively short span of time, and they continued to function, with the notable exception of Hazor, the largest urban center in Palestine in the second millenium. If we hypothecate that the Israelites were responsible for this destruction and at the same time assert that the Israelites were newly arrived nomads, historical analogies would suggest a general nomadization of the non-Israelite population rather than a rapid Israelite settlement of the Canaanite territories. However, this did not occur. On the other hand, it would be incorrect to claim on the grounds that our analogies tell us something different that the invading Israelite nomads could not have decided to settle down as peasants in the space of only a few years.

In any case, one would first have to attempt to demonstrate that there were

---

[279] On this see especially Richard 1980:25-26. Richard stresses both climatic conditions and the collapse of international trade. Like Dever 1980 and, in part, Kamp and Yoffee 1980, Richard operates with a concept of the nomad based on Luke 1965 and especially Rowton (specifically Rowton 1974 and 1976A). Thus she regards the "nomadization" of Palestine as a development which was internal to the Palestinian people undisturbed by significant immigration into the country. A third explanation for the decline of the urban culture has been suggested by Thompson, who reckons the crisis to have been brought about by over-population which in turn had caused an ecological crisis when the land was no longer able to feed itself (Thompson 1978C).

nomads in the regions in and around Palestine during the period in question. Next, one would have to evaluate the sort of information about such nomads which is contained in the sources. The former task is realizable, since in the case of the Late Bronze age we are well informed about the presence of a nomadic population in this part of the Near East. Egyptian texts refer to šasu nomads, while Akkadian ones speak of sutu nomads. Information about the aforementioned has been collected and published by R. Giveon. These materials have been evaluated by M. Weippert, among others, and included in his reformulation of Alt's hypothesis about the Israelite immigration[280]. The sources mentioning the šasu range from the reign of Thutmosis II (c.1512-1504) to that of Rameses III (c.1198-1166). Only Egyptian texts refer to šasu nomads[281]. Lest anyone should be tempted to postulate that this period of time is significant because the nomads first emerged from the desert around 1500 and then disappeared into the arable land in the 12th century, one should note that it was largely in this period that the Egyptians exercized sovereignty over Palestine. In other words, silence about the šasu does not mean that they did not live in this part of the Near East both before and after the sources which mention them become silent. On the other hand, it cannot be determined that they did live in the region in these silent periods. The texts attest that the šasu-nomads dwelled in the regions south of Palestine, in the northern part of Sinai, possibly in some parts of the Negev, as well as in the southern part of the region east of Jordan[282]. Other texts refer to the presence of šasu farther to the north in Palestine, on the plain of Dothan, and even farther north in Syria. Weippert concludes that the šasu were simply omnipresent in the Egyptian Asiatic provinces[283].

As far as the economic system of the šasu is concerned, as well as their migratory routes, and so forth, the sources are utterly silent. We know that they kept small-cattle, that their peregrinations sometimes took them as far as the Nile Delta, and a few hints suggest that they had a traditional family structure[284]. Apart from these facts we are entirely ignorant, unless the šasu are to be identified with other nomadic groups known to have dwelled in the Near East in this period. On this question the sutu nomads come to mind, since during the last half of the second millenium their territory was largely identical with that of the šasu as far as the Egyptian territories in the Middle East are concerned. However, according to M. Heltzer the sutu territories also included

---

[280] See Giveon 1971; cf. Weippert 1974, as well as his revised immigration model in Weippert 1979:30-34.

[281] Giveon 1971:1.

[282] Weippert 1974:270-273; cf. Giveon 1971:236-237.

[283] Thus Weippert 1974:273. Thus W. Helck's attempt to demonstrate that the šasu were only known in the southern part of Palestine collapses; by the same token, this also destroys his chance of showing that the šasu were newly-immigrated desert tribes (Helck 1968B).

[284] Cf. Giveon 1971:255-258 and Weippert 1974:27 on the use of the Egyptian term mhwt, "family", to refer to the social structure of the nomads.

large parts of the territories which were periodically under Hittite dominion[285]. The identification of the šasu with the sutu is not a new suggestion, as
it was actually suggested by earlier scholars whom Giveon is inclined to follow[286]. This enlarges considerably the scope of the sources available to us;
furthermore, a number of important monographs have dealt with the subject[287]. Among these studies, that of M. Heltzer on the sutu is among the most
recent and thorough, and it would be appropriate to use his work as the basis
for our description of these nomads, who dwelled virtually everywhere in the
Fertile Crescent throughout the whole of the second millenium, ranging from
the southern part of Mesopotamia to the southern part of Palestine and Trans-
Jordan. Furthermore, the origin of the sutu is to be sought among a nomadic
group known as the dit/danu, who already appear in Sumerian sources around
the middle of the third millenium[288]. Around the beginning of the first
millenium the sutu fused with the Aramaeans, although their name was preserved through the following centuries as a "historical" epithet for the
Aramaeans or Chaldaeans[289].

Unfortunately, the sources from the western part of the Near East, that is,
from Alalaḫ, Ugarit, and Palestine (the Amarna letters) contain only sparse
information concerning the presence of the sutu apart from references to
military matters such as complaints about Sutaeans engaged as freebooters or
references to their services as mercenaries[290]. If more information is to be
had, it must come from sources from the first part of the second millenium,
and in particular from the Mari archives, which date to the 18th century[291].
In the city-state of Mari the Sutaeans appear alongside two other groups of
nomads, the Ḫanaeans and the Banujaminu. It seems that sutu is a collective
designation for an entire group of tribes. The Mari archives do not permit us
to draw extensive conclusions as to the social organization of the sutu. Heltzer,
at all events, feels able to demonstrate that among the sutu the term ḫibrum
referred to a tribe within the tribal coalition, while bitum may have characterized a lower unit[292]. Like other nomadic groups, the sutu of Mari were lar-

---

[285] Heltzer 1981:83.
[286] See Giveon 1971:4f.
[287] In addition to Heltzer 1981, I shall confine myself here to referring only to Kupper 1957:
83-145 and Luke 1965:105138.
[288] Heltzer 1981:1-10.
[289] Heltzer 1981:96.
[290] Heltzer 1981:79-94. The Amarna sources have been studied by Heltzer 1981:81ff.
[291] Heltzer 1981:13-39.
[292] Heltzer 1981:14 on the ḫibrum. Here Heltzer notes a distinction between the Sutaeans
and the Hanaean, in that the latter appear to have used the term ga'um to refer to the tribe (1981:
21). Matthews (1978:63-66) comments on both terms, defining ga'um as "a tribal section", and
ḫibrum as "a group of families probably linked together by communal wanderings" (after a suggestion of J. Sasson). However, he has not noticed, as Heltzer has, that the Sutaeans and the
Hanaeans may have referred to their tribal sections differently. On bitum, see Heltzer 1981:17.

gely keepers of sheep[293]. There is also evidence that they were used as auxiliaries by both the king of Mari and other Mesopotamian princes. They seem to have been associated with trade, which will presumably have been the caravan trade, and they were used by the crown as messengers[294]. However, other sources suggest that the activities of the *sutu* were not always approved by the authorities; there are a number of references to *sutu* nomads who engaged in illegal slavetrading and kidnapping[295]. Other information implies that their main territory did not lie within the borders of the state of Mari, since a few sources may be taken to suggest that the *sutu* did not pay taxes to the state and instead paid only transit imposts for the privilege of passing through Marian territory[296].

Outside of the ambit of Mari we have Babylonian sources which provide us with more information; these sources are particularly revealing about conditions in the region around Sippar in northern Babylonia[297]. These texts derive from the latter part of the Old Babylonian period and speak of *sutu* who are at least partially preoccupied with agriculture as well as some who are in the employ of private individuals[298]. To a certain extent, the same may be said of a group called *Rabba'um*, who were once understood as a *Banujaminu* tribe. Heltzer, however, has demonstrated that they in reality belonged to the Sutaean group[299]. The territory of the *Rabba'um* extended from Mari, and

---

[293] Heltzer 1981:38. The total dominance of the sheep as the domestic animal of Mesopotamia is noted in Matthews 1978:49. The lexical series ḪAR.ra = *ḫubullu* contains no less than 182 designations for sheep (this may be compared with the many terms used by camel bedouins such as the Šammar for their camels; cf. Stein 1967:49f.).

[294] Heltzer 1981:34.

[295] Heltzer 1981:41-46.

[296] Heltzer 1981:38.

[297] Heltzer 1981:57-75.

[298] Heltzer 1981:70 on the private employment of the *sutu* in Sippar.

[299] Heltzer 1981:48, on the basis of ARM VII:165:15: "*5 šiqil Ra-bi-ú-um Su-tu-ú:* "five sheqels to the Rabbaen, the Sutaean". With respect to the reading *Banujaminu*, "Benjaminites", it should be noted that it would be unreasonable to understand DUMU.MEŠ as other than a logogram for *banū* when it figures together with Northwest Semitic *jaminu*, in spite of the fact that logograms are not otherwise used in place of Northwest Semitic terms in the Mari archives. Some scholars would instead prefer to read "jaminites" and thus to understand DUMU.MEŠ as *marū*, that is, generically. Against this, however, is the fact that neither the Sutaeans nor the Hanaeans in Mari are described as *marū* NN. Heltzer's study has reopened the old question of the relationship between the Marian *Banujaminu* and the OT Benjaminites. Since the Sutaeans were present in the entire region stretching from the Euphrates to southern Palestine, it is not impossible that the *Banujaminu* (who disappear from our sources with the closing of the Mari archives) were also represented elsewhere in the Near East in some kind of fusion with the Sutaeans. For example, it is conceivable that they changed their migratory route from a southeastern course to a purely southerly one, thus abandoning their summer camp site at Ǧebel Bisri. Of course, this can be no more than a loose hypothesis which is only faintly supported by the Priestly view in the OT according to which Benjamin, too, was born in Paddan Aram (Gen 35,26). It would also be possible in this connection to make use of the acknowledgement by Alt and Noth of the fact that the Conquest tradition in the Book of Joshua really only has to do with Benjaminite territory, especially if we disassociate this event from the "magical" date of 1200 (on this date, see further, below).

was situated near the Euphrates around Tuttul, and into northern Syria all the way to Ugarit[300].

Compared with the data which may be gleaned from any modern ethnographic study of a nomadic group, the data about the *sutu*-nomads are so few as to be virtually fragmentary. Moreover, they are completely onesided, since we have no sources which derive from a member of a *sutu*-tribe. Our sources do, however, reveal that the repeated complaints in the Amarna letters about the *sutu* are more biased than the older sources from Mari, since the Amarna correspondence is restricted to references to warlike conditions. The Mari archives and the Babylonian texts also describe such things, but at the same time they also inform us as to peaceful relations between the state and the nomads and imply the integration of nomads and individuals from other sectors in the region.

For our purposes there remains the question as to which situation was the normal one, that is, the peaceful symbiosis described by Gottwald, or the bellicose complications caused by the razzias of the nomads, which were sometimes directed against entire city-states[301]. A situation in which an uncertain coexistence obtained, that is, in which the state may have had the upper hand for long periods of time, but with no assurance of a durable peace, is also conceivable. In this event one could justifiably claim that the peaceful symbiosis between tribal society and state power was not a fact of life, but instead the result of political conditions which enabled a central instance to prevent the nomads from exploiting their advantage in mobility and so to take advantage of other groups within the society.

Of course, the information about nomads in the Marian archives is not confined to references to the *sutu*; they refer numerous times to two other nomadic groups, the Ḫanaeans and the Benjaminites. The materials concerning these groups have been described several times from a variety of viewpoints[302]. It will not be possible here to go into these matters in detail. However, three major treatments should be mentioned in this connections, namely those by J.-R. Kupper, J.T. Luke, and V.H. Matthews. Kupper's fundamental monograph on the Marian nomads was written without knowledge of modern studies on nomadism, although he did cite a number of early works, especially from the period between the two world wars[303]. On the other hand, Kupper's treatment contains a very learned examination of the cuneiform materials from Mari which remains valuable in spite of Luke's attack on Kupper's method and fundamental outlook[304]. Luke is probably right to claim that Kupper is still dependent on the classical view of

---

[300] Heltzer 1981:47-55. In this connection it should be noted that Heltzer does more than merely imply that the Ugaritic royal family was of Sutaean descent (1981:51-55) on the basis of III Krt 13-15 and especially KTU 1,161:2-10, where the king's ancestors are besought to aid Ugarit. Among these are the *rpi arṣ* and the *qbṣ ddn*, that is, "the Rpi(m) of the country" and "the assembly of the Didanu", respectively. Heltzer identifies the Didanu with the mother-tribe of the *sutu, Did/tanu*, and the *Rpim* with the Rabbaeans (naturally he also takes into account the problem of b/p in Ugaritic).

[301] Or, more precisely, against their herds of sheep; cf. Heltzer 1981:25.

[302] Cf. Kupper 1957; cf. also Kupper 1959 and 1973. Reference should also be made to Luke 1965, and to Matthews 1978. See further Klengel 1972:49-74.

[303] Cf. Kupper 1957:XIVn.

[304] Luke 1965:16ff.

the question of the origins of the Semites, that is, that they emerged from the desert and always attempted to settle in the arable land[305]. Kupper has no doubts on this issue, and, oddly enough, if one bases one's views on climato-historical and ecological studies one would be forced to admit that Kupper's ideas have something to recommend themselves. G. Buccellati's study of the Amorites in Mesopotamia towards the close of the third millenium and the beginning of the second millenium is also based on similar views, as are H. Klengel's various studies of the nomads in antiquity[306]. To return to Kupper, there is no question that he regards the main difference between the *Ḫanu* and the *Banujaminu* to reside in the degree to which the respective groups are settled. According to Kupper, the Ḫanaeans were farther along the way to sedentarization than were the Benjaminites. Thus the city-state authorities had an easier time of it controlling the Ḫanaeans than the Benjaminites, and his general impression is that at least in the time of Zimrilim (i.e., the first half of the 18th cent.) relations between the Ḫanaeans and the state of Mari were predominantly friendly, while the Benjaminites were a perpetual source of disquiet. In modern terms the Ḫanaeans had become incapsulated within the state, while the Benjaminites were still not subject to state control. Ḫanaeans had lost the signal advantage inherent in their mobility, while the Benjaminites were still able to depart if pressure from the authorities necessitated it.

Against this view, Luke, who adheres to Mendenhall's and Gottwald's basic understanding of the relationship between nomads and sedentary dwellers (he was Mendenhall's pupil) contends that this view on the differences between the Ḫanaeans and the Benjaminites is false. Like Mendenhall, Gottwald, and Rowton, Luke regards the nomads of the ancient Orient as *enclosed* rather than *incapsulated* within the ancient states. Thus the differences between the Ḫanaeans and the Benjaminites are to be understood on the basis of the viewpoint of the state which has described them for us, which is to say, Mari. Seen from this vantage the Ḫanaeans belonged to the settled population of the state, whereas the Benjaminites were never so considered[307]. The explanation of this fact is that the main parts of the traditional grazing areas of the Ḫanaeans were within the territory of the state of Mari, while those of the Benjaminites lay outside of the state borders[308]. Thus for the Benjaminites Mari was never more than a stopover, so that hostilities must have arisen between the nomads and the state when the state attempted to regulate or entirely prevent the nomads' migrations. Therefore the Benjaminites saw no advantage in allying themselves or subordinating themselves to the authority of Mari. Unlike them, the Ḫanaeans were dependent on the existence of good relations between themselves and the rest of the society.

Luke's criticism of Kupper maintains that Kupper was beguiled by now-antiquated conceptions of the role of the nomads in the Orient. Ironically, Luke himself has been accused by Matthews for not including anthropological materials in his treatment of the situation in Mari[309]. Matthews attempts to correct this situation by subjecting the sources to a sociological analysis on the basis of a number of modern studies, and is thus in a position to describe the realtions between the tribal societies and the state of Mari more thoroughly than does Luke; for this reason he goes much farther in the direction of characterizing the social structure of the region than other earlier writers had done[310]. Matthews is able to demonstrate that agriculture was very important to these nomads, and that this fact was exploited by the state authorities. Other

---

[305] Cf. e.g., Kupper 1973:25: all of the tribes from the Mari period "belong to the great complex of 'West Semitic' peoples commonly called 'Amorites', who had originally come out of the Syrian Desert."

[306] Cf. Buccellati 1966:336. However, it should not be overlooked that in his description of the Amorite settlement of Mesopotamia Buccellati stresses its peaceful nature, so that it seems at times to have been in complete accord with the local population (1966:355-362). Thus also Liverani 1970 and 1973C.

[307] Note Zimri-lim's title of "king of the Hanaeans"; cf. Klengel 1972:55-57.

[308] Cf. Luke 1965:69-75 on the territory of the Benjaminites, and Luke 1965:155-160 on that of the Hanaeans. See Luke 1965:243-290 on the comparison of them.

[309] Matthews 1978:9. This is essentially precisely the same objection raised in this work against Lukes' teacher, Mendenhall.

[310] Matthews 1978:2f.

sources reveal yet another well known type of coordination between nomads and peasants, since we in this connection have to do with nomads who allow their livestock to graze on fields which have been harvested. Furthermore, it appears that the nomads were able to work as day-laborers in the villages, that they engaged in commerce with the villagers, and that to a certain extent they were employed as mercenaries [311]. However, Matthews also emphasizes the less peaceful side of the relations between the nomads and the peasants, namely the fact that there was an everpresent risk that the nomads would attempt to enrich themselves by means of razzias [312]. Concerning the relationship between the state and the tribal society, Matthews thinks to detect an increasing formalization of the political structure of the nomads, since he presupposes the feature mentioned previously that such contacts often entail the enhancement of leadership functions in a tribal society.

Methodologically speaking, Matthews' procedure is decidedly deductive. In answering individual questions he takes his point of departure in a model of the pastoral nomad which is to be understood as a synthesis of a number of modern studies. After this he attempts to find information in the Marian archives which fit into his paradigm. For example, in the course of his study of the political integration of the tribal society and the state he first stresses that such integration ordinarily signifies new functions for the tribal leaders, who thereby lose their unofficial status within their own groups. Matthews subsequently examines the archives with a view to finding documents which agree with the paradigm. The same approach is also evident in questions of detail such as those concerning the economic contacts between the nomads and the sedentary dwellers. Whatever qualities Matthews' study otherwise possesses, one cannot avoid the impression that his paradigm for the pastoral nomad is simply used as a blueprint to guide his account of the nomads of Mari.

If we compare the two recent studies of the nomads in antiquity which have been presented by Heltzer and Matthews, we quickly get some idea of the problems which failure to make use of socio-anthropological analogies entails; we also see what happens if reliance on such analogies is exaggerated. Heltzer was able to write an entire monograph on the Sutaeans without a single reference to anthropology, while Matthews allowed his account of the Marian nomads to be dominated by a predetermined paradigm which may be understood as a synthesis of a number of socio-anthropological studies of nomadism. In Heltzer's case the question is whether he has succeeded in gathering all the relevant information available in his sources, since he had no frame of reference with which the sources could be compared. Thus it is possible that Heltzer has overestimated the references to hostilities between the nomads and the settlers which the Marian archives contain. On the other hand, one feels impelled to ask whether Matthews has not underestimated such references, since he is under the spell of the modern peacefully symbiotic relationship between various social groups in the Orient, a relationship which is at least partially dictated by political considerations. Similarly, Matthews apparently does not realize how complex the situation in the Orient actually is today. This means that he makes use of a general model of the pastoral nomad in the same way as Gottwald and Mendenhall (although he directly criticizes both figures) [313]. I have previously declared my doubts as to the usefulness of this sort of

---

[311] On nomads and agriculture: Matthews 1978:85-92. On their allowing their animals to graze on already-harvested fields, see Matthews 1978:90-92. On their trade with the sedentary population: Matthews 1978:92f. On their military service, see Matthews 1978:95-101.

[312] Matthews 1978:104-107.

[313] Matthews 1978:7f. and 158.

general model if one intends to use it as a point of departure for the study of the nomads of antiquity.

To return to Palestine and its environs in the period in question, that is, the last half of the second millenium, if we deny that there is any general paradigm of the pastoral nomad, this also means that it is impossible simply to transfer the picture of the Marian nomads to this region. There are ecological, chrono-logical, and political reasons to be cautious about drawing parallels between Mari and Late Bronze age and Early Iron age Palestine. Regarded as an eco-logical zone, northern Mesopotamia is fundamentally different from Pale-stine, since it consists of vast contiguous steppes as well as a mighty complex of rivers. Admittedly, Luke has pointed out in his study of the migratory routes of the Marian nomads that at times at least some of them frequented some low mountainous regions (around *Gebel Bisri*), and, furthermore, that their graz-ing areas were interrupted in many places by agricultural territories. There are nevertheless significant differences with respect to the southwestern part of the Fertile Crescent, especially Palestine, where the geography is much more fragmented by disparate ecological zones in which mountains are replaced by valleys and steppes by desert, all within a region of limited physical extension. With respect to time there are a number of centuries between the archives of Mari and the documents which tell us about the presence of nomads in and around Palestine. Even though there is no doubt that there were in fact nomads in the latter area throughout the second millenium, and even though it is possible that the nomads of the southwest belonged to the same or related tribal groups as the nomads of Mari, there is no reason to believe that they pre-served their way of life and social structure without change during the inter-vening centuries. We have literally no information whatsoever about these matters in the Late Bronze age. It is possible that conditions were analogous to those prevailing in the Middle Bronze age, but we simply cannot presup-pose that this was the case.

Finally, it would be appropriate to point to some significant differences be-tween the political structure of Palestine in the Late Bronze age and that in northern Mesopotamia during the Old Babylonian period. Both areas were initially characterized by the existence of a number of city-states, but the size and resources of these states were vastly different in the respective regions. Palestine contained a number of microstates. The number of independent states in Mesopotamia was likewise considerable, but these states controlled sizeable territories. Each state dominated a territory which was vastly larger than that controlled by a corresponding Palestinian state. Subsequently in both periods the city-state system was subdued by other political forces, but also in this case it is impossible to compare the respective developments. In Mesopotamia Hammurabi's policies resulted in the actual unification of Mesopotamia under a single leader, but to begin with this leader was ruler of only one of the great states in the region. In Palestine the city-states were conquered by a foreign imperial power, namely Egypt. In Mesopotamia Hammurabi's conquest of the possessions of his brother kings led to their elimination and the physical destruction of other political quantities than Babylon. By contrast, in Palestine the old political system was retained, but on the conditions laid down by Egypt. In Mesopotamia Hammurabi's policies led to the consolidation of the potential of the central administration, also with respect to the non-sedentary groups (Heltzer's description of the situation of the Sutaeans in Mesopotamia during the latter part of the Old Babylonian period must be seen in the light of this fact). By way of contrast, the Egyptians pursued a policy of divide-and-rule with respect to their vassals, so that the individual petty kings were played off against one another, with the result that they wasted their resources in useless competition with each other. The Palestinian city-states were unable to defend themselves against, for example, the depredations of nomads, and when the Egyptian grasp on the region weakened during the Amarna Period, it is to be supposed that also the Egyptians' ability to contain such nomadic razzias was very limited.

The question is whether this weakening of the central power was synonymous with an attempt by the nomads to immigrate into the arable land, that is, did the Egyptian collapse allow foreign nomadic groups to invade the country? Our sources have nothing to say about the matter. The Amarna archives speak of generally chaotic conditions in which the *sutu*-nomads were also contributors. However, since there is good reason to believe that these *sutu* had been present in the region long before the 14th century, they may hardly be regarded as foreign immigrants. It appears instead that we have to do with a change of political balance between the city-states and the nomads. The city-states became unable to control the nomads, with the result that the latter were able to exploit their mobility in order to secure advantages at the expense of other parts of the society.

Chapter 2

FARMERS AND URBAN DWELLERS

§ 1

Introduction

If one intends to use socio-anthropological materials to shed light on the Israelite social system in the pre-national period, one's analysis of nomadic societies must be supplemented by a corresponding examination of sedentary societies. Since we have determined that the Near East reveals a socio-economic continuum which ranges from the so-called pure nomad to the absolutely stationary peasant, the best approach would be to concentrate on studies of the interactions between the various social groups on the local or regional plane.

The traditional approach has been to concentrate on a small society which is apparently easy to define, and then to describe such a society as an *isolated unit*, that is, as a society in equilibrium. Questions about the changes taking place in such a society are usually relegated to a brief concluding review. Most of the descriptions of Near Eastern peoples are of this type. However, in recent years a number of anthropologists working in the Middle East have acknowledged that such a procedure is not particularly appropriate, since "complex societies" are omnipresent in the Near East; they are only rarely isolated units. In other words, instead of devoting one's attention to a detailed study of, for example, an individual village, it would be more useful to attempt an analysis touching on the role of the village in question within the economic, political, and social system of which it is a part. However, the nature of the ethnographic materials available presents difficulties to the attempt to expand our horizon from a small society to the wider context, since these materials mostly contain studies of individual societies. Thus, for example, J. Gulick, who has recognized the need to produce more broadly-based studies in future, emphasizes that it is not feasible to utilize earlier individual studies for regional descriptions, since the relevant information contained in them is scanty and randomly collected. Accordingly, his own useful survey of socio-anthropological studies in the Middle East also follows the usual scheme in which nomads, peasants, and villagers are treated as isolated phenomena[1]. Fortunately, within the last fifteen years a handful of monographs have appeared which attempt to repair the earlier deficiencies; some of these will be cited in what follows[2].

What method is to be pursued in the study of Middle Eastern societies? P.C. Salzman lists three possibilities[3]. He characterizes the first of these as "the socio-economic strategy", an approach which emphasizes the connections between the individual group and its surroundings[4]. The second method consists of regional analyses which do not single out any group in particular; instead, equal attention is devoted to all the parts of a territory[5]. Finally, Salzman

---

[1] Gulick 1976:53-100. For regional studies, see Gulick 1976:56 and see the criticisms of Fernea 1972:75 and E. Cohen 1977:323.

[2] English 1966; Gubser 1973 and Stöber 1978. Fernea 1970 concentrates on southern Iraq, while Burja 1971 deals with conditions in Yemen. A number of the culture-geographical studies briefly referred to previously could also be assigned to this category (Hütteroth 1959; Ehmann 1975; Jentsch 1973; Grötzbach 1973; cf. also Scholz 1974).

[3] Salzman 1978D:540ff.

[4] Salzman 1978D:540f. Salzman assigns, among others, Barth 1964A, Asad 1970, and Bates 1973, to this type.

[5] Salzman 1978D:541f. As examples, Salzman mentions English 1966 and Evans-Pritchard

suggests that we direct our attention to those fields in which the various groupings intersect, with a view to demonstrating which processes govern the territory in question[6]. A historian would no doubt regard the lastnamed method as the most fruitful; however, the question in this connection is whether the past has in a given instance bequeathed us data which are sufficiently extensive and of such a nature as to be useful. In short, will the study of such social processes be so unambiguous as to yield an integrated model for the historian's use? I shall return to the latter question in the following chapter because a number of scholars have proposed general theories about social development, and these theories have been employed by several OT scholars to describe the emergence of ancient Israel. In this chapter it will not be possible to do more than to present and evaluate some examples of such theories.

One factor which militates against our efforts in this direction is the lack of historical depth of our knowledge of Oriental peasant cultures. Despite the fact that more than two thirds of the population of the Orient are peasants, they have not caught the imagination of early European travellers in the same fashion as the picturesque nomads and the "mysterious" Oriental cities have done. This means that even though it is possible to describe Near Eastern peasant cultures today, we do not have many sources which can tell us much about earlier conditions. On the one hand, the peasant cultures of the Near East are significantly different from those in Europe, particularly in Central and Northern Europe. On the other hand, it would be unreasonable to maintain that ancient Oriental peasant societies were basically the same as existing ones; it is, after all, entirely possible that the present configuration of such societies is the result of the Islamization or Arabification of the East.

Thus, for example, B. Zuber's attempt to employ J. Weullersse's description of Syrian peasants during the period of the British Mandate as a paradigm for the peasant population of ancient Palestine[7] is unsatisfactory. Zuber, too, suffers from the pervasive misconception that particular ecological conditions create a particular type of culture. He ignores the significance of political factors which may intervene and prevent the optimal exploitation of available economic resources. I offered examples above in which rich arable land was not properly exploited because policies favorable to a nomadic way of life enriched the nomads at the expense of the peasants, just as one today sees well-suited pasturage abandoned because of the displeasure of contemporary Near Eastern states with the nomads, of whom they are ashamed and whom they

1949, and others. F. Barth's use of the concept of *"scale"*, by which he presumably means a combination of both level and extent, would seem to belong in the category of regional analysis. The general idea is that a group of people, such as, for example, the inhabitants of a village, at one and the same time belong to different levels in different areas. The social structure may be a variety which does not encompass the whole of the village in question, whereas the economic sphere may necessitate a broader system which may even include several villages, and perhaps also a local town. In political terms it is possible that the villagers may belong to an even more extensive system. Cf. Barth 1978A (and see already Barth 1969:16f.). Analyses along these lines may also be utilized to show which sorts of processes take place in the society in question, as has been emphasized by R. Grönhaug (1978:81).

[6] Salzman 1978D:542f. In this connection Salzman is referring specifically to institutions which serves a mediators between two different social groups in a given area. For example, as presented above, tribal chieftains may be described as such mediatory channels.

[7] Zuber 1976:108ff.

regard as survivors of their own technologically underdeveloped past[8]. These considerations conjoin to suggest that any description of Oriental peasants will be of strictly limited value for our purposes. Thus my reason for offering the following account is a desire to avoid, if possible, a number of fallacious concepts about peasant culture in the Orient so that they will not be utilized in a fictive and worthless paradigm for ancient cultures.

§ 2

N.K. Gottwald's Theory of Village and City as Anti-Morphemes

As will be apparent from my remarks above, I am unable to accept the picture of the situation of the peasant presented by Gottwald. Gottwald describes city culture and peasant culture as *anti-morphemes*, that is, as two types of socio-political life which stand in sharp contrast to one another so that tension obtains between them[9]. It must be stressed that neither Mendenhall nor Gottwald ever offers a coherent description of the characteristics essential to a peasant culture; nor do they present an evaluation of the significance of such characteristics for the socio-political organization of an Oriental society. The reasons for this failure are not difficult to discern: neither has troubled to study the literature on the subject. This applies to both the general literature published by such figures as M. Weber, R. Redfield, and E.R. Wolf, as well as the specialized studies of individual peasant societies[10]. In other words, neither studies which describe the relations between peasants and townsmen in the Middle East nor those which describe individual village societies are mentioned at all[11]. In consequence, Gottwald, too, leaves his reader with the impression that he operates with ideal types which lack all connection with the real situation. For this reason Gottwald fails to rescue his version of the revolution hypothesis from the taint of unreality which he claims poisons Mendenhall's account[12].

---

[8] Thus Von Renesse and Graf Sponeck 1969:165ff.

[9] Gottwald 1979A:467: "we also posit the 'antimorphemes' of city and countryside as two contrasting and clashing forms of sociopolitical life" (see further Gottwald 1979A:467-473).

[10] In this connection I shall confine myself to only mentioning Weber 1976, Redfield 1956, and Wolf 1966A. More specific references will appear in the following notes.

[11] In fact, the only treatment cited by Gottwald which deals with peasant culture is that of Wolf 1966B (Gottwald 1979A:780 n.518). While I have no intention to belittle Wolf's knowledge of the subject, it is significant that Gottwald makes use of an authority who has not himself worked in the Middle East, but in Central America. Mendenhall cites only Sweet 1960 and, later on, Wolf 1966A; cf. Mendenhall 1976C:146 n.6.

[12] Cf. Gottwald 1979A:325. In an article (i.e. Gottwald 1976), which was written later than Gottwald 1979A, but which nevertheless appeared before it, it seems as if K. Marx' "asiatic production model" was leading Gottwald to abandon his basic understanding of town and country as antimorphemes, on the condition that the concepts inherent in this model as to the differences and conn ctions between the econ   of a city (state) and a village should prove fruitful.

In Gottwald's opinion the situation of the peasant society of Palestine around 1200 was such that the free peasant society, consisting of peasants who owned their own land (which Gottwald, like many earlier scholars, terms *ḫupšu*) was gradually destroyed by exploitation on the part of the central states in their efforts to finance both a costly military apparatus and a demanding central administration[13].

In this connection Gottwald takes issue with my interpretation of the term *ḫupšu* as signifying *"clientela"*, that is, either the clients of private individuals (known from Nuzi and the OT) or state authorities (in Ugarit, Alalaḫ, and Byblos)[14]. Without adding additional evidence to the discussion Gottwald compares this social class with the Roman *coloni*, whose free status he stresses, understood in such a manner that they were free to abandon the lands given them by the state if they so chose. This understanding of *coloni* is correct, as far as it goes, but they were nevertheless the clients of the Roman state as long as they remained tenants on their lands. Gottwald's discussion of the *ḫupšu* is, generally speaking, somewhat confused, which is probably because he does not understand the term "client" (as described by R. Syme[15]) correctly. Modern analogies from the Middle East – where, to be sure, we only have analogies and not exact parallels to the Roman system – in which the client system is pervasive among both the peasant and village populations, also reveal that client groups of copyholders are not by definition bound to their proprietors for life. They are instead bound by contracts of a definite term which both they and their proprietor may refuse to renew after expiration. Naturally, this does not mean that it was feasible for the copyholder to do so, owing to a lack of alternatives (nomads, too, have a similar system, which includes herdsmen who are clients attached to wealthy nomads by shepherding contracts). In recent times the picture has changed to some degree because of the possibilities for alternative employment which the great cities of the Middle East offer.

Admittedly, my understanding of the *ḫupšu* has enjoyed a mixed reception ranging from total rejection by T. Willi and Gottwald to clear acceptance by O. Loretz[16]. It is, however, substantiated by materials from the Middle Assyrian kingdom which have been treated by I.M. Diakonoff[17]. Diakonoff adds additionally that the Middle Assyrian texts regard *ḫupšu* as equivalent to the Babylonian *muškēnum*[18]. Finally, one may mention some texts from Alalaḫ which list a number of occupations of the *ḫupšu-namē* (i.e., "*ḫupšu* from the country"): there is a "doctor", a "potter", an "extipex", and so forth. On the other hand, there are no peasants, but there is a single shepherd in the list[19].

As a result, the Palestinian peasant was subjected to ever more onerous taxes and imposts which dragged the free peasant into economic difficulties, so that to begin with he had to acquire debts in order to survive, and ultimately was reduced to an existence as a debt-slave or corvée-peasant[20]. Therefore in psychological terms around 1200 the impoverished peasant class is held to have been well motivated to take arms against the "feudal" system which enslaved him. This was the immediate social presupposition for the emergence of "revolutionary Israel"[21]. Now, it would be impossible to deny that since

---

[13] Gottwald 1979A:210ff.,391ff., and, above all, 480ff.
[14] Gottwald 1979A:481f. and n.408 (1979A:767f.). Cf. Lemche 1975.
[15] Syme 1949:10-27.
[16] Cf. Willi 1977; Gottwald 1979A:767f., and Loretz 1977.
[17] Diakonoff 1969:231.
[18] Cf. also Lemche 1975:144n. It is regrettable that I was not at the time familiar with Diakonoff's contribution.
[19] Dietrich and Loretz 1969A:87.
[20] Gottwald 1979A:480-484.
[21] Gottwald 1979A:214 and 660-663.

time immemorial peasants have on occasion responded to exploitation by a call to arms. However, one should not overlook the fact that no natural law is involved. By this I mean that there are at least as many cases in which an impoverished peasant class did not use arms to defend its existence; instead, it has often silently bent its neck and attempted to muddle through even under extremely poor conditions in the event that no obvious alternative was available. Another factor which is not to be overlooked is that armed uprisings have seldom been initiated by peasants in rural districts; it has often been the case that other forces have urged the peasants to revolt. In this connection it might be added that it is likely that most of the reforms intended to improve the lot of the peasants have originated in the circles of the élite, that is, among well educated intellectuals whose base was in the cities, or among the class of proprietors, who often resided in the cities. Indeed, it is characteristic of the revolutionary phase of the last few centuries in Europe that revolutions have virtually always been introduced in the cities, after which they spread to the rural districts. In this sense there are no significant differences between the French revolution of 1789 and the many efforts at revolution in many European states throughout the 19th century. In fact, even the Communist assumption of power in Russia in 1917 was first effectuated in the cities, and only subsequently, and even then with considerable difficulty, did it spread to the rural districts. This was the case in spite of the fact that these districts were characterized by poverty, exploitation, and sporadic and uncoordinated revolts against individual landowners, revolts which quickly subsided once the exploiter in question was removed[22].

If we turn our attention to the Near East in antiquity it is difficult to find evidence of peasant revolts. However, the lack of examples of peasant uprisings in the later history of the Orient is so striking that some scholars have suggested that Oriental peasants simply have no temper for revolt, which is a dangerously general conclusion. The most extensive mobilization of a Near Eastern peasant population against its rulers was perhaps the Arab revolt against the Turks during the First World War. However, also in this case it is significant that the impulse to revolt did not originate among the peasants, but among the non-implicated élite who resided in Mecca, with the support of a few nomad chieftains and some English gold. Furthermore, even during a general uprising such as the one in question the participation of the *fellahin* was strictly on the local plane. The revolt was conducted in such a manner that the only constant element was the leadership and a small military cadre, while the main body of the revolutionaries consisted of elements of the local populations who were activated in turn as the uprising spread northwards, but who returned home once the movement had passed beyond their own territories[23].

---

[22] On this see especially Stief 1969:28ff. From the time of Nicolai I we know of over 700 oprisings, of which half took place between 1845 and 1854.

[23] The primary source for this uprising is of course T.E. Lawrence's own account (Law-

This short survey is, of course, by no means exhaustive. Naturally, great hordes of rebellious peasants have appeared from time to time, in European history not least during the late Middle Ages and the Renaissance. Nevertheless, it would be unwise to draw all too general conclusions on the basis of these efforts, which, incidentally, were largely futile, as they either ended in bloodbaths or dissolved of their own accord. For this reason one must be sceptical of any hypothesis which claims that Israel arose through a peasant revolt against a feudal urban culture. The Middle East today has a similar feudal system, which is not to be confused with the great fiefholder system of the European Middle Ages in which the individual feudal society functioned as a state within the state. Rather, in the Middle East the system is primarily of local significance. It is also significant that we do not find efforts on the part of the peasants today to throw off the bonds of this system; moreover, there has been strikingly little participation by the peasants in the many revolutions which actually have affected Arab societies since their independence. In this connection, we should note L.E. Sweet's description of the reactions to a revolution which took place in Syria while she resided at Tell Toqaan. Tell Toqaan is a village which was then completely owned by a very small group of landowners; it is also situated in the vicinity of a major Syrian city, namely Aleppo. The inhabitants of the village were concerned with the question of who held power in Damascus; they discussed politics, but played no active part in political life[24]. In other words, Sweet's account implies that Middle Eastern revolutions come from above, i.e., that they have their basis in the urban populations, which is to say, in the élite rather than the proletariat. Thanks to the pervasive client system in these societies the élite are able to mobilize the proletarian element in the population as their support parties when a political breach occurs.

It also seems to be the case that land reforms which seek to improve the lot of the *fellahin* have been imposed on the village societies from above. This applies to the Turkish attempts to redistribute land during the latter half of the 19th century (which in reality were a boon to the already most wealthy part of the population), to the more recent Persian reforms under the aegis of the last Shah, and the Egyptian attempts to regulate property rights after the revolution in 1953. Most of these efforts failed because the élite had as little insight into the forces operative at the village level as the average European Orientalist possesses.

---

rence 1935), but see also the latest thorough study of these operations – and particularly the campaign against 'Aqaba in 1917 in Morsey 1976:170ff. The nucleus of the group which started this campaign consisted of only about 30 persons, who, however, were in possession of 22,000£ in gold!

[24] Sweet 1960:192.

§ 3

Village and City, I: Examples of Village Societies

It is my intention in this section to undertake a close examination of village societies in the Near East. Unfortunately, the sources available are confined to the 20th century, since earlier accounts are sporadic at best and usually represent the views of urban dwellers towards the peasants. I have once again chosen to base my examination on materials deriving from ethnographic descriptions of village societies. I am forced to make some reservations with respect to this study of the situation of the peasants because of the selection of materials available. I have preferred to base my account on conditions in the Middle East. It may perhaps be objected that this choice is tendencious, since we have no guarantee that the structure and function of these village societies corresponds to those of societies in the same region in antiquity. As mentioned above, it is conceivable that the Islamization of the Orient significantly influenced the peasant societies; this will most likely have been the case in connection with the strictures governing inheritance, which play a fairly decisive role in the social and economic structure of the contemporary Near East, and which are rooted by tradition in Islamic law. In reality, one would be justified in selecting materials from traditional peasant societies (i.e., pre-industrial agricultural societies) from the entire world, in order to arrive at as broad a spectrum of variations as possible. However, even my very selective choice will be sufficient to illustrate the fact that even in the Middle East conditions are so various that we must admit the impossibility of insisting on a single ideal type of an Oriental standard peasant who has behaved in one and the same way in all places and at all times. My contention is that we cannot claim without convincing source materials that the Palestinian peasant population will necessarily have behaved in one single way in reaction to a conjectural economic pressure from the urban culture. I shall subsequently address myself to the question as to whether we have such sources either in or outside of the OT.

By way of introduction and illustration I shall here present some of the differences between a number of village societies. This procedure will demonstrate that in spite of many similarities, there are numerous differences with respect to familial relations, property rights, and economic policies. I shall be concerned with three examples, namely *Tell Toqaan* in Syria, *al-Munsif* in Lebanon, and *Kufr el-Ma* in Jordan[25].

I have deliberately chosen to ignore A.M. Lutfiyya's well known study of *Beitin* (Bethel) because of the special role played by the "westerners", that is, those villagers who have lived abroad for

---

[25] See the basic studies of Sweet 1960, Antoun 1972A, and Gulick 1955.

some time and now have reinhabited the village[26]. I have also chosen to ignore AB. Cohen's study of another Palestinian village, the cover-name of which is *Bint al-Ḥudūd*, since Cohen is concerned with a village which is to be understood on the basis of its close proximity to modern Israeli urban society, in particular Tel Aviv[27]. I have not chosen three Arab village societies because of any preconceived notion of their especial relevance. This will become clear below when our investigation widens its focus from individual societies to an examination of examples of regional studies. Nor have I chosen these three societies because they happen to be situated within (Kufr el-Ma) or near the borders of ancient Israel. The number of studies of individual societies which are sufficiently detailed to give a reasonable impression of them is not overwhelming, and if we turn our gaze to other parts of the Middle East (not including Egypt and North Africa) they are few indeed. With a few rare exceptions such as P. Stirling's study of two Turkish villages in the province of *Kaysari*, the non-Arab societies have generally been described within a broad context[28]. This makes it difficult to excise the individual village from the various treatments in order to describe it in the same manner as in the three examples cited here.

Tell Toqaan is a little village in the vicinity of Aleppo; its peasants do not ordinarily own their own land. The population are Moslems. Al-Munsif is near the Lebanese cities, the influence of which is powerfully felt in the village. The inhabitants of Al-Munsif usually own their own land; the population are Christians. Finally, in Kufr el-Ma we have an example of a sizeable village with few connections with the cities; its population are Moslems who generally own their lands. It goes without saying that this description of the three villages in question is applicable only to the time these villages were the objects of ethnographical study. As far as Tell Toqaan is concerned, this date was 1954; al-Munsif was studied in 1952, and Kufr el-Ma mainly between 1959 and 1960[29].

1:

Tell Toqaan (Syria)

Tell Toqaan is a so-called *šorba* ("soup"), that is, a complex village; its population is composed of the descendants of both nomads and old peasant families. Some individuals are descended from urban society. The majority are of Arab descent, but there are also some representatives of non-Arab groups. The families which are descended from nomads are organized along the lines of their tribal affiliations. Naturally, the rest cannot be so classified. However, not just one, but fourteen Arab nomadic tribes are represented in Tell Toqaan; they consist of thirty-five families and comprise one hundred eighty-seven per-

---

[26] Lutfiyya 1966.

[27] Ab. Cohen 1965.

[28] Cf. Stirling 1965. On the Kurdish village societies, see Barth 1953; on the Pashtun villages, see Barth 1959; on the Iranian ones see English 1966.

[29] In addition to his actual period of fieldwork, Antoun mentions visits to the site until 1967, even though his report is primarily concerned with conditions as they were in 1960.

sons. The complex demography of the village is the result of the turbulent history of the region during the settlement period, which took place towards the close of the 19th century[30]. It is also a result of the proximity of the village to nomadic territories which are presently from seventy to eighty kilometers from the village. Although over half of the inhabitants of the village are organized along tribal lines, with a single exception this has nothing to do with the internal structure of the village. Instead, it links the individual families with corresponding families in other villages, or with families which are still nomadic. The single exception is the group around the sheik who resides in the village. The fact that this individual bears the title of sheik does not automatically entail that he is the leader of the village; the title is an honorary one deriving from the position of this individual within his tribe. It is quite another matter that he is de facto the village leader, but this is the result of two related and cohesive factors, namely, first, that he is one of the four proprietors who own most of the land in the village, and, second, that he is the only one of the four who resides in the village, as the others are wealthy residents of Aleppo. Thus in actuality the sheik plays the role of the patron of the village, and it is to him that the other residents are connected by a sort of client status.

The main body of the rest of the village is divided into two strata. One of these is a group of families who are copyholders of the proprietors, the other is composed of day-laborers. The distribution of land is not immediately related to the presence of proprietors in the village. The lands are still subdivided into small plots whose existence dates back to the time before all land came into the hands of a few. No copyholder cultivates a collected territory; rather, he has the charge of a number of parcels spread throughout the lands belonging to the village. These lots date back to the time of the petrification of the earlier *muša'* system, according to which the village fields were regularly divided among all of the peasant families of the village. In other words, the lands belonging to an individual family were spread out into a series of small fields so as to distribute fairly the varying qualities of land in the entire area[31].

The pattern of settlement in the village wholly corresponds to the complicated social structure of the village in that the various families are randomly distributed throughout the village instead of comprising, for example, a single group of non-tribal affiliates living in one place, while the families of the fourteen tribes dwell each in its respective area. There are so many groups repre-

---

[30] As its name indicates, the modern village is situated beside an ancient *tell* (which is, incidentally, only about 15km. from Tell Mardiḫ-Ebla; cf. Matthiae 1980B:173). This also shows how the settlement pattern in a given region in the Near East can be transformed from sedentary agrarian and urban culture to a nomadic culture and back again in the course of time. In modern times the nomadization of the district of Aleppo in Syria first became significant after the establishment of Turkish rule in the 16th century (see above p. 135,n.).

[31] The *muša'* system will be treated thoroughly in an excursus below in which I shall deal with the question as to whether there is any connection between this system and the nomads.

sented in the village that such a form of organization would be impractical. Also in this case the single exception to the rule is the group around the sheik; these are the only sizeable element of the population who belong to the same tribe. Their houses are collected in an easily-definable quarter of the village.

One result of this random distribution of families, as Sweet observes, is that tribal affiliation does not mean anywhere near as much to those of tribal descent as the village fellowship does[32]. This fact is reflected by the marital practices of the villagers. Villages are often regarded as small islands, that is, as self-sufficient and isolated from the rest of the world. Thus one would expect endogamy to prevail within the village. Such a preference for endogamy cannot be detected in Tell Toqaan, since in fact half of the marriages are exogamous with respect to the village[33].

Another result of the distribution of the families is that kinship linkages at higher levels than the family, that is, lineages – which otherwise seem to dominate Oriental social structure – play no significant role in Tell Toqaan. There is accordingly only a single – and popularly elected – official in the village, the *muhtar* (traditionally rendered "mayor"), who is selected from among the wealthier inhabitants of the village. The office of *muhtar* is not respected in Tell Toqaan, as is proved by the fact that the sheik has no interest in holding it. This is a recurrent feature in village societies, because the *muhtar*'s job is an unpleasantly ambiguous one. On the one hand he is to represent the village in an official capacity to third parties, which usually means the authorities. On the other hand he also represents such foreign interests to the villagers in such matters as, for example, taxation. In practice this double responsibility naturally entails that the *muhtar* is the scapegoat of both the villagers and the authorities.

2:

Al-Munsif (Lebanon)

Al-Munsif is a Lebanese village whose population is almost twice that of Tell Toqaan, that is, five hundred eighty-one versus the three hundred nineteen of Tell Toqaan. The main part of the inhabitants of the village belong to a single basic group consisting of over five hundred individuals; this group is, on its

---

[32] Sweet 1960:179.

[33] There are some differences with respect to the pattern of inhabitants of nomadic origin and those of peasant origin. Among other things, there is a higher percentage of marriages which are exogamous among the former group. On the other hand, it develops that the main part of the first-mentioned group's marital connections outside of the village are endogamous, as far as tribal affiliations are concerned (Sweet 1960:173-178).

own self-evaluation, identical with the village. The members of the basic group all regard themselves as the descendants of a single forefather whose name they have preserved, and who is supposed to have immigrated to the present site of the village (the *al-Qurni* district north of Gabal, i.e., Byblos) thirteen generations ago. The inhabitants of the village adhere to this description of the prehistory of the village.

J. Gulick describes the social structure of the inhabitants of Al-Munsif as a "superlineage" which encompasses all the descendants of this remote ancestor; it has segmented into three so-called "maximal lineages" which are themselves subdivided into a number of "minor lineages". In other words, we have to do with a form of organization which in many respects resembles that of an actual tribe; however, the inhabitants regard themselves to be members of a *family* rather than a tribe, which is composed of a number of families. Furthermore, the villagers have no information as to the tribal affiliation (if any) of their ancestor.

Despite the fact that the village behaves as a single individual with respect to foreigners, its political structure does not correspond to its familial subdivisions. Gulick emphasizes that there are obvious signs of division of the village into two parties; this division seems to be implicit in the pattern of habitation. These parties cross the traditional kinship division into minimal and maximal lineages. Otherwise the society is characterized by the fact that there is no proprietor who dominates the economic life of the village. Gulick regards the social structure as egalitarian, although he does not offer a close description of ownership of property of the village. Finally, Gulick stresses that the villagers regard themselves as an integral part of the entire district of al-Qurni; this association is reflected in the pattern of marriage, which does not display any interest in village endogamy, since, as mentioned above, only half of the marriages are conducted with members of the village. On the other hand, within the district as a whole marriage is decidedly endogamous.

Al-Munsif differs in many respects from Tell Toqaan. The differences are most obvious in the case of the occupational pattern. While the inhabitants of Tell Toqaan were all employed in connection with agriculture or with unskilled side employment[34], the occupations in al-Munsif reflect the proximity of the village to Beirut and Tripoli. This means that the single greatest economic factor in the village consists of the incomes brought to the village by those villagers who have employment in the cities. This situation is a relatively recent development, and we should expect that the village was much more economically self-sufficient in earlier times. Gulick, however, points out that the village was not wholly self-sufficient even in earlier days, since it can hardly have been able to produce sufficient bread grain and thus must have relied on imports.

---

[34] Sweet 1960:157.

It is to be emphasized that there is no opposition between village and city in this society. The villagers are well aware of the economic potential offered them by the cities, but this has not entailed that villagers who have resided in the cities have broken socially with their village. It is further emphasized that these modern developments have had little influence on the traditional kinship structure in the village, as more than one scholar has noted[35].

3:

Kufr el-Ma (Jordan)

Of much larger dimensions than the previous examples is the village of Kufr el-Ma in the *Ağlun* district of the kingdom of Jordan; its population is about 2,000 inhabitants. Like the other villages, Kufr el-Ma is not tribally organized, and, as in the case of al-Munsif, its inhabitants are not the descendants of nomads. In this respect Kufr el-Ma resembles a village like Beitin, in which the modern village was not founded by nomads, even though the inhabitants regard themselves as the remote descendants of immigrants who came from the Arabian Peninsula[36]. Both the village and the subdistrict within which it is situated are of interest, since the inhabitants of many of the local villagers think to have the same origins, even though they cannot be called a tribe in any traditional sense. They are the *"people of Tibne"*; but *Tibne*, however, is merely one of the many villages in the district. The background of this designation is to be found in the history of the region. Until the end of the last century Ağlun was plagued by bedouin razzias, and large parts of the district were bound to various bedouin tribes by *ḫūwa* obligations. The exception to this picture was *al-Kura*, whose political center was Tibne, which itself was remote and inaccessible to the nomads. R.T. Antoun's description of the settlement conditions of the time is somewhat unclear, in that he does not say unambiguously whether the main part of the villages were founded before the second half of the 19th century, or whether they were first founded in this period. If I understand Antoun correctly, most of the villages, with the exception of Tibne, were founded some time after 1850 by people from Tibne. These "colonists" originally left Tibne in order to cultivate land elsewhere in

---

[35] Gulick 1955:155. In the society described by Ab. Cohen, the developments after 1948 took a different course than we should have expected, in that the traditional kinship system was strengthened, rather than weakened during the period of the Mandate. Cohen's account has, however, been criticized by H. Rosenfeld, who feels that the kinship system in Bint el-Ḥudūd also played an important role during the Mandate, but that other factors made its significance more visible after the incorporation of the village into the state of Israel. Nevertheless, Rosenfeld himself indirectly corroborates Cohen's observations in a different context, namely a study of Galilean Arab villages (Rosenfeld 1976; cf. Rosenfeld 1972:69f., against Ab. Cohen 1965).

[36] See Lutfiyya 1966:14 and 36f.

the district, on the assumption that they could always seek refuge in Tibne's inaccessibility. At some point towards the close of the 19th century the villages were founded, among them being Kufr el-Ma, by inhabitants of Tibne. The connection to the parent village was strengthened by the simple device of inviting the sheikal family of Tibne, who were the actual leaders of the district, to allow some of their members to establish residence in the various villages. This process created a political cohesion which provided for the possibility of common defense against external enemies (at that time, the nomads; after the First World War, the Jordanian government).

One result of this history is that the "people of Tibne" regard themselves as the descendants of a single ancestor, even though the populace have varying ideas as to what he was actually called and who he was. In practice this means that the main body of al-Kura's inhabitants regard themselves as a single people, namely the "People of Tibne", and they express this conviction of community via the notion of common descent. The descendants of this eponymous ancestor now inhabit nine of the twenty-nine villages in the district; furthermore, they retain their sense of community in spite of the fact that they have not coordinated politically since 1922.

There are three *maximal lineages* and four *minimal lineages* in Kufr el-Ma itself; most of the lineage members belong to the group known as the "people of Tibne". However, none of these lineages lives exclusively in Kufr el-Ma; their membership is distributed over a number of villages. Admittedly, Antoun refers to these lineages as clans, but since he does not define a clan with respect to a lineage, I am inclined to regard the structual level in question as "lineages" or "maximal lineages"[37]. Antoun himself operates on the basis of the clan as the highest level in Kufr el-Ma, after which comes the lineage (which is most often defined in these societies by the word *ḥamūla*, although it is not used by the inhabitants of Kufr el-Ma). A lineage further subdivides into *luzūm* divisions, which Antoun describes as "the close consultation group", i.e., that political unit which is of most importance to daily political life[38]. A *luzūm* consists of a number of households, all of which dwell together in their own part of the village. If one examines the various subdivisions of the system, one discovers that in general in Kufr el-Ma association with a lineage is expressed in the pattern of habitation, whose result is the division of the village into quarters. The lineage system was once of decisive significance for rights to land ownership, since Kufr el-Ma, too, once had a *muša'* distribution system. This system was annulled as recently as in 1939 by government decree, but to this day there is in the village a distribution pattern corresponding to that of

---

[37] For definitions of clan vs. lineage, see below, pp. 231ff.

[38] As far as *luzūm* is concerned, it is derived from Arabic *lazima* meaning "to grip tightly", "persist", but also "to stick together", "be indivisible", as well as "to be obliged", "be forced to" (Wehr 1966:864). *Luzūm* is translated by Wehr as "necessity", "need", and so on (1966:865). The *"close consultation group"* of Antoun seems to correspond to Marx' *"coliable group"* (1967:64ff.).

Tell Toqaan, with the difference that the land is in the hands of the individual peasants. There are neither proprietors nor copyholders.

Nevertheless Antoun refuses to describe Kufr el-Ma as an egalitarian society, since he emphasizes that the village contains many differences in status. These differences have historical roots which are still evident thanks to the freeze on land distribution in 1939. The various lineages own land today on the same pattern as their status within the system back then.

The presence of several mutually competing lineages, each enjoying different hierarchical status, within the village is a decisive factor for the internal political life of the village. This is the case even if the village is able to act in concert in encounters with foreigners, and even if the society displays a considerable degree of village endogamy (more than seventy-five percent, with extra stress on marriages between male and female cousins on the paternal side). A village with a social structure like that of Kufr el-Ma may be expected not to possess a common meeting place, that is, a common forum for political life. Similarly, the individual lineages elect their own *muḥtar*, although in practice the lesser lineages tend to ally themselves with the representatives of mightier lineages. The *muḥtar*, we should recall, represents his lineage to the rest of the village, but he also represents the village to third parties such as other villages or goverment authorities. It should be noted that in Kufr el-Ma the *muḥtar* has no formal power. He is, in the main, a mediating factor in the society.

The three examples offered above should be sufficient to show that peasant societies in the Near East are not the one-dimensional quantity Weullersse's treatment might lead one to expect[39]. It may additionally be pointed out that there are also local differences between individual villages even within the same district or subdistrict. This is implied in Antoun's work on Kufr el-Ma, when he mentions the relationship between Kufr el-Ma and its neighboring villages. In this connection at least one village, namely *Deir Abu Said*, is quite striking. There are no natural supplies of water in Kufr el-Ma, which means that in a year of extreme drought the inhabitants of the village are forced to buy water from a neighboring village, which in this respect is better off economically speaking than is Kufr el-Ma. This economically favorable position is reinforced by the fact that the district representation for the central government is located in Deir Abu Said, which is now in the throes of abandoning the village phase and evolving into a small town[40].

Our three examples also show that there is no reason to accept Gottwald's claim that there is a social and psychological barrier between village and town/city which must inevitably lead to a collision between them.

---

[39] Weullersse 1946.
[40] Cf. Antoun 1972A:6 and 40. Antoun uses "town" of Deir Abu Said (1972A:104).

12

If one turns to Tell Toqaan, one might get the impression that we there have to do with a dichotomy between village and city. However, this distinction becomes immediately less obvious when we discover that it is city-dwellers who own most of the land in the village, and, furthermore, there is no reason to believe – as far as Sweet's analysis is concerned – that they exploit their privilege to the economic detriment of the villagers. Any attempt to define the relationship between Tell Toqaan and the group of proprietors in Aleppo must approximate the following description: in economic terms the village is very dependent on the city, while its daily social life is influenced to a much lesser extent.

The situation in al-Munsif is very different, for we here encounter a lively interchange between city and village, although this is not directly motivated by economic dependence as far as property rights in al-Munsif are concerned. There is no pronounced psychological barrier between city and village in this society, which might be described as economically autonomous (the villagers are their own landowners), but which is extremely influenced at the social level by the city.

Kufr el-Ma differs from the two previous cases in not having pronounced connections with any sizeable urban society with respect to either property rights or social development. In both an economic and a social sense Kufr el-Ma is autonomous Naturally, this is not to say that there are no interconnections between state, city, and village in Jordan, but it does mean that these factors do not determine daily life in the villages.

The preceding analysis has shown that in dealing with the Middle East the relationship between city and village is not a dichotomy, but rather a continuum. Not all peasant societies in the East have the same relationship towards urban culture, as there are apparently many types of connections between city and village. These types pertain to such spheres as the economic, political, and social realms. Our examples indicate that the interconnections between village and city are not necessarily equally intense in all three spheres at the same time. Thus we have seen an example of extremely narrow economic ties in which a village was owned by the villagers and partially governed by them, while the social ties were virtually invisible. In another example we saw that a village was autonomous in social respects, but economically independent, and in a third example we noted a combination of economic independence in the village (as far as ownership of land was concerned) with relatively narrow social ties to the cities because of the sizeable numbers of villagers who at least periodically dwelled in the cities.

§ 4

Village and City, II: Examples of Interaction between City and Country

Our study of the three villages has shown that it would be unwise to preselect a single definite view of the relationship between city and village in the Orient. This analysis may be extended with the aid of a couple of so-called "area studies". I have chosen two studies, P. Gubser's description of the *al-Karak* district in Jordan, a region corresponding to the heartland of Biblical Moab, and P.W. English's study of the province of *Kerman* in Iran[41]. Other examples are available, but the districts mentioned seem with respect to ecology not very different from Palestine, at least until the formation of the modern Jewish state[42]. The political and economic center of al-Karak is a town, whereas that of Kerman is a city. This should make it possible for us to study the relationship between a town and its surrounding area as well as that between a city and its sub-district. However, it will be necessary to recall that these two examples are not universally valid; they apply only to the two societies in question at the time they were studied.

1:

Al-Karak

The district of Al-Karak is of limited extension, as it covers less than 3,000 km² and is inhabited by a population of only 45,000 individuals (according to a census of 1961). Of these, about 7,400 live in the town which has lent its name to the district, that is, al-Karak[43]. The vast majority of the populace of the town are members of the countless tribes which people the district. As it is today, the district is the result of a course of development which was inaugura-

---

[41] Gubser 1973 and English 1966.

[42] Here I have decided not to include two otherwise highly-praised studies of R.A. Fernea (1970) and A.S. Burja (1971). Fernea's territory is characterized by the irrigation-culture of southern Iraq. The intention of his study is to show that also a tribally organized society is able to maintain such an agricultural system; thus it serves as a valuable corrective to K. Wittfogel's famous "hydraulic theory", which linked the emergence of centralized states in Mesopotamia to the emergence of the canal system (Wittfogel 1957). The importance of such a study as that of Fernea for an understanding of how the tribally organized areas in Mesopotamia may have functioned in antiquity has been emphasized by R. McC. Adams (1974). On the other hand, Burja's study of the Ḥureidah of South Yemen in mainly concerned to illustrate the counter-measures which the élite stratum of a stratified Middle Eastern society may utilize in order to retain its position of leadership in spite of altered political and economic circumstances.

[43] Gubser's fieldwork took place in 1968.

ted after the consolidation of Turkish sovereignty over the area in 1893; this development has led almost to the tripling of the population between 1920 and 1960. This has also meant a decisive change in the pattern of settlement. In the 19th century the district contained a single town and three villages, but already in 1920 the number of villages had grown to 32, and in the 1960's it was 82. The area reveals the same tendency as the district of Aleppo to the extent that the majority of its inhabitants are sedentary peasants; nevertheless, tribal organization has been retained completely. A village is normally inhabited by whole sections of a tribe, which entails that all the members of a single tribe within a single village belong to the same unit of the tribe. However, it is unusual for a village to contain only a single section of a single tribe. We discover more often that a village is to be seen as the home of from two to three tribal sections, but where this is the case they are invariably sections of different tribes. Thus a tribe is usually divided into a number of sections which dwell in different villages.

It is on this point that Gubser's account is inadequate, in that it does not clearly inform us as to the role of the village in the consciousness of the villagers. On the one hand he emphasizes that the village is predominantly endogamous, while on the other hand he maintains that there is no community feeling in the village. It is merely a place where people dwell together[44]. However, our experiences from Teel Toqaan reveal that such marital practices by the populace of a village clearly suggest that they feel the village to be more than just a random aggregate. The village headman is usually also the leader of a tribal section which dwells in the village. If there are several sections in the village, then it will also have several leaders, a pattern we also observed in Kufr el-Ma.

If we turn from the villages to the town in the district, we discover that it, too, is largely inhabited by tribally organized individuals. However, the town also contains representatives of all the major tribes in the region. The town is accordingly the common forum for all the tribes. Agriculture is the main occupation in the district, as 68% of the population are so employed. In the town itself a sizeable percentage, indeed, probably the largest single group (over 12%) works in the agricultural sector[45]. Thus there is no significant occupational difference between village and town, which highlights the correctness of the concept of a continuum. This concept is further supported by the fact that the town-dwellers and the villagers have common origins[46].

The history of the district reflects the presence of the many tribes in it.

---

[44] Gubser 1973:61.

[45] Gubser 1973:33.

[46] Gubser himself emphasizes the utility of this concept (1973:2). According to his description, one end of this continuum consists of the extended family, the tribal section, the tribe and the village; in the middle are the district capital and the district itself, that is, in an official capacity, corresponding to our "county"; at the opposite end is the state.

There is no reason for us to discuss the individual tribes and their prehistory, but it is worth noting that throughout the period from the close of the 16th century up to 1893, a period in which the district was in reality politically independent, the evolution of the district was determined by the continually shifting alliances of the tribes. A special role was played in the 18th and 19th centuries by the dominant line known as the *Maǧali*. The Maǧali were the descendants of traders who had immigrated into the area from Hebron. Clever manipulation of the volatile tribal coalitions enabled this extraneous and originally far from numerous group to grasp the reins of political power in the district and become accepted as its de facto leaders[47].

The district is characterized by the absence of a proprietor class. The peasants mostly own their own lands, but in this connection it should be noted that the *muša'* system was unknown in the al-Karak region, even though a large portion of the inhabitants of the villages were once nomads or are the descendants of nomads. The agricultural sector is completely dominated by peasants who own their lands and who are tribally organized. Commerce, however, is not controlled by the same circles; instead the *sūq* of al-Karak, which is the economic center of the district, has traditionally been in the hands of foreign merchants who in earlier times came from Hebron or Jerusalem, and who nowadays come from Damascus[48].

Clearly, in this context there is no natural antagonism between town dwellers and villagers. On the other hand, it would be incorrect to claim on the basis of this single example that this is not the case elsewhere, since the close entente between town and rural district in the province of al-Karak could well be the result of the fact that in both sectors the inhabitants are of common descent. Another contributory factor could be the fact that control of the market economy located in the *sūq* of the town has always been in foreign hands. Thus the town dweller has never enjoyed a position of economic power sufficient to enable him to exploit the rural districts for his own purposes. On the other hand, the merchants who dwell in Damascus, Jerusalem, or Hebron have had no reason to seek political power within the al-Karak district. For this reason private ownership remains the most common form of ownership in the area. The Maǧali family demonstrate that it is possible for a group which is economically well off to achieve political leadership in al-Karak.

---

[47] Gubser 1973:14ff.

[48] On the lack of a *muša'* system, see Gubser 1973:26, and on the role play by foreign traders, see Gubser 1973:37f. In this connection Gubser adds that the local inhabitants regard the practice of trade as "shameful".

2:

Kerman

If we turn our gaze to the Kerman basin in the southern part of Iraq we speedily discover that conditions differ considerably from al-Karak. While al-Karak was a town of around 7,000 inhabitants, Kerman is a moderate city with over 60,000 inhabitants[49]. The peasants usually own the arable land in the district of al-Karak; in the Kerman region this is quite exceptional. Furthermore, as we saw, in al-Karak commerce was controled by foreign merchants, whereas in Kerman it is the city élite who run all facets of the economy. Finally, the inhabitants of the al-Karak district were organized into tribes, while according to English the areas most closely surrounding Kerman are not characterized by a tribally organized population. G. Stöber, however, counts no less than thirty-three tribes dwelling in the vicinity of Kerman, some as nomads, others as peasants[50]. Nevertheless, it is clear that the tribally organized population live farther away from the city than do the other peasants; in most cases they reside in the bordering mountainous regions.

Kerman is an old city; it was founded under Sassanide rule in the hopes that a city at this location would effectively be able to brake the *Baluchi* nomads. The city is not situated on one of the main trading routes (although it is not wholly cut off from international trade), which means that it does not function as an inter-regional trading center. Instead, its economy is completely based on local production[51]. The traditional city of Kerman was divided into a number of named subdivisions. Its inhabitants were mostly divided into two classes, of which one was the élite who were (and are) the dominant factors in the political and economic life of the city; the other was the rest of the population, who exercized a number of trades, such as handicrafts, small-scale trading, and agriculture. This pattern is retained in contemporary Kerman, although, as elsewhere in the Near East, in modern times a middle class consisting of administrators (Kerman is the regional capital) and merchants has made its appearance. It should also be noted that as late as in 1961 as much as 13% of the city population were still engaged in agriculture[52].

Thus in the traditional Kerman there were only two sharply distinguished strata in the population; these consisted of a wealthy élite and a large lower

---

[49] Thus English 1966:103. Stöber notes that the figure had grown to 85,000 already by the time English' monograph appeared (1978:186).

[50] Stöber 1978:213 (cf. 1978:277-286). As late as the 1970's the nomadic population was close to 70,000 individuals, that is, about 8% of the total population. Around the turn of the century they numbered over 130,000, around 44% of the total (Stöber 1978:178).

[51] English 1966:67 and 111.

[52] English 1966:71.

class who mainly just managed (and still do) to muddle through. This social pattern is also discernible outside of the city in the two sub-centers of the region; however, in them the distinction between rich and poor is nowhere near so pronounced as in *Kerman* (they are small towns with populations slightly over 4,000). Groups of large villages (pop. from 2,000 to 4,000) exist outside of the regional centers; these are normally divided into two occupational classes, namely copyholders and those engaged in the local carpet-weaving industry. We first discover societies which are not divided along class lines in small villages and remote nooks-and-corners (the population of the former ranges from 100 to 1,000 inhabitants, while the latter ranges from 50 to 100)[53].

It is interesting to note that from the smallest village to the regional sub-center we have no societies which are autonomous units in the sense which has been traditionally suggested for mini-societies in the Near East. Instead, all phases of their economical and political life is controlled by the city élite, who dominate virtually all the means of production, from arable land to the weaving industry. The élite of Kerman manipulate the economic and political life in the district to their own advantage via chains of dependent clients and by controlling the leadership strata in the subcenters on all levels, from the city to the country peasant. Thus they are in a position to prevent the lesser towns from developing into independent centers capable of rivalling Kerman's position; they are also able to prevent the individual peasant from becoming independent of the élite. Kerman's is thus a society which has many features in common with those upon which Gottwald has based his hypotheses, so that we should expect the Kerman district to be fertile ground for revolutionary peasant movements. It is, after all, difficult to discern alternative possibilities for the impoverished peasants in the district.

However, English's study fails to demonstrate that there is any reciprocal antagonism between the city and its surrounding countryside. There is a social barrier between the city élite and the rural population, but not between the rural population and the city proletariat. Furthermore, there is no psychological barrier between villages, subcenters, and Kerman; quite to the contrary, the city attracts the village population like a magnet. Stöber confirms this impression in the case of the tribal populations, and he expressly mentions that the leadership stratum of the nomads prefer to settle down in the city, not least by reason of the potential for social advancement the city is able to offer. It is also true of the nomads that the towns in their district are their most

---

[53] See English 1966:79-86. The "nooks-and-corners" are located in marginal areas in the territory, that is, in remote hinterlands. According to English their significance for the economy of the region is minimal. This means that the élite in Kerman see no reason to invest in them. Stöber informs us that the sedentary part of the tribal population is to be sought in such small settlements (1978:181).

important markets, where they are able to sell considerable quantities of nomad products[54].

English further mentions that there have been no peasant uprisings in the 1500-year history of the city. He also claims that the social structure is not based on tribal relations, but on an old peasant culture whose basis is the patron-client relationship[55]. This entails that the vast majority of the inhabitants in the district are each and severally bound to one particular family or individual among the élite. For the peasant the chain of command does not ascend from a village fellowship and its leader to the official chief figure of the district, that is, a governor who has been appointed by the Persian government. It ascends instead via the representatives of the individual élite families upwards throughout all levels of the hierarchy. This social structure recalls the system of the Roman republic, in which a number of patrician families divided the rest of the society among themselves and dominated it via their respective groups of clients. In connection with Rome, scholars have often spoken of political parties, but it should be noted that these, too, were based on the special relationship between patron and client[56]. It would be possible to press this analogy much further, since one could compare the emergence in the East of a middle class with the appearance of the Roman knights. This event contributed to the fall of the Republic by dissolving the traditional social structure. One might also compare these events with the appearance of a third class in European societies, which took place from the late Middle Ages to the bourgeois age. It is conceivable that such a class might have existed in antiquity in the Mesopotamian urban cultures, but we have no sources to show that it existed (at any event in any significant numbers) in the Canaanite city-states in West Asia[57].

§ 5

Village and City, III: Concluding Remarks

These examples should be sufficient to show that it is risky to attempt to apply stereotypical generalizations to modern Near Eastern societies, not to speak of

---

[54] Nearly 50% of all the meat sold in the urban markets and about 33% of the milk production derives from the nomads (Stöber 1978:250). On the nomads who settle in the towns instead of becoming peasants, see Stöber 1978:131ff.

[55] Stöber's work indicates that English is only partly right on this score; there is indeed a considerable tribally organized peasant population in the province. However, they dwell for the most part in the marginal regions and therefore have little significance for the organization of the patron - client system.

[56] On Rome: see Syme 1949, and cf. N.S. Hopkins' description of conditions in traditional Tunis (1974:431). On the political possibilities of the system, see Gulick 1967:71-73 and 137, as well as Lapidus 1969A:49ff.

[57] See below, p. 191.

ancient ones. It is important to realize that the examples offered above by no means exhaust the potential variations available. We could easily include a number of other examples which would reveal yet new combinations of the given conditions.

Our examples demonstrated that there is no distinct borderline between tribal and non-tribally-organized peasant societies. Of course, there are differences between individual societies, but these have nothing to do with whether the societies in question are tribal or not. In fact, the differences often cut across the grain of tribal distinctions. With respect to property rights there is no significant difference between Tell Toqaan and the villages in the Kerman district. Both societies are dominated by a proprietor class of which the majority of members dwell in the towns. In Tell Toqaan tribesmen dwelled alongside of of non-tribal townsmen, whereas the villages in the immediate vicinity of Kerman are not tribal at all. Peasants who owned their lands were present in both Kufr el-Ma and al-Munsif, but neither of these villages could be said to be inhabited by tribes in the traditional sense.

In the two areas in question, al-Kura in Jordan and al-Qurni in Lebanon, either other ways of maintaining the extensive private ownership of land by the peasants have been found, or else the areas in question have been too remote for the city élite to take the trouble to attempt to control them. This is a reasonable conclusion in the case of al-Kura, but not for that of al-Qurni; there is a great difference between them with respect to their attitudes towards urban culture. Al-Qurni reflects the fact that a large part of the population seeks employment in the towns, whereas this is quite unusual in al-Kura. Furthermore, there are differences between the individual villages within the same region. Barth's study of the Kurdish villages in northern Iraq reveals examples in which there are significant differences between tribally organized villages and non-tribal ones within one and the same territory. A distinctive characteristic is the fact that the tribally organized villages dominate the rest[58].

These observations show that we must unconditionally demand that scholars investigate a given society on its own terms rather than on the basis of some general conception of the ways societies at a particular cultural level behave. In conjunction with ancient Israel, this means that one must attempt to describe its social structure and its economic and political life on the basis of the sources we happen to possess, whether these be written sources (mainly the OT) or archeological ones. In order to conduct such a study as rigorously as it is at this time possible to do without using generalizing models, it will be

---

[58] See Barth 1953. The tribally organized villages belong to sizeable confederations which date from the times the tribes in question lived a nomadic existence. Thus the tribal system in southern Kurdistan did not disintegrate when settlement took place. Since the tribally organized Kurds still maintain their political fellowship, they have had an easy time of it with respect to the non-tribally organized villages, which they have simply dominated, using force where necessary. The non-tribally organized population have been reduced to copyholders, while the tribal members have become estate owners.

imperative for us to use a model so flexible that it will enable us to situate Israelite society within the Near Eastern cultural continuum.

Attemps have been made to erect typologies of village societies which may then be used as tools for other types of studies. I shall confine myself to mentioning two such systems here, one simple and one complex. Neither of the models may be considered to be exhaustive, and none of the types contained within these models may be taken to be integral. Their creators are X. de Planhol and R.A. Fernea, respectively[59]. De Planhol's model is simple; he recognizes three basic types of Middle Eastern village societies: one in which the towns dominate the society, one in which the peasant society is autonomous, and one in which the peasant society has a nomadic past. The first category is characteristic of the oldest of the Islamic lands; in these the town city has complete control over the rural districts and is to be seen as a parasite which devours the surplus production of the agricultural sector. It gives nothing in return in the form of reinvestment in the villages societies, with the exception of the once-and-for-all transactions necessary to establish possession of the land. The second category, that of the autonomous village societies is generally to be expected in mountainous areas. Here property rights will generally have been influenced by previous *muša'* systems, which in modern times have normally been replaced by private ownership. The independence of these villages is usually a result of their remoteness; on the one hand the cities have not had the possibility to control them effectively, while on the other they are secure from nomadic encroachments. The social structure of this sort of village is traditionally hierarchical[60]. Finally, it is the case with villages of nomadic origin that the hierarchical structure of the population is prominent, since the social structure of the nomads rigidifies during the collision with sedentary culture because of the new possibilities for class differentiation which the division of labor essential to village life creates.

De Planhol's model is to be seen against the background of his primary basis, that is, Turkey, where we apparently find remote and isolated mini-societies in the mountainous regions in eastern Turkey. However, it is doubtful whether the Levant has in historical times produced similarly isolated villages, when we consider that the network of cities has always been much denser than is the case in Turkey, plus the fact that the terrain is much more passable. Also, if we evaluate de Planhol's model on the basis of the examples cited previously certain problems arise, since our examples show that villages may display numerous common features irregardless of whether they are inhabited by tribesmen or *fellahin*. In short, de Planhol's tripartite model is an insufficiently precise tool because it distinguishes entirely too sharply between the three types, and because it allows no room for variants. The single virtue of the

---

[59] Planhol 1972 and Fernea 1972.
[60] Cf. Planhol 1972:108.

model is its clarity, but it is a deceptive clarity which may lead the insufficiently informed reader astray, if such a reader intends to base his hypotheses on the model rather than on the existing conditions. Finally, I must admit that I disagree with the assertion that a dichotomy exists between village and city. Near Eastern cities are not merely parasites which live off the agricultural sector without offering anything in return. The majority, if not all of such societies, are characterized by a lively exchange between city and country, not least within the economic sector. This is because it is the towns and cities which provide markets for the villagers' surplus production (if any). Similarly, the villagers seek in the cities and towns goods which cannot be produced local-ly[61]. Finally, especially in the event that a city or town is a site of central authority or its representatives it has an obviously defensive function with respect to the villages, since it is the urban societies and the states whose task it is to bring about political centralization sufficient to ward off nomadic encroachments (with the exception of the few occasions when the local peasant population is able to manage for itself because of its own political integration, as was the case with the "people of Tibne").

R.A. Fernea also envisions three basic village types. His point of departure is not the relationship between town and village; it is instead the social struc-ture of the village. Fernea distinguishes between villages which are tribally organized, villages which are not so organized, and finally villages in which there are both tribal and non-tribal elements.

We have discussed above villages of the third type (Tell Toqaan), the second type (al-Munsif and the villages in the province of Kerman), and the first type (the villages in the al-Karak district). However, our analysis also showed that we would be forced to ignore a number of significant features if our classifica-tion depended on this distinction alone. Fernea is well aware of this fact since he also proposes two subtypes within each of the main types. It is at this level that he is concerned with the relationship between city/town and village. All villages are divided into two categories, one in which the villages are much influenced by the urban societies, and one in which they are relatively inde-

---

[61] On the general significance of the towns for the rural districts, see Gulick 1969 and 1976: 54ff. For an explicit evaluation of the town/city as a parasite see E. Wirth (1973) and Stöber (1978:266ff.). Among other things, Wirth emphasizes the role of the town as the organizer of the economic life of the region; at the same time, however, he mentions that the only parasitic group is the élite class. But if this is the case, it should be noted that the victims of this class are just as frequently the lower classes of the town itself as they are members of the rural population. In recent years a number of other scholars have preoccupied themselves with this issue, among them R.B. Serjeant (1980B) and N.S. Hopkins (1974), On the question of the town-dominated economy and its importance for the economic strategy pursued by the villages and the nomadic societies in the Middle East, reference should be made to Barth 1973A. An important difference between the Middle Eastern societies and those of, for example, the African regions south of the Sahara, is the presence of urban societies in the Middle East. This has traditionally made it possible for economic surpluses to accrue when the agricultural societies and the nomads pro-duce goods for the comsumption of the towns.

pendent of such influences (the distinctions are only a matter of degree). In villages which are dominated by a city, or so Fernea holds, it is possible to distinguish additionally between two basic types within the class of city-dominated and tribally-organized villages. These types are villages which are economically controlled by the cities, and villages which are politically controlled by the cities (it should be obvious that these two elements will most frequently be inseparable). In villages which lack tribal organization but are dominated by urban culture, one must differentiate between villages which are politically administered by the cities (such as the villages in the Kerman district) and villages in which control is confined to the economic orbit. Fernea does not distinguish further within the category of mixed villages.

Among villages which are relatively independent we must, in connection with those which are tribally organized distinguish between villages in which there are common (cooperative) economic interests, and those in which the individual household (or the section) governs the economy. This means that the political life in such villages takes place in different *fora*, since also in political terms the economic unit, such as the *hamūla* is independent with respect to the rest of the village, as was the case with Kufr el-Ma[62]. The same distinction applies to villages which have no tribal organization, as seems to be the case in al-Munsif. Fernea's scheme contains ten subdivisions in all.

Without regarding Fernea's system as exhaustive or the only one possible, it does seem to apply to the main part of the Near Eastern agrarian societies. Of course, there are variations with respect to the model, but it is at least possible to locate most societies somewhere in the scheme. However, it may prove to be difficult to locate a society which has been studied without reference to Fernea's or a similar paradigm. This problem becomes acute when we include studies which are only a few decades old, and it becomes catastrophic when we have to do with a society about which our source materials are inadequate, so that we lack information sufficient to enable us to assign the society in question its correct place within the scheme. It is therefore important that we not jump to conclusions with respect to any society about which we are poorly informed, since this would entail a distortion of the information we actually do possess. Naturally, these remarks apply equally to the study of ancient societies. Our goal must be an analysis which is solely based on facts which emerge from the sources. Then, and only then, is it relevant to attempt to draw further conclusions concerning the society in question. It is indeed conceivable that we might not be able to reach any clear conclusion but must instead content ourselves with a list of possibilities. Other approaches must be written off as futile; they approach sheer guesswork.

It will be necessary briefly to bring the traditional Middle Eastern town into the discussion in the interests of arriving at a decision as to whether it is

---

[62] Antoun 1972A; 1972B.

reasonable to regard the relationship between city and rural district as a socio-economic continuum, or whether this view is a distortion. I shall in the main confine my remarks to the results of a scientific symposium held in 1966, the subject of which was the Middle Eastern city[63]. This symposium was concerned with Near Eastern urban societies from antiquity to today, although its main emphasis was on Moslem urban culture in the Middle Ages and especially in modern times. It is difficult to determine the extent to which A.L. Oppenheim's Babylonian example is representative for the whole of Mesopotamia. Indeed, Oppenheim admits that the sources dealing with Babylonian urban culture are somewhat onesided (they are concentrated on a single class, namely the administrative stratum which consisted of wealthy families, scribes, and lawyers). Moreover, the sources do not inform us sufficiently as to the composition and way of life of the ordinary population both within and outside of the cities and towns; nor do they inform us as to the interactions between the élite and the lower stratum, or tell us about social conflicts or the like[64]. There are, nevertheless, a number of common features uniting Sippar in the 19th to 16th centuries and later Oriental cities. Sippar was divided into three quarters, the city itself (ālu or libbi āli), the suburbs (uru.bar.ra), and the merchants' area, that is, the mart or quay known as the karum, within which extra-urban trade was concentrated. There was a rich network of connections between the suburbs, which were not satellite towns of the capital, but rather extensive fields which supplied the city with food and with grain for export. The city élite owned this circle around the city and administered its cultivation by copyholders. The élite also dominated the quay and its trade, while there was no connection between the lower stratum and the karum[65].

The various quarters of Sippar were all named; some of these names suggest an association with tribal society, even though Oppenheim feels that it was characteristic of Babylonian cities, in contrast to later Moslem cities, that tribal elements were only slightly represented in them. In any case, Sippar contained two subsections whose names contain tribal designations, namely Sippar-Yaḫruru and Sippar-Amnānum, both of which suggest West Semitic tribal groups on the Middle Euphrates[66]. Oppenheim gives us no other information as to the possible connection between these two quarters and the tribal groups, which did not dwell in the city. This sort of information is probably not contained in the cuneiform records from Sippar, but it must be emphasized that since the city was in the vicinity of the tribal territories the connections in

---

[63] See Lapidus 1969A. Recent important contributions are Laruffa 1974 and Serjeant 1980A.

[64] Oppenheim 1969:4.

[65] Oppenheim 1969:6.

[66] Oppenheim 1969:11-12. R. Harris (who follows Kupper 1957:52n. and 76) offers a completely different explanation of these two names; in here opinion these were not quarters of the city of Sippar, but quasi-independent towns in the suburbs of Sippar (Harris 1975:10-12).

question will probably have existed. We are also informed that Sippar contained a market for the local trade, to which villagers from out of town must have had access, as is suggested by the placement of the marketplace at the city gate[67]. It is accordingly reasonable to conclude, with Adams, that Sippar displays at least as many resemblances to the Near Eastern urban societies as it does differences. The fact that the differences are usually so prominent in Assyriological studies of village and urban cultures is explained by Adams as a result of the fact that scholars have not included modern socio-anthropological analyses in their studies of the urban societies of antiquity[68].

It is important to note that there are only a limited number of studies of the same type concerning West Semitic society in the second millenium. In this connection mainly Ugarit and Alalaḫ are of interest, since they are the only sites which until the present have yielded documents enabling us to develop our insights into the social structures of the states in question. On the other hand, we have very little information about these factors in connection with the Palestinian city states in this period, and the information we have is mostly of very general character. This also applies to the Amarna correspondence, which, as is well known, is predominantly concerned with international politics. Social features are only mentioned *en passant* in conjunction with references to crisis situations. For this reason the picture of social relations emerging from the Amarna letters is probably somewhat onesided, as it tends to concentrate on the *ḫabiru* problem[69].

In the case of Ugarit and Alalaḫ a number of detailed studies of social relationships have been carried out by A. Alt and by M. Dietrich and O. Loretz[70]. However, these studies are mainly concerned to investigate matters of detail such as occupational designations, military titles (especially *marjannu*), and certain class designations. Communications among the various sectors of the society in question are only slightly discussed. However, Dietrich and Loretz feel able to demonstrate that a number of systems of landleasing, which provided income for the palace administration, were in use in Alalaḫ[71].

One of the more valuable studies for our purposes is M. Heltzer's investigation of the agricultural sector in Ugarit[72]. Heltzer has succeeded in describing the types of obligations which were incumbant upon the village population in Ugarit; these were both physical, such as military service and corvée labor, and financial, in the form of a variety of taxes and imposts. He also informs us as to the punitive measures available for use against the peasant population

---

[67] Oppenheim 1969:12. Presumably just outside of the gate, like corresponding markets in Islamic towns; cf. Chalmeta 1980.

[68] Adams 1969:191.

[69] On this issue, and further references, see below, pp. 426ff.

[70] Alt 1956; 1957; 1958; 1964; Dietrich and Loretz 1966; 1969A; 1969B; 1970.

[71] See especially Dietrich and Loretz 1970.

[72] Heltzer 1976.

if they neglected their tasks; he further explains the peasants' possibilities of avoiding their obligations. Heltzer provides us with a sketch of the lines of communication connecting the local society and the palace, which includes mention of the local assemblies (councils of elders) and of the connection of the village leader (title: *ḫazānu*) to the palace. Heltzer reveals that there were many connecting lines between the city and the countryside in Ugarit, but he does not tell us whether the relationship between the two spheres is antipathetic, nor does he conclude that the agricultural sector was an integrated part of the society. However, he does expressly conclude that the basic source of the state's income was the agricultural sector[73].

To turn to other studies of social structure in Ugarit, A. R. Rainey operates with a number of different strata in the society. The highest is the royal dynasty, the middle level is the power apparatus of the dynasty (i.e., the bureaucracy, the military, and the instances governing the economy), while the lowest level consists of the various artisans and "the foreigners". On the other hand, according to Rainey, this society lacked an independent élite[74]. Against this, Heltzer's analysis admits of only two strata; these are, apart from the royal family, the *ardē šarri*, "royal servants", and the *ardē ardē šarri*, "royal servants' servants". One also encounters a third designation, *mārē Ugarit*, properly "citzens of Ugarit", but this group was identical with the peasant population of the kingdom[75]. Similarly, there is no indication that the Phoenician coastal cities contained an independent third class during the second millenium and the beginning of the first millenium. During this period, as in the great states to the north and east, and in the Palestinian city-states, these cities were ruled by royal dynasties. The monarchy was later replaced by local oligarchies when the wealthy assumed the leadership of these states. This élitist leadership stratum ruled over an under-class, but there was no middle group[76].

A more systematic evaluation of the social relationships in question has been undertaken by M. Liverani, who has presented two different models for social study, one which he terms the "bottom-up-model", and one called the "top-down-model" (to use Gottwald's terminology[77]). A "bottom-up-model" entails that one take his starting point in the lowest and most elementary groups, while a "top-down-model" signifies that one begins at the top of the society and then investigates its relationships down through the ranks. Also Liverani's sources are primarily derived from Ugarit and Alalaḫ. Liverani attempts to demonstrate that these regions knew two different types of land ownership. One of these was private ownership of the fields, which were cul-

---

[73] Heltzer 1976:102.
[74] Rainey 1962.
[75] Heltzer 1969A. See also Oelsner 1971. In this connection the most important information is to be found in PRU IV: RŠ 17.238.
[76] Harden 1962:71ff.
[77] Cf. Liverani 1973A ("top down"); 1975 ("bottom-up"). Cf. Gottwald 1979A:327.

tivated by "free peasants" who dwelled in villages. The other type consisted of royal estates. Both sectors yielded revenues to the royal administration; the first type paid via taxes, while the entire revenues of the latter group went into the royal coffers[78].

It is similarly possible to distinguish between two categories of population within the two states, the "freemen", who inhabited villages and practiced private ownership, and the "royal servants". The former group produced their own incomes, while the latter received theirs from the palace. However, it is important not to understand these two categories as classes; nor may we misunderstand the term "free". While the "freemen" were mainly ordinary peasants, the group of "royal servants" included everyone from the highest offices in the country to the slaves of the state[79]. The "freemen" dwelled in villages with an average of 125 to 150 inhabitants, whereas most of the "royal servants" lived in the capital[80]. Some information from Alalaḫ indicates that the ratio of "freemen" to "royal servants" was 10 to 1[81].

The villages will have enjoyed only very limited self-government. This was mainly restricted to relationships within the local society in question, and its main task was to distribute to the inhabitants a job which had been imposed on the village. This would be such matters as the enrollment of a certain number of villagers for military service or corvée labor[82].

Some of Liverani's other views are extremely interesting in this connection, even though they are rather more speculative. These have to do with the breakdown of the traditional family system based on familial ownership and its replacement by a market-oriented economy, plus the establishment of great estates (in part royal estates, in part property of the highest echelons of the "royal servants"). The capitalistic economy led to the accumulation of debts and to the debt-slavery of the individual peasant, and ultimately to a situation in which the social problems of these states became acute in the last part of the Bronze Age, not least because of the disquiet caused by refugees from the agricultural sector, in other words, the ḫabiru[83].

I agree with Liverani's description of the relationship between the agrarian and palace sectors in West Asia in many respects, and in particular with respect to his demonstration of the many connecting lines among them. I declared my satisfaction with his evaluation of the ḫabiru problem long ago[84].

---

[78] Liverani 1975:146.
[79] Liverani 1975:147.
[80] Liverani 1975:152. The section on the village covers variations with respect to size ranging from 15 to 900 persons; the figures derive from data from Alalaḫ. Heltzer presents only averages, that is, 125 per village, with an average family of 6.5 individuals; this seems to correspond to the situation in Alalaḫ (1976:102-112).
[81] Liverani 1975:152.
[82] Liverani 1975:155.
[83] Liverani 1975:159ff; further, Liverani 1965B; 1973A:352ff.
[84] Cf. Lemche 1975:138n; 1979:1; 1980:179.

On these issues Liverani's reconstructions are based on data which are preserved in the sources. In other areas, however, I would advise the utmost caution. Thus, for example, Liverani's account of the social development from the Middle Bronze age to the transitionary point between the Late Bronze and Iron ages is not unchallengeable. In particular I would mention the question of the changes in the system of production and the dissolution of the kinship system. On the last-named point Liverani assumes that the extended family was the basis of the social structure at the beginning of the period. Such an extended family will have produced goods and crops for its own consumption. Familial solidarity will have enabled it to retain its lands in its own hands and to protect them against hostile encroachments. In the latter part of the period this method of production based on solidarity was replaced by a capitalistic money economy, so that familial ties were dissolved and the extended family was replaced by the nuclear family. The question is whether Liverani has any sources at all to support his assumption of a change of social structure. In reality he refers only to documents from the third millenium which seem to suggest that the extended family dominated *Mesopotamian* society around 2000[85]. We have no sources of a comparable nature from the West Semitic ambit. In the next place, Liverani neglects to investigate the possibilities for an independent market economy on the local level. In other words, it is possible that the so-called free villagers were able to supplement their incomes by sale to markets which were not controlled by the state. It is conceivable that there was no room for such a private market in such states as Ugarit and Alalaḫ. It is also possible that we have no information whatsoever about such markets, since the various royal palace administrations were totally uninterested in them. However, to the best of my knowledge no one has ever made an attempt to investigate this aspect of trade in West Asia during the second millenium[86].

Yet another reason why a private economic sector for agricultural products did not exist could be that the so-called "free" peasants were even less "free" than Liverani's account suggests. In this connection it would be appropriate to mention that Liverani's still labors under the impression that such free peasants were termed *ḫupšu*[87], but this view is, as mentioned previously, most likely fallacious[88]. However, if Liverani has incorrectly understood the meaning of *ḫupšu*, then his hypothetical private sector becomes severely limited at least in the case of Alalaḫ, where the group called *ḫupše namē* predominate. In this case there were no free peasants, but only "clients". This in turn would suggest that the palace administrations had greater control of the peasant populations than they would have done had these populations been

---

[85] See Liverani 1975:156.
[86] On the significance of such local markets for the maintenance of some kind of independence (in this case) by a tribal society, see Dostal 1974 (concerning conditions in Yemen).
[87] Cf. Liverani 1965A:272; 1965B:325; 1975:152.
[88] See above, p. 167.

"free" in a technical sense. It also suggests that we should not distinguish between free individuals and those in the service of the state, but between those who were directly paid by the administration and others who were dependent on the authorities, but who did not receive any income from them in the form of rations from the public storehouses.

Thus Liverani's account of conditions in Ugarit and Alalaḫ, which, as he freely admits, is not without more ado to be applied to other parts of the Near East, is in part a collection of brilliant textual analyses and in part what seems to be a rather rough-and-ready Marxist evolutionary model, which serves as a blueprint[89]. Naturally, I do not criticize Liverani for utilizing a Marxist model, but for allowing his model to squeeze his theoretical evaluations in a particular direction without regard to the data made available by his sources.

Yet another point may be briefly mentioned in this connection. Liverani pleads for the diligent application of anthropological insights to the study of the Near East (moreover, in this connection he accuses – correctly – both Dietrich and Loretz of neglecting the sociological aspects of their studies of Alalaḫ and Ugarit). Liverani has himself offered some fine attempts in this direction[90], but in reality his anthropological horizon is probably every bit as limited as is that of Mendenhall and Gottwald.

If we turn to the Arab city of the Middle Ages, our impressions of the significance of the interactions between city and village are further reinforced[91]. There are no major differences between such large cities as Aleppo and Damascus and the towns. All of these urban societies have the same general structure, in that an Oriental town or city was traditionally divided into a number of quarters (ḥāra); it was also governed by an all-powerful élite. The élite consisted of families which were endogamous within their own class. Like the quarters in the villages, the quarters of the cities were divided according to a variety of criteria, among which were such features as family ties, client relationships (entire quarters might be understood as the clients of a single élite family), ethnic or religious fellowships (e.g., sects), but only occasionally common occupation. Therefore we do not find in the Orient divisions into guilds, as we know them from Europe[92]. The quarters had an official leader (numerous titles were employed); he was a native of the quarter in question who was appointed by the élite, not so much with a view to protecting the well-being of the inhabitants, as to furthering the interests of the élite, since he was

---

[89] Liverani makes no attempt to conceal the fact that he follows such a developmental scheme. See also the introduction to Liverani 1979:1.

[90] Cf. e.g. Liverani 1972, where anthropological studies of the significance of the "exchange of gifts" contribute to his evaluation of certain features in the trading pattern we see reflected in the Amarna period and its sources.

[91] See Lapidus 1969B.

[92] Lapidus 1969B:49.

responsible for taxation and was charged with the maintenance of law and order[93].

I.M. Lapidus does not deny that there were conflicts between city and village which were mainly ideologically conditioned (i.e., one society regarded itself as better, cleverer, more moral, more honest, or more orthodox than the other). However, he points out that such disagreements were also present between village and village, city quarter and city quarter, and between village and nomads in the same district[94]. Lapidus accordingly emphasizes that the stereotyped picture of Near Eastern urban culture as sharply divorced from the countryside is possibly the result of the ignorance of the European observer, whose view derives from North African societies. It is possible that such a dichotomy once existed in North Africa, but it was the product of special ethnic conditions, as the towns and cities are generally inhabited by an Arabic-speaking population, while the rural districts are populated by Berbers. This characteristic, however, is the result of a special situation brought about by the Arab conquest of North Africa[95].

Lapidus emphasizes the necessity not to focus on details within a region, but on the entire district in order to investigate the interactions between the various components of the district. If one undertakes an analysis on this basis, the continuity between the individual groupings in the region becomes visible. We discover that the city or town is not so much a *composite unit* as a *geographical collection of disparate units*. In other words, Near Eastern cities are in reality conglomerates of socially discrete village societies in geographical proximity to one another. This applies even to such metropolises as Cairo and Baghdad as late as the 19th century A.D., and to a certain extent even today; that is, it applies to urban societies with a population of between 200,000 to 300,000 individuals[96]. Many sections display great affinity to groups which are not located in the same city, but out in the countryside, especially if there is question of tribal units or sections which are composed of immigrants from a single village. Thus both the political and the social structuring of urban and village societies reveal numerous common features. There are also numerous economic resemblances, such as the fact that a city usually contains a sizeable agricultural sector, and that at least in the larger villages we find mechanisms of the marketplace such that these villages resemble urban societies *en miniature*, even including a hierarchical class structure which recalls that of the city.

---

[93] Lapidus 1969B:49. P. Magnarella informs us of similar conditions in the Turkish provincial town of Süsürluk; here the leader of the quarter is called the *muḫtar*, and he performs similar functions, although there are now representatives of the central authority in the town as well as a common police (1974:45-50).

[94] Lapidus 1969B:73.

[95] Lapidus 1969B:57.

[96] Lapidus 1969B:61ff; cf. Gulick 1969:126ff., and Gulick and Gulick 1974:442, where Isfahan is called "the largest village in Iran."

Therefore Lapidus feels justified in concluding that "cities... were simply the geographical locus of groups whose membership and activities were either smaller than or larger than themselves"[97].

Excursus

Community Property, or the Mušaʾ System

It is sometimes assumed by Orientalists that the presence of communally owned land which is distributed among the individual members of a society is a survival of the communal ideology which is claimed to underlie the common access of nomads to their pasturage. Most recently, W. Thiel has utilized the indications that land was owned in common in pre-national Israel as an indication that Israelite society had its roots in a nomadic past[98]. The system of property owning in question is the so-called *mušaʾ* or *mašaʾ*.

The basic lines of this system are as follows: the land is owned by the entire local society (most often a village) and by regularly re-allocating plots of land the lands are distributed among the various families in the village. The key to the system is the principle of division of which it makes use. As with other agricultural societies the Near Eastern village lands are not all of equal quality. Therefore the *mušaʾ* distributional system attempts to compensate by ensuring that every family owns a parcel of each type of land available. The result is a subdivision of village land into very small parcels indeed. In order to avoid or to repair occasional injustices, the *mušaʾ* area of the village is re-allocated on a regular basis, which is usually of two years' duration[99].

The sources available to me inform me that the area in which the *mušaʾ* system appears or has played a part in the Near East is confined to the western region, where it occurs on the prairies on the landward side of the coastal mountains, on the coastalplains, and in mountainous regions[100]. The system seems to be confined to societies whose economy is based on the cultivation of grain. But what is the origin of this system?. In those societies which are of nomadic or partially nomadic origin which have been discussed here, there was once a *mušaʾ* system in Tell Tòqaan, but not in the al-Karak district[101]. In the villages which are of peasant origin, the system has been an important factor in the economy of the society in question, such as in Bint el-Ḥudūd in the Palestinian coastal plain, in Beitin in the mointains of central Palestine, and in Kufr el-Ma in the Aǧlun province in Jordan[102]. In Beitin the *mušaʾ* system was first intro-

---

[97] Lapidus 1969B:73. Among OT scholars the connection between the town and its surroundings has been emphasized by F.S. Frick (1977:91-97). Frick focuses on the town as a place of refuge for the peasant population, as well as on the economic interaction between town and country. Thus he concludes that "The city in ancient Israel is only part of a total rural-urban system which included the 'mother city' together with its 'daughter villages' and the city's fields" (1977:92).

[98] Thiel 1980A:94; cf. also Thiel 1980B:133-141.

[99] A general description of the system is to be found in Weullersse 1946:99-109, and especially in Granott 1952:213-248. See also the important discussion of the system in Antoun 1972A: 19-25.

[100] Weullersse limited the extent of this system to the hinterland along the coast of the Levant (1946:98), but this stipulation is entirely too narrow, as already our own examples show. According to Fernea one also finds a practice closely related to the *mušaʾ* system in the territory described by him (largely a tribal area) – if it is not in reality simply a *mušaʾ* system (1970:44f.). Fernea understands this situation as a survival of the property system which obtained *before the el-Sabana seized control of their present territory* at some point in the course of the 19th century. In other words, the system is also able to thrive in an agricultural society based on irrigation.

[101] See Gubser 1973:26.

[102] Antoun 1972A:19ff.

duced after the founding of the town in the 19th century, and not in connection with the first settlement of the town in recent times[103]. Bint el-Ḥudūd was founded by peasants from the region around Nablus[104]. Special conditions obtained in Kufr el-Ma because of the peculiar political structure of the al-Kura district. Thus none of these societies has a nomadic past. Finally, it is to be emphasized that in countering the suggestion of a connection between the *mušaʿ* system and nomadism already A. Granott pointed out that the grain-cultivating nomads of Beersheba did not use it[105].

But if the *mušaʿ* system does not have a particular historical origin, how did it in fact begin? It is impossible to answer this definitively. One might be tempted to suppose that since the *mušaʿ* is strongly reminiscent of conditions in Western Europe, where its parallels were practiced until the 19th century – it is still in use at some spots on Corsica[106] – that it was exported from Europe to the Orient. However, it is more likely the case that the appearance of this system in both the Near East and in Europe was the result of the fact that related agricultural conditions give rise to related social practices[107]. However, this remark does not answer the question of the origin of the *mušaʿ* system. Some scholars have maintained that the system serves to support the egalitarian social system of the villages. Naturally, they also maintain that it is a secondary form of this system we encounter when we discover it in societies in which the *mušaʿ* distribution subserves, not an egalitarian ideology, but status differences[108]. To this it must be objected that the materials investigated here offer no certain evidence of a change from one principle of distribution to another. Sweet claims that in Tell Toqaan the distribution took place on an egalitarian basis, whereas Antoun does not suggest that distribution in Kufr el-Ma has ever been so; instead, it follows differences both with respect to the individual lineages in the village and with respect to their individual families[109].

The *mušaʿ* system will probably have had a defensive function against two fronts. On the one hand the system will doubtless have served to strengthen solidarity within the framework of the village. It was necessary to cooperate in order to carry out the distribution, if the village in question was in any way to survive physically. The fact that the lands belonging to an individual lineage were apportioned helter-skelter in small plots will no doubt have strengthened lineage solidarity. It was practically impossible to avoid working together. Outwardly, the system must have functioned as a defensive mechanism against the wealthy. Since the land was at one and the same time private property, or at least the possession of the individual lineage, while at the same time being owned in common by the entire village, the individual peasant could not freely dispose of his land. In other words, it could not be used as security by the moneylender. This is an important point, which is confirmed by the fact that after the gradual retirement of the system during the last century, much land that was previously *mušaʿ* land has come into the possession of the proprietors. This has contributed greatly to the reduction of the numbers of peasants who practice private ownership in the Middle East[110].

As for the question of Israelite community property, we do not know whether the system was only practiced in the pre-national period, or whether it also continued to function during the

---

[103] Lutfiyya 1966:105.

[104] See Ab. Cohen 1965:5f on the *mušaʿ* practices which were retained in this district until the Mandate. On the origins of the villages in this region, see Cohen 1965:9ff.

[105] Cf. Granott 1952:213.

[106] On a similar allocation system on Corsica, see Chiva 1963:103.

[107] Cf. Weullersse 1946:107.

[108] Thus Weullersse 1946:99f. Weullersse operates with three forms: *le village en propriété mouchaa*, in which division of the land which is owned in common by the village takes place; *le village en tenure mouchaa*, in which the village has lost its collective ownership; the land is in the hands of land-owners, even though it continues to be cultivated in small plots; and finally *le village à parcellement mouchaa stabilisé*, in which the *mušaʿ* system has petrified into permanent individual ownership, but in which the fields of each individual peasant are interwoven with those of other peasants just as in the true *mušaʿ* system.

[109] Cf. Sweet 1960:61 and Antoun 1972A:23.

[110] The main reason for the abandonment of the *mušaʿ* system was the Turkish land reform of 1868, which prohibited the communal ownership of land. This compelled the individual peasant to register his plots as private property.

monarchy. Conditions in the later history of the Middle East show that communal ownership of property *can be maintained* even in areas which are governed by some central authority, unless such a government opposes the continuation of the system. The OT informs us that not all lands were common property during the Monarchy; indeed, in many cases land ownership seems to have been private, since wealthy men had the possibility to appropriate arable land in the agrarian societies (that is, if we assume that the social criticism of the prophets refers to some socio-historical reality). On the other hand, it is also evident that members of the various lineages were expected to contribute to the retention of lands belonging to the lineage[111]. I accordingly feel that a *mušaʕ*-like system must also have existed in Israel during the Monarchy, although it is impossible to say anything as to its extent. Furthermore, we cannot assume that all land was common property during the pre-monarchical period, that is, not if there was any continuity between landownership practices in antiquity and in more recent times, since not all land was suitable to the type of apportionment in question. For example, it would be appropriate to be sceptical as to the usefulness of the system in the case of orchards and vineyards. The last-mentioned are in private ownership at present, whereas the former, even in areas which are owned by proprietors, are often in private hands and are physically contiguous with the habitations of the individual families[112].

§ 6

Conclusion: Nomad, City-Dweller, and Farmer in the Middle East

Two chapters have been devoted to an evaluation of some of Gottwald's conceptions of the cultures of the Middle East. Their mutual relations have been examined; thus in what follows I shall rehearse our conclusions, as they must necessarily form part of the basis for a discussion of Israel's origins.

Gottwald still makes use of a conception of Near Eastern society as divided into three spheres, that is, nomads, peasants, and city-dwellers. Admittedly, he emphasizes that there are no social barriers between nomads and peasants, while the peasant and urban societies have little to do with one another. They are *antimorphemes*, that is, separate cultures which are characterized by reciprocal antipathy. However, as we have seen, Gottwald's conception of such a tripartite division of the Oriental societies is hardly adequate, even if he also claims that a community of interests links the nomads and the peasants to each other. In these chapters I have argued that the Near East is to be understood as a socio-economic continuum. This continuum embraces a polymorphous society which ranges from the city-dweller who never passes through the gates of his city, to the pure nomad, whose entire life is an endless trek[113]. This does not mean that there are no differences between the two extremes; indeed,

---

[111] Compare on this point the Israelite גאל institution, concerning which see Lemche 1976: 46ff. The *locus* classicus of this institution in the OT is Jer 32.

[112] We have evidence concerning vineyards from Alalaḫ (15th c.); cf. Dietrich and Loretz 1969B. The vineyards were apparently to some extent in private hands, while others were leased out to tenants (who were members of the ḫupšu class, which, however, still does not make of the ḫupšu a class of free peasants).

[113] Cf. English 1973.

there is no doubt but that very considerable differences do separate them. The city-dweller would have a hard time adjusting to a life as a pure nomad and vice versa, but even these extremes can be bridged by a number of common interests. The peasant is traditionally placed in the middle, but this does not mean that his position is a necessary evolutionary middle stage between the nomad and the city-dweller. In many places in the Near East contact between the cities and the nomadic tribes takes place without middlemen in the peasant class. However, the peasant is in the middle in the sense that he has a number of features in common with the nomad, and others which he has in common with the city-dweller. He is sedentary like a city-dweller, but his economy is in many cases based on the same strategies as the nomad pursues (especially if the peasant keeps flocks of livestock). This means that all local societies may in principle be assigned to a single position on the continuum line if one has sufficient information about them. However, this line is not divided into delimited sections, which would enable us to say that up to such and such a point we have to do with peasants, whereas the nomads start here. Instead, the overlappings between peasant and nomad at this point on the line are so numerous that demarcation would be meaningless. The same is true of the relationship of the village societies to the cities and towns. There is no absolute limit distinguishing the village from the town. Both villages and towns have distinctively different functions, but where they meet on the continuum line there are so many points of agreement that one cannot be certain in individual cases whether we have to do with a village or a town.

Therefore Gottwald's conception of *antimorphemes* is based on a stereotyped concept of the structures of, and the functions contained within, Near Eastern societies. Accordingly, his account cannot be considered a paradigm for a historical investigation of an ancient society such as Israel.

There is no doubt that Gottwald's account of the relationship between nomads and sedentary dwellers contains many insights which have been helpful to OT scholarship. However, he makes use of an ideal type of the "pastoral nomad", which he employs as the paradigm for the relationships obtaining in Palestine at the close of the second millenium. It has been the aim of this study to examine in depth the interactions beween nomads and agricultural societies as an aid to OT scholarship. We have seen that the ideal type of the pastoral nomad is a fiction, at least as it is described by Gottwald. Not one of the features which he held to be important to the understanding of this type has proven to be decisive. All are very general. There is not a single case in all of the many examples derived from the ethnographic literature in which Gottwald's conception of the pastoral nomad actually corresponds to the actual situation. This even applies to the Yörük, who in some respects best approaches the conception of the cowed, egalitarian and peaceful nomad. Although they live in a symbiotic relationship to societies which are not of Yörük descent, this has to do with the *immigration* of the Yörük into their present territory in the last half of the 19th century.

As far as nomadic types are concerned, there are countless varieties. They do not however, exist in delimitable categories, but in a veritable *pot pourri* of hybrid types. Naturally, there are differences between, for example, the Yörük and the al-Murrah. It could be claimed that they occupy opposite ends of the continuum line, and that their material culture is different in practically all respects (but only practically). However, these are the extremes. If one approaches the middle ground with a view to defining the pastoral nomads in contradistinction to camel nomads (who are also pastoral, since they, too, keep livestock) one quickly discovers that there are so many common features that it would be meaningless to distinguish between them as separate groups.

It would be no less unreasonable to attempt to assign the various types specific characteristics as do Gottwald and Mendenhall today, and as Alt, Noth, Albright, and their predecessors and disciples have done. It is a banal psychological insight that men tend to behave in agreement with the possibilities available to them. By this I mean to say that of course Near Eastern societies are filled with conflicts, in spite of the fact that I have spoken of a socio-economic continuum. On the other hand, it would be quite wrongheaded to maintain that these conflicts are the result of any general antipathy among three distinct social types. There are conflicts between and among the various groups, but these conflicts are not in principle different from the conflicts of interest between two nomadic societies, or two peasant societies, and which normally have to do with the distribution of the economic resources of a given region.

It has been pointed out that the small-cattle nomads are every bit as belligerent as the camel nomads, on the condition that they have the possibility to obtain booty and avoid retaliation. The migratory routes of the small-cattle nomads may be just as long and difficult as are those of the camel nomads if the ecological situation requires such routes. There is therefore no natural law which says that one way of life produces heroes, while another is preferable for weaklings. On the other hand, it is correct that in collisions between small-cattle and camel nomads in regions where both are well represented, the small-cattle nomads normally draw the short straw. This is a result of their inferior mobility, a consideration which also applies to the relationship between small-cattle nomads and peasants. It is also correct that small-cattle nomads are more easily outmanouvered by determined central authorities than is the case with camel nomads, although this is not necessarily the case in regions which are inaccessible to the camel nomads, such as the mountains.

These considerations lead us to the third point in Gottwald's account, which deserves to be emphasized. It would be incorrect to utilize the present ecological conditions or the distribution of the contemporary inhabitants of a region as the basis for a study of the same region in antiquity. It would be incorrect to presuppose that the ecological conditions have remained the same, and then to maintain that for that reason the sociological situation has also done so. The

Near East may well have been better off with respect to its ecology, at least in some periods. Thus the ratio between the sedentary and the nomadic population can at times have been quite different than it was in, for example, the Turkish period. In this connection other factors must have played a role; the most prominent of these will have been politics. This means that the ratio in question may have been to the nomads' advantage in spite of reasonably favorable conditions for farming. It was emphasized previously that in many respects the situation of the nomads is better than that of the *fellahin*. Therefore the nomad has no reason to settle down as a peasant unless political developments so require. For this reason there is no easy yardstick for measuring the ratio between nomads and sedentary dwellers. It is simply not the case that a given set of ecological conditions corresponds to a given ratio between nomads and peasants. External conditions are an important factor, but the political situation is far more decisive.

Chapter 3

EGALITARIANISM AND SEGMENTATION

§ 1

Introduction

C.H.J. de Geus' work on Israel in the period of the Judges was presented above as a counterweight to earlier research, which primarily regarded the Israelite social system as a survival of a nomadic past. De Geus' starting point was precisely that we should abandon the notion of ancient Israel's nomadic origins, and, further, that we should altogether surrender the idea that Near Eastern tribal societies must have begun in a previous nomadic existence.

On the other hand, de Geus does not contest the view that in the period of the Judges Israel was a true tribal society composed of three main parts: the extended family, the endogamous clan, and the tribe, the last of which was in Israel primarily a geographical denomination. On this point de Geus does not differ from earlier scholars; indeed, it is possible that he is closer to J. Pedersen that he is aware of being. This applies not least to his emphasis on the connections linking tribal and urban society in ancient Israel, in which in the Israelite territories the towns and villages were often the centers of clan activity[1].

According to de Geus, a tribal system may have many possible origins, of which nomadism is merely a single example. A system may be imported from other societies, or it may arise because of changes in the presuppositions for existence of a given society. Moreover, de Geus recognizes that a tribal system is not an evolutionary stage en route to the formation of a state; in fact, since he follows the views of M. Fried on the place of the tribe in socio-political development, de Geus even maintains that in reality the tribe may well present obstacles to state formation[2].

De Geus' sketch of the Israelite tribal system merely leads to a few general remarks as to the historical development of ancient Israel; it does not permit him to offer an evaluation of the forces which were active in this society. His division of the Israelite tribe into family, clan, and tribe is unsatisfactory. My survey of the family and tribal structures in the Middle East indicates that it is unwise to insist that a single factor, such as the extented family, dominated the Israelite society (i.e., to suggest that several generations lived together,

---

[1] Cf. Pedersen 1958:23ff.
[2] De Geus 1976:131, and see below, pp. 214ff., on Fried.

either matrilocally or patrilocally[3]). Nor is it clear that de Geus' description of the clan as an endogamous unit corresponds to the accounts of this structural level one usually sees in the anthropological literature. Finally, taking our point of departure in the preceding section, one would be justified in questioning whether de Geus or any other OT scholar is fully aware that the social structure of traditional societies may contain more levels than the three which are generally assumed (i.e., family, clan, and tribe). Moreover, one must take into account the fact that there are other socio-political formations in the Near Eastern societies which do not follow the corresponding unilinear descent system[4]. Other interests than purely familial ones, such as, above all, economic interests, may serve to bind people together, even in traditional societies, without this entailing that the members of such linkages have a common genealogical system at a lower level than a whole tribe. It is possible that the OT sources do not tell us whether such groups actually existed. There may be two reasons for this. Either such systems did not exist, or the sources which concentrate on the various genealogical relationships have not preserved evidence of them. It would be appropriate to compare with Gulick's previously mentioned study of al-Munsif in Lebanon, in which even a trained ethnographer is forced to admit that he has probably not managed to identify all the political and economic groupings in this society, in spite of the fact that there are numerous indications that they are present[5].

Thus any analysis of the Israelite tribal system will necessarily be fairly complicated, and it is conceivable that it will prove to be heavy going. On the other hand, it must be stressed that it would be methodologically unsound to preselect a single model of a traditional society in order to allow this model to be reproduced in one's description of ancient Israel. Here, too, it is essential that we allow room for the manifold possible variations. We cannot rule out in advance the possibility that Israelite society may have developed in a direction to which we have no parallels elsewhere. Nor is it inconceivable that we lack the sources which would explain to us just why Israel developed as she did. There are, for example, a plethora of kinship terms in the OT, a phenomenon which may be variously explained. One possibility is that Israelite society was not precise as to the use of these terms, at least not as we should demand[6].

---

[3] In modern times in the Near East (as well as earlier) *patrilocal* residence is the norm as far as extended families are concerned. By "patrilocal" is meant that the married sons continue to dwell in their father's house or in some other way continue to be a part of the father's household. *Matrilocality* offers numerous possible variations, dependent upon whether the kinship system of the society in question is *matrilinear* (i.e., is one in which descent follows the maternal line) or *patrilinear* (thus following the paternal line). *Neolocal* residence simply entails that the sons abandon their father's household in order to establish their own.

[4] *Unilinear:* meaning that the group in question traces its descent along a single line from the common tribal ancestor.

[5] Cf. Gulick 1955:131.

[6] Cf. Fox 1967:240ff. Fox explains the differences between the observations made by a con-

Another possibility is that in the course of the transmission of the OT source materials the contents of such kinship terms may have been changed in periods in which tribal organization no longer existed; or, they may have been preserved in circles which were ignorant of such organization. This would, for example, be possible if the tradents belonged to the élite in the urban societies. A third possibility is that the Israelite societies did not represent a single system, but innumerable ones instead, namely at least the twelve "official" Israelite tribes, plus an unknown number of "unofficial" groupings[7].

§ 2

N.K. Gottwald's Description of Israelite Tribal Society

Unlike other scholars who have concerned themselves with the social structure of the Israelite tribes during the pre-monarchical period, Mendenhall and Gottwald attempt to introduce a dynamic element. In their opinion Israelite society did not arise in the course of time practically as the result of a series of accidents. Instead, they maintain that this occurred as part of a conscious attempt to establish a political alternative to the Canaanite system, which they simply define as both feudally and hierarchically structured. Both Mendenhall and Gottwald have treated with this question at great length, but in what follows we shall be mainly concerned with Gottwald's account for our continued discussion[8].

In Gottwald's opinion, Israel was a unique tribal society since he attempts to prove on the basis of what he describes as "current anthropological theory about tribalism" (i.e., the descriptions of primitive or traditional societies and their evolution which have been proposed by M. Fried, M.D. Sahlins and E. R. Service) that the Israelite tribes were not tribes as such. Rather, he holds that they represented a very singular sociological phenomenon, in that they were *secondary* tribes. In other words, they represented an attempt by a non-tribally organized Canaanite population to establish a different political system from the one already existing in the country.

However, it is important to realize that Gottwald broadly accepts Noth's

---

temporary European observer of the kinship terms used in a traditional (i.e., primitive) society and that society's own understanding of them. Cf. however Stöber, who proposes all of three different models for the social structure of a traditional society. Stöber's models, it is to be noted, derive from information provided by informants from the society in question, but belonging to different strata within it (1978:47-50).

[7] Once again, it is to be stressed that the OT 12-tribe system has only provided us with the names of a *selection* of the tribal units which once existed in pre-monarchical Israel (Lemche 1972:81).

[8] See Mendenhall 1973:174-197, and Gottwald 1979A:228-341.

classical amphicyony hypothesis, not, however, in the form Noth gave his theory, but as a religious confederation which did not have a preestablished number of member-units, but which nevertheless possessed a centralized cult and was in a position to manifest itself politically via, for example, collective military action[9]. The following comments on the internal relations of the Israelite tribes presuppose this understanding of the union. Furthermore, Gottwald's analysis of the forces which were active among the Israelite tribes is dependent upon his understanding of the ideology which prevailed in the tribal federation. The ideology underlying the union is easily described with the classical revolutionary concepts of equality, freedom, and brotherhood. It is to be understood in the light of Israelite Yahwism, the ethical norms of which bound the Israelites together in a covenantal relationship[10].

Therefore the egalitarian ideology penetrated on all levels throughout Israel, including relations among the tribes, among the individual familial groups, and among individuals. For this reason the Israelite tribes were in principle of equal worth. Gottwald claims that the Israelite tribes are to be understood as *segments* of the whole of Israel, and that an Israelite tribe only existed at all because it was a member of the Israelite league[11]. In the opinion of many anthropologists, segmentation is identical with egalitarianism[12]. Therefore, this hypothetical Israel did not give rise to any movement which could lead to the establishment of new political systems, by which Gottwald primarily means the rule of chieftains. To the contrary, the entire ideology of ancient Israel was hostile to the rule of any single individual[13].

Gottwald's description of Israelite tribal society utilizes an analysis of the various levels lower than the tribe, namely the family, בית אב, and the "clan" משפחה[14]. It is here that battle is to be joined, if Gottwald is to succeed in demonstrating that the Israelite tribes differed radically from other tribal societies. The fundamental question confronting Gottwald is whether it can be shown that the *exogamous clan* existed in Israel, since this characteristic feature dominates the entire structure within *true* tribal systems. On the basis of a number of OT marital regulations (Lev 18,6-18; 20,11-12; Dtn 22,30; 27,20), further supported by a number of individual traditions, there seems to be no question but that the individual family or "father's house" was an exogamous unit, while a number of "father's houses" conjoined to make up a משפחה. The question, however, is whether this משפחה was endogamous or exogamous. Gottwald's conclusion is reminiscent of that of de Geus: the Israelite משפחות- were endogamous, which means that marriages were contracted between

---

[9] Gottwald 1979A:376-386.
[10] See below, Ch.5, on Gottwald and the tribal league.
[11] Gottwald 1979A:245.
[12] Cf. e.g. Sahlins 1968:21.
[13] Gottwald 1979A:298.
[14] Gottwald 1979A:257-292.

father's houses which belonged to the same משפחה, whereas marriages between different משפחות were rare. In a true tribal system, so Gottwald holds, these משפחות ought to be *exogamous*, meaning that marriages would be contracted between different משפחות. Gottwald points out that it is nowhere stated in the OT that a father's house contains representatives of more than one משפחה, and he emphasizes that this is decisive for an understanding of the structure of Israelite society (although Gottwald never actually reveals just *why* it is so decisive).

The lowest organizational level was the father's house[15]. In Israel this unit was *extended*, meaning that up to five generations dwelled together and were attached to a single household.

This reconstruction of the Israelite tribal system is to be seen against the background of a number of ideas about Canaanite society which Gottwald never develops at length in his work; they are allowed to serve as simple postulates. The writer first maintains that Canaanite social structure was hierarchical and feudal, that is, based on systematic inequality at all levels. It is synonymous with a monopoly of all political and economic power. Gottwald's second claim is that we do not find the traditional organization of the units in the Canaanite society in a familial and tribal system; nor do we find clans in Canaanite society[16]. These postulates can neither be corroborated nor falsified, as not a single Palestinian document from the second millenium tells us anything about family structure in Canaanite society. The most informative documents concerning social structure in the West Asiatic societies in the Late Bronze age come from Ugarit and have been thoroughly treated by M. Heltzer[17]. However, these materials consist solely of administrative documents, so that they reveal only fragmentary details about family structure in the Ugaritic local societies. Moreover, they apparently contain no information about the regulation of marital contacts in this society. Ugaritic families appear to have been generally small. In most cases they must have been *nuclear families*, although there are a few indications to suggest that extended families existed as well[18]. The materials tell us only a very little about whether individual families belonged to lineages or clans, and in all cases the genealogical depth is poor[19]. It should be noted that Heltzer emphasizes that we cannot compare the Ugaritic data with data about other societies in the Middle East in antiquity, since the ethnic composition and economic structure of Ugarit differed significantly from those of her neighbours[20]. It is difficult, if not

---

[15] Gottwald 1979A:285-292.

[16] Gottwald 1979A:230ff. and 317.

[17] Heltzer 1976.

[18] There is reason to believe that we have to do with extended families when we learn that brothers inherit land in common; cf. Heltzer 1976:96ff.

[19] Heltzer 1976:100 and 102. Heltzer mentions that the genealogical information becomes unclear when one goes back only three generations. Of course, this is by no means an unknown phenomenon in Near Eastern genealogical systems; see also below, p. 229.

[20] Heltzer 1976:102.

impossible, to derive the structure of the Canaanite societies in Palestine from these materials; the information from Ugarit is not to be superimposed upon the Canaanite mini-societies, the diminutive size of which should alone be sufficient to warn us against drawing parallels irresponsibly.

§ 3

The Logical Structure Underlying Gottwald's Description of Israelite Tribal Society

If we thoroughly analyze Gottwald's description of the Israelite tribal system we discover that it is in reality based on a number of logical conclusions which, taken together, make up the foundation of his model of pre-monarchical Israel. It is my intention in this section to scrutinize this foundation very carefully. This should enable us to determine which of Gottwald's theses are essential to the validity of his model. In the following subsections these theses will be our point of departure for further discussion.

The premisses of Gottwald's first logical conclusion are the following: first, it is presupposed that segmentary systems are egalitarian; second, it is claimed that Israel was a segmentary system. Thus he concludes that since Israel was a segmentary society, it will necessarily have been an egalitarian one. None of the premisses in question is at all obvious. In connection with the first premiss, it is necessary to ask whether all segmentary systems are in fact egalitarian. In other words, the question is whether all tribal systems which are organized in segments also are dominated by an egalitarian ideology which manifests itself in the political and economic life of the systems in question. The second premiss is dependent on the first premiss of the fourth conclusion, mentioned below, which has to do with the concept of an Israelite tribal league during the period of the Judges. However, it may also be studied in isolation, since the OT materials which pertain to the period of the Judges must be decisive in determining whether the Israelite tribes were valued equally.

The second conclusion has the following premisses: first, the exogamous clan is the *sine qua non* of tribal organization. Second, the exogamous clan did not exist in Israel. Therefore Israel was not a normal tribal society. The first thesis must be examined; if it proves to be incorrect, it is irrelevant whether there were exogamous clans in Israel or not, although if the practically identical and independently-arrived-at conclusions of Gottwald and de Geus were to prove correct, this would naturally be of importance in and of itself. If the first premiss is false, there would then be no reason to suppose that Israelite tribal formation differed fundamentally from other corresponding social phenomena in the Middle East. Should this prove to be the case, the revolution hypothesis of Mendenhall and Gottwald would then be in serious difficulties.

The first premiss in the third conclusion assumes that the Levites were disseminated throughout Israel[21]. The author also claims that the Levites were *fanatical* worshipers or Yahweh. For this reason one is forced to conclude that *all* of Israel were *fanatical* adherents of Yahweh. In this case, even if the premisses are correct, there is no reason to believe that the conclusion is as well. The correct conclusion would be that a *fanatical* Yahweh-worshiping element was everywhere present in premonarchical Israel. One would then have the task of trying to determine the impact and meaning of such an element.

The fourth conclusion is attached to the third and, as mentioned above, it is also the basis of the first conclusion. Israel is said to be unified by a covenantal relationship according to the first premiss. The second claims that a covenantal relationship requires the presence of a council of elders (i.e., to administer the obligations incumbent upon the contracting parties). Therefore Israelite tribal society must have been led by a council of elders. Now, this premiss in reality stands or falls with the first premiss, which presupposes that it is demonstrable that a tribal league existed in ancient Israel. The second premiss is irrelevant if the first cannot be verified; the conclusion would accordingly also be irrelevant.

Finally we arrive at the fifth conclusion, which is the logical corrollary of the preceding one; it is also the basis for the understanding of the monarchy advocated by Gottwald and Mendenhall, and, in reality, by many others as well. This conclusion claims that a monarchy is not the same as a tribal league, and Israel was incontrovertibly a monarchy from the time of David onwards. Therefore there was no tribal system in Israel during the monarchy. Yet another corollary would be that there was no interest in creating or retaining traditions about an Israelite tribal system during the monarchy. While there is no doubt that both premisses are correct, the conclusion is not necessarily true, since the contents of the two premisses are not on the same level. One of these speaks of a type of society, while the other speaks of a type of government. If one were to claim that Israel was ruled by the administrative council of a tribal league during the period of the Judges, while she was ruled by a monarch during the monarchy, then of course she cannot have been ruled by a tribal council during the monarchy. This is obvious; however, it does not mean that there were no Israelite tribes during the period of the monarchy. It would be naive to suppose that monarchies do not sometimes contain tribes (one has only to cast a glance at the social organization of such Near Eastern states as Jordan or Saudi Arabia. In both states the local form of organization lives on, if not completely healthily, then at least relatively so.). On the other hand, if Gottwald can succeed in demonstrating or arguing convincingly that

---

[21] Gottwald remains neutral with respect to the question of the original status of the tribe of Levi (1979A:320).

in connection with the period of the Judges the Israelite tribes can only be understood as segments of a tribal league, he may be right to claim that the tribes had to disappear when the league no longer existed, that is, after the introduction of the monarchy. However, one could also argue to the effect that the social units at the point of time in question (*in casu* the Israelite tribes during the period of the Judges) could also survive under a different type of government, if the source materials so suggest.

The following discussion of Gottwald's account will attempt either to verify or to falsify these five logical conclusions, or at least the more central among them. It is to be recalled that if a single one of the premises is incorrect, the conclusion derived from it collapses with it. However, if a single one of the logical conclusions is false, this fact will have grave repercussions for the rest of them, since they conjoin to form a single distinct model.

In the first instance our control procedure will be concerned with the socio-anthropological basis for Gottwald's (and Mendenhall's) reconstruction of ancient Israelite society. In this phase, statements based on the OT source materials will not be surveyed, although they will be studied later. The following discussion will be concentrated on two statements: first, that *segmentary systems are egalitarian ones*, and, second, that the *characteristic element in tribal organization is the exogamous clan*. Both statements are hugely important to the revolution hypothesis, since if they cannot be verified one is forced to turn to the OT sources in order to investigate the expressions found in these sources about Israelite society. This review is necessary, since it would be unreasonable to confine ourselves to the understanding of primitive or traditional societies promulgated by the small circle of anthropologists cited by Gottwals and Mendenhall, if we are unable to accept their views as definitive of current theory about tribalism. Finally, we may not rule out the possibility that in the works of Gottwald and Mendenhall we discover a highly idiosyncratic use of the views of the anthropologists in question.

§ 4

Segmentary Societies

The revolution hypotheses of Mendenhall and Gottwald are based, as mentioned previously, on an entirely too limited circle of American social anthropologists. Thus when Gottwald refers to *current theory about tribalism*, he has in mind the views of such anthropologists as Fried, Sahlins, and Service; other views are not taken into account. Gottwald reveals his position already in his definition of a segmentary society: "Segmentary tribes are composed of two or more primary segments which are structurally and functionally equivalent

14

and also politically equal". In so saying Gottwald refers to Sahlins' description of the concept of tribe and not to the English functionalistic anthropologists, who originally developed the theory of segmentary societies[22].

Sahlins and Service, and perhaps also Fried, are members of a long list of earlier – mainly American – anthropologists, whose views may be summarized under the designation *cultural evolutionism*[23]. This branch of research has been thoroughly described by J.J. Honigmann, for which reason I shall confine myself here to a brief general presentation, plus a closer discussion of the evolutionary models proposed by, in particular, Service, Sahlins, and Fried. This branch of study is rooted in the evolutionistic ideas current in the 19th century. Its main purpose is to demonstrate the existence of laws which are both general and determinative of the development of human societies from the most primitive stage to that of the developed state. Evolutionary scholars rejected the notion that anthropology was to be a sort of "apothecary science", in which detailed studies of individual societies are ranged alongside one another with no attempt being made to utilize these materials for the construction of comparative evolutionistic theories. Naturally, the factors on which the individual evolutionist bases his efforts at reconstruction vary considerably. They may be technological, demographical, biological, or psychological factors. Nevertheless, this circle was convinced first, that such general determining factors existed, and, second, that use of the comparative method would enable us to demonstrate which factors are relevant at any stage in human development[24].

In this connection if we turn our attention to the interesting figures of Sahlins, Service, and Fried, our starting point is necessarily Service, since his general introduction, *Primitive Social Organization*, has been a sort of textbook for the movement[25]. Service seems to summarize the entire movement, in that he declines to select any single factor as the sole determinant of evolution. He regards development as a continuing process in which man successively accomodates himself to new conditions, selects new forms of cultural organi-

---

[22] Gottwald 1979A:322, which refers to Sahlins 1968:20-23.

[23] See Honigmann 1976:273-373; see also Hastrup and Ovesen 1980:163-182.

[24] To use but a couple of examples from Honigmann's survey: Darwinistic biology, as used by L.A. White, J. Steward (and Service); technology, as used by V.G. Childe (and also by White).

[25] Service 1971: I have unfortunately only had access to the 2nd edition. Honigmann's brief summary, as well as a number of remarks by Fried (1967) seem to indicate that some of the views adumbrated by Service in the 1st edition of his work appear in modified form in the 2nd edition. However, it was the 1st edition which was the basis for Mendenhall and Gottwald. One of the points which seems to be of greater significance in the 2nd edition than in the 1st is the assignment of the "chieftainship" to a mediatory position between the tribal society and the state. Moreover, there appears to be some change of emphasis with respect to the development from band to tribal society to state. In the 1st edition this seems to have been a fairly mechanical developmental scheme, while in the 2nd the organizational scheme is more sophisticated, so that evolution proceeds from an egalitarian society to a hierarchically ordered one and ultimately to a stratified society. This model is clearest in Service 1975.

zation, or modifies old forms in order to survive as a social being [26]. Should we single out one factor in particular which plays a decisive role in Service's views, it would be *war*, not in the military and technical sense of the word (which, of course, also has importance) but in a modified version of Hobbes' view of man's basic situation as "everyone's battle with everyone else". Man lives in a continuing competetive relationship to other people. This competition brings about a variety of interventions in man's situation; these lead him through a number of sociostructural levels (one could also speak of levels of integration), each of which assures him the best possibilities available for survival[27]. We possess sufficient materials to compose an evolutionary scheme this very day; moreover, they are practically free, since all of the levels are represented in our world, so that they may easily be studied (which they have been). In this connection Service straightforwardly speaks of *our contemporary ancestors*[28].

The lowest level of organization is that of the local *band*[29], which is either matrilocal or patrilocal (Service himself is in no doubt that the patrilocal band is oldest in the evolutionary scheme of things). The patrilocal band consists of a father plus his children and their families. Thus it is in the first instance structured as a nuclear family, and in the second instance as an extended family (including grown sons and their respective nuclear families). The entire group makes up a band, and is exogamous[30]. In this society the self-understanding of the individual may be defined on the basis of three variations in status. The individual is able to distinguish beween *ego* and *the others*, where his cognition is guided by whether nor not a person belongs to his band or is a foreigner. Within his band the individual distinguishes between generations and sexes[31]. A band is a numerically insignificant group of scarcely more than twenty-five persons. The composition of a band is dependent on the way it provides for itself (in a society of hunters and gatherers). However, ecological factors may create difficulties for *band-solidarity*. If the food resources available in a region are thinly dispersed, the members of the band will be so spread out from each other that Service speaks of this sort of band as a *sodality*, by which he means a group of individuals who do not dwell in the same place, but who have some functions or goals in common[32]. Since the only status differences are the previously mentioned ones, there is no need for either political functions, which are monopolized by individuals, or for a system of laws to cover the norms which regulate family life, and which would be administered by the

---

[26] Cf. also Honigmann 1976:279.

[27] Thus Service 1971:103ff.

[28] Service 1971:6. In the same section Service asserts that ethnology possesses a sort of "time machine".

[29] Service 1971:97; further on this social level, Service 1979.

[30] Service 1971:38f.

[31] Service 1971:41f. and 65.

[32] Service 1971:13.

head of the family or by some *ad hoc* appointed individual. Similarly, at this level there are no noteworthy religious institutions[33].

Why does man abandon the band stage, and what leads to the development of the tribe?. Service points to a number of individual factors which act conjointly to bring about a change in the form of organization from that of the primitive band society to a more integrated society. One major factor is the "neolithic revolution", that is, the change from hunter-gatherer societies to societies which produce their own food. This change makes it possible for a much higher concentration of population than was possible previously. Man's internal competitive tendency plays a part in this connection. Already at the level of the band the rivalries between individual families create difficulties, since there are no authorities empowered to bring about a compromise. The same problem manifests itself at the level of the tribe, which lacks formal political leadership and central economic and social control. Tribes arise because of hostilities among groups, that is, as the available remedy. The tribe retains the ideology of eguality. By the same token, the tribe has greater means to assure the safety of the individual person, family, or group[34]. Tribal solidarity requires institutions which cut across the grain of family structures, since the tribe is not merely a random aggregate of bands. Such institutions, or sodalities, may be based on kinship, but this is not essential[35]. The *clan* is the characteristic sodality which is based on kinship. The clain need not necessarily be based on *genealogical descent*; it is sufficient that the clan be able *ideologically* to claim descent from a common forfather (who, it should be observed, need not be a human at all, as he may well be a totem figure of some sort such as an animal or plant). The clan is not a residential unit; it distinguishes itself as a sodality by being spread through the whole tribe. It is not a permanent sociological group (i.e., its members do not function on all occasions as one body). Nevertheless, the awareness of belonging to a clan creates a feeling of solidarity which binds the tribe together. Other sodalities are not organized according to kinship; they may be so-called *secret societies*[36]. If such *sodalities* did not exist, there would be reason to ask what forces hold the tribe together, if it is able to make do without official leadership.

There are a variety of types of tribes such as the *"lineal"* and *"amorphous"*, or composite tribes[37]. Service regards the latter type as a dissolved form of *lineal* tribe. This type occurs when a tribal population is affected by a catastrophe (normally of a political nature)[38]. The normal tribe is *lineal*. It is composed of single-stranded *(unilineal)* families or kingroups *(lineages)* and has

---

[33] Service 1971:98.
[34] Service 1971:100ff.
[35] Service 1971:105.
[36] Service 1971:102 and 107. We shall return to the clan below.
[37] Service 1971:108.
[38] Service 1971:109 and 123-131.

established rules for contracting marriages. Marriages are either *virilocal* (the wife moves in with her husband) or *uxorilocal* (the reverse). The tribe further- more forms either *matrilineal* or *patrilineal* groupings (lineages); these are *residen- tial* units[39].

Although Service is not concerned with the process of segmentation in his *Primitive Social Organization*, it is clear that he regards the individual *residential* units as structurally identical. They are self-sufficient and largely autono- mous[40]. There is agreement on this point between band societies and tribal societies[41]. Certain changes in the understanding of status take place within tribal societies. In a band society, status is *egocentric*, since the individual locates himself within the social context according to the "I - them" principle. A different type of status, namely the *sociocentric* type, appears in tribal societies. In other words, we have do do with a status which the society bestows on the individual: so and so is a good speaker in the assemblies, so and so is generous, so and so is an able warrior, and so forth[42]. This means that a leader is appointed *ad hoc* to manage an existing task. The qualification of the leader are his personal abilities. Thus the type of leadership in egalitarian societies may be described as charismatic, as described by M. Weber[43].

The crucial question is whether a segmentary social system is egalitarian under all conditions. Service's model might lead one to believe so. He himself says, "We will therefore reserve the term segmental in the Durkheimian sense, for the kinds of societies composed of equal and similar component groups". In short, Service defines this system as an *egalitarian segmented society*. This is a very narrow definition of tribal society, as a report by his fellow-evolutionist, Sahlins, illustrates[44].

Sahlins has the same general view of the origins of tribal organization and the reasons for its emergence as Service. Also, he is rather more cautious than we might suppose after perusing Gottwald's application of his introduction to the study of tribal peoples. Sahlins emphasizes that the segmentary tribe is merely one type among many, and that it is at the opposite end of the spectrum from the rule by chieftainship. Between rule by the segmentary tribe and rule by a chieftain there exists a continuous series of other types. Characteristic for the segmentary type is its *extreme decentralization*, whereas the chieftainship is earmarked by *centralization*. The chieftainship includes a superstructure, a hierarchical administration which reduces local units to *subdivisions* with respect to economics and politics. The segmentary tribe contains at a given

---

[39] Service 1971:109-123.
[40] Service 1971:103.
[41] Further on the egalitarian system, see Service 1975:47-70.
[42] Service 1971:40ff. and 65ff, on bands, and 1971:121ff. and 129ff. on tribal levels.
[43] Service 1971:103, plus 1975:55-56.
[44] Cf. Sahlins 1968:14-17; also Sahlins 1961, where he defends his and Service's views against those of (largely) English anthropologists mentioned below.

level collection of units which are both identical and equivalent as far as structure and function are concerned. On the lowest level we find the family, above which are the kinship group (lineage), the village, tribal subsection, and the tribe itself. Otherwise Sahlins' description of this system is not noticeably different from that of Service. He defines leadership in connection with these groups as Service does, although he does additionally stress the significance of informal leadership personified by the so-called "big-men", who are the actual leaders by reason of their personal qualifications.

In the same societies we find ranged alongside the "big-man" the "petty chief", that is, the official leader of the society. His powers, however, are limited by the lack of appropriate instances to enforce his decisions[45]. Although Sahlins does not use the term "egalitarian", he does appear to agree with Service that this feature characterizes segmentary societies, whereas chieftain-ships are organized by degrees of rank (so that Service calls them hierarchi-cal)[46].

None of the information offered above is sufficient to tell us whether the definition of *segmentary organization* offered by these two anthropologists is adequate. They describe the various segments as kinship categories such as family, kinship group, perhaps also clan, section, and so forth. Does this mean that non-egalitarian tribal organizations are not structured according to the same basic principles as those applying to egalitarian societies?

Now, both Service and Sahlins agree that whether or not a tribal system is described as a single category or a continuum of forms the form of government is egalitarian up to a definite point, so that all members of the society in question have the same rights; they have no other obligations than the ones they personally assume or those the unwritten norms of the society force upon them[47]. That this is hardly a satisfactory account of the segmentary society is obvious if we turn to the views of Fried, since Fried does not hesitate to assert that tribal systems are ranked societies[48]; on his view, only bands are egalitarian[49]. In demographic terms, egalitarian societies appear in regions

---

[45] Sahlins 1968:21f.

[46] Sahlins 1968:24: "A chiefdom is a ranked society. The descent and community groups of a segmentary tribe are equal in principle, but those of a chiefdom are hierarchically arranged, the uppermost official superior in authority and entitled to a show of deference from the rest."

[47] However, Sahlins' description of the sorts of societies in which one finds segmentary lineage systems is narrowed considerably in his conclusions concerning them: "The segmentary lineage system is an institution appearing at the tribal level of general cultural evolution; it is not characteristic of bands, chiefdoms, or the several forms of civilization. It develops among socie-ties with a simple neolithic mode of production and a correlative tendency to form small, auto-nomous economic and political groups" (1961:117). In the same section Sahlins emphasizes that this system especially develops in tribal societies which have entered into previously populated areas, that is, as a political reaction to the competition they encounter.

[48] Fried is not so categorical in his own statements, but this must nevertheless be his inten-tion, as is indicated by the fact that his treatment of tribal systems is included in his chapter on *"ranked societies"*; cf. Fried 1967:109-184, esp. 154-173.

[49] Fried speaks of both *simple egalitarian societies* (1967:51) and *band egalitarian societies* (1967:106).

which are very thinly populated, and where the various groups do not seem to compete for the available resources. The difference between an egalitarian and a ranked society is related to the difference between the supply of and demand for prestigious positions in the society. An egalitarian society contains just as many positions as it has people to fill them (this is to be compared with Service's concept of *egocentric status*), while a ranked society has fewer positions than potential applicants for them[50].

Otherwise Fried does not diverge significantly from Service in his description of egalitarian institutions. The differences between them become clear, however, when Fried addresses himself to the ranked societies, since Fried's description of these societies overlaps the definitions of Service (and Sahlins) with respect to both tribal societies and chieftainships. Fried assigns to the ranked society a major part of the functions which Service assigns to the chieftainship[51]. Fried is correspondingly unable to accept Service's evolutionistic paradigm. As an alternative he suggests that the egalitarian band society develops into the ranked society, which ultimately develops into the stratified society. In reality the tribal organization is a non-essential element in this evolution. Thus in a general perspective both the band and the tribe are on the same organizational level. The stage which replaces this level is that of the chieftainship, which leads further to the state[52]. Tribes are *ad hoc* creations; they are secondary political systems which arise as "a reaction to the formation of more complex political structures"[53]. If Gottwald's works lead one to believe that Fried distinguishes between *primary* and *secondary* tribes in such a way that the primary tribes are conceived of as a natural developmental stage between the band society and the chieftainship, whereas the secondary tribe arises because of the pressure of external forces, it would be appropriate to consult Fried himself. It is namely clear that in Fried's opinion it is the fact of tribal organization in and of itself·which is secondary[54]. Thus Gottwald's

---

[50] See Fried 1967:33 on egalitarian societies, and 1967:109 on ranked societies.

[51] That is, centralization of control and transition from charismatic (temporary) leadership to permanent (and usually heritable) rule. Next is the introduction of a central system of "redistribution" into the economic life of the society, as well as the introduction of a limited division of labor, and so on; cf. Service's definition: "Chiefdoms are redistributional societies with a permanent central agency of coordination" (1971:134). See further Fried on the question of redistribution (1967:110f.). The centralization of control and the beginnings of the division of labor are present in the ranked society (Fried 1967:129ff. and 133f.).

[52] Fried 1967:186-226. A stratified society is defined by Fried as one "in which members of the same sex and equivalent status do not have equal access to the basic resources that sustain life" (1967:186). Fried sees the background for the emergence of the stratified society precisely in the differences with respect to these rights, and he regards the most important reason for this as "population pressure" (1967:191f.).

[53] Fried 1967:170; also Fried 1968:15ff. Fried's conclusion is often quoted: "Tribalism is an evolutionary cul-de-sac" (1967:173; 1968:17; cited by, among others, de Geus 1976:131).

[54] This is clearly indicated in Fried 1975:114, where he adds that the view of *"pristine tribes"* as different from existing *"secondary tribes"* is no more than a myth whose origins are to be sought in modern romanticism about the "noble savage".

account represents a peculiar mixture of the views of Fried with those of Service. While Gottwald regards Israel as a segmentary, egalitarian, and secondary tribal society, it is clear that Fried never even speaks of egalitarian tribes[55].

Excursus

On Evolutionism, the "Systems" Approach, and the "New Archeology"

What are both more dogmatic and more orthodox applications of Service's evolutionary model have been presented by two American OT scholars, F.S. Frick and J.W. Flanagan[56]. Both figures attempt to describe pre-national Israel within the sequence of *band society*, tribal society, chieftainship, and state. Both maintain that chiftainship best characterizes the "Israel" of this period. They disagree, however, as to the dates of Israel's pre-national existence, in which this purported transition from an egalitarian and segmentary tribal society to a stratified chieftainship took place. Frick regards the OT Judges as chieftain figures, which means that chieftainship must have been the normal type of leadership during the period of the Judges[57]. Against this, Flanagan feels that this transition in the sociopolitical system first occurred in the time of Saul and David. In company with both Mendenhall and Gottwald, Flanagan regards Israel in the period before the reign of Saul as governed by a tribal league[58]. Both Frick and Flanagan are of interest, in that, unlike Gottwald – and absolutely unlike Mendenhall – they are both adherents of the "New Archeology". Thus they base their conjectures as to the existence of the chieftainship on the archeological evidence regarding dwelling conditions[59].

There is accordingly reason to examine this type of archeological research, if only briefly. The "New Archeology" has arisen in the United States during the postwar period, and it dominates American prehistoric archeology today. It is connected with social anthropology, a connection which in part has its roots in the organization of the archeological departments in American universitites; they are often attached to anthropological, and not, as in Europe, historical, departments[60]. L.S. Binford, one of the spokesmen for this branch of study, thus even finds it possible to claim that in reality archeology *is* anthropology[61]. It is to be noted that the type of anthropology in question is the variety we have termed *cultural evolutionism*. This means that the starting point for many of the scholars pursuing this line of investigation is one or more of the hypothetical reconstructions of cultural development which the cultural evolutionists have pro-

---

[55] It is obvious that Gottwald's "cocktail" of the evolutionistic ideas of both Service and Fried must lead to a degree of imprecision. This fact emerges from a comparison of the views of the two scholars in question, but it is to be noted that they have themselves noted the differences between their views (Service 1978:27, and especially Fried 1978:38ff., in both cases with special attention paid to the selection of factors which lead to the formation of the state). It is particularly important to note that while Fried concentrates on internal conflicts as the main reason for social change (the basic hypothesis in Fried 1967), Service denies that this can be the primary factor (1978:32).

[56] Frick 1979; Flanagan 1981.

[57] Cf. Frick 1979:241 and 248.

[58] Flanagan 1981:55f., with reference to Noth 1930 and Gottwald 1979A. Frick, however, regards the idea of the league as *passée* (1979:233).

[59] Frick 1979:242ff. Cf. Flanagan 1981:51f. (a review of the 20 categories proposed by C.Renfrew for identifying chieftainships, cf. Renfrew 1974:73).

[60] Cf. Trigger 1978:2ff. for a general evaluation of American archeology in relation to European archeology.

[61] Binford 1972:20-32.

posed, not only with respect to the general course of development, but also in their interpretations of the individual stages (and not least the interpretation of Service). This paradigm is then used for the construction of a "General Systems Theory", which, in the words of R.J.C. Munton, is an effort "to construct general theories relating to systems irrespectively of the real world situations to which the systems refer"[62]. This theory is subsequently utilized as the basis for a "systems analysis". This procedure is borrowed from sociology; the New Archeology uses it to study *entire* cultures as functional units in which every single element, also the ideological and religious ones, have a part to play which can be reconstructed through the archeological analysis of the excavational materials[63].

Of course, this approach is beset with difficulties which are frequently ignored by the advocates of the New Archeology when they present the bases for their study in such condescending surveys as, for example, that of K.V. Flannery[64]. Thus it is refreshing to read contributions such as that of F. Hole, which appeared in the comprehensive collection of studies by representatives of the school which was published by C. Renfrew in 1974. Hole is fully aware just how hypothetical are many of the basic concepts of the movement[65]. In attempting to utilize the "systems approach", one attempts to select a number of variable factors which one in advance assumes will be present at a given stage of cultural evolution. These may be such factors as ecological conditions or the socio-economic pattern of the stage in question, or the like. Then one would ideally attempt to relate, for example, the socio-economic structure of a chieftalnship (in the event that one has determined that one has to do with a chieftainship) to the existing ecological conditions in the region in which the hypothetical chieftainship is thought to have existed. If one operates with fixed conceptions as to the economic structure of such a society, one will then also be able to conclude how resources were exploited and distributed in the case under study.

This procedure is fraught with difficulties: the two factors mentioned must be constants, if the analysis is to provide a useful result. Thus, for example, if one is confronted with a Near Eastern pre-historic culture and claims that it was organized along the lines of a chieftainship, it would naturally be of great assistance in one's analysis if the ecological conditions during the period in question corresponded to those which obtain today. Thus one notes that such a "new archeologist" as C.L. Redman determinedly rejects the notion that the ecological conditions may have changed because of climatic changes during the last six or seven thousand years[66]. The other decisive point is the claim that chieftainships are always organized in the same way. However, it is people who create the systems in question, and one would have imagined that scholars were prepared to acknowledge that this factor is entirely unpredictable. But no, "new archeological" scholars ignore this concern in favor of an ecologically oriented determinism which reduces the individual to an automaton who always behaves in a particular way when confronted with particular challenges[67]. However, the human factor is incalculable, as Leach insists in his conclusions in Renfrew's collection (mentioned above)[68]. Leach criticizes the entire branch of study severely for overlooking the possibility for variations; he is particularly critical of its use of social anthropology (and thus he also rejects the socio-anthropological school on which the New Archeology is dependent).

To return to our example of the chieftainship, the new archeologists maintain that a particular

---

[62] Munton 1973:685.
[63] Munton 1973:685.
[64] Flannery 1972.
[65] Hole 1973.
[66] Redman 1978:18.
[67] On concentrates on variables which one feels able to test, and consciously ignores those which cannot be tested on the (correct) assumption that a hypothesis which can neither be verified nor falsified is not a hypothesis, but a postulate.
[68] Leach 1973. It speaks very well indeed of C. Renfrew, who edited the congress volume in question, that it was decided to allow a determined opponent of *cultural evolutionism* to fire an all but annihilating broadside against the "New Archeology". There is also well supported criticism of this approach in Trigger 1978:2-52, incleading Leach's argument that historical events (including the emergence of social types) are unique events (Leach 1973:764; cf. Trigger 1978:43).

pattern of settlement is indicative of its presence[69]. However, the reason such a settlement pattern can indicate this is that this has been demonstrated by the socio-anthropologists in advance. To this Leach can only reply that the socio-anthropologist have *not* done so, and that a chieftainship is only one of perhaps half a dozen possibilities which the archeological results could be taken to indicate, that is, seen from the viewpoint of a social anthropologist[70].

Leach's extremely critical contribution thus presents a number of views which also form the basis for the theme of this work, namely that the fathers of the revolution hypothesis have not constructed their hypothesis on a socio-anthropological foundation, but on evolutionary hypotheses which are predominantly speculative and which have no claim to general applicability, as its proponents otherwise assert. The problem in this chapter is primarily the connection between segmentary socio-political systems and egalitarian ideologies at the level of the tribe. For this reason it is naturally of interest if it is possible to raise doubts as to the validity of the dogma that a band society is invariably egalitarian. I therefore note with considerable satisfaction that there are archeologists who think to have found evidence of bands which are not egalitarian, since such examples demonstrate precisely how empty the general theories are if one omits to take account of the endless number of variations which the human factor makes possible[71].

The models of Service and Fried were examined above. Naturally, these models are not the only ones of their kind; others have appeared which differ from them, and the differences are most pronounced when it comes to demonstrating the hypothetical factors which give the impetus to a new evolution. These may be such things as conflicts internal to the society, external influences resulting from hostilities with neighbouring cultures, population pressure, and so forth[72]. The manifold possibilities have been clearly expressed in recent studies into the origin of the state, since scholars are now prone to emphasize, as they were not earlier, that evolution is not unilinear, but *multilinear*. This means that we are no longer to search for a *single* cause, as there will be numerous interconnected reasons for change within socio-political systems[73]. However, this awareness of multiplicity is not actually a reinforcement for this hypothesis. It is more in the nature of a sign of its imminent collapse, since the possible variations are so numerous that it is no longer legitimate to rule out the decisiveness of the human factor. This brings us back to Leach's argument that this factor is moot if we cannot study it in detail, which we never can in connection with prehistoric societies, but only in contemporary or historical societies where the written records can to some extent substitute for the necessary ethnographic fieldwork.

I would by no means rule out that in particular Frick understands the pre-national Israelite society correctly; indeed, to the contrary, he is probably right to claim that the Judges were chieftains. However, this claim is not entirely new, as W. Richter has given voice to similar ideas,and in all modesty I should perhaps mention that I have previously published such ideas also[74]. However, neither Richter's nor my own point of departure was archeological, but textual, in nature, since our analyses of the narratives in the Book of Judges dealing with these figures led to this conclusion. It is entirely possible that Frick interprets the settlement pattern of an Israelite village like Tel Masos (*Ḥirbet el-Mšāš*) correctly, namely to the effect that this Iron Age village was the seat of a chieftainship in pre-national Israel[75]. But if we did not have other sources which might support such a suggestion (in casu the OT), Frick's interpretation would not be the only one possible. Tel Masos contains a uniform pattern of construction in which only one complex distinguishes itself from the others by being larger and otherwise constructed than the rest of the

---

[69] E.g., in the apportionment of secondary settlements in respect to a given center, as well as the presence in a settlement of architectural structures of distinctive size and design. This type of analysis is exemplified in Renfrew 1973B.

[70] Leach 1973:767.

[71] See King 1978.

[72] Thus Carneiro 1970; 1974; and 1978.

[73] See explicitly Sanders and Webster 1978; cf. also R. Cohen 1978A:8ff; H.T. Wright 1978, and esp. R. Cohen 1978B. However, all of the figures mentioned still adhere to the *"systems approach"*.

[74] Cf. Richter 1965:59 and 71; Lemche 1972:87. However, neither Richter nor I has placed as great weight on the chieftainship as an institution as has Frick.

[75] Frick 1979:242ff.

houses in the village. Frick regards this structure as the residence of the chieftain[76], but one would be equally entitled to regard it as the dwelling of the provincial governor. In this connection one might point out that the dwelling in question represents a different architectural tradition from the others in the village. Thus it is possible that it was the local representative of a Canaanite state who dwelled in the village in question, a conclusion which may be supported by the pottery found in the house[77]. If we did not possess other – written – sources, this explanation would have to be regarded as at least as relevant as that of Frick. It is precisely because we do have written sources which suggest that the area was not dominated by the Canaanites or Philistines that Frick's interpretation recommends itself.

Up to this point this section has shown that the basis for Gottwald's notion of an egalitarian, segmentary society is uncertain. It should also be stressed that the terms "egalitarian" and especially "segmentary" are used so frequently in the ethnographic literature that it would be reasonable to point out that Service's definitions are not the only available, and thus to attempt to clarify the contents and possible limits of these terms in relation to each other.

One reason for these terminological problems is possibly that scholars have used the term *segment* since the days of É. Durkheim without making its precise definition clear. Scholars have generally understood "segmentary" as synonymous with "egalitarian". However, "segment", derived from Latin *segmentum*, is not so much a qualitative as a quantitative term. *Segmentum*, from the verb *seco*, "to cut", actually means a "slice" or a "piece which has been cut off", but it is also applicable to a farming plot of limited size, a "stip of land". However, the term does not suggest anything as to the relationship between the sliced-off piece to the main body from which it has been removed, or to other segments taken from the same body[78]. In certain ethnological circles the term has acquired the meaning "a piece taken from the main body which closely corresponds to other pieces from the same body" with respect to both form and contents. It is understandable that this definition of *segmentum* has added new qualities to the term. In actuality the term *"segmentary society"* merely means that, for example, a tribe has been subdivided into a number of components, a clan into a number of family groups (lineages), or a lineage into a number of families. But it is also claimed that segmentation is synonymous with structural and functional identity on any given level. If one understands segmentation in this sense alone, one will probably fail to note that the social structure of non-egalitarian societies resembles that of egalitarian societies to the point of confusion. By this I mean to suggest that a tribe in a non-egalita-

---

[76] Frick 1979:244. The reference is to structure 314 in Area H (see Aharoni, Fritz and Kempinski 1975:107-109, and the plan in Kempinsky and Fritz 1977:152). The structure belongs to stratum IIB-A (further on Tel Masos, below pp. 403ff.).

[77] Fritz explicitly calls attention to the quantity of imported pottery, both *"Midianite ware"*, as well as wares from the coastal towns (Aharoni, Fritz'and Kempinski 1975:108-109); he also notes that the plan of the house "is characteristic of dwellings throughout the Middle Bronze II to the Late Bronze Age". He therefore maintains that the house is to be regarded as "a throwback to the Canaanite structural tradition" (Kempinsky and Fritz 1977:151).

[78] See OLD 1717, and cf. also LD 1661, which mentions *fragmentum* as a synonym for *segmentum*.

rian society may also be segmented in clans, lineages, families, and so on, although this does not necessarily entail that such subdivisions are of equal value. In such societies as those which Fried has described as "ranked", the order of rank follows the segmentation through all the various components, as for example, in the case of rules for primogeniture, which ensure that the segment of the eldest son always takes precedence over those of his younger brothers. Here we have a segmentary system which is termed either a *ramage* or *conical clan* system[79]. In this connection it would be appropriate to refer to Fried's remark that the use of kinship terms in a society says nothing whatsoever about its political system[80].

The term "segmentary society" ultimately derives from É. Durkheim's *"sociétés segmentaires à base de clans"*[81]. Durkheim himself used the term in three senses: *"sociétés polysegmentaires simples"*, *"sociétés polysegmentaires simplement composées"*, and *"sociétés polysegmentaires doublement composées"*, which describe, respectively, societies consisting of individual tribes, tribal confederations, and leagues between tribal confederations. In other words, these are three different levels of integration[82].

The definition of the segmentary society now in use is mainly the product of a number of English social anthropologists who have been inspired by Durkheim, in particular E.E. Evans-Pritchard and M. Fortes; in its basic lineaments it was presented by these two scholars in the introduction to their *African Political Systems*[83]. According to Evans-Pritchard and Fortes, a segmentary society is a society which is divided into segments which function in complementary opposition to one another and which are of equal value with respect to structure. This signifies that in segmentary societies no one segment dominates at the expense of other segments on the same structural level. Finally, these societies contain no administrative authority beyond the segmentary system itself, which entails that there is no external mechanism capable of mediating conflicts among the segments. Conflicts are resolved with the aid of "the sum-total of intersegment relations"[84]. This system is ordinarily to be found in stable and homogeneous societies[85]. Segmentary societies are organized as *"segmentary lineage systems"*. We have to do with complicated societies on a level higher than that of huntergatherer groups, and the members of which belong to genealogically structured lineages. The political,

---

[79] Examples of a social structure utilizing the conical clan are provided by Sahlins 1968:25, and Service 1975:80.

[80] Fried 1967:121.

[81] Durkheim 1922:150.

[82] Durkheim 1919:104.

[83] Fortes and Evans-Pritchard 1940:13-14.

[84] With the exception of the notion of "complementary opposition", this has been derived from Fortes and Evans-Pritchard 1940:13-14, but see also Fortes 1953:27 ("complementary relationship with/or in opposition to like units").

[85] Cf. Fortes 1953:27 and 36.

social, economical, and ritual life of such societies is related to its components, that is, its lineages[86]. The system may be termed "egalitarian" in the sense that its lineages are equipoised – on the same level –; but it should be noted that both Fortes and Evans-Pritchard generally avoid the term "egalitarian" in their description of these societies.

Fortes and Evans-Pritchard have proposed their model of segmentary societies on the basis of African societies, most of which are situated south of the Sahara. They never seriously inquire as to whether their definition is applicable to other cultures, nor do they claim that the segmentary is the only type of social structure one encounters in traditional African societies, as is also demonstrated by their choice of examples in *African Political Systems*, of which five are characterized as "primitive states", that is, societies with centralized political systems[87]. It is evident that Fortes' and Evans-Pritchard's description of the segmentary society is not that of a specific social structure, but of a political system in which units which are organized by kinship comprise the political forum itself, while the individual lineages are the political combattants. The question in this connection is then whether a segmentary society reveals its existence solely through the presence of a segmentary kinship system, or whether it shares its form of social organization with other political systems. If the latter should prove to be the case, it would then be appropriate to discuss where the borderline runs which separates segmentary political systems from centralized systems. This issue is illustrated by other attempts to describe segmentary societies in other circumstances, which reveal that a society which is termed "segmentary" by some is elsewhere called a "segmentary state"[88].

If we turn our attention to the selection of segmentary societies provided by J. Middleton and D. Tait, we discover that these scholars distinguish between three main types. There are not only significant differences between the individual main types, but also between the various societies they present as belonging to a given main type[89]. This lack of definition, which could easily be illustrated by reference to other examples, has also made questionable the usefulness of this classificatory system[90]. Thus A.R. Richards has pointed out

---

[86] On the lineage, its role, composition, underlying ideology, and so forth, see especially Fortes 1953.

[87] Fortes and Evans-Pritchard 1940:5.

[88] I am referring to the *Alur*, which Richards deals with under the heading of "segmentary societies" (1960A:311-325); however, the ethnographer who described the *Alur*, A. Southall, calls this system "a segmentary state". C. Sigrist prefers the phrase *"zentralisierte Gesellschaft"* (1967:19), whereas Middleton and Tait assign it to their group III, that is, among the segmentary societies (1958:15), together with e.g. the *Mandari*. Sigrist terms the *Mandari* a *"Grenzfälle des segmentären Gesellschaftstypus"* (1967:19).

[89] Middleton and Tait 1958:12ff. It should be emphasized that it is impossible to delimit the individual types with precision. They are three main types within a continuum of forms; this is best illustrated by Middleton and Tait's diagram illustrating the similarities and dissimilarities between 6 different societies.

[90] Cf. Sigrist 1967:32ff.

that the main part of the societies described by Pritchard and Fortes are ranked and not egalitarian (in the sense advocated by Service and Fried) societies[91]. Similarly, J.A. Barnes asserts that segmentation is not only to be found in stateless societies, as it also appears in "primitive states"[92]. Thus one ought not to become fixated on apparent differences between segmentary and centralized societies; both may contain segmentary systems which have the same formal structure. It is impossible to distinguish sharply between the two categories of African societies proposed by Evans-Pritchard and Fortes and then claim that one is lineage - structured while the other is not. The second category, too, is lineage-structured. What is decisive is the degree of influence the lineage structure has on the society in question.

This formal similarity between both the primitive state and the stateless society with respect to social structure has led some scholars to inquires as to whether there are not logical fallacies in the segmentary lineage model. M.G. Smith emphasizes two separate sides of the model, one of which is the formal structure, that is, the lineage system, while the other is "a substantive concept" which has to do with the political system[93]. Smith maintains that in formulating the theory of segmentary societies scholars have confused both aspects; he accordingly claims that we are confronted with a segmentary society only when these aspects are united. This means in turn that it would be insufficient to focus on the presence of the formal structure alone (i.e., segmentary lineages) in order subsequently to assume that the political system automatically corresponds to it. To put it in Smith's words, a lineage cannot serve as its own explanation[94]. Thus Smith refuses to distinguish between stateless – segmentary – societies and centralized states; he prefers instead to distinguish between the types of government which are present in the individual cases[95].

A corresponding procedure is advocated by C. Sigrist, who emphasizes the indication as to whether we have to do with an *acephalous* society (which is probably a better designation than is "segmentary society") is *"das Fehlen einer mit einem Segment assozierten Zentralinstanz...."*[96], since by "acephalous society"

---

[91] Richards 1960C. Richards emphasizes how the historical tradition (most often preserved in various myths and legends concerning the origin of an individual clan or lineage) is used as a *"charter"* – quite apart from questions of historical accuracy – to demonstrate the legitimate claim of an individual group to superiority over other corresponding groups (whether politically or morally is unimportant). The limited utility of such a concept as that of the "segmentary society" is further expressed by the following remark by Richards: "In classifying these African societies we now distinguish not only acephalous from centralized systems of government...but multi-kingdom tribes, segmentary states, snowball states and segmentary tribes of three different kinds" (1960C:175).

[92] Cf. Barnes 1954:47ff., and see also Barnes 1955; Barnes emphasizes that it is necessary to distinguish between a long series of related processes within the individual society.

[93] Smith 1956:43.

[94] Smith 1956:78.

[95] Cf. Smith 1956:50.

[96] Sigrist 1967:29. By *"Instanz"* Sigrist means *'eine Person oder eine Gruppe von Personen, deren sozialen Rolle durch ein spezifisches Recht oder ein spezifischen Pflicht, das Verhall anderen Gruppen Mittglieder zu kontrollieren, konstituirt ist"* (1967:30).

he understands a system *"...deren politischen Organization durch gleichrangigen und gleichartigen unterteilte mehr- oder vielstufiege Gruppen vermittelt ist"*[97]. In other words, our criticisms of the theory of segmentation must not lead to the conclusion that there are no societies which are not centrally governed. It is undeniable that decentralized social systems may exist without the society in question necessarily ending in chaos. Rather, the discussion has led to a recognition of the fact that segmentation and the existence of lineages are not sufficient criteria for differentiating between acephalous and centralized systems. Centralized societies may well be segmentary, whereas acephalous ones usually are so. If an acephalous society were not constructed of equivalued segments, it would hardly be able to survive, for sooner or later a single segment would gain control of the rest (which is what actually happens in the societies Fried has described as "ranked"), or else the inequality between the segments will cause the disruption of the acephalous system.

In short, as defined by Service and others, and as utilized by Gottwald, the expression "segmentary societies are egalitarian ones" has little to recommend it. One ought rather to use the term"acephalous" than "segmentary". Instead of speaking of egalitarian societies it would be more appropriate to speak of societies which are dominated by an egalitarian ideology[98]. This would allow for the fact that a society whose ideology is egalitarian need not in fact *be* egalitarian, since in some cases ideology is not the determinative factor for the behavioural pattern; other factors may substitute for the ideology[99]. This leads to the recognition that in the study of traditional or primitive society, *in each individual case one must determine whether the society in question is segmentary, and then whether it is egalitarian.*

§ 5

Segmentary Societies in the Near East

The next step towards a description of the social structure of ancient Israel in this section will be directed towards the Near East. It is my intention to examine closely how the model of segmentary societies fares when compared with materials which have not been derived from African societies of the 19th

---

[97] Sigrist 1967:30.

[98] This ideology is analyzed in Sigrist 1967:185ff. Sigrist understands it as the most important internal means of control within such societies; its function is to ensure that no single "instance" achieves dominion over the others. There is some question, however, as to whether this ideology is confined to acephalous societies alone (cf. also Lefebure 1979A:10).

[99] Of course, this last statement should be readily intelligible to Scandinavians, who dwell in societies which have been permeated by an egalitarian socialistic ideology in recent generations, but which nevertheless are fully stratified societies.

and 20th centuries, most of which are geographically situated south of the Sahara. It would in advance be reasonable to be somewhat sceptical as to whether it is at all relevant to concern oneself with a model which is based on societies which at the time of their first contacts with Europeans were at a "neolithic" stage in many respects, and whose economic systems, both internal and external, may be described as primitive or underdeveloped with respect to the societies of the Near East in historical times[100]. Sigrist correctly remarks that it is inviting to make use of the African materials, since in connection with their use one is not obliged to to take account of a long and in many respects known historical development (in most cases in Africa we have no sources relating to such development)[101]. In the Middle East we are confronted with societies which are, as Weullersse puts it, "overcivilized" in the sense that they are the products of millenial developments[102]. Similarly, it should be noted that also Israelite tribal society did not belong within a historical and cultural – one is tempted to say, a "neutral" – situation[103].

If we turn briefly once more to Fortes' definition of a segmentary society, we note that such societies are said to be characterized by a number of so-called *unilineal descent groups* which are exogamous and corporative units. They are exogamous, which means that such marital contacts create the connections among the individual groups which protect the society from dissolution. They are corporative in the sense that a member of a unilineal descent group has "no legal or political status except as a member of a lineage", and because "the perpetual exercise of defined rights, duties, offices and social tasks (is) vested in the lineage as a corporate unit"[104]. This lineage structure is the decisive factor for the organization of the entire society.

On the other hand, one will not have studied the Middle East for very long before being struck by a notable discrepancy between reality and Fortes' definition: the traditional Middle Eastern society is markedly endogamous, rather than exogamous, as is most often the case in the African societies. By "endogamy" is meant that, beyond the confines of the family one seeks to contract marriages with partners who are among one's closest kin; one does not seek beyond this circle. This endogamous marital system is most emphatically expressed in a type of alliance which has been alternately called "the Arabian marriage", "*bint al-ʿamm* marriage" (i.e., marriage with the father's brother's daughter), and "parallel cousin marriage". Since the system is also patrilineal, all connections are in theory at least formed in the father's line, while affinal

---

[100] The same question is also posed by Barnes, only he does so in connection with the use of the segmentary model to describe societies in Australia and New Guinea (Barnes 1971:262) which are presumably at a lower developmental level than the African societies.

[101] Sigrist 1967:10.

[102] Weullersse 1946:55. Admittedly, Weullersse is talking about the Syrian *fellah*, but there is no reason to assign this quality to the Syrian peasant alone.

[103] Cf. Mendenhall 1973:176.

[104] Fortes 1953:25-27.

ties would be exceptions. This system is dominant from Morocco in the west to Baluchistan in the east, from Turkey in the north to the Sudan in the south; moreover, it includes not only Moslem populations, but also Christian and Jewish Oriental populations[105]. The custom is so extensive in the Mohammedan world that some scholars have been led to believe that it came into the world with the advent of Islam. Against this supposition is the fact that it is nowhere prescribed in the Koran or in Ḥadīṯ[106], as well as its usage in Christian populations, whose religion in fact warns against or forbids such consanguineous alliances as those between cousins.

Although one should be careful not to overemphasize the continuity between the modern, but nevertheless traditionally organized part of the Near East and the pre-Islamic Orient (to do so would be to obscure any changes which may have arisen in the course of the last two millenia[107]), it would be equally rash to claim that Near Eastern endogamous marriage regulations are to be understood without further ado as a continuation of pre-Islamic Arab bedouin practices, and that there is no connection whatsoever to usage in antiquity, especially if we can find even hints of similar conditions in antiquity[108]. I shall return below to OT information as to Israelite marital practices; I shall content myself here with adding a few observations of J. Renger, who has attempted to demonstrate the practice of exogamous marriage among Semitic nomads during the second millenium B.C.[109]. Renger's reason for supposing that these nomads practiced exogamy is that some of them used names in which ḫāl, figures (derived from Akkadian ḫālum, mother's brother; it is preserved with similar meaning in other Semitic languages such as Arabic, in which ḫal may be used of the mother's kin)[110]. However, the existence of this sort of name is not by itself sufficient to prove the existence of exogamous marriages beyond the circle of the family, for example, within a lineage. It would also be necessary to demonstrate that the mother's brother referred to by the name in question actually belonged to a foreign lineage (or clan). The materials in question offer no information on this. It is more likely that we have to do with a special relationship, often described in the anthropological literature, which has been observed in some societies to obtain between male offspring and their maternal uncles. Moreover, it is here we find the source of Renger's misapprehension, since this type of relationship is most often found in connection with exogamous marriages. Thus Renger has simply assumed that it was evidence for the existence of exogamous marital relations. However, the custom is well attested among the endogamous societies of the Middle East today[111].

[105] See the materials presented in Patai 1955, which may be supplemented by additional materials from the countless subsequent ethnographic descriptions of Middle Eastern societies. In particular I should like to refer to an example of the survival of this system in a Jewish Oriental society in contemporary Israel, as depicted by H. Goldberg (1967), and to similar cases in Lebanese Christian societies, as described by E.L. Peters and R. Creswell (Peters 1976; Cresswell 1976). Striking exceptions to this custom are to be found among the Berbers of North Africa, and in particular among the matrilinear Tuaregs (cf. Nicolaisen 1963B:448ff.).

[106] See also Hilal 1970:73.

[107] In my opinion, Patai has fallen into this trap, particularly in his monograph on Israelite familial relations (Patai 1959).

[108] Against de Geus 1976:138n., whose idea is in turn based on Hoebel 1972:406-408. Since the Arabs appear in Assyrian sources in the first half of the first millennium, it would be appropriate to ask de Geus whether they were endogamous back then, and, if so, we would want to know where they got the system.

[109] Renger 1973A; cf. de Geus 1976:138n. Note, however, how cautiously Renger expresses himself elsewhere with respect to the existence of a "custom of preferential marriage" (1973B: 273).

[110] On this see Huffmon 1965:194-195, and Muntigh 1974:55.

[111] Fundamental on this issue is Goody 1959, whose work, however, is based on West-African conditions. However, corresponding conditions do exist in the Middle East as well; cf. Barth 1973B:14, and Peters 1965:134-135.

15

The discussion concerning this type of marriage has been quite intense during the last quarter of a century. There would be no reason to refer to this discussion if it were not for the fact that it reveals some of the central problems which we confront when we attempt to analyze the forces which are operative within the social structures of the societies in question. First, however, one must be aware that the traditional Middle Eastern societies are apparently constructed as segmentary lineage systems analogous to those in African societies. Moreover, it would be reasonable to describe these lineages as unilineal, as does R. Patai[112]. These lineages are not merely present; in Patai's opinion they are the decisive element in the social structure, irregardless of whether they form part of a tribal society or a village which is not tribally organized, or even a traditionally Oriental urban society.

A functional explanation for the fact that the African segmentary lineage systems are exogamous is that such marriages create alliances between different lineages which prevent the dissolution of the society. This type of marriage does not lead to the fusion of two lineages, since these are unilineal (whether or not they are matrilineal or patrilineal). An endogamous segmentary lineage system thus appears to be impossible as well as self-contradictory, since one may assume beforehand that if the lineages within a society do not establish kinship ties, no solidarity is established between its various components, so that the society in question would dissolve as soon as conflicts arose within its membership. This would be an extreme rarity in the Middle East, where we have evidence of societies which may well have survived for more than a millenium without being held together by such external forces as, for example, a state (e.g., Arab bedouin tribes).

What is the purpose of endogamous marriage in the Orient? If we could say something definitive about this, we would probably also be in a position to explain the origin of the custom. In actual fact, scholars have suggested more than a few reasons for the system, all of which differ considerably from each other. Individual explanations concentrate on political, economic, ecological, cultural, psychological, or ideological aspect either singly or in combination[113]. Advocates of the "political" position advance two arguments: first, that endogamy strengthens and preserves a lineage. Thus a man's position in his society is assured, since his position is dependent on his relationship to a particular lineage, concerning which it should ideally be impossible to raise doubts[114]. Second, this system also guarantees that the optimal number of

---

[112] Patai 1965.

[113] Cf. C. Pastner 1979:45.

[114] Cf. Barth 1954:171; Peters 1963:110-111. It is usually claimed that membership of a particular lineage is a sort of visiting-card which is first presented when one encounters strangers. Thus in the attempt to weaken the traditional social structure, some modern states have forbidden the use of family names by individuals. This was the case under Atatürk in modern Turkey; however, one should also note I.M. Lewis' entertaining description of the results obtained by the anti-lineage edict of a frustrated socialist government in Somalia. The result was that individuals

males will always be available to a lineage in conflict situations, since no one could be in doubt as to where he belongs, if there should arise conflicts between the mother's and father's lineages[115]. The "economic" argument is concerned with property rights and emphasizes that endogamy enables a lineage to retain its possessions within the lineage. If one married women off to foreign lineages, they would naturally take some family property with them, in part as their dowries, and in part as their share of their inheritance[116]. The "ecological" explanation is related to the "economic" one, and has to do with the preservation of the resources available to the family. The "cultural" or "ideological" explanation maintains that the matrimonial pattern enhances the feeling of unity within the kinship group, while at the same time being the best guarantee that the women do not bring shame over their ancestral family. In other words, it is easier to control the women if they remain within their parents' lineage than it is if they marry outside of the lineage[117]. The "psychological" explanation is closely related to the previous one, in that it emphasizes that familial conflicts are reduced if both parties to a marriage belong to the same lineage. The respective parties are used to one another, and no changes occur with respect to the status of individual members of the family, so long as foreign ties do not enter into the lineage in question[118].

Unfortunately, all of the explanations offered above may be questioned. Against the "political" argument it may be said that alliances across lineage boundaries would be able to mobilize more personnel for war than intra-lineage marriages do, and that there is no need to strengthen individual lineages, since the patrilineal ideology is sufficient to ensure that the various lineage members are aware of their obligations. Similarly, one might say that while a lineage does not lose goods or gold if it does not marry its daughters off, if it fails to do so it also renounces all possibility of obtaining economic advantage through marital alliances with wealthier lineages[119]. Finally,

---

proceeded to introduce themselves as ex-member NN of ex-lineage NN, until at last "ex²" too, was forbidden (Lewis 1976:326-327).

[115] See Barth 1954:171. Yet another aspect touched on by Barth is the fact that it is often cheaper to enter into parallel cousin marriages, since the bride-pride is then lower. This enables a lineage to retain its economic potential (1954:167f.).

[116] See Barth 1954:170 and Peters 1963:111. However, it must be added that while women are entitled to inherit at a ratio with respect to their brothers of 1:2, they are normally ignored (cf. Cuissenier 1975:424ff.; 1976:138ff. on conditions in North Africa; and 1975:239ff. on conditions in Turkey). Cf. therefore also F.I. Khuri, who emphasizes that since women do not actually inherit, their inheritance rights can hardly be considered a reason for the endogamous marital system (1970:600).

[117] This is the view of I.M. Hilal (1970). Yet another kind of ideological explanation is to be found in the work of J.M.B. Keyser (1974), who, however, instead of focusing on parallel cousin marriages for their own sake regards them as a metaphorical expression of a dominant endogamous ideology.

[118] Thus Khuri 1970. It is perhaps symptomatic that Arab ethnologists tend to concentrate on this explanatory model or on the related psychological one (Hilal), since in this fashion they reveal their own cultural standpoint.

[119] Cf. Khuri 1970:600; Hilal 1970:75-76.

against the ideological and psychological explanations it could be objected that Near Eastern lineages tend to fission, so that in reality the matrimonial pattern does not contribute to lineage solidarity; it may just as easily be understood as contributing to the process of division[120].

Thus there is is scarcely a single particular explanation of the endogamous matrimonial pattern of the Near East, or, perhaps more correctly, if such an explanation actually exists, it is apparently impossible to isolate it among the many conceivable contending arguments. Therefore it may be appropriate to try another path in the effort to determine whether there is agreement between endogamous ideology and the actual circumstances. For example, is it the case that parallel cousins are preferred as marital partners in the Near East, or is this just a *metaphor*, as has been suggested by J.M.B. Keyser. One might also stop placing special emphasis on concrete examples of this marital praxis, and instead expand the scope of the investigation to include other alliances which are typologically related. In the last analysis this would entail that one included all marital connections contracted with women in the paternal line.

The percentage of marriages with the father's brother's daughter varies considerably from place to place; at some sites it is perhaps very limited (under 10%), while it may dominate at others. However, the tendency towards endogamy is evident even in the former case, as, for example, in a village in which the actual occurrence of real parallel-cousin marriages is rare, and in which lineage endogamy is indeed frequent, but hardly the only practice observed, but in which by the same token the entire village functions as an endogamous system, despite the fact that there are perhaps several lineages represented in it[121]. In such a case it is clear that other factors are active than an ideologically based endogamy within a given lineage, or, one might say that this ideology is manipulated by the existing ecological conditions, that is, by the interaction between a given number of families who dwell in the place in question and the resources available to these families. The best exploitation of these resources, as well as the defence of the access to them results in alliances between the implicated lineages, which thus cross the boundaries separating them, the result being a noticeable village endogamy.

E.L. Peters has recently demonstrated the ways marital alliances are manipulated in a bedouin society. It appears that the members of such a society are always able to modify the kinship system in the society in such a way as to

---

[120] Cf. Murphy and Kasdan 1967:2; 1959:26; and cf. Peters 1960:132-133.

[121] Cf. also Antoun 1972B:129-133. Important exceptions are places where we find what Antoun calls "two communities of social control", that is, two competing "strata" within a single village (such as the one described by Peters 1963), which do not practice intermarriage. Among the villages mentioned above we find three variations: in Tell Toqaan the village did not practice village-endogamy; in al-Munsif there was district-endogamy, but not village-endogamy; and in Kufr el-Ma village endogamy predominated, as over 75% of the marriages contracted were within the confines of the village.

ensure the best exploitation of the potential available in the region[122]. In the example investigated by Peters, affinal connections (i.e., cross-cousin marriages) are also emphasized. The reasons for this are not difficult to discern. Endogamous practice creates no changes of status within a lineage, whereas affinal connections tend to do so, for example, if the woman comes from an important family. As one might expect, a given lineage within this society is segmented along the lines which are drawn up by cases of exogamous connections[123].

These examples indicate that endogamous marital practices in the Middle East are not a frozen system; rather, this tendency is only pursued by the lineages in question as long as nothing better presents itself. Exogamous alliances serve to provide advantages to a given lineage, and so to open new possibilities for its membership. This pattern is clear when we examine conditions among groups which primarily pursue political possibilities; such groups tend to exploit marital relationships to forward their own political interests and to secure for themselves political support in other circles[124]. As a result, in the study of marital connections in the Near East one should in future not be so concerned with the types, as with the intentions and results in each individual case. By this means we may manage to grasp what Barth has termed "the dialectical relation between concepts and norms, and social reality"[125].

For our purposes the decisive issue is whether all of this has to do with a segmentary lineage system. Are lineages which behave in the ways described above kinship groups at all, or are they not better understood as political interest groups which manifest themselves as kinship units? The problem is by no means a simple one, even though we might prefer to consider the well-known practice according to which genealogies are composed which are intended to correspond with the conditions obtaining at a given time[126]. This means that when the frame of reference of a society has to be expressed in kinship terms, the genealogical system is the means available for concealing actual lapses in the kinship system. It is in this sense also characteristic that such manipulation of a genealogy is not masked by doctoring the lowest and still-living stage, nor the generation immediately preceding it; instead, "corrections" are undertaken from three to five generations in the past, that is, in the period when memory presumably begins to fail[127]. The purpose of all this is that the politically and economically active unit will also be seen to

---

[122] Cf. Peters 1960. See also Murphy and Kasdan 1967:2.

[123] Cf. Peters 1960:395.

[124] Examples are the so-called "learned families" described in Peters 1963, as well as the families from suburban Beirut which have been studied by Khuri (1976).

[125] Barth 1973B:18.

[126] See Peters 1960.

[127] "The area of ambiguity"; Peters 1960:382; 1963:106; cf. Cresswell 1976:104-105. Patai calls this system "lineage camouflage"(1965:342).

be in agreement with a patrilineal ideology, whatever its actual composition may be. Thus, at least on the formal level a lineage always retains its appearance of being a unilineal paternal descent chain[128]. This implies the conclusion that while the underlying ideology insists that we have to do with unilineal lineages, this need not necessarily be the case in actuality. Of course, this does not mean that unilineal lineages do not occur in the Middle East, but it does suggest that in many cases what we are really confronted with is a matter of approximations to an ideal quantity. Our considerations must accordingly be directed towards the study of the relationship between ideology and practice.

This relationship has been especially stressed in Peters' analysis of the relationship of the politically active groups to the dominant ideology of the segmentary lineage, as we meet it among the Cyrenaika bedouin[129]. Peters is forced to conclude that the political formations among these bedouin do not follow lineage ideology. For this reason he feels that he has demonstrated that the segmentary lineage model is inapplicable as a basis for the study of the bedouin of Cyrenaika, and presumably of other traditional Near Easter societies[130]. Peters' conclusion is the starting point of an investigation by P.C. Salzman, who has attempted to determine the relationship between lineage ideology and the actual conditions more closely[131]. Salzman correctly inquires as to whether there actually is any lineage ideology in these societies, on the grounds that they apparently do not follow it in practice and tend instead to be guided by other considerations, among which the economic ones predominate[132]. Salzman concludes that the lineage model is to be understood as a sort of "folk ideology" which may be described as as "asserted ideology". He also claims that in reality it is a socially-structuring strategy which is kept in reserve within systems which perhaps were based on segmentary lineages earlier, but which because of special ecological circumstances (which, presumably, are not necessarily the only possible causes) have been forced to adapt themselves otherwise than is prescribed in the "folk model"[133]. However, the model is always latently present, so that it may be utilized if altered circumstances permit or necessitate it[134]. Salzman's idea is worth paying attention to, as it offers a potential explanation of the fact, noted

---

[128] Cf. Murphy and Kasdan 1959:24.

[129] Peters 1967.

[130] Peters 1967:278-279.

[131] Salzman 1978A; 1978C.

[132] Salzman 1978C:55; cf. 1978A:626.

[133] A common feature of all of Salzman's many studies of the Near Eastern nomadic societies is that he regards their many and various political and social systems as responses to challenges which have been presented them by a variety of ecological conditions. However, Salzman cannot be regarded as an ecological determinist who claims that the same conditions always produce the same responses.

[134] Cf. especially Salzman 1978A:619; cf. also Lefebure 1979A:10.

by others, that lineages may sometimes be reintegrated in the presence of certain enabling conditions[135].

This brief sketch of some of the topics in the debate concerning the so-called segmentary lineage structured societies in the Near East should be sufficient to show that an extremely complicated analysis is required if one intends to utilize this lineage model in connection with complex societies. It was mentioned above that already in the Middle East in antiquity there were societies which were considerably more complex than are the African societies on which the model in question was constructed. This indicates that we should also expect this model to fail if it is used in unmodified form for the study of ancient societies which at first glance resemble the segmented African societies. On the other hand, Salzman's concept of an "asserted ideology" opens new possibilities for the understanding of the hypothecated process of retribalization which Mendenhall and Gottwald claim once led to the emergence of the Israelite tribal society.

§ 6

The Exogamous Clan and Tribal Organization

The previous section demonstrated that it was incorrect of Gottwald *a priori* to claim that a segmentary society is *ipso facto* an egalitarian one. This section will deal with yet another of his *a priori* assumptions, namely *that a true tribal society contains exogamous clans*. As was shown in the previous section, the Middle East is dominated by endogamous marital practices. For this reason alone it would be possible to claim that Gottwald's claim is illegitimate. It would be possible, if absurd, to object to this that we then have no true tribal societies in the Middle East, as they are all secondary tribal formations! To counter this sort of assertion it would be useful to comment on recent ethnological discussions concerning the situation of the clan organization within a traditional social structure.

In this section I will not deal extensively with the "family" as a sociological concept. The traditional Middle Eastern family has often been regarded as an extended one; thus the frequency of nuclear families in village and especially urban societies has been seen as the result of intensified urbanization[136]. Everything now suggests that this view is to be modified. J. Gulick has presented some statistical materials which show that in both villages and towns the families

---

[135] Salzman's examples include, among others, Aswad 1971*, where reference is made to a Turkish agrarian society in which an old lineage structure had lain dormant for over a century, but which quickly proved to be still viable under new circumstances. Thus the society in question was speedily able to conform to the traditional model.

[136] See e.g. Van Nieuwenhuijze 1971:386.

average between six and seven persons; he further emphasizes that these are nuclear families[137]. We have cited above examples of nomadic societies which show that the average number of members per family is not radically different from that obtaining among town and village families. The number of extended families makes up in all an average of about ten percent of the total. The reason there are not more extended families is probably economic, as only the wealthy in society are in a position to support large (and in rare cases, polygynous) families. In most societies the families fission before they can develop into large families. A contributory reason for this, which is sometimes mentioned, is the role of the women in such fission processes; in particular, attention has centered around the conflicts between mothers-in-law and daughters-in-law, which sooner or later makes impossible the familial solidarity so dear to the ideology of these societies, and separation occurs to preserve peace in the household[138].

Gottwald's definition of a clan maintains that a clan is not a group which dwells in the same place or has the same occupation. To the contrary, it is a sociological formation which cuts accross the local groups. In every individual family there are at all times members of two or more clans, since the clan is invariably exogamous, for which reason man and wife necessarily come from different clans[139]. Gottwald regards this definition of the clan as the laudable product of the "father" of American ethnology, L.H. Morgan. According to Gottwald, Morgan succeeded in demonstrating that this organization exists everywhere on earth; it is a universal human constant. Thus it is of decisive importance to Gottwald that this organization does not figure in Israel[140].

If we accordingly turn to Morgan's definition of the clan (which, incidentally, he used in connection with matrilineal societies, while reserving the designation *gentes* for patrilineal "clans"), it is correct that Morgan regarded this type of organization as having *almost* universal significance. The true scientist, however, always acknowledges his doubts, however few, as to the universality of his conclusions by inserting this little *'almost'*[141]. Morgan defined a *gens* (clan) as a unity consisting of blood-related individuals who descend from a common tribal forefather, and who distinquish themselves from other such groups by means of their clan name[142]. The clan is exclusively understood in such a way that it distinguishes between those who are members of it and who are outside of it. It accords common rights and privileges to all of its members, while at the same time attempting to reinforce itself by regulations making exogamous marriages obligatory[143].

This definition of the clan, on which Gottwald is largely reliant, appeared in a major socio-anthropological work which appeared in 1877. Let us therefore turn to a definition of the clan from a work which appeared in 1977[144]:

[137] Gulick 1976:128ff (note that according to Heltzer the villages in the kingdom of Ugarit had an average family size of 6.5 individuals).
[138] Cf. Cuissenier 1975:435; 1976:147f.
[139] Gottwald 1979A:299.
[140] Gottwald 1979A:298.
[141] Morgan 1877:60.
[142] Morgan 1877:60.
[143] Morgan 1877:320.
[144] Glatzer 1977:105. The same definition is to be found in Radcliffe-Brown (1950:40) and

"Unter Clan ist eine soziale Einheit zu verstehen, deren Mitglieder sich durch unilineare Descendenz von einem gemeinsamen realen oder fiktiven Vorfahren verbunden fühlen, deren Mitglieder aber im Unterschied zur Lineage die genealogischen Stufen zum gemeinsamen Vorfahren und die verwandtschaftlichen Verbindungen untereinander nicht lükkenlos angeben können... Heiratsnormen mache ich nicht zum Bestandteil der Clan-Definition".

As was the case with our discussion of segmentary societies, this description of the clan derives mainly from the English social anthropologists, especially once again Evans-Pritchard and Fortes. Its basis, however, was already laid by E. Durkheim[145]. Durkheim was able to differentiate between social groups which actually are related by blood, and others which are united by an impression of blood-relatedness. For Durkheim, the clan was a *horde* which has ceased to be independent and has become part of a larger whole. Durkheim does not define this larger whole in this connection, but it is apparent that he had the tribe in mind, as his example (the Cabyles) indicates[146]. According to Durkheim's description the clan is without question a group which reckons itself to consist of blood relations, but it is not a "family" in the sense that it may function as a conglomerate containing elements which in reality are not connected by common descent. The solidarity of such a group is present the moment the individuals of which it consists acknowledge that they are represented by a common name or symbol[147].

However, Durkheim did not distinguish between real and fictive kinship within the clan, that is, whether the familial solidarity derived from real descent or not. Therefore we find in Durkheim's works the classical tri-partite division into family, clan, and tribe, with a superstructure as a fourth level which consists of the tribal coalition. It was the achievement of Evans-Pritchard and Fortes to have demonstrated that middle groups exist between the clan and the family, namely the much-discussed lineages. With respect to structure lineages resemble clans, as a study of their respective family trees reveals. In other words, both lineages and clans are unilineal groups which

---

Middleton and Tait (1958:4). de Geus (1976:136n.) cites a definition of E.A. Hoebel (1972: 691), according to which the clan is "a unilineal kinship group that maintains the fiction of common genetic descent from a remote ancestor, usually legendary or mythological." This definition is unsatisfactory because it does not distinguish sufficiently clearly between clan and lineage. The lineage, too, is able to count its ancestors back to a tribal ancestor who may be fictive or legendary, but need not be so; this is not the decisive issue. What *is* important is that unlike the clan, in which there may be only a vague feeling that such reckoning is more or less possible, in the lineage the membership can recite such a reckoning. Thus de Geus has not recognized the problems inherent in the Israelite social structure in the event that it possessed lineages side by side with clans, if it possessed any clans at all. Yet another matter is that de Geus (1976:136) wrongly defines the clan with respect to the extended family: "The exogamic extended family must form part of a larger endogamic unit, the clan". Although this applies to the Middle East, it is by no means an apriori truth, since in most places outside of the Middle East today the clans are exogamous.

[145] See Durkheim 1922:149-157.
[146] Durkheim 1922:153.
[147] Durkheim 1922:151.

reckon themselves to be descendants of a particular individual. The members of both groups are able to recite the number of generations which has elapsed since this ancestor lived, as well as a number of branchings-off the family tree, and so forth. The difference between lineages and clans is that while the family tree of a lineage is permanent and reflects either a real or a postulated kinship between its members, concerning which all members are able to recite the details, in the case of the clan its family tree varies according to the portion of the clan where one seeks one's information[148].

Scholars speak of different levels of lineages.Thus, for example, they often differentiate between three stages of kinship consisting of, at the top, the maximal lineage, in the middle the lineage proper, and at the bottom the minimal lineage. There are also societies without clans; in such cases a tribe is generally held to be identical with a maximal lineage. A well-known example is that of the *Tiv* in northern Nigeria[149]; the Tiv regard themselves as a single maximal lineage which is segmented through twelve generations down to the present one. Thus all members derive from a single ancestor. It should be added that the Tiv as a tribe are rather numerous (800,000 individuals)[150].

I shall briefly discuss yet another definition of the clan. In G.P. Murdock's opinion to be a clan an organization has to fulfil three conditions. It has to have "a unilineal rule of descent"; it has to be "a residential unit"; and, finally, it has to function outwardly as an "actual social integration"[151]. Murdock's definition has only the first condition in common with those of his English colleagues. I shall not deal more extensively with Murdock's description of the clan, which he also designates "a compromise kin group"[152]. For one thing, it does not seem to have been followed by very many anthropologists – and in particular not in the USA – and for another it has not influenced Gottwald's concept of the clan which it directly opposes, especially as far as the second point in Murdock's definition is concerned. De Geus apparently uses a similar concept of the clan without being aware of it, since he conceives of the clan as a unilinear descent group which consists of people (obviously) who function in "a real community of living and dwelling". It should be clear that in reality de Geus is referring to lineages, not to clans[153].

Thus we see that clans are found in many, but not all, places. The next issue is the question of endogamy or exogamy. Evans-Pritchard constructed his lineage theory on the basis of the African Nuer society, which is unambiguously exogamous. Clan A marries off its daughters to clan B, which give theirs in return to clan A[154]. Hence a nuclear family among the Nuer always

---

[148] Cf. Radcliffe-Brown (1950:39). Other examples: Southall 1970A:65; Fried 1966:289.

[149] On the Tiv, see Bohannan 1958.

[150] Cf. also Murphy and Kasdan 1959:21, who mention that in ideal terms all Arabs are members of a single "superlineage", that is, the descendants of Abraham.

[151] Murdock 1949:65-78.

[152] Murdock 1949:66.

[153] Cf. de Geus 1976:137.

[154] Naturally, one will also find many variations of this scheme. A simple variant would entail that clan A gives its daughters in marriage to clan B, whereas B does not give its daughters to A, but to clan C, which in turn gives its daughters in marriage to clan A. Thus Fox 1967:208f. Other models are illustrated in Hastrup and Ovesen 1980:218ff.

consists of a husband from one clan and a wife from another. The ideas underlying such a system have been extensively discused; these, however, are of no
interest here, since we are concerned with endogamous clans. When Evans-
Pritchard delimited clan and lineage in relation to one another, he simply
assumed that clans are exogamous[155]. This is a characteristic example of how
an ethnologist's fieldwork determines his general theories. In Evans-Pritchard's case, however, he was in a position to make amends for his onesided-
ness, since he later studied the Sanussi society of the bedouins of Cyrenaika.
We learn from Evans-Pritchard's study of the Sanussi that after having made
acquaintance with this Near Eastern social system he dropped exogamy from
his definition of the clan; he subsequently regarded the use of "fixed" and
looser kinship convictions as alone decisive in determining when we have to do
with a clan[156].

In this connection also the last part of Gottwald's definition of a clan proves
to be inadequate. According to Gottwald, exogamous matrimonial practices
ought to entail that at least two clans would always be represented in every
family. This is correct in cases in which the woman in a patrilineal society is
still reckoned to be a member of her own clan. Thus Glatzer is able to assert
that this is the case among the pashtun groups he has studied[157]. On the other
hand, if on entering into the marriage the woman loses her status within her
parents' clan and so is incorporated in her husband's clan, then we no longer
find evidence of the presence of both clans. They do not become integrated
into each other as a result of such marital connections. On the other hand,
there will always be a certain degree of integration because of the affinal ties
which are created by marriage, and if a contractual agreement is enacted between two clans (A and B) to the effect that they will exchange daughters in
future, then the presuppositions for further political cooperation are present.
This sort of political alliance is known in the Middle East despite the fact that
the matrimonial system is regarded as endogamous. However, in the event
that the OT fails to mention in connection with a particular family that two
clans were represented in it, it is impossible to say whether the family in
question belonged to an exogamous or endogamous system, since the
woman's affiliations are only rarely mentioned in genealogies, even if she
remains a member of her paternal lineage[158].

As mentioned previously, Gottwald assumed *a priori* that *a true tribal system
has to contain the exogamous clan;* as we have seen, this assumption derives from

---

[155] Cf. Evans-Pritchard 1940B:284: "The segments <among the Nuer> are genealogical
structures, and we therefore refer to them as lineages and to the clan as an exogamous system
of lineages which trace their descent to a common ancestor." See also Fortes' description of the
system among the Tallensi (1940: 242ff.).

[156] Cf. Evans-Pritchard 1949:54-61.

[157] Glatzer 1977:107

[158] Cf. Murphy and Kasdan 1967:10-13.

a dated definition of the clan. Thus Gottwald's dictum cannot be used as the premiss of a logical syllogism intended to prove that the Israelite tribal system was unique. Further, the formal similarities between the clan and the lineage make it difficult to determine in the case of ancient Israel whether Israelite society tribal society contained clans, or whether it was solely a question of (maximal) lineages. I shall return to this issue below when I address myself to the question as to whether Israelite lineages were composed of extended or nuclear families.

There is at any rate no doubt that there were tribes in ancient Israel. However, any discussion of the nature of these tribes must be conducted in isolation from a conjectural Israelite tribal league. Gottwald claims that a שבט is only a שבט by virtue of its being a שבט ישראל. Of course, this is not an argument, but a mere postulate. The argument must necessarily entrail, for example, that the tribe of Manasseh was only a tribe if it belonged to שבטי ישראל, that is, if it was a member of the Israelite tribal league. This is to confuse two phenomena which scholars as early as Durkheim were able to keep separate. The tribe of Manasseh was a tribe irregardless of whether it belonged to a tribal league, but it is conceivable that it was not regarded as an *Israelite* tribe unless it also belonged to a Israelite league of tribes. The question in the latter instance would then be whether or not such a league actually existed, and what "Israel" signified in pre-monarchical times *if* such a league did not exist.

The question as to the relationship between all Israel and the individual Israelite tribes has also been addressed by de Geus who, interestingly enough, has arrived at a conclusion reminiscent of Gottwald's. De Geus emphasizes that in the OT the Israelite tribal names are used as territorial demarcational terms[159]. On the other hand, or so he claims, an Israelite tribe was always a branch of the whole Israelite people[160]. Since de Geus does not understand pre-monarchical Israel as a tribal league, these views force him to offer a historical explanation for Israel's conviction of solidarity. Israel was, on his view, a "Gesellschaftsnation", like that of the Hellenes[161]. In other words, already in the period of the Judges the Israelites were able to distinguish between what was Israelite and what was not. One might add that this identification of what was specifically Israelite was expressed in the form of a genealogical system which encompassed all Israelites[162].

In reality, de Geus is very close to accepting the revolution hypothesis, since he is forced to accept the notion of an awareness of ethnic unity which distinguished Israelites from Canaanites. This cannot have been a political

---

[159] De Geus 1976:144-145; cf. 1976:156.

[160] De Geus 1976:149-150.

[161] De Geus 1976:164.

[162] De Geus does not say this directly, but it would be the logical result if there actually existed some sort of Israelite conviction of unity during the prenational period which was based on some notion of blood ties (in this connection de Geus even speaks of racism, 1976:163).

unity, at least not on a level higher than that of the tribe. Nor, according to de Geus, did the Israelites have a nomadic past. Thus he is forced to hypothecate a type of cohesion of national or "ethnic" character as the cause of the emergence of an Israelite conviction of community; otherwise, his description of Israel as a "Gesellschaftsnation" would be meaningless.

De Geus' description of the Israelite society apparently suffers from some terminological confusion. This is more apparent when we examine his attempt to describe the Israelite tribe, since at least this writer is never quite sure when he is referring to a single Israelite tribe, or to the Israelite tribes understood as the people of Israel. It is apparent in de Geus' discussion of the criteria which may be used to determine what makes a people. In this connection de Geus cites Herodotus' three points (namely blood, language, and religion), but he rejects these in favor of *connubium* (by which he means the territory within which marital alliances are formed) and *forum* (the area in which "fellow tribesmen" and "fellow countrymen" acknowledge the same norms)[163].

At this stage in the discussion it would be appropriate to attempt to define the word "tribe" more closely. If the concept is to be useful at all, any definition of it must be able to distinguish the tribe from the "people" or "nation", but it is here that the difficulties truly arise. A different definition from that employed by Gottwald emphasizes that a tribe may be part of a "nation" (not in the sense of a state, but a "people"), or it may be identical with a whole nation. In practically all cases a tribe will be segmented into at least two sizeable subdivisions (*moieties* or *subtribes*). The form, function, and significance of such subdivisions corresponds in virtually all respects to those of the tribe, but they are confined to apply to only a section of it. A section may be segmented into a number of clans which once again in terms of structure and function resemble both the sub-tribe and the tribe. On all three levels of integration it is more the concept of blood ties than actual blood relations which motivates common activities. Familial ties which may but need not be substantive are to be found on the next level, that of the lineage, since a clan is segmented into a number of maximal lineages which are in turn composed of lineages and minimal lineages. Finally, the lineages themselves are subdivided into families. This is the fundamental structure of the segmentary tribe[164].

---

[163] De Geus 1976:163. De Geus has borrowed the concept of *connubium* from G.E. Dole (1968:96). Dole does not, however, use the term *forum*, although in principle it corresponds to Dole's description of the autonomous unit (1968:96). De Geus' description of the *forum* corresponds to many descriptions of tribal systems. Thus, for example, Lienhardt (1958:117): "It < the tribe > is also, in their theory, the largest group of people among whom it would be possible and desirable to settle cases of homicide by the payment of compensation in cattle...."; further, Tait (1958:168): "The tribe is the largest unit of common values...."; finally, Middleton (1958 208): "The tribe is the largest unit within which it is said that dispute should ultimately be settled by discussion." *Connubium*, on the other hand, is not normally used as a characterization of the tribe.

[164] To be sure, this description is only a rough model; in actual practice there may be even

This model tells us only about the structural organisation of the tribe; it says nothing about the forces which bind a tribe together. Mendenhall adds that modern anthropology describes the tribe as "an association of a much larger number of kinship segments which are each composed of families... it is composed of economically self-sufficient residential groups which because of the absense of higher authority take unto themselves the private right to protect themselves"[165]. In this sense the tribe may also be defined as the maximal "protective association", to employ a term utilized by Gottwald (although he especially uses this description of the Israelite clans)[166]. Of course, none of this explains *why* a tribe functions as a "protective association". In spite of the assertions of Mendenhall and Gottwald that they use a broad "matrix" to describe pre-monarchical Israelite society, the fact is that they have isolated a single aspect and allowed it to explain the Israelite feeling of community, namely the Yahwistic religion. Moreover, as of this time their claim is a mere postulate, since an independent analysis would be required to demonstrate that the Yahwistic religion actually played the role ascribed to it in Israel during the period of the Judges by these two scholars. Thus for the present the question of a common religion must be assigned a place among the numerous factors which may have led to the emergence of the Israelite tribes.

Mendenhall's and Gottwald's description of the tribe as a *protective association*, which they have borrowed from Sahlins and Service, also assumes that it contains a number of "cross-cutting associations" which bind the tribe together. This definition is frequently attacked for being too narrow, since it only applies to a limited number of societies which one would be justified in calling tribes. These criticisms usually appeared in conjunction with a general opposition to the developmental scheme of Service, since it confines tribal societies to a single socio-economic level (the neolithic method of production, coupled with the segmentary system)[167]. Any ethnologist who is worth his salt will be able to point to an extensive number of societies which one would be fully justified in calling tribes, but which do not live on this stage[168].

We must accordingly begin at the beginning. A useful point of departure is the five criteria mentioned by de Geus: common blood, common language, common religion, *connubium*, and *forum*[169]. However, it must be borne in

---

more stages from the family to the tribe. For example, the sub-tribe may be subdivided into sub-sub-tribes (to use a jargon which is, unfortunately, not wholly foreign to the anthropological literature), the clans into sub-clans, maximal lineages into sub-maximal lineages, and so forth.

[165] Mendenhall 1973:184; the definition, however, is naturally derived from Service (1971:100 and 103).

[166] Cf. Gottwald 1979A:330-331.

[167] See especially L.S. Lewis 1968; Dole 1968:89-90.

[168] Cf. L.S. Lewis 1968:101-104, and Dole 1968:90. See also the survey of research in Naroll 1964:283ff.

[169] Other criteria may be such things as physical appearance, the name (of the society), or history.

mind that it is difficult to find a definition of "tribe" which would not be equally applicable to other social units, by which I mean primarily those of the "people" and the "nation". De Geus himself regards the *forum* as the decisive criterium, but it is clear from his confusion of "people" and "tribe" that this criterium is inadequate to distinguish, in the case in question, an Israelite tribe, since a number of tribes may have a common forum (or all tribes may do so). The same problem besets several of the inclusive models which have arisen in recent times as bases for the evaluation of a society, whether one terms such a theoretical basis a *"cultunit"*, with R. Naroll, or a *"culture unit"*, with G. E. Dole. These models, too, are unable to isolate a single section from the entire people[170].

Concepts such as blood, language, religion, and so forth are generally rejected as sufficient grounds for isolating a society in respect to its surroundings[171]. Thus S.F. Nadel points out that the *Nupe* are characterized by a common language and ritual, but their bloodties are a doubtful criterium, since the *Nupe* are a heterogeneous society consisting of at least three different ethnic groups[172]. Nadel also rejects the concept of the *protective association* (which he does not use himself) as characteristic of the *Nupe*: "Save for the vague obligation of offering hospitality to every Nupe, there is no factor of actual co-operation which would embrace the tribe as a whole"[173]. To mention only a couple of other African examples, the *Alur* are not homogenously organized; rather, they are a heterogeneous population consisting of a dominant stratum and a helot class, and each has its own traditions as to its origins[174]. Similar conditions obtain among the *Kiga* in the same part of Africa[175]. The general problem is that any single society may prove to fulfil some of the criteria of definition, such as, for example, those of common language and religion, but it will not pass the test with respect to other features, such as *connubium* and blood relationship. Yet another society may lack the common language but still fulfil some of the other qualifications. In other words, a broad definition of the concept of "tribe" tends to be so circumstantial that no single society could satisfy its requirements. Another way of putting it would be to say that in this case the definition does not apply to any individual example of a tribal society.

To illustrate this fact with a well documented example, we shall briefly discuss the *Nuer*. This society, which in the 1930's consisted of approximately 300,000 individuals, is divided into a number of tribes; these may be subdivided into three families or tribal groups which, however, are not to be confused with tribal coalitions[176]. The Nuer nation as a whole included a variety of individual tribes whose size ranged from 5,000 to 45,000 members. Each of the tribes is economically autonomous, which also applies to the means of production. Each tribe has its own name, which is also the symbol of the tribe. Each

---

[170] Cf. Narroll 1964; Dole 1968.

[171] See among others Hymes 1968, and in particular Fried 1975, who deals with each of the criteria mentioned above without, however, being able to arrive at any clear basis for the definition of a tribe.

[172] Nadel 1967:313.

[173] Nadel 1967:314.

[174] Richards 1960A:313.

[175] Baxter 1960:280.

[176] Evans-Pritchard 1940B:276 concerning the entire Nuer society (Evans-Pritchard 1940A: 3 gives the number of members of this socity as 200,000). On these tribal groups, see Evans-Pritchard 1940A:5. Like their neighbors, the Dinka the Nuer may be characterized as "a congeries of tribes, which sometimes form loose federations" (1940A:5).

tribe has a dominant clan, and each organizes its members into age-group classes[177]. Evans-Pritchard points out that these factors are not sufficient to distinguish a tribe from its sections, since they may all be applied to the individual groupings within the tribe. Thus he includes such other criteria as the notions that a tribe is a field in which it is felt that conflicts must be peacefully resolved and that a tribe is a society which feels impelled to undertake joint action against external opponents[178]. In practice, however, these rules are of limited validity, since feuds between the individual sections of a Nuer tribe are frequent and bloody. Accordingly, every decision as to what a Nuer tribe actually is is quite arbitrary; naturally, this also applies to the distinction between them and other tribes[179].

It is evident that it is quite difficult to isolate a Nuer tribe from the whole of the Nuer nation; it is similarly difficult to define it with respect to its subsections. This means that it is impossible to point to a tribe as a cultural unit distinct from other tribes. If we take the first criterium, that of blood relationship, as our yardstick, we discover that the entire Nuer nation is comprehended by a genealogical system. Admittedly, this system is fictive, but it nevertheless plays an actual role in things, since it serves to determine who is and is not, a Nuer. Language is apparently also the common property of all Nuer (or at least Evans-Pritchard never says the opposite), so that this criterium also fails as an indicator that we have to do with a single tribe. Evans-Pritchard does not use religion as a criterium, and it is hard to imagine that it could be useful in distinguishing between two Nuer tribes. If we turn to the criteria of *connubium* and *forum* it is clear that to a certain extent a Nuer tribe may be regarded as a *connubium*, although in practice this is not decisive, since the actual *connubium* exists on a lower level than that of the tribe, namely between two clans which are linked by marital alliances. *Forum*, however, has some usefulness, but it should be recalled that this is a relative term in the sense that while there may exist a body of norms regulating such things as, for example, the extinguishing of feuds between members of a tribe, these norms are not necessarily observed in practice[180]. Similarly, such norms need not apply only to a single tribe. There may exist a series of commonly agreed-upon regulations dealing with the mutual relations between tribes; there may also be some which are not held in common. Additionally, one discovers that the sub-tribes within a tribe may be able to agree on a series of rules, but they will in addition

---

[177] Evans-Pritchard 1940B:278. In addition to the division because of sex, division into age groups determines the rights and duties of the individual members of the society.

[178] Evans-Pritchard 1940A:142; 1940B:278 and 283.

[179] Evans-Pritchard 1940A:148; 1940B:283f.

[180] A *forum* may be very simply defined as the territory within which the *possibility* exists to resolve conflicts between two or more parties. On the other hand, it must be acknowledged that the reality is frequently quite different, meaning that feuds and disagreements are in fact quite frequent within the unit which composes a *forum*; see e.g. Peters 1967 (on the bedouins of Cyrenaica) or Irons 1974 (on the Yomut of Iran).

also possess their own rules. Thus a sub-tribe also possesses its own forum.

Evans-Pritchard's characterization of a Nuer tribe also includes *territoriality*, by which he means that a tribe is a localizable quantity. It resides on its own territory and is autonomous with respect to its exploitation. This is also only partially true, since we have considerable evidence that tribal territories are not closed-off areas to which only a single tribe has access. There will especially tend to be a considerable degree of overlap with the territories of other tribes around border regions. This means that one can never be sure when one has left one tribal area and entered another.

Therefore, in our efforts to arrive at a definition of the concept of "tribe", we shall never be able to propose a definition which has more than a restricted validity. Of course, it is impossible to generalize on the basis of Evans-Pritchard's study of the Nuer. There may well be other societies in which other factors manifest themselves, and in which it would be easier to distinguish the individual tribes from each other or to demonstrate that there indeed are tribes in the area in question. Nevertheless, our discussion of the concept of "tribe" indicates that while we have a number of definitions which have analytical usefulness when confronted with an object of study (a society) which has not yet been explored, we are nevertheless unable to determine in the event that a society does not behave as our definitions prescribe that it is not a tribal society. For this reason I cannot but admit that Evans-Pritchard is right to describe his definition of a Nuer tribe as relative and arbitrary, and to believe that it would also apply in other cases.

Uncertainty as to how to demarcate the various social units of the Nuer was brought into relief during the 1970's in the discussion in the English journal, *Man* concerning the relationship between the Nuer and their neighbors, the *Dinka*. In this connection A. Southall questioned whether there ever was a discrete ethnic unit known as the Nuer before the colonial period (or, for that matter, the Dinka), or whether these peoples were not in a manner of speaking "created" by the colonial authorities[181]. Southall points out that the name "Nuer" is not actually used by the Nuer themselves; rather, it is the Dinka term for them. He implies that when the English arrived they simply decided without consulting the local population who belonged to the Nuer and then applied to them the term used for them by their neighbors. However, Southall also asks how it was possible for the parties involved always to be able to determine who belonged to which group[182].

This brings us to yet another discussion which has currency today, namely how one is to isolate a society from its context. A well-known attempt to propose an analytical model for this purpose is Naroll's "cultunit", consisting of six different factors[183]. Once again, as has been stressed by R. Cohen, the problem is that "no set of criteria fits all cases"[184].

Yet another path would entail that we simply chose to give up the old designations, in particular the concept of "tribe", since it is impossible to arrive at an unambiguous idea as to the

---

[181] Cf. Southall 1976:464.

[182] Cf. Southall 1976:465.

[183] Naroll 1964. Naroll mentions such features as territory, political organization, language, adaptation to ecological conditions, and local social structure (1964:284).

[184] R. Cohen 1978C:382. Naroll's idea has been criticized for presenting a fallacious understanding of the phenomenon of the tribe; thus, for example, Southall 1970B:44f.

contents of the term. Thus some scholars have concentrated on introducing such terms as "ethnicity" and "ethnic" in order to avoid the many connotations (and misapprehensions) associated with the word "tribe" in daily speech[185]. An example of such a new effort, associated with the concept of "ethnicity", is F. Barth's proposal for new approaches to the study of "ethnic groups"[186]. According to Barth, earlier ethnographers emphasized four elements, namely the ability of a population to reproduce itself biologically (self-perpetuation), their propensity to hold certain cultural values in common, to create an internal network of communications and actions (interaction), and their ability to constitute an organization whose members are able to identify themselves and who are so identifiable by foreigners. Barth prefers to use a model which emphasizes the processes which take place in a given society. He seems to regard "ethnicity" as the result of the self-understanding of a group, the means by which they describe themselves in the context of their relationships to others. This proposal enables Barth to relativize the concept of the borderlines between societies, since on his view these are not territorial demarcations, but subjective differences which the society in question interprets as a we-they relationship. At the same time Barth stresses that this barrier is constantly being modified to agree with changes of circumstance[187].

I shall not delve into the question of "ethnicity" further in this context. The usefulness of such an analytical construct for the purposes of historical investigation would seem to be limited, since we are only very rarely indeed in a position to see where the divisions are to made between two societies except in the cases where these are indicated by territorial boundaries. However, the debate concerning the concepts of "tribe", "ethnicity", and so forth underlines the fact that we must be prepared to describe tribes as flexibly as possible. It also shows that what Gottwald and Mendenhall regard as "current theory" is only an epiphenomenon in the on-going discussion. To use Barth's definition, *"ethnicity"* in the case of Israel would signify the process which enabled people who understood themselves to be Israelites to distinguish between themselves and others. We must seek the reasons behind such an ability to differentiate in the available source materials. To focus in advance of such an investigation on a single element, especially the notion of a specifically Israelite religion, could well prove to have fatal consequences.

The possibilities for survival of tribal societies in the event that they become encapsulated within the political system of a nation-state is a special problem. It is often held that when this occurs it is merely a matter of time before a tribe collapses and disappears[188]. As we have seen, this is not completely wrong as far as the Near East is concerned. In large sections of the Near East, however, tribal societies do continue to exist, although they are exposed to extreme pressures from the nation-states, in the form of the efforts of these states to eliminate the tribal societies by removing or destroying their economic basis. In many cases this is connected with the fact that most of these tribes live a nomadic existence. One must not ignore the fact that most of the existing tribal societies in the Middle East are either still nomadic or once were so[189].

---

[185] See the survey of research by R. Cohen 1978C. On the traditional "popular" understanding of the concept of tribe, see Southall 1970B:31-33; Lewis 1976:354-355, and R. Cohen 1978C:384. For the beginnings of the use of the term "ethnicity" in a study of ancient Oriental cultures, see Kamp and Yoffee 1980.

[186] Barth 1969.

[187] Barth 1969:25. One recognizes this basic understanding in Barth's study, in which an ideology is modified in order to fit in with the existing conditions (cf. above, p. 299).

[188] This is the reason why e.g. Gottwald asserts that the Israelite tribal system did not exist during the monarchy. See also Dole 1968:91-94 (esp.p.94).

[189] Sweet 1960 cannot be taken to tell against this fact. In Tell Toqaan there dwelled some peasants who were tribally organized as well as some who were not, but, as is clearly indicated

This might lead a superficial observer to believe that this situation applies to all the tribal societies in the Near East, including the Israelite tribes in antiquity. However, this is not a necessary conclusion, since the difference between the the tribes of Israel and contemporary Near Eastern nomadic tribes has to do with territorial and political circumstances. The Israelites dwelled in a territory which at least in a transitional period was not controlled by a centralized political system. Their tribes were therefore autonomous units who dwelled in their own tribal areas, and it would presumably be best to describe them as an alliance of sedentary local mountain peasants who held a common territory. In the period of the Judges the Israelite economy was no doubt based on agriculture. We do not find many parallels to this situation in the Near East today, although one would not have to go all that far back to find similar conditions aplenty, not least in Persia. Virtually all of the agrarian societies in the Middle East are now subject to centralized political control.

It would be worth noting that the social form of organization at levels lower than that of the tribe is rather similar whether we have to do with a tribal society, non-tribally organized peasants, or non-tribal urban dwellers in the Middle East. The reason for this is possibly that when external political forces have not dominated the situation, tribes have appeared or reappeared to compensate for this lack in order to defend the territorial rights of the local inhabitants. Thus in a stateless society a tribe could serve as a "protective association". On the other hand, in the event that some external political power dominated the tribal territory, the tribal organization would accordingly lose this function, even though the tribe itself would continue to exist. In any event, both lineages and families would continue to have a number of functions, above all on the local level. This reinforces the significance of the lineage and we have observed in recent times the fact that Arab village family groups have been strengthened within the context of a centralized system such as that prevailing in Israel, since it is ordinarily they who own the land. In other words, the lineage replaces the tribe as the unit which has territorial ownership rights; political and economic life is a function of the private possessions of the various local groups. Also other functions associated with a lineage are preserved, such as marital policy and, to a certain extent, the resolution of conflicts among family groups. This implies that lineages tend to survive whether or not there is a higher level of (tribal) organization present. If the political conditions in the area in question should change, that is, if the central authority breaks down or weakens, the lineages are able to (re-)organize themselves as tribes. As we have seen, an example of this phenomenon is provided by the emergence of the "people of Tibne" in the Jordanian province of Aǧlun

---

in Sweet's account, the tribal members of the village were descendants of nomads who had settled down, and they still had tribal kinsmen who continued to live as nomads. On the other hand, at least in Yemen there are sedentary tribes which appear to have been sedentary for thousands of years; cf. Sergeant 1980B:127.

towards the end of the 19th century, when a number of village societies began a process of political integration which could have led to actual tribe-formation. Historically, they did not achieve this goal, but this is connected with the fact that the system was not allowed to develop more than fifty years. The members of the "people of Tibne" simply did not achieve sufficient chronological distance from their system to enable them to construct a genealogy encompassing the entire area. This example shows that secondary tribal formations are possible in the Middle East, although this is certainly not to be regarded as the only valid model for the emergence of new tribal societies (although some scholars would no doubt prefer to argue this position).

Chapter 4

SOCIAL STRUCTURE IN ISRAEL
IN THE PRE-NATIONAL PERIOD

§ 1

בית אב: *Family, Household, Minimal Lineage, Lineage*

Taking into account the insights we have gained in the previous chapter, it should now be possible to undertake a new analysis of the social structure of Israelite society. The goals of our analysis will be two: on the one hand I shall attempt to test whether earlier scholarship has correctly described the Israelite "father's house", "clan", and "tribe"; on the other I shall attempt to demonstrate that Israelite society contained more levels than is usually assumed. One could begin either, with Gottwald, at the highest level, that of the tribe, or, with de Geus, at the lowest level, that of the family. For that matter, one could just as well begin with the משפחה, which is ordinarily taken to refer to the clan, a unit many have held to be the most important social unit in the society, and then attempt to locate the other levels in relation to it. In what follows, however, I shall begin with the family in the traditional manner.

The Israelite family is often held to have been extended, that is, a *Grossfamilie* composed of a number of generations who dwelled together and functioned as a social and economic unit. According to Gottwald the family contained up to five generations who made up a *residential unit* (in practice, however, it is more than difficult to imagine that more than three generations lived together, when we take into account the short lifespan prevailing at the time). Within this unit the patriarch, the head of family, his wife or wives plus, perhaps, one or more grandparents dwelled as pensioners. There will have been other members of the father's family who had not married, such as brothers or uncles; other member of the extended family were the unmarried and married sons of the patriarch and their wives, unmarried daughters, daughters who had been returned by their husbands or were widows[1]. There may also have been children of the married sons of the patriarch[2]. Normally, the extended family was synonymous with the dwelling of these individuals in the same house or tent. They will also have had a common economy governed by the patriarch.

---

[1] Examples in the OT in which childless widows were returned to their parents are provided by Gen 38, in which Judah sends Tamar back, and by Ruth 1, in which Naomi tells her daughters in law to return to their kin.

[2] Gottwald 1979A:285; cf. de Geus 1976:134, and De Vaux 1961:39.

Finally, the extended family was an exogamous unit[3]. Some scholars have supposed that this form of organization was a survival of Israel's hypothetical nomadic past. They have suggested that after the Settlement, during which process Israel changed occupation, the extended family gradually became dissolved. Others have argued that the extended family in fact is most commonly present in sedentary agrarian societies.

Among those who regard Israelite social structure as a survival of Israel's nomadic past is A. Causse, who emphasized that the institution of the family survived better than other features of nomadic life. Therefore we still discover in sedentary Israel that *"la bayit apparait encore comme un groupe relativement étendu...."*[4]. M. Noth and R. de Vaux are on the same wavelength[5]. This view has even been clearly expressed in quite recent times by W. Dietrich, as it is in reality the basis of Dietrich's monograph on the encounter between the social systems of Israel and Canaan[6]. W. Thiel also argues for a nomadic background for the extended family, although he also claims that it is characteristic for semi-nomads, whereas bedouins normally have nuclear families[7]. Against this, de Geus maintains that "the bet 'ab can also be said to be an institution typical of a sedentary population whose economy is mainly agrarian," and adds that the urbanization of the agrarian society destroyed the extended family[8].

In reality, these assertions are simply the results of the adoption of conclusions based on observations in Europe of changes in the family structures of European societies during the transition from agrarian societies to industrial states. Since no industrialization or only a very little has as yet taken place in the Middle East – measured with a Western yardstick – it is more than doubtful that these observations are at all applicable to the traditional family system of the Orient. In connection with Israel in pre-national times they are directly misleading.

None of the views mentioned above are confirmed by the ethnographic materials available, as the limited statistics we have suggest that extended families appear with equal frequency in all sectors of society. Therefore this familial institution cannot be taken as evidence either for or against Israel's hypothetical nomadic past.

It is to be seen that the idea of the extended family as the basis of Israelite society does not completely correspond with the use of kinship terms in the OT. It is invariably pointed out that the Hebrew term בית אב, "father's house", designates the family, but a few scholars have noted cases in which this term does not describe the same phenomenon. I shall refer in this connection to only two authors, J. Pedersen and N.K. Gottwald. Pedersen's great work on Israel, which is occasionally anathematized by some, contains despite valid criticisms of his methodology a number of observations which are still useful today. This is not least the case since Pedersen expresses himself much less

---

[3] The Israelite family is occasionally described as endogamous, as, for example, by Patai (1959:17f.). This is a misunderstanding. The individual family is exogamous because its members cannot contract marital relations with one another. However, it is *endogamous* to the extent that the lineage of which it is a part is so.

[4] Causse 1937:15; cf. on this Kimbrough 1978:43ff.

[5] Noth 1962B:58f.; De Vaux 1961:28f.

[6] Dietrich 1979.

[7] Thiel 1980A:37ff.

[8] De Geus 1976:136.

dogmatically than a number of later authors have done who have been concerned with the issues in question.

By this I mean that Pedersen frequently expresses himself much more cautiously than his critics sometimes seem to suggest. Indeed, Pedersen's account of the somewhat labile kinship relationships in ancient Israel is a good example of this. Of course, this by no means contradicts the criticisms which have been launched against Pedersen by J. Barr and, recently, P. Addinall[9]. Addinall's critique has to do with Pedersen's attempt to describe a specifically Israelite *psyche*; he is able to demonstrate some confusion in Pedersen's work, since Pedersen failed to explain the relationships obtaining between "the fundamental psychological conception", "the old Israelite conception", and "the transformed conception". Addinall's example of this confusion is well chosen. Pedersen claims that Amos and Hosea represent the old conception, while their contemporaries represent the transformed conception. But what, then, is the fundamental conception, the views adumbrated by Amos and Hosea, or those held by the rest of the Israelites? If the old conception was identical with the fundamental conception, then it would presumably be shared by the main part of the Israelites, but it is obvious that this was not the case in the time of Amos and Hosea. Logically, then, the transformed conception must have been identical with the fundamental one at this point. The fact that Pedersen's notion of a "Folk Psyche" was a feature of his relationship to V. Grønbech is well documented and should not require further discussion[10]. Grønbech depicted the psyches of the Nordic and Greek civilizations in the same way Pedersen approached the mentality of Israel[11].

In other words, if we discount Pedersen's discussion of the psychological feelings of solidarity which no doubt were and are present in the various social groups, but which in practice are difficult to make use of as a tool for historical analysis, his description of the structure of Israelite society nevertheless still contains a number of important observations. Pedersen emphasized that the borderline between such concepts as "tribe" and "family" was fluid in ancient Israel, and that there was no sharp demarcation between "lineage" and "father's house". He added that we "Sometimes discover the word 'lineage' where the system would lead us to expect 'father's house'"[12]. This is no doubt correct. Pedersen also added that one cannot quantitively conclude that a certain number of families comprised a lineage, or that a certain number of lineages comprised a tribe. On his view, this was a result of the fact that kinship, that is, blood ties, was the constitutive element; moreover, it was of significance at all levels in the society[13]. Pedersen's observation is in reality completely a jour in terms of contemporary research, since it corresponds rather well to the fact that a number of the proponents of the concept of *"ethnicity"* regard the self-identification of a given population as the most important criterium for identifying the population in question.

On the other hand, Pedersen did not recognize that this uncertain use of the

---

[9] Cf. Barr 1961:181-184, and Addinall 1981.

[10] See also Nielsen 1972:11.

[11] Cf. Grønbech 1909 and 1961.

[12] Pedersen 1958:35.

[13] Pedersen 1958:35-36. Thus Pedersen is able to write, "Where the concept 'household, institution' is not expressly emphasized, the two words (i.e., בית אב and משפחה) are used practically indiscriminately." (1958:40). See also Noth 1962B:58, and De Vaux 1961:39-40.

terms בית אב and משפחה conceals a middle term which distinguishes these two concepts as "pure" types with respect to one another. This middle term may be either the lineage of the minimal lineage. It is not unlikely that in Israel the same term was used of both the family, the minimal lineage and the "ordinary" lineage, and that משפחה was only used of the maximal lineage and the clan (if it actually existed), or else it applied to both the "ordinary" lineage and the maximal type. There are sufficient examples to indicate that Near Eastern traditional societies as well as others elsewhere use this sort of confusing terminology, so that only a detailed ethnographic analysis of an individual kinship system is able to clarify the levels within such a system. This supposition is confirmed by Gottwald's description of the family[14]. Gottwald maintains without hesitation that a בית אב is an extended family, and that it is *"primarily a living group"*, by which he means a *residential unit*[15]. However, in the same passage Gottwald calculates that as described by him the extended family will consist of from fifty to one hundred individuals. Thus it would naturally be impossible for this group to dwell together under the same roof (an observation which is also confirmed by archeological excavations of the residential sections of Israelite villages, the houses in which were entirely too small to contain such numbers). In other cases, however, as Gottwald notes, there is evidence of father's houses which only consisted of a few individuals[16].

It is to be observed that anthropologists regard a social group consisting of more than fifty persons, and who dwell as separate family groups, as a lineage or minimal lineage, but hardly an extended family. In other words, Gottwald confuses the concepts of lineage and family, for which reason his account of the family is rather murky, since he seems to speak of both groups interchangeably in the same terms. For example, Gottwald mentions that the "father" is the oldest living male in a lineage, and that this is import of the term בית אב[17]. He also points out that the "father" of a בית אב is not its founder, but only its chief at the time he is called its "father"[18]. It is only in the event that the בית אב functioned as an economically united structure, that is, where its chief singlehandedly determined its economic and familial transactions, that it would be reasonable to regard such an overgrown "family" as an extended one. Modern relationships in numerous village societies in the Middle East indicate that a *ḥamūla*, which is more of a lineage than a clan, is the actual possessor of property, especially in areas where the *mušaʾ* system once prevailed. However, in practice the administration of the common property of a *ḥamūla* is con-

---

[14] Gottwald 1979A:285-287.

[15] Gottwald 1979A:285.

[16] Gottwald 1979A:286.

[17] Gottwald 1979A:286-287. Therefore an extended family does not have a name which lives on in the family. This is correct; it is first with the lineage that we find name-bearing social units. A lineage bears its name from generation to generation, as long as it persists as a social reality.

[18] Gottwald 1979A:287.

fined to the reapportionment of plots of land encompassed by the system. Between the times when reapportionment takes place the *ḥamūla* does not intervene in the husbandry of the plots by the individual members of the family except in cases where a member attempts to sell his plot to foreigners. When this occurs the entire lineage then steps in on behalf of the family in question and redeems the land, since it is regarded as the communal property of all members. The leader of the *ḥamūla* also has some limited influence in the village. He may serve as a mediating factor in conflicts between members of his *ḥamūla*; he is often the most wealthy member as well (though this need not be the case), but he has no authority to dispose of the *ḥamūla*'s property as he desires. There is no reason why the situation in Israel should have been identical to this. However, since Gottwald succeeds (perhaps without knowing it) in demonstrating the existence of the lineage system in the structure of Israelite society, he is not without more ado entitled to assume that its leader, the "father", is also its patriarch, that is, in the sense that he has absolute authority over all the members of his lineage. Such an assumption must be proved by practical examples.

In actuality, when Gottwald describes some "father's houses" as containing only a couple of members, he is not speaking of extended families, even though the same Hebrew terminology is used; these are obviously nuclear families. The widow from Tekoa who was alone in the world with but a single son, is not a member of an extended, but a nuclear family (2 Sam 14,5-7). She would nevertheless still remain a member of a lineage. Thus in my opinion Gottwald's analysis shows that ancient Israel possessed both nuclear families, extended families, and lineages, and that all three were referred to by the same term, בית אב. Nevertheless, there is no reason to assume that in every case we shall be in a position to determine which of these phenomena we are dealing with, which naturally limits the analytical value of this insight. The subsequent sections of Gottwald's treatment of Israelite social organization emphasize that בית אב is also used of the lineage, since, as he notes, the term בית אב sometimes figures metaphorically instead of משפחה, and, in a few cases, it even substitutes for שבט, "tribe". The reason why this is possible is not that בית אב is a metaphor for משפחה, but that the two concepts overlap because they are both used of the same structural level in Israelite society.

Two other factors are decisive for the existence of both extended and nuclear families in a traditional society. The first of these is the question on the distribution of wealth; the other has to do with the domestic cycle. If a society contains extended families the domestic cycle of such a society must be relatively slow in the sense that married sons remain for a number of years in the family residence. If the society is governed by *neolocal* practices, extended families will be rare, since the individual family constantly segments off into new and independent families. However, even societies which strive to retain familial solidarity have to contend with the fact that it may be quite difficult for the parent family to provide for a sizeable number of members. Logically, this would seem to support the view that Israel had extended families in her nomadic past, while the nuclear family began to replace them after the Settlement, since this would correspond to the economic circumstances of nomadic and sedentary life, respectively. Nomads are able to stay together since the only limit on the amount of property an individual family may possess is its herds of animals, which is, naturally, a variable quantity. The larger the family, the greater the number of sons necessary to watch over the herds, which in turn provides optimum conditions for the flourishing and growth of the herds. Nevertheless, it is interesting to note that such families always divide anyway, since sooner or later married sons depart from their family and begin to work on their own account. As mentioned above, the reason is usually conflicts between the female members of the household, although of course conflicts between the father and his sons are also sufficient to result in such fissioning[19]. As far as the peasants are concerned, other rules apply from the moment a society proves unable to lay claim to more land. If there is question of a poor family with a modest plot of land it would be quite impossible to provide for a numerous group, not to speak of a polygynous family, which is ordinarily found only in the wealthier reaches of the society. In modern times the rules of inheritance have entailed that the poor become even more impoverished, since the *neolocal* family is entitled to demand its share of the inheritance the moment it abandons the family residence. This leads to even further division of the property accorded to the individual family, and so to even more severe poverty. Until modern times, when medical advances began to make themselves felt in such societies, this sort of development was limited because especially infant mortality was very great.

The study of the Near Eastern traditional societies indicates that even in pre-national times in ancient Israel the society contained both nuclear and extended families, and that the last - mentioned must have been in the minority[20]. The only way to avoid this conclusion is to postulate that there were no poor Israelites, but only rich ones, which is quite impossible because of the limited resources available in Palestine. There is no reason to be surprised that we seldom encounter poor families in the OT, since in this respect the OT does not differ importantly from other literary works in antiquity. An example would be the Homeric poems, which are notorious for being solely interested in the fates of the great, while the "average man" is simply subsumed under the rubric of "the people". It is necessary to keep this feature in mind when analyzing the use of בית (אב) in conjunction with the patriarchal narratives,

---

[19] On this see e.g. Antoun 1972A:55. A third reason mentioned by Antoun is poor harvests, which may compel a father to eject his sons, since he no longer can support them. In the case of a nomadic society, see Bates 1973:93-95.

[20] See above, p. 231f.

since not to do so would be a serious distortion of the picture. It is reasonable to suppose that the Israelite patriarchs are depicted as great men. My reason for introducing my discussion of the use of בית and בית אב in the OT with an evaluation of the materials in Genesis is that Genesis is largely concerned to seem as if it recounts familial histories. Thus if we have any possibility to catch a glimpse of especially the domestic cycle in Israel, the patriarchal narratives offer the best materials available[21].

There can be no doubt that בית אב may be a designation for the extended family. There is an example which, although it is in the Primeval History, nevertheless gives us some idea of what the Israelites used this term to signify. In Gen 7,1, Noah is told to enter the Ark together with his entire בית; in Gen 7,7 Noah, his sons, his wife, and his sons' wives obey the order[22]. Another passage, this time from the Joseph Novella, describes the "house" of Jacob as consisting of Jacob, his sons, and his grandsons (Gen 45,10-11). If grandsons are members of Jacob's household, then his married sons naturally are as well. These are the two clearest examples. There are, however, a number of other passages which are not completely clear as to whether they refer to extended or nuclear families, just as there are some in which it is unclear whether we have to do with extended families or lineages.

We shall begin with the last-mentioned group. First, it would be a practical measure to prove that בית אב really can be used of the lineage; it is therefore necessary to point to passages which unambiguously describe such families. The first example of this is in Gen 18,19, where the text distinguishes between Abraham, his children, and "his household after him". It would be meaningless to claim that ביתו אחריו refers to the grandchildren of the still-living Abraham; the verse clearly refers to his descendants, that is, his lineage (implicitly the people of Israel, who, according to the OT, descended from Abraham). The other example which is relevant in this connection is Gen 24,38 and 24,40. Abraham's servant has been ordered to seek a wife for Isaac among the members of Abraham's "father's house", his משפחה. At this stage we shall not attempt to determine whether בית אב and משפחה represent the same genealogical level. However, it would not be reasonable to suppose that in this context

---

[21] The materials are used here without reference to literary critical or traditio-historical considerations. This approach may be defended since, whether we have to do with J,E, P or the materials in the Joseph Novella, all of the units of tradition are chronologically quite removed from the period about which they presume to speak. Thus we may conclude that such materials express a later ideological understanding of the earliest ancestors of the Israelites; they are not historical sources about them.

[22] In this paragraph the term בית אב is used in spite of the fact that by no means all of the examples cited use the full term. We frequently encounter only בית, or even אב alone (which usually occurs in the membership rolls in the plural, אבות), although there is no reason to belive that different emphases are represented by this. In this connection, other meanings of the term בית are quite irrelevant, although it should be noted that it is used of a building, of the activities which take place within it (the household), as well as of the persons who dwell in it (the family).

בית אב represents Abraham's extended family, since there is neither reference to common residence or to a common economy. Thus בית אב may be used of both lineages and extended families, even though in sociological terms these are two distinct levels in societal structure. The extended family is a residential group, while the other, the lineage, is a descent group which is composed of a number of residential groups.

This evidence may be supported with a long series of other examples, although in these cases it is impossible to say with certainty whether reference is made to a lineage or to an extended family. One such ambiguous case is present already in the narrative of the commissioning of Abraham (Gen 12,1). Abraham is told to abandon his מלדת and his בית אב [23]; in this context בית אב could acceptably be rendered by both "family" and "lineage"[24]. The same is true of Jacob's remark that he desires to return to his "father's house" from which he had absented himself (Gen 28,21). This could equally well refer to his lineage, which still resides in the land of Canaan, or to his family, in which his father Isaac rules as patriarch. In Gen 31,14, Laban's daughters deny that they belong to their "father's house", since they have been "sold". One might be tempted to believe that the reference is to Laban's family, which they have abandoned because of their marriage to Jacob. However, when we consider that Israelite marital practice ordinarily entailed that the bride left her family in connection with marriage, this notion would be a banality. It is therefore possible that the two women are here referring to their paternal lineage. In other words, in spite of the fact that Jacob's marriages with Lea and Rachel belong to the not-unknown group of cousin marriages, and that, further, they are contracted within Abraham's *patrilineage*, which is traced back to Terah, the two women are nevertheless here expressing their doubts as to whether the relationship between their paternal line and Jacob's.

A likewise uncertain passage is Gen 38,11, where Judah sends his daughter-in-law Tamar back to her paternal family. In the Joseph Novella one could point to Gen 41,51: the birth of Manasseh leads Joseph to "forget" his "father's house". It is possible that Joseph is referring to his family, which at the time resides in Canaan, or the passage could simply be a sentimental statement to

---

[23] It is to be observed that Abraham is nowhere said to belong to any tribal unit. This is a difficulty for which those scholars who reckon the patriarchal narratives to be of worth as historical sources owe us an explanation. If one conceives of Abraham, as many scholars have done, as an Amorite nomad from the upper regions of Mesopotamia, then he would simply have to be a member of a tribe. In this connection it would be an unworthy and *ad hoc* argument merely to claim that the OT has "forgotten" to mention Abraham's tribal affiliations. The reason may have been that at the stage of oral tradition Abraham was not regarded as a member of a (foreign) tribe), but as *the* tribal ancestor par excellence, that is, of the Israelite nation. Oral tradition, however, is not history; it is instead composed of *stories;* cf. also Westermann 1981:30.

[24] Gen 20,13 refers to Abraham's absence from his בית אב. In this case Abraham is described as wandering about in a foreign land with his family. Thus in this context it would be most appropriate to take בית אב to refer to his lineage.

the effect that he will be able to manage without his family. However, it is also conceivable that Joseph means that by marrying an Egyptian he has broken with his lineage, so that the birth of Manasseh means that the newly-created family has proved its viability and thus may become the origins of a new lineage. In this sense there may be some sort of parallel to Esau's marriage, since his marriage was also contracted outside of his own paternal line. Moreover, it resulted in the fact that Esau was bypassed in favor of Jacob, so that in the end he chose to break with his family (Gen 26,34-35 (cf.27,46); 36,1).

It should be emphasized that if we had not succeeded in demonstrating that בית אב may designate "lineage", we would have been logically forced to adhere to the usual understanding of all these passages, and of others in Genesis. However, now that we know that בית אב is used of both the family and the lineage it will be necessary in individual cases to undertake an analysis to determine in which sense the term is used. The previously so proudly adhered-to definition of "father's house" as "family" is impossible to retain.

The next question is whether בית אב is also used of the nuclear family. This is a more thorny problem to solve, since our information is limited, and every single relevant example contains some uncertain aspects. The clearest example of the existence of the nuclear family is in Gen 34,19.26, but it is possible to object that the reference here is not to Israelite, but Canaanite families. According to Gen 34,19, the most important son in Hamor's house was Shechem, who was unmarried. This probably signifies that the married sons in the town did not continue to reside in their fathers' households, but formed their own instead. This is confirmed by v 26, since Dinah is removed from *Shechem's house*. This suggests that the newly-married Shechem must have formed his own household. In this case the settlement pattern is clearly neolocal[25]. I am likewise inclined to regard the information concerning Esau's household in Gen 36,6 as evidence of a nuclear family which was, incidentally neolocal, since this household consisted of Esau, his wives, sons, and daughters, whereas his daughters-in-law and grand children are not mentioned. This family was also polygynous.

Yet another complex of traditions is of interest in this connection; it is found in the Joseph Novella. We have to do with a number of passages which apparently distinguish between the family of Joseph's brothers and Joseph's

---

[25] If one prefers in this connection the classical solution of the traditio-historical problems, and thus assigns Gen 34 to J (Eissfeldt:L) and E, so that J informs us about Shechem and Dinah, while E tells us about Hamor and Jacob (cf. Wellhausen 1963:314-322; Gunkel 1917:369ff., and Eissfeldt 1922:23ff. and 69*ff. Further developed by Lehming 1958 and De Pury 1969; cf. now also Westermann 1981:651-654. This approach has not, however, been followed by Nielsen 1959: 240-259 or Otto 1979:170-175, each on the basis of his own particular understanding of textual analysis (Nielsen pursues a traditio-historical course, while Otto's approach is literary critical, with traditio-historical leanings), it is to be seen that this procedure separates Hamor from Shechem. This would possibly prevent our drawing the above-mentioned conclusion as to the familial system in Shechem.

"father's house". In Gen 42,19.33 Joseph's brothers are instructed to take provisions back to their households, that is, their respective families, and in Gen 45,18 they are told to fetch both their father and their households, that is, their families. The individual families of Joseph's brothers are apparently regarded as autonomous units with respect to Jacob. Finally, in Gen 50,8 the text distinguishes between Joseph's house (which, since nothing more is said, must be understood as a nuclear family, for the simple reason that it was established in isolation of Jacob's house), his brothers, and his father's house; these groups are ordered to accompany Jacob's funeral procession to the cave of Machpelah. Even though we cannot in this instance be sure that the text implies that the families of Joseph's brothers were understood as units which had separated off from their father's house, this interpretation is very tempting. However, at this juncture I shall not press this point, but will defer dealing with it until we have tested it in comparison with materials from other parts of the OT.

The first section to be included in our discussion is the Gideon narratives in Jdg 6-8, plus the supplementary Abimelech narrative in Jdg 9[26]. Gideon was the youngest in his father's house, which belonged to the smallest אלף in Manasseh. In this context, "father's house" may refer to Gideon's family, that is, the group over which his father presided, or it may refer to his lineage. אלף may apply to the same level as משפחה or to an independent level.

Following Mendenhall's attempt to trace the census lists in Num 1 and 26 back to the premonarchical period[27], Gottwald defines the term אלף as the military unit which is based on a משפחה[28]. Since in reality this attempt has no firmer basis than the fact that Num 1 and 26 pretend to be a military roster of all the men in Israel who are capable of bearing arms, this theory can hardly bear critical scrutiny. Any list of men who are capable of bearing arms could hardly be more than a list of juridical persons who have reached adulthood. I have previously rejected the notion that Num 1 and 26 contains materials from the pre-monarchical period[29]; it would be difficult to convince me that the opposite is the case, even though Mendenhall reduces the figures somewhat, when we consider that three main sections of Ephraim (משפחה is used) only yield the figure 32,500 (or, according to Mendenhall's reduction, 325) warriors, while the same census assigns to Dan, which has only a single section, the figure of 64,400 (or 644) warriors. It is impossible to determine what were the considerations underlying the figures in Num 1 and 26, but the notion that these figures are based on data from the period of the Judges is quite out of the question (the difference between Num 1 and Num 26 is that the figures in Num 1 are slightly smaller than those in Num 26. This may be explained by the redactional interests of P:

---

[26] As was the case with the materials in Genesis, this discussions is undertaken without reference to the traditio-historical problems caused on the one hand by the linkage between the possibly originally independent figures of Jerubbaal and Gideon, and on the other hand the addition of the Abimelech narrative to the Gideon-Jerubbaal tradition. On these issues see Richter 1963:300ff. and Haag 1967. As in the patriarchal narratives these problems are of only secondary interest, since it is the use of the terms בית אב and משפחה, as well as other kinship expressions, which, preserved by the tradition, form the basis for our analysis. We can determine how the tradents understood these terms, but we have no way of knowing what their meaning was in prenational times.

[27] See Mendenhall 1958.

[28] Gottwald 1979A:270-276.

[29] Lemche 1972:109f.

a considerable period of time had elapsed between the two censuses, so of course there are more Israelites).

It is correct, as noted by de Geus, that some of the names in the Manasseh section (Num 26, 29-34) can be traced back to the period of the Monarchy, in particular to the period around 800, on the basis of information in the ostraca from Samaria[30]. However, this only gives us information about two facts: first, that there was some continuity in the Israelite pattern of settlement, as mentioned by de Geus, and, second, that at least some of the materials in Num 26 which have been reworked by P reflect actual settlement patterns. These, however, are from the period of the *Monarchy*, and we have no indication as to whether this information may be traced back to the pre-national period. On the other hand, it is clear (and if we did not have other evidence to this effect, Jdg 6,15 would be sufficient by itself) that אלף signified an organizational level in the Israelite society. Pedersen points out that the root אלף I means "to be on a confidential footing with"[31], while Noth emphasizes the connection with the figure 1,000, so that אלף must be considered an old designation for an Israelite tribe in sections of 1,000 men each[32]. This suggestion has no logical implications in Jdg 6,15, since how on earth could the group-of-one thousand to which Gideon belongs be smaller than others? Gottwald is probably right that at a later time the roots אלף I and אלף III must have become confused in, for example, David's military system. He points to parallel occurrences in Ugaritic and Akkadian; Akkadian lim, "one thousand", is usually held to derive from the same root as Northwest Semitic לאם. However this may be, it appears certain that אלף signifies a higher level of organization than בית אב in Jdg 6,15 (but not necessarily elsewhere). However, it is by no means certain that it is the same level as משפחה.

This means that בית אב may be used of all levels below the level of the אלף, or, perhaps, of the משפחה. In the same chapter it appears (v 11) that Gideon's family is an extended one, as Gideon is occupied in cultivating the lands of his father. Nevertheless, in Jdg 6,27 the "lineage" meaning of בית אב is possibly better expressed than is the case in v 15, since v 27 distinguishes between two groups in Ophrah, namely the בית אב of Gideon and the rest of the inhabitants of the town. Of course, it is conceivable that the text merely means that Gideon has reason to fear for the reactions of his father and brothers, that is, for a punishment that is confined to the framework of his family. But there is also the possibility that "father's house" in Jdg 6,27 refers to Gideon's lineage; in this case the implication would be that Gideon has reason to fear the consequences of his actions with respect to his relationship to his lineage. If this is correct, then it is certain that Gideon's lineage is not identical with the population of the town of Ophrah, since a distinction is made between his lineage and the rest of the town. It is quite another matter whether or not the rest of the town belongs to Gideon's maximal lineage (or clan), that is, Abiezer, but this possibility might be taken to suggest that the Israelite tribes (or at least Manasseh) possessed both lineages and maximal lineages. However, the materials in Jdg 6,27 do not permit any certain conclusion on this point.

It is clearer in other passes in the Gideon narratives that Gideon's lineage,

---

[30] See de Geus 1976:138-139; cf. Noth 1927:164-172 (and the map on p.177); cf. also Lemche 1972:109-110.

[31] Pedersen 1958:37-38. In this way the term אלף seems to have a number of connotations in common with Arabic *luzūm*, which in Kufr el-Ma in fact composed the circle of "close consultation" within a lineage (see above, p. 176 and 38n.).

[32] Noth 1950A:103.

rather than his extended family, is intended, irrespective of whether this unit is governed by Gideon or his father. I am referring a Jdg 8,27, in which the ephod becomes a snare for Gideon and his house. If it were not for the fact that this passage is to be understood in the light of the succeeding story of Abimelech, Jdg 8,27 could well be taken to refer to Gideon's extended family. However, it is obvious that this passage is transitionary between the narratives of Gideon and Abimelech, and also that Abimelech's adventure first begins after the death of Gideon, so that it must be Gideon's descendants who are affected by the "snare", that is, his lineage, since, of course, Gideon's extended family would have disbanded at his death. The reference to Jerubba'al's house (i.e., Gideon's) in Jdg 8,35 must be understood analogously. In extension of this, Gideon's kin are referred to in Jdg 9,2, but in terms which imply dynastic tendencies within the line, since the sons of Jerubba'al are said to be 70 in number. This figure could well be symbolic like other similar figures in the Book of Judges. Nevertheless, the leading conception is obviously that Gideon (Jerubba'al) founded a dynasty which was subsequently destroyed by Abimelech (just as the later kings of the Northern Kingdom founded dynasties which were annihilated by usurpers; it is possible that the stories of Gideon and Abimelech are intended to serve as the paradigm for this process).

To mention another dynastic line, there is no question but that "David's house" signifies David's lineage, and it is conceivable that already the designation "Saul's house" is not used of his extended family, but of his descendants understood as his lineage, the members of which trace their origins to Saul. It is an entirely natural development of the basic concept of the lineage system that in a monarchy in which the king is selected from the circle of his lineage, this unit develops into a dynasty whose membership will be much more extensive than that of ordinary lineages, and yet retains the genealogical principle of the lineage.

One interesting feature of Abimelech's revolt against his paternal line is his use of the affinal ties to his mother's kin, since it is with the aid of the משפחת בית אבי אמו (Jdg 9,1) that he carries out his "coup". There is no reason to believe that the text merely suggests the moral support of Abimelech's mother's kin. The coup which Abimelech is prepared to launch requires a sizeable support group, and in fact it is this role that is played by Abimelech's mother's lineage which dwells at Shechem. Although the texts condemn Abimelech's actions and describe them as unnatural, they can hardly be said to be surprising for anyone who has studied family politics in the Middle East. It is precisely the relationship to one's mother's kin that provides an alternative to someone who is at odds with his own, and we have descriptions of the ways people pursuing their own political ends have manipulated their affinal kin to obtain them[33].

---

[33] Peters 1976 (cf. also other studies by Peters of corresponding meanings of affinal ties, such as 1965:145 and 1967:274ff.) is instructive in this connection.

Thus Jdg 6-9 confirms the fact that בית אב may be used of both the extended family and the lineage, as in the patriarchal narratives. However, there is no information concerning the existence of nuclear families alongside of extended families in the Gideon traditions. It will accordingly be necessarily to unearth some other examples to this end. The first narrative which will prove useful in this connection is the Samson story, and within this cycle especially the account in Jdg 14. According to Jdg 13 the familial relations in the house of Manoah are decidedly those of a nuclear family, as the family consists of the husband, Manoah, and his wife, but there are no children until Samson arrives on the scene. When Samson begins to explore the world a bit, he always devotedly returns to his father and mother, which is to say, to his nuclear family. On one occasion we are simply informed that he returns to his father's house, in Jdg 14,19. In this connection בית אביה can scarcely mean anything but "father and mother", who are in fact mentioned in Jdg 14,2 and 14,9. In other words, there is no suggestion in Jdg 14 that Samson's family was anything but nuclear.

It could be objected that this argument is weakened by Jdg 16, 31, which relates that Samson's brothers and כל בית אביו participated in his funeral. If this is to be harmonized with Jdg 14, one could stress that other brothers were born to the family after Samson was born, and that they have no role in the story until Jdg 16,31. Alternatively, one might simply postulate that in Jdg 16,31 אח is used in the extended sense of "kinsman", without being more closely specified. One could also point out that the notice in Jdg 16,31 is unique in the Samson narratives from a traditio-historical point of view, since it is a "Judge-notice" like those describing other Judges such as the lists of "small" Judges in Jdg 10,1-5; 12,(7)8-15. However, in terms of contents there is no difficulty reading Jdg 16,31 in connection with the rest of the Samson traditions, since the notice informs us that Samson's adventures have taken place over a considerable period of time; thus Samson's father Manoah has been dead for quite some time when Samson joins him. Thus in Jdg 16,31 בית אב does not refer to Samson's family, but to his lineage, to which his brothers also belong.

A narrative in the Book of Ruth also confirms the existence of nuclear families which are parts of a greater kinship system. The family which left Bethlehem in order to settle in Moab consisted of a husband and wife and their two unmarried sons. It never managed to develop into an extended family because of the early death of Elimelech. Later, both sons contracted marriages, but since the father was out of the picture one would at most be able to say that a social unit was created which consisted of two nuclear families, both of which were childless, and in which the mother of the male members resided as a widow. When Naomi returned to Bethlehem, however, the family had ceased to exist, since only the mother and one of her daughters-in-law was left. Therefore we should expect that the two widows would settle down in Naomi's familial circle, that is, that they would seek the shelter of her paternal lineage. However, the plot in the story maintains that unlike what seems to have been normal practice the two women wished to remain within the kin of Naomi's deceased husband in order to re-establish their own family through new marital connections with this family. With respect to kinship terminology the Book of Ruth tells us nothing new, but it does show that the nuclear family was well known in Israelite society. In the OT the emphasis is rather on extended rather than nuclear families, but, as mentioned above, this has to do with the fact that the figures we encounter in most of the narratives are great men. Even today one discovers a preference for the extended family in the Near East, since it represents the ideal of maintaining solidarity between a father and his sons, and between and among the sons themselves, even though it is universally recognized that in practice this ideal is only occasionally realizable.

These considerations permit us to suggest some conclusions concerning the domestic cycle in ancient Israel. A number of references in the narratives studied above suggest that neolocal residence was not out of the question. Esau abandoned the house of Jacob after his marriage, just as Elimelech took Naomi with him to Moab and thereby separated off from his father's family. Some of the dubious cases mentioned above may also be explained by the difference between ideology (i.e., the ideal of the extended family) and praxis (the frequent occurrence of new residence for married sons). It is conceivable that one such example is the disagreements between Gen 45,10-11 and Gen 45,18. In Gen 45,10-11 Jacob's family is described as an extended family consisting of fathers, sons, and sons' wives, while in Gen 45,18 we apparently have to do with Jacob's family on the one hand and on the other the nuclear families of his various sons, understood as independent units. It is possible that a number of passages in the OT in which the extended family appears in reality have to do with nuclear families, although the tradents of these materials have described them as if the familial fellowship has not come to an end.

In this connection it would be appropriate to examine the conception that it is of vital importance that a man's name survives in Israel. We encountered this notion as the guiding theme of the Book of Ruth, with obvious allusions to the narrative of Judah and Tamar in Gen 38.

It is remarkable that the subsequent genealogy actually contradicts the intentions of Ruth's and Naomi's strategy with respect to Boaz, since it is not the name of Ruth's husband and Naomi's son that is preserved through the birth of Obed, but rather Boaz' name that is transmitted. We have no information as to the precise connection between Boaz and Elimelech, except that they belonged to the same מִשְׁפָּחָה. It would be wrong simply to reckon Boaz as a brother of Elimelech on the grounds that the genealogy only describes a single line. Instead, it is more likely that we have to do with the phenomenon anthropologists call "telescoping" and manipulation of a family tree[34]. In constructing a genealogy for David's ancestry, it was described as a single line without noting a break between Salmon and Boaz or, alternatively, between Boaz and Obed. We could discuss this genealogy at great length without being able to arrive at any assured result. For that matter, it might be based on a genealogy deriving from the period of greatness of the Davidic dynasty, that is, the Monarchy, but it could just as easily be a post-exilic construction. The genealogy in Ruth 4,18-22 may well have been added secondarily to the book as a result of confusion between the Boaz mentioned in the Book of Ruth with the Boaz in the genealogy of

---

[34] See also Wilson 1977:33-36.

David in 1 Chron 2,11f., as E. Würthwein has suggested[35]. On the other hand, it would not be unreasonable to suppose that the Book of Ruth has survived only because of the link between it and the house of David. Furthermore, if David really was of Moabite descent (if only partially), this would explain why he took his family to safety from king Saul in Moab (1 Sam 22,3), a point worth noting[36]. According to Ruth 4,18-22 (and Gen 38,30), David was an eleventh generational descendant of Judah. If this level of tradition uses a chronology like the official one found elsewhere in the OT, then at least eight hundred years will have elapsed between Judah and David. There is no doubt but that the intervening nine generations are all too few[37].

There is also a clear allusion to Deut 25,5-10, which contains regulations concerning punitive measures to be used against anyone who refuses to honor his obligation to "redeem" the name of a deceased relative. The same idea is also at the root of the passages concerning the daughters of Zelophehad (Num 27 and 36). Although it is usual to do so, these passages cannot be used to fill out our understanding of extended families in Israel. Rather, it is quite logical that they aim at the preservation of nuclear units. If a man is the patriarch of an extended family, there would ordinarily be no problem connected with the preservation of his name, since his married sons would also be members of the family. Accordingly, the rule in question (including the injunction to perform the duties of Levirate marriage) cannot be used as a criterium applicable to the extended family. On the other hand, if a married son is still a member of his paternal extended family, then it is irrelevant to the survival of the extended family in question whether or not the son begets any heirs, as long as their are other living sons in the family. As long as the extended family exists, it is not a son's name that is important, but the father's. Thus if this custom has any meaning, it is that it points to the existence of nuclear and neolocal families, since it is the nuclear family that is threatened by extinction when the father of the house dies without having left sons behind him. Such a nuclear family simply ceases to be an autonomous unit.

In Gen 38, when Judah gives his second son to his daughter-in-law Tamar, the reason is perhaps that because Tamar had formed an autonomous nuclear family via her first marriage Judah attempts to rescue his deceased son's nuclear family by providing it with offspring with the help of his second son. The reason Judah does not have congress with Tamar after having fathered a son with her is probably that the son in question is not Judah's in the first instance, but his deceased son's child. Thus Tamar and her son form their own nuclear family, and it would be impossible for Judah to marry his daughter-in-law without dissolving this family. Although this narrative does not permit us to say anything about the frequency of nuclear families, understood as neolocal segments of extended families, our observations nevertheless suggest that a domestic cycle was well known in Israel in which married sons abandoned their paternal families and established families of their own.

---

[35] Würthwein 1969:24.
[36] Cf. Gerleman 1965:7-9; cf. Stoebe 1973:406-407.
[37] Cf. Rudolph 1962:71f.

§ 2

מִשְׁפָּחָה: Clan, Maximal Lineage, Lineage

It is clear the the traditional literature of the OT employs a very loose terminology to describe the lower levels of the society, since "house" and "father's house" are used indiscriminately of the nuclear family, the extended family, and also of the higher kinship group, the lineage. Therefore in this section it will be our goal to attempt to delimit the term בֵּית אָב with respect to its "upward" orientation to the מִשְׁפָּחָה. מִשְׁפָּחָה has been held by virtually all scholars to be the Israelite definition of the clan; they have generally based this view on Jos 7,17, the narrative of Achan's theft and punishment. In this narrative the lot-casting procedure follows the order of tribe, מִשְׁפָּחָה, בֵּית אָב, and finally the man himself (and his immediate family)[38]. מִשְׁפָּחָה is thus held to signify the level between the family and the tribe, and according to the classical sociological descriptions (above all Durkheim's), this level is identified with that of the clan. However, no scholar has troubled to define precisely what he meant by the word "clan". As recent a scholar as de Geus simply announces that the father's house must have some kind of superstructure, since it is unable to survive by itself, and that this superstructure is the מִשְׁפָּחָה. He never seems to ask whether this conclusion is as simple as all that, and in reality he merely says that there is a general consensus on this issue. De Geus also dismisses the apparently vague borders between the terms בֵּית אָב and מִשְׁפָּחָה as inessential to the understanding and description of the Israelite clan and its functions[39].

Gottwald's definition of the מִשְׁפָּחָה takes a different pathway, but it is dependent on his incorrect definition of the clan. According to Gottwald, מִשְׁפָּחָה is to be rendered *"protective association of families"* or of *"extended families"*. It is composed of related persons, and with respect to residence it is a unit[40]. However, Gottwald does not trouble to argue at any length for this definition, unless we should be inclined to accept his description of the instition of the גֹּאֵל as a sufficient basis for his understanding of the term מִשְׁפָּחָה[41].

---

[38] De Geus indeed says that "It is a widespread misunderstanding that Josh. 7,16-17 provides a realistic and reliable picture of the social organization of the ancient Israelites" (1976:133). Thus it is really quite surprising that he later states that "In reality ancient Israel only had the tripartition: extended family-clan-people" (1976:146). In spite of the fact that de Geus interprets בֵּית אָב as "extended family" and speaks of the people, he nevertheless retains an extremely undifferentiated model of Israelite social structure which in the main is not different from a number of earlier studies, such as, e.g., that of Causse 1937:15-31. As mentioned previously, the tripartition in question was already to be found in Durkheim 1922:149ff. However, Durkheim's theory-formation was based on ethnographic materials which were anything but satisfactory. With respect to his understanding of ancient peoples, Durkheim was in fact influenced by just such a passage as Jos 7 (cf. Durkheim 1922:153f. and 154n.).

[39] de Geus 1976:137.

[40] Gottwald 1979A:257.

[41] See Gottwald 1979A:262-267.

It is clear that in his discussion of the institution of the גאל that Gottwald has overlooked Jer 32, in which Jeremiah fulfils his גאל responsibilities with respect to a family property in Anathoth. In this case the property in question is a plot of land which belonged to his paternal uncle, and which accordingly is the community property of Jeremiah's lineage. Jer 32 bears witness perhaps more clearly than any other passage in the OT that the lineage system still existed in Israel after the formation of the state in spite of the fact that the political significance of the tribes had declined after the creation of a central authority. This provides clear evidence that the lineage institution was able to survive independently of the tribes. This remains the case in the Near East today, as we have seen, and it appears to have been the case in ancient Israel.

It is conceivable that we have another example of the significance of the family group for the individual in the story of Naboth's vineyard, since in this narrative Naboth refuses to sell his property because he had inherited it from his forfathers (1 Kgs 21,3)[42]. Thus the passages in Leviticus and Numbers which touch on the institution of the גאל need not necessarily reflect circumstances in pre-monarchical times (in casu Lev 25 and Num 27 and 36). These sections may easily be understood as retrojections of practices which obtained during the Monarchy or later. On the other hand, it is very likely indeed that similar regulations will have been in force even in pre-national Israel, since the institution in question is, so to speak, an integral part of any society which is constructed on the lineage principle[43].

The apparent overlap between בית אב and משפחה is dismissed; moreover, בית אב tends to be used metaphorically[44]. However, most scholars, including both Gottwald and de Geus, are prone to believe that the משפחה was the most important social and political group in the Israelite tribal system in the pre-monarchical period.

Thus it is quite surprising that in reality this term does not often figure in the OT. Of course, if we open a concordance we will discover that the word is used a considerable number of times, but this statistical consideration is deceptive since a great many of the occurrences of the word are in genealogies such as the one in Num 26, in which the term appears 92 times, or in the description of the apportionment of the land in Jos 13-21, where it appears 41 times. In the Book of Genesis משפחה only figures 12 times, of which half are in the genealogies in chapters 10 and 36. These statistics show that the vast majority of the occurrences of the term are confined to a single type of literature, and also that it tends to appear in bunches. In other words, משפחה is only used in a very limited number of passages. We find some examples in Gen 24, 38.40(41). Isolated occurrences also occur in Gen 12,3 and 28,14 (which, however, quotes 12,3), and in Gen 8,19 where, however, משפחה distinguishes taxonomically between the various types of animals in the Ark. In the Book of Exodus the term is used in a bunch in chapter 6 (a genealogy); otherwise it only occurs once more, in Exod 12,21. The term is concentrated in Lev 25 in connection with the regulations governing the jubilee, but otherwise occurs only in Lev 20,5. Indeed, this is the case with the entire Pentateuch, but this situation also obtains outside of the Pentateuch. I have already referred to Jos 13-21, but the term displays the same uneven distribution in the Book of

---

[42] Thus Gray 1964:389.

[43] Cf. Lemche 1976:46-51, where it is pointed out that there are some survivals of such early regulations in the Priestly fiction known as the Yobel Year or Jubilee.

[44] Gottwald 1979A:287-288.

Judges. מִשְׁפָּחָה occurs 8 times in the Book of Judges, of which four occurrences are in chapters 17-18 and designate the tribe of Dan. It is attached once more to Dan in Jdg 13,2. If we follow the use of מִשְׁפָּחָה forwards from the Book of Judges, we discover that it occurs sporadically, with occasional bunches such as those in Zech 12 and 1 Chron, especially chapter 6. מִשְׁפָּחָה occurs fairly frequently in the Book of Jeremiah, but in only a single case (Jer 3,14) does it have anything to do with the theme of this chapter. It never occurs in the Book of Isaiah, once in Ezekiel, twice in Amos, once in Michah, but never in Hosea, Jonah, Obadiah, and so forth. It should also be added that if we ignore the uses of the term in genealogies we discover that some of the remaining examples prove to be metaphors for nations or peoples[45].

Gottwald discusses the use of the term מִשְׁפָּחָה as a designation for the tribe of Dan in Jdg 17-18 and concludes that although in a technical sense Dan was a שֵׁבֶט, political circumstances had reduced it to the status of a מִשְׁפָּחָה[46]. This is merely one possibility among several; another would be to relate the use of מִשְׁפָּחָה in conjunction with Dan in Jdg 17-18 (and Jdg 13,2) to the presence of only a single מִשְׁפָּחָה in Dan in Num 26,42-43 (which Gottwald claims to be the result of a lack of information by P about Dan). Since Jdg 17-18 are part of the post-deuteronomistic addition to the Book of Judges (Jdg 17-21, eventually 13-21)[47], it is possible that the use of מִשְׁפָּחָה-in the Dan section in Jdg 17-18 reflects P's lack of knowledge about the tribe of Dan, which at the time of the incorporation of Jdg 17-18 into the deuteronomistic Book of Judges can hardly have existed as an independent tribe. A third explanation could simply be that the Danites in fact used מִשְׁפָּחָה rather than שֵׁבֶט or מַטֶּה of their tribe as well as of its primary sections.

Although this survey of the use of מִשְׁפָּחָה in the OT has been of some value, a literary critical evaluation of the materials in which the term predominates shows that these are mainly lists, and that the provenance of these lists is Priestly. Nor should we forget that back in the heyday of literary criticism large sections of Jos 13-21 were also thought to be of Priestly origin[48]. Our survey also shows that מִשְׁפָּחָה only rarely occurs in isolated contexts in which the term figures as some sort of kinship term. Scholars have most often taken their starting point in lists such as the one in Num 26, plus the scheme of "tribe-clan-family" which seems to emerge from Jos 7,14. On the basis of these considerations, scholars have arrived at a particular understanding of the term מִשְׁפָּחָה, which they have then subsequently forced onto what might be called the practical examples of the use of the term in daily speech. This is a methodologically dubious procedure, since the stereotypical use of מִשְׁפָּחָה in the lists need not by any means be an expression of anything other than a Priestly systematization of the kinship units which has no relation to the sociological contents

---

[45] E.g., Gen 10,5.18.20.31.32; 12,3; 28,14; Jer 1,15; 2,4; 10,25; 25,9; Amos 3,1.2; Nahum 3,4; Zech 12,12; 14,17.18; Pss 96,7; 22,28.

[46] Gottwald 1979A:249-251.

[47] See Noth 1943:54n, and cf. already Wellhausen 1963:227-233. Further, Weiser 1966:141-143; Eissfeldt 1965:242 (although Eissfeldt never accepted Noth's hypothesis about the Deuteronomistic Historical Work). Finally, see Noth 1962A.

[48] See Eissfeldt 1922:227*244* and 75-79.

the term once possessed. It should also be noted that the Priestly traditions are reluctant to employ the term בית אב, which is not normally used in the Priestly genealogies and census lists. In other words, unless we can determine with certainty the level within the Israelite tribel system to which the actual "living" usage of the term משפחה refers, its use in the Priestly traditions and in the allocation-of-land traditions in the Book of Joshua must be regarded as secondary in relation to the original meaning of the term. It is accordingly necessary to isolate the examples which occur in the narrative parts of the OT in which the term is unambiguously used to refer to a social unit.

The first complex of examples to be studied is in Gen 24, in which figures three times (vv 38.40.41). Abraham's command to his servant in Gen 24,38 entails that the latter is to seek a bride for Isaac among Abraham's בית אב, in his משפחה. In v 40 the sequence is reversed, and in v 41 we encounter only the term משפחה. Neither בית אב nor משפחה is used in Gen 24,4, the passage in which the command is originally issued, but מולדת (and ארץ). The parallelization between בית אב and משפחה is absolutely worth considering, but this is usually rejected because of preconceived notions as to the significance of משפחה which assume that the term refers to a higher level of integration than does בית אב[49]. Thus it is maintained that Abraham's servant is told to seek a bride in his master's בית אב, which is a part of Abraham's משפחה. It is conceivable that this is the intended meaning, but it is nevertheless impossible to rule out that the two terms may instead by synonymous. משפחה does not figure elsewhere in the patriarchal narratives.

There are other passages in the OT in which משפחה occurs in conjunction with בית אב. The first such example, Jdg 9,1, was mentioned previously. Abimelech goes to his משפחת בית אבי אמו, a phrase which may be compared with the characterization of Shimei as belonging to the משפחת בית שאול, 2 Sam 16,5. While the first example may be taken to suggest that Abimelech addresses himself to the clan or lineage of his mother in Shechem for assistance (meaning that the expression "the משפחה of his mother's father's house" is to be rendered "the משפחה to which his mother's father's house belongs"), a corresponding rendering of 2 Sam 16,5 is more problematical. Does Shimei belong to the house of Saul or not? If one takes the phrase to mean, "Shimei belong to the משפחה of which the house of Saul is also a member", then he is a distant relation of Saul's kin, that is, he does not belong to the house of Saul. On the other hand, if we translate "Shimei belongs to the משפחה which consists of Saul's house", then in terms of kinship Shimei is rather close to Saul himself. Both possibilities are grammatically possible, as is also apparent when we consider the juxtaposition of משפחה and מטה in Num 36, 6.8.12. Here we read משפחת מטה אביהם (with variants), "(the daughters') father's tribe's משפחה"; here

---

[49] Cf. de Geus 1976:137n, against Pedersen 1958:35. In close agreement with Pedersen is also De Vaux 1971B:228.

מטה is necessarily higher ranked than is משפחה.

At this point, we have not yet succeeded in proving that בית אב and משפחה are, or can be, synonyms, even though the materials we have studied so far do not rule out the possibility of their semantic coincidence. Thus our next move will be to examine a number of examples in which משפחה is used by itself. These examples may be cited as an independent collection, since they may be understood as a counterpart to Jos 7,14ff, which lists the sequence of שבט, משפחה, and בית (אב) and Achan himself. I am referring to Deut 29,17, 1 Sam 9,21 and 1 Sam 10,21. In the sermon against idolatry in Deut 29,15ff the units which are envisaged as potentially falling into apostasy are a man or a woman, a משפחה, or a tribe. בית אב has either been left out, or else the text does not acknowledge it as a unit discernible from the משפחה. The same phenomenon is observable in two other texts. In 1 Sam 9,21 Saul describes himself as a Benjaminite from a משפחה among the משפחות of Benjamin. Here, too, the "father's house" is not mentioned. 1 Sam 10,21, however, is more decisive for our purposes. Here lots are cast to determine who is to be king in Israel. First the lot falls on the tribe of Benjamin, then on the משפחה of Matri, and finally on Saul. The closest parallel to this passage was precisely the lot-casting in Jos 7,14ff, although the occasion was undeniably less positive. However, in Jos 7,14, בית אב appears between משפחה and the person in question, Achan.

Naturally, it would be possible to explain the absence of בית אב from these three passages as the result of a desire for brevity which resulted in the omission of one of the stages. However, one would be equally justified in claiming that in these passages משפחה represents the same level as do בית אב and משפחה in Jos 7,14. If the latter assumption is correct, then it will have been possible to refer to any of several levels within Israelite social structure as a משפחה. I have shown above how בית אב is used of the steps leading from the family to the lineage; thus it would be possible to formulate a hypothesis to the effect that משפחה covers the areas of the lineage and the maximal lineage. However, none of our examples suggest that there were clans in ancient Israel which were definable as משפחות. Indeed, it is doubtful whether the OT materials offer us the possibility to decide whether there were clans in Israel, or whether the highest level of integration below that of the tribe was the maximal lineage, perhaps supplemented by the sub-tribe, or *moiety*. Our difficulties in this respect have to do with the fact that we have defined the clan as a descent group which has no fixed genealogy. The pervasive OT mania for describing the entire Israelite nation within the compass of a single genealogical system might lead one to think that clans did not exist in the Israelite system. However, when we consider that this genealogical scheme is no doubt the result of a secondary and fictive systematization – no matter when it may have been composed – then it is clear that the genealogical tables round about in the work do not offer conclusive evidence of the genealogical recollections of the average Israelite.

R.R. Wilson has dealt with the genealogical narrative in Gen 29,31-30,24; 35,16-20[50]. The genealogy in Gen 29,31-30,24 cannot be separated from the rest of J's narratives about Jacob and his wives, since it has been assembled with the others in mind. Nevertheless, Wilson feels that the basis for the list of Jacob's sons is older than J, since, or so he maintains, these lists ultimately derive from the conclusion of the period of the Judges. His argument for this position is based on the concept of the favorization of the sons of Rachel, which he takes to be unthinkable in a system developed during the reign of David, who was a Judaean. I do not find this argument persuasive. Wilson himself is well aware of the political aspects of the twelve-tribe genealogy; thus he should be aware as well that any preference given to the great central-Palestinian tribes in a genealogy worked out during the reigns of David or Solomon would have considerable pro-pagandistic value for the relationship between Judah and these tribes. It would have facilitated the inclusion of these tribes in the political system created by David. Furthermore, Wilson underrates the significance of the traditional tribal structure after the introduction of the Monarchy, as is indicated by his understanding of the lineage structure[51]. According to Wilson, this structure lost its political relevance after the introduction of the Monarchy, for which reason it was impossible to establish "segmentary genealogies" (i.e., genealogies which reflect the existence of a segmentary society) after the emergence of the Monarchy. This view cannot possibly be correct; as we have seen previously, there are numerous examples which suggest that the lineage structure continued to play a part. This part will not have been at the national-politi-cal level (at least not normally, and in any case only for the lineages of individual great figures), but at the local level, and it will have continued to do so even after Israel became a monarchy. As we have also seen, lineage structure has cheerfully persisted in the contemporary centralized states of the Middle East.

If one decides to define the מִשְׁפָּחָה as a social solidarity group which encom-passes familial property (the גֹּאֵל institution), blood revenge, or cult, it is still impossible to determine whether the term refers to clans or lineages, since in a society without clans the lineage can perform all of these functions[52]. There is accordingly no reason to devote more time to this question, although it will be necessary to examine briefly the kinship designations and the perikopes dealing with the allocation of the land in order to find out how the terms בֵּית אָב and מִשְׁפָּחָה are used in these passages.

The natural point of departure for an investigation of these late genealogical materials is Num 26, if for no other reason than that a high percentage of the occurrences of מִשְׁפָּחָה are to be found here.

It would be a methodological error of some dimensions to regard P's lists in Numbers as evidence about tribal structure in the pre-national period. These records tell us mainly some-thing about how P conceived of the organization of the tribes. Thus it would be incorrect to reason on the basis of the use of מִשְׁפָּחָה, which occurs in the Pentateuch mainly in P-sections, plus its continued use in Joshua (especially chs. 13-21), Judges, and Samuel and so conclude that the reason the term occurs frequently in these parts of the OT and only rarely elsewhere (and later) is that the clan (lineage) system fell into desuetude after the introduction of the Monarchy. It would be more appropriate to investigate the scarcity of the term in the following parts of the OT on the basis of the horizon which characterizes these works. This horizon proves to be the con-ception of the whole nation as a single (or dual) centralized society (societies). Moreover, the

---

[50] Wilson 1977:184ff.

[51] Wilson 1977:194.

[52] In 2 Sam 14,7, the מִשְׁפָּחָה is referred to as a blood-revenge group, while in 1 Sam 20,6.29 it is a cultic unit. On the latter aspect, see Gottwald 1979A:282-284.

interest in these works is concentrated on the leadership level, while the tradents often do not concern themselves with the local units[53].

It is furthermore interesting that it is P who is so interested in lists of membership, since Oriental traditional societies are virtually notorious for their aversion to censuses (note, for example, the uncertainty concerning the population of Saudi Arabia even now). The OT also records one particular tradition which powerfully reflects this attitude, namely the narrative of David's census in 2 Sam 24, which had such catastrophic consequences[54]. How on earth, then, could anyone ask us to believe that the census lists in Numbers date from the sojourn of the Israelite nomads in the desert? Instead, everything suggests that here, too, we have proof that P's intentions do not correspond to the norms of ancient Israel.

The task assigned to Israel's leaders is to take a census of the people לבית אבתם, according to Num 26,2. This is the sole reference to the בית אב in Num 26; subsequently, in conjunction with the census itself we encounter only the משפחה. Logically, this suggests that a census which is to be taken by father's houses actually takes place by משפחות. Clearly, this means that if the information in the Book of Numbers is to be taken to support a definition of משפחה, the only permissible conclusion is that משפחה represents the same basic unit as בית אב does. Moreover, from a sociological perspective it is irrelevant whether or not there are traditio-historical or literary critical reasons to excise לבית אבתם in v 2 from the context in the introduction to the chapter.

According to Noth[55], Num 25,19-26,4a. is to be understood as the introduction of the final tion to the earlier tribal list in Num 26,4b-51. As mentioned above, I see no reason why the materials in question should be earlier than the Israel of the Monarchy at the earliest. Moreover, these materials seem to be of a very heterogeneous nature. We have already seen that in the Manasseh section (Num 26,29-34) a number of names represent localities which are presumably villages or small towns. Gilead, which also figures in the Manasseh section, is either a regional name or, more probably, a tribe which fissioned at some point from either Manasseh or Machir and so became a new tribe, Manasseh. The daughters Zelophehad also stand for localities, as we are informed by the Samaritan ostraca nrs. 44; 50; 43; 45-47: Noah and Hoglah. Nor can Tirzah be legitimately separated from the city of the same name (*Tell Fara'*). The meaning of the remaining names in the section is uncertain. In at least some cases we obviously have to do with town or village names, such as, for example, Elon in the Zebulon section in Num 26,26[56]. We cannot be sure in other cases. The two משפחה in Issachar, that is, Tola and Puah (Num 26,3), can hardly be separated from the lesser Judge, Tola ben Puah in Jdg 10,1. Thus it is conceivable that they represent two family groups named after these two personages. The question, however, is then, why two משפחה? Conversely, if these two משפחה are original, it is conceivable that Tola ben Puah was a secondary personification of these family names; this possibility would then have serious consequences for the understanding of the Judge list in Jdg 10,1-5. The other names in the Issachar section, Shimron and Jashub in Num 26,24 may well be family names, but they might just as easily refer to localities. Of course, it is possible that Shimron is identical with the Shamir mentioned in Jdg 10,2, but this would not aid our understanding of Jdg 10,1-2, since Tola ben Puah was buried in Shamir. We cannot devote more space to this issue here, but it is at any rate obvious that P's materials in Num 26 are not homogeneous. In my opinion, this suggests that these materials can scarcely have been collected prior to P.

---

[53] This is particularly directed against Andersen 1969:37.

[54] Cf. also Hertzberg 1965:339, who emphasizes that to the author of this section there was no need to explain the criticism of the census; it was *"selbstverständlich"*.

[55] Noth 1966B:178 (cf. Noth 1930:122-132; 1948:232f.).

[56] On the minor Judge Elon, see Lemche 1972:85f.

Both לבית אבתם and משפחה in the rest of Num 26 belong to the Priestly framework around the census materials presented in the chapter. The organizational level which is the basis of Num 26 is, incidentally, confined to the tribe and its primary sections, which in sociological terms means the sub-tribe or *moiety*. In isolated cases segments of these units are referred to, while the lower levels are not included as independent units in the census. For this reason it may be maintained that Num 26 implies that the Priestly systematization did no more than to identify the בית אב with the משפחה; furthermore, it uses these designations only of the highest levels of an Israelite tribe. I propose therefore that, like the Deuteronomists in Jos 7, P has systematized the kinship terms. In other words, P has adopted traditional terms and fixed their semantic fields, possibly under the influence of the Deuteronomistic use of the tripartite scheme of משפחה, בית אב, and שבט It is possible that P's use of משפחה is based on earlier usage, but it could just as easily be the result of a secondary isolation of the respective terms from their historical use in earlier Israelite society. To mention an example, scholars have been given reason to pause by the fact that the משפחה of Saul, which is called the משפחה of Matri in 1 Sam 10,21, is not mentioned in the Benjamin section in Num 26,38-41. Attempts have been made to avoid this difficulty by correcting משפחת המטרי in the MT to משפחת בכרי, with reference to 1 Sam 9,1, where we read בן בכרת, and בן בכרי in 2 Sam 20,1 (Sheba). However, it is clearly best to retain the reading in the MT of 1 Sam 10,21 as the *lectio difficilior*[57]. Similarly, attempts have also been made to harmonize 1 Sam 9,1 with 2 Sam 20,1 by reading בן מטרי instead of בן בכרת in 1 Sam 9,1. This, too, is a poor idea[58]. The reason Matri is not mentioned in Num 26,38-41 is either that the text simply does not penetrate to the level which Matri's משפחה belonged to, or else Matri's משפחה no longer existed when the materials in the census in Num 26 were collected.

If we turn to the other great census in Numbers, namely Num 1,1-47 (with an addition which is concerned with the tribe of Levi in vv 48-54), we do not find the same use of בית אב and משפחה as in Num 26.

Num 1 is P material in its entirety, as practically all scholars agree. Disagreements have only been concerned with the list of tribal leaders in Num 1,5-15. Noth thought to find older materials here, and held that the list was a record of the officials of the amphictyony[59]. His argument was that the forms of the names are old and can in some čases be traced back to the second millenium since, among other things, they contain elements with which we are familiar from the Mari texts[60]. In reality, Noth's method is the same as that employed by other scholars in their attempts to provide an early date for the Israelite patriarchs, and for Abraham in particular. The moments of uncertainty inherent in this approach (i.e., the confusion between a *terminus a quo* and a *terminus ad quem*) have been unravelled by Thompson[61]. Noth's argument is therefore not decisive.

---

[57] Cf. already (and correctly) Stoebe 1973:213.
[58] See Stoebe 1973:193.
[59] Noth 1966B:19-21. .
[60] See already Noth 1928:16; 1953B:229f.
[61] 1974:17-51; see especially 1974:22-36, on Abraham.

In this case Moses is instructed to take a census of the Israelites למשפחתם
לבית אבהם (Num 1,2). A group of assistants, one from each tribe, make up a
new element in the list; each is the leader of בית אביו, "his (tribe's) father's
house" (Num 1,4). These leaders are further characterized in Num 1,16 as the
נשיאי מטות אבותם ראשי אלפי ישראל. For each tribe, the census which follows is
conducted למשפחתם לבית אבתם. Unlike Num 26, this census does not penetrate
below the level of the tribe, which means that the first segments of the tribes
are not mentioned here, as they are in the other great list in Numbers. There
is therefore no difficulty with the terminology used in Num 1; the idea is
simply to ascertain the number of grown men in the various tribes according
to the various subdivisions of the tribe in question. However, the text is not
especially interested in the details of these tribal subdivisions. This disinterest
in the social structural levels below the tribal level cast a pall of unreality on the
whole narrative. It feels as if a traditional usage has settled onto a census text,
or, better, as if the text never departs from a conventionalized conceptual
world. The terms "father's house" and משפחה seem to have no connection with
reality in this section. This means that Num 1 provides us with no additional
information as to the designations בית אב and משפחה which might enable us to
delimit them with respect to one another and to the various other levels in the
Israelite tribal system.

We may perhaps be able to derive more information from Num 3,14-39, a
list of the members of the tribe of Levi which descends to the third level in the
genealogy of the tribe, that is, to the grandsons of Levi the founder of the tribe.
This level is characterized in Num 3 within the individual tribal sections as
משפחה; each is named after one of the sons of Levi, Gershon, Kohath, and
Merari. Of course, one could rightly object that this text, too, is very late and
that for this very reason it need not be anything but a secondary systematization of the kinship terms in the OT. However, the text does nevertheless cor-
roborate our earlier impression that משפחה tends to be used more of the higher
levels in society than of the lower ones. Late though they may be, the census
texts in the Book of Numbers also show that even at this stage in the formation
of Israelite traditions there was considerable uncertainty as to the demarcation
of the terms משפחה and בית אב with respect to one another. Once again, this
implies that these two terms overlap one another to a certain extent, as I have
already suggested was the case on the basis of the other occurrences of משפחה in
the OT. Our analysis of the kinship terms בית אב and משפחה has accordingly
also emphasized that Pedersen understood matters correctly when he suggested that the boundaries between them were fluid. However, our study has also
shown that the Israelite kinship system, that is, the genealogical structure of
the Israelite tribes, does not contain evidence which indicates that the Israelite
tribal society was in any way unique. Admittedly, this system no doubt contained a number of distinctive features, but then most tribal systems do so. How-

ever, none of these features is so remarkable as to warrant the conclusion that the system as a whole had a historically unique origin.

It would be appropriate to attach some further remarks to the Israelite מִשְׁפָּחָה. I feel it would be incorrect to regard this social unit, which was described above as the maximal lineage (or, possibly, the clan), as the most important social or political factor in Israelite society. The references to the מִשְׁפָּחָה in the OT are entirely too sporadic to warrant this hypothesis, even though it has been repeated so often that is has become conventional. The most important social unit was the father's house, but it is important to recall that this designation was applicable to a variety of groups, and it would be a precarious undertaking indeed to point out the one which was of signal importance to the life of the average Israelite.

However, as far as the daily life of the Israelite was concerned, his family must have been of decisive importance, whether or not it was a nuclear or extended one. All families will have been economically independent, just as they must also have able to decide for themselves with respect to the marital alliances the family decided to form.

Accordingly, the Israelite lineage must first have been of significance when irregular factors entered the picture, for example, if economic misfortune entailed the loss of lands which were ultimately the common property of the lineage, or if the society to which the lineage belonged was subjected to external political pressures, irrespective of whether these came from other groups or from a centralized political authority[62]. A lineage would also have had a role to play if conflicts arose between its members. In this event it could, for example, serve as a blood-revenge organization, as we learn from the narrative of the widow from Tekoa (2 Sam 14,5-7). Finally, it must be regarded as an established fact that the Israelite lineages dwelled together. In other words, a lineage composed a village or the population of a small town, as Pedersen recognized long ago, and as de Geus has recently reiterated[63]. There is no reason to be surprised at this fact, since it is a natural consequence of the agrarian mode of production which was established in the country already in the pre-national period. It would be unthinkable for an individual living in a society without an established central authority simply to settle down somewhere at an arbitrarily chosen spot. In the short run, he would not even be able

---

[62] Gideon's מִשְׁפָּחָה assembles precisely in the face of an external enemy, namely the Midianite nomads who apparently attempted to extort the agrarian Abiezrites. This resembles the ḫūwa practices of modern times, in which villages are liable to pay certain imposts to nomadic groups. It was long ago recognized that only the Abiezrites actually participated in the battles in question; see e.g. already Wellhausen 1894:40, as well as two recent analyses of the Gideon tradition, namely Beyerlin 1963 and Lindars 1965. See also Lemche 1972:82f.

[63] Cf. Pedersen 1958:26f.; de Geus 1976:138. However, this need not always have been the case. In the case of Simeon, the tribal area of which included portions of the Negeb, it would be most reasonable to suppose that parts of the tribe must have had a nomadic economy, which means that in many cases there was no coincidence of lineage and town.

to survive physically. It requires only a minimal knowledge of the conditions of settlement in the Near East to assure one that no one in this part of the world lives alone, whether he dwells in a tent or a house. Furthermore, there is no special settlement pattern characterizing nomads who have become peasants which would allow us to distinguish them from ordinary peasants. Therefore in ancient Israel the settlement pattern is neither an argument for or against the notion that Israel had nomadic origins[64].

Finally, my argumentation against the commonly held idea that the משפחה was the most important social and political unit in ancient Israel is also supported by the fact that this term is never used in conjunction with any of the leadership designations in the OT. To mention only the three most common leadership titles, namely נשיא, ראש, and זקן, none of these is ever defined as זקן המשפחה, ראש המשפחה, or נשיא המשפחה This is quite astonishing, when we consider how much emphasis has been placed on the importance of the Israelite משפחה in pre-monarchical times. Brief examination of the designation זקן reveals that in the OT it is much more often cited as זקן ישראל, or, more frequently, זקני ישראל, than used in any other fashion (apart from the cases in which the title is not defined more precisely)[65]. It occurs a single time in 1 Sam 2,31-32 in conjunction with בית (אב); however, here it is possible that it does not refer to a position of honor, but to a designation of age[66]. One often encounter the title זקני העיר[67]. However, any attempt to link the designations זקן and משפחה with each other is only possible if one has decided in advance of any evidence that a village is necessarily inhabited by a משפחה. However, as we have seen, this can hardly have been the case, since it is much more likely that villages were inhabited by one or more father's houses, understood as lineages.

Thus it is extremely brash of de Geus to declare that, "Like the townlets, the clan was ruled by a council of elders, the z°qēnîm"[68]. This statement assumes that the town and the family group were identical, a notion which rules out the possibility that several families may have dwelled in the same town or village. However, de Geus' reason for making this identification is merely that in Num 26 we discover the names of some משפחות which the Samaritan ostraca identify as village

---

[64] It would be more correct to stress that the settlement pattern in prenational Israel does not allow us to draw any conclusions as to Israel's origins than to emphasize – with de Geus 1976:156 and 165 – that this pattern cannot prove that Israel came from the desert. It is not completely clear whether de Geus feels that the agrarian culture in ancient Israel provides us with an argument *against* the notion of an Israelite immigration. If this is his view, it is incorrect, since, as mentioned, it speaks neither for nor against the immigration hypothesis.

[65] Examples: Exod 3,18; 12,21; 17,5; 24,1.9; Lev 9,1; Num 11,16; Deut 31,9, etc.

[66] As a result of the judgment to be visited upon Eli's בית אב, it will not again contain a זקן. This could be taken to suggest that this "father's house" will lose its autonomy and thus no longer be represented by its own זקן. However, the intention of the text could just as easily be to stress that in future no male heir of the house of Eli will live to be old, a prophecy which was fulfilled when Eli's sons fell in the battle against the Philistines (1 Sam 4,11).

[67] Examples of the זקני העיר: Deut 21,19.20; 22,15.17; Jos 20,4; Ruth 4,2.

[68] De Geus 1976:139.

or town names. Admittedly, the scholarly ancestors of de Geus' viewpoint are numerous, although their error is relatively easy to point out. On the one hand they have confused the clan and the lineage, while on the other they have confused the family and the lineage. In segmentary societies the clan is frequently on a level at which is has no daily functions, but where it is instead the lineage that comprises the framework for the live of the average family. It is possible that the official leader of a lineage was called a זקן, but it is equally conceivable that this title was applied to leaders on a wide variety of levels in the social structure. Unfortunately, the information contained in the OT on these matters is so ambiguous as to prevent any certain conclusions.

If we examine the title ראש, we discover that it is never linked with משפחה, but often with the father's house; in fact, by far the majority of the occurrences of this title associate it with the בית אב[69]. The title is sometimes ranged alongside the אלפי ישראל; however, it is by no means clear that in such contexts אלף is the same stage as the משפחה or is instead a special capacity of the משפחה (i.e., the military one). For this reason it would be unwise to associate the ראש with the משפחה. It would be far more natural to use the occurrences of ראש בית אב and ראש אלף to indicate the identity of the בית אב and the אלף[70].

There remains, finally, the much-discussed title נשיא. Like the others examined above, this title is never linked with משפחה, but it is occasionally associated with בית אב.

Numerous scholars have built imposing theses on the title נשיא; this has especially been the case since Noth proposed that the figure in question was a member of the college of officials of the amphictyony[71]. Some criticism of this view has, however, been voiced in recent times by such scholars as A.D.H. Mayes and de Geus. The latter simply states that "any person holding a high office in ancient Israel could be called nāśī"[72]. This is a reasonable conclusion on the basis of the occurrence of this title in Exod 22,27, since this text makes no effort to identify this official. Furthermore, in the OT the title is not confined to Israelites. We may adduce Gen 34,2, where Hamor the Canaanite is designated נשיא הארץ, and to Jos 13,21, which speaks of נשיאי מדין in a passage which alludes to Num 22, where וקיני מדין is used (Num 22,4.7). When נשיא is used of an Israelite, the context is Priestly in by far the majority of cases. The exceptions to this rule are, in addition to the ones mentioned previously, Ezek 19,1; 21,17.30; and 22,6, in all of which we read the formula נשיאי ישראל; 1 Kgs 8,1, where נשיא is associated with both מטה and בית אב); and in Jos 9,15.18; 22,30, where the term always appears in the form of נשיאי העדה (with possible P influence). It seems probable that we have to do once again with a situation in which P has elevated and standardized a title to give it pan-Israelite significance which in earlier times was used in a variety of nuances. P can scarcely have possessed special information concerning the meaning of the word נשיא, not even when he juxtaposes the title to בית אב, since, with the exception of Num 1,16 and 25,14 he invariably uses it of the Levites. Thus the use of the term נשיא in

---

[69] Examples Exod 6,14.25; Num 7,2; 17,18; (25,15); 31,26; 36,1; Jos 21,1; 22,14; etc. There are also 16 attestations in Chron. Most of the examples in question are found in late contexts. Of all the texts containing a juxtaposition of בית אב and ראש, a single passage clearly shows that ראש was associated with the בית אב level. See Num 36,1: ראשי האבות למשפחת בני גלעד. Naturally, this P passage subordinates the בית אב under the level of the משפחה. However, this example also shows that P associated the leadership function with the father's house rather than with the משפחה.

[70] For the juxtaposition of ראש and אלף: Num 1,16; 10,4; Jos 22,21.30. Other passages refer to the ראש המטה or to the ראש השבט. Such a ראש השבט is present in Jdg 10,18, in the form of Jephthah (in the passage in question juxtaposed with קצין).

[71] Noth 1930:151-162; cf. also Speiser 1963.

[72] Quoted from de Geus 1976:157. See also Mayes 1974:54-55.

Numbers reflects its use in Levitical circles, to which P may have belonged. However, P may also have been influenced by the phrase נשיא ישראל in Ezek 19,1; 21,17; and 22,6 (or *vice versa*).

These observations underline the hypothesis presented in this section, namely that the most important political unit in Israel was the father's house and not the משפחה. At all events, we have definitely seen that the משפחה was not a social group with any significant *political* role[73].

Excursus

Marriage in Israel

It was determined above that Israelite marital praxis was endogamous, which means that at the level of the lineage marriages were contracted within the same lineage. On the other hand, de Geus is quite right to point out that there are a number of exceptions to this rule. Nevertheless, like several other scholars, de Geus maintains that endogamy was the normal custom in Israel[74]. While I see no grounds for challenging this widespread opinion, it would be appropriate to point out that it might be more accurate to say that there was a preference for endogamous marriages, but that exogamous ones were not unheard-of. On the basis of the OT materials alone it is quite difficult to obtain more precise knowledge of Israelite practices, owing to the scarcity of the data. By this I mean that it is impossible for us to follow an individual lineage through a number of generations in order to check its marital pattern. We have no such data, with the exception of the lineage of Terah. Naturally, it would be absurd to claim that Terah's lineage was a typical example, since it was also the genealogical basis of the entire nation. On the other hand, it could be maintained that the understanding of marriage underlying the patriarchal narratives must reflect the ideology behind the marital practices of the Israelite society in which such narratives were created.

If we examine Terah's genealogical table closely (fig.1) from Terah to Ephraim and Manasseh, that is, the patriarchal line, it is clear that the table reveals a lineage or, possibly, a maximal lineage, which it illustrates over a period of about six generations. This table also shows that within this lineage there was a dominant tendency to contract marriages within the lineage. Terah's son Abram marries his half-sister Sarai according to the information in Gen 20,12. Abram's brother Nahor marries his brother's daughter Michah. Subsequently, it is to be noted, we have no information with respect to the marital practices of the line of Nahor-Haran. The names of women are not recorded, but of course this has to do with the fact that they are irrelevant to the line of Abraham/Abram.

If we turn to Abraham's line, we discover that Isaac marries his cousin's daughter Rebecca. Later on, Jacob marries Lea and Rachel, the daughters of his maternal uncle[75]. Esau, however,

---

[73] For the same reason, it is possible that scholars have been too quick to affirm that the משפחה was a local unit such as a clan, the members of which were held to be identical with the inhabitants of a given Israelite town. A very interesting confirmation of the suspicion that not all the members of a משפחה need necessarily have dwelled in one and the same place is provided by Samaria ostraca nrs. 13 and 28. These contain the name אישד, which Noth corrected to אביעזר (Noth 1927:167). It is a reasonable assumption that א<ב>יעזר was a village or a town like the other names figuring on these ostraca. However, if Gideon belonged to the משפחה of Abiezer, it is to be seen that he did not dwell in a town or village of this name, but in Ophrah. Of course, it would be out of proportion to rely too heavily on an emendation like the one mentioned here, but on the other hand the hypothesis according to which Israelite "clans" had a common dwelling place is based on no more than an antiquated sociological convention.

[74] De Geus 1976:137.

[75] It is important to realize that even if the patriarchal narratives do not provide us with

drops out of this endogamous unit thanks to his connections with Canaanite women; he soon moves his tents to other pastures. After Jacob's marriages with the daughters of Laban, the connections with the line of Nahor-Haran cease, and the scanty information we have left as to the marriages of Jacob's sons suggests exagamous connections.

In order to interpret the information provided by this scheme it will be necessary to distinguish between ideology and praxis. As far as the three most important patriarchs are concerned, that is, the tribal ancestors of the entire nation, the scheme insists that they contracted marriages which conformed with the dominant preference for endogamous alliances. However, at the next level, which is concerned with the origins of the individual tribes, the sources suggest exagamous marriages. At the level of the fifth generation we discover rather numerous exogamous marriages, as is confirmed by a study of the line of Levi. In this connection it is wholly irrelevant whether we have to do with a totally a-historical reconstruction of this line, or whether the table in fact preserves ancient information which really does reflect earlier fission within the tribe of Levi (fig.2).

Starting with the fifth generation exogamous marriages pervade the scene, even though we have little concrete information. When we arrive at the brothers Moses and Aaron, it is noteworthy that both contract marriages with women who do not belong to the tribe of Levi. Moses marries the Midianite Zipporah, while Aaron marries Elisheba, a Judaean. An important conclusion which may be drawn from these observations is that in composing their genealogical tables the tradents in question did not hesitate to include exogamous connections; this, in my opinion, means that such marriages cannot have been unknown to the tradents in the society in which they lived. This should hardly be surprising, when we consider that it is nowhere attested that marital practices must be only endogamous, even in the contemporary Middle East. Of course, this is the preferred sort of marriage, but it is not the only one. In most Near Eastern societies we find at least some exogamous marriages in spite of the dominant ideology. Therefore Israelite marital praxis will hardly have differed fundamentally from current Near Eastern praxis. Also here we discover that there is no basis for any theory according to which Israel enjoyed – from a sociological point of view – a unique status. In fact, this study proves the opposite: that in general terms Israelite society (not the society of the nation-state) may be classified as a tribal society not unlike types which are still to be found in the Middle East. However, these remarks do not imply that Israelite society was *identical* to any particular Near Eastern tribal system, but only that it belonged to a category which was not unique with respect to its basic social structure.

The law in Lev 18,6-18 (cf. also Lev 20,11-12 and Deut 27, 20.22-23) has often been interpreted as a set of norms, and even as perhaps once having been a dodecalogue which was constructed on the basis of an even older decalogue[76]. This decalogue is supposed to have regulated the sexual contacts within an Israelite extended family[77]. In other words, these regulations applied to incest. However, others such as De Vaux, Pedersen, and Gottwald find rules governing the contracting of marriage in Lev 18. They have held that these rules show that the father's house was an exogamous unit. They have dismissed exceptions to these "rules" despite the fact that these are not uncommon in the OT, on the theory that they either represent breaches of the rules or the practices of other periods[78]. De Geus has used this section to argue that the extended family was the constitutive basis of ancient Israelite society; other and earlier scholars had argued a similar position, although they generally regarded this institution, and thereby also the decalogue underlying Lev 18,7ff, as a survival of Israel's past[79].

However, this is clearly a case of incest prohibitions rather than marital regulations, since they do not inform us as to which marital relations are in fact permitted, and which are preferred. By this I mean that the preference for lineage (or clan) endogamy is not expressed in this section.

---

examples of marriages with the father's brother's daughter, the classificatory marriages with the father's brother's sister's daughter nevertheless belong to the same type.

[76] Cf. Elliger 1955, and the reconstruction in Elliger 1955:238-239.

[77] Thus Elliger 1955:240; Noth 1966A:116; Nielsen 1965:22-23; de Geus 1976:135-136; and, recently, Halbe 1980.

[78] Cf. De Vaux 1961:56; Pedersen 1958:48-49; Gottwald 1979A:302.

[79] De Geus 1976:136. On the concept of these rules as a survival from nomadic times, see emphatically Gerstenberger 1965:110-117.

We have only to do with forbidden degrees of marriage or sexual relations, and in this respect there is naturally some coincidence between incest rules and marital prohibitions. As to whether the text actually alludes to the extended family, the decisive question is the relationship between Lev 18,18 and Lev 18,6-17. We should note that Lev 18,18, which prohibits simultaneous marriages with two sisters, actually goes beyond the limits of the extended family, since unmarried sisters are unknown in patrilocal families. Thus the *forum* implied by Lev 18,6-18 is not that of the extended family, but of the exogamous circle in Israelite society. The starting point for the establishment of this circle is an *"ego"*, understood as an adult married Israelite, under consideration of his patrilineage in a single ascending and descending generation. However, the section nowhere indicates that it envisions a group that dwells together (nor is this the case even if we excise Lev 18,18 as secondary). However, it is likely that Lev 18,18 is secondary to its context, for form critical reasons, even though the scholars who have suggested this were motivated by the fact that the verse contradicts the notion of the extended family[80].

§ 3

מטה, שבט: *The Tribe*

There is no doubt that an Israelite tribe was constructed on the basis of a number of segmentation levels which ranged from sub-tribes (or *moieties*) at the top to nuclear families at the bottom. However, this does not tell us anything decisive about the principles of tribal leadership or the reasons for the solidarity of the tribe. We must reject the notion that the Israelite tribes were governed by a self-regulating egalitarian ideology, if the sources do not permit us to conclude that this sort of political organization existed. One cannot claim the authority of the predominantly Priestly data in the Tetrateuch concerning the structure and leadership of the tribes, since these data are both late and schematic and in all probability reveal little understanding of actual conditions in the pre-national period.

The materials for an investigation of leadership in Israelite tribal society are to be found in the Book of the Judges. We may be able to unearth some helpful data in the Books of Samuel, but if we go back to the Book of Joshua we must conclude that the traditions it contains have been so extensively reworked by later tradents that they offer no concrete information as to the political leadership of the tribes. I shall not reproduce here my earlier work on the period of the Judges, most of which I am still prepared to defend today[81]. There is therefore no reason to concern ourselves at any length with the individual traditions; instead, we may concentrate on the attempt to discover how the various types of leadership appear in the sources pertaining to the period of the Judges.

---

[80] See further Elliger 1955:237; Kilian 1963:23; and Halbe 1980:60ff. It is generally agreed that v 17 is to be excised from this context because of its contents alone (an exception is supposed to be K. Rabast 1948*, but I have unfortunately not been able to gain access to his work. However, see explicitly on this Feucht 1964:32).

[81] Lemche 1972:74-93.

The conclusion I arrived at in 1972, which was based on the investigation by W. Richter of the period of the Judges, was a rejection of the notion that there was more than one "type" of Judge in the Israel of the period. The Judges were renowned local figures, in spite of the fact that special traditions concerning them are preserved in only a few cases[82]. There is no information which suggests that any Judge managed to establish a dynasty, or that the narratives refer to a succession of pan-Israelite rulers[83]. Nevertheless, the traditions concerning a number of the Judges do preserve some dynastic features. Such features appear in the concluding remarks about Gideon (Jerubba'al) in Jdg 8,30, and in the notices concerning such "small" Judges as Jair (Jdg 10,4), Ibzan (Jdg 12,9), and Abdon (Jdg 12,14). These four Judges are all depicted as the fathers of a considerable number of sons, and we are additionally told in connection with Jair and Abdon that each son rode upon an ass – no doubt symbolic of rulership.

While we have no reason to believe that the various round numbers of the sons of the Judges are accurate, it is at least obvious that the tradition represents these men as possessing unusual significance. Associations are attached to them which exceed by far the expectations of the average Israelite to his own existence. Thus there is very good reason to believe that the traditions of the period of the Judges tell us about a number of individuals who are definitely not to be seen as normal leadership figures in an egalitarian society. Instead, the concept of the Judge is characterized by ideas concerning the presence of what must be at least a rudimentary hierarchy[84]. The narrative of Gideon's election to leadership could also be cited as further evidence that pre-monarchical Israelite society was not averse to the idea of being governed by a chieftain figure. This impression is further confirmed by the narrative about Jephthah.

Gottwald expresses the matter as follows: "Tendencies toward the chiefdom and monarchy are clearly evidenced in Saul and even earlier in some of the diverse functionaries called obscurely

---

[82] Lemche 1972:87; cf. Richter 1965, and also Hauser 1975 and de Geus 1976:206. Contra: Rösel 1980, who insists on the distinction between the major and minor Judges. According to Rösel the major Judge is a (military) leader, שׁפט , while the minor Judge is the local ruler, or See further Rösel 1981:202-203, where the writer maintains that Jephthah was incumbant in two offices at once; thus he was the "transitionary figure" who enabled the title of שׁפט to be associated with the various "Retter" figures.

[83] Lemche 1972:87.

[84] Gottwald claims that we are unable to assert of Ibzan that he was a leadership type who exceeded the norms adhered to by the Israelites, since the tradition would otherwise no doubt have accorded him the same "honors" as those heaped upon Abimelech (1979A:307). This is a classical *argumentum e silentio*; Gottwald's argument has no force whatsoever. In the first place, Ibzan (or any of the others mentioned in this connection) need not have behaved as Abimelech did, even if his position was extremely eminent. In the second place, Gottwald has ignored the significance of Abimelech's association with Shechem. It is more likely that it was not Abimelech's career, but his association with this important central Palestinian city and sanctuary which provided the reason for the preservation of the traditions in Jdg 9.

"judges", notably Gideon and Abimelech, and perhaps also in some of the socalled minor judges such as Ibzan"[85]. Of course, it is frequently claimed that Abimelech was not a king of an Israelite state as such, but of a Canaanite city-state[86]. However, there is no doubt that his kingdom included central portions of Manasseh. The possibility that Abimelech may at some point in the development of the tradition about him have been understood as an Israelite prince would harmonize well with E. Nielsen's observation that the original tradition about Abimelech will once have been much more positive towards him than the last redaction of Jdg 9 allows us to suspect: "After all, Abimelech gets an exit worthy of a hero: in the battle, at the head of his Israelite men...Certainly a true predecessor of the noble chieftain and king, Saul"[87]. Even the present redaction of Jdg 9 is pre-Deuteronomistic and reveals a different understanding of Shechem from that of the Deuteronomists[88]. B. Otzen finds evidence in the account of Abimelech's activities of a sort of symbiosis between the Israelites and the Canaanites, and in this connection he refers to the understanding of Israel's origins of Mendenhall and Gottwald[89]. However, in this case Otzen has misunderstood the intentions underlying the revolution model, which in fact has no room for a figure like Abimelech[90]. According to Gottwald, after the death of Abimelech Shechem was probably incorporated into Manasseh, but this will not have occurred before the early days of David's reign. The precise association between Abimelech and Gideon-Jerubba'al is not entirely clear, and will hardly become more so. On the other hand, there are obvious points of contact between Jdg 8,22-23 and Jdg 9. Jdg 8,22f shows us the righteous figure of Gideon who rejects monarchical rule, while Jdg 9 demonstrates how bad things can get, if one ultimately falls for the temptation to establish a monarchy. Thus the connection between the traditions concerning Gideon and Abimelech is clearly redactional and reflects a strongly negative view of the institution of monarchy, as is stressed by Crüsemann[91]. T. Ishida, however, feels that Jdg 8,22f were interpolated in order to acquit Gideon of participation in the establishment of despotism by Abimelech[92].

A detailed description of the powers accorded to such local petty princes is impossible because of the deficiencies in our sources. A number of Judges are associated with traditions dealing with military functions; concerning others, however, we lack such information. We are told concerning Samuel (that is, if we reckon Samuel among the Judges) that he performed juridical functions (1 Sam 7,16-17), which presumably means that he served as an intermediary in cases of conflict between the central Palestinian tribes, above all that of Benjamin. A secondary tradition also associates a military feat with Samuel's activity (1 Sam 7,7-14)[93]. Also, a legendary account of the election of Saul to the kingship (1 Sam 9,1-10,16) describes Samuel as a local prophet.

In addition to traditions recording the military feats of Gideon, we also have some which inform us of his activities as a cultic organizer (Jdg 6,24.25ff;

---

[85] See Gottwald 1979A:297-298; cf. also Soggin 1967:11-15.
[86] Cf. on this point Alt 1930:6f.; cf. also Reviv 1966; Mayes 1977:316; Hermann 1973:164, and Soggin 1971.
[87] Nielsen 1959:168.
[88] Nielsen 1959:171.
[89] Otzen 1977:128.
[90] Cf. also Gottwald 1979A:552.
[91] Crüsemann 1978:42. The question as to whether or not Gideon became king is irrelevant in this connection, but see Davies 1963 and compare with Nielsen 1959:143n.
[92] Ishida 1977:184-185.
[93] On Samuel's victory over the Philistines, see Lemche 1972:104, and especially Weiser 1958. Stoebe maintains that 1 Sam 7,7-14 is a Deuteronomistic creation *without* use of earlier sources (1973:170-171).

8,27). The titles which are associated with the Judges are, besides, of course, שפט [94], קצין and ראש (used of Jephthah), while משל is employed in the narrative of the election of Gideon (Jdg 8,22-23). The title of king is only used of Abimelech, who, however, is usually accounted a pariah among the rest of the figures in the Book of the Judges. This rather poor harvest may be supplemented with some information which suggests that these figures had their various centers of power in small towns or towns, but it is worth noting in this connection that there is nothing remarkable here, since in the pre-national period the entire Israelite tribal system dwelled in fortified small towns or unfortified villages.

It would be fruitless to attempt on the basis of the available materials to go deeper into the question as to the highest level of leadership in the Israelite tribes especially because we only possess information concerning the central and North Israelite tribes. We have no data which informs us about the frequency of chieftain figures, nor do we have any which might be used as evidence to suggest that such rulers were mainly the exceptions to this picture. It would be a serious mistake to imagine that tradition has bequeathed to us the names of all the chieftains in pre-national Israel in the books of Judges and 1 Samuel. If this were the case, we should have very few to distribute throughout the Israelite tribes during the period we have traditionally thought the period of the Judges to have been. One could with equal justice argue that the phenomenon of the chieftain was quite common in these tribes, since virtually every tradition concerning the period in question tells us about such figures. The sole exceptions are confined to the additions to the Book of the Judges (Jdg 17-21). Thus we must conclude that chieftainship was a well-known form of leadership in pre-monarchical Israel, and that the individual Israelite tribes did not resent this institution at all as long as it did not trespass against certain norms, of which process the story of Abimelech appears to offer a negative example. For this reason we have no information about the Israelite tribal society which could be taken to suggest that this segmentarily structured society was governed by an egalitarian ideology. Even the Deuteronomists have no objection to this rule by individuals, with the exception of their remarks about the monarchy (and in spite of Jdg 8,22-23). Instead, they simply conclude the various episodes with a neutral notice according to which the savior in question "judged", that is, ruled over Israel for so and so many years.

This conclusion is not contradicted by the fact that in the sources we are informed a single time about a lower level of leadership than that of the whole tribe, namely the so-called council of elders, who are mentioned in conjunction with Jephthah's accomplishments[95].

---

[94] See Lemche 1972:74-76, and, further, de Geus 1965:82. The classical account is Grether 1939, esp. Grether 1939:111ff. See also Richter 1965:58-70.

[95] Jdg 11,5-11.

Deborah's leadership designations are characterized by an unusual degree of opaqueness. The greatest difficulty is offered by פרעות in Jdg 5,2(see also Deut 32,42), which may mean "chieftain", "leader", or "the fair-haired one". It would also be appropriate to include the difficulties connected with Jdg 5,7.11; in Jdg 5,7 we find the term פרחון and in 5,11 פרזני. Since Luther the traditional translation has been "Bauern", since scholars have derived the term from the root פרז, with which we are familiar because of the term פרזות, meaning "the open land", 'villages'[96]. Naturally, Gottwald desires to retain the traditional understanding because of his basic view of the nature of premonarchical Israelite society[97]. However, this term was problematical even in antiquity, as we can see from the fact the LXX[A] simply transcribes φραξων in v 7, but there is also a rather strong traditional tendency to translate the term as "prince", "potentate", "chieftain", or the like. This is apparent in the text in LXX[B] of Jdg 5,7, where we read δυνατοί; this is followed by the Vulgate, which reads *fortes*. The latter translational tradition has gained ground in recent years, although the philological basis for this is not especially convincing. Thus Gray sugges that we read <רוזנים> that is, "rulers", instead of פרזון, since he reckons פ to have arisen through dittography (פ resembles ר in protohebraic script). This is a completely arbitrary suggestion which violates the modern rules governing the use of the *lectio difficilior*[98]. M.S. Seale's suggestion that פרזון has arisen via metathesis from פזרון is hardly better. Seales derives פזרון from פזר, which he translates to "distribute generously"[99]. P.C. Craigie renders פרזון "warriors" on the basis of Arabic *baraza*, "going forth into battle"[100]. However, this is a derivative sense of *baraza*, the basic meaning of which is "to come out", "to appear", with no military implications. In the III form *baraza* may be used in the sense "to meet in combat or duel", which explains the derivatives *mubāriz*, "Combattant", "fighter"[101]. Craigie's second argument is likewise uncertain, although it is more reasonable, since he points to Hab 3,14, where we read פרזו, rendered in the LXX as δυναστῶν (cf. also the Vulgate and the Peshitta). Here a translation like "chieftain" or "leader" would be more natural because of context. In connection with Hab 3,14 Albright's suggested translation "followers" has nothing in its favor except the fact that, as Albright pointed out, a peasant can in fact follow someone[102]. As his third argument Craigie points to and emphasizes the context of Jdg 5,11. A. Weiser arrives at a similar conclusion; he speaks of an abstract form meaning something like *"Führung"*. A similar view was later arrived at by Albright[103].

Thus the problems seem to be far from solved. In philological terms the translation "peasants" would seem to be the best substantiated, but the use of the derivative of פרז in Hab 3,14, where "peasant" would be a more than peculiar rendering, means that we cannot reject the possibility that פרזון may be used of a leadership group in the Song of Deborah.

On the other hand, it is certain that חקקי ישראל in Jdg 5,9 and מחקקים in Jdg 5,14 refer to a leadership group. These leaders are said to have been present; but then, what function did they have? Since neither חקק nor מחקק appears elsewhere in the OT, and since the other titles are likewise unclear, any attempt to characterize them more fully would be futile, even though חקק and מחקק seem to be derivatives of חק, meaning "rule", or "norm".

The most reasonable course would be to examine the fragmentary information we have about the activities of the council of elders in the light of the descriptions of the titles which have been presented previously. It is most likely

---

[96] Cf. Burney 1918:115-116, who reads "villagers" and "peasantry". Compare Moore 1895: 143-144, and the classical German commentaries of K. Budde (1897:42) and W. Nowack (1902: 44-45).

[97] Gottwald 1979A:779-780 n.516.

[98] See Gray 1967:278.

[99] Seale 1962.

[100] Craigie 1972:350.

[101] Cf. Wehr 1966:52.

[102] Cf. Albright 1950A:17 n.SS, followed by F. Horst in Robinson and Horst 1964:182 *("Gefolgschaft")*.

[103] Cf. Weiser 1959:76-77, and Albright 1968:43n, who refers to the Papyrus Anastasi I 12:4.

that we have to do with the chiefs of family groups, where by "family" I intend בית אב and not משפחה[104]. In most cases, the activities of this group have been suppressed by the traditions, presumably because they have "drowned" when the old tradition was made Pan-Israelite. Thus, for example, the group which is active in connection with the election of Gideon to the kingship is not a council of elders, but all Israel. However, we must bear in mind that information as to the activities of the council of elders in the pre-national period is quite limited. Also, the main part of the views which scholarship has historically pronounced concerning the council of elders in Israel have either been based on the late traditions of the Tetrateuch and the introductory sections of the Deuteronomistic Historical Work, or they have been based on general "ethnological" observations which have no basis in the OT. It is impossible to conclude on the basis of any OT text that, for example, a council of elders once existed in a given Israelite tribe which met regularly, perhaps once a year, in order to resolve conflicts between the various parts of the tribe. We cannot even be sure that such councils existed even at lower levels of the society, that is, beyond the local group. On the other hand, there are good reasons to believe that the local societies were "governed" by the leaders of lineages by the ad hoc facticity of their mere presence as, for example, in the much-discussed "law in the gate". This sort of administration of justice will not have been confined to juridical functions alone. It must also have been important as a regulator of numerous other relationships in such mini-societies, to the extent that there were matters of common interest to the whole society[105].

We encounter such ad hoc functions in Gen 23, where Abraham addresses himself to the leaders of Hebron collectively, but with the intention of getting them to mediate between him and Ephron. Ephron himself is sitting among the other elders of the town, and is thus in a position to deal with Abraham directly. True to his lights, H.J. Boecker understands the court of the elders, that is, the courts which consisted of *"Sippenältesten"*, as a survival from the nomadic past[106]. As we shall see in the following materials, this is incorrect. This sort of legal practice is rooted in the family-lineage social organization, whether we find it among nomads (who do not sit in gates) or sedentary dwellers. Moreover, it is also found in tribal societies and in societies which are not organized in tribes.

The presence of a chieftain in a tribe does not mean that this figure will have been forced to govern on the basis of a council of elders. There is sufficient

---

[104] משפחה appears 8 times in the Book of Judges, of which 4 occurrences have to do with the tribe of Dan: Jdg 13,2; 18,2.11.(19). משפחה appears twice in connection with kinship groups from Canaanite towns; Jdg 1,25 refers to a group from Bethel/Luz, while Jdg 9,1 refers to one from Shechem. משפחה is also used in Jdg 17,7, in which a young Levite is described as belonging to the משפחת יהודה; here it would be most natural to regard משפחה as a synonym for שבט or מטה, analogous to its usage in connection with the tribe of Dan. It is only in Jdg 21,24 that the בני ישראל return home, each to לשבטו ולמשפחתו, that we find משפחה used in its actual sense, as referring to a level of Israelite social organization.

[105] On the phenomenon of law in the gate, see Deut 21,19; 25,7; Isa 29,21; Amos 5,12.15; Zech 8,16; Prov 22,22; Job 5,4, and Ruth 3,11.

[106] Boecker 1976:22-25.

ethnological evidence to indicate that in traditional societies chieftains may very well function without the use of other support-organizations than their own immediate circles. The connections linking the various leaders to the individual groups in their tribes may be based upon personal ties and contacts between the chieftains and the individual family leaders[107]. If there is no chieftain in the tribe, there is no reason for an alternative council of elders. It is only on special occasions and particularly in times of crisis that we should expect to see the local leaders of a region meet at the supralocal level. In fact, it is only in such extraordinary circumstances that we meet the elders in the sources which describe pre-national Israel. An example is Jdg 11, where the elders of Gilead are compelled by force of circumstance to seek the aid of a local robber baron by the name of Jephthah.

Thus an Israelite tribe had only an ephemeral political organization. It may have had a chieftain as supreme leader, although this fact does not make it easier to tell whether this sort of organization entailed a greater context in the daily political manifestations of the tribe. It need not have been organized as a hierarchically structured chieftainship, since our sources seem rather to suggest that such political organizations were short-term affairs. In any case, we have no indication that chieftainship-dynasties arose in ancient Israel, with the single exception of the line of Gideon and Abimelech. However, it is important to point out that in pre-national Israel there does not seem to have been any resentment in principle to a centralized type of leadership. There does not seem to have been any common political forum for a whole tribe except in cases of hostilities with foreign groups. Furthermore, not even in such cases is it clear that a whole tribe would necessarily be involved in the fighting. Thus, for example, the texts which most likely comprise the nucleus of the Gideon traditions imply that it was only the group of the Abiezrites who resisted the encroachments of the Midianite nomads.

We have no information to suggest that there was any sort of common juridical forum, not even, for example, in connection with Samuel's activities as a Judge, since Samuel seems rather to have served as a local mediator to whom two clashing family groups could address themselves than as a judge in any classical sense. It is possible that judgements affecting a whole tribe took place in conjunction with pilgrimages to sanctuaries, as Deuteronomy implies. However, the legal ordinance in this work regarding the location of the place of judgement obviously refers to extraordinary situations (Deut 17,8-9). Moreover, the situation described in Deut 21,1-9 suggests that such legislation is concerned with events in which more than one local society is involved.

In Deut 17,8-9 it is local judges who send the case along to another venue, rather than the accused. According to Deut 17,9 certain cases are brought to the sanctuary in order to be presented to the "Levitical priests" and a "judge". In this passage it is probably correct to regard

---

[107] On the tribal chieftains, see above, pp. 119ff.

אל סזגים הלים as a secondary element (as is also suggested by the stereotypical use of the plural form)[108]. On the other hand, P. Merendino has proposed that only הלים is secondary to its context[109], while G. Seitz claims that השפט is secondary, since the text must originally have presupposed a divine judgement. Thus in adding a "judge" a later tradent in reality had the king in mind[110]. However, the formulation of Deut 17,8-9 is clearly Deuteronomistic, which is also true of the phrase identifying the site where the judgement is to take place אל מקם אשר יבחר יזה אלהיך ם. The Deuteronomists also embraced the centralization of the courts (as they did the cult)[111]. In a pre-Deuteronomistic tradition it would be possible to maintain that the text originally only referred to a local application to a judge who, like Samuel (1 Sam 7,15-16) served as a supralocal mediator. In Deut 21,5 it is the Levites who function as mediators, but this too is a secondary element; indeed, all of v 5 is to be excised as secondary to the older tradition[112]. Merendino claims, though, that v 5 belongs to an earlier layer in Deut 21,1-9, but not to the oldest[113]. Seitz, too, regards v 5 as redactional[114].

Admittedly, Deut 17,8-9 refers to a judge (and some Levites), and Deut 21,1ff refer to judges in the plural, but since the context is the pre-national period the function referred to can hardly be other than that of mediator. The function of a supralocal *ad hoc* juridical mediator was no doubt to prevent the occurrence of *vendettas* between two mini-societies within an Israelite tribe. Opposition to allowing bloodfeuds to spread is a familiar feature of many traditional societies. It cannot be regarded as the result of a change in the society's way of life such as a transition from a nomadic to a sedentary social system.

There is a time-hallowed scholarly notion that tribal societies are prevaded by bloodfeuds. Ordinarily, this is by no means the case. Most of the so-called "primitive" societies have a variety of rules as to how one is to prevent conflicts from developing into feuds, that is, as long as the problem is one of conflict *within* the society. However, between rival tribes one might almost say that the feud would be the normal situation. Normally, even murders would be the object of mediation to prevent a *vendetta* from spreading throughout a society. Thus the payment of bloodmoney (*dija*) is standard pratice even among 'asil bedouins like the Šammar and the Rwala[115]. Lutfiyya has described other varieties of mediation, but among sedentary societies, and Antoun and H. Ammar have presented actual case-studies of the procedures involved[116]. M. Gluckman has published a general evaluation of the numerous mediating factors[117]. The rules concerning blood-revenge in the Old Testament cannot by any means be considered a survival of the desert period, as scholar after scholar has supposed[118]. If the rule of talion is seen in conjunction with OT apodictic law, the apodictic law loses its *Sitz im Leben* in Israel's hypothetical nomadic past. Instead, we have to do with legal practices originating in a particular type of social structure which was not that of an organized state,but these practices were not dependent on a specific way of life (i.e. nomadic or sedentary).

It is doubtful whether possibilities for mediation between blood-feuding

---

[108] Cf. Von Rad 1964:84-85.
[109] Merendino 1969:176.
[110] Seitz 1971:201-202.
[111] See also Von Rad 1964:11.
[112] Thus Von Rad 1964:97.
[113] See the synopsis in Merendino 1969:240.
[114] Seitz 1971:158.
[115] Cf. Stein 1967:129; Musil 1928:491-493.
[116] Lutfiyya 1966:92-100; Antoun 1972A:36ff.; Ammar 1970:126-128.
[117] Gluckman 1965:169-215.
[118] See e.g. Boecker 1976:21ff. This is also the basic view in most of the contributions in Koch 1972, not least in that of Preiser 1972.

Israelite tribes existed. Instead, our sources for the period of the Judges seem rather to suggest that conflicts arising between two tribes were resolved quite differently and very violently[119].

Thus with relation to the internal structure of the Israelite tribes, it is possible to agree with the views of a number of recent accounts of these societies, although the sketch presented here differs from these in maintaining that the Israelite tribes had a considerable potential for political integration in the form of the rule of a single individual. However, since there were no instances within the daily life of a tribe which were capable of unifying it as a political group, and, further, since such solidarity only arose in times of crisis, it would be appropriate to examine yet another aspect of Israelite tribal society. We shall see that there were in fact durable political constellations even though there was no cooperation between the various parts of the tribe in daily life. In this connection it is accordingly important to emphasize that the Israelite tribes were also territorial units, which means that the individual tribe identified itself with its geographical territory to such a degree that many of the references to the tribes in the OT are actually more in the nature of geographical notices than references to a particular society which existed in a particular region. Already Noth was able to show that a number of tribal names in reality were geographical names, an observation whose validity is not confined to the less important tribes, but also to such quantities as Judah and Ephraim. Especially in the case of Ephraim it is certain that the name is frequently used as a geographical designation and not as a reference to the Ephraimites who dwelled on the הר אפרים[120].

However, not all tribal names were geographical designations; indeed, there is good reason to suppose that the greater part of them were personal names[121]. Thus we cannot conclude merely on the basis of a name that an Israelite tribe must have arisen as the sum of the individuals who dwelled in a given region. These tribal names contain no information as to how the tribes in question were formed, or concerning the reasons for their emergence. To put it another way, the tribal names do not suggest circumstances which might be taken to distinguish the Israelite tribes from the other tribal societies of the

---

[119] Cf. Jdg 12,1-6: the battles between the Gideadites and the Ephraimites, plus the related matter of the *shibboleth*.

[120] Cf. Noth 1950A:54ff., and with particular reference to Ephraim 1950A:60f. On the הר אפרים, see Jos 17,15; 19,50; 20,7, etc. It would be appropriate to mention a couple of passages in which "Ephraim" is mentioned geographically. In 2 Sam 2,9 Ishba'al is mentioned as the ruler of Ephraim (among other areas). Manasseh presumably was also a part of his kingdom (as it will earlier have been part of Saul's), but it is not mentioned in this context. It is therefore reasonable to regard "Ephraim" here as a designation for Central Palestine. The independent citation of "Benjamin" here is presumably the result of the fact that Benjamin was especially associated with the house of Saul. In 2 Sam 13,23 "Ephraim" is unquestionably a geographical designation.

[121] This applies to Simeon, Manasseh, and Zebulon; "Ashur", however, is probably a divine name (cf. Noth 1950A:58ff.).

Orient and elsewhere. The fact that individual tribes suffered displacements with respect to political importance or site of habitation, indeed, even the fact that some entirely disappeared or were assimilated into other tribes also corresponds to the normal political development of many traditional societies.

On the other hand, the fact that the Israelite tribal society was organized in a fixed twelve-tribe system, with local variations, is quite unusual. I have dealt with this problem in my earlier book; accordingly, in these pages I shall merely touch the attendant problems en passant, among other things because a number of other scholars have arrived at similar results, above all the conclusion that the *terminus a quo* of the twelve-tribe system was the establishment of the united Monarchy around 1000[122]. We do not know whether geographical displacements continued to take place after the introduction of the monarchy. Although scholars often dismiss this possibility, usually on the grounds that they do not believe the Israelite tribes continued to exist after the formation of the state, there are no theoretical reasons why this could not have taken place on the local plane. The reason for this is that a central authority will not have been overly concerned with whether Israelite NN belonged to tribe A or to tribe B, as long as he paid his taxes and did not exploit his tribal affiliations to undertake political activities detrimental to the state. In political terms there is no doubt that at the time of the appearance of the state or at the latest shortly after its partition into two independent states the tribal society must have exhausted its political role. It is clear that this did not occur without commotion, as the narrative of Sheba's revolt (2 Sam 20,1-22) suggests, but this development was nevertheless unavoidable[123].

It is possible that local conditions may have enabled a minitribe like Simeon to survive until the beginning of the national period, if contemporary Israeli scholars are correct in their claim that the list of Simeon's territorial possessions in Jos 19,1-9 is not merely a carbon copy of Judah's districts, but a notice which in its original form demarcated an independent Simeonite territory, perhaps in the western part of the Negev[124]. It is difficult to determine just

---

[122] Cf. Lemche 1972:106-113.119, and now also de Geus 1976:118, as well as Gottwald 1979A: 362: "The terminus a quo (i.e., for a twelve-tribe system) is the rise of the monarchy... The terminus ad quem must be the division of the kingdom." Mayes goes no further than to date the oldest of the lists in question to a later date than the Song of Deborah (1974:31), which he dates to the 12th century (cf. Mayes 1969). Concerning List A, which contains the name of Levi, I should prefer to reemphasize my previously-adumbrated view that this is not an independent list, but the postulate of a Priestly redaction.

[123] It is significant that the last time the tribal affiliations of an important figure are mentioned is in 1 Kgs 15,27: Ba'asha, a man of בית יששכר. The many subsequent usurpers in the Northern Kingdom do not seem to have had other support than that of the military (Zimri, Omri, Jehu, and Pekah). For this reason alone Alt's theory about a putative North Israelite elective monarchy (Alt 1951) has no basis in reality, especially as concerns the dynastic complications which arose after the fall of the dynasty of Jeroboam. It would be equally appropriate to call the Roman Empire during the time of the "Soldier Emperors" an "elective monarchy".

[124] On this see Talmon 1965, and most recently Na'aman 1980. Kallai-Kleinmann dates the

when Gad began to expand in the territory east of the Jordan, since the history
of Reuben in the southern part of the region is only very poorly intimated by
our sources. It would be reasonable to assume that the Rubenite family groups
had fused with those of the Gadites prior to the introduction of the monarchy.

The *terminus ante quem* for the conclusion of the southward expansion is the middle of the 9th century, since the stele of Mesha (KAI 181:10) mentions Gad. However, since it is doubtful that the
OT actually knows anything at all of an independent Reubenite tribal territory, it would be
natural to assume that the fusion of Gad with Reuben had been concluded prior to the formation
of the state[125]. We find the territory of Reuben described in Jos 13,15-23, that of Gad in Jos
13,24-28, but also in Num 32,33-38.
    Noth held that there was originally only a single tribal territory which was redactionally divi-
ded up at a later date into the territories of Reuben and Gad, a division which followed different
principles, so that the division is not identical with respect to Jos 13 and Num 32. M. Wüst
argues that the description in Num 32 is the older of the two, and that it reflects political conditions before 900. He also maintains that in delineating the border between Gad and Reuben,
Jos 13 actually follows the historical border between Israel and Moab; thus, in including the
territory of Reuben, which in reality was Moabite territory, the text represents an ideal, not a
historical, situation[126]. Accordingly, there is reason to question whether Reuben was actually
associated with the territory east of the Jordan at all, and indeed some have maintained that
Reuben may originally have dwelled in the region later occupied by Benjamin[127]. The explanation of this fact may well reside in the possibility that as an integrated tribe Reuben never existed
in the region east of the Jordan. It is conceivable that Reubenite family groups who were
expelled from the area west of the Jordan by the Benjaminites trickled across the river and then
subsequently became fused with the Gadites, who already dwelled there.

Of course, such tribal fusions will have been possible before the introduction
of the monarchy. This is why it was possible for Manasseh to assimilate both
Gilead and Machir, but in such a way that Machir became a sub-tribe of
Manasseh, while Gilead became a main section subordinated under Machir.
We also have an example of fission instead of fusion in the division of the house
of Joseph into Ephraim and Manasseh, as Noth maintains. However, in this
case de Geus is probably right to claim that this was more likely to be a case
of the political fusion of two independent tribes, and that this fusion can hardly
have taken place before the monarchy arose[128]. Finally, it seems as if the
parallel fusion of the house of Judah may have taken place via a sequence in
which a single large tribe assimilated a series of small tribes from the region
around Hebron: Caleb, Jerahmeel, and Othniel. This may first have taken
place in the time of David, as De Vaux has claimed[129].

---

list in Jos 19,2ff. to no later than the time of Solomon (1958:158-160). It is not completely clear
in Cross and Wright 1956:214-215 whether they hold the list in Jos 19,2-7 to be older than that
in Jos 15,26-32 (against Alt and Noth), and perhaps just as old as 1 Chron 4,28-32 takes it to be
(1 Chron 4,28-32 supposes it to be pre-Davidic).
    [125] On Reuben and Gad in the territory east of the Jordan, see Noth 1944:423-433.
    [126] Wüst 1975:180-185.
    [127] On this see Noth 1950A:63-64.
    [128] Compare this with de Geus' convincing presentation of the materials concerning the
בית יוסף (1976:70-96); cf. de Geus: "The expression 'house of Joseph' first crops up in the early
time of the kings, and it has an anti-Davidic sound...We find that the O.T. gives us no occasion
to think there was an ancient independent tribe of Joseph...The earliest traditions have only
Ephraim and Manasse" (1976:95).
    [129] De Vaux 1971B:509f. Cf. also Mowinckel 1967:141 and 147f.

Countless similar processes may have taken place at any point in the history of the monarchy, although we have no information on the matter. Similarly, local reshufflings of tribal affiliations between two tribes are conceivable for both the pre-national and the national periods. A classical example of such a reorganization is to be found in the description of the border between Manasseh and Ephraim in Jos 17,8, which informs us that Ephraimites dwelled in the town of Tappuah, while Manassites dwelled in the region around the town. This notice has often been taken to suggest that there was Ephraimite expansion into Manassite territory during the period of the Judges. I feel instead that this placement of the two populations with respect to one another rather suggests the intrusion of Manassite elements into Ephraimite territory (that is, if one is at all inclined to reckon with some sort of "intrusion", which as an explanatory model is a survival of the old mania for explaining almost anything as the result of "invasions"), since we may assume that it will have been more difficult to gain control of a town (whether or not it was fortified) than of the lands around it[130]. I would categorically reject the notion that this sort of process could not have taken place after the formation of the state, for the simple reason (already mentioned above) that the state would not be concerned as long as such displacements and alliances had no influence on the administration of such areas. A change in tribal affiliation would have little or no significance for the state if such a change meant in practice no more than that the local population of a town or a rural area stopped reckoning themselves members of one tribe in favor of another. In other words, the state would not be involved as long as such changes in tribal borders had no demographic consequences, but only consequences for the internal loyalties of the peoples in question.

Excursus

The Tribal Boundaries

The presupposition for state control of its territories no matter what tribal relations obtain is the existence of a national administrative subdivision of the territory as a whole. Such a type of administration existed in Israel at least since the days of Solomon. The record of this system is preserved in 1 Kgs 4, which clearly shows that the royal authority only took heed of the existing tribal areas to a limited extent[131]. We do not know whether a similar administrative system existed in the southern part of the kingdom of David and Solomon, although some scholars have

[130] Cf. on this Alt 1927:200f.; Noth 1935:249-250 and 1953A:103. On Tappua in particular see Elliger 1930:298-301; 1937 and 1938. See also Jenni 1958:38; Kuschke 1965:102-103; Aharoni 1967:194, and most recently Otto 1979:236-237.

[131] Thus Wright 1967; otherwise: Alt 1913; Aharoni 1967:280; Noth 1968:67, and Mettinger 1971:118-119, who feels that Solomon's district subdivision was undertaken on the basis of existing tribal borders and also with reference to the recent incorporation of Canaanite towns.

attempted to back-date the district-subdivisions in Judah which Alt had assigned to an earlier period in the history of Judah[132].

We find other dates suggested by Y. Aharoni, who dated this subdivision to the time of Hezekiah, and by F. Cross and G.E. Wright, who dated it to the time of Jehosaphat[133]. The reason for dating this division to the time of Jehosaphat is a couple of notices in 2 Chron 17,2.19 and 19,5. However, P. Welten has argued persuasively that with the exception of individual notices such as 2 Chron 26,6a.10; 32,30a; and 11,5b.6a-10a β the Chronicler does not actually use old materials about the kings of Israel which are not present in the Books of the Kings. Instead, the Chronicler seems to pursue a midrash-like treatment of the monarchs who had received a "gold star" at the hands of the Deuteronomists, which is the case in connection with Jehosaphat in 1 Kgs 22,41-51[134].

With respect to the purported Judaean district system in the time of David or Solomon, the question is contingent on whether the catalogue of Solomon's districts in 1 Kgs 4,7-19 lists eleven or twelve districts. T.N.D. Mettinger has argued that this text in reality only refers to eleven districts, since he regards 1 Kgs 4,19 as a doublet of v 13, which he feels contains reminiscences of an earlier subdivisional system[135]. On the assumption that there were supposed to be twelve districts in all, this observation means that one is missing, and Mettinger claims that it must have been Judah. Numerous earlier studies, however, propose the opposite position: that twelve districts are in fact enumerated in 1 Kgs 4,7-19. In other words, the text only refers to the northern and eastern parts of Solomon's Israelite possessions, Judah not being included[136]. M. Ottoson, though, also feels that 1 Kgs 4,19 contains information which is older than Solomon's administrative system.

In recent times scholars have been inclined to maintain that this Solomonic administrative system, which is assured with respect to the Northern Kingdom, and which has been hypothecated for Judah, in reality replaced an earlier subdivisional system. This system, which may have been introduced under David, will have divided the central parts of the Davidic empire into districts on the basis of the existing tribal boundaries. Scholars have held that the remains of this Davidic subdivision are to be found in the older parts of Jos 13-19, specifically in the *"Grenzfix-punkte"* lists discussed by Alt and Noth[137]. Admittedly, Alt and Noth held that this earlier system derived from the period prior to the formation of the state, but we should not overlook the fact that Noth's reason for insisting on this point – not least in his polemic against Mowinckel – was connected with his amphictyony hypothesis, which made it possible to provide a *Sitz im Leben* for the description of the tribal boundaries, namely the central instance of the amphictyony[138].

With the disintegration of the amphictyony hypothesis, however, the basis for dating the description of the tribal borders in Jos 13-19 to an early date has also disappeared. Scholars are now prone to posit a date at some point in the history of the monarchy; in particular, they have emphasized the time of the united monarchy as the only period in which such a description of the territory of the twelve tribes of Israel would have been topical[139]. I do not intend to offer a

---

[132] Cf. Alt 1925A.

[133] See Aharoni 1959, and Cross and Wright 1956:202ff., followed by Aharoni 1967:302-304.

[134] Welten 1973:191-194; cf. Donner 1977:392.

[135] Mettinger 1971:121ff.

[136] Cf. Alt 1913, followed by Noth 1968:74; Aharoni 1967:279. See also Ottosson 1969:218-220.

[137] See, above all, Noth 1935:229-241, and also Alt 1927.

[138] On the date of the *"Grenzfixpunkte"*-system, see Alt 1927:201. See also Noth 1953A:13-14, and further, Noth 1950C. In the last-mentioned work, Noth's then-current interest in equipping the central office of the Judge with functions led him to allow the Judge to undertake to control the border contours. Noth's polemic was also directed against Mowinckel (1946); cf. also Mowinckel 1964:51-75.

[139] Thus Mayes 1974:73, and Gottwald 1979A:157. De Geus is an exception to the presently-obtaining rule, since he regards the monarchy as *a terminus a qua*. De Geus separates out a prenational tribal list in the form of a border list covering Benjamin, Ephraim, Zebulon, Asher, and Naphtali, which he compares with the description of Ishaba'al's kingdom in 2 Sam 2,9 (1976:81). De Geus does not press this argument any futher so as, for example, to suggest that

detailed description of the problems connected with the dating of the geographical information present in Jos 13-19, nor a traditio-historical analysis of the section. However, it will be necessary to examine some of the main arguments for the various dates.

It is possible to object against the notion that the period of the Judges was the background for the emergence of the accounts of the tribal territories on the grounds that it has no "holes" in. it. In other words, it does not take into account the conditions which actually prevailed during most of the period of the Judges, when a sizeable part of the later Israelite state was not in Israelite hands. This objection cannot be countered by, for example, arguing that there is no question of actual borders, but only of ideals. We would then be forced to ask, with Mowinckel, as to who could have been interested in such an ideal demand, when the twelve-tribe amphic-tyony did not exist[140]. In favor of a Davidic date is the fact that there are no holes connected with it, not even as far as Jerusalem is concerned and, further, the fact that the borders of several of the central tribes extend to the coastline[141]. Against this date is the fact that the western border of Judah can hardly have been the Mediterranean, unless the Philistine territory was incorporated into Judah. Jos 15,1-12 does not in any way reckon with the existence of a possibly quasi-independent Philistine society in southwestern Palestine. Thus Jos 15 either suggests that the Philistines were part of the Davidic empire, concerning which we have no information, or it implies that they became independent again later on. Alternatively, it is possible that the description of the tribal boundaries – at least as we have it now – is not from the time of David. Yet another argument against a Davidic date is the lack of information concerning the borders of Ephraim and Manasseh towards the coast. When we get to upper and lower Beth Horon, we discover that we lack further information as to the last 15-20 km of densely populated territory leading to the coast. If these borders derived from the time of David, we should expect that they contained precise details about this part of the borders. Finally, a third objection to be aired is that it is inexplicable that materials concerning the various tribes should be so variously reprodu-ced in Jos 13-19, and that in particular the lack of information concerning Issachar is striking.

The result of these general observations concerning the age of the system in question is that we do not have to do with a system from the early part of the monarchy, because we are not always presented with actual, but sometimes ideal, boundaries. The era in which it would have been appropriate to work out such a system, and when there would have been some political basis for doing so, was the time of Josiah, when such a system will have served as a program for Josiah's policy of national renewal. This is not to reject the notion that Jos 13-19 contains a wide variety of materials, of which some may be much older than the final system; nor does it deny that even younger tradents (I am thinking primarily of the Priestly Writer, of the circle who

this group of tribes *were* the actual prenational Israel, although on the basis of his dating of the borders in question this would be a tempting idea. Alternatively, one could claim that Saul first established lasting political connections among these tribes (cf. also Grønbæk 1971:226ff., who holds that in reality 2 Sam 2,9 describes Saul's kingdom). De Geus claims that the older border list was later supplied with an account of Jedaean territory which was not based on the settle-ment pattern of the historical tribe of Judah, but on the basis of the southern border of the king-dom (or of Canaan). Thus de Geus, following Aharoni 1967:233.

[140] See Mowinckel 1946:64-65. Mowinckel's sharp clash with the studies of the tribal borders of Alt and Noth is usually dismissed without argumentation. This was Mowinckel's own fault to some degree, since his manner of discussion could sometimes be unnecessarily sarcastic. Another reason, however, is that scholars have correctly understood the irony in Noth's reply (1950C:158-159, especially concerning Mowinckel's dating of the border descriptions to the post-exiic period, as well as because of his ideas about oral tradition: namely that the written account had perished during the destruction of Jerusalem in 587). Nevertheless, in spite of his clearly assailable theories concerning Jos 13-19, Mowinckel's attack on Alt and Noth contains all of the important arguments *against* dating the border lists to the period of the Judges.

[141] This also applies to the border between Benjamin and Judah; see Jos 15,5-11 and 18,15-19. Thus there is no room for a city-state (Jerusalem) between Benjamin and Judah. These data no doubt contain information from the time of the monarchy, and they implicitly contain the most important arguments against Alt's hypothesis according to which the city-state of Jerusalem continued to exist in the period of the monarchy as the private possession of the Israelite king; see Alt 1930:45ff.

followed in his footsteps) may have reworked parts of the Josianic tradition in order to retain the
twelve-tribe system as the ultimate goal of the boundary lists.

The earlier literary critical analysis of Jos 13-19 cannot bear closer scrutiny either (Wellhausen
held that Jos 13-19 consisted mainly of Q-materials, i.e., P-materials, plus only limited sections
of J and E[142], while Mowinckel maintained that P composed the lot on the basis of earlier
materials). No matter when the final redaction of these texts came about, there is no doubt that
the border-system ultimately dates from the pre-exilic period, if for no other reason, then simply
because there was no *Sitz im Leben* capable of producing it in the post-exilic period, when there
were no tribes.

Noth's traditio-historical analysis of Jos 13-19 simply rejects outright the notion that P is
present in the section; he held that the final redactor was the Deuteronomist[143]. On the other
hand, O. Eissfeldt held that Jos 13-19 contained elements of J, E, and P[144] (W. Rudolph, however, accepts only J and P, plus a number of notices which have nothing to do with the Pentateuchal "sources")[145]. Eissfeldt was probably on the right track when he insisted that it was not P
who composed Jos 13-19, but an author who wrote in P's style[146]. Eissfeldt was unable to find
traces of J and E in Jos 13-14. In this writer's opinion, Eissfeldt's theory is worth testing, since
the problem is not whether Jos 13-19 contains materials by P or someone like him, but whether
there are other Pentateuchal sources present. At the same time one might inquire as to whether
there are Deuteronomistic sections, and since this is unquestionably the case, the ultimate
problem is whether it was the Deuteronomists who collected the various materials in Jos 13-19,
or whether it was P who did so. It is also possible that P or the P-like author reworked Jos 13-19
in order to fulfil an expectation which was the basis of the tribal census in Num 26, namely that
the Num passage would be the basis of the later allocation of the land of Canaan to the Israelite
tribes. With reference to my proposed Josianic date for the border-system, I shall merely add
that this is now accepted by a number of scholars[147], all of whom, however, also hold that it contains older materials.

Thus the conclusion of this excursus on the tribal-boundary system is regrettable. It would
have provided an excellent confirmation of my theory that the twelve-tribe system derived from
the era of David and Solomon. This would have been the case if list type B (i.e., the list which
contains Ephraim and Manasseh, but omits Levi) actually corresponded to a district administrative system from the Davidic era which followed this twelve-tribe system. The notion that
such an administrative system was introduced at this time must remain a postulate. By the same
token, the idea that the Davidic era was probably the only one in which all the tribes mentioned
in twelve-tribe system B could have existed at the same time if briefly must also be admitted to
be purely hypothetical.

The significance of established borders within a politically autonomous tribal
society like the Israelite one is an interesting question. If the tribal borders had
something of the character of state borders, so that one could, for example,
precisely distinguish Ephraimite from Manassite territory to one side and
Benjaminite to the other, the Israelites will then have been in a position to
regard all connections across these boundaries as illegitimate trespasses
against political divisions. If this was the case, then Israel could certainly be
held to be a rare case. In antropological terms it is virtually an a priori truth
that tribal territories are only relative geographical demarcations. In other
words, while a sedentary tribe is able to define its region with respect to the

[142] Wellhausen 1963:127-132.
[143] Noth 1943:183-189.
[144] Eissfeldt 1922:75-79 and 227*-241*.
[145] Rudolph 1938:211-238.
[146] Cf. Eissfeldt 1965:251.
[147] Cf. Bächli 1973, and also Strange 1966:139.

territories of its neighbors in general terms, in practice there proves to be a broad belt of no man's land separating them. This is not wasteland, but simply a middle ground in which the connections between two neighboring tribes are intense and in which the demarcation between the two societies is elastic. Such connections are usually of both a political and an economic nature. By this I mean that in general tribes may be regarded as communities of common interests, but on the local plane there may be more interests held in common between an Ephraimite dwelling on the Benjaminite border and his Benjaminite neighbor than there are between the Ephraimite and other Ephraimites who dwell in the northern part of the tribal territory. Thus in the daily life of a tribe an official tribal border has no great significance as a social, economic, or political line of demarcation. It first becomes significant the moment an external instance threatens a tribe's hold on its territory and attempts to expel it from it. Thus, as is indicated by the sources on the period of the Judges, the tribe was capable of acting as a corporate unit, and numerous tribes were capable of coordinating their activities in the form of ad hoc coalitions against external enemies.

Of course, none of this provides us with a definitive answer as to what was the nature of an Israelite tribe, since such an answer is not practicable[148]. Almost all the definitions proposed as yet have a tendency towards circularity. It would be reasonable to regard an Israelite tribe as a territorial, or territory-possessing, unit which acted corporately when its territory was in jeopardy. However, if we then ask why the tribe acted in this manner, the definition bites its own tail, as it were: the tribe did so because it was composed of the people who dwelled in the region in question. Only a historical explanation is capable of breaking this circle, namely in the event that the tribe in question had migrated as a separate tribal unit into its territory while at the same time possessing recollections of the tribe's common past. Unfortunately, no such separate traditions concerning the individual Israelite tribes are preserved in the OT, not even in Jdg 1[149]. Rather, the preserved traditions concern all of the Israelite tribes.

Thus we still have the thorny problem as to what actually distinguishes a tribe from another. Once again it would be tempting to reply that it was the

---

[148] Note de Geus: "The tribes were geographical entities, groupings of related clans, with but a few functions of their own. This vagueness is a characteristic of the notion of tribe" (1976: 211). This definition is beset with difficulties, since it fails to explain how endogamous clans are related except through their common territory; in other words, this is circular logic.

[149] With respect to Jdg 1, I am able fully to agree with de Geus' evaluation of it (1976:85-86), which holds the chapter to be a late collection of traditions which reflects the existence of the monarchy, and which has no value as a source with respect to the Israelite immigration. Jdg 1 also receives this treatment in Gottwald 1979A:163-175. The chapter has been composed by a redactor writing during the time of the monarchy, but only the basis of individual traditions concerning individual tribes (Gottwald speaks of "tribal annals"): "But the focus and fulcrum of Judges 1, as it lies before us, is the Davidic monarchy...."(1979A:175).

tribes of the individual territories. If we assume that the Israelite tribes were first constituted as such after the immigration, this conclusion inevitably presents itself. A conception of the process of immigration which presupposes that the tribes immigrated separately into Palestine and settled in territories which they continued to regard as their own offers the possibility for a historical explanation of tribal solidarity. So also does the notion that the immigration took place in such a way that tribes which once dwelled in marginal areas on the borders of the arable land infiltrated into the new areas and then reestablished their tribes. We cannot deny that such immigrations could have taken place in theory; this remains true when we consider the evidence concerning the tribes of Israel. Moreover, it is not difficult to point to parallels.

If the archeological evidence can be taken to support one or the other of these alternatives, it would accordingly be far from unreasonable to retain one of these classical conceptions of Israel's origins. This must be emphasized even in spite of the arguments of de Geus and Gottwald to the effect that there are no elements in the Israelite tribal society which prove that the Israelites came to Palestine as foreigners (nomads). On the other hand, if the archeological materials definitely argue against the notion that foreigners immigrated into Palestine, then we would be forced to accept that there is no satisfactory definition of the constitution of an Israelite tribe. This situation is by no means unique, since numerous other tribal societies in the Middle East and elsewhere offer similar difficulties.

To put the matter another way: it is possible that we shall conclude that the Israelite tribes arose in Palestine as a result of the entry of new peoples into the country, or on the basis of already indigenous Canaanites who had withdrawn from the dominance of the city-states, or as an amalgam of these two forces (or even more). If this proves to be the case, we shall then lack an explanation of the Israelite tribe, and if we should fail to find an explanation on the basis of the premisses contained in our sources, we shall be obliged simply to acknowledge this fact.

Chapter 5

THE "PERIOD OF THE JUDGES" AND THE ALL-ISRAELITE TRADITION

§ 1

Introduction

As the preceding chapters have hopefully demonstrated, sociological methods are useful only to a limited extent in connection with the interpretation of phenomena which are poorly illuminated by the available sources. Sociological study has shown that societies develop in a fantastic variety of ways. Thus they are impossible to categorize without an intimate knowledge of the societies in question. For this reason, very little is actually said about Israelite society in the pre-national period by emphasizing that it was a tribal society. It is simply out of the question to superimpose one or another conception of the nature of tribal societies upon the data concerning Israel and then to conclude that its structure was so and so, its ideology had this and that contents, and that its historical origins and development must have taken such and such turns.

It is possible that Gottwald would subscribe to these observations, even though he himself is on the wrong track in methodological terms, as, for example, in his definition of tribal societies as egalitarian. Gottwald would presumably also emphasize the importance of the fact that we are virtually confined to a single group of sources which may be able to tell us something about Israelite society in the pre-national period, that is, the OT sources. A lengthy presentation of these sources namely makes up the introductory section to his *The Tribes of Yahweh*[1].

The basic question here concerns the context of the OT sources: at what point in time did the idea of the common prehistory of the Israelite people become the point of departure for Israel's history-writing? What historical presupposition enable the creation of a pan-Israelite ideology? Could this have been anything but a united Israel? Most scholars would answer the last question in the affirmative, but this neverthess does not solve our problem, for the question is really, when do we first encounter this united Israel? Prior to the immigration? In the period of the Judges? Or during the United monarchy under David and Solomon?

---

[1] Gottwald 1979A:25-187.

For at least a generation scholars were not much preoccupied with this last question, since they thought themselves entitled to assume the existence of the Israelite amphictyony during the period of the Judges. They held that this twelve-tribe league was the Sitz im Leben of the amphictyonic ideology, and was thus the birthplace of the "centralistic" tendency within Israelite tradition. Traditions about periods prior to the establishment of the twelve-tribe system in Palestine, following the immigration, came under the influence of the later league during the period of the Judges, for which reason they could not be held to be authentic sources about Israel's prehistory. This was emphasized by M. Noth, and this insight was his reason for introducing his study of the history of Israel with an examination of the period of the Judges, which he regarded as the first tangible part of Israel's history[2]. The amphictyony hypothesis has been found to be so extraordinarily satisfactory that earlier adherents of the hypothesis have reacted against the many criticisms of it which have emerged during the last twenty years by maintaining that the critics are merely destructive figures who lay waste but do not themselves build anything. Indeed, O. Bächli seems prone to contest whether or not it is legitimate merely to criticize the value of the amphictyony hypothesis as a heuristic model for understanding the formation of OT tradition unless one is also prepared to substitute another model in its place[3]. In the same vein, we have also seen scholars who have attempted to "save the appearances" of the amphictyony hypothesis by dating the amphictyony to the period just before the introduction of the monarchy, since we must search in vain in the Book of Judges to find a pan-Israelite *forum* in it. In other words, scholars have attempted in desperation to manoeuver the pan-Israelite ideas into a hypothetical hiatus between the period of the Judges and the sources of the beginnings of the monarchy; to this end they have proclaimed that, for example, Gilgal was the central sanctuary at this time[4]. Historical counter-arguments to this position are not difficult to produce; naturally, they center on the possibility of finding sources which might suggest traces of Israelite-Judaean cooperative action during the initial phases of the formation of the state[5].

---

[2] Cf. Noth 1950A:105-130.

[3] Thus Bächli 1977:181.

[4] Thus, for example, the position of Gilgal has been elevated from anonymity to virtually *the* Israelite sanctuary during the period of the Judges by E. Otto (1975). Admittedly, Otto emphasizes that none of the twelve-tribe traditions is earlier than Saul (1975:331), and that it was thus Saul who created the pan-Israelite twelve-tribe league. However, he did not do so from scratch, since precisely Gilgal was the common meeting place of the northern and southern tribes prior to Saul. Otto claims that since Judah was a Leah tribe it was originally a Central Palestinian tribe or was connected with the other Leah tribes, an association which, however, was terminated by the immigration of the Rachel tribes. However, the southern tribes and the 10-tribe amphictyony continued to maintain a cultic fellowship; cf. Otto 1975:332f. and 340. On earlier scholarship and especially the notion of H.Kraus concerning Gilgal as a cult center, see Lemche 1972:45-51. Gottwald, too, is in favor of the view that in premonarchical Israel the Israelite tribal confederation had a common cult – even though this confederation was scarcely an amphictyony. See Gottwald 1979A:359-360.

[5] Cf. Lemche 1972:99-101.

But if we are unable to demonstrate evidence of such a premonarchical union of Judah and the northern tribes, that is, if there is no room for a pan-Israelite tribal league during the pre-national period, then it is inevitable that scholars should attempt to localize the *Sitz im Leben* of the pan-Israelite idea to a different period in the history of Israel. This ideology presupposes the existence of a united Israel either as a still-existing reality or as a recollection which is still influential for subsequent attempts to depict the history of Israel as the history of the entire people until the partition of the monarchy after the death of Solomon. It is accordingly not difficult to point to the presupposition for the emergence of this pan-Israelite ideology. If we dispense with the notion of a tribal league, the only possibility remaining is the eighty years of united monarchy under the rule of David and Solomon. Of course, this is not the last word on the date of the appearance of the pan-Israelite view of history. It is entirely possible that this view was a product of the united monarchy and served as a historical and ideological legitimation of it. Nor can we rule out the possibility that this ideology was the product of a Judaean reaction to the partition of the kingdom in 926, and that it functioned in this context as a Judaean apology for the notion of a united state. It may also have come about as an attempt to form an ideological basis for Josiah's policies during the late 7th century. Finally, of course, it would also be possible to maintain that the Exile itself provided the motivation for the emergence of a pan-Israelite view of history, since it gave rise to expectations of the reestablishment of the Israelite kingdom after the end of the Exile.

It will be my intention in the following chapter to explore more thoroughly these ideas concerning the formation of the OT historical traditions; there, as elsewhere, my point of departure will be Gottwald's work. Gottwald maintains unambiguously that the pan-Israelite traditions arose within the centralized cult of the pre-monarchical Israelite tribal league. Thus my first task will be to determine whether Gottwald has found new arguments to demonstrate that this tribal league in fact ever existed at all. In this connection it would be methodologically wrong to employ the fact of a "centralized" tradition as one's starting point and then to undertake a sociological analysis of it on the basis of a preconceived notion of its date. Instead, the only fruitful approach would be to undertake a historical analysis of the sources of the period of the Judges in order to arrive at reasonably assured conclusions as to the existence of the hypothetical pan-Israelite tribal league. Only then would it be appropriate to perform a sociological analysis of the relevant traditions in order to form an idea as to their *Sitz im Leben* in the "league", and at the same time determine the date of the collection of the various individual traditions.

At this point I shall be in a position to utilize the earlier criticisms which have been presented of the amphictyony hypothesis as the basis for controlling Gottwald's hypothesis. On the basis of the views and analyses of traditions I have previously adumbrated concerning the period of the Judges I shall assert that if Gottwald is unable to add new aspects to the discussion of the tribal league, then he has not succeeded in establishing a legitimate defense of a pre-monarchical date for this historical tradition, no matter what sociological analysis he employs. In other words, the league hypothesis cannot be used to explain the formation of the tradition, for which reason we shall be obliged to examine later phases in Israel's history to explain this phenomenon. The *terminus a quo* of our search will necessarily be the unification of Israel and Judah by David into a single political system, despite the possibility that in structural terms this kingdom may have had the form of a dual monarchy. However, a *terminus a quo* is by no means necessarily identical with a *terminus ante quem*. In this case the *terminus ante quem* was the appearance of the Deuteronomistic literature and the final redaction of the Tetrateuch, that is, the time of the Exile and subsequently. Of course, a *terminus ante quem* is not identical with a *terminus a quo*, for which reason we shall be obliged to discover criteria which may help us to determine at what point between the two extremes the formation of the traditions in question must have taken place. This can be done in a number of ways so as to provide numerous controls on our results. It may be done in a system-immanent manner, as emphasized by H.H. Schmid[6], which entails an examination of the various masses of tradition contained within the Tetrateuch itself. It may also be done via external control, which in this case would entail that we investigate materials datable to the periods between our *termini a quo* and *ante quem*, and which refer to Israel's early history, but which are located in literary contexts outside of the Tetrateuch.

A thorough treatment of these questions would be much more extensive than our purposes require, and the results of such an analysis would have only limited relevance to our break with the revolution hypothesis. Thus I shall content myself with a mere sketch in which I shall point out a number of possibilities and attempt to formulate a logically structured approach to some of the main problems in the discussion of the formation of Israelite historical tradition.

§ 2

N.K Gottwald's Understanding of the Tradition

Both Mendenhall and Gottwald unambiguously assume that those parts of the OT historical tradition which deal with Israel's earliest history were already fixed before the conclusion of the period of the Judges. Furthermore, both definitely assert that a common or pan-Israelite tribal league existed

---

[6] Cf. Schmid 1976:12.

prior to the formation of the state of Israel. The reason both adhere so tenaciously to the league hypothesis in spite of the thorough criticisms of it during recent decades is not difficult to discern; it has been distinctively formulated by Gottwald himself: "...if we were to strip away analytically the cultic, military, socioeconomic, and jural structure of the Israelite confederacy, Israel would simply fall apart into autonomous tribes without any discernible defining relationships among them and without any distinguishable consciousness or culture"[7]. We shall later have occasion to consider whether Gottwald has not actually offered here a fairly accurate characterization of pre-national Israel. In other words, we shall see that the Israelites had no consciousness of unity before Davidic times; this is a possibility which up to now only a very few scholars have been willing to entertain seriously. The reason why this has been the case is quite clear. Any working hypothesis which asserts that there was no pan-Israelite fellowship, no pan-Israelite religion or ideology, and no pan-Israelite historical tradition in pre-national times would have serious consequences for our understanding of both the developmental history of Israel and her religious development until late in the period of the monarchy. It must be emphasized that both Mendenhall and Gottwald, as well as their supporters, have been forced to adhere to an entirely traditional picture of the superstructure of Israelite tribal society in the period of the Judges, since the revolution hypothesis (as they have propounded it) can only be maintained by asserting the existence of the tribal league. If there was no pan-Israelite political or religious institution in the period of the Judges, it would be impossible to claim that Israel came into being because rebellious Canaanite peasants (or proletarians) joined in Yahwism to form an anti-Canaanite society, since there would then have been no Israelite society they could possibly have joined.

In Mendenhall's works, arguments in favor of the existence of a tribal society are hard to find. Thus I intend here to examine more close the argumentation of Gottwald, who attempts to show that as it is represented in the Pentateuch and the Book of Joshua the pan-Israelite historical tradition must ultimately derive from the pre-national era. Gottwald's starting point is his criticism of earlier scholarship for not being prepared to recognize that Israel was "a social totality" already in the prenational period. Of course, by this he means that scholars have not been willing to use sociological method to analyze both the Israelite society and its traditions[8]. Naturally, some tendencies in this direction are already present in Noth's work. Gottwald is willing to admit this, but there is nevertheless some question as to whether Gottwald

---

[7] 1979A:383; cf. also 1979A:101: "Without the existence of the cult as the centralized organ of the social system of Israel, no basic themes would have developed at all, and there would have been no occasion for the agglomeration of disparate traditions of proto-Israelites into the harmonized tradition of united Israel."

[8] Gottwald 1979A:18; cf. 1979A:386 (on Noth).

is correct to claim that these are only preliminary tendencies. I think one would be justified in claiming that that Noth's amphictyony hypothesis is a sociological model which lends itself to use as a unitary conception of Israel in the period of the Judges, since it applies to Israel's daily religious life, her political activities, and provides a framework for the structuring of the traditions about the tribal league.

Examination ot Gottwald's use of his sources reveals that he would hardly have gotten very far with his analysis of the OT materials if he had not been able to make use of the insights of earlier German research, in particular that of Noth and von Rad. It is namely the work of precisely these two scholars on the Mosaic books which has composed the basis for virtually all serious research into the Pentateuch and the Deuteronomistic Historical Work[9]. We shall shortly see that when Gottwald goes further than Noth (and von Rad), which he actually does only occasionally, the quality of his argumentation also suffers thereby. I shall briefly illustrate this point with an example. Gottwald claims that the monarchy cannot have provided the background for the formation of the Israelite historical tradition, because the "historians" of the monarchy were content merely to collect earlier traditions without significantly changing their contents. Furthermore, the author maintains that these traditions conflicted with what he regards as "the presuppositions and impulses of the monarchic traditionists"[10]. In other words, Gottwald is unable to imagine that the collectors of the historical traditions who worked during the period of the monarchy might have belonged to circles which did not support monarchic ideology. Nor does he seem able to imagine that the lack of interest in the institution of monarchy which seems to emerge from the sources dealing with Israel's earliest history could possibly be explained by their having been composed first *after* the dissolution of the monarchy. On this as on other issues, the fathers of the revolution hypothesis operate with a remarkably uniform picture of Israel during the monarchy; this picture rules out the possibility that this society may have contained a variety of levels. The possibility is never entertained that more than one tradition may have existed, that there was, conceivably, one official tradition based on the royal administration, and an unofficial one based on circles which either opposed the royal power or were neutral with respect to it. Such centers could have been local sanctuaries; they could also have been circles rooted in Israel's traditional social structure, or there might have been question of a rural, so-called "little" tradition, as opposed to the official "great" tradition of the state.

Another point to be dealt with below has to do with Gottwald's at least partially justified criticism of the amphictyony hypothesis. In spite of the author's sceptical attitude towards the idea of an Israelite twelve-tribe league

---

[9] Namely Noth 1948 and Von Rad 1938.
[10] 1979A:42.

during the period of the Judges, he confines himself to describing his own version of Israel's historical point of departure as follows: "we simply state that the peculiar structure of Israel consisted in its being a social movement with a well-articulated religious cult"[11]. Gottwald assumes in part that the formulation of the traditions concerning Israel's earliest history took place within this cult, and in part that the cult in question was centralistic, so that the tradition-formation taking place around the cult had to lead to a pan-Israelite historical tradition, which subsequently became the common property and guideline of the Israelite people in the pre-national period[12]. Of course, these are mere postulates, but they are so interwoven with the rest of Gottwald's work as to form a totality which ultimately forms the basis of his analyses.

Naturally, it would be more methodologically correct first to analyze the OT materials in order to determine whether the sources for the period of the Judges indicate that a league existed. Should such an examination prove successful, it would then be appropriate to describe the function of the historical traditions within the league. If such an analysis actually led us to conclude that the confederacy idea deserved to be retained, it would be reasonable to suppose that the main lineaments of Noth's sketch could be sustained, and we would also have to conclude that Gottwald's sociological analysis of the sources was a valuable supplement to Noth's earlier traditio-historical observations. On the other hand, if a historical analysis of the OT sources cannot demonstrate that Israel was united in some form of pre-national tribal confederation of a permanent or semi-permanent nature, then it would be illegitimate simply to postulate that such a confederation must have existed and subsequently undertake a sociological analysis presupposing the existence of this confederation. This procedure is ineluctably circular: the sources are centralistic because there once existed a pan-Israelite tribal league, and the centralizing tendency of the sources proves that such a league did in fact exist.

In Gottwald's opinion the nucleus of the tradition was a number of

---

[11] 1979A:27.

[12] 1979A:25-31. Cf. Gottwald's reconstruction of the formation of the tradition (1979A:88-99 and 100-114). It is worth noting that the materials which Gottwald imagines belong in a cultic context include "liturgies, poems, myths, sagas, legends, and genealogies" (1979A:28). The association of some of these materials to a cultic context is surely somewhat suspect. This certainly applies to significant parts of the genealogical recollections in the OT, as these are much more likely to have had their origin in kinship contexts, that is, as parts of the private traditions of a number of families. Cf. Wilson 1977, especially the general introduction on pp. 38-45. Wilson distinguishes between "domestic functions", "politico-jural functions", and "religious functions". In connection with the last-named of these functions, Wilson mentions that it is primarily to be found in societies with well-developed ancestor cults, and in societies with "divine kingship", in which the royal dynastic genealogy is fostered by the royal cult (cf. Wilson 1977:44-45). As for the connection between myths, sagas, and legends and a single, particular *Sitz im Leben*, reference shouls be made to Long 1976A, who quite correctly points out that, for example, in a given society a *saga* may have a number of different *Sitze*, and that variations occur from society to society. Thus no neutral law links such things as saga and cult; indeed, the reverse is probably the case.

complexes of traditions, each of which had a prehistory of its own prior to the collection of them in the various literary strata in the Pentateuch and the Book of Joshua[13]. This assumption also makes it possible to date the assimilation of the individual complexes into the Israelite tradition which is preserved in the early literary layers of the Mosaic books. Thus it is possible to point to a number of basic traditions which have been integrated into the Exodus narrative and the tradition of the Settlement. These were later expanded by the addition of a number of other complexes of tradition, including the story of the Sinai event. It should be noted on this point that Gottwald accepts the separation of the Sinai and Exodus traditions suggested by von Rad[14]. However, Gottwald draws on Noth's views in arguing against von Rad that the connection between the Sinai complex and the Exodus narrative was created before the Yahwist had composed his historical work in the early years of the era of the monarchy[15].

Gottwald's preconceived understanding of ancient Israel once more forms the basis for his date for and evaluation of the collection of the individual complexes of traditions since, according to him, it was precisely the establishment of Israel as a socially remarkable society which made possible a normative view of history. This view was then later developed in the cult in the course of the pre-national period[16]. Again and again we discover that the textual materials are analyzed on the basis of a particular and preconceived notion of the Israelite society in the period of the Judges. Gottwald does not consider whether it is at all possible to arrive at an understanding of Israel's political system in the era of the Judges solely on the basis of the existing traditions. By locating the formation of the traditions in the cult, Gottwald (like Noth before him) has found what one might be tempted to call a *Deus ex machina*, that is, an analytical model which permits every sort of conclusion as to the formation of the tradition, not least because this cult is without further ado elevated to the status of a pan-Israelite institution. I have no intention of rejecting the possibility that the process in question may have evolved as Gottwald or, for that matter, Mendenhall, has suggested. However, it is out of the question simply to assume that this is the only possible matrix for the understanding of the formation of the tradition.

---

[13] See the presentation of the problem (whose point of departure is Noth 1948) in Gottwald 1979A:72-82.

[14] Gottwald 1979A:72ff., and on the Sinai-Exodus traditions, see Von Rad 1938:20ff., which is followed by Gottwald 1979A:88ff.

[15] 1979A:89f. See also 1979A:81, and Noth 1948:63-67. Noth felt that the entry of the Sinai tradition into the Pentateuch was the result of the fact *"dass auch bei diesem Vorgang noch einmal die Südstämme zur Bereicherung der Pentateuchüberlieferung beigetragen haben"* (1948:66).

[16] See especially Von Rad 1938:41ff. Von Rad held that the cultic background was the result of a festival of covenant renewal. He also claimed that other parts of the "Hexateuchal traditions" had a cultic background, such as the emergence of the immigration traditions, which he labelled *'eine Heiligtumsüberlieferung"* (1938:49). Further on the role of the Sinai traditions, see Noth 1948:64ff.

In this connection it is important to note that Gottwald accepts that the traditions of the Exodus and Sinai were linked together already in the days of the league, and that he also maintains that even if they are two separate complexes of traditions, they are primarily different by reason of their different functions. These functions may well have been performed within one and the same cultic event, or in connection with different cultic arrangements at the same central sanctuary. This means that even if Gottwald emphasizes the necessity to distinguish between a rudimentary covenant and law tradition which was nurtured within the original Moses group and the well developed covenant ideas and complexes of laws of the later tribal league, he nevertheless believes that these central parts of the Pentateuchal traditions existed already in pre-national times. The writer never questions their presence at this date, or it would perhaps be more accurate to say that he simply ignores other possibilities for the emergence of the OT legal traditions and the concept of the covenant[17].

Thus in Gottwald's opinion the pre-national centralized cult contains four different aspects. The first of these is a "manifestation of the deity", by which he means the Sinai theme, with which the sub-theme of the theophany is associated. The other is a "constitution or reconstitution of the community" meaning the Sinai theme plus a sub-theme consisting of conceptions of the covenant. The third is a "recital of the actions of the deity", which entails a rehearsal of the basic historical themes of the Exodus and the Settlement. The fourth and final aspect is the "declaration of the will of the deity for the community", meaning the Sinai theme, whose sub-theme is the Law[18]. It should be obvious – and Gottwald himself emphasizes the fact – that the total unification of these themes would only be relevant in a likewise united Israel. However, the conjoining of these various themes in a centralized tradition in the OT does not prove that the tradition dates from the pre-national period.

The main part of Gottwald's treatment of the traditions dealing with the history of Israel before the establishment of the tribal league is devoted to a thorough analysis of the connections between these traditions and the central cult. However, it will hardly be necessary to examine this argumentation in detail, since it is not yet clear that Gottwald has provided us with a precisely formulated and convincing defense of the league hypothesis. It will accordingly be necessary to investigate whether *The Tribes of Yahweh* in fact contains a historical analysis of the source materials relating to the period of the Judges. If there is no such analysis, then we have no decisive argument in favor of dating the centralistic tradition to the time of the Judges.

---

[17] See Gottwald 1979A:35-41 on the religion of the "Moses group", and 1979A:36f. on the difference between this religion and that of the later tribal confederation.
[18] 1979A:90f.

§ 3

Is There Anything New in Gottwald's Understanding of Israelite Tribal Society in the Period of the Judges?

I mentioned above Gottwald's literary analyses and their basis in the concept of a confederation which was presented by Noth. In this section it is my intention to study more thoroughly Gottwald's sociological matrix for understanding ancient Israel by examining his attitude towards the concept of the Israelite twelve-tribe amphictyony in the period of the Judges.

An appropriate place to start would be Gottwald's rejection of the amphictyony hypothesis, and in particular his rejection of the analogical value of the Greek amphictyony[19]. In Gottwald's opinion, the similarities between the Greek and Israelite leagues are only superficial, since the confederations in Hellas and Israel had quite different functions. In Greece the amphictyony had only limited significance with respect to societies which had found their form independently of the league; by way of contrast, or so Gottwald maintains, in Israel the confederation was the forum which shaped pre-national Israelite society[20]. This way of approaching the matter is new and apparently decisive, above all when we apply Gottwald's views to the later developments of the idea of the amphictyony from the hand of Noth[21].

Nevertheless, although it involves a slight digression from our main goal, it must be mentioned that Gottwald's understanding of the Greek amphictyony is somewhat imprecise. At the time he had written the main part of his work he could not have been familiar with my presentation of the Greek amphictyony, but he ought perhaps to have been cognizant of the separate publication of this part of *Israel i dommertiden* by the time his additional work appeared[22]. Had he seen the article in question, he would have realized, first, that there was only one amphictyony in ancient Hellas, namely the Delphian league, and, second, he would have known that the members of this organization were *not* city-states, as he claimed, but "nations", such as the Dorians, Ionians, Locraeans, and so on. In other words, the Delphian amphictyony may have been formed *prior to* the establishment of "the cultural and political entities"[23]. On the other hand, Gottwald is right in claiming that the

---

[19] Cf. Gottwald 1979A:345-357 on the criticisms of the twelve-tribe hypothesis in general, and 1979A:376-386 on the Greek amphictyony in particular.

[20] Gottwald 1979A:377.

[21] On this see Lemche 1972:25-30; cf. also Bächli 1977:61-70.

[22] Cf. Lemche 1977 (and compare Lemche 1972:20ff. and 39ff.).

[23] There have been attempts to date the Delphian Amphictyony back to the earliest period of Greek history; see, for example, Wüst 1954. However, the existing materials by no means allow Wüst's hypothesis to stand; they do not indicate a date for the founding of the amphictyony earlier than the 8th or 7th centuries.

Delphian amphictyony enjoyed only limited functions within Greek society, that it only contributed slightly to the formation of a pan-Hellenic ideology, and that at least in the classical period it was forced to compete with a long series of other Greek sanctuaries in this role, such as those of Olympia and Corinth[24].

This subject will not delay us more here, but it should be emphasized that Gottwald's criticism of the use of the Greek amphictyony as an analogy to the Israelite organization does not bring him a single step closer to proving the existence of an Israelite league. It is no help at all to conclude, as he does at the end of his section on the Greek versus the Israelite amphictyonies, that we must retain the concept of a confederation in the case of Israel, since without it we should be unable to explain intra-Israelite solidarity before the monarchy[25]. It is simply out of the question to maintain that Israel must have comprised this sort of union in the era of the Judges; rather, the task of the researcher is and must be to demonstrate that this was (or was not) the case.

Furthermore, it should be added that Israel could well have functioned as a cultic, military, socio-economic, and juridical structure without necessarily having belonged to an integrated confederation. With all the weaknesses de Geus' study otherwise reveals, he nevertheless demonstrates this point adequately. This fact is also supported by a close examination of a number of traditional societies such as that of the much-discussed Nuer (also mentioned in this work), the solidarity of whom is not regulated by law, but only by an awareness of the fact that all Nuer are Nuer. A non-organized Israelite tribal society which consisted of a greater or lesser number of individual tribes could have been likewise characterized by feelings of solidarity, irrespective of whether the individual Israelite tribes enjoyed any cultic, political, or economic fellowship. Another point is that we cannot simply presuppose that they enjoyed such solidarity. Only an analysis of the historical traditions concerning the period of the Judges can provide us with a legitimate basis for such a conclusion.

What are Gottwald's other arguments for claiming that a tribal league existed during the period of the Judges? Once again it is necessary to examine his criticism of the amphictyony hypothesis, and specifically his rejection of the back-dating of the twelve-tribe ideology to the pre-national period[26]. On this point Gottwald is quite emphatic, and, in my opinion, perspicacious. There are no pre-Davidic references to a twelve-tribe scheme, nor do any of the sources for the period of the Judges have to do with this ideology. On the other hand, Gottwald's conviction that the twelve-tribe system derives from the era of David and represents that monarch's administrative system is less well

---

[24] See Lemche 1977:52ff.
[25] 1979A:383.
[26] 1979A:358-375.

founded, since his argumentation for such administrative renewal during the reign of David could at best be described as a qualified guess. Gottwald requires two separate administrative subdivisions to have taken place during the united monarchy in order to explain the presence in the OT of two different editions of the twelve-tribe lists: one which leaves out the tribe of Levi, and one which includes it. Gottwald asserts that the latter of these two lists came about as a consequence of the fact that in the time of Solomon the "Davidic" subdivision lost its significance; the number twelve was no longer politically relevant, so that it continued to figure only in cultic-ideological contexts as an expression of the unity of Israel[27]. No lengthy argumentation is necessary on this point, since I can confine myself to reiterating my observation (published in *Israel i dommertiden*) to the effect that while the list-type which includes Levi is no doubt secondary with respect to the list which excludes Levi, in reality the difference between the two lists is literary and reflects the redaction-historical interests of the redactor of the Pentateuch[28]. The fact that the twelve-tribe system may be dated to the period of the united kingdom can never be an argument *in favor of* an all-Israelite tribal confederation in the era of the Judges. In fact, it can only count as an argument *against* the hypothesis of the existence of such a confederation, whether one regards the confederation as a twelve-tribe amphictyony or as a greater permanent tribal league with less than twelve members. Gottwald's remark to the effect that precisely at the time when the monarchy was introduced there existed by pure coincidence an Israelite confederation of twelve tribes is incomprehensible in this connection, for how on earth can he permit himself to claim that it existed just after having admitted that we have no sources which indicate this?[29].

It is accordingly necessary for Gottwald to present more concrete views and arguments if we are to admit that a league of the type he suggests once existed. One searches in vain for decisively new views on this point in the *Tribes of Yahweh*. There is nothing whatsoever in the work which even tangentially resembles an evidential argument in favor of the confederation; instead, one finds everywhere only presumptions or unsupported postulates. This judgement may be substantiated in many ways, but the clearest evidence is possibly provided by Gottwald's criticism of the attacks of A.D.H. Mayes and R. Smend on the amphictyony hypothesis[30]. In Gottwald's opinion, Mayes and

---

[27] 1979A:373.

[28] Cf. Lemche 1972:106-113.

[29] 1979A:363. Gottwald nowhere attempts to explain his assumption of the existence of a twelve-tribe confederation at this date. There can hardly be any other defence for the twelve-tribe confederation's necessary connection between the northern and southern Palestinian tribes than that provided by R. Smend (1967), but on this see Lemche 1972:99-101, and of the literature mentioned there see especially De Vaux 1970A.

[30] Gottwald 1979A:382 (on Smend 1966, Mayes 1973, and Mayes 1974). It is significant that Gottwald lumps Smend and Mayes together, since, unlike Mayes, Smend is a convinced adherent of Noth's amphictyony hypothesis; cf. Smend 1971A. Gottwald refers to Smend 1966,

Smend only succeed in demonstrating that there was no twelve-tribe amphictyony in pre-national Israel, but they have not been able to show that there was no Israelite tribal league at all. His argument against Mayes and Smend is as follows: "Nevertheless, a social-structural bond, more encompassing than separate suballiances for warfare and for cult and more precise than widely diffused belief in Yahweh, is necessary to account for the emergent unity of premonarchic Israel under the turbulent and hostile conditions of Late Bronze-Early Iron Canaan"[31]. Now, how can Gottwald possibly know this? Is he not in actuality simply saying that in his own opinion he does not feel that this can have been the case?

Now, if an analysis of the historical tradition fails to prove that the league existed, are we not then obliged to accept this datum and on the basis of it attempt to describe the formation of the Israelite state precisely as a result of the political life of a number of separate social units? Such units will at times have been in partial accord with one another, while at other times they must have clashed in direct contradiction; at all times, however, they will have been under pressure from other parts of Palestinian society and its neighboring societies. It is necessary to take Gottwald seriously to task on this point, since he insists on retaining the hypothesis of a central tribal cult in spite of the very considerable criticisms which have been launched of the confederation hypothesis. In my earlier work on the period of the Judges I dealt with one of the central issues in this connection, namely the question as to whether it is possible to identify a central sanctuary in pre-national Israel[32]. My conclusion was, in all simplicity, that we cannot do so. On the other hand, it is possible to say that there were a number of sanctuaries with extra-regional significance in the country. However, none of these was venerated by all of the Israelite tribes, not even Shechem. But if there was no central sanctuary, then there was likewise no *Sitz im Leben* for a centralized cultic-historical tradition in the Israel of the period of the Judges[33].

---

in which Smend correctly rejected Von Rad's theory that the Israelite "holy war" was an amphictyonic institution (Von Rad 1951). However, Smend's work was intended to be a rescue-action for the amphictyony hypothesis, since Smend recognized that the military traditions of the period of the Judges had no association of any kind to any *permanent* tribal federation. On the other hand, Gottwald correctly points out that it would be unrealistic to conceive of a Yahwistic tribal confederation which did not wage "the wars of Yahweh". Of course, this is but one more indication that the league hypothesis rests on an extremely weak foundation.

[31] Gottwald 1979A:382.

[32] Lemche 1972:44-75, but see also Mayes 1974:34-55, and de Geus 1976:195-201.

[33] This is also my main objection to Gottwald in my "review" of Gottwald 1979A (see Lemche 1982). For the same reason there is no point in concerning ourselves with L.L. Thompson's "positive" criticisms of Gottwald's understanding of the preservation and transmission of the tradition as an ideological or mythological expression of Israel's socio-economic experiences in prenational times (L.L. Thompson 1981). I have no difficulty in following Thompson's description of Jos 1-5 as "myth", understood as an ideological *raison d'etre* for Israel's right to possess the land. However, Thompson errs on two vital points. In the first place, he makes no attempt whatsoever to date Jos 1-5. In the second place, he never attempts to explain what he takes this

I shall not attempt a thorough discussion of the tribal league at this juncture, but will instead confine myself to referring to my earlier treatment of this issue, as well as to my recent survey on the status of the amphictyony since 1970[34]. However, in passing it would be worth mentioning that no decisive new moments have been added to the discussion, with the single exception of de Geus' work on the Israelite tribes in 1976. The subjects which have been discussed have been concentrated around such traditional topics as the question of the central sanctuary, the value of the Greek amphictyony as an analogy, holy war, the office of the "Judge" (and other amphictyonic officials), and so forth[35]. With reference to the matter of the central sanctuary, scholars have come no closer to showing whether Shechem may really be regarded as the pan-Israelite center of an Israelite league consisting of both northern and southern tribes, in spite of the claims of H. Seebass and others[36]. There has also been a tendency to weaken Noth's view of the significance of the central sanctuary, not least in the form of efforts to distinguish between a central sanctuary and an ark-sanctuary[37]. In this direction, of course, much is conceivable. Thus, for example, it is possible to deny that the sanctuary or sanctuaries where the ark resided functioned as a central sanctuary. This would strengthen the candidacy of Shechem,since, as is well known, the ark can scarcely have been located there[38]. One could equally well attempt to argue for the existence of a number of separate ark-sanctuaries, by, for example, distinguishing between a Gilgal-ark and a Shiloh-ark[39]. None of these attempts has proved convincing, since no one has troubled to draw the consequences these suggestions would necessarily entail with respect to the location of the ark-sanctuary in the Pentateuchal sources.

Concerning the status of the Greek amphictyony, scholars have more or less correctly maintained that Noth understood it to be only an *analogy*, and not a *model*[40]. In fact, generally speaking, a number of researchers have stated that the amphictyony hypothesis which should be debated is the one Noth originally proposed, which should be dealt with in isolation of later developments of it[41]. All of these tendencies have contributed to the lessening of the importance placed by scholars on the role of the amphictyony in premonarchical Israel; the proposition has increasingly been felt to be superfluous. On the other hand, it is still regarded as important

"Israel" to be (i.e., what sort of political quantity it was). S. Tengström, on the other hand, does this, but to Tengström the prenational Israel is still a twelve-tribe amphictyony; he dismisses the modern criticisms of the amphictyony as not decisive (1976:88). Like Gottwald, Tengström is forced to retain the concept of a collected Israel in the period of the Judges, since this is the essential presupposition for his hypothesis about an ancient basic narrative. It is also to be noted that Tengström goes even further than Noth and Gottwald, in that he not only speaks of a prenational origin for the Hexateuchal traditions, but of the existence of an early "Israel-saga" of considerable dimensions (1976:14).

[34] See Lemche 1972; 1984.

[35] Important works from the period subsequent to 1970: A) opponents: De Vaux 1971A; Mayes 1973; 1974; 1977; de Geus 1976. B) adherents: Smend 1971A; Bächli 1977; Seebass 1978.

[36] Cf. Seebass 1978:205.

[37] Thus Smend 1971A:629; Seebass 1978:207; Bächli 1977:117, as well as Tengström 1976:88. In this connection Bächli asks whether there is not a question of some completely different cultic implement as pan-Israelite cult object.

[38] Jos 8,30ff. is a late addition; cf. Lemche 1972:50, following Nielsen 1959:77ff., and Noth 1930:93. Noth nevertheless maintained that the Ark must have been there.

[39] Thus Otto 1975:360f.

[40] Thus Bächli 1977:178, and Seebass 1978:201. Seebass apparently feels that the analogy is uninteresting (cf. Seebass 1980), while Bächli, in a manner of speaking, wants to have his cake and eat it too, in the sense that he is prepared to discount the value of the Greek amphictyony as an analogy, while at the same time he asserts the significance of a rather dubious questionable Polynesian "amphictyony" which he cites on the authority of W. Mühlmann (1938:82). However, this "amphictyony" idea is based on a more than suspect oral tradition, as well as on a written tradition which is even more questionable (cf. Lemche 1984).

[41] Cf. Smend 1971A:623, and Seebass 1978:196, both with some justice, since individual writers have added their own speculative developments to the theory so as in the course of time to have reconstructed a "United States of Israel" in the premonarchical era; see thus Bright 1960:142-151, and Kraus 1969:414f. and 452ff.

whether we should continue to distinguish between the so-called "holy war" in Israel and the sacral tribal league, or whether there existed one or two offices of "Judge"[42]. Both of the last-mentioned elements belong to the expanded version of the amphictyony model, but both are results of the tireless pursuit by scholars of some functions which the tribal league might have had in order to explain its presence at all. Therefore, no matter whether scholars are prepared to abandon such concepts as the existence of a pan-Israelite lawspeaker, or defensive war as the task *par excellence* of the league, none of these matters could ever become arguments in favor of the retention of the amphictyony hypothesis[43]. Various *ad hoc* strategic retreats have been undertaken to strengthen the hypothesis, but the problem is that the starting point of these efforts has been that the hypothesis is valid until the opposite has been proven[44]. Against this, I would most earnestly maintain that since the reservations which Fohrer, Herrmann, and others have voiced since the 1960's, it has been amply shown that Noth's working hypothesis was misleading from the beginning[45]. Thus if one intends to retain the hypothesis, it will be necessary to discover new and decisive arguments in its favor. There is no question but that at present the burden of proof is on the shoulders of the adherents of the twelve-tribe league.

---

[42] On the theory of a connection between "holy war" and the tribal league, see Von Rad 1951; on the office of the Judge, see Noth 1950B.

[43] On the divorce of the "holy war" from the amphictyony, see Smend 1966, but see also the more radical attitudes towards the very concept Stolz 1972 and Weippert 1972. F. Stolz regards the "holy war" as the result of a Deuteronomistic or in any eventa late Judaean idealization of the war, while Weippert insists that in the ancient Orient all wars were "holy" ones (on this point see already Pedersen 1960:3-27). On the respective offices of the Judges, consult the criticisms of Noth in de Geus 1965, Richter 1965, Lemche 1972: 74-87, and Hauser 1975. Noth's hypothesis has been defended most recently by H. Rösel 1980 and 1981.

[44] See Bächli 1977:181.

[45] Cf. Herrmann 1962 and 1969; Fohrer 1966, and the survey in Lemche 1972:31-38.

Chapter 6

ANOTHER PATH? THE FORMATION OF THE ISRAELITE HISTORICAL TRADITION

§ 1

Historical Tradition and the Prophets

The following study of the problems connected with the emergence of the "canonical" understanding of the earliest history of Israel will be, as mentioned previously, only a sketch. I intend to place special emphasis on the question of the covenant traditions, and in particular on the Sinai tradition and its linkage with the complexes dealing with the Exodus and the Settlement. This should help us to discover when it would be reasonable to say that the covenant and Exodus traditions became conjoined in the history of the development of Israelite tradition. My emphasis on precisely these materials is not at all accidental, since the entire conception of the establishment of an anti-Canaanite, Yahwistic league of tribes in the period of the Judges either stands or falls by the question of whether this process of tradition-formation may be dated to the pre-national period. For this reason it is extremely disappointing that on this issue Gottwald has chosen to make use of Lord Nelson's method: he has set his telescope to his blind eye, and completely ignored the current debates concerning not only the placement of the Sinai traditions in the Pentateuch, but also those concerning the date of the Pentateuchal sources, and in particular the date of the Yahwist and his possible connection with Deuteronomism. For chronological reasons, much of the professional literature which I shall cite below was not available to Gottwald when he wrote the main part of his work (it seems to have been concluded around 1974). However, he did have occasion to respond to these contributions in his addition to *The Tribes of Yahweh*, but instead completely failed to take account of the new radical departures in the field of Pentateuchal research. Both the programmatic works of H.H. Schmid and R. Rendstorff have been left out of account in Gottwald's monograph. This may well prove to be fatal, since if the views of these two scholars (and others) establish themselves, the revolution hypothesis will be relegated to a footnote in future research. If this should occur, it would be most regrettable, because then the previously mentioned *relevant* criticisms of the earlier research into Israelite prehistory which both Gottwald and Mendenhall have presented would be overlooked. Scholars would run the risk of continuing to tread the familiar pathways without taking account of the obvious faults which the studies of Israelite history of Alt and Noth really do contain[1].

The best materials available for undertaking a control of the date for the emergence of the traditions concerning the earliest history of Israel – that is, understood as a *canonical* whole – are presumably in the prophetic books of the OT. These are the only writings in which a traditional analysis utilizing literary critical, form critical and traditio-historical methods can issue in reasonably assured dates for the earliest materials, since these will not ordinarily be traceable to much further back than the time of the prophet whose name is associated with the book in question. Of course, this does not mean that this is a minor task, since there is no assurance in advance that such a traditional textual analysis will lead to unambiguous results. In other words, there will inevitably be a margin of uncertainty left when we ask as to whether one or another prophetic oracle is authentic or not. Nor is my analysis of the prophetic materials undertaken without its own presuppositions, since a number of scholars have concerned themselves with the prophets' use of historical motifs. In particular the names of E. Rohland, S. Herrmann, L. Perlitt, and J. Vollmer come to mind[2]. Of these four figures, Perlitt's treatment of covenantal theology in the OT contains the most striking presentation of the problem. Perlitt deals with the prophetic materials in a chapter expressively entitled *"Das Bundesschweigen bei den Propheten des 8.Jh.s"*[3]. By way of contrast, Herrmann's study is not so much concerned with the prophets' use of history as with their proclamations about the future, and Vollmer presupposes quite a lot which in reality has not been satisfactorily established, meaning that his is a quite traditional understanding of the early history of Israel.

Perlitt puts his finger where the wound itches already in his introduction: *"Nähme man die Spruchsammlungen der Propheten Amos, Jesaja und Micha, aber selbst die des Hosea für sich und läse sie nicht von vornherein durch die brille ihres kanonischen Kontextes, käme kaum jemand auf die Idee, dass in ihnen beschriebene, geforderte oder auch als zerstört beklagte Gottesverhältnis auf den Begriff Bund zu bringen"*[4]. The writer's subsequent survey of the covenant motif, or rather, of the lack of allusions to covenantal concepts is accordingly only offered in illustration of this initial remark, and is actually superfluous, as Perlitt himself admits[5]. However,

---

[1] I am primarily referring to Schmid 1976 and Rendtorff 1977A. see further in this chapter, below pp. 367ff. It should be mentioned here, however, that neither these two scholars nor any other, Van Seters included, has addressed himself seriously to the question of Israel's actual historical origins.

[2] See Rohland 1979; Herrmann 1965; Perlitt 1969, and Vollmer 1971.

[3] See Perlitt 1969:129-155. The more radical of the *"Dielheimere"* not only speak of *"das Bundesschweigen"*, but of *"das grosse Schweigen"*, by which they mean the general silence concerning Israel's prehistory in prenational times. See Diebner and Schult 1975*, with which I am unfortunately only acquainted thanks to a short summary in Schmid 1976:166.

[4] Perlitt 1969:129.

[5] Ibid.

Perlitt also acknowledges that we have to do with more than just a *"Bundes-schweigen"* in the writings of these four prophets, since in reality they also keep silent with respect to the Pentateuch understood as a "'mosaisch' geprägten und abgerundeten Pentateuch...."[6]. Vollmer's study does not bring us any further, although he does supply the detailed analyses which are lacking in Perlitt's volume. In many cases Vollmer's evaluation of the attachments of the various prophetic passages with which he deals is surely correct. However, one might be inclined to ask why he (or, for that matter, Perlitt) has not pursued his study later than the 8th century prophets and thus, for example, has not undertaken a similar analysis of the Book of Jeremiah. As we shall see, here, too, there are surprises in store for those scholars who may believe in advance that this late pre-exilic prophet had a well established covenant theology.

The materials in question will be presented below, and emphasis will be placed on the question of authenticity. Following this it will perhaps be possible to evaluate the significance to the prophets of the traditions concerning Israel's earliest history, as well as the extent of their knowledge of Israelite prehistory, and possibly form an idea of the shape of these traditions from the 8th century until post-exilic times. However, I have no intention to undertake traditio-historical and form-critical evaluations of the various oracles in depth.

1.

Amos

Brief perusal of the Book of Amos gives the impression that Amos had an extensive knowledge of traditions concerning Israel's earliest history. If the references to the sojourns in Egypt and the desert are authentic Amos oracles, we could say with certainty that, generally speaking, this prophet was familiar with these traditions in the same version as that preserved in the Tetrateuch.

Amos 4,10 and 7,9. Of the seven passages in the Book of Amos which it would be relevant to consider in this context, Am 4,10 and 7,9 may be discarded immediately. They are not evidence as to the use by this prophet of historical motifs. Am 4,10 could conceivably refer to one of the plagues of Egypt, but scholars have more often been prone to regard the pestilence as a disease it was still possible to contract in Egypt in Amos' time[7]. Am 7,9 and 7,16 tell us no

---

[6] 1969:152.

[7] Among other suggestions, scholars have taken this for a reference to a hypothetical defeat suffered by the forces of Jeroboam II at the hands of the Egyptians, but comparable to the fate of Sancherib's army in 701; thus e.g. Rudolph 1971:179. This is pure guesswork. Others have simply excised v 10a as a gloss from late, perhaps post-exilic, times; see thus Vollmer 1971:11. Perlitt, however, reckons the whole of v 6-13 to be an addition to the authentic word of Amos, Amos 4,4-5 (1969:135n).

more than that Amos was familiar with the name of the patriarch Isaac; but is this the patriarch mentioned in the Book of Genesis? By this I mean to say that the juxtaposition (identification) of Israel and Isaac can only be taken to imply a North Palestinian location for the "Isaac" in question. In other words, the reference to Isaac in the Book of Amos is a reminiscence of quite different Isaac traditions than those which are preserved in the Book of Genesis[8].

Amos 2,9ff and 3,1b. Are these two passages, both of which reveal considerable influences from formulaic language, authentic words of Amos? Am 3,1b can hardly be so[9]. The following considerations argue that this passage is secondary: in the first place, there is a change from third to second person with reference to Yahweh in v 1a and 1b; in the second place there is the expression עַל כָל המשפחה (אשר העליתי), which has been borrowed from Am 3,2[10]. Third, there is demonstrable tension between the stereotype expression election in v 1b and the original in v 2[11].

As far as Am 2,9-12 is concerned, a close scrutiny of the relationship between v 9 and 10 is decisive for the question of the authenticity of v 10. In v 9 the Amorites are described as giants; this is not explicitly stated in many other OT passages. Gigantism is usually ascribed to the "sons of Anak" or to the "inhabitants of the land". It is accordingly possible that v 9 contains a special tradition[12]. Of more importance is the fact that v 10 does not seem to be the original sequel to v 9. In favor of this judgement is the repeated introduction, ואנכי (v 9 and 10); also, v 10 interrupts v 9 and returns to events which chronologically precede v 9. Therefore v 10 must be regarded as secondary, as is suggested, but not proven, by its traditional language[13].

---

[8] Naturally, in this connection scholars have referred to the special connection between the Northern Kingdom and the sanctuary at Beersheba; cf. Amos 5,5; 8,14, and the oft-quoted dissertation of Zimmerli (1932). However, it is impossible to follow Wolff's view that it was pilgrims to Beersheba who were responsible for the identification of Isaac and Israel (1975:348; see also Rudolph 1971:237).

[9] On this point see Wolff 1975:212. Wolff emphasizes the Deuteronomistic character of the passage, as does W.H. Schmidt (1965:172f.). Rudolph (1971:152) and Robinson (1964:81) both also reckon it to be secondary. See also Vollmer 1971:43n.

[10] Thus Schmidt 1965:172f., who refers to the connection between Amos 3,2 and Gen 12,3; 28,14, and Jer 33,24 and 31,1.

[11] Thus Schmidt 1965:172f; cf. also Perlitt 1969:13n., who regards both Amos 2,10 ans 3,1b as Deuteronomistic interpolations.

[12] Cf. Schmidt 1965:179 and Vollmer 1971:23ff.

[13] See n.11. This view is also shared by Vollmer (1971:24). S. Herrmann, however, seems to view Amos 2,10; 4,10, and 5,15 as authentic words of Amos (1965:119n). Admittedly, such approaches as that of Vollmer (and, for that matter, my own) may be criticized for being too narrowly literary critical (see e.g. Grønbæk 1975:91n.), but it remains necessary to determine just what parts of the Book of Amos (or any prophetic book) actually derive from the prophet himself if we are to evaluate his use of historical retrospects (or those of any other prophet). If we do not pay due attention to the redactional problems, we should unavoidably be compelled to operate with too many unknown factors to allow a useful conclusion. In other words, Amos' use of history may well prove to be significantly different from that of the Book of Amos, since

It should, however, be mentioned here that there is impressive congruence between the expressions employed in v 10 and expressions which appear in "assuredly" Deuteronomistic passages: v 10bα, שנה ארבעים במדבר אתכם ואולך; cf. Deut 29,4a, במדבר שנה ארבעים אתכם ואולך; v 10bβ, האמרי ארץ את לרשת; cf. Jos 1,11; Jdg 2,6; Deut 9,4.5, etc.: הארץ את לרשת. On the conunction of האמרי ארץ and ירש, see Jdg 11,21. We may perhaps ignore v 11f, since the passage refers to conditions after the Settlement, whether the allusion is to Judges, the later prophets, or possibly both groups[14].

Amos 5,25. The passage is a cult polemic in the course of which reference is made to the lack of sacrifices during the sojourn in the desert. The logic of the argument corresponds to that used by the Deuteronomists to explain why David was not allowed to construct his temple in 2 Sam 7,6. The problems connected with this passage are legion. In the first place, one may ask whether v 25 was an original part of the anti-cultic torrent beginning in v 21ff. Second, it may be held that the unquestionably secondary v 26 pulls v 25 with it in its wake. Moreover, if one nevertheless insists that Am 5,25 is an authentic oracle of Amos, it would still be appropriate to ask whether this also applies to the last element in Am 5,25 – or are the "forty years" a Deuteronomistic addition which is dependent on the similarly Deuteronomistic Am 2,10?[15]. Of course, it could be argued that the secondary v 26 does not pull v 25 with it, since v 26 is concerned with a completely different subject (the worship of foreign gods) than that which preoccupies v 21-25 (corruption of the cult of Yahweh). But if this is the case, then v 25 is anticlimactic with respect to v 24. The rela-

---

the book is the work of a redactor, rather than the prophet himself. The result of Herrmann's failure to test his materials is that his study is not very helpful in this particular connection; indeed, it is largely irrelevant to it.

[14] It could be held that both v 11 and v 12 are Deuteronomistic, but that their usage differs from that typical of the Deuteronomists on one point. In v 11 אקים is probably Deuteronomistic (cf.e.g. Deut 18,15, and 34,10, with נביא). However, within the Deuteronomistic literature מיד is otherwise only used in connection with Samson (Jdg 13,5.7; 16,17; i.e., on the assumption that the Samson narratives are to be reckoned part of the Deuteronomistic Book of Judges).

[15] Since the time of Wellhausen scholars have reckoned v 26f. to be secondary, since the Babylonian astral divinities referred to will hardly have been worshiped in Palestine before 722. I am unable to accept Hammershaimb's objection to this argument (1967:89f.). J. McKay has attempted to demonstrate that foreign cults did not get a foothold in Palestine as easily as scholars have been prone to imagine, especially since there is reason to believe that, like the later Macedonians and Romans, the Assyrians made no attempt to force their own religion onto their vassals (McKay 1973). It is likely that McKay exaggerates to some extent, since he bases his evaluation of the question of Assyrian influence on the "official" Assyrian attitude. However, alongside this "official" influence, it would be wise to assume that from the close of the 8th century and throughout the entire 7th century there was considerable Assyrian cultural influence in Palestine, as this almost invariably occurs whenever a superior culture comes into contact with a cultural backwater. In the OT this indirect Assyrian influence manifests itself in the phenomenon of Deuteronomism, and it undoubtedly played a role in the composition of Deuteronomy. On this issue see McCarthy 1963:122ff. (on Deut 28); Frankena 1965, and above all Weinfeld 1972, who attempts to demonstrate a large number of points of contact between Akkadian and Deuteronomistic phraseology.

tionship between this section and the contents of Jer 7,21ff must be taken into account. The scheme in Jer 7,21ff is as follows: a) rejection of the sacrificial cult b) reference to the sojourn in the desert, and c) summons to follow Yahweh's commandments and his way. Jer 7,21ff is part of what is clearly a Deuterono-mistically reworked section running from v 21 to 29[16]. The Amos section reveals the following sequence: a) rejection of sacrifices, b) demand for law and justice, and c) reference to the sojourn in the desert. This reference to the period in the desert is formulated in Deuteronomistic style and is related to the Deuteronomistic Jer 7,21ff as well as Am 2,10[17].

Amos 9,7. This verse has also been accepted by both Wolff and Vollmer as an authentic Amos oracle[18]. I am far from convinced that this is the case. הלֹא את ישראל העליתי מארץ מצרים is, in the first place, verbally identical with Am 2,10 and 3,1b, which, as we have seen, are Deuteronomistic. Next, one feels compelled to ask whether ופלשתיים מכפתור is an authentic recollection of Philistine origins as seen through the eyes of the other inhabitants of Palestine. Or is it not more likely to be a secondary conclusion made on the basis of Gen 10,14; Deut 2,23, and Jer 47,4? Third, one must ask whether וארם מקיר is not simply a short-circuit; cf. 2 Kgs 16,9 and Am 1,5. 2 Kgs 16,9 says that Tiglath Pileser III deported the Aramaeans *to* Kir (ca. 734); Amos is thus supposed to have predicted this about forty years earlier[19]. Finally, in Isa 22,6 Kir is also mentioned along with Elam and Aram (MT reads, however, אדם) as sending contingents af troops. This combination in Isa 22,6 suggests a location some-where in the north-eastern part of Syria; thus Am 9,7aβ could well be a late - perhaps very late - gloss on the rhetorical question in Am 9,7aα.

Amos 3,2. In other words, the only tradition concerning Israel's prehistory in the Book of Amos which we can be reasonably sure derives from the prophet himself is Am 3,2: רק אתכם ידעתי מכל משפחות האדמה. Even in this case, however, there is good reason to inquire as to whether the text refers to the events of the Exodus at all, as it could just as easily be held to be an echo of the promise to

---

[16] Cf. Thiel 1973:121-128.

[17] Amos 5,25 as a Deuteronomistic passage: thus Wolff 1975:309f. Cf. also Thiel 1973:127 and Vollmer 1971:41-43. Even Rudolph has acknowledged that v 25 is not appropriate in its pre-sent context, but he does maintain that it is nevertheless authentic (1971:208ff.).

[18] Wolff 1975:398ff. and Vollmer 1971:33-37.

[19] LXX[B] on 2 Kgs 16,9 lacks קירה. Many scholars, including, most recently, Strange (1980:75n) reckon קירה in 2 Kgs 16,9 to be a gloss. However, Amos 1,5 implies that קירה is to be retained in 2 Kgs 16,9. Gray attempts to circumvent the problem by interpreting קירה in 2 Kgs 16,9 as *"the city"*, that is, Nineveh. Unfortunately, this is out of the question since, as far as I am aware, the Assyrians did not refer to Nineveh or any other city in Mesopotamia in this fashion (Gray 1964: 574). Gray also attempts to explain קיר in Amos 9,7 away as a corruption of *qᵉrārîr* on the analogy of Arabic broken plural forms, and thus reads *"waterholes"* or *'oases"*. Gray's emendations tell us more about the ingenuity of their author than they do about the text of the Book of Amos.

the patriarchs in Gen 12,3 and 28,14 (J)[20]. Of course, these observations imply that there is only scant material in the Book of Amos which may be taken to express Amos' knowledge of the earliest history of Israel. Moreover, the authentic expressions (including Am 2,9) make use of formulations which clearly differ from the traditional terminology of the Pentateuch (the Amonites are giants and the verb is used of the election of Israel).

2

Hosea

The references in the Book of Hosea to Israel's prehistory are more accessible and intelligible than are those in the Book of Amos, since the authenticity of the main part of them may be readily sustained.

Hosea 2,16f. There can be no doubt as to the authenticity of this passage, since it is clear that we have to do with independent expressions in v 16 and 17. However, v 17bα, וכיום עלתה מארץ מצרים, may be understood as a gloss on כימי נעוריה, whereas the positive understanding of the period in the desert is also expressed elsewhere in the Book of Hosea (Hos 9,10; 11,1ff.).

Hosea 8,13; 9,3 and 11,5. Hos 8,13 presumably derives from the hand of the prophet himself[21]. The degenerate sacrificial cult is to be punished with a new exile. In Hos 9,3 and 11,5, Egypt is parallel to Assyria in both cases and is to be understood as the τύπος of exilic existence as such. In other words, it is difficult to accept that these two cases can be taken to imply that the Israelites fled into Egypt at some point between 732 and 722, just as many Judaeans were later to do after the events of 587[22]. In agreement with this view, I am also inclined to regard Hos 11,5bα, אשור הוא מלכו as authentic[23]. This is to say that in some respects we must regard Hosea as a forerunner of Deutero Isaiah, who saw a new Exodus in the departure of the Jews from Babylon.

Hos 9,10. As mentioned previously, Hosea 9,10 and 2,16f have in common the

---

[20] Perlitt stresses that precisely Amos 3,2 would serve in the context of a covenant procedure to nullify the covenantal implication of a reciprocal obligation between God and man: *"Nicht ein Vertrag mit gegenseitigen Verpflichtungen stand für Amos am Anfang des Gottesverhältnisses sondern die freie Tat Jahwes."* (1969:135).

[21] Thus also Robinson 1964:33; Wolff 1965:187, who with respect to form compares with Hos 3,1; 4,14; 6,7. Vollmer, following a suggestion of K. Marti, proposes to excise Hos 8,13bγ (המה מצרים ישׁובו) as a *"Zusatz"*, but he offers no reason for this (1971:68n).

[22] Against Robinson 1964:35f.

[23] Against Robinson 1964:42, and Vollmer 1971:60.

feature that they entertain a positive opinion of Israel's stay in the desert. There is no doubt as to the authenticity of Hos 9,10 since, in the first place, it contains original material, and in the second, it does not employ formulaic expressions. Wolff thinks to find an isolated tradition in Hos 9,10 which dates Yahweh's election of Israel to the desert period rather than during the sojourn in Egypt, as the Pentateuchal sources imply[24]; in this connection he refers to Deut 32,10; Jer 2,2f; and Ezek 16,1ff. While it is conceivable that Deut 32,10 knows a different election tradition than that which is usual in the Pentateuch – even though the mentioned passages in Jeremiah and Ezekiel hardly support Wolff's view – Hosea otherwise knows the usual conception of Israel's stay in Egypt. See above all Hos 11,1 and perhaps Hos 12,10.

Hosea 11,1ff. In terms of contents this passage is closely related to 2,16f and 9,10, and the section must derive from the prophet himself. The same reasons apply to this passage as to Hos 2,16f and 9,10.

Hosea 12. Large parts of this chapter are from Hosea's own hand, although it is possible to question especially v 13-14. It is difficult to see what was the purpose of adding these two verses, unless it was to explain the somewhat doubtful verses 10 and 11. The "prophet" referred to in v 14 can hardly be other than Moses, although the designation נביא was first attached to him by the Deuteronomists[25]. Nor is v 11 from the hand of Hosea, as it would be strange indeed if Yahweh had already announced in the time of Hosea that דברתי על הנביאים ואנכי חזון הרביתי ; we should expect this instead at a later date. But if it is likely that Hos 12,11 is secondary, v 10 must be so as well, since it is the first part of the historical retrospect consisting of verses 10-11. The usage in v 10 is conventional in part; its contents are even more so, at least as far as v 10a is concerned. Both v 10a and 10b give voice to ideas which are otherwise much more poetically expressed elsewhere in the Book of Hosea[26].

Hosea seems to be familiar with that portion of Israelite tradition which is also preserved in the Pentateuch. This judgement applies to both the patriarchal narratives and the Exodus traditions. On the other hand, it is clear that the Settlement traditions play only a modest role for Hosea, if any. Further, it is far from certain that the patriarchal and Exodus traditions which Hosea knew had the same form and contents as those with which we are familiar. It was

---

[24] 1965:213.

[25] See Deut 18,15.18 and 34,10.

[26] In connection with v 10b compare 2,16f.; 10a is to be compared with Hos 11,1. Vollmer offers an thorough analysis of the Jacob traditions in Hos 12 (1971:105-115). His analysis is consciously literary critical; it allows only v 3-4 and 8-9 to survive as the original nucleus. But if this is the case, they can only be a fragment of such a nucleus, since it is hard to see any internal connection between v 4 and 8, or between v 8 and v 9.

mentioned above in connection with my survey of Hos 9,10 that it is possible that Hosea there refers to an isolated election tradition. However, he does know the sojourn in Egypt (Hos 11,1; cf. also Hos 8,13; 9,3, and 11,5). The traditions of Israel's wanderings in the desert were not unknown to him either, or at least this seems to be implied in Hos 9,10 by the reference to Israel's apostasy at Ba'al Pe'or (Num 25). On the other hand, the Book of Hosea knows nothing of Moses, since Hos 12,14 is secondary.

Of the three patriarchs, Hosea mentions only Jacob; Abraham and Isaac were apparently completely beyond his ken. The Jacob traditions in Hos 12 differ somewhat from those we know from the Book of Genesis. Nevertheless, we are able to recognize the materials in Genesis which correspond to events in Jacob's life as recounted in Hos 12: Hos 12,4a = Gen 25,22; Hos 12,4b = Gen 32,25-33; Hos 12,5b = Gen 28,10-22. In all three cases there are divergences from Genesis. Gen 25,22 does not record that Jacob deceived Esau in their mother's womb. Gen 32,25-33 does not refer to weeping, and, finally, the chronological sequence of sojourn at Bethel and battle at Penuel is different in Hos 12 from the sequence in Genesis. This fact may have one of two causes: either Hosea knew different versions of the Jacob traditions, or else he made use of the traditions available to him very freely. On the basis of the Book of Hosea alone it will hardly be possible for us to determine which of these alternatives is correct. At least one thing is certain, however, which is that at least in the form in which we know them today, the Pentateuchal traditions did not have normative significance in Hosea's own time.

3.

Isaiah

Unlike the northern prophet Hosea, it is more than doubtful that the Judaean prophet Isaiah refers at all to the history of Israel before the introduction of the monarchy. The only even relevant materials are confined to Isa 10,23-26 and 11,15-16. There is no reason to devote space to discussion of these passages, since there is general agreement that both Isa 10,23-26 and 11,15-16 are late and inauthentic; they may even be of postexilic date[27].

Egypt is mentioned a number of times in Isa 1-39, but it is remarkable that even the oracles against Egypt in Isa 19-20 do not refer to the Exodus traditions, nor do the reproaches which are directed against those seeking shelter among the Egyptians and the Assyrians in Isa 30,1-5 and 31,1-3. There is accordingly good reason to believe that Isaiah had only a distant knowledge of

---

[27] Cf. thus Wildberger 1972:418f. and 466f., and Kaiser 1963:119 and 131ff.

the Exodus traditions, if he knew them at all. These comments seem also to apply to the patriarchal traditions. "Jacob" is apparently only used generally to refer to Israel, as is presumably also the case in Isa 29,22, where Jacob figures together with Abraham; it should be noted that this passage is part of the obviously secondary section Isa 29,16-24[28].

4.

Micah

An examination of the use of historical motifs by Isaiah's contemporary and fellow Judaean, Micah of Moresheth brings us to similar conclusions.

Micah 6,4-5. It is bewildering that there is any discussion at all considering the "authenticity" of this passage[29]. V 4a, כי העלתיך מארץ מצרים ומבית עבדים פדיתיך is entirely Deuteronomistic in style. In the OT the verb פדה is only used to refer to the liberation of Israel from Egypt in Deuteronomistic literature (Deut 7,8; 9,26; 13,6; 15,15; 21,8; 24,18; in fact, in Deuteronomy this verb is *only* used in this connection. See further the excursus below). בית עבדים is also a specifically Deuteronomistic expression (cf. Deut 5,6; 6,12; 7,8; 8,14; 13,6.11; Jos 24,17; Jdg 6,8; Jer 34,13)[30]. V 4b, the reference to Moses, Aaron, and Miriam, corresponds in terms of contents to the secondary Hos 12,14. This is the only passage among the pre-exilic prophets which mentions Miriam and Aaron. As mentioned previously, Moses is also not mentioned by the pre-exilic prophets[31]. E. Nielsen has characterized v 5, which refers to Balaam and the passage over the Jordan as a sort of chapter superscription which presupposes the Deuteronomistic edition of Jos 3-5[32]. It is hard to say

---

[28] Compare Eissfeldt 1965:317, who discusses Isa 29,16-24 on the same level with, among other passages, Isa 11,10-16. See also Vollmer 1971:169, who regards Isa 29,17-24 as dependent on Deutero Isaiah, and therefore post-exilic.

[29] There are in fact a number of scholars who treat Micah 6,4-5 as authentic. Cf. Eissfeldt 1965:411 and Vuilleunier 1971: 70ff. The passage is regarded as inauthentic in the main part of the earlier commentaries, including Robinson 1964:145, Nowack 1903:205, and Marti 1904:291 (whereas Sellin 1922:260 argues for its authenticity). Perlitt simply maintains that the entire section Mi 6,1-8 presupposes the collected Pentateuch (1969:137). These evaluations of the authenticity of Mi 6,4-5 may be offered without reference to the century-long discussion as to the authenticity or inauthenticity of Mi 4-7; see Jeppesen 1978 and 1979.

[30] Exod 13,3.14 and 20,2 are often regarded by the classical Pentateuchal scholars as Deuteronomistically reworked parts of the Pentateuch. See for example Eissfeldt 1922:270*.173*. On Exod 13,1-16 one may also consult Noth 1948:32n and 1965:79. Others have reckoned this passage to be "proto-Deuteronomistic"; see e.g. Childs 1974:184. However, B.S. Childs himself assigns Exod 13,2-16 to the D-stratum. Noth has a different view of the redactional situation of Exod 20,2; see Noth 1948:51. See also Nielsen 1965:36 and Stamm and Andrews 1967:16.

[31] Jer 15,1 can hardly be authentic; see below.

[32] 1959:297.

whether Micah 6,4-5 is to be ascribed to a Deuteronomistic redaction which took place during the Exile, or to a postexilic redactor who wrote in Deuteronomistic style. The positive evaluation of Miriam and Aaron in v 4b, that is, as being on a par with Moses, is not fully congruent with the descriptions of Miriam and Aaron in Deuteronomy[33]. Thus it is possible that Micah 6,4-5 is of post-exilic date and has been influenced by concepts which are also evident in the Priestly traditions.

Micah 7,15. This verse is part of the passage running from Micah 7 v 14 to v 20 (possibly 7,7(8)-20; there is some disagreement with respect to the precise delimitation of this last part of the Book of Micah), which is a liturgy or "psalm" of presumably post-exilic date[34]. The terminology in v 15 is entirely traditional. It is not necessarily Deuteronomistic, but this does not mean that it may be pre-exilic.

All this goes to show that neither of the two Judaean prophets that is, Micah and Isaiah, from the close of the 8th century, refers to the traditions of the Exodus. If they were somehow familiar with these traditions, it is fair to say that they were of no importance either to them or their audience. It should also be noted that the *fora* of these two figures were not identical, as it is well known that Isaiah was active in Jerusalem, where he apparently had access to the highest figures in Israelite society, while Micah was active in a Judaean province. Thus it would be reasonable to claim that the Pentateuchal traditions were foreign to the Judaean horizon in the 8th century.

5.

Jeremiah

The only one of the writings in the OT which contains prophetic oracles from the 7th century (namely the close of the 7th cent.), and which contains references to the Exodus traditions, is the book of the prophet Jeremiah. Here, however, the references to the Exodus from Egypt and the period in the desert are quite numerous[35].

---

[33] Miriam: see Deut 24,9 (cf. Num 12); Aaron: see Deut 9,20 (the golden calf). Deut 10,6 and 32,50 are burial traditions.

[34] See Robinson and Horst 1964:151f. Also Weiser 1966:229.

[35] As far as the Book of Jeremiah is concerned the following survey is mainly based on Thiel 1973 and 1981. Thiel reckons the "C" source to be Deuteronomistic (cf. already Mowinckel 1914). H. Weippert 1973 is far more reticent with respect to the extent of Deuteronomistic redaction in Jeremiah. On this see Thiel 1981:98, and on this question E.W. Nicholson is practically in agreement with Thiel (1970:20-37, esp. pp.28ff., against Bright 1951). J. Sturdy has recently expressed views similar to those of Bright and H. Weippert (Sturdy 1980).

Jer. 2,2-3. There is no doubt that this is an authentic oracle of Jeremiah. The passage displays no signs of Deuteronomistic influence. On the other hand, the passage clearly refers to Hos 2,17, a fact which has convinced most commentators of Jeremiah's dependence on Hosea[36].

Jer. 2,6-7. It is difficult to assign these verses with precision. On the one hand, they contain numerous obvious reminiscences of Deuteronomistic style; on the other, however, they also contain materials which obviously come from elsewhere. Even W. Thiel is only inclined to ascribe Deuteronomistic redaction to v 5bγ, וילכו אחרי ההבל ויהבלו, which recurs word-perfect in 2 Kgs 17,15[37]. V 6b, המולך אתנו במדבר בארץ ערבה ושחה, seems to be closely related to Deuteronomistic formulations (cf. Deut 8,15). The description of the desert in both Jer 2,6 and Deut 8,15 may be dependent, not necessarily in literary terms, but in traditio-historical ones, on Isa 30,6. There is traditional language in v 6aβ. In other words, although v 6-7 cannot be wholly Deuteronomistic, the passage seems to reflect the influence of Deuteronomistic redaction. The description of the desert makes use of terms which are not used in the Deuteronomistic sections of the OT. If the origins of v 6-7 can be traced back to Jeremiah, then it appears that the prophet here presents a picture of the desert period which reveals some tensions with Jer 2,2-3. Jeremiah seems to be more dependent on Isaiah than on Hosea, as is the case in Jer 2,2-3.

Jer. 3,18. It will not be necessary to use much space on this passage, as its usage is Deuteronomistic, its ideational content is late, and the association with the traditions of the Exodus and Settlement is secondary[38].

Jer. 3,19. The promise concerning possession of the land seems to derive from Jeremiah. The reference to Yahweh's sons points to Hos 11,1. A keyword in the verse is צבי in 19bβ, which is also used of Palestine in Ezek 20,6.15[39].

Jer. 7,7. A part of the famous Temple Speech, but the product of a Deuteronomistic tradent, or, perhaps better, clad in Deuteronomistic garments. Note the phrase בארץ אשר נתתי לאבותיכם, which corresponds to Jos 21,43 and 1 Kgs 8,48.

Jer. 7,21-27(28). The introduction in v 21a is Deuteronomistic, whereas v 21b may contain original material comparable to Jer 6,20. On the other hand, the main part of v 22-29 is Deuteronomistic, even though some original fragments may be present in the conclusion of the passage. In terms of contents and

---

[36] Cf. e.g. Rudolph 1958:12.
[37] Thiel 1973:80f.
[38] In this connection it is therefore of no importance whether the author of Jer 3,18 is Deuteronomistic or later (thus Thiel 1973:91ff.).
[39] See also Dan 8,9; 11,16.41.

understanding of history the passage is comparable to Am 5,25, which, as we saw above, has been reworked by the Deuteronomist. Actual polemic against the Yahwistic cult is extremely rare in Jeremiah, and when he does so (cf. Jer 6,20) he is presumably dependent on the far more pronounced criticisms of Isaiah (Isa 1,11f). The fragment Jer 7,21b is possibly dependent on Hosea (Hos 8,13)[40].

Jer 11,2-5. This section, too, in a Deuteronomistically-formulated text. There is no need to go into the matter in detail, since מכור הברזל in v 4 is sufficient evidence of the provenance of this section. The Deuteronomistic literature has the patent on this description of Egypt (Deut 4,20 and 1 Kgs 8,51)[41].

Jer. 14,21. I have only included this passage for the sake of completeness. V 21b is full of ambiguity. The connection with the Ark in the temple in Jerusalem is clear, but it is uncertain whether the covenant referred to is that of Sinai or the one with David. Probably the latter, since the Sinai covenant is only mentioned in the Deuteronomistic parts of the Book of Jeremiah[42]. On the other hand, it would be a mistake to regard v 21b as secondary, that is, Deuteronomistic, since this supposition would make the passage the only one in the Book of Jeremiah where the Deuteronomists make Yahweh the cause of the breach of covenant[43].

Jer 15,1. Thiel holds that the entire section Jer 14,1-15,4 has been reworked by the Deuteronomists, which also applies to Jer 15,1-4[44]. The introduction in Jer 15,1 is identical with Jer 14,11.14. According to Thiel the expression שלח מעל פני is only found in the Deuteronomistic literature (1 Kgs 9,7). This understanding of Moses and Samuel as intermediaries is only expressed in sections with a Deuteronomistic flavor. On Moses, see Exod 32,11.14 and Num 14,13-20; on Samuel see 1 Sam 7,5-11 and 12,19-23. Also, as mentioned previously, the pre-exilic prophets do not mention Moses at all. Thus if we are to attempt to evaluate Jeremiah's knowledge of or interest in these historical traditions, we must disregard Jer 15,1.

Jer 16,14-15. It is generally assumed that v 14-15 are post-exilic. They have probably been inserted by a late redactor as a loan from Jer 23,7-8. The

---

[40] See further Thiel 1973:121-128.
[41] Again, Thiel 1973:139ff.
[42] See Jer 11,1 and 31,32f.
[43] Cf. Jer 11,10; 31,32; 33,20 (Deuteronomistic?), as well as (Hophal) 33,21 (Deuteronomistic). See Deut 31,16.20. In Jdg 2,1 Yahweh promises to the contrary that he will not break his covenant.
[44] 1973:178-194. Otherwise H. Weippert 1973:163f.

section contains ideas which are otherwise mainly expressed by Deutero
Isaiah (Isa 43,16-21)[45].

Jer.17,4. This verse derives from the hand of Jeremiah, but is otherwise of no
great interest in this connection, since it merely reveals knowledge of the
promise of the possession of the land.

Jer 23,7-8. This passage is perhaps quoted in Jer 16,14-15. Once again we have
to do with Deuteronomistic usage, although it is uncertain whether 23,7-8
ultimately derives from the Deuteronomistic redaction of the Book of Jeremiah or post-exilic redaction. W. Rudolph feels that v 7-8 are post-exilic, while
Thiel insists that they derive from the Deuteronomists[46]. Thiel admits that
the Deuteronomists normally use the verb יצא, in conjunction with the Exodus, while v 7-8 in our passage use עלה in the Hiphil. However, closer examination of the use of יצא and עלה in the Qal and Hiphil shows that Thiel's
problem is a superficial one[47]. Nevertheless, the phrase מארץ צפונה ומכל
האָרצות אשר הדחתים שם does seem to point to a post-exilic situation.

Jer 30,3. This verse is to be evaluated analogously to Jer 7,7; also, note that
שבת (עמי) is Deuteronomistic terminology[48].

Jer. 31,2-3. This passage is no doubt an authentic oracle of the prophet Jeremiah. It is characteristic of Jeremiah's use of the Exodus traditions that traditional phraseology is not employed; the desert is not a place of horror, as in Jer
2,6 (at least not when Jer exploits the tradition of Hosea). Furthermore, the
prophet emphasizes the close relationship between Israel and her God during

---

[45] Cf. Rudolph 1958:102f., and most recently Thiel 1973:201.

[46] Rudolph 1958:137; Thiel 1973:248f.

[47] Scholars have traditionally distinguished between two types of description of the Exodus
event, one of which employs the verb יצא, while the other prefers עלה, יצא is found in J-contexts
in the Pentateuch, whereas in E-contexts we find עלה (although in every case it is necessary to
consider whether the Deuteronomists have not had a hand in the formulation). P restricts himself almost exclusively to עלה, but, unlike J, who uses יצא in conjunction with מצרים, P uses עלה
together with ארץ מצרים (E has been held to use both מצרים and ארץ מצרים). Within the Deuteronomistic literature some nuances are detectable. With a single exception (Deut 20,1) Deuteronomy uses יצא in conjunction with both מצרים and ארץ מצרים, whereas in the Deuteronomistic
Historical Work and in Jeremiah יצא and עלה occur with roughly equal frequency. In the Historical Work both verbs are attached to either מצרים or ארץ מצרים. In the Book of Jeremiah they are
associated with ארץ מצרים alone.

[48] Cf. Deut 30,3. The evidence for this is particularly rich in the Deuteronomistic rescension
of the Book of Jeremiah; cf. Jer 29,14 (which Thiel ascribes to the Deuteronomists, although he
will not rule out a post-exilic date (Thiel 1981:20); cf. Jer 23,7-8 and 31,23 (others have, however,
dealt differently with this verse; see thus Rudolph 1958:199 and Thiel 1981:20, who regards it as
a late "Judaean" gloss); 32,44; 33,7.11.26. Thiel reckons Jer 30,18 to be Deuteronomistic (1981:
15), although he admits the possibility of authenticity. Hos 6,11 and Amos 9,14 also seem to be
from the hand of a redactor, but one working from within the Deuteronomistic tradition.

the desert period. Here Jer 31,2-3 agrees closely with Jer 2,2-3, so that the heritage of Hosea shines through both.

Jer 31,31-34. We are once more on solidly Deuteronomistic ground. There is no reason to go along with Rudolph and excise ואת בית יהודה(v 31bβ as a later addition; nor is there reason to claim that בית ישראל only refers to the Northern Kingdom, or to associate v 31-34 with v 18-22, which derive from Jeremiah[49]. Already the designation בית ישראל in v 31ff is in sharp contrast with the repeated אפרים in v 18ff. As far as v 32 is concerned, it is sufficient to refer to Weippert's table, in which the verse is ranged together with Deut 29,24; 1 Kgs 8,21; Jer 11,4, and Jer 34,13[50]. As far as I am aware there is no parallel to ברית חדשה in v 31; it is to be understood in the context of the passages in the Book of Jeremiah which refer to a new Exodus (from the north), and which are either Deuteronomistic or later. In other words, the new covenant is a new "Sinai covenant", a restoration of Israel's pre-historic – and now revoked – covenant. There is no precise parallel to the phrase נתתי את תורתי בקרבם ועל לבם אכתבנה in v 33bα. The conjunction of נתן and תורה is quite remarkable in the OT[51], and v 33 bβ seems to be overloaded. These may be indications of the clumsiness of a late post-Deuteronomistic scribe. As far as I can see, the closest parallels to v 33bα are Deut 11,18 (ושמתם את דברי אלה על לבבכם) andt Deut 6,6 (והיו הדברים האלה...על לבבך). The so-called "covenant formulary" in v 33bβ (והייתי להם לאלהים והמה יהיו לי לעם) is only found in Deuteronomistic passages in the Book of Jeremiah (7,23; 11,4; 24,7; 30,22; 31,1.33, and 32,38; see also 13,11)[52].

Jer 32,20-23. A part of the section running from v 17 to v 25. This section (v 17-25) is thoroughly impregnated with Deuteronomistic terminology. Rudolph maintains that only, אהה אדני יהוה in v 17aα, plus v 24-25, are pre-Deuteronomistic[53]. Rudolph compares this section with the long prayer in Neh 9,6ff and speaks of "den Ton des Gemeindegebets[54]". It will be unnecessary to go into this passage in great detail, as for our purposes it will suffice to refer only to the phrase in v 20: אתות ומפתים The conjunction of these two terms is a Deuteronomistic specialty as may be seen from inspection of Deut 6,22; 13,2-3; 28,46; 29,2; and 34,11[55]. In v 21 the combination of אתות ומפתים ccom-

---

[49] 1958:184f. On Jer 31,31-34 as Deuteronomistic, see also Thiel 1981:23ff., and Nicholson 1970:82ff. See also Perlitt 1969: 145n.

[50] 1973:98. Admittedly, H. Weippert's scheme is intended to show that Jer 34,13 is not Deuteronomistic.

[51] Otherwise only in Exod 24,12 (possibly a P addition; see Noth 1948:192f., or from a redactor who has linked J and P, and who therefore inserted this verse to build a bridge to Exod 25ff. This appears to be Childs' opinion (1974:499 and 507)), and Neh 9,13.

[52] See also Thiel 1973:122.

[53] 1958:193. Thiel 1981:31 reckons the whole section v 16-44 to be Deuteronomistic.

[54] 1958:195.

[55] This combination is otherwise only found in Exod 7,3 (P) and in Isa 20,3, the authenti-

panies the Exodus event (described in Deuteronomistic terms) and also includes the phrase ובזרע נטויה וביד חזקה ובאזרע, as in Deut 7,19 and 26,8 (which also includes ובמרא גדל). את הארץ הזאת אשר נשבעת לאבותם לתת להם in v 22a recurs almost
verbatim in Deuteronomy with relentless monotony (Deut 1,8.35; 6,10.18.23;
7,13; 8,1, etc.). ארץ זבת חלב ודבש(22b) also has an extraordinary number of
parallels in Deuteronomy (Deut 6,3; 11,9; 26,9.15; 27,3; 31,20; Jos 5,6). Because of the frequent occurrence of this phrase in the Tetrateuch (Exod 3,8.17;
13.5; 33.3; Lev 20,24; Num 13,27; 14,8; 16,13.14) H. Weippert holds that it is
"alttestamentliche Allgemeingut", for which reason it cannot be taken as an
indication of Deuteronomisms in the Book of Jeremiah[56]. It is conceivable
that this phrase is common property, but the rest of the Deuteronomisms in
Jer 32,20ff show that in this case the phrase is most likely also Deuteronomistic.

Jer 34,13. This passage occurs in the account of Zedekiah's decree concerning
the slaves in Jer 34,8-20. It is possible that an older narrative underlies Jer
34,8-20, but it is impossible to deny that in the form it now possesses the section is Deuteronomistically reworked, and that the contents of v 13 are
Deuteronomistic pure and simple. The fact that the section as such is Deuteronomistic is shown by the quotation from the slave law of Exod 21,2ff (via Deut
15,12-18) in v 14[57]. The law in question has nothing whatsoever to do with the
events depicted in Jer 34,8ff. Deut 15 implies a concern with the manumission
of individual slaves, while Jer 34,8ff have to do with a collective manumission
with a view to including the slaves thus released in the ranks of the military[58].
Admittedly, the law in Deut 15,12-18, which has been "borrowed" from the
Book of the Covenant (Exod 21,2-6) is already interpreted in a collective sense
in Deuteronomy and is attached to the *šemiṭṭa* rules in v 11ff, concerning the so-
called "Sabbatical year". However, this redactional association was undertaken by the Deuteronomists, and the use of the slave law in the collective
interpretation in Jer 34,14 is dependent on the Deuteronomistic interpretation
of the law in Exod 21,2-6. H. Weippert claims that the text of Jer 34,13 is not
wholly Deuteronomistic, but her argument to this effect is oversubtle[59].

Jer 35. Jeremiah's encounter with the Rechabites. This chapter is only of
indirect interest, since neither Jeremiah nor the Rechabites refer to the Exodus
traditions. Nevertheless, the Rechabites' views of an ideal existence (i.e., they
dwell in tents and do not drink wine) must be the result of their consciousness

---

city of which is still in doubt (see Eissfeldt 1965:307; However, Eissfeldt himself felt that Isa 20,3
is authentic (1965:314)). Further below in our examination of Ps 78 and 135.

[56] 1973:228n.
[57] Cf. Lemche 1976:51-53; cf. also Thiel 1981:39ff.
[58] Cf. Lemche 1976:51n.
[59] See above on Jer 31,31-34, and n.50.

of Israel's past in the desert. In other words, like Hosea and Jeremiah himself, the Rechabites understand this part of Israel's past as an ideal time. Although this picture of the Rechabites coheres with the other sources we possess which mention them, we are nevertheless forced to assign Jer 35 to the Deuteronomistic redaction of the Book of Jeremiah[60].

A review of the passages in the Book of Jeremiah which can with certainty be assigned to the prophet himself, and which are relevant to the present study, are Jer 2,2-3; 3,19; 17,4, and 31,2-3. These passages all indicate that Jeremiah's understanding of the Exodus traditions was on the same wavelength as Hosea's. For Jeremiah and Hosea, the desert period was a time when there was an especially close relationship between Israel and Yahweh. Thus it did not connote some form of punishment. Jeremiah's language is reminiscent of Hosea's, a feature which is most evident when he represents the relationship between Yahweh and Israel in terms of the sonship of the latter. The existing materials make it difficult for us to determine just what version of the Exodus traditions Jeremiah was familiar with. He alludes to both the escape from Egypt and the sojourn in the desert, and also to the possession of the land, which he describes as Israel's possession, but also as the gift of Yahweh. This means that Jeremiah must have known traditions which corresponded broadly to those now preserved in the Tetrateuch. It is characteristic of Jeremiah, and of Hosea, that the language of his references to the traditions of the Exodus and the wandering in the desert have not been borrowed from the Pentateuch. Jeremiah is independent in this respect. It is surprising that when we compare the authentic Jeremianic materials with those in the Book of Hosea we discover that there is no sign of a development in the direction of a more comprehensive collection of the Pentateuchal traditions so as to form a single view of the past, in spite of the almost one hundred and fifty years separating these two prophets. In short, these traditions concerning Israel's past cannot have been the common property of all Judaeans around 600. If they had been collected earlier, the various tradents and redactors did not pass them on to the circles to which Jeremiah belonged, and to whom he addressed himself. If the Josianic reform was carried out under the influence of pressure from Deuteronomistic circles, then it is striking that the historical contents of this reform message are not reflected in Jeremiah's proclamation. This is very strange indeed, when we consider that this prophet is otherwise represented as the voice of these reformist circles.

---

[60] Cf. e.g. Rudolph 1958:207-210; Thiel 1981:44-48.

6.

Ezekiel

With the prophet Ezekiel we have arrived at a figure who was active at approximately the same time the Deuteronomistic Historical Work was collected. It will not be possible in this connection to discuss the problems attaching to Ezek 16 and 23 or to the authenticity of Ezek 20. In the main I shall confine myself to the views which have been presented in W.Zimmerli's monumental commentary on Ezekiel[61].

Ezek 16 and 23. It is not of crucial importance whether we accept or reject the authenticity of these two chapters. Zimmerli regards Ezek 16 as a redactional work because of the parallel in Ezek 23, the nucleus of which at least derives from the prophet himself. This means that the stark description of Israel's unfaithfulness with Egypt in Ezek 16,26 is to be understood along the same lines as Ezek 23,8.19. Zimmerli does not feel that these passages refer to the Pentateuchal traditions concerning Israel's sojourn in Egypt, but instead to the flirtations of the Israelite monarchs with Egypt, even though Ezek 20 actually mentions the apostasy of the people prior to the Exodus[62]. Ezek 16,60.62 is part of the secondary appendix running from v 44 to v 63[63]. In terms of usage, Ezek 16,60ff are more reminiscent of P than of Deuteronomistic language: v 60: חכרתי אני את בריתי אותך; cf. Gen 9,15.16; Exod 2,24; 6,5; Lev 26,42.45; V 62: והקימתי אני את בריתי אתך: cf. Gen 6,18; 9,9.11; 17,7.19.21; Exod 6,4; Lev 26,9.

Ezek 20. The date is 591. In this connection it is unimportant whether we divide between v 31 and 32 or between v 32 and 33 in our demarcation of the two parts in Ezek 20[64]. It is also relatively unimportant that v 27-31(32) may be an addition to the nucleus consisting of v 5-26. The main part, v 5-26, derives ultimately from the prophet[65]. Zimmerli feels that the terminology employed in this section has more to do with the language of P than with that of the Deuteronomists (based on a comparison with Exod 6 (P)). As far as

---

[61] Zimmerli 1969.

[62] 1969:548f. Otherwise Fohrer 1955:132f.

[63] Zimmerli 1969:369ff.; Fohrer 1955:92.

[64] See Zimmerli 1969:437ff. (between v 31 and 32); others divide between v 32 and 33 (thus also Fohrer 1955:114).

[65] It will be seen that this investigation follows Zimmerli's very precisely. As far as the interpretation of ch.20 is concerned, unlike Zimmerli I would exclude the so-called "little credo" (Deut 26,5-9). The credo begins with the Aramaean "tribal ancestor", who lies beyond the horizon of Ezekiel. In terms of usage the credo in Deut 26,5-9 is Deuteronomistic; cf. Rost 1965 (contra Von Rad 1938:11), and there are very few reminiscences of this in Ezek 20.

contents are concerned, I shall confine myself to my review of Ezekiel's statements below.

Ezek 33,24. This statement is part of the passage running from v 23 to v 29, which probably consists of expressions composed by Ezekiel, and which derive from the period after 587 (note the reference to the ruins in the land of Israel)[66]. Here, too, the passage in question recalls the language of P, in particular v 24b, לנו נתנה הארץ למורשה, which is strongly reminiscent of Exod 6,8b (ונתתי אתה לכם מורשה). Exod 6,8a mentions Abraham, Isaac, and Jacob, whereas Ezek 33,24 refers to Abraham alone. Since the authenticity of this passage is not to be doubted, this is the first time Abraham is mentioned by a prophet[67].

Ezek 36,28. This verse is part of the secondary section Ezek 36,16-38; its language mimics that of the Deuteronomistic passages in the Book of Jeremiah[68].

Ezek 37,25. This verse is part of the secondary section consisting of v 24b-28. Zimmerli points to numerous similarities to Ezek 28,25f and, further, to linguistic affinities with Lev 26[69].

What remains of Ezekiel is Ezek 20,5-26, which is the primary source as to the understanding of Israel's prehistory held by this prophet. It is to be emphasized that the promises to the patriarchs and, indeed, the very patriarchal traditions themselves are ignored here (unless לזרע בית יעקב in v 5bα can be taken to indicate some interest in the patriarchal stories). However, in Ezek 33,24 the prophet does state that during the exilic period Judaeans set great store by the promise to Abraham.

Ezekiel's treatment of the Exodus tradition differs notably from that of Hosea and Jeremiah. For Ezekiel the period in the desert was not characterized by an especially close relationship between Israel and Yahweh; instead he emphasizes the "murmuring" motif which signals the people's rebelliousness in the Pentateuch[70]. Ezekiel is most closely related to the P source, especially Exod 6, but he also reveals knowledge of Jeremianic terminology, as in Ezek 20,6.15, צבי היא לכל הארצות, which is closely related to Jer 3,19. The fact that the references in the Book of Ezekiel to the Pentateuchal narratives are so detailed suggests, but does not prove, that these traditions were first collected in

---

[66] Thus Zimmerli 1969:818, and Fohrer 1955:188, contra Noth 1953D: 359n.

[67] Isa 29,22; Mi 7,20, and Jer 33,26 are all secondary passages.

[68] For details see Zimmerli 1969:872ff. and 880; cf. Jer 11,4; 24,7; 30,22 (see also Thiel 1973:253ff.).

[69] Zimmerli 1969:909.

[70] Cf. Noth 1948:134-143.

Ezekiel's day. However, it is at least clear that these traditions had a completely different validity and authority for Ezekiel than they did for his earlier colleagues. With respect to language, Ezekiel is much less original than are his predecessors. His usage approximates that of the Pentateuchal sources, and especially that of the terminology of P[71].

7.

Deutero Isaiah

Deutero Isaiah also includes a number of expressions which seem to reflect the Pentateuchal traditions. The patriarchs Abraham and Jacob are mentioned. "Jacob" is mentioned in Isa 41,8 but the reference is probably not to the patriarch of the same name in spite of v 8b (זרע אברהם אהבי), but to the Israelites, as in other passages in Deutero Isaiah. In addition to Isa 41,8b, Abraham is mentioned in Isa 51,2 together with Sarah; this passage also directly alludes to the theme of the promises[72]. A lengthy series of passages include motifs from the Exodus cycle, although the delimitation of these passages is by no means unproblematical. K. Kiesow has presented the most extensive analysis of the Exodus texts in Deutero Isaiah; he lists six passages: Isa 40,1-11; 43,16-21; 49,7-12; 51,9-10; 52,7-12; 55,12-13[73]. Of these, however, only two are held to be unambiguous Exodus texts, namely Isa 43,16-21 and 51,9-10[74].

I shall not attempt a thorough discussion of these passages at this juncture. Instead, I shall confine myself to an account of Kiesow's views, since he has pointed to an important feature which agrees fairly well with the views presented in this chapter, namely the late combination of *Exodus* and *mythos*[75]. If we compare Isa 43,16-21 with 51,9-10, some important differences in the treatment of the Exodus theme are immediately obvious. In Isa 43,16-21 the theme has not been clad in mythological garb, while this is the case in Isa 51,9-10. It

[71] There are a number of possible explanations. First, Ezekiel may have known the P source or an early version of it. Second, Ezekiel may have been contemporary with circles whose activities eventually were recorded in the P source. Third, as far as terminology is concerned, the P source may well be dependent on Ezekiel.

[72] On the probability that Isa 41,8b is secondary, see Elliger 1971:138 (emphatically); Elliger also demonstrates that Isa 51,2 is secondary, like the other passages in which the prophets mention Abraham (Ezek 33,24; Isa 29,22; Jer 33,26; and Mi 7,20).

[73] Kiesow 1979:21. Kiesow additionally deals with Isa 62,10-12 and Isa 35. He characterizes Isa 35 as *"Eine Mosaik von Anspielungen und Zitaten aus Jes 40-55"* (1979:189).

[74] The clear reference to the prehistory in Isa 52,3-6 is unquestionably secondary (a prose text).

[75] Kiesow 1979:174.

is interesting that Kiesow finds it necessary to make use of a complicated redactio-historical sketch of Isa 40-55. He presupposes the presence of a fundamental writing consisting of Isa 40,13-48,20, and with two redactional strata, namely Isa 49,1-52 and 52,13-55,13, plus a prologue to the entire corpus, Isa 40,1-11[76]. On this view, the mythologization of the Exodus theme first occurs in the earliest of the two redactional strata as a development of the theme. Kiesow dates this redactional activity to the time of the Exile[77]. There is no need to pursue this issure further here, as we shall return to it later in connection with our examination of the Exodus theme in the Psalms. However, the implications of Kiesow's study may tend to suggest that in the course of the Exile the Exodus motif was transformed from "history" into "myth"[78]. It is sufficient here to note that Deutero Isaiah uses these historical themes in a completely original manner with respect to the ways they are formulated in the Pentateuch; this applies not only to the mythologizing parts, but also to Isa 43,16-21, where we observe a "free" quotation of Exod 15,21.

8.

The Post-Exilic Period

The post-Exilic prophets only refer to the earliest history of Israel in a very few passages.

Isa 63, 7ff. This follows the events of the Exodus fairly closely, especially in v 11f, where Moses and the crossing of the Sea of Reeds are mentioned.

Haggai 2,5. On the occasion of the reconstruction of the temple Yahweh proclaims that his spirit will be with the covenant that was concluded during the Exodus from Egypt. The terminology is late, and Deuteronomistic style is involved. The date must be around 520.

Malachi 3,22. The legislation on Mt. Horeb. The dates assigned to this prophet range between 520 and 400, though probably earlier than later. The

---

[76] Cf. Kiesow 1979:165.

[77] 1979:197ff.

[78] This observation is important whether or not one is prepared to follow Kiesow's redactio-historical sketch. The differences between the contents of Isa 43,16-21 and 51,9-10 are so striking that even if one wanted to argue for a *unitary* view of Isa 40-55 (i.e., one prophet, one document, and no thorough-going redactional layer) one would be forced to admit that two completely different views of the Exodus event are expressed in Isa 40-55. One would perhaps be forced to conclude that in the course of his career the prophet altered his interpretation of the Exodus event in a radical manner.

main reason for this date is the lack of references to the P traditions even though Deuteronomistic reminiscences are present, as also in Mal 3,22. This is, of course, not a decisive argument, since already Ezekiel, writing a century earlier, used many terms similar to those appearing in P.

Zechariah 10,10-11. The text may possibly refer to the Exodus event in conjunction with the concept of a new Exodus. It is very difficult to date, but can hardly be pre-exilic[79].

9.

Conclusion

Perhaps already Amos, but in any case the prophet Hosea, made use of the traditions concerning Israel's oldest history; thus these prophets (or, again, at least Hosea) were the only prophetic figures of the 8th century who display any knowledge of the narratives of the patriarchs and the Exodus. Both prophets were solely active in the Northern Kingdom prior to the fall of Samaria in 722, even though Amos was a Judaean by birth.

Against this, Isaiah and Micah, who were active in Judah towards the close of the 8th century and possibly at the beginning of the 7th century, never refer to the Pentateuchal traditions. Thus it seems reasonable to conclude that the Pentateuchal traditions were of no importance in Judah in the 8th century, while they must have been a living reality for at least some groups in the Northern Kingdom at this time.

It is difficult to determine what form these traditions about Israel's past had in Hosea's day and earlier. Thus it is difficult to be sure whether Hosea reproduces such stories as those about Jacob as they were known in the 8th century, or whether he relates them quite freely.

In seventh century Judah, the only allusions to the Pentateuchal traditions are to be found in the Book of Jeremiah. It is characteristic for the parts of the book which may be traced back to the prophet himself that he seems to be following the proclamation of Hosea rather than the Pentateuchal traditions in

---

[79] This passage is generally dated without further discussion to the post-exilic period; see thus F. Horst (in Robinson and Horst 1964:250). Horst's sole difficulty is the question of how late in the post-exilic period the text is to be dated. Against this, B. Otzen has attempted to date the passage to the pre-exilic period on the basis of a *"zeitgeschichtliche"* analysis of the text (1964: 38-45). One should note E.Nielsen's thorough criticisms of this view (1970:34-40). Nielsen only accepts Otzen's date to the time of Josiah as a *terminus a quo*; nor does he hesitate to point to the post-exilic period as the time this passage, which he assigns to a prophetic poet-taster (Epigon), was assembled.

the form in which they now exist. This means that on the basis of the original
sections of the books of Hosea and Jeremiah it cannot be shown that the Exodus and especially the Settlement traditions existed in a form corresponding
to the present Pentateuch plus the Book of Joshua.

Of the later prophets from the 6th century, Ezekiel is quite independent of
his predecessors, although he may have had some knowledge of Jeremiah
(note צבי as a designation for the Holy Land). Ezekiel's use of Israel's early
history is concentrated in his preaching in Ezek 20. At least according to
Zimmerli this chapter reveals affinities with the terminology of the P source,
and demonstrates a detailed knowledge of traditions concerning Israel's prehistory which agree largely with those preserved in the Pentateuch.

Deutero Isaiah differs from Ezekiel in that he is much freer with respect to
these historical traditions, which he normally only uses indirectly in order to
illustrate the new Exodus, without explicitly referring to the Exodus from
Egypt. Deutero Isaiah apparently had materials available which differed to
some degree from those available to the pre-exilic prophets, even though it is
doubtful that Isa 41,8 and 51,2 may be assigned to this prophet.

After the Return from the Babylonian Exile, the Exodus traditions and the
patriarchal narratives were not as topical for the prophetic proclamation as
they were for Hosea prior to the fall of Samaria, or for Jeremiah before the fall
of Jerusalem, or for Ezekiel and Deutero Isaiah during the Exile. With a few
exceptions, the later prophets do not refer to traditions from Israel's earliest
history. Furthermore, the few references to the Exodus traditions in Haggai,
Malachi, and, perhaps, (Deutero) Zechariah may be regarded as a late phase
of the "Deuteronomistic" tradition.

These conclusions are rather negative, as far as the prophets' relationship
to Israel's earliest history is concerned. This fact was apparently already realized by the Deuteronomists, as they did the best they could to make good the
deficiency by inserting a considerable number of formulaic additions into the
prophecies of Amos, and into the Book of Jeremiah, towards which they seem
to have felt especially close. It would not be appropriate to go into the matter
of the Deuteronomistic redaction of the prophetic literature here. Instead, it
would be more useful at this time to abandon the OT prophets in order to investigate other materials in our search for historical perspectives outside of the
Pentateuch.

§ 2

Historical Tradition in the Psalms

With the exception of the Hexateuch (understood as the first four of the Mosaic books plus the two first parts of the Deuteronomistic Historical Work) plus the prophetic books and, to a certain extent, the remainder of the Deuteronomistic Historical Work, interest in Israel's earliest history is not especially prominent. The relationship between the Tetrateuch and the Deuteronomistic literature will be discussed below. Only one textual corpus remains for our study, that is, the Psalms. Other parts of the OT, notably the extensive corpus of Wisdom literature, are generally silent about Israel's early history. This cannot be taken to suggest that the Wisdom authors were unfamiliar with the Pentateuchal traditions. It is very likely that several of the writings in question, including Ecclesiastes and presumably also the Book of Job, were first composed at a time when most or all of the Pentateuch existed in its present form. The reason for this silence as far as history is concerned is therefore to be explained by the respective σϰοποί of these works. The subject of these Wisdom compositions is the individual, whereas Israel's history concerns the entire nation, that is, the Israelite-Jewish people. This supposition is confirmed by the Psalms, for in the Psalter we do not find much in the nature of historical motifs among the psalms for individuals, but in the collective psalms in which these motifs are distributed over a number of different genres.

The problems to be dealt with in attempting to include the Psalms in this discussion are more than numerous. We are not concerned with how and in what connection historical motifs appear, nor with why they are employed. Instead, our approach is chronological; the question is when these motifs appeared and how they have been incorporated into the psalm in question. In other words, there is no need for a synchronous analysis of the historical motifs. Our desideratum is a diachronic placement of the individual motifs in order to determine their evolution in the course of development of Israel's hymnic literature. Of course, the main difficulty in this enterprise is the fact that dating the individual psalms which contain historical motifs is often somewhat subjective. One's evaluation of the individual sources as being pre-exilic, exilic, or post-exilic is often in part based on circular reasoning, since the historical motifs involved are frequently used to provide the basis for such dates.

However, the task is not impossible, and it has in fact been attempted previously by A. Lauha in his monograph which appeared in 1945[80]. Lauha's

---

[80] Lauha 1945.

book is primarily devoted to an analysis of the Psalms on a motif-by-motif basis. He proceeds chronologically, which means that he begins with the most ancient times and proceeds systematically to the post-exilic period. A collected appreciation of the use of historical retrospects in the Psalms is reserved for an appendix-like chapter in Lauha's book[81]. Thus Lauha's "chronological" sequence presents the Creation, the Primeval History, the patriarchal traditions, the Exodus, the crossing of the Sea of Reeds, and so forth as they appear in a number of psalms. Lauha is above all interested in revealing the sources on which the use of the individual historical themes in the respective psalms was based. His discussion is accordingly with whether one or another psalm makes use of the Exodus motif as it appears in P, J, or in the Deuteronomistic materials. He also asks whether the structure of a given psalm reflects such things as Deuteronomistic or pre-Deuteronomistic ideas. Lauha's book is therefore highly relevant to our purposes, since we are interested in the history of individual motifs in the Psalter, even though he is only secondarily concerned with this question and nowhere presents a synthesis of his detailed analyses. Thus no synthesis was available to this writer as a basis for his own evaluations as to the sequence in which the various themes were incorporated into the Psalter. I am particularly interested in the question as to whether the Exodus traditions were assimilated into the Psalms already before the fall of the Northern Kingdom, or whether the presence of this theme in the Psalter presupposes Deuteronomistic tradition and is accordingly to be assigned a later date.

Lauha has elsewhere dealt more extensively with one of the themes in question in a manner which is directly relevant to this study. In the work in question he has concentrated his attention on the miracle at the Sea of Reeds and attempted on the basis of traditio-historical considerations to determine the development of this motif in the Psalter, as well as in the OT literature outside of the Psalms[82]. Lauha's conclusion in this connection is remarkable, since he has found it probable that it was first very late, that is, not before the time of the Exile, that this motif began to play a dominant role in the Israelite understanding of history[83]. This observation of Lauha's is very significant, and it may be supported by another observation which one cannot fail to make when one has examined the prophetic literature and discovered that the theme of the events at the Sea of Reeds is never mentioned by any pre-exilic prophet. Other scholars have commented on this phenomenon, not least among them being B.S. Childs. G.W. Coats has also written in express disagreement with Noth, who regarded the miracle at the Sea of Reeds as the nucleus of the Exodus theme, and who also held that the two motifs taken together comprised the

---

[81] Luaha 1945:128-144.
[82] Lauha 1963.
[83] Lauha 1963:42.

basis of the Israelite concept of election[84]. S.I.L. Norin has argued for a very early conjoining of the motifs of the Exodus and the Sea of Reeds. He holds that this union plus the victory hymn in Exod 5,1b-18 date from the period of the Judges, that is, from a period less than a hundred years after the original historical event[85]. Norin's point of departure for his study is a series of rather dubious religio-historical observations concerning the religious conceptions of the Semites in Egypt at the time of the Exodus events. He maintains that these religious conceptions achieved written form in the interpretation of the miracle at the Sea of Reeds which was promulgated by the Exodus-group during the period after the release from Egypt[86]. To Norin, the interpenetration of historical and mythological motifs to form an understanding of the miracle at the Sea of Reeds was a reality at a very early point in the history of the tradition. Against this, numerous other scholars have held that the mythologization of the historical tradition first came about in exilic times and was manifestly expressed in Deutero Isaiah's use of the theme[87].

The mythological motifs associated with the miracle at the Sea of Reeds continued to live on in North Israelite tradition, or so Norin maintains, and are expressed in, for example, Ps 89,6-19. He holds that the Deuteronomistic reform movement undertook what was in reality a demythologization of the Reed Sea theme. In Norin's opinion, a number of psalms which he dates to the period of Josiah illustrate this fact. It was first during the period of the Exile that the interweaving of myth and Reed Sea event reappeared, whereas the entire theme disappeared from view after the Exile. In Norin's words, no new Exodus psalms were composed after the Exile[88]. The last-mentioned observation is supported to a certain degree by the detail mentioned above, namely the fact that post-exilic prophetic literature is not only uninterested in the miracle at the Sea of Reeds, but also in retrospective references to Israel's early history altogether. Finally, it should also be mentioned that Norin finds himself unable to support the hypothesis once presented by J. Pedersen concerning an ancient association between the "Passover legend" and the Exodus event[89]. He is surely right in this, since the Exodus psalms never refer to the Passover; the linkage between the Passover and the Exodus event was a creation of the Deuteronomistic theology, and it continued to develop after its emergence[90].

---

[84] See Childs 1970; also Childs 1967 and Coats 1967, contra Noth 1948:50ff.

[85] Norin 1977.

[86] Norin 1977:46ff.

[87] On this see most recently Kiesow 1979:105ff. (in connection with Isa 51,9f.). For his part Norin asserts that during the 7th century a thorough demythologization of the Exodus traditions was carried out under Deuteronomistic influence (1977:167).

[88] 1977:170.

[89] Cf. on this point Pedersen 1934 and 1960:549-555. Norin's rejection of this thesis is in Norin 1977:172ff. Cf. already Noth 1948:70, and most recently Steingrimsson 1979.

[90] Norin argues for the separate existence of an ancient cult of the Exodus which was inde-

The weakness in Norin's hypothesis is not so much his religio-historical studies of the religion of the Semitic-language speakers who dwelled in the Nile Delta, as it is the conclusions he draws from this analysis. Is it reasonable to suppose that it is mainly Egyptian mythological material which figures not only in Israelite, but also Ugaritic conceptions of the chaos battle? Norin supports his argument with the hypothesis that it is possible to distinguish between a Canaanite-Northwest Semitic myth of the battle of the god with the sea (Yam and Nahar) and Egyptian conceptions of the serpent-monster, *Apep*. Norin is able to find a not entirely implausible etymology for *Rahab*, one of the names of the chaos beast, but in the case of *Leviathan* there is no question but that that this name is of Semitic origin[91]. It is first in the Book of Job that we find an identification of Leviathan with an Egyptian monster (in reality, the crocodile)[92].

Now, the concept of the seamonster as a *hydra* with many heads is a widespread one indeed. We encounter it in the Greek myths, in the story of Hercules' battle with the hydra, and in the Babylonian chaos battle narrative, *Enuma Eliš*, where Tiamat is also understood as a serpentlike monster. In other words, although in the nature of things Norin's hypothesis cannot be ruled out as impossible, it is nevertheless by far the least likely. In any event, it is entirely unnecessary as an explanation of the concepts of the chaos monster which are present in the OT. Finally, it might be added that even if Egyptian ideas underly the Israelite concepts, this would not give us a date for their assimilation into Israelite tradition, since Israel's knowledge of Egyptian cul-

---

pendent of the פסח - מצה festival(s) (1977:189ff.). He further maintains that the various festivals were first connected with one another during the post-exilic period (1977:201ff.). However, Norin's demonstration of the existence of an ancient Exodus festival is dependent on a somewhat implausible exegesis of Exod 32, which he associates with the existence of an ancient bull cult in the Sinaitic peninsula (1977:189ff.). It would be appropriate to enquire as to the possible *Sitz im Leben* of such a bull cult in Sinai during the second millennium. Anyone who has ever visited this wasteland, whether we are speaking of the northern desert areas or the moonlike landscape of the south, would have no difficulty in acknowledging the absurdity of the notion. As has long been recognized, Exod 32 is nothing but a polemic against the royal bull cult in the Northern Kingdom; cf. Aberbach and Smolar 1967, and, most recently, Van Seters 1981:170-174. Admittedly, Van Seters claims that the narrative in 1 Kgs 12,25ff. is a purely Deuteronomistic fabrication, and thus instead reckons Deut 9,8ff. to be the oldest edition of the Deuteronomistic criticism of the bull-calf cult in the Northern Kingdom. However, Van Seters does recognize that literary dependency connects the Deuteronomistic description of Jeroboam's calves with the polemic against Aaron's calf in Exod 32. Other explanations of the bull calf cult, such as those of Eissfeldt 1940 and Weippert 1961 (which take the "calf" to be, respectively, a cult standard and a pedestal) may be disregarded here, but they do nevertheless contradict the OT understanding of the calves, that is, as evaluated by the Deuteronomists, or in passages which accord with Deuteronomistic polemics and are perhaps dependent on them, such as Exod 32 and Ps 106,19f.

[91] On Rahab see Norin 1977:71ff., where the author suggests an Egyptian etymology: *r,' ḥ,'ḥ*, "the convoluted serpent". Of course, the Semitic etymology of Leviathan is לוה, as Norin acknowledges (1977:68). With respect to Norin's etymology of Rahab it must be admitted that it is possible; by the same token, however, Norin is unable to provide a single example in which *r,'* (a rare word for "serpent") and *ḥ,'ḥ* (convoluted or bent) were conjoined in Egyptian.

[92] Cf. Job 40,25, and cf. on this Driver 1956.

ture and religion did not cease with the Exodus event. Not least from the time of the United Monarchy do we have evidence of considerable Egyptian influence on the newly-emerged state. Norin's colleague at the University of Lund, T.N.D. Mettinger, could have pointed this out to him, since Mettinger has written of such influences in his work on the administrative system in the young Israelite state[93]. Furthermore, Egyptian influence is detectable outside of the administrative field above all in Judah in the form of, for example, royal ideology, namely the notion of the god-king, which is expressed in Ps 110, and perhaps also the practice of anointment of kings[94].

It would also be appropriate to ask whether the motif of the chaos battle really is present in the hymn of the Sea of reeds, Exod 15,1b-18, or whether this hymn is not in actuality quite reticent in its use of mythological material[95]. Finally, Norin paid too little attention to the relationship between the Exodus tradition and the miracle at the Sea of Reeds; thus he has failed to deal with the very relevant problems which Childs and Coats have noted concerning the traditio-historical connections linking the Exodus event and the miracle at the Sea of Reeds on the one hand and the traditions of the desert wandering on the other. It would be fair to say that instead of meeting these factors head-on, Norin has tried to avoid them via the agency of his religio-historical observations. Nevertheless, the problem remains, and it may be attacked traditio-historically, as Childs and Coats have done, or form critically, as J. Kühlewein has attempted[96]. In the opinion of this writer, the conclusion of Childs and Coats (i.e., that the miracle at the Sea of Reeds was in traditio-historical terms originally attached to the traditions of the desert period and was part of the Yahwist's scheme of paradigmatic narratives, all of which illustrate how Yahweh preserves Israel from impending danger. They also hold that it was first P, the later reworker of the Exodus and desert period materials, who attached the miracle at the Sea of Reeds directly to the release from Egypt) is

---

[93] Mettinger 1971. See also Bernhardt 1971, who emphasizes the parallelism between the Egyptian administration of Palestine during the New Kingdom and during the period of the Davidic Empire (1971:145).

[94] Cf. Kutsch 1963:34ff. However, Kutsch regards the Israelite anointment rite as a cultural loan from the Hittites (1963: 36ff.). On the other hand, De Vaux sees it as a borrowed Egyptian practice (De Vaux 1964). Mettinger sees the problem of anointing differently however, since he compares it with a Near Eastern ritual associated with the conclusion of contracts of various types (1976:212ff.).

[95] Of course, it could be held that there are mythological motifs in Exod 15,8. Norin, however, regards this verse as secondary (1977:95). Others maintain that there is no disagreement between the description of the miracle in the Yahwistic accoun t in Exod 14 and that in the hymn in Exod 15,1b-18. Thus most recently Kiesow 1979:108: *"Die Darstellung des Schilmeerwunders in Ex 15,8ff. wäre dann nicht mehr als eine poetische Ausgestaltung der Ost-Wind-version von J"...."Das Meer trägt in Ex 15 keinerlei personhafte Züge"*.

[96] Cf. Kühlewein 1973. Unlike Lauha (1945), whose analysis follows the various themes, Kühlewein employs the opposite approach, in that his analysis follows the various psalmic genres in which historical motifs appear. He reserves his study of the various historical themes to the last part of his treatment.

well substantiated; this suggests that Lauha saw the problem more clearly than Norin when he assigned the mythologization of the miracle at the Sea of Reeds to a late phase in the history of the tradition.

A problem which is closely related to the above is the question of the date of the hymn in Exod 15,1b-18 and its relation to the Song of Miriam in Exod 15,21b. Numerous scholars, among whom Noth is but the most illustrious, regard the strophe Exod 15,21b to be the nucleus of the preceding victory hymn, Exod 15,1b-18, to which they assign a late date. Others, such as Albright, Cross, and D.N. Freedman, reckon the hymn to be one of the oldest if not the oldest text in the OT[97]. A thorough examination of the arguments for an early date has been carried out by Norin, who has also troubled to examine the linguistic evidence. Archaic usage permeates the *entire* song; it includes such things as the demonstrative pronoun זו , which also appears in numerous much younger texts in the OT[98], the suffix מו , which, however, is quite common in poetic literature, and the syntax used in the song, especially the use of prefigured verbal forms even in the section running from v 16 onwards. Cross and Freedman originally translated this section in the future tense, although Cross has since returned to an understanding of it as an imperfect sequence (for this reason Childs correctly questions the relevance of the syntactic argument)[99]. As we have seen, archaisms are evenly distributed throughout the entire hymn; Norin, following D.A. Robertson, takes this to signify that the psalm has been written in an archaic and not an archaising style[100].

A linguistic analysis such as that of Robertson also arrives at the conclusion that the Book of Job is one of the oldest parts of the OT; such conclusions may be difficult for us to agree with. A presupposition for this early date for the Exodus passage must be that the poem was written down at an early date. However, if it had been transmitted orally for perhaps several centuries and then written down at a late date, we should expect that the non-archaic usage of a later period would have established itself in at least a couple of passages,

---

[97] For a late date for Exod 15,1b-18: Noth 1965:98, who held that it was a later extension of the Song of Miriam, Exod 15,21b (cf. on this Norin 1977:93.101). For an early date see Cross and Freedman 1955, and, following them, Albright 1968:10 (13th century).

[98] Thus Isa 42,24; 43,21. It also occurs in a number of psalmic passages such as Ps 9,16 and 10,2 which are to be assigned to the time of the monarchy in Jerusalem at the earliest (and concerning which post-exilic dates have been suggested cf. Kraus 1966:79). It also occurs in a number of individual laments, such as Ps 17,9; 31,5; 32,8; 142,3; 143,8, in connection with which a precise date is impossible, as well as in Ps 68,29, concerning which, see below.

[99] Cf. Cross and Freedman 1955:242: v 17: *"Thou wilt bring them, thou wilt plant them, in the mount of thy heritage...."*. This is to be compared with Cross 1973:131: *"You brought them, you planted them in the mount of your heritage"*. Both are attempts to render Hebrew ...תבאמו ותטעמו בהר נחלתך. Naturally, the reason for this *volte face* is that Cross changed his views as to the date of the hymn (cf. Cross 1973:124: the close of the 12th or the beginning of the 11th century). For criticism of the methods involved see Childs 1974:242.

[100] Cf. Robertson 1972. With particular reference to the distribution of archaisms and their significance see Robertson 1972:135-146. Compare Norin 1977:82ff.

as, for example, in the secondary passages which Norin proposes to excise. As far as I can see, Norin does not comment on this circumstance. Instead, he follows his linguistic study up with a "form critical" analysis which is more in the nature of an examination of individual concepts. This analysis allows him to claim that the hymn reflects the Northwest Semitic Ba'al myth[101].

If Norin's analysis of the psalm is to be accepted, it must be possible for the psalm to be traced back to the event itself or to a period shortly thereafter. Therefore a number of features are excised from the hymn as secondary anachronisms. This applies especially to v 14b, חיל אחז ישבי פלשת since at this time the Philistines could not have been Israel's opponents[102]. The crucial factor for this early date is the conclusion of the hymn in v 16ff. If Norin's interpretation is to be regarded as valid, one must naturally reject the notion that these verses refer to conditions in Palestine after the Settlement. Thus Norin compares the reference to בהר נחלתך מכן לשבתך with the references to Ba'al's temple in the Ugaritic texts[103]. I shall not discuss Norin's exegesis of this passage more closely here, and prefer instead to follow Childs' somewhat more reasonable interpretation. Childs points out that it would be far more natural to understand בהר נחלתך מכן לשבתך and מקדש אדני as references to conditions after the immigration, since the reference is clearly to something as late as the temple in Jerusalem[104]. In terms of the interweaving of the motifs involved, Childs' observations are quite important, since he has pointed out that the hymn contains features in its description of the miracle at the Sea of Reeds which are distributed throughout both J's and P's accounts of the crossing of the Sea of Reeds. He concludes that this does not prove that the hymn presupposes the existence of a collected Pentateuch, but that it represents an independent tradition with respect to the Pentateuchal traditions[105]. This in turn suggests that although it is possible that the hymn was added during one of the last phases in the redaction of the Pentateuch, as G. Fohrer has argued[106], this fact still tells us nothing decisive about the age of the poem. The only date we can assign to it would then be at some point in the history of the monarchy after the construction of the temple by Solomon. If the text is not to be dated to the period of the united monarchy, as proposed by Mowinckel, then its time of authorship must be assigned to some point after 722, that is, after the incorporation of the Exodus theme into Judaean tradition. Since the text does not reveal Deuteronomistic features and its terminology is distinctively different from that of the Deuteronomists, it might be reasonable

---

[101] Norin 1977:84-93. Both the hymn in Exod 15,1b-18 and the old Ugaritic Ba'al epic have the same fundamental structure, according to Norin (1977:91): *"Konflikt, Tempelbau, Königtum"*.
[102] 1977:96. He also regards v 15 as secondary (ibid.).
[103] 1977:88ff. (esp. pp.90f.).
[104] 1974:246.
[105] Cf. Childs 1970:411f.
[106] 1964:112.

to suggest a date of some time in the first half of the 7th century for the composition of the hymn. Thus the hymn would provide evidence of the "neutral" attitude towards the Exodus materials which Norin maintains characterized this period. These observations imply that it might be possible to use Exod 15,1b-18 as the starting point for an analysis of the use of the Sea of Reeds theme in the Psalms, but not to provide more dramatic conclusions.

However, I initially proposed that the materials would be presented as a diachronic account of the appearance of the Exodus motif in the psalmic literature. Thus in what follows I shall attempt to examine the various materials with a view to dating the occurrences of the Exodus motif in order to determine whether it may be detected in Judaean tradition from the period preceding the fall of Samaria in 722, or whether it is first evident in psalms whose provenance was the temple in Jerusalem - and Jerusalemite tradtion - from the close of the 8th century. Such a chronologically based study will also serve to illustrate how the Exodus motif became intermeshed with other motifs in the course of the development of the psalmic literature. Obviously, the individual dates arrived at below are conjectural and subjective to some extent; thus it would be naive to imagine that my analysis is the last word on this sobject.

1.

Psalm 80

The Exodus motif is clearly touched on in Ps 80,9-10, where the connection with the idea of the Settlement is also apparent. This psalm is ordinarily dated to the period immediately preceding 722, although a few scholars have dated it to the time of Josiah[107]. It is claimed that the picture of Israel in the psalm reflects the decline of the Northern Kingdom (indeed, the Northern Kingdom is the only part of "Israel" with which the psalm is concerned). The reason for dating the psalm to the period immediately following 722 is that it nevertheless expresses the hope that events will be reversed so that Israel, that is, the Northern Kingdom, will be restored. Those who date the psalm to the later part of the 7th century base this decision on the fact that the three northern tribes which are mentioned are Ephraim, Benjamin, and Manasseh, since, as H.-J. Kraus has pointed out, it was the territory of these three tribes which was

---

[107] For a date for this psalm to the time of Josiah, see Kraus 1966:557. See also Bentzen 1939:457. Gunkel, however, felt that the psalm derived from the Northern Kingdom, but from some time after the events of 722 (1929:353).

affected by Josiah's expansionary policies[108]. However, the last-mentioned date is debatable. In the first place, the psalm contains none of the motifs associated with psalms deriving from Judah in the 7th century, or from exilic or post-exilic times. Further, the psalm is not only completely devoid of Deuteronomistic terminology, it also contains only a single point of contact with the Deuteronomistic view of history, namely the concept of the wrath of God with his people in v 5 (עַד מָתַי עָשַׁנְתָ בִּתְפִלַּת עַמֶּךָ). The notion that it is God who punishes Israel because of his anger towards her is, of course, a fixed element in the Deuteronomistic literature. However, it is to be observed that this motif is not attached in Ps 80 to the further concept that the cause of Yahweh's wrath is Israel's sin. Thus it would be more appropriate to claim that Ps 80,5 represents one of the concepts which led to the development of the Deuteronomistic theology of history. We have to do with the pan-Oriental view that the gods direct history and punish their respective peoples if they become angry with them, as B. Albrektson has shown. Naturally, in this context the most appropriate parallel is the remark of Mesha of Moab that Moab had been humiliated by Israel because Chemosh was angry with his country (כי יאנף כמש בארצה)[109]. This observation means that we may date Ps 80 to an early stage in the history of Israel, so that a date in the 8th century would not be unreasonable. For that matter, the contents of the psalm itself would make a date in the latter part of the 9th century plausible, so that one could also hold that the difficulties alluded to in the psalm are those the land experienced during the reign of the first kings of the dynasty of Jehu, which were caused by the Aramaeans[110].

The heart of the problem is whether the psalm is to be dated to the period before or after the conquest of Samaria by the Assyrians. Although it is impossible to be sure on this issue, the psalm nevertheless suggests that the Northern Kingdom still exists, though in an enfeebled condition. Not all of the tribes of the Northern Kingdom are referred to, but only those in central Palestine. These tribes are described as being exposed to danger, but not to the threat of extinction or subjection to foreign powers. Accordingly, there is reason to support O. Eissfeldt's date for Ps 80, which places it between the conclusion of the Syro-Ephraimite war in 732 and the fall of Samaria in 722[111]. In this period the three tribes in question were the only ones remaining after the new organization of the Assyrian provinces in western Asia undertaken by

---

[108] Kraus 1966:557.

[109] KAI 181:5-6. Cf. Albrektson 1967:101f. See also Albrekson's résumé (1979:32f.).

[110] In other words, to the period which is reflected in the traditions contained in 1 Kgs 20 and 22, which have been wrongly, though possibly intentionally, assigned to the monarchy of Ahab in Kings (on this see Schmitt 1972). On the other hand, a date to the first half of the 8th century would be meaningless, since from the Assyrian conquest of Damascus in 802 until the accession of Tiglath Pileser III Israel was relatively untroubled by both the Aramaeans and the Assyrians, and thus was able to consolidate her power in this period.

[111] Cf. Eissfeldt 1953, and see also Eissfeldt 1964.

Tiglath Pileser III in conjunction with the conclusion of his war' with Aram and Israel. The image conjured up in v 13f in fact suggests the exposed position of the Israelite rump-state after it had been divested of the main part of its territories[112]. The metaphor which figures in v 9f.15b-16a points to a traditio-historical connection with the Northern Kingdom; this picture of Israel is, as is well known, also used by Hosea in Hos 10,1, and it recurs, as we have seen, in Jer 2,21, which is dependent on Hosea[113]. The metaphor of the grapevine in Hosea, Jeremiah, and Ps 80 differs considerably from the motif of the vineyard in Isaianic tradition. Of course, one could always maintain that if Jeremiah was able to make use of a metaphor from Hosea towards the end of the 7th century, the psalmist responsible for Ps 80 could have done so as well. It would nevertheless still be more natural to regard Ps 80,9ff as a reflection of North Israelite tradition, since the motifs which are associated with the Exodus motif in Judaean psalms are completely absent from Ps 80. It is also remarkable that there is no connection with other aspects of Hosea's proclamation such as his theme of rejection; it is equally noteworthy that the connection between the theme of the Exodus and the Settlement is already well established in Ps 80. On the other hand, the motif of the events at the Sea of Reeds is wholly lacking, but Ps 80 is insufficient by itself to prove that this motif was unknown, since the compact metaphor in v 9ff does not allow room for the inclusion of other events from Israel's past.

2.

Psalm 68

Norin claims that there are no references to the Exodus event in Ps 68, and that instead v 8f represent the same picture of Yahweh going off to war as the one present in the Song of Deborah, Jdg 5,4-5[114]. Norin also discusses Ps 68,7, which he maintains has nothing to do with the Israelite travails in Egypt, but with the release of prisoners instead[115]. In my opinion, Norin's attempt to dismiss Ps 68 as an Exodus hymn is poorly founded. It is correct that the motif in v 7 does not immediatley refer to the Exodus event. Nevertheless, there were

---

[112] Seen in this light, Ps 80 is a Northern counterpart to Isa 8,23-9,6. Cf. Alt 1950.

[113] CF. Ps 80,9: חמטעה...גפן ממצרים תסיע ...; Hos 10,1 גפן בוקק ישראל. However, in Jer 2,21 שרק , is used; cf. Jer 2,21aα ואנכי נטעתיך שרק, but one should note הגפן נכריה in Jer 2,21bβ. Jeremiah's vocabularly is, however, no doubt influenced by a line strectching back to Isaiah; cf. Isa 5,1ff. (and esp. Isa 5,2 aβ: ויטעהו שרק). The post- exilic Isa 27,2ff. is also based on Isa 5,1ff.

[114] 1977:161-164. Cf. also Kraus 1966:469f. and Mowinckel 1953:34f.

[115] Ps 68,7b מוציא אסירים; cf. Norin 1977:162.

good reasons for including the theme of the prisoners at this juncture in the psalm, as I shall attempt to show in conjunction with my discussion of the assimilation of themes from individual psalms of lament into the collective (national) psalms of lament. Here it will suffice to point out that if we read v 8-11 as a unit, then it is impossible not to observe that we are confronted with the same conjunction of Exodus event (without reference to the miracle at the Sea of Reeds) and the Settlement as we found to be expressed in Ps 80. Natu-rally, it is necessary to join אלהים בצאתך לפני עמך in v 8a to חיתך ישבו בה in v 11a so as to form a coherent sequence. This sequence is united by the theme of the desert wandering in v 8b. The reference to Sinai in v 9 supplements these elements and suggests that the author of this part of Ps 68 knew the complexes of tradition which are now preserved in the Pentateuch and was able to use them to form a continuous description of Israel's path from Egypt to the Promised Land.

It is important to note that the theme of the covenant, which is the central element in the Sinai traditions in the present Pentateuch, is completely absent from Ps 68. Also the linking of the Exodus, the wandering in the desert, the theophany on Sinai, and the Settlement in Canaan provides no indication whatsoever that the psalmist had at his disposal the Pentateuch or one of its fundamental sources such as J.

Unfortunately, Ps 68 is among the most difficult psalms to date in the entire collection. Suggestions in this direction have ranged from the 13th-12th cen-turies to the time of Saul, the period of the monarchy, and all the way to the post-exilic period[116]. Verses 29-32 seem to show that the final redaction of the psalm was first completed at a very late date; it is also possible that they reflect ideas which were pregnantly expressed by Deutero Isaiah. In other words, the present form of the psalm may reasonably be dated towards the conclusion of the period of the Exile[117]. Of course, this is not the last word on the date of the psalm, since it also contains many passages which seem to go much further back into Israel's history. It would be appropriate to mention Albright's attempt to describe Ps 68 as a collection of superscriptions of individual old psalms, which he dated to the pre-national period[118]. Today, however, scholars

---

[116] A variety of dates have been suggested for Ps 68. Albright, for example, assigned it to the period of the Judges (1950B; see also 1968:23f.). The same date has been advocated by Cross (1973:100ff.). Mowinckel dated the basic form of the psalm to the time of Saul (1953:72; see also 1953:68-73, which contains a detailed critique of Albright's treatment of this psalm. Kraus, how-ever, (1966:470ff.), followed by Norin (1977:163f.), dates it to the end of the 8th century and loca-tes it in Jerusalem (even though Kraus also notes that v 31f. suggest some post-exilic redaction). Gunkel found Ps 68 to be a late and post-exilic work (1929:286f.).

[117] With respect to the post-exilic section v 29-32 reference should especially be made to Gunkel 1929:286 and Kraus 1966:476f; both scholars compare the section with Isa 18,7; Zeph 3,10; Zech 14,16ff.; Gunkel adds Isa 45,14 and 60,3.

[118] 1950B:1ff. Contrariwise, Mowinckel regarded Ps 68 as a liturgy associated with the Enthronement Festival of Yahweh (1953:16ff.). Mowinckel had earlier regarded Ps 68 as a victory hymn: *"das aber nach dem Aufzug des Thronbesteigungsfestes stilisiert ist"* (1922:332).

doing research on the Psalms are not much in favor of dividing individual psalms up into a number of independent parts. This procedure is nevertheless relevant to Ps 68, since it has proven to be extremely difficult to find any unifying theme connecting the various parts of this psalm. The introduction in v 2-7 is a song of praise containing Wisdom motifs. The second part, v 8-11, contains a historical retrospect over Israel's earliest history. The third part, v 12-15 is a victory hymn containing references to concrete events. The fourth part, v 16-19 is a doxology, that is, a hymn in praise of Yahweh, whose provenance would seem to be the temple in Jerusalem. The fifth part, v 20-24, is yet another hymn to Yahweh, which describes him in quite general terms as a victor. The sixth part, v 25-28, describes a festal procession. The seventh, v 29-32, contains an injunction addressed to *Elohim* to exercize his mastery of the world from his temple in Jerusalem. Finally, the eighth part, v 33-36, contains an injunction to praise *Elohim*, although it provides no reason for offering such praise. The closest parallels to this part are in Ps 95-99.

Of course, one could maintain that the many different forms employed in Ps 68 imply that we have to do with a liturgical composition. However, even though the present form of this liturgy may be late, it may very easily contain elements which are much older than the final redaction of the psalm. It is practically impossible to date the strophe in v 8-11, but there is nothing to rule out a date towards the close of the 8th century. It cannot possibly belong to the latter part of the 7th century, since it does not contain even reminiscences of a Deuteronomistic nature. The notion that Israel has ever been estranged from her God is very distant from this psalm.

3.

Psalm 81

This psalm contains numerous references to Pentateuchal motifs; its emphasis is on the Exodus event, but it does not allude to the miracle at the Sea of Reeds. The psalm also seems to play on the Sinai themes in both the first part of the psalm, v 5-6, חק לישראל and עדות ביהוסף, and in its second part, v 8a. The psalm also contains a reference to the events in Meribah which are related in Num 20,1-13. However, the psalm's understanding of these events is quite peculiar, since v 8b, אבחנך על מי מריבה suggests a positive view of the episode in Num 20,1-13, whereas the Pentateuchal account emphasizes that these events were Moses' misfortune (Moses is, incidentally, nowhere mentioned in Ps 81). In order to understand this motif it would be appropriate to point out that literary criticism has divided Num 20,1-13 into respective J and P versions. The understanding of the events as a crime committed by Moses against

Yahweh is only present in the P account, while the J version relates how the people attempt to test Yahweh, a thematic parallel to Isaiah's demand of Ahaz that he test Yahweh (Isa 7,10-11)[119]. Thus Ps 81,8b corresponds neither to the Yahwistic nor the Priestly versions of the Meribah incident. However, the fact that we encounter all of three different views of this miracle in the OT suggests that the motif was well known and that it must have been employed prior to its incorporation in the Pentateuchal sources. This is in turn emphasized by the fact that this event is frequently referred to in the Psalms[120].

The question as to the significance of the Sinai theme in the psalm is dependent upon the connection between the prologue, v 1-6a, and the main part, v 6b-17. It is not without further ado clear that v 6ff presuppose the introduction. Several scholars have pointed to the connection between שמע עמי in v 9a and prophetic judgement oracles and Deuteronomistic parenetic passages[121]. This could be taken to suggest that the second part is rooted in traditio-historical terms in some other milieu than the celebration presupposed by the introduction. At all events, the present *form* of the psalm seems to presuppose the style of the prophetic judgement oracle. As far as *contents* are concerned, the motif of guilt and punishment also recalls prophetic judgment oracles in traditio-historical terms. Thus it would be reasonable to date the psalm to the pre-exilic period, and to locate it in Judah in the 7th century. This date is by no means as obvious as might at first seem to be the case, since the psalm is unambiguously laden with Deuteronomistic themes and phraseology. This is clear in the main part, and especially in the quotation in v 10 from the Decalogue; however, the Deuteronomistic quotation which is present in both Exod 20,2 and Deut 5,6 (אנכי יהוה אלהיך הוצאתיך מארץ מצרים) follows the quotation in Ps 81 (namely in v 11). Admittedly, the psalm employs המעלה instead of הוצאתיך, which might be taken to suggest that this is a non-Deuteronomistic (i.e., E) passage, but the use of the root עלה in this context is in fact well attested in the Deuteronomistic literature, not merely in Deut 20,1, but also in the Deuteronomistic passages in the Book of Jeremiah and in the Deuteronomistic Historical Work[122]. Now, the linkage of the Ten Commandments, the so-called covenant formula, and the historical scheme with which we are so familiar from the Deuteronomistic literature shows that the psalm must have been

---

[119] Cf. Eissfeldt 1922:177*f. According to Eissfeldt's division of Num 20,1-13, P is to be found in v 1a.2.3b.4*.6.7.8a (with the exception of קח את המטה). 10*.12-13. Eissfeldt assigned J (which he called L) to v 3a.5.8a(קח את המטה).8b.9.11. He took v 1b to belong to E. See further Noth 1966B: 127, who assigned the following verses to P: v 2.3b.4.6.7.8anβn.10.11β. 12. Noth regarded the rest of the materials as a late accretion of motifs borrowed from Exod 17,1-7 which were added to the Priestly narrative in Num 20,1-13.

[120] Kraus 1966:562 emends אבחנך to תבחני, with reference to Exod 17,7; Num 20,13; Ps 77,13ff.; 95,9. He maintains that this is a clear attempt at harmonization. However, the MT is to be retained as the *lectio difficilior*.

[121] Cf. Kraus 1966:566f.; Norin 1977:142.

[122] See n.47, above.

composed by circles which were extremely close to the Deuteronomistic movement[123]. It is possible that Ps 81 not only presupposes the existence of Deuteronomism as a phenomenon, but also the existence of the final collection of
Deuteronomy, since v 17 in Ps 81 very closely resembles a quotation from Deut
32,13-14[124].

Thus this psalm in unlikely to be pre-exilic. My reasons for hesitation with
respect to dating it to the Exile or later are that the situation of the Exile is
nowhere presupposed in the psalm, and that cultic festivals are referred to in
the introduction. Thus a post-exilic date would be possible. An argument
against a post-exilic date would have to rely on the fact that there is no evidence
of knowledge of the Pentateuchal sources, especially P, in Ps 81. This is an uncertain argument, however, since it is a typical *argumentum e silentio*. The fact
that the psalm does not utilize P material does not necessarily signify that the
psalmist was unfamiliar with P; it only tells us that he did not quote it. Nevertheless, for want of better arguments, this argument has played a major role
in the discussion of the dates of the individual psalms. My own conclusion,
however, is necessarily that a post-exilic date is not excluded; moreover, this
date would explain the linking of the Sinai motif and the Exodus event. On the
other hand, a date in late pre-exilic times cannot be completely ruled out, in
part because of the above-mentioned - and unconvincing - argument concerning P material, and in part because of the historical reason that the Exile
is not mentioned among the lists of punishments affecting Israel because of the
people's apostasy (which is, once again, an *e silentio* reason).

4.

Psalm 77

Once again, in the case of Ps 77 we observe that the attempts to date this psalm
have ranged from a provenance in the Northern Kingdom before the fall of Samaria to the post-exilic period[125]. The psalm resolves into two parts. The first

---

[123] Thus also Norin 1977:142f.

[124] Ps 81,17: תנובה שדי וינקהו דבש מסלע ושמן :32,13 cf. Deut ,ויאכילהו מהלב חטה ומצור דבש אשביעך
מחלמיש צור ירכבהו על במותי ארץ ויאכל , cf. also v 14b: עם חלב כליות חטה. It could be maintained that even if the "Song of Moses", Deut 32, is not Deuteronomistic in literary critical
terms, the "quotation" from this text may have been borrowed prior to the incorporation of the
poem in Deut. In this as in other matters one's final decision will be guided by the question of
dates. Thus Deut 32 has been evaluated quite variously. Albright claimed that it derived from
the premonarchical period, to be precise around 1025, after the fall of Shiloh (1968:15). This is
to be compared with von Rad, who insisted that the poem is postexilic and displays clear points
of contract with Deutero Isaiah (1964:143). E. Nielsen regards Deut 32 without further discussion as a Deuteronomistic "fare-well address" (1959:49 and 107).

[125] Dates assigned to Ps 77: Gunkel assumed that its provenance was the Northern King-

section, v 2-11, is a psalm of lament; in terms of form it is an individual lament, but, taken together with the second part, a hymn to Yahweh as the God of the Exodus and the victor of the Chaos Battle, it may be characterized as national lament. It is related in terms of motifs with Ps 89, which also contains a corresponding hymnic part, v 6-19 (which, however, does not contain motifs from Israel's earliest history)[126].

Like Ps 89, the poet behind Ps 77 does not understand the situation he describes, whether the issue is the personal status of the poet or the state of the entire nation. If the psalm is really an original unity, this might suggest a period in which the Deuteronomistic view of history had not yet won the day. On the other hand, v 2-11 do not contain any motifs at all which would legitimate the transition from the individual to the national plane. Furthermore, since historical retrospects are ordinarily associated with the national perspective, and since in Ps 77 we are actually confronted with a mixture of two different forms, it would not be unreasonable to suppose that we have to do with two distinct psalms which became unified at some point. This implies that whatever date we arrive at for the first part need not necessarily apply to the second part of Ps 77. Thus, even though v 2ff should prove to be derived from the close of the 8th century, as H. Gunkel suggested (which, however, requires one to prove that the divine designation עליון in v 11 was a North Israelite divine epithet or a North Israelite divinity)[127], this would not prevent the second part from being dated to the exilic or post-exilic periods.

Norin reckons this psalm to be exilic since it contains both references to P traditions and to Deuteronomistic terminology. He also claims that v 14 is best

---

dom (1929:335), although it is not clear whether he thought the date to be prior to or after 722. Kraus, however (1966:530) regarded it as post-exilic (again followed by Norin 1977:121).

[126] It is impossible for me to agree with Norin 1977:114ff. (which is in turn dependent on Ahlström 1959:69ff.), who thinks to find the Exodus motif in the hymnic section v 6ff., while at the same time denying that v 10-13 contain a creation motif for the reason *"dass diese Motive in der Regel nicht mit der Schöpfung kombiniert werden, sondern mit dem Exodusmotiv"* (Norin 1977:114). Norin is overtrumping himself on this point, as a glance at his commentary on Exod 15,13.17 (1977:91) shows, since Norin there maintains in connection with the motifs in the Reed Sea hymn that the hymn contains the same scheme as is present in the Ugaritic Ba'al epic. The royal motif in Ps 89,6-19 (and in this connection one ought solely to be concerned with v 6-19) is to be found in v 15: צדק ומשפט מכון כסאך; cf. Ps 96,10.13; 97,6; 98,9; 99,4f. Compare further with the combination of צדק and משפט in conjunction with the royal ideology in Lemche 1979B and Liverani 1971B. There is no doubt but that Ps 89,6-19 illustrates the well known fact that the Israelite religion displays the same conjunction of chaos battle with creation as is present in the Babylonian religion, but which is not attested at Ugarit. On the description of creation in Ps 89 see also Kraus 1966:620.

[127] Within Scandinavian tradition it has been virtually a dogma that a hypothetical divinity known as אל עליון was also worshipped in pre-Israelite Jerusalem, and that it was this divinity's attributes which Yahweh eventually assimilated. On this issue see already Nyberg 1938:352, and, further, Nyberg 1938:357: *"Die Hauptstätte dieses vielnamigen Gottes wenigstens im Süden des Westlandes, vielleicht überhaupt muss Jerusalem gewesen sein; nur so versteht man die politische Bedeutung dieser Stadt sowohl vor wie nach der israelitischen Eroberung".* It is accordingly rather disappointing that Norin does not comment on this tradition.

understood as a close relation of Exod 15,11. The Deuteronomistic materials
are especially evident in v 15-16, although v 16 also contains one feature which
is prominent in P, namely the use of גאל to speak of the release[128]. I am not
sure that the use of גאל in this passage actually proves a knowledge of Priestly
usage. I shall attempt to comment below on the use of this term in parallelism
with another which many scholars have held to be a typical example of Deuteronomistic terminology, namely the use of פדה to describe the liberation from
Egypt. Characteristic Priestly expressions seem to appear first in v 21, where
Moses and Aaron are mentioned as the shepherds of Israel, to which it would
be appropriate to compare Num 33,1; Micah 6,4; and Ps 99,6. In its present
context the passage in v 17ff definitely refers to the miracle at the Sea of Reeds;
thus Ps 77 shows that the theme of the Exodus was first attached to the Reed
Sea event at a late point in the formation of the tradition. However, it has been
pointed out that v 17-20 do not in and of themselves refer to the miracle at the
Sea of Reeds. This association is established by the framework around these
verses, so that it is possible to regard v 17-20 as a fragment of an old description
of the Chaos Battle. This in turn shows that the Exodus motif was connected
with the miracle at the Sea of Reeds precisely via the inclusion of Chaos Battle
motifs which provided a mythological extension of the original motif[129]. If
this connection was first established during the Exile the reason for the
phenomenon in question might have been that the Chaos Battle motif, which
was once associated with the New Year Festival, lost this association during the
"a-cultic" (at least in Jerusalem) situation of the Exile. Having become
"unemployed", it was much easier for this traditional motif to migrate into
other contexts. This possibility would also explain why an examination of the
prophetic literature shows that this motif first occurs in conjunction with the
historical Reed Sea theme in the writings of Deutero Isaiah.

Excursus

גאל and פדה and the Exodus from Egypt

An examination of the use of the root גאל as both verb and substantive (גאל and גאלה) in the OT
indicates that it is possible to distinguish between four major areas of meaning[130]. The basic
sense is the idea of the "redeemer" of land or persons, possibly in combination with one another.
However, the expression "redeemer of blood", גאל דם, is also well known in the OT. The use of
the term in connection with the paying of substitute fees instead of the obligatory dues to the
temple is related to this notion. Both of the latter usages are mainly found in the Psalms and in
the prophetic books. The root גאל is used in the Psalter in both individual and collective contexts.

---

[128] See the excurses on גאל and פדה below.
[129] Cf. Kraus 1966:533.
[130] It is to be emphasized that the root גאל is unknown outside of Hebrew.

It ordinarily appears in laments or songs of thanksgiving, but in connection with collective (national) psalms it is possible to distinguish between two subtypes. These are psalms which do not contain historical retrospects, and those which do so; the latter group refer either to the Exodus event or to the miracle at the Sea of Reeds.

The original use of the word in Israelite tradition was no doubt the legislation concerning the Jubilee in Lev 25, or, more precisely, in the גאל sections, v 23-54. These rules are incorporated into a Priestly context and have been expanded by this circle of tradents; they also figure in the so-called "Holiness Code". Nevertheless, there is no doubt that behind such legislation we glimpse an institution with ancient roots in the Israelite society, as H. Graf Reventlow has argued[131]. The elements in the גאל institution are in two parts which can hardly be distinguished from each other. These are the rules concerning the redemption of lost family property and those which apply to the redemption of relatives who have had to sell themselves as slaves because of debts. The fact that these two areas in reality make up a single facet is clearly exemplified by the practical demonstration of the גאל institution in the Book of Ruth. This example is in no way connected with the Jubilee year, which shows that the origins of this institution were independent of the Priestly framework concerning the Jubilee in Lev 25[132].

The phrase גאל דם to designate the "redeemer of blood" in Lev 25,23-54 is secondary to the גאל regulations. But it is obvious that the origin of this special designation was the existence of the institution of the "redeemer"; it signigies a specialization whose background was the same concepts of the unity of the lineage which are also the basis of the גאל institution[133].

A further specialization of the term is to be found in the Priestly legislation in Lev 27, which has to do with substitute fees which are to be paid in lieu of a number of dues to the priesthood. This is no doubt a secondary application of the concept of the גאל, since, while there is indeed a question of property which a man is forced to surrender, or, more correctly, which he desires to avoid surrendering, these are not payments which are indissolubly connected with the person in question, that is, they do not have to do with the basis of his existence, namely his property or his person. In fact, it is doubtful whether Lev 27 is at all based on an old technical use of the term גאל ; it might be preferable to regard this usage as a construction placed upon the term[134].

If we turn to the Psalms and inquire as to the original use of the term, that is, whether it is basically associated with individual or collective psalms, the considerable number of psalms as well as passages in the prophetic literature which use it solely in a collective sense might lead us to believe that the term was fixed in its collective sense[135]. Only a few examples of the individual use of the root גאל are attested in the Psalter, to which should be added a couple of occurrences

---

[131] See Reventlow 1961, and cf. Lemche 1976:46-51. However, Reventlow does not speak of the institution of the גאל, but of the existence of ancient מד -regulations (based on the verb which introduces the various regulations). Further on this institution see Pedersen 1958:62ff., and De Vaux 1961:40f.

[132] The narrative in Ruth 4,4ff. is instructive in this context. Here the widow, Naomi, attempts to sell a field she has inherited from her deceased husband. She offers it to the most closely related "redeemer". However, accruing to the right to take possession of the field in question is the obligation to "redeem" the young widow Ruth, Naomi's daughter in law.

[133] Cf. De Vaux 1961:26ff. and 41; Pedersen 1958:294ff. Both regarded this as a survival from the bedouin culture.

[134] Perhaps it would be more accurate to suggest that the connection between property donations and the institution of the גאל in Lev 27,14-24 has terminologically influenced the other redeemer transactions. Noth furthermore emphasizes the secondary nature of the chapter with respect to the Holiness Code, just as he also points to the peculiar tension in Lev 27 between payments in kind and payments in cash, which also suggests that at any rate large sections of Lev 27 must be quite late (1966A:178ff.).

[135] See Ps 74,2; 107,2 (but note the related usage in Ps 77,16 and 106,10). Among the prophets see Isa 44,22 and 23; 52,3 and 9; 62,12; 63,9; Jer 31,11 (parallel with פדה); Hos 13,14 and Micah 4,10. Of this whole range of prophetic passages only Hos 13,14 and Jer 31,11 are pre-exilic (one should also note the distinctions as to who or what Israel is to be redeemed from). See also Isa 35,9 (post-exilic); 43,1; 48,20; 51,10.

in the Book of Job, and a single occurrence in Genesis[136]. The psalms in question nowhere refer specifically to the old גאל institution; nevertheless, there are clear signs that this complex of concepts underlies the present use of the term. The first example to be mentioned is in Ps 72,14, מתוך ומחמס יגאל נפשם[137]. Here the meaning of the phrase it unambiguous, but in the psalm the obligation to redeem has been transferred to the king in his capacity as the highest legal instance. In other psalms in which the term is used in individual contexts, such as Ps 69,19, the redeemer in question is Yahweh, in whom the troubled psalmist places his confidence[138].

It would accordingly be reasonable to claim that in cultic contexts the origin of the root גאל must be assigned to the individual psalms of lament and thanksgiving. By the same token, there is no doubt the use of this term in the Psalms presupposes the institution of the גאל, so that it has not derived its meaning from a cultic context, but from the legal practices of an agricultural society. This observation is confirmed by the fact that the use of the term in collective psalms is even more rare than is its appearance in the individual ones. Also, in two of the four examples of collective usage there seems to be some connection to the Exodus event (Ps 77,16 and 106,10)[139]. The phrase ויגאלם מיד אויב in Ps 106,10b, however, indicates that the psalm contains a collective understanding of גאל *without* reference to the Exodus; it is only through the framework provided by the surrounding verses that this redemption motif has been connected with the Exodus event, although this motif has not influenced the text in v 10. גאלת בזרע עמך in Ps 77,16 is unmistakably related to Exod 6,6b, וגאלתי אתכם בזרע נטויה (P)[140]. In fact, these are the only passages in the OT in which גאל and זרוע are found together. It would be most reasonable to suppose that the Exodus passage is the older, and that Ps 106,10 is only a weakened quotation of it.

If we seek outside of the Psalter and turn to the prophetic literature, we quickly discover how the connection between the Exodus event and the concept of the גאל came about. It is impossible to determine whether Hosea or Jeremiah originated the usage of the root גאל in collective psalms which do not refer to the release from Egypt, or whether they are both dependent on the cultic use of the term. However, there is no question but that Deutero Isaiah is largely responsible for the linkage of the Exodus motif with the concept of the גאל, since in the writings of this prophet the root גאל plays a very prominent role. The term is used all of sixteen times, both as verb and substantive. Furthermore, in the passages in question the connection between the release and the Exodus is either expressly present, or one is forced to admit that the concept of the Exodus underlies the usage discussed in the great majority of passages. The only remaining problem is whether Deutero Isaiah was the author of this linkage, or whether he presupposes Exod 15,13. Chronology seems to speak in favor of the latter assumption, since it is probable that the hymn in Exod 15,1b-18 is older than Deutero Isaiah. For this reason it would be reasonable to suppose that Deutero Isaiah found a point of departure in Exod 15,13 for his use of the term גאל, although it must be admitted that he interprets his "loan" in so original a manner that one could justifiably claim that it is his use of the term that has determined its use in younger literature.

As far as the root פדה is concerned, Norin offers only a superficial review of its use in the OT[141]. In Norin's opinion, the use of פדה in the Psalms may be traced back to an ancient North Israelite cultic tradition. This tradition is held to be reflected in Hos 7,13 and 13,14 (in the latter passage together with גאל) and in Micah 6,4 (sic!). Norin's conclusion is quite misleading, and he himself presents a good objection to his own view in the form of UT 1006, a slave contract

---

[136] Ps 69,19; 72,14; 103,4; 119,154; cf. Gen 48,16 and Job 3,5. Ps 72 is admittedly a royal psalm, but the usage in v 14 refers nevertheless to the redemption of the individual.

[137] Note, however, the phraseology in v 14b: ויקר דמם בעיניו. The connection with גאל דם is not very remote from this.

[138] See also Ps 19,15 and 78,35, which use the substantive. In Ps 19,15 it is an epithet of Yahweh, while in 78,35 it is an epithet of אל עליון. In Ps 103,4 and 119,154, Yahweh is the one who "redeems".

[139] This association is especially evident in Deutero Isaiah and in texts dependent on him. See Isa 43,1; 48,20; 51,10, and Isa 35,9, which is dependent on Deutero Isaiah. Trito Isaiah, however, seems to avoid this association; see Isa 62,12 and 63,9.

[140] Cf. Childs 1974:111.

[141] 1977:154.

from Ugarit[142]. If Norin had not so hastily anchored this contract in a cultic context, he could not have avoided discovering a background similar to the use of the root פדה in the OT. The relevant passage in the OT is presumably the oldest example in the work; it is the law of the "Hebrew slave" in Exod 21,8, which has to do with the redemption of a Hebrew woman[143]. However, this use of פדה is not unique in the OT, as it also occurs with corresponding contents in Lev 19,20, where the person in question is a slave, and in 1 Sam 14,45, where Saul's army "redeems" Jonathan from the sentence of death which his father had pronounced[144]. It would be much more reasonable to point to a juridical, rather than a religious *Sitz im Leben* for the use of the root פדה in the Psalter. Admittedly, the root פדה is also used in connection with the redemption of the firstborn in the perhaps Deuteronomistically reworked passage in Exod 13,13.15. This passage may be dependent on the formulation in Exod 34,20. The root is also used in the Priestly legislation in Lev 27,27.29 and Num 18,15.16.17. However, it would be reasonable to suppose that in these cases we have to do with a secondary application of פדה analogous to that observed earlier in the case of גאל[145].

If the semantic background of the term פדה is to be sought in the realm of forensic language, it is not difficult to imagine why the verb is used frequently in the individual psalms of lament and thanksgiving[146]. On the other hand, פדה only rarely appears in collective contexts, and it only occurs once in the Psalter in connection with the release from Egypt in Ps 78,42[147]. The semantic extension from the individual to the national fields may already have taken place in the temple cult in the Northern Kingdom, as Hos 7,13 and 13,14 may be taken to suggest. Alternatively, the prophet Hosea may have freed the motif from its individual associations and conferred national significance upon it. The latter solution is the more likely, since the three examples we possess in which there is a national application *without* reference to the Exodus event (i.e., Ps 25,22; 44,27; and 130,8) are all quite late, that is, they are exilic or post-exilic[148]. This implies

---

[142] UT 1006 (i.e., RŠ 16.191+272; see PRU II:18f. (= KTU 11.2.12). The question, however, is whether Norin has understood this text. In reality it is a ransom contract in which a citizen of Ugarit ransoms (verb: *pdi*) three brothers plus their sons and daughters for 100 shekels of silver from the service (i.e., slavery) of foreigners (1.15: *bertim*, "Beyroutheans"). This transaction received official status by the impression of the royal seal, possibly because it was an agreement with the citizens of another state. Thus the record of the transaction was kept in the royal archives. There is nothings whatever to suggest that the event had a cultic character. Further on this text, Liverani 1962:148f.

[143] On Exod 21,7-11 see Lemche 1975:143. In contradistinction to Lev 19,20, this is a technical law which has to do with *ḫabiru* slaves.

[144] Again, there is nothing whatsoever in 1 Sam 14,45 to suggest a cultic activity, unless one wishes to maintain that every legal act had a cultic character. Saul has pronounced a sentence of death, but his army "ransoms" Jonathan from the punishment. It has been suggested that another person may have been killed in place of Jonathan; cf. Stoebe 1973:270. Stoebe is rightly critical of this interpretation, and suggests that in the passage in question פדה is used in an absolute sense.

[145] In Exod 4,24-26, which is presumably the oldest and no doubt the most difficult text having to do with circumcision, פדה is not used as a technical term. Of course, this does not prove that the term cannot have been used in such a sense prior to its adoption by P. On the other hand, neither does it support the possibility that פדה and the circumcision may have been conjoined to each other prior to P.

[146] Note the contexts in the psalms in which פדה figures: Ps 26,11, in connection with a prayer for assistance in court (thus Kraus 1966:218); cf. Ps 31,6 and 49,16 (see also Ps 34,23, a psalm of confidence and assurance of protection, which refers to Yahweh as he who *ransoms* עבדיו נפש). In Ps 49,8 פדה is used specifically with reference to ransom money. See further Ps 55,19; 69,19, and also Jer 15,21. The connection between imminent danger to life and limb is particularly clear in these passages, and thus it would not be unreasonable to suppose that the technical expression for such a ransom procedure was פדה נפש (compare also Ps 49,9: פדיון נפשם), which means that a translation of "pardoning" would be approximately correct.

[147] Ps 72,42b: יום פדם אשר מני צר (reading with the LXX, which has ἐκ χειρὸς θλίβοντος in v 42bβ). For more on Ps 78, see the special section below.

[148] V 22 is an addition to Ps 25, which is an individual psalm. Ps 44,27 is part of a collective

that when the Deuteronomists use the term and insert it in contexts which have to do with the Exodus,it does not thereby refer to the language of the cult, but to a tradition which had already been established by Hosea, a tradition which, however, lacked reference to the release from Egypt. The path subsequent to Deuteronomism leads to the cultic poetry of the exilic or, more probably, the post-exilic period.

Our analyses of the uses of גאל and פדה in the OT have suggested some interesting possibilities. The root גאל appears to have developed within the tradition of cultic poetry, although its background was in a juridical institution. פדה was probably employed within the "individual" cultic tradition against a corresponding background. However, it was first through the Deuteronomistic use of the term, which was dependent on Hosea, that it became secondarily transferred to the national field and was associated with the Exodus conceptions. From this point on the psalmists used the root פדה to refer to the national liberation[149]. The motifs can scarcely have been borrowed the other way around, since the term which is most frequently used of national salvation in the Psalter (גאל) never won a place in the Deuteronomistic literature. This is an interesting *memento* for those who assume without more ado that the Deuteronomistic view of history was based on motifs derived from the cult, especially from the national laments and songs of thanksgiving. The evolutionary pathway may have progressed from the Deuteronomistic tradition to the temple cult, but cultic poets had other materials available than Deuteronomistic ones in their development of historical retrospects. Also, they were in a position to exploit the possibilities inherent in the individual laments and psalms of thanksgiving on an independent basis.

We are left with the unresolved question as to whether the point of departure for the special Deuteronomistic view of history was the "individual" psalm tradition. It is possible that the Deuteronomists borrowed motifs from this tradition and combined them with the old idea of the wrath of the god against his people, which is well attested in Oriental tradition[150]. It might be more appropriate simply to point out that the Deuteronomists continue an evolutionary course which had been already with the pre-Deuteronomistic prophets. Its basis was the concept of Israel's disobedience of her God, a concept which is clearly absent from such an old lament as Ps 80.

5.

Psalm 66.

This psalm may date from either pre-or post-exilic times. An exilic date is, however, out of the question, since v 13-15 presuppose the existence of a temple. Scholars have argued for post-exilic date because of the presence of Priestly terminology in v 13-15 (עלות, נדרי, and קטרת), Norin has rejected this

---

psalm which, however, presupposes the existence of the Deuteronomistic covenant theology (see below). Ps 130,8 is more difficult to evaluate. Both Kraus (1966:870) and Gunkel (1929:562) regard it as post-exilic.

[149] פדה appears twice in Deutero Isaiah, namely in Isa 50,2 and 51,11. In Isa 50,2 a connection with the Exodus motif may be implied (cf. v 2b), but Isa 50,2a seems rather to depend on 50,1b, which speaks of "debt-slaves". Thus in this context Deutero Isaiah is using פדה in its old sense, that is, as referring to ransom from slavery, and not primarily in connection with the concept of the Exodus. Isa 51,11 (ופדויי יהוה) refers unequivocally to those ransomed from Egypt. See v 10. However, Kiesow reckons v 11 to be part of a redactional layer in company with Isa 50,2 and Isa 35,10, since he regards the use of פדה in both passages as evidence of the influence of Deuteronomistic terminology (1979:150).

[150] See the works of Albrektson mentioned in n.109.

argument on the assumption that P had borrowed these terms from the temple services, which means that they must have been employed in pre-exilic worship as well. Norin's argument would be more convincing if the terms in question were the only indications of P material in Ps 66. However, other parts of the psalm tend to set the psalm in relation to late linguistic usage than to conceptions of the Exodus; I refer specifically to הפך ים ליבשה in v 6a. The use of יבשה in this context is paralleled in a very young passage in the OT, namely Neh 9,11, where we read ויעברו בתוך הים ביבשה. The background of both Neh 9,11 and Ps 66,6a is probably Exod 14,16.22.29 and 15,19. The occurrences in Exod 14 derive from the Priestly additions to this composite chapter, whereas Exod 15,19 belongs to the possibly very late redactional framework around the hymn about the Sea of Reeds in v 1b-18[151]. P's motive for using this terminology is his desire to compare theologically the miracle at the Sea of Reeds with the creation. As is well known, P uses the same term in connection with the separation of the wet elements from the dry elements in Gen 1,9-10[152]. It is also impossible to separate the formulation in v 6a from the description of the crossing of the Jordan in Jos 4,22b (ביבשה עבר ישראל), But instead of reflecting an ancient terminology associated with the Passover festival postulated by Kraus to have taken place in Gilgal, the passage is a young stratum within Jos 3-5, which are unusually complicated in traditio-historical terms[153]. V 6a contains a unique juxtaposition of the verb הפך and the substantive ים. However, this is not an original passage, but a weak reflection of a number of passages in Exodus, foremost among them being Exod 7,17.20, where the waters of the Nile are transformed into blood. This formulation recurs in further quotations of the narrative about the plagues of Egypt (e.g., Ps 78,44 and 105,29)[154]. Thus the most probable conclusion is that Ps 66 presupposes the existence of the Pentateuchal traditions as well as the fact of the Priestly redaction. This requires a date for the psalm at some point in the post-exilic period. Thus it is of no importance whether v 2 describes the miracle at the Sea of Reeds or the crossing of the Jordan, as some scholars have held, or whether ים and נהר are to be understood as synonyms as in the Ugaritic depictions of the Chaos Battle, as argued by M. Dahood[155]. In all events the Exodus event and

---

[151] Exod 14,16.22.29 are generally assigned to P; cf. Noth 1965:83 and Childs 1974:220. However, Noth reckoned Exod 15,19 to be 'ein prosaischer Zusatz nach 14,23.28.29 P" (1965:100). See also Childs 1974:248, who assigns it to the final Priestly redaction of the Pentateuch.

[152] יבשה in P contexts: cf. Exod 4,9 (Noth 1965:32). Occurrences in other passages are likewise late. Cf. e.g. Isa 44,3; Jonah 1,9.13; 2,11; Neh 9,11.

[153] Cf. Lemche 1972:45-51 (with references); see also Otto 1975.

[154] Exod 7,17.20, which is usually assigned to J.S.Ö. Steingrimsson, however, assigns it to his narrative "B" (1979:58ff.). General evaluation of this in Steingrimsson 1979:195-201. Steingrimsson assumes three layers, A,B,C, but assumes that all three are reworkings of a basic tradition (1979:210). Although Steingrimsson's "B" layer is the oldest of the three, he holds all of them to be later than 587; they are "Homilien" (1979:219-220). Thus Steingrimsson is among the growing ranks of the scholars who prefer a late date for the Pentateuchal sources. See further below.

[155] Dahood 1968:120f.

the miracle at the Sea of Reeds are joined together in this psalm, as we see from the correlation of v 6 and 12; but this was also to be expected in view of the late date of the psalm.

6.

Psalm 78

This psalm contains virtually the entire OT historical tradition including the covenant theme in collected form until the time of the united monarchy. Gunkel therefore held it to be a didactic poem from the post-exilic period analogous to such psalms as 106 and 136[156]. Others have suggested dates ranging from the 8th to the 7th centuries[157]. However, there should be no doubt whatsoever that all dates before the post-exilic period are out of the question. In terms of contents Ps 78 presupposes both the existence of the Deuteronomistic Historical Work (up to the Second Book of Samuel) and the collected Tetrateuch. It also quotes almost verbatim from the Mosaic books as, for example, in the list of the plagues of Egypt. Thus ויהפך לדם יאריהם in v 44a is an example of a free quotation of Exod 7,19-20. In particular the word יאריהם is revealing, since this word points to a direct relationship to Exod 7,19. On the other hand, v 44b is an independent contribution from the hand of "Asaph". Ps 78 also contains quotations from the Deuteronomistic literature, as, for example, in v 43, where we read אשר שם במצרים אתותיו ומופתיו בשדה צען; this is to be compared with Deut 6,22; 7,19; 13,2.3; 28,46; 29,2; 34,11; Jer 32,21; and so forth. The preceding verse (42b) employs one of the Deuteronomist's favorite verbs (פדה) of the release from Egypt.

Thus the psalm is post-exilic, and we should perhaps be prepared to go fairly late in the post-exilic period in order to find its right place. Psalm 78 accordingly tells us no more about the Israelite historical tradition than we

---

[156] See Gunkel 1933:326; cf. Gunkel 1929:341, where he maintains that the author of Ps 78 possessed no sources concerning Israel's earlier history which are not present in the historical narrative complexes in the OT. See also on the evaluation of Ps 78 Mowinckel 1951:375ff.

[157] Thus e.g. Robertson 1972, who dates Ps 78 to the period between 930 and 721, and describes its usage as the Standard Hebrew of this period (see his linguistic survey of Ps 78 1972: 43-46). However, the contents of this psalm makes Robertson's assessment of its language as paradigmatic for the 8th century – and his undertaking in general – more than suspect. Robertson's approach to Ps 78 would equally well justify the claim that since the psalm is post-exilic, then other texts which contain archaisms, such as Exod 15,1b-18, must be earlier, but how much earlier? It could also be claimed that other literature in the OT which is on the same linguistic level as Ps 78 (this unquestionably applies to the main part of the OT) must be post-exilic or exilic at the earliest. It would be more appropriate to question the relevance of Robertson's method. It is symptomatic that Norin does not follow Robertson's date, but instead dates Ps 78 to the time of Josiah because of the clear points of contact with Deuteronomistic literature (1977:133).

already knew in advance, namely that in the post-exilic period this tradition was closed, all of its motifs were indissolubly connected in both the Tetrateuch and the Deuteronomistic Historical Work. It is also to be observed that the historical retrospect in this psalm plays a mere didactic role and is not anchored in any kind of cultic context.

7.

Psalms 104-106

Some scholars prefer to differentiate between the dates of origin of these psalms; thus, for example, they would assign Ps 105 to the time of the Exile and relegate Ps 106 to the post-exilic period. However, I find it most correct to deal with the use of historical motifs in these three texts in a single analysis[158]. Admittedly, Ps 104 falls somewhat outside of the concerns of this study, since its theme is God as the creator of the world and the maintainer of life. However, even if Ps 104 is concerned with myth instead of history, this is surely an irrelevant modern distinction. In reality Ps 104-105-106 comprise a triad which traces the history of the world from the creation to the time of the Exile. In other words, taken together they cover the same time span as the Tetrateuch and the Deuteronomistic Historical Work up to the conclusion of the Second Book of Kings. In all probability, these psalms also presuppose the existence of these historical works. This is most clearly evident in Ps 105 and 106, but it would also be reasonable to suppose that it is also true of Ps 104, which in reality resembles a free composition based on the Priestly creation narrative in Gen 1. If Ps 104 is to be assigned to the post-exilic period, this suggests that this period, too, was able to compose poetic works of high literary quality (which ought actually to be evident because of the existence of a number of important Wisdom writings from this period, such as Ecclesiastes, Job, and so on). Also the other two poetic works, Ps 105 and 106, are artistically impressive reformulations of the history of Israel in pre-exilic times. If these psalms are to be evaluated on the basis of their use of historical themes, then it should be clear that they are not cultic poetry, but didactic literature (on this point, too, they correspond well to the postexilic Wisdom compositions). It would probably not be wholly wrong to ascribe as their *Sitz im Leben* the congregational hymnody of the post-exilic synagogue. In formal terms it would be appropriate to compare these psalm with the later Christian Church psalms.

If we turn specifically to Ps 105 and 106, we note that their contents are quite different. Ps 105 has the form of a doxology consisting of a list of great deeds Yahweh has performed on Israel's behalf. The psalm emphasizes in particular the divine covenant, the land of Israel as god's gift, and the release from Egypt.

Ps 106 is the negative corollary to Ps 105, so that in reality the two psalms complement one another in terms of contents. The psalm focuses on the pre-history of the Israelite people, but here emphasis is placed on all the negative aspects, although the theme of salvation history is still the yardstick by which the crimes of the Israelites against their God are to be evaluated. The psalm does not stress the miracles God performed in Egypt, but the Israelites' apostasy. The miracle at the Sea of Reeds is described as a salvific action, but what did it lead to in the case of Israel? Apostasy and unbelief in the desert. The episode of the golden calf is singled out as the most important parenetic example of apostasy. A number of subsequent events are similarly cited and evaluated in terms akin to those employed in the historical books of the OT.

8.

Psalms 135 and 136

These psalms may also be treated together, since they may be understood as comprising a counterpart to the triad of Ps 104-106. However, they also show that not all post-exilic poetry was of high literary merit. Ps 135 feels like a somewhat anemic reworking of Ps 104-106, while Ps 136 contains a single original element, namely its antiphonal structure. Unfortunately, the psalmist in question was so impressed with his "innovation" that he seriously misused this stylistic device, so that in the present form of the psalm the twenty-seven repetitions of כי לעולם חסדו seem like a parody. The historical themes are all interconnected; they stretch from the creation, the account of which un-questionably quotes directly from the narrative in Gen 1, to the Settlement in the land of Canaan. However, these themes have no independent function and seem to be used to form the background for the repeated use of the refrain. Both psalms are accordingly to be characterized as late post-exilic poeta-stry[159].

---

[158] Thus Norin 1977:137, who dates Ps 105 to the time of the Exile. Compare Norin 1977: 122, where Ps 106 is assigned to the postexilic period.

[159] Gunkel dated both psalms to *"das späteste Zeitalter der Psalmendichtung"* (1929:575 and 577, respectively). Kraus assumes that both psalms were employed in the Passover celebrations of the post-exilic congregation, and of course assigns them a cultic function (1966:896 and 901).

9.

Psalm 114

The last psalm to be included in our review of the motifs of the Exodus and Reed Sea traditions is Ps 114. Unlike the psalms immediately preceding, there is considerable disagreement as to the date of this psalm; suggestions have ranged from the pre-exilic to the post-exilic periods[160]. The motifs which are conjoined in the psalm are those of the Exodus and the Settlement (v 5b), as well as the incident at Meribah (although the name is not mentioned). The historical materials employed have been used quite freely, which makes it difficult to date the psalm with precision. Thus the date would seem to depend on one's construction of v 8, which in terms of contents is to be compared with Isa 41,18. The question is then whether the psalmist is dependent on Deutero Isaiah or the reverse, or whether both are dependent on a common *Vorlage*. This issue cannot be settled with certainty, but it is at any rate apparent that in Ps 114,8 the motif in question appears to be extraneous to the rest of the text. The motif is not functional, so that one senses the psalmist included it simply because he thought it ought to be included, and did not bother to legitimate his decision. This is different from Deutero Isaiah, who employed the motif organically in its context and used it as an integral part of it. Thus Ps 114,8 has the feel of a free quotation from the exilic prophet. If this supposition is correct, then Ps 114 is probably to be dated to the post-exilic period, although it is impossible to assign a more precise date to it[161].

The preceding analysis of twelve psalms which contain retrospects of Israel's earliest history permits a number of conclusions which may be of importance for our attempt to arrive at an idea of when this prehistory was collected and inserted into the special historical scheme in the OT. These

---

[160] Bentzen held that Ps 114 probably voices "the religious atmosphere of the late pre-exilic period", and also claimed that it was contemporary with the Deuteronomistic movement and the prophet Jeremiah (1939:575). Kraus seems to wobble a bit between the post-Deuteronomistic date suggested by Gunkel and a late pre-exilic date (1966:780f.). Norin, on the other hand, oscillates between a Davidic date and the time of Josiah (1977:127).

[161] Bentzen argued for a date previous to Deutero Isaiah, and held that Deutero Isaiah was dependent on the formulations in Ps 114,8 and 107,35. This is an alternating possibility, since these two psalmic passages taken together reproduce the contents of Isa 41,18. However, there are differences between the respective contexts of the prophetic passage and the two psalmic passages in question. Ps 107,35 corresponds almost verbatim to Isa 41,18b: אשים מדבר לאגם מים וארץ ציה למוצאי מים; cf. Ps 107,35: ישם מדבר לאגם מים וארץ ציה למוצאי מים . In this connection it is to be noted that Isa 41,18a and Ps 114,8 are only parallel in terms of contents. Thus it is most likely that Ps 107,35 is a direct quotation of Isa 41,18b; cf. Kraus, who regards the section v. 33-43 as "*Zusatzdichtung*" from the post-exilic period (1966:740). Isa 41,18 is not to be seen as a "quotation" from the two psalms, since how should we then explain the differences in the methods of quotation? Both psalmic passages are instead dependent on Isa 41,18, although each uses this prophetic passage in its own way.

psalmic materials may also be able to tell us something about how these historical traditions were collected, and in what stages the process took place. Only two of our texts proved to be pre-exilic, namely Ps 80, which possibly derives from the Northern Kingdom just prior to its extinction in 722, and elements of Ps 68. It is characteristic of these two texts that the themes of the Exodus and the Settlement are already united in them; it is also notwworthy that the motif of the miracle at the Sea of Reeds is absent from both. Ps 80 also lacks any mention of the traditions of the desert wandering. Ps 68 contains an allusion to this cycle of motifs, but it is not specific. On the other hand, Ps 68 does contain a reference to Sinai, but this is apparently only an allusion to an event which was understood as a theophany. Neither psalm touches on covenantal conceptions, nor do they contain any traces of the Deuteronomistic view of history. The historical traditions contained in these psalms correspond to the results of our analysis of the prophetic materials. Thus our review of these two complexes arrives at approximately the same result, to the extent that we are dealing with the pre-exilic period. The prophets, however, must be held to be those who created the presuppositions for the emergence of the Deuteronomistic view of history, that is, the understanding of national catastrophe as a well-deserved punishment sent from Yahweh. This view of history does not require a historicizing garb which cloaks the past in the mantle of salvation history, as such early Judaean prophets as Isaiah and Micah attest.

It is accordingly possible to conceive of two developmental lines in the evolution of the Israelite understanding of history. One of these may have been North Israelite, and it will have explained Yahweh's punitive judgements on historical grounds. The other will then have been Judaean, and it either did not employ or else underplayed the historical argument. If, as I have suggested, Ps 80 derives from the Northern Kingdom, this might be taken to imply that the North Israelite tradition mentioned above was more likely to have been developed within prophetic circles than within the compass of the official cult. Contrariwise, a cultic background for the Judaean tradition seems very likely.

These traditions first became mythologically colored during the Exile. It was suggested above that the reason for this may have been the fact that the mythological cycle of materials, which were once associated with the New Year Festival, lost their *Sitz im Leben* during the Exile, and so became available for reuse in a new and different context. The inaugurator of this new use of the mythical materials was Deutero Isaiah. He was accordingly directly responsible for the fact that the historical retrospects became equipped with mythological materials in the postexilic psalms. Deutero Isaiah's use of historicizing mythology probably also had consequences for the Pentateuch, if it is correct, as some scholars have argued, that the Yahwist's description of the miracle at the Sea of Reeds is naturalistic, while that of the Priestly tradition has been in-

fluenced by conceptions of the Chaos Battle[162]. It is possible that P was drawing on the same tradition as the post-exilic psalms.

It is first in the clearly post-exilic psalms (Ps 78; 105-106; 135-136) that we
find a collection of historical tradition comparable to that contained in the
Pentateuch. Moreover, it can be shown that the background of this collection
was the psalmists' knowledge of the Pentateuchal traditions as these were preserved in, it should be noted, the collected Pentateuch. Gunkel called these
psalms didactic poems, and A. Jirku suggested on the basis of the retrospects
contained in them that there was an erudite tradition in Israel which produced
what might be termed short accounts of the historical tradition. These views
are probably correct, but the date of the emergence of this erudite tradition
was the post-exilic period[163].

We are left with the question of the covenantal concepts in the Psalter and
their relationship to the rest of the historical themes. As mentioned previously,
the only examples of such psalmic references are all post-exilic. Nevertheless,
it is still unclear whether the pre-exilic psalms provide us with unambiguous
evidence that the Sinai event (which Ps 68 seems to reflect) was understood as
a covenant-making event and not "just" as a divine theophany. I should like
to stress as urgently as possible that the term ברית, "covenant", figures all of
twenty times in the Psalter, but *not a single time in connection with Sinai or Horeb*.
Several of the psalms in question are very difficult to date; this applies to such
psalms as 55, 83, and certainly also 25. These psalms may accordingly not be
used as evidence to the effect that there was a silence in the pre-exilic psalms
concerning the concept of the covenant. However, the opposite is also true, as
these examples are also insufficient to prove that the concept played any significant role in the pre-exilic psalms. Only a single psalm which uses the term
ברית is presumably pre-exilic, namely Ps 132 (v 12), but this psalm refers to the
covenant between David and Yahweh, as does Ps 89, the date of which is, however, much more controversial. Neither of these two psalms seems to presuppose Deuteronomism, not even Ps 89, which is thematically linked to such
an old psalm as Ps 80, since it merely regards the national disaster as a punitive
act on the part of Yahweh, although Yahweh does not supply his reasons for
doing so. In other words, it is Yahweh who has broken his covenant. A further
point of comparison would be 2 Sam 7, the Deuteronomistic edition of the
dynastic promise to the Davidic line. However, it should be observed that ברית
does not figure in the promise in 2 Sam 7, nor does שמר, which is the Deuteronomists' favorite verb to describe how one "keeps" the covenant. Rather
than claiming that Ps 89 and 132 introduce the concept of ברית because of

---

[162] Cf. Childs 1974:228, and compare with the "reconstruction" of the J narrative and the P
version in Childs 1974:220-221.
[163] Contra Jirku 1917; cf. Jirku 1917:159, who remarks concerning this tradition, *"...dass sie
daher als selbständige Quelle für die mosaische Zeit neben den betreffende Kapiteln des Bücher Exodus und
Numeri anzusehen sind"*.

Deuteronomistic influence, it would be more appropriate to regard 2 Sam 7 as a Deuteronomistic *break* with the covenant concepts which were associated with the ruling dynasty in Judah during the monarchy[164]. ברית is used in a few passages in the Psalter (Ps 55,21 and 83,6) with no reference to a divine covenant, but it is most often used in this sense. Most such passages are late, that is, exilic, as in Ps 44,18 and 74,20, or post-exilic, as in Ps 50,6.16; 78,10. 37; 103,18; 105,8.10; and 106,45. Ps 44 is of especial importance in this connection, since this psalm testifies to a thorough familiarity with the Deuteronomistic view of history. This is made particularly plain by the phrase ולא שכחנוך ולא שקרנו בבריתך in v 18aβ b. However, it is clear that the psalmist refuses to accept the Deuteronomistic view of history, and instead emphatically insists that "we have not broken your covenant"; his opposition to the Deuteronomistic position simply could not be more powerfully stated[165].

I shall not press the matter further at this juncture, but the views adumbrated above should serve to demonstrate just how unreasonable it is of A. Weiser to make a hypothetical festival of covenant renewal the main event of the pre-exilic Israelite temple cult in Jerusalem. The only covenant of significance at this time was the covenant with David, but it was clearly not of the type Weiser and a number of others have imagined[166].

Finally, it should be noted that as far as the inclusion of the covenant theme in the historical retrospects is concerned, and indeed, its role as the constitutive element in the relationship between Israel and her God, there is once again considerable agreement between the OT psalms and the prophetic books. When I address myself to the on-going debate concerning the age of the Pentateuchal sources below, the results of my analyses of the prophetic and psalmic materials must be allowed to have their say. However, at this point it would be methodologically incorrect to use the results arrived at thus far as evidence that all of the Pentateuchal sources must be young since they contain a collection of historical traditions. This would be a logical circle, since it was precisely the collection of the Pentateuchal sources which was the most important presupposition for dating a number of psalms to the post-exilic period. However, if there is well-corroborated evidence within the Pentateuchal materials to suggest that even the oldest of these socalled "source documents", J and E (if an actual E source ever really existed) are perhaps to be dated to the

---

[164] In other words, I can fully support R.A. Carlson, who emphasizes that the relationship between Ps 89 and 2 Sam 7 does not alter the fact that the formulation of the Nathan oracle is Deuteronomistic (1964:124). On the other hand, the use of חסד in 2 Sam 7,15 is probably to be seen as a survival of covenant usage (but not, however, everywhere חסד happens to appear). This indicates that the background of the formulation of the dynastic promise in 2 Sam 7 was an actual legitimation of the Davidic dynasty during the time of the monarchy. Thus it is really quite striking that the Deuteronomists failed to mention ברית in this connection.

[165] Cf. Kraus 1966:327-328.

[166] Cf. Weiser 1966:81ff. Weiser's theory of a festival of covenant renewal is the basis for his explication of quite a number of psalms in his commentary on the Psalms (1950).

close of the monarchy or even to the exilic period, then these assumptions would be supported by the results of my review of the prophetic and psalmic materials[167].

§ 3

The Yahwist, Deuteronomism, and the Israelite Historical Tradition

By way of introduction it would be appropriate to attach some critical remarks to the attempt of H. Vorländer to employ a method which in many respects resembles that utilized here in order to lower the date of the collection of the Yahwistic Historical Work[168]. The greater part of Vorländer's work is devoted to a catalogue-like correlation of Pentateuchal motifs with allustions to the same motifs elsewhere in the OT[169]. With no exceptions, Vorländer's conclusion is that none of the themes in the Pentateuch, from the creation to the patriarchs to the sojourn in Egypt or the wandering in the desert, is found in any pre-exilic text in the OT. For this reason Vorländer concludes that these themes were not collected or known in pre-exilic Israel or Judah.

As far as the majority of Vorländer's examples are concerned I am prepared to admit that he is correct. However, the cataloguelike quality of his work is the result of the fact that Vorländer does not trouble to substantiate his late dates for the prophetic and psalmic texts in question; he goes no further than mere suggestions. Thus Vorländer has in reality missed the possibility that especially in the Book of Hosea as well as in a very few individual pre-exilic psalms there may be motifs which are also to be found in the present Pentateuch. He rules out even Hosea's references to the Jacob traditions as late with undo haste, when the text itself does not provide decisive reasons for so doing[170]. This is very odd, since Vorländer himself does not reject the possibility that the late commission of the traditions concerning Israel's past to writing may have taken place on the basis of pre-exilic traditions, which he apparently understands as having been mainly orally transmitted[171]. Thus even on Vorländer's presuppositions it is possible that the fairly general references to the desert wandering, the sojourn in Egypt, and the Exodus in the writings of, for

---

[167] It remains to be added that other "historical" personnages and events are mentioned in the Psalms, but this is virtually always in very late psalms or passages in psalms. Also, while some figures, such as Moses, are mentioned, others, such as Joshua, are not.

[168] Vorländer 1978.

[169] Vorländer 1978:23-283.

[170] See Vorländer 1978:69-71. This is not to claim that all of Hos 12 derives from the prophet himself. See also above, p. 313.

[171] Cf. Vorländer 1978:348. Vorländer repeatedly refers to the views of the so-called "Uppsala School", and in particular takes his point of departure in Nielsen 1954.

example, Hosea, were based on a knowledge of such non-literary traditions. Indeed, it is possible that the special character of the Jacob traditions preserved by Hosea is the result of the fact that this cycle of tradition had not yet been finally fixed in writing by the middle of the 8th century.

Vorländer's contribution, which is corroborated in its main lines by the present work, does imply that the burden of proof must rest with those scholars who would date the formation of a quasi-canonical Pentateuchal tradition such as, for example, a Yahwistic Pentateuch, already to the earliest period of the monarchy. I shall not pursue my commentary on Vorländer's work at this point; the later parts of it will come in to focus below. It is not necessarily the most annihilating criticism of the classical arguments for an early date for the Pentateuchal sources, but it is in any case the most sharply formulated[172].

To characterize the general situation of the present discussion as to the process by means of which the Pentateuch was collected, it is possible to distinguish between three groups within contemporary Pentateuchal research. The first group is composed of a long list of scholars who adhere to the classical form of the source hypothesis, or a variant of it. A smaller group have quite a different view of the question of the age of the sources in question, since its members regard the written fixation of the sources as having taken place at much later dates in the history of Israel. This group may be divided into a variety of sub-groups, dependent up on whether they employ the idea of collected documentary sources (such as, e.g., the "Yahwist"), or prefer some variation on the fragmentary hypothesis, which would also rule out the existence of a collected Yahwistic source. The third group consists of a number of scholars whose goal is a middle position; this position aims to differentiate between a Yahwistic *"Grundschrift"* and subsequent Yahwistic elaborations. It is the case with all three groups that it is difficult to find any two representatives who are wholly agreed with one another except on some entirely general issues.

As is well known, the classical position states that in the beginning was the Yahwist, who possibly made use of an earlier source-Vorlage (Noth's *"Grundschrift"*)[173]. The Elohistic work will then have been a source document independent of the Yahwist. This triad was completed by the addition of the very late Priestly Work. The respective dates of the three collections were estimated to have been around 900 (but most often assigned to the period between 950 and 850) for the Yahwist, around 800 for the Elohist, and the time of the Exile (some preferred the postexilic period) for the Priestly Work. Most variations

---

[172] Vorländer 1978:285-335.
[173] Cf. Noth 1948:40-44. Other scholars have also assumed some sort of pre-Yahwistic "source", although not necessarily in the same sense of "source" Noth intended with his *"Grundschrift"*. Note, for example, Eissfeldt, who spoke of a *"Laienquelle"* (with the siglum L) (1965:191-194), or Fohrer, who referred to his own version as a *"Nomadenquelle"* (with the siglum N) (1969:173ff.).

of this hypothesis also entail numerous phases of redaction. At this point I shall omit discussion of the various rescensions proposed in connection with J and E. Instead, it would be appropriate to mention the idea of a pre-Deuteronomistic redactor known as RJE who was held to have combined the two "old" source documents, J and E. This redaction was to have taken place during the Exile and to have been followed by a Deuteronomistic revision of RJE. Finally, during the post-exilic period this revised Pentateuch was combined with the independent Priestly Work by redactor RP. This short resumé has been borrowed from P. Weimar, who (sometimes accompanied by E. Zenger) is among those who currently are attempting to retain the main lines of the documentary hypothesis as promulgated by Wellhausen[174]. Broadly construed, it is also this account of the process of redaction one encounters in W.H. Schmidt's new introduction to the OT[175].

W.H. Schmidt's work additionally contains the most recent thorough list of arguments in favor of an early date for J[176]. I shall restate it briefly here, in order to examine it more closely subsequently. In the first place, it is assumed that the national consolidation of the Israelite tribal society under David also entailed a lively literary activity. This activity was additionally concerned with history; an attempt was made to collect the traditions concerning the prehistory of the nation. Argumentation on this point involves a number of nuances. Some scholars have insisted that one of the reasons for the production of the Yahwistic History was the concern to legitimate the Israelite monarchy. this means that the Yahwist is to be assigned to Judah, with residence in Jerusalem. However, other scholars have maintained that the interest displayed by the Yahwist were current in Judah, but not in Jerusalem; this could be taken to indicate that the Yahwist was perhaps not even especially interested in providing a refense for the young Israelite monarchy[177]. The literary technique of the Yahwist is also held by Schmidt to have been akin to other literary products of this period, such as the narrative of "David's Rise to Power" and the

---

[174] Cf. Weimar 1977:162-172.

[175] Schmidt 1979:47-48.

[176] Schmidt 1979:74; cf. Schmidt 1981. Schmidt's point of departure is to a large extent the collection of arguments in favor of an early date for the Yahwist which was amassed by Müller 1969:52n. These are as follows: a) J's special interest in Judah. b) Gen 34,30f. and 35,21 as an explanation for the disappearance of Reuben, Simeon, and Levi. c) the emphasis on Hebron. d) the claim that Gen 27,40b presupposes the attempt of Hadad to rebell against Solomon (1 Kgs 11,14.22.25a). e) the claim that Exod 14,13 derives from the period prior to the fourth year of the reign of Rehoboam, that is, prior to Pharoah Shishak's Palestinian campaign. f) the claim that the description of the North Israelite sanctuaries at Shechem, Bethel, and Penuel was not possible subsequent to the cultic innovations of Jeroboam. g)finally, the claim that Gen 31,46ff. shows that the hostilities with the Aramaeans had not yet been joined.

[177] Thus Schmidt himself (1979:75). J.A. Soggin, however, regards the Yahwistic History as an apologetic work intended to legitimate the Israelite monarchy. Although Soggin is hesitant to attempt to date J with precision, in the final analysis he nevertheless advocates the traditional 10th-century date (1976:102).

"Succession Narrative". However, this is a dangerous argument which is not substantiated by other dates arrived at for the story of David's rise, as for example, that of J.H. Grønbæk (the time of the Divided Monarchy)[178].

Second, it is emphasized that the peoples mentioned in connection with Israel's early history, that is, the Canaanites, the Philistines, the Aramaeans, the Ammonites, the Moabites, and the Edomites were precisely the groups with whom Israel was in particular contact in the time of David and Solomon. A related viewpoint is one which emphasizes the peoples Israel was *not* in contact with in her past as providing grounds for a *terminus ante quem*. In this connection Assyria is usually mentioned, as Israel's first serious contact with the Assyrians took place in the time of Ahab at the battle of Qarqar in 853. Thus this date is held by some to provide a *terminus ante quem* for the emergence of the Yahwistic History[179]. A corollary to this is Schmidt's third argument, which is the point that Gen 9,18-25 expresses a curse upon Canaan, while the Philistines (Japheth) are stated to be especially dependent upon Shem (i.e., Israel). Naturally, this argument is only meaningful if one is able to maintain that the original Yahwistic narrative started in Gen 2,4b, that is, that the Yahwistic Primeval History is just as old as the rest of the Yahwistic History.

Schmidt's fourth argument has to do with Judah's position in the Yahwistic traditions, since in them Judah is accorded pride of place among the tribes, as is shown by, for example, the fact that Abraham, the patriarch of Judah, has the first place. This situation agrees well with the time of the united monarchy. Furthermore, the narrative of the Israelite period of forced labor in Egypt seems to presuppose knowledge of similar conditions in Israel, which immediately directs our interest to the time of Solomon. However, does this not mean that it is no longer possible to claim that the Yahwist is pro-monarchical?

Schmidt's sixth argument is a restatement of von Rad's well known view that the period of Solomon was a period of "enlightenment". This period is supposed to have been characterized by a theological and national *Aufklärung*, the tendencies of which are held to be discernible in the Yahwistic traditions[180]. In furtherance of this position, one frequently also encounters the view that the Solomonic age was especially internationally oriented, or, perhaps better, that its horizons were universalistic rather than particularistic (i.e., parochially Israelite)[181].

The last-mentioned argument for a date for the Yahwist to the time of the united monarchy is perhaps the weakest link in the chain of arguments, since it is extremely circular. What other *ancient* sources do we have which tell us

---

[178] Cf. Grønbæk 1971:277, who dates the History of David's Rise to the reign of Ba'asha.

[179] See especially Schmidt 1979:74 and 1981:96. On 853 as a *terminus ante quem*, see Kaiser 1969:75-76.

[180] Schmidt 1979:73-74. Cf. Von Rad 1944:187-188, and esp. von Rad 1957:62-70 (called *"Der neue Geist"*).

[181] See again von Rad 1944:187, and Schmidt 1981:94.

anything decisive about the international horizons and the enlightened view of the world during the Solomonic age than precisely the Yahwistic traditions? These traditions may be supplemented by the much late legendary accounts of Solomon's wisdom which have been incorporated in the Deuteronomistic Historical Work and even later in the post-exilic and early Judaic Wisdom materials. But none of the data available can make up for the fact that it is first a much later (perhaps as much as three hundred years) tradition that is able to tell us about conditions at Solomon's court. Not even the "Succession Narrative" is any help on this point in part, since there are some scholars who have expressed their disagreement with L. Rost's classical hypothesis, which assigns an early date to this work[182], and in part because it is possible to argue that while this narrative complex is a story of high literary quality, this does not prove that it derives from a period of *enlightenment*. Finally, there is also good reason to question whether the author of the "Succession Narrative" really was a member of Solomon's court[183].

The notion that the era of David and Solomon was especially suitable for the composition of an Israelite work of history has been criticized from a number of vantage points. J.A. Soggin's arguments concerning the various possibilities for dating such historical writing may actually be considered to provide indirect against this view, even though Soggin himself is prone to retain the Solomonic date. Soggin points out that the presence of a palace culture with its related scribal tradition in itself does not warrant the further claim that such scribal capacities were employed in the writing down of historical narratives. In this connection he points to Mycenaean culture and emphasizes the fact that the decipherment of *Linear B* did not mean that we suddenly had the sources of the Homeric poems in our grasp, but only a corpus of inventory lists[184]. To the contrary, as Soggin says, it was most likely in periods of crisis in

---

[182] See Rost 1926. Against this, both Carlson (1964) and Van Seters (1981) regard the "Succession Narrative" as a late (Deuteronomistic) account of the reign of David.

[183] Rost held that the Succession Narrative was written *in majorem gloriam Salomonis* (1926). Carlson saw the matter differently, since he regarded the Succession Narrative as part of the description of David under "the curse". Even without advocating very late dates for the Succession Narrative, other scholars have questioned its pro-Davidic *Tendenz*. Thus notably Delekat, who sees the narrative complex as anti-Salomonic (1967), but see also Würthwein 1974:49-50. R.N. Whybray is less radical; he feels that the criticisms in the text are less directed against Solomon than against David, since the "loyalty" of the author to the Davidic dynasty was unquestionable (1968:50ff.). Crüsemann (1978:180-193) is generally on the same wavelength, since he assumes that the narrative was composed at court. Thus his only reservation is that the work contains criticisms of the activities of the king, but not of the institution as such.

[184] Soggin 1976:59. In connection with the relationship between Homer and Mycenean palace culture, it should be noted that a number of classical philologists have emphasized the extraordinary differences between the milieu presupposed by the Homeric poems and the historical Mycenean social organization. See above all Finley 1977:44ff.; a similar evaluation is to be found in Kirk 1962:23-39. Note also Kirk's discussion of the possibilities of literary activity in these Mycenean palaces (1962:105-125; 1976:19ff.). Kirk stresses the fact that with the exception of some small and isolated fragments which may derive from Mycenean times (but need not necessarily do so), the Homeric poems have no feeling whatsoever for the specific character of Mycenean culture.

which scribes attempted to preserve their heritage by committing ancient oral traditions to writing. In the case of Israel he points to three periods which might come into consideration, namely the period from 1200 to 900, the era of the Exile, and the second century B.C.[185]. Even though, as mentioned previously, Soggin prefers to focus on the first of these periods, his description of the time of the united monarchy as a period of crisis simply has to be regarded as a break with the notion that this time was a harmonic era of enlightenment.

Vorländer's criticisms of this argument, which result in a date for the Yahwist to the 10th century, are several[186]. The writer's first point is that the presuppositions of the Yahwist do not confine his activities to only a single period in the history of Israel. Other periods could be claimed with equal justice to have provided the necessary background, such as the time of Josaphat, Jeroboam II, or even, for that matter, the 55 years of apparently uneventful rule under Manasseh. His second point, which he has borrowed from such scholars as H. Holzinger and Mowinckel, is more decisive. Vorländer points out that it is not only times of prosperity and peace which might have provided the background for the production of such national histories as that of the Yahwist, but also periods of crisis or of national catastrophe. This argument is correct, although Vorländer's choice of examples is unfortunate, since he maintains that Titus Livius wrote his Roman history after the fall of the Republic. This is correct, but it is nevertheless also the case that Livy's writing took place during the reign of Augustus in one of the very few periods in which peace reigned throughout the Roman Empire. Similarly, Saxo Grammaticus did not write his *Gesta Danorum* during a time of national crisis, as Vorländer maintains, but during the Danish High Middle Age under the rule of Valdemar the Great. On the other hand, it is not difficult to find other parallels which would fit his point more accurately, that is, which would show that situations of actual national crisis can produce an extremely lively and valuable literature (in which class I would personally reckon traditional history writing). For Europeans the *exemplum instar omnium* is the emergence of Romanticism after about 1800 A.D. Romanticism expressed itself differently according as the countries in which it appeared were experiencing times of peace and prosperity or of national disaster, but the movement did manifest itself virtually everywhere nonetheless. The Danish example is in fact illustrative.

Denmark's unfortunate foreign policy in the period 1802–1815 almost resulted in the eradication of the country. The greater part of the kingdom (i.e., Norway) was lost, bringing as its consequence national bankrupcy on its heels; at the same time of series of military defeats also took place which entailed,

---

[185] 1976:59.
[186] Vorländer 1978:296-321.

among other things, the ruin of the capital city, and so forth. Nevertheless, in Danish tradition this period is regarded as a golden age in which historical research, the study of the sagas, and all of the arts and sciences in general flowered as never before, or since, in this country[187].

Of course, such an example cannot possibly prove that a similar situation was the presupposition for the emergence of a nationally self-conscious literature in ancient Israel. However, it does serve to show that the existence of a given literary work cannot lead to any particular date for this work, or, perhaps more accurately, the example shows that in terms of scientific method it is a very dubious undertaking to attempt to reason from the contents of a literary work to the context which produced it.

This argumentation may also be stood on its head as far as the reasons (to be discussed below) for a late date for the Pentateuch are concerned. We shall see that when a number of scholars attempt to describe the situation of the Exile as precisely the one which must have given rise to the composition of the basic traditions of the Pentateuch, in reality they are on just as shaky ground – methodologically considered – as their opponents. This is obviously the case because there are unquestionably many cases in which periods of literary productivity and national prosperity do accompany one another[188]. There is no natural law stipulating the sort of situation which produces artistic accomplishment. Thus, even though Vorländer correctly argues against an early date for the Yahwist as far as this issue is concerned, he nevertheless fails to disprove the classical hypothesis as to the time of origin of the Yahwistic History. It goes without saying that this argumentation naturally also applies to any other attempt to use a history-of-culture basis to date the Yahwist, or, for that matter, the Elohist, to, for example, the 9th or 8th centuries.

The other points in the defense by Schmidt and others of the early date of the Yahwist are examined and rejected en bloc by Vorländer[189]. It is shown that none of these arguments permits us to point to a single point in Israel's history at the exclusion of all others. In other words, it seems as if almost any date which may be suggested for (in this case) the Yahwist may be supported by numerous observations concerning Israel's cultural history; unfortunately, they may be countered by an equal number of entirely relevant explanations to the contrary. To take but a single example, we shall consider the problem of

---

[187] References to this period would be superfluous for Danish and – presumably – other Scandinavian readers, as it is covered in the ordinary grammar school curriculum. For non-Scandinavians reference should be made to Oakley 1972:166ff. and Lauring 1976:206ff.; both of these are popularizations, but they are sufficient to give some general idea of the period.

[188] This is my main objection to H. Friis' attempt to describe the era of the Exile as the period in which an Israelite national literature must have arisen. Friis argues that precisely this period was characterized by repristinatory tendencies throughout the ancient Orient (Friis 1975).

[189] 1978:296ff. It should be added that Vorländer offers a similar treatment to attempts to date J to the 9th, 8th, and 7th centuries (1978:321ff.).

the preeminence of Judah. In the time of David and Solomon this exalted status would be wholly intelligble, since both kings were Judaeans and clearly favored their Judaean fellowcountrymen[190]. After the partition of the kingdom, the preeminence of Judah could be the result of the fact that the Yahwist himself was a Judaean, whether he was active in Jerusalem or in the country. What else could one expect of a Judaean than that he would value his own national group above all others? We must also take into account the probability that the claims of the Davidic dynasty to rule over the Northern Kingdom did not cease with the accession of Jeroboam ben Nebat, but that they instead lived on as part of the self-legitimation of the Davidic dynasty. After the fall of Samaria Judah's preeminence would be a matter of course, once the North Palestinian tribes had definitively lost their political significance. Judah's importance will have been equally intelligble during the Exile, since by this date the Northern Kingdom had ceased to exist for more than 135 years. The exiles were Judaeans, as were those who remained in the land, and the Deuteronomistic Historical Work gives ample information as to how Judaean circles regarded the previous population of the Northern Kingdom at this time[191]. Also as far as the post-exilic is concerned it is possible to explain Judah's precedence, both with respect to the late eschatological expectations which attached to the restoration of the Davidic dynasty and to the emphasis on the position of Judah during the history of the monarchy. The best example of this is the treatment of Israel and Judah during the monarchy in the Books of Chronicles, since the traditions concerning Israel in the Deuteronomistic Historical Work have been largely excised by the Chronicler. It is interesting to note that only a single period is excluded as the possible background for the Yahwist, namely the pre-monarchical period. Judah's precedence in this period would require the existence of a tribal league this time which encompassed both the South and North Palestinian tribal groups, and such a league is, as we have seen, indemonstrable.

The other facets of the argumentation for a early date for the Yahwist are susceptible to similar treatment. In consequence, these arguments for an early date for the Yahwist are worthless. We are left with a vague feeling that the Yahwist seems to be somewhat more archaic than the Elohist. However, such feelings do not have much evidential value, and especially not when they are often misleading. To take a well known example which is often cited to "prove" that the Elohist is younger than the Yahwist, scholars have maintained that while the Yahwist makes extensive use of anthropomorphisms, the Elohist replaces these with other devices (he introduces a mediatory element, the מלאך אלהים[192]. There is no reason to take this point seriously, since the neces-

---

[190] Cf. Vorländer 1978:305.

[191] Cf. 2 Kgs 17,24-41.

[192] Weiser still maintained this as late as 1966 (cf. Weiser 1966:107); cf. Soggin 1976:106. Other more recent introductions avoid direct use of this argument for dating E, but it never-

sary rebuttal was already pronounced by J. Pedersen as early as 1931[193].

In his most recent contribution to this discussion, W.H. Schmidt has attempted to add an additional argument for an early date which he has borrowed from Noth[194], which is that there is nothing in the Yahwistic literature which requires a date for this author later than the era of David and Solomon. Apart from the fact that Noth himself was able to reveal considerable uncertainty with respect to the possibilities for dating the Yahwistic source[195], there is only one thing to say to this argument, which Schmidt supports with virtually the same observations as in his *Einführung*. This is, that even if this observation is correct, there is nothing in the Yahwistic literature which prevents us from assigning it to a later period in the history of Israel.

Schmidt also states that there is no reason to be surprised that the Yahwistic literature is not quoted in the late sections of the OT, since not even P, which presumably presupposes both J and E, reveals to any significant degree *"wörtliche Übereinstimmungen mit ihm (auf)"*. To this we may reply that it is not this fact which is so striking, as the fact that the *traditions* which are contained in the Yahwistic History are so very rarely mentioned elsewhere. Moreover, then they are mentioned, they appear in North Israelite sources, but not in Judaean sources until after the fall of the Northern Kingdom (i.e., in the Book of Jeremiah, more specifically in those passages in Jeremiah which are clearly extensions of earlier North Israelite tradition). Finally, Schmidt also owes us an explanation of how we are to determine whether P is *quoting* Yahwistic passages. Such an approach would open up new vistas in the study of the Pentateuch, or rather, it would actually be more in the nature of a return to an idea once prominent in Scandinavian research, namely the notion that as the sole author of the Tetrateuch P quotes a vast number of earlier traditions. How-

---

theless haunts the corridors of Fohrer's argumentation (1969:171), when he claims that in E we find, *"..eine stärkere Betonung des Abstandes Gottes von Welt und Mensch".* This must refer to *"eine stärkere Betonung"* in E *than in J.* See also the accounts of Schmidt (1979:83) and Kaiser (1969: 85) on this issue. In this connection it would also be appropriate to refer to Jaroš 1974, since it is precisely Jaroš basic hypothesis that E represents a later phase of the Israelite break with Canaanite religion than J does, since, according to Jaroš J had no difficulties in this respect, at least as far as the issues against which E directs his polemic were concerned. Finally, it should be added that Jaroš presupposes completely traditional dates for J and E, the last-mentioned of which he assigns to the 8th century.

[193] See Pedersen 1931:178.

[194] Schmidt 1981:96-97; cf. Noth 1948:249.

[195] Cf. Noth 1948:248 for his date for J. Noth maintained that the date when the traditions were collected at the preliterary level was the pre-monarchical period. On the other hand, he held that the formation of the state was the precondition which enabled the emergence of the written sources. Noth further adds: *"Für die genauere Datierung der einzelnen Quellen fehlt es viel stärker an sicheren Anhaltspunkten, als man gemeinhin wahrhaben will".* However, this merely means that Noth regarded the time of the United Monarchy as a *"durchaus möglich"* date for the first literary concretization of the traditions about Israel's prehistory. This dating cannot be separated from Noth's amphictyony hypothesis and his ideas concerning the formation of the tradition in connection with the amphictyony.

ever, one doubts that Schmidt intends to make this sort of admission to Scandinavian research.

For the moment we must be content to admit that in spite of an extremely long tradition within OT studies which dates the Yahwist to the early monarchy, there is not a single decisive, not to say, "objective", argument in favor of this date. If the Yahwist was a Judaean, as most seem to agree, he can hardly be dated to the period prior to 722, since the historical traditions in the present Yahwistic literature cannot be demonstrated in any earlier Judaean context.

The problems are somewhat different with respect to the date of the Elohist, since scholars differ widely as to their understanding of the nature of this work. There is disagreement as to whether the Elohist represents a source document analogous to that of the Yahwist, which is the traditional view, or whether the "Elohist" is not more accurately described as an independent redaction of the basic Yahwistic source, as a number of scholars have suggested[196], or, ultimately, whether we would not be best served by a concept of an "Elohist", but one which differs considerably from the Yahwistic source. It is also conceivable that the source in question is more in the nature of a fragmentary collection of individual traditions than a collected description of Israel's past like that of J. However, as R. Smend seems to feel, these traditions nevertheless reveal some common redactional and theological features, which would entitle us to describe them as an independent source[197].

However we should decide the matter, very few scholars feel that the Elohist is older than the Yahwist (but why, actually? Is it because we find it impossible to shake off the feeling that this "work" is a conscious supplement to J?). There is an impressive consensus to the effect that no matter what its character, E must be later than J. This means in turn, if J cannot be localized to any historical context previous to 722, that the Elohist must be even younger. Already earlier researchers argued that there were connections between the Elohist and North Israelite tradition, connections deriving from Elijah and Elishah and which may be associated with the activities of a prophet like Hosea[198]. Other scholars have seen no difficulty whatsoever in dating the Elo-

---

[196] The question as to whether the Elohist was a redactional layer rather than a "source" was raised by P. Volz and W. Rudolph (1933; cf. Rudolph 1938). This view has played an important role in various Scandinavian approaches to the Pentateuch, such as those of J. Pedersen (1960:546; cf. 1931:178) and especially I. Engnell (1945:186-209 and 1970: 51ff. Engnell attempted a general break with the notion of continuous sources in the Pentateuch). Among those advocating a late date for the Yahwist there is also considerable scepticism with respect to the existence of an independent Elohistic source. Such scholars include a circle who were influenced by F.V. Winnett (cf. Winnet 1965), including N.E. Wagner (1967;1972) and Van Seters (1975:125-131). As an indication that similar views are also making headway among scholars with a different understanding of the redactional situation, H.-C. Schmitt 1980:178-190 should be mentioned.

[197] Cf. Smend 1978:82-86.

[198] On this see Jaroš 1974:67-68. Jaroš regards the time of Hosea as the *terminua ante quem*. Criticisms of this view, as well as a list of scholars sharing the same opinion is to be found in Vorländer 1978:329-330.

histic stratum in the Tetrateuch to even later times such as the period of the Exile; some have even labelled it a Deuteronomistically inspired product[199]. However, although this problem is not unimportant, it does not concern the conclusions to be presented here, as they have primarily to do with the value of these traditions as historical source materials. In this connection it is once again the problems connected with the Yahwistic literature which are decisive.

The question in a nutshell has to do with the status of the Yahwist as an independent author. The crucial issue is whether we are able to agree with R. Rendtorff's attempt to combat the conception of J as a theologian, that is, an author who, no matter when he was active, composed his work from one end to the other with a particular intention, or whether we prefer to retain the more traditional understanding of the Yahwist as an independent author who composed a history of Israel from the creation to just before the Settlement, as stressed by, among others, J. Van Seters and H.H. Schmid[200]. The investigation may be pursued, as Rendtorff has done, by inquiring as to whether it can be demonstrated that there ever existed any independent version of the Pentateuch prior to its final redaction. In other words, is it possible to show that there are connections between the various complexes of traditions at, for example, the Yahwistic stage? Rendtorff himself denies this possibility. In his opinion, each of the narrative complexes in the Pentateuch were originally independent of one another and has had its own particular history of tradition. On the one hand this applies to the Primeval History and the patriarchal narratives in Genesis (the latter provides the main evidence in Rendtorff's proof), while it applies, on the other, to the various thematic cycles in Exodus-Numbers, the "Passover legend", the Sinai narrative, and the narratives concerning the desert period. The most important break in the chain is that between the patriarchal narratives and the traditions in Exodus-Numbers. Rendtorff's main argument is the lack of "Yahwistic" cross-references intended to link these two collections of traditions, and, further, the total lack of mention of the patriarchal traditions in Exodus-Numbers, apart from in passages which do not belong to J, but to later redactions[201]. The patriarchal narratives and the other narrative cycles, respectively, do not display any reciprocal interests or take account of one another before the final stage of redac-

---

[199] Vorländer clearly argues that the Elohist cannot possibly have been pre-exilic (1978:335). On the other hand, he is rather vague with respect to the relationship between the Yahwist and the Elohist; see his introduction (1978:15-21). In this connection one should also note R. Rendtorff's corresponding remarks (1977A:82). On the possible familial resemblance between the Elohist and the Deuteronomists, see Smend 1978:86, who, however, does not without more ado date the Elohist to the time of the Exile. He confines himself instead to remarking that there are no certain indications that the Elohist may be dated to the Northern Kingdom before 722, and emphasizes that a later date (after 722) and a Judaean provenence would be equally conceivable.

[200] Even though it should be noted that the authors mentioned naturally do not accept the traditional early date for the Yahwist.

[201] Rendtorff 1977A:65-70. Compare Rendtorff 1977B:9f., and cf. already Rendtorff 1969:9.

tion. In fact, there are not even originally Yahwistic connections between the traditions of the three patriarchs, especially not between the Abraham and Jacob traditions, since the former are based on the theme of the promise, while the latter is a *"Führungsgeschichte"*[202]. Furthermore, or so Rendtorff holds, if we go even deeper into things we discover that even the Abrahamic stratum does not rely on a single promise; instead, it contains a number of individual promises which in form critical and redaction critical terms are to be assigned to various levels. They will finally have been connected into a comprehensive promise to the patriarch at a relatively late redactional stage[203]. Thus in Rendtorff's opinion it would be absurd to continue to adhere to the concept of an extensive Yahwistic source document. The connections between the various cycles of narratives were first established by the final redactor, and not by the Yahwist[204].

As far as a precise description of the final redaction is concerned, Rendtorff has been hesitant to speak. In 1974, when he presented his break with the documentary hypothesis of traditional Pentateuchal research, he still regarded P as the collector of Genesis to Numbers, but in his monograph on the subject which appeared in 1977 he both abandons the notion that P was a continuous source document and denies that P could have been the final redactor. In recent times, Rendtorff has preferred to speak of a *"deuteronomisch geprägte"* redaction[205]. He has also been hesitant to specify the date of such a redaction; in his monograph Rendtorff suggests thay an early Deuteronomistic circle may have been behind the collection of the Pentateuch, but in a response to his critics in another contribution which appeared in the same year it appears that he was increasingly prone to regard an actual Deuteronomistic redactor as the collector of the Pentateuch[206]. This seems to agree with his further suggestion that it is perhaps impossible to disassociate the Tetrateuch and Deuteronomy from one another, since both may have been created by an early Deuteronomistic redactor[207].

Rendtorff's insights concerning the formation of the Pentateuch were presented in 1974, but they were first the object of a thorough discussion in connection with a special number of the *Journal for the Study of the Old Testament*. This issue contains contributions by R.N. Whybray, J. Van Seters, N.E. Wagner, G.W. Coats, and H.H. Schmid, plus a lengthy review of his monograph by

---

[202] Cf. 1977A:49-51; 1977B:6-7. On the joining of these materials see Rendtorff 1977A:57ff.
[203] Cf. Rendtorff 1977A:37-65. In his analysis of the individual promise motifs and the interrelations among them via redactional phases Rendtorff is largely continuing the initiatives of his colleague at Heidelberg, C. Westermann, who has undertaken thorough form critical studies of these materials (Westermann 1976:123-149).
[204] 1977A:158-173.
[205] Cf. 1977B:9, and compare with 1977A:164.
[206] Compare Rendtorff 1977A:169ff. with Rendtorff 1977C:45.
[207] 1977A:167f.

R.E. Clements[208]. In what follows I shall attempt to present the quintessence of this discussion, although I shall reserve my remarks about Rendtorff's sharpest critic, J. Van Seters for separate treatment. As far as the main issues are concerned, Whybray, Wagner, and Coats do not appear to be far from sharing Rendtorff's views; all three emphasize the necessity to deal with the various complexes of tradition in the Pentateuch in isolation from each other[209]. Wagner is particularly concerned with the question of the relationship between the "Yahwist" responsible for Gen 1-11 and the one responsible for Gen 12-36. His main desideratum is a degree of clarity as to what is meant by the term "Yahwist". As he points out, this term is in many contexts simply a relic from the days of the classical documentary theory, in spite of the fact that modern discoveries have voided it of contents[210]. For their part, Coats and Whybray emphasize that the connection between the narrative themes in Exodus and Numbers is primary in relation to the connections between them and the patriarchal traditions (it should be added that neither writer was at the time familiar with Rendtorff's monograph of that year, in which Rendtorff reveals that he is fully aware of this situation)[211]. At the time he composed his contribution, Schmid seems to have had access to Rendtorff's monograph, since he emphasizes that it is more fruitful to ignore the difference between the Deuteronomistically inspired collection of the various themes and the earlier redactional phases of the individual themes[212]. This Deuteronomistic linkage of the various themes seems to suggest that the "Yahwist" is to be seen in relation to the Deuteronomistic movement, that is, as a reaction which occurred parallel to the Deuteronomists' production of their own version of the historical traditions[213]. Clements' position is from the other side of the coin, since he maintains that in spite of Rendtorff's criticisms of earlier Pentateuchal research it remains possible to retain the notion of a pre-Deuteronomistic corpus of traditions[214]. However, Clements also asserts that this pre-Deuteronomistic corpus can scarcely have had the same contents as those it possessed

---

[208] Rendtorff 1977B, and cf. Whybray 1977, Van Seters 1977, Wagner 1977, Coats 1977, Schmid 1977, and Clements 1977.

[209] Cf. Whybray 1977:12f., and Coats 1977:30f. (however, both address themselves to the two main parts, the patriarchal traditions and the traditions of Exodus to Numbers), plus Wagner 1977:22.

[210] Wagner 1977:21f.

[211] Coats 1977:30f. and Whybray 1977:12f. Cf. Rendtorff 1977A: 70ff. It is precisely Rendtorff's point that both the patriarchal traditions and the Exodus to Numbers complex had their own independent courses of development until the final phase of the redaction of the Pentateuch. Both complexes were assembled without reference to each other.

[212] Schmid 1977:36.

[213] Schmid 1977:39; this is also the main theme of Schmid 1976. See below on the effort of Schmid's student, M. Rose, to clarify the relationship between the Deuteronomist and the Yahwist.

[214] Clements 1977:52 and 56. On p.56 Clements even goes so far as to insist that there once existed *"an early epic history of Israel"*.

24

after its later reworking. Thus it is possible that this collection was not the unitary account of Israel's earliest history scholars have thought it to be until recently. It may have been something more in the direction of an anthology of legends from Israel's earliest times[215]. Nevertheless, Clements feels that this collection must have been consciously structured, so that it is still possible to retain the idea of an early Yahwistic author who, however, did not manage to smooth out the disparities and unevennesses between the various sagas and legends he incorporated into his work[216].

In reality, Clements and Rendtorff are not on the same wavelength, since Clements simply presupposes an early date for J and supports this with arguments of the sort rejected previously, that is, vague presumptions which allow him to state that it is conceivable that such an early J existed. In favor of this Clements is only able to point out that the tradition history of the Pentateuch was long and complicated. No serious scholar would be inclined to disagree on this point, nor, for that matter, does Rendtorff (although Rendtorff's use of tradition history has been criticized for not attempting to see the development of the tradition in a historical and sociological context)[217].

It is important that we should not lose sight of Rendtorff's entirely correct basic assumption, which is that if a "Yahwist" existed who was responsible for the main body of the Pentateuch, a body containing parts of all of the Pentateuchal themes, then it must be possible to follow this "Yahwist" throughout all the these originally separate themes. However, if cross-references and connective links between such sections prove to be clearly very late, then the connection between these narrative cycles to demonstrate the existence of both an early phase of redaction, during which the various themes were joined together, and a later reworking of this redaction by means of which its linkages were strengthened. But Rendtorff's argument is precisely that we cannot do this, and on this issue he has not been challenged by his opponents. On the other hand, it is possible to ask as to how we are to regard the final phase of

---

[215] Clements 1977:51.

[216] Clements 1977:52ff.

[217] Cf. Van Seters 1979 (an extensive review article on Rendtorff 1977A and Schmid 1976; see esp. pp.666f.). In the light of the criticisms offered above of attempts to base a date for the Yahwist on sociological and historical criteria it should not be surprising that the present author does not share this critical attitude towards Rendtorff, since I, following Vorländer's lead, am inclined to reject all *Zeitgeschichtliche* explanations. I have no doubt that such analyses are relevant, but they become so *only after one has successfully dated a literary stratum on other grounds*. It should be superabundantly clear, after more than a century of critical discussion of these questions, that virtually any period in the history of Israel and Judah can be made to harmonize with a given document (in this case the Yahwist). Thus I have no doubt whatsoever that Van Seters' *Zeitgeschichtliche* observations, as formulated, e.g., in Van Seters 1972A, are correct. However, they cannot be one's point of departure for a date for the Yahwist, as they ought rather to be a result of such a date. In all scientific work, and even in a discipline which is as "subjective" as OT studies tend to be, it is methodologically correct to proceed from what is certain to that which is less so, and not to follow the reverse procedure. This banal observation loses none of its actuality when it is applied to the present discussion of the age of the Pentateuchal traditions.

redaction; as far as I can see, it is a matter of taste as to whether we are to speak of a "Yahwistic" redactor or of a Deuteronomistically-inspired one. For this reason Rendtorff rightly regards Van Seters' criticism of his position as a misunderstanding, since Van Seters seems to believe that Rendtorff assumes the existence of ancient *written* sources which have been integrated by the redactor. Thus Rendtorff is able to maintain that in reality he and Van Seters are in closer agreement than the latter supposes[218].

We are left with the question as to whether it was an early (proto) Deuteronomistic redactor who unified the Pentateuchal themes, a Deuteronomistic redactor whose work paralleled the other redactional activity of the school, or a late Deuteronomistically inspired redactor who was responsible for this. One seeks in vain for some clarification of these questions in Rendtorff's works. There may be a number of reasons for this; one may be that the writer himself has not yet made up his mind on this issue, as is indicated by a comparison of his remarks concerning P in his address at the I.O.S.O.T. congress in 1974 with those on the same subject in his 1977 monograph. Another reason may be related to a methodological weakness in Rendtorff's work to which several of his critics have called attention, namely the fact that he does not include materials external to the Pentateuch (for example, from the Deuteronomistic Historical Work) as a basis for comparison. Without comparing the materials in the Tetrateuch with those in the Deuteronomistic literature, Rendtorff is unable to decide the question of the relationship between the Yahwist and the Deuteronomist[219].

To exemplify this criticism, it would be appropriate to turn to Rendtorff's analysis of the theme of the promise into a number of individual promises: one dealing with possession of the land, one with progeny, and one with blessing. According to Rendtorff, these various elements belong to different stages in the tradition of the Abraham narratives, which were first assembled in the familiar comprehensive formula (Gen 12,1-3; 13,14-17; 22,16-18; 28,13-14) during the final process of redaction[220]. The counter argument of Schmid and Van Seters is that no part of the promise theme is pre-Deuteronomistic; all of the elements belong to the stage which Rendtorff has called the final redaction but which they prefer to call the "Yahwist"[221]. Admittedly, some scholars, such as Noth[222], have regarded the promise of progeny in Gen 15,4 as ancient, but as a whole Gen 15 can hardly be a very old text, as was demonstrated long ago by O. Kaiser[223]. Thus it would be more correct to regard

---

[218] See Rendtorff 1977C:43f.

[219] Cf. Schmid 1977:34-35; Van Seters 1979:664.

[220] Cf. Rendtorff 1977A:40ff.; Rendtorff distinguishes between the promise of land, the promise of progeny, the motif of blessing, and the motif of divine guidance.

[221] Cf. Schmid 1977:35f., and Van Seters 1975:249-278 and 1977:16.

[222] See 1948:252n.

[223] Cf. Kaiser 1958, and see also Westermann 1981:256, who declares that both texts in Gen 15, that is, v 1-6 and 7-21, belong to *"einem späten Stadium der Geschichte der Väterverheissungen"*. Cf.

Gen 15 as the text which integrates the promise of the birth of a son with the promise of innumerable offspring, as maintained by Schmid. E. Otto has protested against this[224] that this combination is known in the Ugaritic texts. However, Otto's counter argument by no means proves that Gen 15 is pre-exilic, but rather the contrary, since the promise of innumerable progeny thus becomes an element in the transfer of the royal ideology onto the patriarch Abraham after the fall of the monarchy. Schmid has pointed out that this seems to be the case with Gen 12,3, which is taken to be an example of a reapplication of the theme of Ps 72,17 to Abraham during the time of the Exile[225]. There are no difficulties connected with the attempt to regard the theme of the promise as a whole as an effort to decorate Abraham with feathers borrowed from the pre-exilic royal ideology. If it had been possible to describe the Yahwist as an author who was active during the united monarchy, a chapter like Gen 15 could then be taken to signify that the description of the patriarch as a "royal" personage was intended to represent him as the *heros eponymos* of the Judaean dynasty[226]. However, in the event that we are forced to conclude that this date for the Yahwist is unlikely, this transfer of ideology to Abraham becomes instead evidence of an attempt to preserve the expectations which accrued to the Davidic kings, in spite of the fact that these kings had long before played out their historical role.

In this connection Otto requires Schmid to specify more closely the relationship between the Deuteronomist and the Yahwist, a relationship he himself has attempted to sketch out on the supposition that the historical résumés in Deut 1-3 and 10 presuppose the basic narrative contents of the Yahwistic literature[227]. Otto has elsewhere maintained that the Yahwist originally included a narrative of the Conquest, and that this narrative is present in the Book of Joshua with Deuteronomistic modifications, instead of having been completely replaced by a Deuteronomistic edition of the story[228]. Otto's claim is based upon a literary critical analysis of Jos 2-11 which he feels reveals the presence of a pre-Deuteronomistic source (which he calls "A"), a source which

---

Westermann 1976:126, where he concludes that with respect to Gen 15,16 and 18, Gen 15,4 is *"eine spätere Formulerung"*.

[224] Cf. Westermann 1976:123, with reference to Krt I, and see esp. the analysis in Westermann 1976:155ff. This study has been noted by Otto 1977:86n.

[225] Cf. Schmid 1977:36, and compare with Schmid 1976:33. See also Van Seters 1975:274.

[226] Thus it is not possible for me to find any value in Clements' attempt to demonstrate that the covenant with David was dependent on the covenant with Abraham (cf. Clements 1967). There is no question but that Kaiser's analysis of this chapter has revealed the extent to which the ideas it contains resemble those advocated by the Deuteronomists. However, it would also be worthwhile to recall that the covenant with David need not necessarily be regarded as an original element in the Judaean royal ideology, as it could just as easily be understood as a very late attempt to restructure that ideology along (possibly) Assyrian lines, in which the king was understood as the servant of Assur.

[227] Otto 1977:87.

[228] Otto 1975:95-103.

he holds to be identical with the concluding part of the Yahwistic work of the Tetrateuch.

Now, it was long ago observed that the goal of the Yahwist's narrative is the Conquest/Settlement of Palestine, as is indicated by a number of notices within the Yahwistic parts of Exodus and Numbers[229]. Also, the description of the conquest of the territory east of the Jordan points to a subsequent conquest of the region west of the Jordan[230]. Otto's methodologically correct (because he has studied a group of texts which overlap or crossreference) examination of the relationship between the Yahwist and the Deuteronomist is intended to establish the chronological precedence of the Yahwist with respect to the Deuteronomist. If his observations are correct, our next task will be to turn to a number of individual arguments set forth by Schmid which might help us to date this pre-Deuteronomistic Yahwist more closely. In particular, one might consider the understanding of Moses as a prophet, which must presuppose the history of classical prophecy, especially in connection with his call in Exod 3[231]. One might also consider Moses' behavior in the narrative of the plagues of Egypt in Exod 6,28-11,10 (and elsewhere), as well as the covenantal ideas in the Sinai pericope[232]. Even though the results of such a study need not entail a return to the classical position regarding the redaction history of the Pentateuch, such a date for J would nevertheless be extremely uncertain.

However, Otto was not to be allowed the last word on the matter, since all of his arguments intended to prove the presence of the Yahwist in Jos 1-11 have been extensively analyzed and categorically rejected by M. Rose in his recent monograph on the relationship between the Deuteronomist and the Yahwist[233]. It should be noted that, like many of the younger scholars active today, Rose assumes that the Deuteronomistic Historical Work was composed in a number of stages; in his case, the writer assumes that the first edition appeared early in the period of the Exile, and was followed by a later redactional stratum[234]. This makes it possible for Rose to propose a model which distinguishes between a Deuteronomist who does not presuppose a Yahwist, and a redactional Deuteronomistic stratum which does. If it can be shown that the Yahwist presupposes this supposed earlier Deuteronomist, then the out-

---

[229] The texts in question in the Tetrateuch (particularly Exod 23 and 34) have been studied by Otto 1975:199-316.

[230] Cf. Otto 1975:98.

[231] See especially Schmid 1976:19-43.

[232] Cf. Schmid 1976:83-118.

[233] Rose 1981.

[234] Rose has previously presented an account of his understanding of the developmental history of the Deuteronomistic literature (Rose 1975). Another group of scholars who have also attempted to divide the developmental history of the Deuteronomistic History into a number of redactional phases has coalesced around R. Smend (cf. Smend 1971B and Dietrich 1972). On the other hand, one ought not to overlook the fact that still other scholars continue to attempt to support Noth's conception of a single, collected Deuteronomistic redaction; see thus most recently Hoffmann 1980:316-318.

lines appear of a new sketch of how the Israelite historical tradition came about.

This is precisely what Rose attempts to do; he concludes on the one hand that the Yahwistic strata in the Tetrateuch aim at an account of the Settlement, and on the other hand that this Yahwistic narrative is not preserved in the Book of Joshua. We are instead forced to reckon with a Yahwist who bases his account upon an already existing tradition of Israel's conquest of Palestine which is preserved in the earlier Deuteronomistic part of the Book of Joshua. The sections which form a bridge between the Tetrateuch and the chapters in the Book of Joshua which are concerned with the Settlement, and which Otto had assumed were evidence of Yahwistic traditions, are instead redactional attempts to create a connection between the Yahwistic literature and the Deuteronomistic account of the Settlement. However, these redactional additions were not added in order to connect the *original* edition of the narrative of the Settlement with an already existing Yahwistic History[235].

Rose tests his basic hypothesis with respect to other materials than the introduction to the account of the Settlement in the Book of Joshua, as he also includes an analysis of the relationship between the historical introduction to Deuteronomy, Deut 1-3, and the Yahwistic parts of the Tetrateuch[236]. His conclusions are analogous to those stated above: the Yahwistic traditions of the Tetrateuch presuppose the earlier materials contained in Deut 1-3. In other words, he concludes that this first anticipatory sketch of the Deuteronomistic Historical Work was in fact the first edition of a history of Israel. Rose accordingly notes that this historical work contains neither any references to the patriarchal age nor, especially, any references to the theme of the promise associated with the patriarchal traditions. Rose suggests that the reason for this was that these matters were simply not relevant to the Deuteronomist. It was first the later reworker of the Deuteronomistic corpus who included these materials in his account. The original Deuteronomist was concerned with such themes as *"Landnahme, Landbesitz und Land verlust"*[237]. Nor did the first Deuteronomist know anything of the Sinai theme, as its related traditions first appear in the redactional stratum[238]. In other words, Rose's model entails that the collection of the Israelite historical tradition presupposes the time of the Exile. Of course, this does not prevent Rose from maintaining that these late historical works contain materials (whose origins may have been both oral and written) which may be much older[239]. Further, Rose's model does not require us to regard the Yahwist as a Deuteronomist, which is a frequently uttered accusa-

---

[235] Cf. Rose 1981:21-169.171-220.316ff.

[236] 1981:221-315. The Tetrateuchal materials in question are Exod 18,13f.; Num 11,4ff.; 13f., which are studied in connection with Jos 14,6-15 and Jdg 1,11.

[237] 1981:325.

[238] 1981:326.

[239] 1981:325.

tion against those who prefer to date the collection of the historical traditions quite late.

It may be said that the Deuteronomist and the Yahwist represent two different ways of regarding Israel's new situation after the loss of national independence. This last point will be of some importance below when I attempt to decide the question of an early versus a late Yahwist, since I shall there address myself to the fact that, among other things, the Yahwist does not have the same view of the problem of sanctuaries, that is, the problem of the centralization of the cult, as that held by the Deuteronomist.

As far as the subject of this part of my study of the origins of the historical traditions is concerned, it is important that Rose's conclusions largely agree with my presentation of the historical tradition in the prophets and the Psalter. Thus I agree completely with Rose that there must have existed older traditions about Israel's past, that is, traditions which predate the Exile. These narratives are not the free inventions of the late period. On the other hand, there is no doubt but that these traditions were first collected and adapted for theological purposes at a very late point in the history of Israel. It accordingly seems possible provisionally to state that the traditions concerning early Israel until the introduction of the monarchy were only slightly known if they played any role at all in Judah prior to 722. Also, it seems certain that the Northern Kingdom was familiar with these traditions before the catastrophe of 722. Unfortunately, it will hardly be possible to say anything definite about the contents and extent of these traditions. Finally, these northern traditions were first collected in Judah by Deuteronomists who were active in the time of the Exile, and by a Yahwist who can hardly have been earlier.

Is it possible to avoid these conclusions? Efforts in this direction have been presented by R. Smend, followed by H.C. Schmitt[240]. Smend is fully aware that it is not possible to maintain the conception of an early Yahwist in the sense of an author of a historical work which began with the creation and concluded with the Settlement in Palestine. He admits that many elements in the Yahwistic traditions must be quite late; this applies to the entire Primeval History and to such novellas as the story of Joseph or the account of the fetching of Rebeccah as a bride for Isaac in Gen 24. Smend accordingly hypothecates the formation of a Yahwistic tradition which spanned most of the period of the monarchy; this tradition was originally an "anthology" of sagas and legends which was ultimately developed by a purposeful Yahwistic redactor who was active towards the close of the monarchy[241].

For his part, Schmitt arrives at similar conclusions on the basis of his analysis of the Joseph novella[242]. Schmitt and Smend differ somewhat on matters

[240] Cf. Smend 1978:86-94. Schmitt 1980:189-190.

[241] Smend 1978:90 and 94.

[242] Schmitt 1980:185ff. It will not be necessary to discuss Schmitt's understanding of the Joseph Novella here; his work may be described as a break with Redford 1970, which in turn

pertaining to the delimitation of the Elohist with respect to the Yahwist. Smend somewhat hesitantly mentions a number of special features in E which he thinks entitle us to retain the concept of an independent Elohistic stratum, while Schmitt is more inclined to regard the Elohist as a redactor, or, more correctly, as a purposeful redactor who left behind him a collected pre-Priestly Tetrateuch, that is, a Yahwistic History[243].

Any criticism of this concept of a lengthy Yahwistic process of compilation must necessarily ask as to the necessity of the hypothesis. By this I mean that if we "empty" the earlier Yahwistic traditions of their theological contents simply in order to regard them as a sort of compilation of heterogeneous individual traditions, as Smend seems prepared to do[244], of what theoretical use is this supposed early Yahwistic tradition? One must require convincing reasons for a pre-exilic collection of basic traditions stemming from one or more "early" Yahwists. If we are unable to produce such arguments, we are forced to conclude that we only have to do with a sort of scholarly inertia which allows the rudiments of earlier academic research to live on long after they have lost their *Sitz im Leben* in the academic debate. If we examine Smend's description of the historical development, we discover that he does not mention any factors sufficient to warrant the assumption of an early Yahwist. Indeed, he is himself able to point to the hollowness of the arguments which have been advanced previously[245]. Even though a number of traditions with the Yahwistic materials seem to be untouched by Deuteronomistic ideas, this is not a decisive argument for the possibility that these traditions may be pre-Deuteronomistic. One often gets the idea from current discussions that at any rate from the time of the Josianic reform and later Deuteronomistic ideas were dominant in the Judah of the Exile. The Deuteronomists themselves would no doubt approve of this idea, but the question nevertheless remains as to whether this is an adequate understanding of this period. It would be much more natural to assume that a number of different theological movements were active in this period which must have existed independently of each other to the extent that each group appears to have had its own special interests. They must naturally also have been related to one another to the extent that all of them were in the same situation and had to find answers to questions such as those the situation of the Exile posed. Thus there is no difficulty in conceiving of an exilic cultural milieu which had room for the Deuteronomists as well as for the mo-

---

may be seen as yet another fruit of the scholarly tradition which may be traced back to Winnet (cf. above n.196).

[243] 1980:190. Schmitt speaks of two different redactions of older Pentateuchal materials, the first "Elohistic", the second "Yahwistic". However, Schmitt emphasizes that his conclusions arise from his study of the Joseph Novella and require to be substantiated by an analysis of sources outside of Genesis. See further on Smend's understanding of the Elohist, 1978:85.

[244] 1978:87.

[245] Cf. Smend 1978:93f.

vements which crystallized in the form of the Priestly and the Yahwistic traditions in the Tetrateuch.

On the models offered by Rose and others the Yahwist does not seem to have
been unaware of the already existing Deuteronomistic literature, since his
narrative is intended to cohere with the Deuteronomistic narrative of the
Settlement. This does not mean that the Yahwist was unable to supplement the
Deuteronomistic traditions with his own views, to which he gave concrete
expression in his theme concerning the promise to the fathers. This theme was
adopted by a later phase of Deuteronomistic redaction and worked into the
Deuteronomistic literature. Finally, the theme was also adopted by the Priestly
tradition. Of course, these remarks are only tentative and highly hypothetical,
but in illustration of my point it would be appropriate to consult the remarks
offered on Ps 44 above, where it was emphasized that this psalm is not Deuteronomistic, and in fact it seems to deny the correctness of the Deuteronomistic theology. Thus it would be naive to suppose that the Exile led to an instantaneous simplification of Israelite-Judaic culture. Instead, we have found
reason to believe that the period catalyzed a process of debate between the
proponents of a number of views concerning Israel's history and religion, all
of which took their point of departure in the catastrophe of 587.

§ 4

Conclusion

This evaluation of the process by which the historical tradition was formed will
necessarily have consequences for our assessment of the value of this tradition
as a historical source for reconstructing Israel's past. The question as to
whether the Deuteronomists, or, more particularly, the Yahwist, made use of
available oral sources, which is the traditional view (but undeniably a view
based on the assumption that the Yahwist was active during the early part of
the monarchy), or whether the Yahwist's materials were already available to
him in written form, or whether he in reality personally composed his narratives with some higher purpose in mind are actually of secondary importance.[246]. What is decisive for a historian's evaluation of these materials is that
they are removed by more than half a millenium from the events these traditions describe. Indeed, if one retains the notion of a patriarchal age, the distance between the patriarchs and the writing down of the sources is easily at
least a thousand years. *The gap between written fixation and the "underlying events"
is too great to permit us to accept the tradition as a primary source for our reconstruction of*

---

[246] Thus in reality Van Seters 1975:309-312.

the past[247]. In reality, there is no reason to discuss this question further. The notion of a special "patriarchal age" has been shown to be a *fata morgana* by the studies of both Thompson and Van Seters. These scholars have thoroughly examined and dismissed the long series of arguments which have been led into the field in order to prove that the patriarchs belonged to the second millennium[248]. However, in spite of these important investigations, one often sees Alt's theory about "*der Gott der Väter*", understood as a special type of religion practiced by his hypothetical small-cattle nomads in the earliest period of Israelite history, advanced in defense of the earlier view of the patriarchal age[249].

This argument, too, is without substance. There is no doubt that Alt's own authority has contributed to the fact that his view of the religion of the patriarchs has been generally accepted, even though the materials upon which Alt based his thesis mainly consisted of very late Nabataean and Palmyrene inscriptions[250]. The decisive break with the theory of a special patriarchal religion appeared in H. Vorländer's comprehensive study of the concept of the personal god (i.e., one connected with the individual) in the Orient. Vorländer concluded that this type of religion was found everywhere in the ancient Near East; it designated private religion in contradistinction to the official variety[251]. It is to be observed that the mistake made by Alt and his followers consisted in failing to distinguish between the various levels in Israelite society. The fact that the patriarchal narratives point to the existence of a form of religion which was closely bound up with the individual does not prove that in evolutionary terms the patriarchs precede the official state religion of later Israel. It merely points to a particular milieu within this Israelite society in which "*der Gott der Väter*" had its *Sitz im Leben*, namely, local tradition. In other words, there are not many relevant scientific arguments which support the assumption that the patriarchs belonged to a special "age" within Israel's historical development[252].

---

[247] Actually, one could continue to assert this evaluation of the source value of these materials even if one associated the activities of the Yahwist with the early monarchical period, since even with such a date the Yahwist would be removed from the events of the immigration by something like 300 years, and from the so-called Patriarchal Age by at least 400 to 500 years.

[248] Thompson 1974 and Van Seters 1975:5-122. However, one should not overlook the fact that Thompson has expressed some reservations about Van Seters' dating of the patriarchal narratives; see thus Thompson 1978B. Thompson's argument is that Van Seters has committed the same error as that committed by earlier scholars, in that he has even undertaken *to date* the patriarchal narratives to a particular age.

[249] Cf. Alt 1929.

[250] See Alt 1929:68-77.

[251] Vorländer 1975. On the OT see Vorländer 1975:169ff., and on Alt's hypothesis in particular see 1975:203ff., and compare with Van Seters recent criticisms of Alt's attitudes towards patriarchal religion (Van Seters 1980).

[252] Otto argues for the existence of a patriarchal age on the basis of sociological features embedded in the narratives. He notes that certain of these special features must have preceded the establishment of the Israelite tribal system. He also maintains that the religion of the patria-

As of yet we do not have studies of the traditions of Exodus-Numbers on the one hand and of Joshua and Judges on the other which may be compared with the monographs of Thompson and Van Seters about the patriarchal traditions. I hope to return to this area myself at a later date, but in this context it should be said that even as far as the period of the Judges is concerned we only occasionally have to do with sources which cannot be understood as originally independent legends which were first inserted into a historical framework and chronology by a redactor (be he Deuteronomistic or pre-Deuteronomistic)[253]. This means that the nature of the sources dealing with the period of the Judges prevent our being able to write a history of this period. We cannot even permit ourselves to use the various traditions of the Judges as historical references to individual events which actually occurred during the premonarchical period. Or at least, in order to do so we should have to analyze the individual narratives thoroughly not only with a view to distinguishing between the original narrative and its redactional accretions, but also in order to evaluate the type of narrative with respect to the various categories of legends. One must always recall that we have no means whatsoever to check the history of the tradition of these narratives prior to their written fixation[254].

Literary critical methods, assisted by the insights of redaction history and form criticism, may perhaps enable us to arrive at the first written edition of

---

rchs reflects the tribe-less shepherd society, the context of which was *"eine familiar strukturierte Gesellschaft"* (1981:89ff.). The religion of this society was first replaced after the formation of the tribes and the occupation of Palestine by an extra-familial solidarity. In reality Otto is very close to the ideas of Mendenhall and Gottwald concerning ancient Israelite Yahwism. Nevertheless, his position is to be rejected. It is obvious that the patriarchal narratives reflect a society without tribes, since the patriarchs themselves are not depicted as members of tribes, but as *tribal founders*.

[253] Cf. Lemche 1972:87. In a sense, S.M. Warner's attempt to date the traditions of the period of the Judges to prior to the immigration on the basis of *"the pattern of social development within early Israel"* (see Warner 1976, and compare Warner 1978) may be taken to support this view of the traditions of the period of the Judges. Warner attempts to find parallels between the social structure in the days of Eli and Samuel and that at the time of the Conquest, and to demonstrate significant differences between the structure at the time of the Conquest, in the days of Eli and Samuel, and in the so-called period of the Judges. I am rather more than sceptical as to whether Warner has succeeded in establishing his noteworthy hypothesis. I am also afraid that he places entirely too much value on the historical contents of his sources. See further below on his view of the patriarchal narratives. Actually, Warner's understanding of the texts is entirely conservative. If one does not share his view, there is no need to feel concern about an apparent sociological difference between Israel at the time of the Conquest, in the period of the Judges, and shortly afterwards, just prior to the establishment of the monarchy.

[254] See Olrik 1921:43: *"It is only occasionally that the scholar may observe the saga in its natural state"*. This is Olrik's point of departure for a chapter devoted to *"The individual tradition (the source criticism of the saga)"* (1921:43-65). It is important to note that even if Olrik frequently attempts to find the historical contents of a saga (e.g., in Olrik 1903, in connection with the legends about Rolf Kraka and the Lejre Kings; but see also Olrik 1910, which deals with the legends about Starkad the Old, where he did not attempt to find a historical nucleus), he nevertheless concluded (1921: 127) that *"to determine the historical basis of a saga on the evidence of the legendary tradition itself is difficult as a rule"*. In this connection he mentions that certain features argue against the historical nature of a saga, such as, for example, if it resembles a popular fairytale, if it is a saga of origins (i.e., aetiological), or if the course of the narrative is associated with several localities.

the narrative about a particular "Judge". But even this edition is not identical with the preliterary stage of the narrative in question. It would be a serious mistake to believe that the oldest literary tradition reproduces the oral tradition. In recent times, folklorists have frequently observed that the major break in the development of an oral tradition occurs precisely when written fixation occurs, because written fixation in and of itself signifies an end to the free poetical elaboration of a tradition. By the same token, the process of writing things down militates against the very nature of the oral tradition[255]. For example, it has been said in connection with the studies by M. Parry and A.B. Lord into the Serbo Croatian epic literature that it has proven to be very difficult for the oral narrators to "fix" the form of their story while it is being written down. Either the recording situation, which is unnatural for the poets in question, has inhibited their poetic tendencies and thus weakened the final result, or else (and this occurred in only a very few cases, and even then when the poet was probably a major talent) the poets exploited the situation and in fact embroidered their performances[256].

The second point to be considered in evaluating the oral tradition is the necessity to acknowledge that we have no means of controlling it. Whether an oral narrative is in prose or in verse, it is always uniquely appropriate to the situation in which it is recited, since the narrator is free with respect to the version of the story he chooses to tell. Thus, for example, the rules for the study of legends and saga recommended by A. Olrik teach us to distinguish between the basic narrative and its ornamentation. Olrik holds that the basic narrative is identical with the *essential course of the event*. Other elements represent elaborations of the basic narrative; such elements include such things as personal names and place names (this can hardly surprise anyone familiar with the discrepancies with respect to details found in the Babylonian and OT versions of the Flood Narrative).

In the traditio-historical research pursued in Scandinavia, the reliability of the oral tradition has been emphasized countless times[257]. In this connection, Scandinavian scholars have been prone to utilize the concept of "schools of tradition", that is, institutional circles who saw it as their task to preserve the oral traditions about Israel's past as carefully as possible. Against this contention it would be correct to point out that this type of argumentation easily becomes too circular, since in order to maintain the notion of the reliability of the tradition one has also to postulate the existence of a circle of tradents who

---

[255] See the discussion in Kirk 1976:113ff.

[256] See Lord 1960:78ff., which notes that the epic of a lesser poet (2294 verses) became tripled in extent in spite of the fact that the more noteworthy *guslar* who was to perform it had not heard the song previously and, indeed, had to sing it immediately after having heard it for the first time.

[257] See on this Engnell 1945:39-44; and Nielsen 1954:18-38, esp.p.37.

controlled each other's results; this postulate must then be used to explain the "fact" that the tradition is reliable.

The question of the verbatim accuracy of oral tradition is hardly so simple; every case it must be answered with studies in detail of the practices within a particular society and at a particular time. The *guslars* who were studied by Parry clearly knew nothing of any demand for accuracy; on the other hand, they proved able to preserve *their own poems* almost unchanged (but, however, only almost) for many years, but as far as the poems of others were concerned there was no verbatim tradition from one poet to another[258]. It would appear that OT scholars have confused two categories of oral poets in ancient Greece, namely the so-called ῥαψῳδός, *rhapsode*, with the ἀοιδός, or *singer*. The former was the preserver of tradition in the time subsequent to Homer. There is reason to believe that the activities of the rhapsode were in principle controllable, precisely for the reason that the Homeric poems already existed in written form (only a very few scholars would maintain today that much time elapsed between the time these poems were composed and the point at which they were written down[259], while the singer was a poet pure and simple, as Homer was[260].

The classical account of Israelite oral tradition was published by Gunkel[261]; in this connection there are considerable differences between the first and third editions of his commentary on Genesis. The third edition has often been held to reveal Gunkel's dependence on the studies of the Danish folklorist, A. Olrik. Gunkel had made acquaintance with Olrik's *epic laws* via the German edition of his work[262]. However, S.M. Warner has recently studied the relationship between Gunkel and Olrik, only to arrive at the conclusion that in reality Olrik's theories had no relation to Gunkel's understanding of folklore materials[263]. This should be obvious, since Olrik was in fact an opponent of the German folkloristic scholarship of his day[264]. In recent times, Olrik's laws have been revived and employed by Van Seters in order to determine whether the traditions about Abraham are of oral or written origin[265]. Van Seters' use of Olrik's laws has been criticized by Warner, who, however, does not object to Van Seters' conclusion, namely that the process of tradition in question was a written one. In fact, Warner agrees with Van Seters on this point[266]; however, he also questions the relevance of Olrik's laws and, much as we might expect, he notes that these laws can hardly be held to be completely valid today[267].

[258] See the discussion of this in Kirk 1976:119ff. and 133ff. Of course, one ought not to overlook the fact that the ideal of the Serbo Croatian *guslars* is verbatim reproduction. Ideals, however, are apparently one thing, and reality quite another.

[259] Cf. Kirk 1976:129ff., but see also M. Skafte Jensen, who stresses that one must not exaggerate the differences between the ῥαψῳδός and the ἀοιδός in Homer's day. In the period of the rhapsode, the poems had already achieved fixed literary form, even though the rhapsode, too, was an oral poet (1980: 121-124).

[260] Kirk reckons the *guslars* to be the closest approximations to the rhapsodes, rather than to the singers (of whose number Homer was one), who were independently creative poets, but once again consult Skafte Jensen 1980:123.

[261] 1917:VIIIff.LVI-LXXX.

[262] Olrik 1909*; I have utilized the latest Danish edition: Olrik 1921:66-82.

[263] Warner 1979:331.

[264] Cf. H. Ellekilde in Olrik 1921:28-29, as well as Olrik's own defense of the "Finno-Danish method" (1921:142-143).

[265] 1975:158-164.

[266] 1979:332ff.

[267] 1979:333f., and see the evaluation of them in Thompson 1946:455ff.

On the other hand, we must be fair to Olrik. One might have wished that instead of merely examining the epic laws Warner had also proceeded to study the practical application of them in folklore research. This is not an unreasonable demand, since Olrik's major work (Dan. title: *Danmarks Heltedigtning*) is readily available in English translation[268]. Had he done so, Warner would have avoided the cheap sort of argument that attributes opinions to Olrik (such as, for example, the contention that the latter was influenced by *"a superorganic anthropological view-point"*[269]) which do not figure in his studies.

Like most of the folklore research of his day, Olrik's work was primarily based on the analysis of texts, which means that he was forced to study *oral* tradition on the basis of *written* sources. Thus, in actuality he had at best a poor knowledge of the practical aspects of oral tradition. Practical field studies of this type of tradition were almost wholly lacking at the time. The situation has changed dramatically since Olrik's day, mainly because of M. Parry's extensive studies of Serbo Croatian heroic poetry. These studies were undertaken in the period between the two World Wars, but they were unfortunately never completed because of Parry's early death[270]. Since this initial effort a number of investigations of the uses of oral tradition in traditional socie-ties have appeared. All of these have been based on actual fieldwork in such societies; they have also covered both prose traditions and epic poetry[271]. Parry's most important contribution is acknowledged to be his proposal of an *"oral formulaic theory"*. In brief, this theory states that an orally transmitted narrative (a heroic poem) is recreated on each occasion when it is performed. However, this is not a matter of original creation, since the individual singer makes use of estab-lished formulas which often make up a very large part, if not the largest, of the epic in question. The contribution of the poet consists mainly of the structuring of his work.

This theory signified a decisive turning point in the study of Homer (Parry's studies of Serbo Croatian heroic poetry were a result of his preoccupation with the Homeric poems), as is indi-cated by the recently released collection of essays on Homer and oral tradition published by J. Lactacz[272]. In this collection both the articles and the table of contents are divided into sections dependent on whether the subjects in question appeared prior or subsequent to Parry's work in Jugoslavia. Within the field of Homer studies, Parry's investigations led to a reappraisal of Homer as a traditional poet. However, it should be noted that the optimistic attempts to under-stand the fixed elements of tradition in the Homeric poems as historical recollections were gene-rally put to shame after the decipherment of the *linear B* tablets deriving from the palace culture of the Mycenaean-Minoan civilization. After the decipherment it speedily became clear that there was a vast difference between the culture reflected in the *linear B* tablets and the social system described in the Homeric poems[273].

In OT research, however, scholars have only made use of Parry's "oral formulaic theory" to a limited extent, and the main efforts in this direction have come from America. These efforts have been only slightly successful, in spite of the fact that already in 1963 R.C. Culley published an account of Parry's (and Lord's) works[274]. What is mostly of interest for our purposes is the question of the historical content of oral traditions, as well as the problem of the relationship be-tween oral and written tradition in the OT. On the latter subject I shall confine myself to referr-ing to the lengthy discussion between D.M. Gunn and Van Seters[275]. On the question of the

---

[268] Olrik 1903;1910; English trans. in Olrik 1919.

[269] 1979:334-335.

[270] In 1935; Parry's notes have only been published in part (Parry and Lord 1953; 1954), but a number of his individual studies have been collected in Parry 1971. There is also a relatively accessible summary by Lord 1960.

[271] These researches have been surveyed by Culley 1976A, and by Long 1976B.

[272] Lactacz 1979. See also Kirk 1976, and above all Skafte Jensen 1980.

[273] See above, n.184.

[274] Culley 1963; Coote 1976; Wittig 1976, as well as the reply by Lord (1976). See also Cul-ley 1976B:20-25.

[275] This was inaugurated by Van Seters' attempt to characterize the OT battle narrative as a scribal convention (1972B). This was countered by Gunn (1974A; 1974B). The discussion con-tinued in Van Seters 1975, which reveals the limitations of Van Seters' understanding of oral tradition; cf. Warner 1979. The debate has continued in Van Seters 1976 and Gunn 1976A, and,

historical contents of oral traditions, Culley has changed direction on a couple of occasions. Culley took his point of departure in a well known study by the Dutch anthropologist J. Vansina[276]; Vansina's view (which Culley shares) is that we cannot *categorically* dismiss the possibility that oral traditions *may* contain relevant historical recollections. On the other hand, Culley is fully aware that it is very difficult to control the historical basis of orally transmitted narratives. He also cites many types of fallacious information found in oral sources, including their propensity to confuse different events and persons, and to have disordered chronologies, not least because of the ever-present tendency to foreshorten (telescope) a lengthy period of time.

I shall not continue this discussion at any greater length, and will instead merely state, own view, namely that when we encounter an oral tradition (which in connection with the OT always means that we find it in written form, which is, in other words, against its nature) we cannot count on the accuracy of other elements in the tradition than the main plot. For example, in connection with the Ehud narrative in Jdg 3,12-30 we should ignore the details, including such names as Ehud and Eglon, or even, for that matter, Israel and Moab. Thus we would no longer automatically be able to assign a particular milieu to this narrative of the period of the Judges. It might just as easily be pre-Israelite, but assimilated into Israelite tradition. It might just as easily derive from the period of the monarchy, although the oral tradition has assigned it to the period of the Judges. In short, we have no way whatsoever, to determine whether any historical tradition at all underlies the narrative in Jdg 3,12-30, as long as we lack other sources. Precisely the same judgement applies to most of the other traditions in the Book of Judges[277]. In other words, I agree with Van Seters' concluding remarks on the Abraham traditions, namely that it is possible that it was first the hand of the Yahwistic author which made Abraham the subject of these stories, since we have no way of associating the figure of Abraham with the stories which are told about him before the phase of Yahwistic redaction[278].

---

in conjunction with the Davidic traditions, in Gunn 1976B and Van Seters 1981. Throughout the discussion, Van Seters has continued to insist that we have to do with written tradition.

[276] Culley 1972; cf. Vansina 1965.

[277] Naturally, this applies especially to the Samson traditions, but also to the Gideon narratives and even to those dealing with the victory of Deborah and Barak over the Canaanites (in spite of Jdg 5).

[278] Van Seters 1975:309. A different evaluation is offered by Warner 1977, who argues for the notion of a patriarchal age, since we have not as yet developed sufficient criteria for judging the relationship of the oral tradition to history. One might be tempted to suspect that one's willingness to use uncertainty as an argument in a historical reconstruction is more of a psychological than a methodological problem. However, it is obviously methodologically preferable to take an "agnostic" position, that is, to maintain that as long as the historical contents of a patriarchal tradition cannot be demonstrated with reasonable certainty, then it would be more correct to ignore the patriarchs and their era as a historically verifiable phenomenon. See also Miller 1977C, with whose evaluation of the study of the sources I am in complete agreement (Miller 1977C:65: "In evaluating written sources, ancient and modern, it is rarely a matter of deciding whether a particular document is trustworthy for historical reconstruction, but of determining its degree of credibility and the kind of historical information which legitimately can be derived from it."

This brings us to the end of our search for an evaluation of the origins and character of the historical traditions of ancient Israel. Earlier in this investigation I posed the question, "In what phase of the history of Israel did the concept of a common prehistory for the entire Israelite people emerge as the guideline for historical writing in the OT?" My first answer to this question is that *on no account were the basic preconditions present for the emergence of the concept of Israel as a unity before the period of the monarchy*. Furthermore, *on no account could this concept of a united Israel have resulted in pan-Israelite historical writing before the time of the Exile*. This does not mean that traditions concerning the prenational period were unknown before the beginning of the Exile. Many such traditions clearly existed, but with a very few exceptions it is extremely difficult, not to say impossible, for us to say anything definite about the appearance of these traditions prior to their written fixation.

Thus we are forced to conclude that as far as the use of the OT historical traditions is concerned, the fathers of the revolution hypothesis have built their castle on sand. Their view that the period fo the Judges was the time when these historical traditions crystallized is quite impossible. On the other hand, this is not the only difficulty confronting the adherents of the revolution hypothesis. It remains to be proved just how much of the information in our late sources may be used to reconstruct pre-monarchical Israel. Such an analysis could only be carried out by a very careful traditio-historical study of all the narratives concerning the pre-monarchical period. It is far from certain that such an analysis would lead to any positive result, in the sense that we may never know whether one or another narrative contains a historical nucleus deriving from a pre-national society. But if this accurately describes the state of affairs, then we are also forced to conclude that the OT contains very few concrete recollections which might be used with confidence to reconstruct Israel's past. To put the matter another way, we cannot write a history of Israel which goes back before about 1000, although this, of course, does not exclude the possibility that we may find information in the late historical materials relating to fundamental features and perhaps individual situations from the pre-national society.

The result of these views could well be the atomization of prenational Israelite society, as Gottwald has claimed, and that we should be unable to propose an integrated model of Israelite society, as Bächli has demanded. It would be possible to criticize my conclusions on these grounds, but such criticism would be unwarranted. My view, which leaves in ruins the OT description of Israel as a society which functioned as a unit, also provides a new model for the social system prevalent in most of Palestine in the period prior to 1000, since it is no longer necessary to maintain that a specifically Israelite immigration took place at this time. If we would retain the notion of an immigration, we should be forced to demonstrate that some such phenomenon actually occurred in Palestine during the second millennium. The nature of the sources preserved in the OT rules this possibility out of court; an archeological argument would be required.

Chapter 7

FROM THE LATE BRONZE AGE TO THE EARLY IRON AGE: THE ARCHEOLOGICAL EVIDENCE

§ 1

The Bible and Archeology

The fundamental problem to be considered in the introduction to this chapter is that of the confusion of Biblical scholarship with archeology. For its part, archeology attempts to interpret the finds made in Palestine in the light of data in the OT, while the Biblical scholar is for his part prone to use the archeological materials as illustrations or even evidence of the "fact" that the Biblical account may be regarded as an authentic source. The result is, all too frequently, that neither the excavational results nor the OT texts are allowed to speak for themselves. That is, neither class of materials is evaluated by means of the methods appropriate to its interpretation. Even though this confusion between archeology and textual study is psychologically easily intelligible, its results remain unfortunate. This miserable situation is reflected in the state in which Palestinian archeology has found itself for quite some time. In spite of the fact that for more than a century scholars have excavated in Palestine more intensively than they have anywhere else in the world, it would be extraordinarily difficult to discern a clear synthesis with respect to the situation during the critical years around 1200, when Israel is supposed to have arrived in the land.

It is symptomatic that few efforts have been made to describe this epoch as an archeological phase rather than a historical period[1]. The reason for this seems to be the fact that some archeologists appear to find it more fascinating to hunt for "proof" of the presence of Israel, since even the most minute changes in architecture, pottery, town lay-out, and so forth, have been taken to show the presence of new (foreign) elements among the existing population at this time[2]. If a destruction layer is uncovered in the towns and cities of the

---

[1] In this respect it is merely a question of degree which separates the two most important surveys of the archeology of Palestine, namely Albright 1949:110ff. and Kenyon 1965:195ff. (1979:180ff.), in spite of the fact that they are frequently taken to be diametrical opposites.

[2] Of course, this is a serious accusation, but no one who has every studied a reference work like EAEHL or the current reports of archeological excavations in a given two-year sequence of Israel Exploration Journal can fail to be struck by the boldness with which many contributors characterize one or another phenomenon as a result of early Israelite activity.

13th century, it is held to be clear that the Israelites were the cause (indeed, it is possible that the very dates assigned to such destruction layers derive from the wish to find a connection with the Settlement[3]). A description of the transition between the Late Bronze Age and the Iron Age in Palestine – seen in an international perspective – is definitely a desideratum, as is emphasized by comparison with the situation in other parts of the Mediterranean area, particularly in Greece, in which a number of archeologically based historical surveys have been published over a considerable period of time. A study of even a few of these accounts would be constructive reading for anyone who is familiar with the current discussion of the origins of Israel. I should above all like to recommend A.M. Snodgrass' description of post-Mycenaean Greece as thought-provoking reading for the historian of Palestine[4].

The historical evolution of Greece has traditionally been interpreted in an analogous way to the problems concerning Israel's origins. It has often been claimed that Mycenaean palace culture was capsized by barbarian immigrants towards the close of the 13th century. These newly-arrived barbarians are supposed to have precipitated this previously highly civilized society back into a thoroughly primitive tribal system, or else they compelled the earlier inhabitants to emmigrate. This picture was held to be archeologically demonstrable in the destruction strata found wherever Mycenaean cultural centers existed during the Bronze Age, supported by the discovery of a new material culture which was clearly distinct with respect to pottery and architecture. Finally, it is not to be forgotten that this new immigration seemed to have left evidence behind it in later Greek tradition[5].

Snodgrass' study presents us with quite a different evaluation of the situation. The study contains above all a thorough review of the material cultural remains of the Dark Age which followed the collapse of Mycenaean culture and which stretched from the 12th to the 10th centuries. Snodgrass' main thesis is that the comprehensively destructive Dorian invasion never took place. Instead, it appears that the Mycenaean world suffered some extreme, if transitory, shocks towards the end of the 13th century, after which it declined of its own accord as a result of internal developments in Greece which lasted more than a century. The data which have been taken to indicate an invasion by a foreign people are more probably an indication of local population movements, since the Dorians may at most be described as a population deriving from remote areas of Greece. While the destruction of Mycenaean civilization probably entailed some lesser degree of Mycenaean emmigration, the great Greek colonization of Asia Minor known as the Ionian migration first began several centuries after the collapse of the palace culture.

Snodgrass is nevertheless prepared to retain the notion of the period subsequent to the destruction of Mycenaea as a dark age, and he accepts the idea that a clear break occurred in the culture at this time. However, he emphasizes that these developments were not the result of foreign elements, but a break brought about by the local population. Its result was a general impoverishment of the society which is discernible throughout the material culture. A new social pattern also arose, as well as changes in the patterns of trade and the industrial system, accom-

---

[3] The exceptions are the sites where it is impossible to deny that we have to do with evidence of the Sea Peoples, particularly in cases in which there is no agreement between a destruction layer and the Biblical Settlement narrative, as is the case in Gezer. In connection with Gezer, W.G. Dever mentions the Israelites as the possible cause of the destruction of the town in the Late Bronze Age, in spite of the fact that the OT knows nothing of this event (1976B:439); this also applies to such coastal towns as Ashdod and Dor.

[4] Snodgrass 1971. One ought also to consult Crossland and Birchall 1974, which also esp. contains Evans 1974; on the transition between the Late Bronze and Iron Ages, see esp. Tritsch 1974.

[5] For an evaluation of the classical tradition, see Snodgrass 1971:2-10.

panied by, above all, a drastic fall in population, which first began to reverse itself in the 8th century[6].

There is no point in continuing my discussion of the merits and possible demerits of Snodgrass' account. I have chosen his study simply as an example of an interpretation of archeological materials which, had it been undertaken in Palestine, could easily have provided the sole basis for a discussion of Israel's origins. Snodgrass does not deny that changes in the material culture occurred in Greece during the Dark Age, nor that towns were destroyed, or that some reconstruction took place according to principles which differed from those previously adhered to, to mention but a few examples. Nevertheless, his main hypothesis is that it was fundamentally the same culture which prevailed in Greece, also during the so-called Dark Age.

By way of comparison, what is the situation of Palestinian archeology? How is the situation with respect to the continuity of the material culture? What relationship obtains between the destruction layers and the continued inhabitation of a number of "Canaanite" towns? Are there indications of new settlements? Finally, what are the demands levied upon those who attempt to find archeological criteria for evaluating Israel's presence in the country? Each of these questions deserves a monograph, but for the purposes of this treatment we shall confine ourselves to a presentation of these questions and a sketch intended to answer some of the main problems.

It is methodologically important to attempt to emphasize the differences between Palestine during the Late Bronze Age and the beginning of the Iron Age in order to arrive at a decision in principle as to whether we have to do with a single culture, which continued in one form or another (perhaps, along different lines than previously), or whether there is reason to believe that Iron Age Palestine reveals evidence of a new culture. In short, our methodological approach resembles Alt's territorial-historical method. Alt attempted to reveal the presence of the Israelites by demonstrating that the pattern of settlement in the country changed during the Iron Age. However, he did not consider whether this new settlement pattern constituted a cultural break with the past or merely continued the earlier Bronze Age culture according to new premises, which perhaps are reflected in the types of settlements of the Iron Age. Naturally, it was impossible for Alt to obtain a clear picture of these matters, since his topographical studies were based on the written sources within and outside of the OT. He did not have access to archeological materials capable of illuminating the demographic differences.

My first point will not require much space: the question of the connection between archeology and the OT text. I have already criticized the pervasive mania within certain archeological circles for corrolating text and excavation before either the text or the excavation has had an opportunity to speak for itself. Already my demonstration in the preceding chapter of this work that the historical tradition was a late phenomenon should caution us against using the

---

[6] Snodgrass 1971:360ff. One of the results of the new situation was a drastic decline in the population during the 11th century; according to Snodgrass, this led to an equally abrupt increase in the 8th century (1971:365-367).

OT as some sort of *checklist*, which might enable us to say whether an event took place or not. This search for external evidence has also been renounced by numerous scholars, including several whose field is the archeology of Palestine[7]. In practice the credibility of this approach has also been undermined decisively by the demonstration that there are numerous disagreements between the OT texts dealing with Israel's immigration and the excavational results. These disagreements have been pointed out in many works, so that I may confine my account here to a brief résumé based on an article by J.M. Miller[8]. Miller mentions only two sites in which it appears to be possible to make the Biblical and archeological data agree with one another, namely Hazor and Lachish, both of which seem to have been destroyed around 1200[9]. However, we should also note that some scholars remain who doubt whether Lachish is really identical with *Tell ed-Duweir.*

Most recently, G.W. Ahlström has argued against this identification[10], mainly on the grounds of the information provided by Eusebius[11]. He also mentions a number of strategic considerations, such as the fact that if Tell ed-Duweir was Lachish, then there must have been a hole in Rehoboam's chain of defenses in the south between Adoraim and Tell ed-Duweir. As an alternative Ahlström suggests *Tell Eitun* (Palestine Grid 1432 0999), although this is a gratuitous suggestion, since nothing is known of this site. Nor does the information contained in the famous Lachish ostracon (Nr.IV) solve the problem[12]. The letter may have been sent to Lachish because its sender, Hoshaiah, wished to receive signals from Lachish but was unable to see any, despite the fact that Lachish was on his line of sight. The letter may also have been sent to Tell ed-Duweir, that is, the town NN, from an outpost who is reporting that he cannot see Lachish and is urgently awaiting the signals from the site. The latter explanation is the more inviting, for why would Hoshaiah request Lachish to send up smoke signals if he was at the same time able to communicate with the town in writing? On the other hand, the letter could just as easily have been sent by an over-cautious picket who is merely reporting back to his base that he is still looking for signals from Lachish (i.e., Tell ed-Duweir), as ordered. Ahlström's final aggument is that one cannot see Azekah (i.e., *Tell ez-Zakerije*) from Tell ed-Duweir. I can personally confirm this point on the basis of observations undertaken in Azekah in extremely clear weather in November, 1974, as well as several visits to Tell ed-Duweir[13]. But what about smoke-signals?.
A study of the terrain based on the map, *Palestine 1:100,000,* explains the problems involved. Azekah is situated 325m above sealevel, while Tell ed-Duweir is 250m above sealevel. As the crow flies the distance between the two sites is 17.5km. Thus it would be possible for the two sites

---

[7] Thus De Vaux 1970B. See also Miller's contribution to the discussion of Albright's methods (Miller 1979). Noth's reservations about the "Bible and spade" approach are collected in Noth 1971A:I:1-51. See also Soggin 1962, who adheres to a "maximalist" view, since he apparently regards the Biblical tradition as a sort of "cross-off list": in some cases it is falsified, while it is confirmed in others. Soggin relies on the (highly questionable) "balance of probability" principle, which he has borrowed from J. Bright. Emphatically against this norm is M.Liverani; Liverani emphasizes that, as such, "data" must be without contradiction; otherwise they are not "data", but opinions about data. Thus it is incorrect to assert the validity of a theory which only accounts for some of the "data", but not all (1980:29).

[8] 1979:39. Other studies of this complex are to be found in Weippert 1967:124-132, and Miller 1977A:252-262; cf. also Miller 1977B.

[9] See further below, pp. 393ff and 400.

[10] Ahlström 1980.

[11] *Onomasticon* 120:20f.

[12] KAI 194:10-13; cf. ANET[3]:322.

[13] And in spite of the fact the G.I. Davies does not rule out the possibility (1982:27).

to be visible to each other, were it not for the fact that the line of sight is blocked by a hill (pt.273 (138 113), *Tell 'Aner*) which is situated precisely on the line 6 km northeast of Tell ed-Duweir. However, this is not an argument against the identification of Tell ed-Duweir with Lachish[14], since the letter in question does not state that it is possible to see Azekah from Lachish; rather, the idea is clearly that it is possible to see both Lachish and Azekah from Hoshaiah's observation post (Tell 'Aner, be a logical candidate in this connection as the site of this post)[15].

In the cases of both Lachish and Hazor it is clear that reoccupation of these sites took place during the Early Iron Age, not, however, in the form of fortified towns, but as unfortified villages. In both cases doubts have been expressed as to the identity of the conquerors in question[16].

A great number of sites reveal direct disagreement between the OT and archeology. Miller mentions Arad, which was not inhabited from the Early Bronze Age to the 11th century[17]; Heshbon, in the territory east of the Jordan, can hardly have been founded before the end of the 7th century[18]; and there was Jericho, which was not a fortified town in the Late Bronze Age[19]. Nor, for that matter, were Ai, Gibeon[20], or Jarmuth[21] fortified towns in this period. Other towns existed in the Late Bronze Age which were not destroyed during the transition to the Iron Age; this applies to Jerusalem, Hebron, and Debir[22]. Finally, Miller mentions such anomalies as Hormah; towns in this

[14] Contra Ahlström 1980:9.

[15] For criticisms of Ahlström's use of Eusebius, as well as his proposal to identify Lachish with *Tell Eitun*, see Davies 1982.

[16] See below.

[17] On this see Aharoni 1975A:82f.

[18] Cf. Horn 1976:514, but see also Boraas and Geraty 1979:13, who claim that there was a town at this site already in the 12th century. To this it should be noted that the only structure mentioned in Boraas' and Geraty's article which is older than the 7th century is a water reservoir from the 8th century.

[19] Admittedly, Kenyon spoke of the existence of a Late Bronze Age town in *Tell es-Sultan* (1957:261ff.; 1966:208ff.; 1976: 563-564). Nevertheless, no matter how you look at it, there was no more than an unfortified village-like habitation in the 14th century. It was mentioned above, p. 56, that it has been held that erosion during the lengthy period in the Iron Age when the site was unoccupied was responsible for the lack of remains from the Late Bronze Age. Against this, however, see Weippert and Weippert 1976, who have undertaken a new analysis of the earlier excavations and have concluded that Tell es-Sultan was inhabited from the 11th century, and possibly as early as the 12th century, since an unfortified village seems to have been present.

[20] As far as Ai is concerned, the results of the excavations of J. Marquet-Krause in the 1930's have been confirmed by new excavations by J.A. Callaway conducted in 1964-1972. See in brief Callaway 1975 and 1976. See further below for the conditions at *et-Tell* during the Iron Age. For Gibeon, reference should be made to the reports by J.B. Pritchard, and in particular to his conclusions in Pritchard 1962:157f.

[21] Jarmuth was identified with *Hirbet Jarmuk* (Palestine Grid 1475 1240). However, the exploratory excavations around 1970 revealed that the tell can scarcely have been inhabited during the Late Bronze Age or in Iron I. It is hardly surprising that this conclusion disagrees with the Biblical account when we consider the similar situation elsewhere. However, if the *"Jaruma"* mentioned in to so-called "Amarna letter" from *Tell Hesi* mentioned by Albright (1942; cf. ANET³:490) is identical with Jarmuth, then Hirbet Jarmuk cannot be identical with Jarmuth, since, as mentioned, the site was uninhabited during the Late Bronze Age. On the excavations see Ben-Tor 1975, and his summary in 1976; but see also Miller, who questions the correctness of Albright's reading of the abovementioned tablet from Tell Hesi (1979:38f.).

[22] Debir is more likely to be identified with *Hirbet Rabūd* than with *Tell Beit Mirsim* (thus Albright), for the reasons proposed by M. Kochavi (1974:26ff.).

class are either impossible to localize, or the relevant candidates could not have been inhabited at the time of the immigration[23]. This also applies to Bethel, which was inhabited furing the Late Bronze and Iron ages, but was destroyed and rebuilt a number of times throughout the entire period[24]. Thus Miller correctly concludes that it is at present impossible to defend the notion of an Israelite *conquest* of Palestine towards the close of the 13th century[25]. On the other hand, he reveals elsewhere that he is still inclined to retain the notion of an Israelite immigration. Miller's model of this immigration follows that of Alt; this orientation seems also to have been followed by some individual Israeli archeologists[26].

Our conclusion is therefore unambiguous: archeology and text may not be subsumed under a single formula. Thus it was correct to dismiss the importance of the Settlement traditions in the OT and to see them instead as expressions of a very late view of the nation's origins which arose in the last part of the monarchical period and particularly in the period after the loss of national independence. The consequences of this fact ought to be taken seriously. It is no longer legitimate to attempt to "save the appearances" of certain portions of the Settlement narratives. Rather, it is the very idea of Settlement, as it appears in the OT, which must be done away with, for historical reasons. In one's reconstruction of the course of events towards the close of the second millennium one ought at least in the first instance to ignore completely the OT traditions, and instead attempt to reconstruct the archeological history of the period without considering whether it was Israelites or Canaanites who were active at one site or another. If an archeological description of the culture of Iron Age Palestine shows that there was continuity between this period and the culture of the Late Bronze Age, then we ought simply to avoid speaking of any concentrated Israelite immigration into the country in the 13th-12th centuries. By "concentrated" I mean the idea of a collected Israelite invasion as well as the notion of an uncoordinated mass immigration of Israelite nomads into the country.

---

[23] Thus, for *example, Tell es-Sab'a* (Tel Beersheba); cf. Simons 1959:145 (§ 137 no.28), which contains no indications of habitation during the Late Bronze Age (cf. Aharoni 1973:1 and 1975B:161), or *Ḥirbet el-Mšaš*, which Aharoni identified with Horma (1967:185) Ḥirbet el-Mšaš (Tell Masos) was also uninhabited during the Late Bronze Age. Aharoni still insisted on this identification in a posthumously published article, but at the same time he drew a number of extensive conclusions concerning the significance of these excavations for the traditions concerning Israel's immigration. Thus he maintained that the narratives in which Horma figures reflect conditions which were much earlier than the Iron and Late Bronze Ages, namely all the way back in the Middle Bronze Age. This means that in the OT we have a collection of traditions of extremely varied age. This in turn entails that it is impossible to reconstruct the Israelite immigration on the basis of the OT traditions. Thus, in the Autumn of his life Aharoni had arrived at a position concerning the Israelite immigration into Palestine which was close to Alt's hypothesis (Aharoni 1976A; cf. also Aharoni in Aharoni, Fritz and Kempinsky 1975:114ff.).

[24] See further below.

[25] 1979:40.

[26] Miller 1977A.

This conclusion leaves two tasks to us. The first of these will be to offer a description of the development of the country prior to the formation of the Israelite state around 1000; the second will be to describe how the ideas recorded in the OT account of Israel's origins came into being. Any confusion between these two approaches will necessarily lead to misleading results.

§ 2

Settlement Pattern I: Introduction

In order to see the developments which occurred during the Iron Age in the right light, one must first take account of the situation in the previous period. In relation to the immediately surrounding periods (i.e., the Middle Bronze and Iron Ages), the Late Bronze Age reveals a notable drop in the number of settlements in Palestine[27]. Not least in the northern part of the central massif, that is, the traditional territories of Ephraim and Manasseh, there is a very clear reduction in the number of sites to perhaps 25% of the previous number; other regions reveal a similar pattern[28]. Thompson suggests that in Late Bronze Age Palestine the rural population moved in the direction of the urban societies; this seems to be correct, and it is not difficult to understand at least one of the reasons for this movement in the population. In relation to the Middle Bronze Age, the Late Bronze period was a difficult one in which to live. Whether it was a matter of the activities of foreign conquerors (i.e., ordinarily the Egyptians during the New Kingdom), or whether it was the continual all-against-all wars among the Palestinian mini-states, the constant wars no doubt made survival in the undefended small societies precarious. This clearly forced the agrarian population to seek the protection of the walls of the cities[29].

During the subsequent period, the Iron Age, this tendency changed dramatically, since we discover at a number of sites that the number of settlements not only equalled, but even surpassed the number existing in the Middle Bronze period. Once again the development in the central mountainous ter-

---

[27] Similar developments have also been observed elsewhere in the Near East during this period; cf. Marfoe 1979:31, fig.9, for *Biqa'* and *Amuq*.

[28] The most important source for the pattern in the central highlands and the Golan region is supposed to be Kochavi 1972*, which has unfortunately not been available to me. This survey may be supplemented by Campbell 1968. As far as the Negev and Sinai are concerned, consult Thompson 1975, and for the eastern side of the Jordan Valley see Ibrahim, Sauer, and Yassine 1976. Fig.9 in Marfoe 1979 arranges the results of these surveys in an easily-grasped scheme.

[29] Thompson 1978A:24ff.; 1979:66.

rain is striking. Thus in connection with numerous recent surveys of the territories of Ephraim and Manasseh we discover that the number of settlements
had increased by 600% already in the Early Iron Age; this tendency continues
into the later Iron Age (the era of the monarchy) until the number present in
the Early Iron period had doubled. Also, the nature of these new settlements
is clear, as most of them were open settlements, that is, villages or only lightly
defended localities[30]. Furthermore, it seems to be characteristic of these
settlements that we encounter them in bunches in the central mountainous
region. Thus there is a bunch northeast of Shechem, another by the Brook of
Kanah, a third near the western edge of the central mountains, a fourth out
towards the coastal plain of the Shephelah, and a fifth in the Ramallah region[31]. The same pattern seems to recur elsewhere in the country, as in the
Galilaean villages discovered by Aharoni[32]. In general it is true of all of the
areas in question (apart from the Negeb and Sinai) that they are characterized
by newly-established village societies. The date of all this activity perhaps falls
towards the close of the 13th century; many are in any case from the beginning
of the 12th century.

§ 3

Settlement Pattern II: the Cities

What was the situation of the larger towns and cities during the period mentioned above? A number of examples will be useful in answering this question.
Every possible reservation should be made in conjunction with the individual
examples, since each description is dependent on the standards adhered to
during the excavation in question, the extensiveness of the excavation reports
(if such exist), and the interpretations of the various sites by the individual
archeologists.

As is well known, the excavator Y. Yadin interpreted the history of Hazor
as an example of the transition between the Late Bronze and Iron Ages on the
basis of the Biblical account of the Settlement, and in particular on the

---

[30] An example of such a sparsely-defended society in the Ephraimite and Manassite territory is the region of Ḥirbet Jānūn, which has been explored by E. Otto (184 173; 184 174; 185 174).
Ḥirbet Jānūn itself, which contains Israelite Janoah, can scarcely have been inhabited before
Iron II; but a "citadel-like" structure slightly to the north seems to date from Iron IA, that is,
from the 12th century; however, it was abandoned before the close of the 12th century. Otto
points to similarities between the pottery found in this structure and that of Hazor XII (1978;
cf. Otto 1979:212-218).
[31] Cf. Garsiel and Finkelstein 1978:193f.
[32] On these see Aharoni 1957; 1967:219-220; and 1976B.

strength of Jos 11. Yadin understood Joshua and his Israelites to be the destroyers of Hazor (stratum XIII)[33]. The date assigned to the fall of the city
was the last part of the 13th century. This interpretation did not go uncontes-
ted, since others, among whom Y. Aharoni was prominent, attempted to up-
date the destruction of Late Bronze Age Hazor to the beginning of the following century[34]. Aharoni based his interpretation on the Galilaean village societies whose presence he had demonstrated; the material culture of these societies is virtually identical with that of the earliest Iron Age inhabitation of
Hazor (stratum XII). In Aharoni's opinion, the villages were founded by
immigrating Israelites; thus Hazor was not destroyed by these Israelites in the
course of their immigration, but as the result of battles, as depicted in Jdg
4-5[35]. Yadin and others, however, do not feel that there is reason to date the
foundation of the villages earlier than the destruction of Hazor. Thus they
regard both the new occupation of Hazor (stratum XII) and the foundation
of the villages as the results of Israelite activity[36]. Thus the problem of the
destruction of Hazor remains unsolved, but it has been additionally complicated by the fact that in the case of Hazor XII the material culture present cannot be described as a complete break with the past. To the contrary, the pottery
tradition of Hazor XII represents a continuation of the tradition of Hazor
XIII[37].

As far as continuity in the settlement pattern of Hazor is concerned, it is to
be seen that on the one hand the lower town was surrendered after the destruction of stratum XIII, while on the other the new construction at the acropolis
of the town did not follow the pattern of Hazor XIII[38]. The reason for these
features may have been that the town was conquered by foreigners who,
having destroyed Hazor XIII, were unfamiliar with the ground plan of the

---

[33] On Hazor: see the excavation reports by Yadin et al.: 1958; 1959; 1961, to which should be
added the important conclusion by Yadin (1972). On the destruction of Hazor XIII (stratigraphy of the upper city), see Yadin 1972:108-109.

[34] See Aharoni 1970:263. He had previously even dated the destruction of Hazor XIII to
the close of the 12th century (1957).

[35] 1957:149f.; 1967:200-208.

[36] Cf. Yadin 1972:131f.

[37] For the relevant materials: in addition to the works of Yadin (mentioned previously), reference should be made to Amiran 1970:191ff. Scholars have placed particular emphasis on the
great *pithoi*; cf. Amiran 1970:pl.77. The model for these is also to be found in Amiran 1970:pl.45
(p.143, which also has a photograph), deriving from Hazor. As Amiran notes, the form in
question is localized to the northern part of the country, and to Hazor in particular, where its
developmental history can be traced all the way back to MB IIC. As far as the Early Iron Age
is concerned this is confirmed by a number or parallels from other sites in the northern part of
the country (Iron I period) cf. Amiran 1970:pl.77). For example, in addition to those found in
Hazor XII there are some from Ḥirbet et-Ṭeleil, Shiloh, Bethel, Beth-Shemesh, Afula,Tell Beit
Mirsim, and *Tell Nasbeh* (one could mention others). On the other hand, only a very few
examples (if any) have been found at Ḥirbet el-Mšaš. General information on the pottery and
the conclusions which may be drawn on the basis of it is available in Franken 1976:8ff. See also
the thorough discussion of the "question of identification" in Liverani 1980:23ff.

[38] That is, if it is at all possible to speak of a structure on Hazor XII.

town and therefore started their rebuilding from scratch. However, other factors could just as easily explain the phenomena in question. When the lower town was abandoned, the survivors of this catastrophe at the end of the Bronze Age might have chosen to settle in the upper town, which might have seemed to offer some hope of security. In Hazor XIII and earlier it is likely that public buildings were predominantly placed in the acropolis. These structures will have been destroyed by the time of Hazor XII; they will in any case have been of only limited usefulness to the society of Hazor XII. Accordingly, the new society would have had little reason to reestablish the structures on the acropolis. Finally, the surviving population did not have the resources to rebuild the city, as is clearly evidenced by the condition of stratum XII[39]. In all likelihood, the rebuilders were relatively few in number; one of the reasons for this was probably a considerable emmigration from the destroyed city. In other words, it would be reasonable to regard the emergence of the same material culture in the newly founded Galilaean villages as the result of the activities of the refugees from Hazor. In conclusion, it should be added that if the connection between the emergence of the villages and the fall of Hazor is established, there is nothing to suggest that the destruction of Hazor XII is to be dated to before 1200. V. Fritz goes so far as to attempt to prove that this can hardly have taken place before 1200-1190; he also emphasizes that this date does not suggest that the Israelites were the authors of the destruction, but more likely the Sea People[40].

My two other examples from the north are Megiddo and Ta'anak. Both display a quite different fate from that of Hazor, since neither was destroyed at the end of the Late Bronze Age, at least, as far as the normal interpretation of the excavations is concerned[41]. Megiddo VIIA is a reconstruction and repairs phase with respect to Megiddo VIIB, which is to be dated to the beginning of the 13th century. Megiddo continued its existence across the divide between the Late Bronze and on into the Iron Age until the middle of the 12th century, when the town was laid waste and subsequently remained abandoned for a period of indeterminate length. The subsequent reconstruction around 1100 made use of new ground plans; the most striking aspect of these was the final abandonment of the *temenos*-area in the new town (stratum VIB). The pottery from Megiddo VIB by no means suggests that it was the Philistines who reestablished the town. Furthermore, the surrender of the previously sacred area implies that the new population were not descendants of the earlier population. It remains uncertain whether it was Israelites or Canaanites from other parts of the country who were behind the reconstruction.

---

[39] Cf. Yadin 1972:129, who lists hut-foundations, hearths, and victual shafts as charactistic of the remains of Hazor XII, although no permanent structures have been discovered.

[40] 1973:134ff. But see also Kenyon 1979:209, which sets the date for the destruction of Hazor to 1275 on the basis of the similarities between the latest LB stratum and the stratum immediately preceding it, as well as the very modest presence of Mycenaean IIIB pottery.

[41] On the stratigraphy of Megiddo in the period 1300-1100, see Aharoni and Yadin 1977.

The date of the destruction of Megiddo VIIA was arrived at on the basis of the discovery of a statue base bearing the cartouche of Rameses VI[42]. Since an early contribution of Albright[43], scholars have maintained that there was an interval between Megiddo VIIA and VIB. This has been emphatically denied by Kenyon[44], who has claimed to the contrary that the city was reconstructed *immediately* after its destruction. Aharoni agrees with this[45]; he additionally dates the destruction to 1130. With respect to the pottery Kenyon emphasizes that Megiddo VIB is a direct continuation of VIIA[46]. This might suggest that it was the inhabitants of the destroyed Megiddo who continued to dwell at the site, but this would nevertheless lead us to ask why the sacred area was abandoned after over a thousand years of continuous use. Was this because it had fallen in disgrace as a result of a social or religious revolution? Alternatively, was it because the inhabitants of Megiddo VIB were not descendants of Megiddo VII's population, but perhaps derived from an area in the vicinity that knew nothing of the sacred area? Finally, is it not also possible that foreign conquerors had desecrated the sacred area in such a way that it was no longer possible to use it? Any attempt to answer this and similar questions would be sheer guesswork. M. Ottoson seems inclined to assign to the Israelites the blame for the nullification of the traditions of sacred areas in such localities as Megiddo, Hazor, Shechem, and Beth-Shan (*Upper Level* V)[47]. As far as the date of the destruction of the city is concerned, it must be recognized that the statue base from VIIA only gives us a *terminus a quo* for this event to around 1150; it does not say very much in the direction of a *terminus ante quem*. The eagerness of Albright and others to find an interval in the period of habitation is presumably explained by the fact that they interpreted the finds in Megiddo on the basis of preconceived notions as to the significance of the events underlying the Song of Deborah, rather than proceeding in the opposite direction.

Unlike Megiddo, it can be said that Ta'anach does not represent continuity between the Bronze and Iron Ages, since this town was in ruins throughout most of the Late Bronze Age. Around 1200 it seems to have been rebuilt as a fortified town which, however, only survived until the close of the 12th century. It is uncertain whether Ta'anach was destroyed at the same time as Megiddo VIIA or somewhat later, but in any case the town was not rebuilt again during the Early Iron Age[48].

Thus there seems to be no established pattern concerning the fortunes of the northern towns around 1200, but before we proceed to draw conclusions from this fact (conclusions which may be supplemented by the inclusion of other sites from the northern part of the country; in this connection Dan, Beth-Shan, and *Tell Qeisan* would be obvious choices) it would be appropriate to examine some other localities. The first such example is Shechem. The problems connected with the stratigraphy of the town have hardly been clarified. Should we follow the opinion of G.E. Wright, the American scholar largely responsible for the excavation of the town, Shechem survived the uneasy period which characterized the beginnings of the Iron Age, only to be burned

---

[42] Cf. Lamon and Shipton 1939:7. Rameses VI reigned from ca. 1156 to 1148.

[43] Albright 1936; 1937. Cf. Wright 1950:233.

[44] 1965:232. In a later publication Kenyon was less inclined to be categorical, and instead merely confined herself to the remark that Megiddo VIB followed the destruction of VIIA (1979: 226).

[45] In Aharoni and Yadin 1977:850.

[46] See already Simons 1942.

[47] 1980:107f.

[48] On Ta'anach reference should be made to Lapp 1964; 1967; 1969, plus 1975:91-103. See also Glock 1978.

down a century later, that is, around 1100. Wright associated this destruction with the depredations of Abimelech in this area[49].

However, there is reason to question Wright's dates, which are mainly based on his excavations in the *temenos*-area in Shechem. Around 1970, Wright's efforts were followed up by a number of excavations in an area adjacent to the *temenos*-area (field XIII); these were undertaken specifically with the intention of clarifying the stratigraphy. Their results suggest that Shechem was more likely to have been destroyed earlier than 1100[50]. As J. Bimson has emphasized, the destruction of the town probably took place around 1200, or in any event not very late in the 12th century[51]. This acknowledgement immediately raises difficulties for the traditions about Israel in the period of the Judges, since Shechem does not seem to have re-emerged as a town (although it may have done so as an undefended settlement) before the time of the Israelite monarchy[52]. Bimson accordingly concludes – probably correctly – that if the events which are related in Jdg 9 have any historical basis, then they are to be assigned to the time prior to 1200.

Alternatively, if there was any compelling reason to do so, one could always maintain that the destruction around 1200 was in fact the result of Abimelech's activities. E. Otto argues additionally that a small layer of destruction in the habitation quarters of Shechem in the 14th century derives from the events narrated in Gen 34, that is, when the "Jacob clan" annihilated Canaanite Shechem[53]. This example is unfortunately typical of Otto's work, in which a minute literary critical analysis is invariably directly associated with the results of archeological soundings. The rationale underlying this method, which in many respects resembles that of Albright, is an unshakeable faith in the notion that once one has arrived at the original nucleus of an OT tradition by literary critical means, one has also arrived at historical information. A similar sort of blind reliance on the accuracy of the OT tradition is evidenced by Bimson, who, however, is more in the nature of a quasi-fundamentalist, as he only occasionally allows for doubt concerning the historicity of the Biblical tradition[54].

Bimson, however, nevertheless manages to present a treatment of conditions in Palestine

---

[49] Cf. Wright 1965:101-102, and compare Campbell and Ross 1963: 285-291.

[50] On field XIII: Campbell, Ross, and Toombs 1971, plus Seger 1972. The most recent summary is that of Toombs 1979.

[51] Bimson 1978:109-110. Wright arrived at his date of 1100 via an analysis of the pottery found in pits which had been dug in the floor of *temenos* 9; this pottery derived from Iron IA. Wright accordingly concluded that this material belonged to the destruction layer. However, it would be most correct, with Bimson, to emphasize that the pottery must belong to the period when the shafts were in use, that is, in the 12th century, for which reason the destruction of *temenos* 9 must have been still earlier. On the stratigraphy see now Toombs 1976 and 1979; Toombs maintains that Shechem was deserted from around 1150/1125 to 975 (see his scheme published in Toombs 1976: 58; 1979:78). Thus also Kenyon 1979:342. Nevertheless, Toombs retains Wright's interpretation of the destruction, and in reality he also adheres to Wright's date. Otto has no hesitation about dating the latest LB layer, that is, stratum IIB, to 1350-1200 (1979: 109).

[52] Cf. Toombs 1976:59. Permanent structures seem first to reappear in the 10th century, in which period it seems as if the architectural tradition had suffered a decisive break. Thus the sacred *temenos* area was used as a warehouse in this period, and a "four room house" was located in the site of the earlier *migdal* temple (Wright 1965:145ff. and fig.73).

[53] 1979:179f.

[54] Bimson 1978.

around 1200 based on archeological evidence which this writer is largely able to follow[55]. The reason he is able to do so is that he attempts to preserve the the notion of a collected Israelite conquest of the country, but one which took place already at the close of the 15th century. This date is arrived at with the aid of a detailled, but strained effort to date the close of the Middle Bronze Age to 1450-1400. However, the problem created by an ultraconservative reconstruction like Bimson's is an old one: if Israel had marched into Palestine with her banners flying as early as 1430 (Bimson's date), then whatever became of this "Israel" fifty years later? It seems inconceivable that we should have no evidence of this "Israel" at all preserved in the Amarna correspondence, which was written during the first fifty years after Bimson's Conquest (it might also be added that Bimson's treatment of the ḥabiru problem is hardly satisfactory; symbollically enough, he has hidden it in an appendix)[56].

In Bethel, somewhat farther to the south, we have a town which tells a different story from that of Shechem, since according to its excavators, W.F. Albright and J.L. Kelso, it appears to have been inhabited throughout most of the Late Bronze Age and the whole of the Iron Age[57]. In the couse of the Late Bronze Age the town was destroyed twice, once at the close of the 14th century, and again at the end of the 13th century. According to the excavators, the second destruction of the town was a complete annihilation of Late Bronze Age Bethel. The newly constructed town in Iron I, the 12th century, was held to represent a completely new culture. However, the excavation report of Albright and Kelso leaves doubt as to whether they mean something more than just that the Iron Age town was a significantly poorer community than its Bronze Age predecessor, or whether this case too is an example of continuity[58]. In this connection it should be noted that the Bethel report observes a decline in the material culture already as early as the youngest stratum from the Late Bronze Age[59]. Finally, it cannot be determined with certainty as to whether the Bethel of Iron I was a fortified town, or whether it was not rather an open village like nearby Ai[60].

---

[55] Bimson 1978:48-65.

[56] Bimson 1978:241-247.

[57] On Bethel, see Kelso 1968; there is also a short survey in Kelso 1975. For Bethel in the Late Bronze and Iron I epochs, see Kelso 1958:28-35.

[58] Note Kelso 1968:32: "We have never seen indications of a more destructive conflagration in any Palestinian excavation...". Unlike the well constructed Late Bronze Age town, the Bethel of Iron I may be characterized as a collection of "ramshackle huts" (1975:192), accompanied by a decline in the rest of the material culture. Thus the cultural break seems to have been total. On the other hand, Albright wrote of the settlements of the "newly arrived" Israelites in Bethel and on Tell Beit Mirsim that, "When they (the Israelites) occupied a Canaanite patrician house, as happened at Bethel and Tell Beit Mirsim, they kept the old ground plan with little change, but the mode of construction and details of the resulting plan were as different as the inventory of the house". In other words, in spite of the frequently described enormous layer of destruction which separates Late Bronze Age Bethel from the Bethel of the Early Iron Age, the *new* settlers nevertheless retained the old Late Bronze Age ground plan from the Late Bronze Age - at least partially - until the close of Iron I (cf. Kelso 1968:35). The pottery has been described by Kelso in Kelso 1968:58-66 (with plates). However, it is immediately obvious both on the basis of the texts and the illustrations, that the Iron I pottery generally continued the tradition from the Late Bronze Age, although the quality was poorer. It is also noted that the quality continued to decline throughout Iron I, phases 1-3 (cf. Kelso 1968:63).

[59] Kelso 1968:31.

There is apparently some agreement between conditions in Shechem and Bethel, since both were laid waste around 1200. On the other hand, Bethel continued to be inhabited down into the Iron Age, whereas Shechem reveals a hiatus, that is, provided the excavator has interpreted his materials correctly. In any event, there seems to be evidence of human activity on the site in the Iron Age, since a number of pits had been dug in the Late Bronze Age layer in the temple area. Other areas contained similar traces dating from the same period; in some cases these are related to at least a temporary inhabitation of the sites in question[61].

We have some notion of the state of affairs in connection with the town of Debir, in the southwestern part of the Judaean mountains[62]. In the western part of the Judaean mountainous region, the Debir of the Late Bronze Age was founded at the transition between the 14th and 13th centuries. However, this town did not suffer the same fate as that of the northern towns. It continued to be a fortified town with a cultural continuum until Iron II, that is, some time in the period of the monarchy[63]. If we press farther on into the Shephelah in order to include *Tell beit Mirsim* which was for many years ordinarily held to be identical with Debir[64], we discover a wholly different situation. According to Albright, who excavated the site, this Late Bronze Age town was founded in the middle of the 15th century, but was completely destroyed towards the end of the 13th century[65]. In the beginning of the Iron Age the

---

[60] The description of the walls of Bethel during Iron I (Kelso 1968:18) is exceptionally unclear. The walls of Bethel were constructed in MB IIB (Albright's division). They apparently continued to be used until Byzantine times, although not at all places (note the remark about an Iron I house which seems to have been constructed across the southern wall). It is further noted that the breaches in the MB IIB wall, which have been held to have arisen in conjunction with the destruction of the Late Bronze Age town, were repaired in places. The authors of these repairs are said to have been Israelites, although no date for the repairs is suggested.

[61] Thus at Tell Beit Mirsim; cf. Albright 1943:1ff. At Lachish this sort of construction figures as an interim stratum, although it is more in the nature of a precursor of the Iron II activity at the site (stratum V) than a direct consequent of the Late Bronze Age town (stratum VI); see thus Ussishkin 1978:26-27.92. At Hazor, however, these constructions are taken to be characteristic of the earliest Iron Age stratum, stratum XII (Yadin 1972:129), and at Tel Dan similar conditions are found at the same time as at Hazor. See also the noteworthy silo in Tel Dan locus 3127, Area Y; see Biran 1977:245 and 1980:173f. (with a photograph of the contents in Biran 1980:176). Note the description of stratum VI (Iron I) in Biran 1976:54: "pits and silos are the main features of the first Iron Age level (stratum VI)". In the same passage Biran also calls our attention to the similarities between Dan VI and Hazor XII.

[62] Sources: Kochavi 1974; 1978. Palestine Grid 1515 0933.

[63] Kochavi 1974:28f., which makes some concessions to the view of the Settlement advocated by Israeli scholars. It is also noted that the Late Bronze Age walls continued in use until the 9th century. On the other hand, the report maintains complete silence about any destruction of Debir in connection with an Israelite "Conquest" of the site. Note further the results of Kochavi's trench A, in which the Iron I layer (A4) immediately succeeds the youngest of the Late Bronze Age strata (LB 1; 1974:12).

[64] This has been maintained since Albright 1924.

[65] Cf. Albright 1932B:53ff.

town was an undefended settlement until around 1100, when it was recon-structed as a Philistine town[66].

A similar fate struck Lachish, situated somewhat farther to the north; this Late Bronze Age town seems to have been destroyed at the same time, or per-haps slightly later than Tell beit Mirsim[67]. In this case no new habitation took place previous to Israelite times, that is, the period of the monarchy[68]. As far as both towns are concerned, scholars were quick to associate the destruction of these Bronze Age societies with the Israelite conquest of the country[69]. However, there is no reason why the agents of destruction in question could not have been the Sea People, even though neither of them was immediately rebuilt by the Philistines[70]. Even farther to the north the Late Bronze Age town of Gezer fell around 1200, but was speedily rebuilt. The American exca-vators of the town have not hesitated to label the following three strata in the town for Philistine[71].

Already this limited selection of sites permits us to draw certain conclusions. There is no doubt that as a whole the period around 1200 was a difficult one for the Palestinian towns and cities. A number of these experienced violent destruction, so that they were abandoned for varying lengths of time, or else they were replaced by materially much poorer constructions. However, as a number of earlier accounts have noted, this materially poorer culture is not synonymous with a new culture; it is instead a result of the far less favorable conditions which characterized the Iron Age societies[72]. The reasons for this will be discussed in the conclusions which I shall draw at the end of this study, but in this context it would be worthwhile to note that Iron Age towns do not contain features which cannot be explained or understood as continuations of features of Late Bronze Age culture, with the exception of the sites at which the presence of the Philistines is indicated by the presence of their special pottery.

In the case of Bethel it was noted that in the second phase of the Late Bronze Age this town was characterized by increasing poverty compared with its si-

---

[66] However, Albright does note (1932B:52) that, "There was no interval of abandonment between C (LB) and B (Jer I)".

[67] The conclusions of the earlier English excavators of the site (concerning which, see Tufnell 1953; 1958) seem to have been confirmed by the recent Israeli excavations in the 1970's; cf. Ussishkin 1978, as well as Ussishkin 1977. On the date of the fall of Lachish, see Albright 1935:13-14. See also Albright 1938:79, where the writer claims that the pottery from graves be-longing to inhabitants who immediately succeeded the destruction of Late Bronze Age Tell Beit Mirsim is contemporary with pottery deriving from Lachish' final phase in the Late Bronze Age. It should also be noted that neither Tufnell nor the Israeli excavators attempt to set so definite a date for the destruction of Lachish as Albright's reconstructions require. See Tufnell 1958:36 and 133, and Ussishkin 1978:92.

[68] Ussishkin 1978:93.

[69] Albright 1935; this subsequently became a recurrent theme in Albright's authorship.

[70] Thus Fritz 1973:135f.

[71] For Gezer: Dever et al., 1970 and 1974. Short report in Dever 1976. Cf. further Dever et al. 1974:5 (fig.I).

[72] See thus Franken 1975:333. Cf. also Bimson 1978:56ff.

tuation in the beginning of the Late Bronze Age. Similar observations apply
to such other sites as Gezer, as has also been observed by a number of archeologists, including Kenyon, Dever, and Albright[73]. Indeed, Kenyon even
speaks of a break in Late Bronze Age culture around 1400 which she holds was
more decisive than the transitional period between the Bronze and Iron Ages.
Albright has also described the pottery from the close of the Late Bronze Age
in Palestine as the most boring one in the archeological history of the country.
However, the break in question is not a transition from one culture to another,
but a dividing line in the material development of Late Bronze Age civilization. A period of relative prosperity was replaced by a period of decline, which
in turn was replaced – at least in many parts of the country – by yet another
decline around 1200. It ought also to be noted that the wave of destruction
around 1200 was not without parallels in the latter half of the second millennium. A series of destructions which was at least equally extensive took place
at the beginnning of this period; it has most often been associated by archeologists with Thutmoses III's Palestinian campaign around 1470. Among the
sites mentioned by this monarch, Gezer, Ta'anach, and perhaps also Megiddo
were laid in ruin at this time, while others, such as Hazor, Shechem, Bethel,
Lachish, and *Tell beit Mirsim*, may have suffered a similar fate even earlier.
More isolated cases of destruction also took place in the period 1470-1200,
although we cannot point to a single specific cause. Finally, it is to be observed
that this pattern continued on into the Iron Age, as Megiddo and Ta'anach
attest.

§ 4

Settlement Pattern III: The Villages

The main part of the materials concerning village societies in the Early Iron
Age have been entirely inadequately published, with the single exception of
Ḫirbet Mšāš (Tel Masos), in the north eastern part of the Negeb. Nevertheless,
I shall attempt to present a selection of these sites and attach to them the few
relevant remarks which may be extracted from the various short reports and
notices which have appeared. From the northern part of the country in Upper
Galilee, reference should be made to *Ḫirbet et-Ṭeleil*, one of the villages which
has been examined by Aharoni[74]; these extend from Central Palestine to
'Izbet Ṣarṭah and Ai[75], and from the southern region to Ḫirbet Mšāš .

[73] Cf. Kenyon 1965:209; Dever 1977:91; and Albright 1949:99-101.
[74] Yet another example from the northern part of the country could well be *Tell Qiri*
(161 227), which is 3 km from Tel Joqne'am, but is not registered in Israel 1:100 000, sheet 3.
Tell Qiri was a village which was inhabited from the 12th to the 8th centuries. It was never
destroyed by force in this period, although the site provides evidence of 12 phases of occupation,
distributed over 5 strata. Cf. Ben-Tor 1979.

Ḥirbet et-Teleil (Palestine Grid 1814 2636) was inhabited from the beginning of the Iron Age. The site was clearly not fortified, although Aharoni was able to discover the remains of at least one foundation-walled building. Ḥirbet et-Teleil resembles Hazor XII with respect to culture, so that Aharoni regarded the village, in company with a dozen similar sites in the same area, as Israelite[76]. As far as the pottery is concerned, the style is a continuation of the tradition of the Late Bronze Age, as Aharoni is aware. The same types found in Hazor XII recur at this site[77]. Nevertheless, Aharoni maintains that Israelite, rather than Canaanite, potters were responsible for the ceramics at the site, and that these figures *imitated* the Canaanite pottery at first, after which they progressed to develop an independent repertoire of types[78]. Of course, this interpretation has forced itself upon its author because of the preconceived notion of an Israelite immigration. Thus it cannot be taken to argue against the fact that there is a cultural continuum in this area spanning from the Late Bronze Age to the Iron Age.

'Izbet Ṣarṭah (146 168) is situated in the westernmost part of the Shephelah, about 100m above sealevel. The site was inhabited from the beginning of the Iron Age, perhaps as early as the close of the 13th century, and down to the middle of the 11th century, when it was abandoned with the exception of a brief reoccupation around 1000. The site contains three strata in all; the first of these lasted from the close of the 13th century until the middle of the 12th century; the second was from the middle of the 12th century until the middle of the 11th century, and, as mentioned previously, there are indications of a rudimentary third stratum from the close of the 11th century[79]. M. Kochavi, who excavated the site, has not hesitated, like other Israelite archeologists, to label the settlement Israelite, despite the fact that no reason is offered for this identification; moreover, it this identification were correct it would mean that already in the early phase of their immigration Israelite groups must have settled on the periphery of the coastal plain[80]. Unfortunately, the few notes which have been published tell us nothing about the pottery tradition at this site. Scholars have instead fastened their attention on a tablet containing what may be a very early version of the Canaanite alphabet, as well as the presence of a so-called "four-room house", which is dated to stratum II[81]. Because of

---

[75] Other examples from Mid-Palestine could be Janoah (cf. Otto 1978) or Jericho (cf. Weippert and Weippert 1976).

[76] Cf. Aharoni 1957:146f. and 1976B.

[77] Aharoni 1957:148, fig.7-10; 1976B:407. Notes the parallels from Hazor (Yadin 1961:pl. CLXVII:8,10 (pithoi), and Yadin 1959:pl.LVI:14 (krater).

[78] Aharoni 1976B:407; 1967:219f.

[79] Kochavi 1977:1-4.

[80] See on this Garsiel and Finkelstein 1978.

[81] On the inscription, see Kochavi 1977:4-13, and Demsky 1977, plus Garbini 1978. Dates: Kochavi: ca. 1200; Demsky: 12th c.; Garbini: beginning of the 11th c. Garbini additionally rejects the possibility that the inscription is an alphabet; on the other hand, he does not rule out the possibility that it is "proto-Canaanite" syllabic script, rather than an alphabetical script.

the western situation of the site, there would be reason to expect evidence of Philistine influence, but Kochavi would presumably hardly have failed to mention indications of Philistine materials. An inscription bearing a *Canaanite* alphabet is naturally unable to prove that the site was inhabited by Israelites[82]. Also, the hypothesis according to which the "four-room house" was Israelite in origin has not been verified, as we shall see below. Thus, as long as other information concerning 'Izbet Ṣarṭah has not been published, it would be reasonable to conclude that in cultural terms this village displays no special characteristics which would entitle us to claim that it was the home of newly arrived (foreign) immigrants.

J.A. Callaway's account of the conditions in the Iron Age village at *et-Tell*, that is, Biblical Ai, is somewhat more informative[83]. A village was located at this site around 1200 on top of a mound containing the ruins of an Early Bronze Age town which had lain untouched for more than a millennium. The settlement, which was an open village, was founded at the same time as a number of settlements, such as those at Gibeon, Mizpah, *Tajibah*, Michmash, and *Tell el-Ful;* it survived until the middle of the 11th century, when Ai was abandoned once more[84]. The Iron Age settlement at Ai falls into two phases with a dividing line around 1150-1125. The latter phase represents a decline with respect to the former one[85]. Callaway's evaluation of the material culture of the site is unambiguous; Ai was an agricultural society from its very beginnings. Its inhabitants were probably peasants already prior to their settlement at Ai, for which reason Callaway points to the possibility that they may have been arrivals from adjacent areas[86].

Finally, we shall turn our attention to a village society in the northern part of the Negeb which has been reasonably characterized by preliminary excavation reports, namely Ḥirbet Mšaš[87]. The village was founded towards the close of the 13th century and survived until the end of the 11th century or the beginning of the 10th century. Throughout this period it was an undefended village of considerable size[88]. Ḥirbet Mšaš contains three main strata plus

---

[82] Cf. Naveh, (1978), who notes similarities between the script type on this ostracon and that of the oldest Greek alphabet.

[83] Cf. Callaway 1965:22-28; 1969:5-9; 1970:12-19; 1975:49-52; and finally, 1976:18-30.

[84] Callaway 1976:19, fig.2; 1976:29f.

[85] Callaway 1976:30.

[86] Callaway 1976:29. Callaway had previously presented some very diffuse theories concerning the inhabitants of Ai at the beginning of the Iron Age (Callaway 1968); among other things, he maintained that the village had been founded by Hivvite immigrants from Anatolia. It is easy for Bimson to ridicule these efforts (1978:60ff.), but hardly fair of him, since this hypothesis seems to have been abandoned later by its own author.

[87] The most important reports have been published in virtually identical English and German-language versions. The English reports will be cited here: Aharoni, Fritz, and Kempinsky 1974; 1975; and Kempinsky and Fritz 1977. Short report by Kempinsky 1977.

[88] Concerning the foundation of the settlement: the most recent date has been proposed by Fritz (in Kempinsky and Fritz 1977:156). For the final phase: Kempinsky (in Kempinsky and Fritz 1977:147).

sub-phases; according to the excavators the first phase reveals signs of the settlement of nomads with the intention of pursuing agriculture as a way of life[89]. However, from the beginning of the 12th century we find a permanent settlement at Ḥirbet Mšaš, a settlement which was dominated by early varieties of the four-room house, although other types are also represented[90]. The excavators describe the settlement as Israelite. However, V. Fritz' latest publications on the subject indicate that a number of factors have led him to question his previously unconditional acceptance of the dates of the conquest suggested by Alt and Noth.

Fritz acknowledges that as far as the technological situation of the village is concerned, both with respect to metallurgy and pottery, the tradition is merely a continuation of the tradition of the Late Bronze Age. Furthermore, as far as the Iron Age pottery is concerned there is kinship linking the pottery at Ḥirbet Mšaš and that found in a number of different localities in the southwestern of Palestine, while the pottery of Ḥirbet Mšaš also differs on numerous points from pottery found in the northern part of the country[91]. Thus Fritz' latest interpretation suggests that the Israelite immigration must have taken place prior to the inhabitation of Ḥirbet Mšaš, that is, earlier than the end of the 13th century, since he maintains that the close relationship between the culture of Ḥirbet Mšaš and the older civilization of the Late Bronze Age, as well as the evolved agricultural techniques of the inhabitants, suggest that these "Israelites" had learned their trade through a length symbiotic relationship to the Canaanite societies in the country[92].

Thus there is reason to ask why Fritz attempts to maintain the notion of an Israelite immigration at all, especially when we consider that he is forced to conclude that it must have taken place earlier than is usually assumed. In defense of his claim, Fritz is in fact only able to point to a single element, namely the four-room house, the Israelite origin of which he supports by reference to some presumptions proposed previously by Y. Shiloh[93]. Now, it

---

[89] Cf. Fritz 1975, which also contains an attempt to reconcile the results of these excavations with the immigration theories of Alt.

[90] On the four room house at Ḥirbet Mšaš esp. Fritz 1980:121ff.

[91] Cf. Fritz 1980:133f., which begins with the following sentence: *"Diese Beobachtungen lassen sich mit keiner der bisher entwickelten Landnahmetheorien in Verbindung bringen"* (p.133). On the pottery see Kempinsky (in Kempinsky and Fritz 1977: 144ff., which in particular compares with the materials from Tel Ṣippor (124 118), cf. on this Biran 1978. Tel Ṣippor was inhabited in the MB, LB, and Iron I Ages, but it was abandoned around 1100. Kempinsky notes that the *collared-rim pithoi* found in most of the northern part of the country are mainly absent from Ḥirbet Mšaš.

[92] Fritz 1980:132-135.

[93] Fritz 1980:132-135; cf. Shiloh 1970 and 1973. At Ḥirbet Mšaš there is no doubt but that the finds represent domiciles for ordinary inhabitants; moreover, the examples discovered there are among the oldest which have been unearthed. Thus G.E. Wright's criticisms of Shiloh (Wright 1978) is therefore untenable. Wright claims that this type of house was mainly concentrated in the northern part of the country, and additionally that it was an architectural loan from Phoenicia. On the other hand, Wright is surely correct in maintaining that the term "four room house" is somewhat misleading since, while there is no question that we have to do with a basic type, the subdivision of it into chambers varies widely.

seems paradoxical to claim that the single gift made by foreign nomads to the land they settled down in was a new type of house. Furthermore, it is to be emphasized that this house type was hardly exclusively Israelite. Admittedly, Fritz claims that the plan of the house is an attempt to translate the structure of the "black tent" of the bedouin into architecturally solid form, as is suggested in C.G. Feilberg's treatment of 1944[94]. Feilberg dated the emergence of the black tent to around 1000, but Fritz has failed to note that Feilberg did so on the basis of evidence in the OT[95]. It is possible that this type of tent is as old as Fritz and Feilberg feel, but this point cannot be proved. Thus Fritz' argument is in reality dangerously close to being circular. Also, the four-room house developped gradually throughout the Iron Age; the examples found in Hirbet Mšaš are some of the oldest, so that we can see how this house type matured to the point where it was often used for official structures during the monarchy. However, it is frequently overlooked that the type is also found elsewhere in non-Israelite contexts, such as at *Tell eš-Šaria*, where the context is clearly Philistine. This find convinced the excavators that this house type represents an architectural renewal imported by the Philistines into Palestine[96]. Thus at present the four-room house is an open question. We are only entitled to conclude that it was apparently a new element in the material culture of Iron Age Palestine, an element whose origins are unclear. Certainly the introduction of this element is insufficient to provide grounds for belief in an immigration theory, especially when the finds made in the houses in question do not reveal exceptional features.

§ 5

Conclusion

This chapter contains only a short survey focusing in part on the changed pattern of settlement which occurred at the beginning of the Iron Age with respect to the previous period. It also includes a review of a number of individual sites which are to be regarded as representative of the development of the Palestinian societies around 1200. The materials speak for themselves to some extent. While it would be correct to claim that they provide evidence of dramatic events in the region in this period, there is no reason to believe that they have anything to do with a specifically *Israelite* immigration. In the Early Iron

---

[94] Fritz 1980:126; cf. Feilberg 1944.
[95] Feilberg 1944:105ff. and 198ff.
[96] Compare Oren 1978:1064.

Age, hardly a single cultural product is preserved which requires the assumption that considerable changes occurred in the ethnic composition of the population, although the presentation of these archeological materials has not been so minute as to allow us to note minimal shiftings of the local populations. It would naturally be impossible to deny that such limited movements of population took place both within and across the borders of Palestine, but it is only very rarely that we have been able to point to concrete features in the material culture which would justify such an assumption[97].

However, it is not the intention of this chapter to evaluate the historical process which resulted in the archeological pattern arising from the development from the Bronze to the Iron Ages. Such an effort will be made in my final conclusion below. Instead, we have simply attempted to discover whether the archeological materials alone, that is, taken in isolation from the Biblical traditions, can be taken to suggest that the Israelites were present in the country in the Early Iron Age. The conclusion is unambiguous: we cannot say this, if the designation *Israel* is assumed to have ethnic connotations. The question as to whether a political entity known as "Israel" existed in the country in the country in the Early Iron Age is quite a different matter. The archeological materials tell us nothing whatsoever about such an entity, so that any evaluation of Israel as a *political* phenomenon of the pre-monarchical period must depend on the use of the OT sources and the analysis to which one subjects them. If such an analysis nevertheless should permit us to conclude that certain political structures existed in pre-national Israel, then the archeological materials may be used to tell us about the material culture of this society; at most, they may be able to tell us something about the social structure of this society.

Finally, we are forced to conclude that unlike the result of our survey of the literary tradition, absolutely nothing in the archeological materials *contradicts* the revolution hypothesis, as von Fritz so confidently maintains[98]. To the contrary, all of the features mentioned above are compatible with the revolution hypothesis in one or another form. In fact, one would even be able to find support for the concept of an originally egalitarian Israelite society in the archeological materials, since it is possible to emphasize the lack of "official" architecture in the strata from Iron I in both towns and villages[99]. Of course, this by no means signifies that this short survey of some of the main lines of the cultural development of the region from the Late Bronze Age to the Iron Age in any way *proves* that the revolution hypothesis, whether in Mendenhall's , Gottwald's, or anyone else's version, is the only conceivable explanation of Israel's origin. This would require a collected evaluation of the materials which have been examined in this section.

---

[97] Cf. Franken 1969:61ff. on the conditions at Deir 'Alla.
[98] Contra Fritz 1980:133.
[99] Cf. Campbell 1979:47, and Albright 1949:119.

Part II

CONCLUSION

In an earlier article I rejected Gottwald's understanding of Israel's origins for two reasons. In the first place, Gottwald has not paid due attention to the age of his source materials. In the second place, Gottwald has personally transgressed against one of the old *domain assumptions* which he himself had criticized so severely: he has isolated a single feature in the Israelite society and elevated it to the status of a central or constitutive element in the developmental history of Israel[1]. My rejection of Gottwald's views has not become less relevant after the examination of the revolution hypothesis in this work. In this part I have isolated some of the most important basic hypotheses in Gottwald's monograph concerning nomads, peasants and urban dwellers, tribal systems, and the date of the pan-Israelite tradition in the OT. In each individual case we observed that Gottwald misleads his readers.

A central part of my rejection of Gottwald's individual hypotheses is the section dealing with the logical structure of Gottwald's description of tribal society, since I was able to falsify all of two of Gottwald's most important premises. Only a premiss the truth contents of which may be held to be evident may be taken to be a useful starting point for an analysis (in this case the analysis of the earliest Israelite society). The two fundamental hypotheses in question, first, that segmentary societies are egalitarian, and second, that true tribal societies contain exogamous clans, may be regarded as statements whose contents are obviously not true. The rest of Gottwald's premisses have not been subjected to an equally thorough evaluation, but as I pointed out earlier, Gottwald's premisses are interdependent. In other words, if the above-cited premisses are false, then their conclusions are as well; moreover, if two of the logical conclusions are invalid, then the rest of Gottwald's analysis of the tribal system cannot be verified and is to be rejected.

Other parts of Gottwald's treatment have not been subjected to a similar analysis of their logical structure, but the reader should note that also these passages are constructed in the same way as the sections I have criticized. This means that *Gottwald makes far too extensive use of postulates whose truth is not obvious*. To mention but a single important example which we touched on previously, Gottwald feels that it is not possible to understand the formation of the OT tradition without a preconceived notion that a united Israel (although this may not necessarily have been a twelve-tribe league) existed even before the formation of the state of Israel around 1000. This, too, is clearly a postulate, and it is one whose truth is not immediately apparent. Our examination of the pro-

---

[1] Lemche 1982:30-39.

cess by means of which the historical tradition came into being in ancient Israel has shown that the pan-Israelite tradition may very easily be understood as the conclusion of a historical development which was already ended or very close to its conclusion when the Babylonians conquered Jerusalem in 587 and the Assyrians conquered Samaria in 722.

In this case, my criticism strikes Gottwald alone, but even though his is a dubious distinction, it is nevertheless a case of *pars pro toto*, since Gottwald's argumentation (or system of postulates) has old and profound roots within the study of the OT. Scholars have generally chosen to approximate as closely as possible to the OT accounts, and they have only departed from them when other sources (either written or archeological) have contradicted them. This criticism applies to the fathers of the revolution hypothesis, since their self-declared goal is to preserve (as verified) the religious tradition while at the same time surrendering the historicity of the historical tradition. This entails that the Mosaic tradition is to be retained as an adequate expression of the ideology underlying the most ancient Israel, even though the historical reality may actually have been quite different from the one depicted in the OT.

Of course, this criticism applies with equal force to earlier scholarship in general, both prior to Alt's articles on the immigration in 1925 and 1939 and later. It applies even more to Albright and his school than it does to Alt, Noth, and the long series of mainly European scholars who have followed in Alt's footprints, and who have had even greater difficulties disassociating themselves from Alt's understanding of Israel's past than their current American colleagues have in rejecting Albright's model[2]. It is also interesting to observe that my criticism additionally strikes the adherents of a late date for the historical traditions in the OT, since none of them has as yet proposed an alternative model for the emergence of ancient Israel; indeed, in several cases they seem to presuppose an entirely traditional understanding for this process (in the sense advocated by Alt).

However, this work is not to be understood as a mere criticism of the central aspects of the revolution hypothesis, a critique which presumably indicates that this hypothesis is not applicable as a "heuristic" model for the study of ancient Israel. This section will hopefully have shown that the OT naturally contains a considerable amount of information about the non-national Israelite society (which is a much better definition than to say "prenational society"), despite the fact that the relevant sources were collected at a very late point in the history of Israel. If we compare the analysis presented here of Israelite social structure with the available ethnographic materials about Near Eastern traditional societies, which are far more relevant in this context than is the *cultural evolutionism* and its epiphenomena employed by Gottwald (and

---

[2] For examples, consult Weippert 1967 and 1979, plus Fritz' discussion with himself in Fritz 1975 and 1980.

others), we possibly arrive at a point of departure for a reconstruction of the process by which Israel came into being. A sketch in this direction will be presented in the following section.

It will immediately be obvious from my sketch that I do not feel that an account of this kind can possibly be very informative with respect to historical details. As of yet we still lack adequate sources for such a reconstruction, which must be able to depict a course of events in which the various individual events in the OT narratives can be located. Naturally, this applies completely to the account of Israel's pre-Palestinian existence, which in its present form can hardly be described as other than a fiction. However, it also applies to the narratives about Israel's pre-national life in the period of the Judges, not to speak of the "Settlement" narratives. The piecing together of the sources dealing with the prehistory of Israel before the year 1000 was the result of a redactional process which took place numerous centuries later than the events mentioned in the sources.

There are long sections in Gottwald's compendious monograph which have not been reviewed in this discussion; this applies especially to his theoretical section[3]. However, these sections are of secondary importance once we have acknowledged that Gottwald's evaluation of his source materials is incorrect. I would by no means reject a *materialistic* approach to the sources; nor, for that matter, would I reject a dynamic-revolutionary model. Nevertheless, the problem would always remain as to the sources such models would rely on. Does not the revolution hypothesis of Gottwald (and Mendenhall) invariably contradict the contents of the historical narratives, while the ideological contents of these narratives are retained as if they were historical? Are we not instead forced to conclude that if the OT description of Israel's earliest period is a fiction then the ideology underlying this description is every bit as late as the historical account itself? Perhaps in the last analysis the greatest weakness of the revolution hypothesis lies in its giving precedence to Israelite ideology in its analysis of early Israel. Both Mendenhall and Gottwald (and, to a lesser extent, Frick, who is one of their students) fail to distinguish between ideology and reality. By this I mean that they confuse Israel's self-understanding with history. Now, anthropologists and archeologists would normally agree that not all parts of human existence are equally easy or equally difficult to analyze. One account has pointed to the fact that it is unquestionably easiest to account for the material culture of a given society. It is more difficult to describe the economic forces active in the same society. Even more problems accrue to the attempt to understand correctly the social structure of the society. Finally, the most difficult task of all is the clarification of religious and ideological conceptions[4]. Yet another modern account suggests that we utilize a production

---

[3] I am referring to such sections as that in Gottwald 1979A:622-649.
[4] Cf. Hawkes 1954.

scale, and thus distinguish between material production, human reproduction, and finally the production of meaning[5]. The result is the same: while it proves to be relatively easy to get some perspective on the first field, the production of material commodities and foodstuffs, the second sector is more difficult to analyze, while the third requires an even greater effort. The latter model is derived from a textbook on ethnography which aims at ethnographic fieldwork; the former was proposed by an archeologist and has to do with the interpretation of excavational finds. The adherents of *cultural evolutionism* and the *new archeology* hope to avoid the difficulties mentioned here with the aid of their *general systems theory*, which attempts to comprehend all of the sectors involved within the compass of a single integral theory. However, as E. Leach has pointed out (and as I mentioned previously), these attempts have excluded a single vague, but nevertheless decisive factor, namely the human propensity for variation[6].

The anthropological sections above were intended to give some idea of the countless possible variations which confront us even in a single region, the Near East. It should be obvious that when even a synchronous study reveals innumerable differences, we shall hardly encounter fewer variations when we proceed to a diachronic analysis. For this reason anthropology does not offer us any universal solutions which the historian has only to collect and exploit. We have instead a number of potential models which may be utilized or rejected as they are appropriate or inappropriate. In some cases we have information about a given historical society which may be able to suggest in what direction we are to seek an explanation. In such a case, the broad spectrum of variations made available to us by anthropology may help to isolate the possible solution (or solutions). In other cases, not even this procedure is possible. In both cases a cautious use of the anthropological materials would be synonymous with a reduction of the many so-called "common sense" explanations which have marred Oriental studies for over a century, and which are best described as "armchair theories" (to use the jargon affected by many anthropologists).

---

[5] Hastrup and Ovesen 1980.
[6] See above, p. 217f.

Conclusion

EVOLUTIONARY ISRAEL: AN ALTERNATIVE EXPLANATION OF ISRAEL'S ORIGINS

§ 1

The Old Testament and the Immigration Theories

Although the hypothesis of Israel's revolutionary origins is to be rejected, this does not mean that it is devoid of scientific merit. The most important qualities of the hypothesis are not contained in its attempt to answer the question of the emergence of Israel, but in its at times very perspicacious objections to the earlier explanations. As mentioned previously, Mendenhall and Gottwald direct their fire at the theory of the Israelite pastoral nomads, who immigrated into the arable land over a lengthy period of time. Both scholars retain the most important part of Albright's view of the rise of Israel, namely the idea that the *prima causa* of this event was a divine intervention in history. But where Albright had maintained that it was the Israelite society as a whole which had received a primeval revelation (the Sinai event), Mendenhall and Gottwald prefer to believe that only a very limited part of later Israel participated in the theophany which preceded the arrival in the land of Canaan.

This part of the revolution hypothesis is to be dismissed, since it presupposes a fallacious understanding of the historical traditions in the OT. On the other hand, the rejection of the theory of the intruding pastoral nomad is still highly relevant. In this connection Mendenhall was able to depict a scheme showing to what extent the earlier interpretations of the immigration were based on the Biblical tradition. He noted that the notion of an Israelite semi-nomad had no basis in the OT accounts of the Settlement. On the other hand, he also felt that the OT account of the origin of Israelite religion was susceptible of verification.

My starting point for these concluding remarks will be a similar attempt to evaluate the relationship between three different conceptions of the immigration and the OT data as well as the non-Biblical information concerning Israel's earliest history. To turn first to the notion of the entrance of an Israelite seminomad into the country, it is first to be observed that this idea has no basis on the OT sources. This is a serious weakness, since this very immigration hypothesis was proposed by a circle of scholars who attempted to maintain the notion that the pre-historic traditions were very ancient. This must be emphasized, in spite of the very solid exegetical research performed by the proponents of this approach. Furthermore, the archeological materials from Palestine force us to conclude that there is no reason to believe that any new and foreign people entered into the country in significant numbers in the period around 1200, with the exception of the Sea People. Moreover, even if one bases one's views on a more radical understanding of the nature of the Biblical sources (as is the case in this work), one is still forced to conclude that the case for this view of Israel's origins is not a good one. We still have no sources of any kind whatsoever which might support this view. Of course, a late date for the Biblical historical tradition just might enable us to retain this immigration hypothesis. This would also permit us to plead for a solution to the archeological problems which permit us to retain the notion of a peaceful Israelite infiltration into the country at the beginning of the Iron Age. It is namely to be emphasized that when the OT historical tradition is revealed to be a fiction written around the middle of the first millennium, this Biblical tradition may then be held to be *neutral*. It no longer provides us with arguments either for or against the immigration, as this has been described by a long series of scholars, from Alt to Weippert. Similarly, one could apparently avoid the problems caused by the lack of archeological evidence of an Israelite presence in the country during the last part of the second millennium. If one takes one's point of departure in Israel's stage of social development (i.e., if one claims that the Israelites were pastoral nomads), one could then claim that they have left no remains behind them, since it is characteristic of nomadic cultures that they neither possess goods nor property which would be available to later archeologists. This would make it possible to sustain the concept of Israel's peaceful immigration into the land of Canaan as sketched out by Alt, no matter how often and vociferously the adherents of the "sociological" revolution theory should happen to protest. As I pointed out previously in my survey of nomadic settlement processes, the notion that peregrinating nomads may settle down in the course of a peaceful and lengthy development and become settled peasants is by no means ruled out by the socio-anthropological materials, which some have held to say the opposite. However, it was emphasized that such a course of development would be unusual, especially if it took place in a political vacuum, that is, in an area without strong central government, which was actually the situation in Palestine when the Egyptian hold on the country failed.

Thus those readers who are convinced that Alt was basically right may stop reading at this point; it is still possible to defend Alt's hypothesis[1]. On the

---

[1] This also applies to Fritz (1980), who appears to have overlooked the fact that Alt's model required a lengthy course of immigration, which naturally took account of the many cultural forms shared by the Israelites and the Canaanites. Salzman (1978B) has presented an account of a modern nomadic people which has won the control of a sedentary peasant population. The result was both the settlement of the nomadic leadership stratum and the beginnings of a process which ultimately led to the formation of a state.

other hand, one wonders whether this thesis is at all necessary in order to understand how Israel came into being. One also wonders whether it is even close to being the most probable explanation. By this I mean that, as described here, this hypothesis still lacks any sort of foundation in the sources, both the written and the archeological ones. Thus it is at best a *construction*. Accordingly, if one finds some material which points to a different model, in terms of scientific method it would then be preferable to discard Alt's immigration hypothesis and turn instead to this alternative explanation of Israel's origins, which can at least claim to have some support in the sources. This course leaves us with two possible working hypotheses: the question as to whether Israel conquered Palestine from *within* or *from without*. The latter possibility was preferred by Albright, who was able to cite the Biblical tradition as his witness. Unfortunately, this possibility collapses pitifully when one considers the archeological evidence from Palestine. Furthermore, if one examines the Biblical tradition with the spectacles used here, one immediately pulls the carpet out from under the hypothesis that an Israelite invasion took place during the transitional phase between the Late Bronze Age and the Early Iron Age. As J.M. Miller has recently emphasized, it is no longer possible to offer even a reasonable defense of the Conquest narratives[2].

We are left with the revolution hypothesis. If we examine this theory in the light of the Biblical tradition, one is forced to acknowledge that it has no basis whatsoever in the canonical account in the OT. On the other hand, it must also be admitted that there are no difficulties connected with the attempt to reconcile the notion central to the revolution hypothesis of an internal conquest of Palestine with the archeological data. This is surely a positive feature; moreover, it is one which could form the basis for a reformulation of the revolution hypothesis so that it contains the idea of an internal development in Palestine stretching from the close of the second millennium until the formation of the state under David. However, in order to do so it will be necessary to divest this hypothesis of its ideological contents. It is a banal but nevertheless ineluctable fact in this connection that once one has said A one is also forced to say B, that is, *once one has dismissed the OT recollection of Israel's immigration into Palestine as ahistorical and late, one is also thereby compelled to ignore the narratives concerning the origins of Israelite religion*. Therefore it is out of the question to regard Israel's hypothetical religious experience as a starting point for a survey of the early history of Israel. This is the sole scientifically acceptable point of departure for an analysis of the process which led to the formation of the state. Instead of acknowledging this fact, we are forced to note that, like countless others, Gottwald and Mendenhall have arbitrarily rejected a tradition which superficially claims to be historical in favor of a late and at least equally dubious tradition concerning the divine theophany at Sinai. They have

---

[2] Miller 1979:40.

furthermore relied on the concept of a covenant established at Sinai between ancient Israel and her God. It should also be observed that this notion of "covenant" is one which is only poorly attested in sources which we may be reasonably certain are pre-exilic.

In this connection the following axiom surely applies: *our most important duty is to acknowledge our ignorance*. By this I mean that we are obliged to avoid composing hypotheses about Israel's pre-national existence in the absence of adequate sources. It is generally the case that the understanding of Israel's history until the year 1000 formulated by traditional OT study has been based on such hypotheses. Already Alt and Noth, but also many of their predecessors – pre-eminent among them being E. Meyer – were aware of the chasm separating the Biblical account from the realm of the historically possible, as far as the narratives from the primeval history of Israel (i.e., before the immigration) were concerned. At present the situation is, if possible, even worse. The demise of the amphictyony hypothesis signifies that also the OT account of the period between the immigration and the formation of the state is to be regarded as a construction of the same sort as the patriarchal narratives, the stories of the sojourn in Egypt, the desert wandering, and the immigration into Palestine. Thus it is entirely legitimate to conclude that at this time it would be foolish to write a history of Israel which begins before the year 1000 without stressing that it is first from the time of David that we have to do with *historical*, rather than *prehistorical*, time.

But our first axiom has an obvious corollary, namely the fact that *once we have acknowledged the state of our ignorance we are in a position to acknowledge what we really do know*. We know that the OT scarcely contains *historical* sources about Israel's past. We also know that the OT contains extensive materials which purport to tell us something about Israel's past, and we are forced to recognize that materials are the stuff of saga and legend. In other words, we only have *certain* data as to how Israel's prehistory was understood around the middle of the first millennium and later; however, this is the only certain information we possess. Having come so far, it would then be appropriate to reuse these legendary materials to reconstruct Israelite prehistory, but on different premises than was formerly the case. Scholars were previously entirely too prone to allow themselves to be led by the Biblical account. In other words, the description of pre-national Israel has been undertaken on the conditions set by the Biblical tradition, even though this tradition has naturally been very critically analyzed and evaluated for the last century or more. In principle, scholars have clung to the OT narrative. In this connection there has been no difference between Alt, Noth, Von Rad, or other European scholars on the one hand, and Albright and his students on the other; it is likewise unimportant whether one group had more faith in the historicity of the sources than another. The result has invariably been an account of the premonarchical history of Israel which has continually had to be modified as soon as new archeological data or new sociological insights have arrived on the scene. In practice this has entailed the creation of a picture of Israel's earliest history from which scholars have gradually retreated after lengthy debates which have showed the picture in question to be based on positions which could not be sustained in the light of new information.

As an alternative to this scenario, I propose that we decline to be led by the Biblical account and instead regard it, like other legendary materials, as essentially ahistorical, that is, as a source which only exceptionally can be verified by other information. To illustrate with a fictive example: in its present Deuteronomistic framework the Ehud narrative is a heroic legend similar to the heroic legends of other peoples, such as the Danish saga of Rolf Kraka or the Greek Theseus narratives. No one would today dream of utilizing the two last-mentioned bodies of material as historical sources unless he possessed other information concerning these two figures deriving from a context which would make it possible to date them with reasonable certainty. We would be much more likely to regard them as myths or romances to which for example, a structuralistic or semiotic analysis would be more appropriate[3]. It would be similarly incorrect to attempt to squeeze the Ehud narrative in order to "reveal" a historical "nucleus" which may not even be present in the narrative. On the other hand, it is not completely out of the question (although hardly very likely) that we shall one day possess information about Ehud which would allow us to date him to the "period of the Judges", in, for example, around 1150. It is equally conceivable that refined excavational techniques or better knowledge of the material culture in Jericho and the territory east of the Jordan may some day allow us to prove that individuals from the land east of the Jordan established a shortlived colony in the region of Jericho around 1150, only to vanish shortly thereafter. This would provide us with some evidence in favor of a historical nucleus in Jdg 3, even though we should still have to accept that many details in the narrative were of younger date. Of course, this is only a conjectural example. One must not overlook the fact that we have no external evidence of this kind from the pre-national period. Thus it is hardly to be recommended that scholars make the search for this sort of evidence their starting point.

Instead, we are better served in our study of Israel's prehistory by following the conclusions which may be drawn on the basis of our knowledge of the social, economic, cultural, and political developments in Palestine towards the

---

[3] See also M. Liverani's *"memorandum"* (Liverani 1973B). Liverani's examples, however, have not been derived from "dark, heroic ages", but from texts which most scholars have previously regarded as historical sources, such as the autobiography of Idrimi (Liverani 1971C), Hittite "historical" texts (Liverani 1973D and 1977), and above all the Amarna correspondence, which reveals the ahistorical dimension of the scribes who appear to have structured their contemporary-historical writings along the lines of ideological or mythical schemes or structures (Liverani 1971A and 1974).

close of the second millennium. Such a procedure would allow us to propose some very general observations on this course of development based directly on materials which in the nature of things are mainly archeological. Of course, such materials also contain countless possibilities for misinterpretations, misunderstandings, and abuses, but these may be corrected without great difficulty as new insights win acceptance and as we become more proficient in the application of the scientific methods in question.

The psychological advantage of such a method is that the scheme I propose is positive, while a scheme based on the OT tradition is necessarily negative. This means that a model of the development of Palestine prior to the year 1000 will become increasingly detailed as our fund of information grows and our analytical methods become more sophisticated. Thus we shall continually be able to *add something to* such a model, that is, to extend it, even while in some cases certain hypotheses may have to be abandoned. Ideally, this would enable us at some future time to offer a fairly exhaustive description of the evolution of the country prior to the formation of the Israelite state.

I described the traditional OT scheme as psychologically negative in the sense that its function all too easily becomes apologetic. Scholars have constantly found themselves to be obliged to surrender parts of this scheme because of new information which is not based on the OT. This leads us to a third axiom, which has to do with the understanding of the OT text as legendary: *a saga or legend is ahistorical until the opposite has been proved; it is not historical until its "historical" contents have been disproved.* This must be our point of departure, in spite of the cautious acceptance by Culley and others of the possibility that legends may contain historical recollections.

§ 2

Palestine in the Late Bronze Age and the Early Iron Age

Since, as we have seen, the period of the Judges is no longer to be regarded as a historical epoch like the period of the monarchy, there is also no reason to regard the interval between 1200 and 1000 as the only period in which Israel's origins are to be sought. If we ignore the conception of a collected Israelite immigration, the year 1200 is no longer a *terminus a quo* for the beginning of the process which was concluded with the formation of the Israelite state. Instead, the possibility is now open to regard the formation of the state as the result of a development which may actually have covered the whole of the Late Bronze Age (or, for that matter, an even longer period of time). As mentioned previously, this means that there is no longer any reason to compress all of the traditions concerning Israel's prehistory into a two-hundred-year period of the Judges. They may very well be regarded instead as typical examples of the mixture of legendary accounts one encounters in popular traditions. Thus they may have had quite different places of origin and once been concerned with events from entirely different periods. In this respect I am quite prepared to follow the suggestion of Aharoni, who recognized the impossibility of localizing the traditions concerning Israel's prehistory within a single epoch[4]. On the other hand, this acknowledgement ought not to become the basis of a new type of fundamentalism in which one nevertheless naively compares the Biblical sagas with historical traditions. There is not necessarily any contradiction between these observations and the position of J. Van Seters, who holds that the process of tradition was a literary one. Thus, for example, he maintains that the Abraham traditions were created by the Yahwist in the time of the Exile[5].

The fact is that such a late Yahwist was able to embue a shadowy legendary hero, in casu Abraham, with new life, when everything indicates that this figure previously was a diffuse one at best. This was done by associating the figure of Abraham with a long series of fairy tales and legends which may have had quite different ages and origins. This process only serves to confirm a feature long ago recognized by students of folklore, namely the fact that the embryonic plot of a legendary narrative is primary with respect to the persons and places which figure in it at a given point in the history of its tradition. Even if the Yahwist was a conscious author who worked on the basis of written tradition, this tradition was still not identical with historical documents; rather, it was presumably just as ahistorical as any oral sagas could be.

The next point which requires clarification applies to the date which may be allowed to serve as our point of departure for an analysis of the processes which led to the emergence of Israel. A date is necessary if we are not to introduce such a description by locating it in a fully gray and unknown past. In this case our task is somewhat facilitated by the fact that the Late Bronze Age in Palestine is not entirely a prehistorical period. This is because we in fact possess some information about the history and social life of the region until the reign of Rameses II, plus some sporadic information subsequently. To a certain extent this information may also be seen in relation to the archeological picture of the Late Bronze Age and the transitional phase to the Early Iron Age. Our most important source is the Amarna archives, which are also to be supplemented by some Egyptian inscriptions as well as a few letters like the recently published one found in Aphek[6]. Moreover, the written sources from

---

[4] Aharoni 1976A.

[5] Van Seters 1975.

[6] Cf. Owen 1981 (a letter from the prefect of Ugarit to an important Egyptian official; dated around 1250.

Palestine may also be supplemented by other textual materials from elsewhere in the Near East (mainly Ugarit and Alalaḫ), all of which may conjoin to give us some insight into the society of the Near East at the time. Of course, it is important to recognize that the variegated picture of social relations we have seen in the contemporary Orient cautions us that it would be unreasonable to suppose that if we find a particular social structure in Ugarit we also have reason to believe the same structure existed elsewhere.

In Ugarit, in fact, we encounter a very heterogeneous population containing elements of all of the peoples of the eastern Mediterranean. There are obvious signs of powerful cultural influences from near and far. Furthermore, Ugarit must be seen as one of the most important transit stations for trade between the Aegean area and the Orient in the Late Bronze Age[7]. Heltzer's study of the rural population of Ugarit shows that this population did not dwell in the large towns in the state, but in a sizeable number of small villages[8]. In Palestine in the Late Bronze Age conditions were quite different, that is, if Thompson's observations are correct, since such a pattern of open and presumably unfortified village societies is not found in most of Palestine. Therefore it is likely that the rural population dwelled within the confines of the walls of the fortified towns, a conjecture which, even seen in the light of modern conditions, is not unreasonable.

The next issue to be clarified is the question of the practical differences entailed upon for the life of the average peasant if he dwelled in some regions in villages which were *extra muros*, while dwelling elsewhere within the protecting but also confining walls of the towns. It seems immediately obvious that Palestinian peasants must have been more dependent on the central authorities than were their Ugaritic counterparts. Indeed, it is entirely conceivable that there were no peasants at all in the mini-states in Palestine who owned their own land, while such self-reliant peasants were the very basis of the agricultural sector in Ugarit. We simply do not have sufficient information to be sure in this matter, even if we are not entirely without data. If my interpretation of the term *ḫupšu* is correct, that is, as referring to class of clients – which in an agricultural context means copyholders – then the example of Byblos offers us some illumination. Admittedly, Byblos is in Phoenicia rather than Palestine, but the Byblian sources nevertheless inform us of the existence of a non-free peasant class and also tell us about the reactions of this class to a number of influences[9]. In this connection it is to be emphasized that the groups of

---

[7] On this see Helck 1979:41, and Heltzer 1977. Heltzer regards Ugarit as the center of the regional metal trade, even though Ugarit itself had no ore deposits (1977:211). See also Klengel 1979:142-153 on Ugarit's general position in the scheme of international trade, including trade with the Aegaean area.

[8] Cf. Heltzer 1976. Heltzer estimates that the state of Ugarit contained throughout its history between 180 and 200 villages (1976:104).

[9] Cf. Lemche 1975:139ff., and 1979A:3ff.

ḫupšu mentioned in the correspondence of Rib-Addu, the king of Byblos, are invariably regarded as clients of the king[10]. This means that in Byblos the *ḫupšu* were a non-free peasant class who, however, were not slaves. On the other hand, they did not own their own lands, and their employer was the king, which in practice must have meant the official authorities organized around the palace[11]. Since the sources are silent on the matter, we have no way of knowing whether this city-state also contained a corresponding sector of privately organized copyholders, or, for that matter, an additional category of peasants who possessed their own lands.' Nor can we be sure that conditions were uniform in all of the small states in the region which consisted of Phoenicia and Palestine. We have the results of some surveys performed in the Beqa' valley in Lebanon which suggest that there were some structural differences between this area and, for example, Palestine. During the Late Bronze Age the Lebanese hinterland seems to have possessed a not-insignificant number of of village societies, even though the area was fragmented by a number of city-states[12]. On the other hand, it is not unimportant that the Amarna letters do not refer to the existence of a class of peasants who owned their own lands. This absence is all the more striking when we consider that information from much later times shows that the peasant population must have comprised by far the largest part of the population, perhaps even as much as 80%. Thus as a working hypothesis we may propose a model of the society of the southern Canaanite territory in which there was no room for independent peasants. Instead, the peasant class must have been attached to the central instances in the states to which they belonged rather than to private enterprize.

We are better informed about other groups within these city-states. We know that in addition to the administrative officials of the palace there also existed a class of professional warriors. These were organized into various special units, of which the chariot troops were the most eminent in the hierarchy[13]. Once again we should note that most of the information on this subject derives from Ugarit and Alalaḫ in the northern part of the region; thus it would be advisable to exercize caution in transferring these data to the far more modest Palestinian states. There is no reason to believe that such a professional warrior class need have been very numerous. This is indirectly implied by the requests for Egyptian troop contingents which are preserved in the Amarna letters[14]. Reference is usually made to very modest figures. For

---

[10] Cf. EA 77:36; 81:33; 85:12; 112:12; 114:22,57; 117:90; 118:23.37; 125:27; 130:42.

[11] On the palace administration of the Late Bronze Age see e.g. Liverani 1973A.

[12] See Marfoe 1979.

[13] The well-known *marjannu*. On these figures and the military in general – based on materials from Ugarit and Alalaḫ – see Heltzer 1969A:42f., and 1971, as well as Dietrich and Loretz 1969A:93 (on the *marjannu* at Alalaḫ). Heltzer emphasizes that not even the *marjannu* may be regarded as autonomous or quasi-autonomous feudal lords, as they, too, belonged to the circle of the *bnš mlk* (cf. already and more thoroughly Heltzer 1969B). Dietrich and Loretz, insist on the traditional understanding of the *marjannu* as *nobles* whose specialty was the war chariot.

[14] Thus ÌR-Ḥepa to Pharoah: 50 soldiers (EA 289:42-43); Rib-Addu to Pharoah: 20 men

example, if king X is at war with king Y and accordingly requests Egyptian reinforcements, and if in doing so he merely asks for 30 men, then we may suppose that this sort of request scarcely belongs in a context in which the local troops employed number in the thousands or even hundreds. This may be plausibly argued in spite of the fact that the Egyptian troops could be considered to be special troops[15], and that they must additionally have been surrounded by the aura of prestige of the Egyptian empire. The reasons for this paucity of numbers are evident. With the possible exception of Hazor all of the Palestinian states were quite small, and they were no doubt also rather poor. The economy of these states was based on agricultural products and probably on the by no means extravagant proceeds of the transit trade, as well as on locally produced products. This means that only very restricted means of coercion can have been available to the individual local potentate.

We do not know to what extent the royal central administrations of the small Palestinian states were counterbalanced by the existence of an independent class of citizens whose independence was based on trade and some form of "industry". Some of the Amarna letters suggest that such a class may have existed, and that in some cases it may have served as a political power factor capable of opposing the local king (as well as the Egyptian overlordship, at least in the eyes of the local king)[16]. In connection with Palestine there is nothing to suggest that such a class of citizens, that is, a sort of city elite, ever managed to achieve lasting control of their respective states before these states were absorbed into the great Davidic empire. However, the form of government in the later Phoenician city-states generally changed from monarchy to oligarchy[17]. We have no information as to whether alliances may have occurred between the non-free peasant class and the citizen class, although we do have some data informing us of connections between citizen groups and parasocial phenomena, that is, groups of *ḫabiru*[18].

At this point our analysis turns away from the central towns and moves in the direction of their periphery. Like Mendenhall and Gottwald, L. Marfoe has attempted to analyze a society from its periphery and in towards its center. However much merit this procedure may otherwise have, it is irrelevant in a Palestinian context, since we lack the essential presuppositions for starting

from Miluḫa and 20 Egyptians (EA 108:67 Rib-Addu is more optimistic elsewhere, in that he requests all of 200 men (EA 71:24)), or Abimelech of Tyre: 20 men (EA 151:15).

[15] Note the frequent references in the Amarna letters to *ṣābē piṭṭatu*, "archers", as, for example, in EA 286:53.57.59; 287:17.

[16] Thus EA 73:25ff. Abdi-Aširta urges the LU.MEŠ *am-mi-ja* to rebel against their prince and join the *ḫabiru*. Note also EA 74:29ff. and EA 128:36ff., where there are problems with the very citizenry of Byblos.

[17] Of course, this was a development which first reached its peak acceleration in the first millennium; cf. Harden 1971:71f.

[18] The best-known example is in EA 289:21-24: the coalition between Labaju, Shechem, and the *ḫabiru*. This difficult situation is repeatedly alluded to in several of Rib-Addu's letters, as, for example, in EA 68:16-18; 74:19-21; 76:33-37.

outside of the towns. Once again the particular settlement pattern of the region is the cause since, as we have seen, Palestine did not ordinarily contain open village societies during the Late Bronze Age[19]. Thus it would be appropriate to adhere to the normal procedure, so that after having examined the Canaanite town and its social composition we shall proceed to study the periphery of the city-state with respect to two factors which were influential there.

Two groups of people were not forced to dwell in the towns: nomads and *habiru*. These two quantities are not to be equated. I have dealt with the *habiru* in a number of earlier publications, so that I shall not devote much space to them here. I accordingly presuppose that my hypotheses concerning the connection between the social designation *habiru* and the social term עברי are well known. This also applies to my view of the *habiru* as a parasocial phenomenon, that is, as a refugee[20]. It is possible to distinguish between three uses of the *habiru* designation in the sources dealing with Palestine in the Late Bronze Age. One of these refers to hordes of outlaw *habiru*'s who dwelled in regions which were not under the control of the city-states. These groups had definite possibilities for action, since most of Palestine is composed of mountainous areas. In the Late Bronze Age these areas were still sparsely populated and covered by forest and scrub growth[21]. The second use of the term *habiru* also refers to a refugee, but one who had sought the protection of a foreign state. Since the region was subdivided into a number of territorial states and no nation-states existed at the time[22], there were no ethnic barriers for a refugee to trespass against. In other words, if a man fled from state M to state N, he soon found himself among people with whom he shared both a common language and a common culture. It seems likely that this group of *habiru* functioned as *hupšu*, that is, the clients of the king or state (no matter what their tasks were). As for the third usage of the term, it seems as if it is used in the Amarna letters in a sense which exceeds its ordinary contents. Thus there are examples in which it is used by a prince as an expletive to describe his colleagues, or to refer to an element in the population with whom the prince is embroiled in conflict[23]. It is essential to determine the precise sense in which the term *habiru* is used in the Amarna correspondence. All three meanings are of significance in determining the role of the *habiru* in the emergence of Israel.

The Amarna letters and some Egyptian sources provide us with considerable information about the nomads in Palestine and adjacent areas[24]. As

---

[19] On this see Marfoe 1979:32-34, with respect to Palestine; for the Late Bronze Age settlements, see Thompson 1979.

[20] Lemche 1979:3; 1980:179, following Bottéro 1954:194, and Liverani 1965B. Cf. also Liverani 1962:86f.; 1963:223f., and Buccellati 1977.

[21] Cf. Rowton 1965; 1967.

[22] See Buccellati 1967 for a characterization of the two types of state in West Asia.

[23] On this see Mendenhall 1973:122f.

[24] See above pp. 155ff.

mentioned previously, the sources in question do not contain much concrete information about these nomads with respect to their political organization, social structure, or economic life. In geographical terms the *sutu-šasu* seem to be associated with regions which cannot be held to be *ḫabiru* territory; thus we are forced to seek them in the marginal areas in the south and to the east. There is nothing to suggest that they composed any sort of threat to the Canaanite city-states; nor do we hear that their wanderings led them to trespass against or even touch upon the territories of the city-states. It is conceivable that the states along the coastal plain were frequently visited by the nomads from the Negeb region, but we have no assurance of this. Nor is there anything to indicate the presence of a nomadic population element in the mountainous regions in the central parts of the country. There is no reason for amazement in this connection since this region was heavily forrested and thus a suitable home for bands of outlaws; it must have been rather uninviting to nomads[25]. The notion that such nomads could have posed a direct threat to the existence of the Canaanite states of the Late Bronze Age is hardly credible; at best it is only a fragile working hypothesis[26]. On the other hand, they may well have had something to do with the decline of the urban cultures towards the close of the period, since in unquiet times they probably helped to cut off the commercial contacts between Egypt and Palestine (to the extent that this traffic was not waterborne)[27]. It is not difficult to imagine that the nomads may also have taken possession of new territory; in some cases they may have settled down after the collapse of Egyptian sovereignty towards the end of the Late Bronze Age. However, it is to be stressed that the nomadic element in question was already in the country during the Amarna period. Thus, if a village such as Ḥirbet Mšaš was founded by nomads, it must have been nomads who had dwelled in the country for centuries[28].

Archeology records a noticeable decline in the cultural level of Palestine from the 14th century and later; this is among other things evident in the small quantites of imported products and in the poor quality of the local pottery. It was also noted above that this declining tendency continued across the dividing line of the year 1200 and far down into the Early Iron Age, although the problems of the Late Bronze Age towns seem to have been acute from the end of the 13th century and later. What reasons can we provide for this decline? Six possibly contributory factors may be mentioned in this connection: war, a trade crisis, epidemic illness, climatic disruptions, social problems, and the

---

[25] Cf. Planhol 1965 on the "relationship" between nomads and the forested mountain regions in Anatolia.

[26] Already the Egyptians were aware of this; see the quotation above, p. 90.

[27] A general description of the positive and negative effects of the nomads on the extra-regional trade is to be found in Klengel 1977.

[28] Cf. Fritz 1980:134.

pressure exerted by the Egyptian empire on the limited resources of the coun-try[29].

In the Late Bronze Age Palestine was under Egyptian control, although at times this control appears to have been more nominal than real. It is well known that an empire consists of a center plus one or more provinces, and that the economic flow of such a social system moves from the peripheral areas towards the center. This means that the provinces are more or less drained of their resources. As is indicated by the remains of the material culture of Pale-stine at this time, this was probably the most important reason why the Late Bronze Age was not a period of prosperity like the Middle Bronze Age. On the other hand, at least at the beginning there are no signs of any noticeable decline in the standard of living, which suggest that at this time Egyptian exploitation was not overly severe; the drain on the country's resources was bearable and so did not significantly inhibit the economic life of the region. However, it must be admitted in this context that although we possess consi-derable information about the Egyptian administration of Palestine and Syria, in reality we have no precise data as to the taxation of the provinces, so that the importance of this factor for the development of the Near East must remain indeterminable[30].

Yet another difficult factor to get a grip on is the problem of climate. Accord-ing to the information presented previously, the Late Bronze Age must be regarded as a relatively unfavorable period with respect to climate, but we have no sources which relate that there was famine because of drought in Pale-stine during the period between 1500 and 1000. We do have information that Anatolia was affected by drought on several occasions, and that as late as the reign of Merneptah the Egyptians sent grain to aid the Hittites. Nevertheless, we should exercize due caution in transferring this information to other regions in the Near East[31].

The patriarchal narratives in the OT often refer to famine in Palestine, and this is even described as the background of the Israelites' journey down to Egypt[32]. However, even though the Biblical chronology assigns these events

---

[29] An ideological crisis might be added to make up a 7th factor. However, since the only materials relevant to this category are to be found in the OT, it would be wise to delay an evalua-tion of this factor until pertinent extra-Biblical material has turned up. It should be obvious that the collapse of the palace culture in the Late Bronze Age must have entailed a crisis of confidence among the populations, but we know nothing about how this came to expression (apart from the purely practical and material consequences).

[30] On the Egyptian administration of Syria and Palestine see Helck 1971:246-255. With respect to the taxation of the provinces, it is represented in some entirely stereotyped graphic illustrations in a number of graves (cf. Helck 1971:246), and they are, of course, also mentioned in a number of royal inscriptions. It remains nevertheless impossible to arrive at a reasonable evaluation of the approximate amounts in question, or to get some idea of what these represen-ted in terms of the percentage of the total economic production of the Asiatic provinces.

[31] On famine among the Hittites, see Klengel 1974. On Mernephtah's assistance to them, see Klengel 1974:167f. Cf. Breasted 1906: § 580 and Wainwright 1960, plus Goetze 1975B:265.

[32] Gen 41; cf. Gen 12,10 and 26,1.

to a time shortly before the beginning of the Late Bronze Age, there is no reason whatsoever to believe that these narratives have anything to do with conditions in the second millennium, especially since the period from 1000 and later can hardly have been more favorable, as is also indicated by some legends from the period of the monarchy[33]. It is virtually certain that drought must have affected Palestine and Syria in the course of the second millennium. However, we have no concrete information which informs us as to periods of bad growth or their effects. Also, there is no reason to regard the remarks of the Egyptian border guards concerning the immigration of nomads from Sinai to the Nile Delta as evidence of famine in Palestine, as they are in reality on evidence of scarcities in Sinai[34]. Thus we are forced to conclude that although it is obvious that such climatic disruptions must have played a part in the development of Palestinian society in this era, it is impossible to regard them as the basis for an analysis, or to single them out as the determinative factor.

A similar judgement applies to our third criterium, that of epidemic illness. We have sources which refer to such epidemics; interestingly enough, they are not Egyptian, but Hittite sources. It is well known that the Syrian campaign of Šuppiluliumaš was abruptly ended by an epidemic which even snatched the Great King himself away[35]. In a lecture to the Vetus Testamentum congress in Vienna in 1980, de Geus attempted to emphasize the role played by epidemics as one of the major reasons for the decline and collapse of Late Bronze Age culture. Nevertheless, although this factor was no doubt also an important one, in the case of Palestine we have no examples which suggest that one or another event was caused by the decimation of the local population because of plague or other epidemic illnesses[36].

We have more concrete information regarding the first-mentioned cause, namely war. We may distinguish between different types of military activities which affected Palestinian society in the Late Bronze Age. In the first place, there were wars of conquest in which Palestine was the prey of a foreign power. The power in question was in this instance Egypt, as the Hittites never got so far south during their advance prior to the reconsolidation of Egyptian power during the 19th dynasty. The second variety consisted of internal struggles between the Canaanite mini-states. We are well informed as to such combats thanks to the Amarna documents, but we have no later information. Finally, the third category has to do with military activities which only concerned Palestine indirectly, which means the rivalry between the great powers, Egypt and Ḫatti. It is possible that the area was threatened during the last part of the second millennium by short-term Assyrian incursions into western Asia,

---

[33] 1 Kgs 17-18.
[34] Papyrus Anastasi VI; See ANET³:259.
[35] See Goetze 1975A:18-19.
[36] The contribution in question had not been published at the time of this writing (1982).

particularly those of Tiglath Pileser I, although Palestine was not directly affected by these[37].

If we turn to the Egyptian royal inscriptions from the time of the 18th and 19th dynasties, it looks as if Palestine was conquered and reconquered endlessly by various pharaohs, from the very first Egyptian possession of the country as early as the close of the 16th century[38]. It can hardly have been as bad as all that. There is very good reason to believe that a number of these "campaigns" never took place, and that at most what actually happened was that a given pharaoh or his representatives accepted the submission of the Canaanite petty kings in connection with a new accession to the throne[39]. Also, even though the Egyptian conquest of the country must have had extensive consequences for the country at the beginning of the Late Bronze Age, there is no reason to believe that similar events took place later on. In short, the Egyptian conquest of Palestine no doubt signified that the country became part of the Egyptian empire, with all of the economic consequences mentioned previously. Nevertheless, in subsequent periods there were both advantages and disadvantages in connection with membership of the Egyptian political system. The disadvantages were a feature of the imposts and tribute payments made to Egypt, while on the positive side of the ledger there were lengthy periods of relative peace. These latter were interrupted by intervals when the Egyptian hold on the region weakened, as it did in the Amarna period. In such a situation a Palestinian power center could not prevent an unfortunate course of development, since it was impossible to establish such a power center under the Egyptian overlordship.

Epochs like the Amarna period must have accentuated the turbulence in the region, since the latent internecine conflicts inherent in the city-state system will then have enjoyed untrammeled possibilities for growth, as the Amarna correspondence so suggestively reveals. In the period following the reconsolidation of Egyptian rule we have no information as to similar civil warlike conditions. However, it is conceivable that corresponding internal political difficulties always played some part, and that they may have escalated when the Egyptian presence declined. This may have happened as early as the later years of Rameses II, and the situation probably became acute under his successors[40]. Although we have little concrete data to this effect, the archeologi-

---

[37] Tiglath Pileser I (1115-1077) reached during his second campaign against the West Phoenicia, Arvad, and Ṣumura (Ṣamuri) – by sea. The campaign also affected both Byblos and Sidon, and was registered as far south as Egypt, which sent exotic presents to the Assyrian Great King. Cf. Weidner 1957 (with texts) and Wiseman 1975.

[38] A selection of these texts are available in translation in ANET³:234ff. (Thutmoses III). 245-248 (Amenhotep II).255-258 (Rameses II). Palestine had presumably been invaded already by Amenhotep I (1546-1526); cf. Helck 1968A:148. The decisive conquest was undertaken by Thutmoses III(1504-1450); cf. Helck 1968A:154ff.

[39] Cf. Helck's evaluation of the first campaign of Amenhotep II in Helck 1968A:162; on that of Thutmoses IV (1425-1417) see Helck 1968A:165.

[40] See also Liverani, who emphasizes that in reality the Amarna period may have been a characteristic of Palestine in the close of the 2nd millennium (1971A:268).

cal picture during the period from the close of the 13th and the whole of the 12th century suggests that the Canaanite city-states were in a serious crisis at this time. This was a time of crisis which was only exacerbated by the arrival of the groups of Sea Peoples such as the Philistines and the Tjekkers[41].

Finally, there is the interval between the Amarna period and the treaty concluded between Rameses II and Hattušiliš III which ended the rivalry of the two great powers. The main events in this interval took place in Syria, but Palestine was the country of transit for numerous Egyptian armies on their way to and from the battle zones. Once again we lack concrete information as to the inconveniences brought about by this situation, so we are reduced to drawing rather general conclusions based on a "normative view" of war and its consequences, seen in historical perspective. Thus it would be permissible to assume that Egyptian military units ordinarily lived off the land. Also, it is well known that war is not an inexpensive undertaking, so that we again have reason to *presume* that the increase in Egyptian military activity also entailed increases in the taxes and imposts which were levied on the Egyptian provinces. Therefore it would hardly be unreasonable to regard the decrease of evidence of international trade (i.e., the lack of imported pottery) from the 14th century and later as one of the consequences of the generally turbulent situation. To put the matter more precisely, the tensions of this era, in which the two great military powers of the Near East vied with each other for supremacy, were contributory to the interruption of trade. Other factors which also militated against peaceful trade will no doubt have included the disintegration which began to affect the Mycenaean world from this time onwards.

The last factor listed above was the social aspect; it may not be considered in isolation from the previously-mentioned factors since its presuppositions are distributed among these. The tendencies towards dissolution among the city-states of the Near East exemplify the brutal conditions then confronting Bronze Age culture. In a previous article I have discussed the significance the political chaos, military confrontations, and falling standard of living must have had for the lowest strata in the various societies involved[42]. At that time I argued that the weakest part of the population would necessarily be forced to shoulder the heaviest burdens in such a situation. However, in the case of Palestine we have no hard facts as to how matters proceeded. Thus we do not know whether the disintegration of the state-run agrarian sector was the result of an economic exploitation of this sector which resulted in insufferable living

---

[41] Even though we have evidence of the presence of Sea People groups already prior to 1200, including especially the *šerden*, who, among other things, supported the Egyptians at the battle of Qadesh (ca.1300; cf. Gardiner 1960:15 (P26)), and even earlier in the Amarna Letters (EA 81: 16; 122:35; 123: 15), this decisive crisis in the movement of the Sea Peoples first took place around the beginning of the 12th century. See most recently Strange 1980:157-160.

[42] Lemche 1980:179ff.

conditions for the populace. However, it is in this connection that the ḫabiru problem is of decisive importance.

We happen to possess one actual example of what could transpire in a state when its agricultural sector became seriously weakened. I refer once more to Byblos during the Amarna period, in which we have the evidence of king Rib-Addu's correspondence which suggests that the non-free clients (ḫupšu) of his state were emmigrating to foreign regions, egged on by the siren-song of the king of Amurru. Thus it seems as if Rib-Addu's most dangerous opponent was playing on a pronounced social resentment in Rib-Addu's state in order to destroy the basis for the existence of Byblos[43]. We have other evidence as to the presence of ḫabiru groups which were beyond state control. In this connection we must examine the settlement pattern during the Late Bronze Age, and in particular those parts of Palestine which were either uninhabited or only sparsely populated. Such regions included the Negeb and the mountainous areas in the central and northern part of the country. Admittedly, there were some individual towns such as Shechem and Jerusalem in this mountainous part of the country, but Shechem came under ḫabiru control already in the Amarna period, and Jerusalem was in acute danger of suffering a similar fate[44]. Therefore, as a working hypothesis I propose the following scenario: at least as early as from the first half of the 14th century and subsequently the mountainous regions were "inhabited" by a para-social element, the ḫabiru, who consisted of runaway former non-free peasants or copyholders from the small city-states in the plains and valleys of Palestine[45]. The Canaanite city-states were not destroyed, but weakened, by this evacuation, which also clearly continued to be a problem after the end of the Amarna period[46]. In the Amarna period there had not as yet arisen any coordinated political or social resistance to the city-states, with the exception of isolated examples like Shechem. The phenomenon was recognized as parasocial by the city-states, which abhorred them to such a degree that they also used the term ḫabiru of other political tendencies which they regarded as illegitimate, such as groups of citizens opposed to the local city-state government, or other rulers seeking to expand their territories at their neighbors' expense. As of yet, archeology does not permit us to localize the presence of these ḫabiru in the mountainous regions, but the reason for this is no doubt that they were not a sedentary ele-

---

[43] Cf. Artzy 1964; Klengel 1964; 1969:253ff. and 276ff., and Liverani 1965A and 1967. Note also the evaluation of Rib-Addu and his "crisis" in Liverani 1971A and 1974.

[44] Cf. EA 189.

[45] The extent of the references to the ḫabiru in the Armarna archives, as well as their geographical distribution, may be seen in Mendenhall's table (Mendenhall 1973:123). At this time we are in the 1st half of the 14th century, but even earlier, during the reign of Amenhotep II, the ḫabiru were mentioned among his Asiatic prisoners of war (cf. ANET³:247). Finally, an Egyptian inscription from the close of the 14th century mentions the presence of the ḫabiru in Palestine (the stela of Seti I from Beth Shan; see ANET³:255).

[46] See ANET³:255, and cf. Albright 1952, and Lemche 1979A:21-22.

ment, but outlaw groups of freebooters. More than a century elapsed after the
Amarna period before we can demonstrate the existence of concrete political
structures outside of the domains of the city-states (that is, if we are willing to
acknowledge the establishment of permanent structures in the form of open
villages as also constituting political entities)[47].

What were the reasons these new political structures arose and manifested
themselves as new settlements? A primary reason for this delayed reaction of
a social movement which is already discernible in the Amarna period must
have been the technical difficulties connected with cultivation of the mountainous regions, which had traditionally prohibited the exploitation of these
areas for farming. These technical problems seem to have been solved by the
beginning of the Iron Age. The first notable novelty in this connection is the
introduction of iron for the production of tools. Earlier scholarship regarded
this as one of the three most important presuppositions for the sudden changes
in Palestine around 1200; indeed, some have additionally pointed to the Philistines as the importers of iron into this part of the Near East[48]. However,
more recent studies have shown that iron was far from playing any dominant
role in daily life until some time *after* the formation of the Israelite state.
Implements of bronze still dominated the picture in the early "Iron Age".
Moreover, as far as the Philistine role as iron-importers is concerned, it is to
be noted that there is now evidence of iron metallurgy in Palestine already
before the arrival of the Philistines in the country[49]. Thus one would do well
to discard iron as the reason for the emergence of agrarian societies in the
mountainous regions of Palestine around 1200.

As mentioned previously, there is reason to believe that the mountainous
areas were covered with forest and scrub growth during the Late Bronze Age.
Such growth had to be removed, if the areas in question were to be cultivated,
which is why scholars imagined that iron tools were essential to such a task.
However, this is simply not the case, as anyone can say who has even witnessed
the ignition and spread of forest fires in Mediterranean regions. It cannot have
been any great task to clear the mountains of undergrowth; a couple of well-
placed torches and a favorable wind will have been sufficient in such arid territory. On the other hand, there were some real problems connected with the
utilization of the newly-exposed mountain slopes for farming; these difficulties

---

[47] See above, pp. 401-405 for these villages and the date of their foundation.
[48] Gottwald still maintained this in Gottwald 1979A:297 and 655-660.
[49] On this see Stech-Wheeler and Muhly, et al., 1981. Note the statistical evaluation of the
respective importance of bronze and iron from 1200 to 900 in Waldbaum 1978:39 (Palestine).
According to Waldbaum, in the 12th century the relationship was 74% bronze vs. 4% iron; in
the 11th c. it was 78% bronze vs. 14% iron, and as late as the 10th c. it was 60% bronze vs. 27%
iron. It should also be noted that this iron was of little practical use until down into the 10th c.,
when steel technology made its appearance (Stech-Wheeler and Muhly, et al., 1981; Strange, as
yet unpublished). Generally on the question of the introduction of iron, see Wertime and Muhly
1980, including esp. Waldbaum 1980 and Snodgrass 1980.

are related to the water supply in the areas in question. In such regions, drought is the rule for most of the year, while torrential rains also fall at certain times. The rain quickly runs off and disappears without the presence of forest vegetation to retain moisture. Even more to the point is the fact that the run-off takes the topsoil with it. None of this is new, but it is interesting to observe that towards the close of the 13th century a technique was evolved in Palestine to counteract the unfortunate results of the deforestation. The inhabitants began to terrace the slopes and hence were able both to retain the earth and to exploit the rainfall available rationally[50]. Is is also frequently pointed out that in the same period ways of preserving the available rainfall were discovered; it was at this time lined water cisterns were introduced[51].

Thus the material presuppositions for the emergence of an agrarian culture in the Palestinian highlands were at hand around 1200 or shortly before.

The next question has to do with the evolution of political integration in the area. I can suggest two models of this process. The first of them corresponds to the concepts of political integration in the Beqa' valley in Lebanon which have been presented by L. Marfoe[52]. It is to be recalled that Marfoe's pattern consisted of a greater or lesser number of microscopic city-states which were surrounded by rings of villages. Marfoe feels that kinship ties must have been poor in the agrarian sections of the city-states in question, so that importance mainly accrued to the most elementary unit, the family (nuclear or extended). The pattern of settlement changed during the transition from the Bronze Age to the Iron Age, in that the number of villages in the valley reaches decreased considerably. On the other hand, a whole series of new settlements sprang up at this time on the mountain slopes; Marfoe holds that these were probably autonomous village societies. A higher degree of social and political integration was achieved than that of the nuclear family in such circumstances, as in the course of time true tribal societies arose which had the potential to develop into tribal states or chieftainships. The presupposition for Marfoe's model is that the Canaanite states lacked social integration at a level higher than that of the local family.

There is reason to doubt the validity of Marfoe's model. Admittedly, we have very little information as to the social structure of the lower levels of Canaanite society, for which reason scholars usually rely on data from Ugarit and Alalaḫ to some degree. However, there are a number of differences already with respect to these two societies. Thus it is hardly acceptable merely to reapply, for example, the results of a sociological analysis of Ugarit to other parts of the Middle East. Nor do the archives of Ugarit contain such extensive materials that we are able to say with certainty that the family was the only

---

[50] On terrassing see Ron 1966 and De Geus 1975; see also Gottwald 1979A:655-660.
[51] See already Albright 1949:113 and 210. Further, Gottwald 1979A:656.
[52] Marfoe 1979.

form of social organization this society possessed. A different model, one which would assert the existence of a lineage structure in Canaanite society (analogous to the structure we find everywhere in the Middle East in the post-Christian period), is at least equally plausible. If lineages were the basic structure in the societies in question, they will also have been the primary factor for the establishment of agrarian societies outside of the Canaanite city-states. Any (re)tribalization of the Canaanite agricultural populace will have followed lineage structure and been related to the political integration of the lineages on the various higher stages, until a fully developed tribal organization was achieved. Thus the formation of the Israelite monarchy was the initial phase of the *detribalization* of this lineage structure. During the monarchy lineage structure will have persisted, although it will no longer have been subordinated to a local political organization, that is, it was no longer part of a tribe.

Both of the models mentioned, which are to be regarded as variants of one and the same basic thesis on the emergence of tribal societies in the Near East at the close of the Bronze Age and the beginnings of the Iron Age, are possible, but as of yet they cannot be regarded as more than working hypotheses. In the case of Palestine we already know the result of the process in question, namely the emergence of the Israelite tribes, or rather, of a number of Palestinian tribes whose various populations became unified in the kingdom of Israel after the formation of the state. In this connection it is entirely appropriate that our first certain reference to the presence in Palestine of a society of non-national character is to be dated to the end of the 13th century; it is no less appropriate that this society is called "Israel". Of course, I am referring to the reference on the "victory stela" of Merneptah to "Israel" as one of the vanquished enemies of the Egyptians who dwelled in the Levant. It has very frequently been pointed out that in the inscription in question this "Israel" is characterized as a different sort of society from those of the three city-states mentioned in the same section of the text (i.e., Askalon, Gezer, and Janoam), since the determinant for "people" is employed[53]. Thus there is no reason not to suppose that the Israel in question was a tribal society. However, the question is, how to define this society? Was there a single tribe by the name of Israel, or was it a coalition of tribes? The former possibility is unlikely, since the OT scarcely speaks of a single tribe named Israel; it refers instead to a tribal ancestor of this name. Against the second possibility is the fact that scholars have been unable to demonstrate the existence of an Israelite tribal coalition during the pre-national period, at least not in the sense of a permanent political organization with a fixed membership circle. It is possible to claim that Merneptah's stela actually implies the geographical location of this "Israel", since the text moves from the southwestern to the northeastern parts of Palestine, that is, from Askalon on the coast to Gezer and Janoam (that is, if Janoam is synonymous with the region around *Jānūn*). If this observation is correct, then it would be

---

[53] The most recent studies by OT scholars: Engel 1979 and Otto 1979:200-205.

natural to seek this "Israel" in the northern part of the highlands of central Palestine. There are a number of hints in favor of this supposition in the OT legendary materials, which unambiguously associate the figure of Jacob-Israel with precisely this territory. Of course, we have no way of knowing how many of the OT Iraelite tribes may have belonged to such a coalition, but it would not be unreasonable to suppose that the three units later described as Rachel-tribes were the basic element. It is similarly an open question as to whether Ephraim, Manasseh, and Benjamin existed as independent tribes within some kind of league, or whether they were secondary segments of a primary unit called Israel. It is likewise impossible on the basis of the OT evidence to say how such fission or fusion processes may have taken place.

The population of the society in question can no longer be regarded as ḫabiru. This society was the result of a movement which owed its origins to the choices made by individual persons, families, and lineages with respect to their way of life. In other words, the parties involved had said goodbye to their previous existences, which had been made miserable by the poor social conditions which were all the Canaanite states had to offer in the Late Bronze Age. It is interesting to note that the OT still preserves evidence that as late as the year 1000, and perhaps later, the term ḫabiru continued to be pejoratively associated with this society. Thus, for example, the OT records that the Philistines termed the Israelites ḫabiru and in the Joseph novella and the Exodus traditions the designation is placed in the mouths of the Egyptians with reference to the Israelites[54]. It is conceivable that these references contain an ancient reflection of the fact that after the societies in question had established themselves in the mountainous regions, beyond the control of the city-states as well as that of the Egyptian empire, they came to be termed ḫabiru by the respective "official" instances. Of course, they will not have referred to themselves as ḫabiru, but it appears that this term for the inhabitants of the mountainous regions was adopted by the Philistines when they in turn assumed control of the Canaanite states along the coast.

The final question in this connection has to do with the autonomy of the villages with respect to the "Canaanite" urban socities. The OT source materials indicate that the Israelite villages were politically independent, although they were also to some extent economically dependent on the city-states[55]. The connections linking town and village may be determined by study of the pottery which has been found in the villages. On the one hand, this pottery represents a further development of the earlier Late Bronze Age tradition, but on the other we can detect the beginnings of an independent tradition in the Israelite villages (the "collared rim" pithoi). Rather than indicating the presence of a *new* people, the pottery indicates that an old tradition was originally retai-

---

[54] Cf. Lemche 1979A:9ff. and 1980:154ff.
[55] Cf. 1 Sam 14,3.19ff.

ned in the new societies in the mountains which then subsequently evolved of its own accord. It did not evolve along the same lines everywhere, as we can see by examination of the local differences within the "Israelite" area itself.

The understanding of Israelite village society presented here is closely related to some of Gottwald's observations[56]. However, in the article in question Gottwald is solely concerned with economic conditions (based on K. Marx' account of an "Asiatic method of production"), whereas I have attempted to broaden the perspective to some extent. For example, Gottwald attempts to explain the ability of the Israelite villages to defend their independence on the basis of the successful attempts of these villages to avoid economic integration in to the Canaanite system. However, in this respect other factors must have been at least equally important (especially when we consider that there are reasons to doubt the health of the Canaanite economic system in the period 1200-1000), such as military and strategic matters. Gottwald has overlooked the fact that the Israelite villages were mainly new settlements, plus the fact that they were geographically situated outside of the immediate political control of the Canaanite states, that is, in mountainous regions which were difficult of access. Also, there is reason to question whether the towns had any interest whatsoever in gaining control of the Israelite mountain villages, when we consider their remote situation. In fact, if we were to attempt to plot these villages on the scheme worked out by Fernea, we should be forced to describe them as extremely independent with respect to the urban centers[57]. It would be much more difficult to determine whether the life of these villages was governed by cooperative interests within the framework of the individual villages, or whether they were ruled by the specific economic interests of individuals or lineages within the villages. There are signs in the OT that both types of influence may have been present.

§ 3

Future Perspectives: Israelite Religion

The explanation of the origins of Israel presented here does not presuppose an Israelite immigration which is archeologically indemonstrable, and which the cultural pattern in the new-founded villages does not seem to require. Thus we conclude that the concept of an immigration is a superfluous hypothesis. Nor have we found it necessary to maintain that an element in Israelite society

---

[56] Cf. Gottwald 1976.
[57] See above, pp. 187f.

which produced meaning and comprehension (i.e., Israelite religion) made this society something unique from its very inception. The revolution hypothesis, as we have seen, links the idea of a unique Israelite religion together with the notion that the Israelite tribal society played a unique role in its own time. This is hardly a reasonable point of departure. It would be far more reasonable to regard Israel as but one among the many stateless societies which arose towards the end of the Late Bronze Age and the beginning of the Iron Age, and which were later to be known as the Aramaean, Moabite, Ammonite, and Edomite tribes and states. The process of (re)tribalization was probably far more extensive than either Mendenhall or Gottwald has imagined, but there is no reason to believe that Israel differed significantly in this respect from her eastern neighbors.

The fundamental mistake has been that scholars have chosen to "theologize" this social process. They have projected the ideas of the Jewish pariah-society concerning its origins back into the past. Therefore they have also failed to interpret this late – that is, exilic and post-exilic – Jewish society on the basis of its own presuppositions, but on the basis of the fanciful picture this society had created of its own past and the origins of its religion. As an alternative, I would emphasize the necessity of an explanation of Israel's origins, which avoids reference to an element productive of meanings until such an element can be located within a context which belongs to the past and which is not a 500-year younger social phenomenon. This opens up entirely new perspectives not only for the understanding of the historical development of Israel, but also for a description of the history of Israelite religion.

It will only be possible in this context to mention some general problems which should be dealt with in this connection. In the first place, it is out of the question simply *a priori* to assume that Israelite religion was unique from its very beginnings, even though it claims this distinction itself. It must be *proven* that this was the case. However, before attempting to muster such proof, it must first be shown that this religion was not Canaanite, which I mean in a sense that is broader than is customary in OT usage. Scholars have focused entirely too frequently on a single element within Canaanite religion, namely the aspect of fertility worship and natural religion. They have generally forgotten that there was another side to the picture also in the Canaanite world. By this I mean that we have massive evidence stretching over a period of more than fifteen hundred years up to the formation of the Israelite state of a different side of the religious life than sex orgies, blood rites, and similar abominations. The entire Oriental tradition contained an additional aspect which was not concerned with sacrifices, but with laws and justice, cosmic and earthly rules for conducting one's life and governing states; in short, all of this was concerned with *social justice*.

Oddly enough, we must turn to such a relatively conservative scholar as E. Hammershaimb to find some understanding of this side of Canaanite religion, since in an article which appeared almost twenty-five years ago Hammershaimb was able to demonstrate the extent to which the social ethics of the prophets were rooted in conceptions which were well known in other parts of the Near East than Israel[58]. Thus it is and will remain an important task of the history of religions to attempt to determine to what extent Israelite religion was independent with respect to this other tradition in the religious life of the Near East. In fact, it may prove to be a fruitful working hypothesis to assume that the phenomenon which came to be the specifically Israelite religion was fundamentally what might be termed an isolation of one particular aspect of Canaanite culture, namely the ethical. The theologians who strove to achieve this isolation seem to have consciously rejected the other side of the coin, namely, fertility worship.

The next phase in this sort of analysis of Israelite religion will be based on the sociology of religion, since it will be essential to attempt to determine whether Israelite ethical religion was an *urban religion* or a *rural religion*. By this I mean that it should be possible to discover what sort of milieu was conducive to an ethical religion like Judaism. Although I cannot prove it, it seems plausible to me that the *ethical religion* derived from urban circles, and specifically from the upper strata, since it was these circles which were in a position to permit themselves the luxury of scorning the forces of nature, and thus to reject the association between rite and fertility. Such groups will have been free to to pursue other norms.

In this context I can do no more than merely to suggest a working hypothesis which, however, if it is used as a starting point, also entails that when we undertake to analyze the individual traditions in the OT we have not previously determined our conclusions. This point of departure will make it possible for us to open our eyes with respect to the sources dealing with Israel's religious life in the so-called "period of the Judges" and the monarchy without automatically evaluating this life as divergences from or approximations to an orthodox Yahwistic religion. Fo example, without dogmatic assumptions, the names of Saul's sons may be taken to suggest that there was a neutral attitude with respect to Yahweh, Ba'al, and El during the period when the monarchy was introduced. It should also be possible to acknowledge that it was possible for a legendary Israelite hero to be called ירבעל, without feeling called upon to distort this name, as was done in later Jewish tradition. It will also be easier to understand the religious developments during the period of the monarchy, and to explain the massive presence of elements of Canaanite religion throughout this period. There will no longer be any reason to speak of syncretism as a mixture of two essentially different types of religion. Instead, using

---

[58] Hammershaimb 1960. It is these expectations which underly the *mīšarum* concepts which were dispersed in both Mesopotamia and the Near East; cf. Lemche 1976 and 1979B.

the perspectives of the sociology of religion, we shall be in a position to reckon with a variety of different levels within Canaanite religion.

With such a working hypothesis as one's point of departure, it will not be necessary to deny that there actually existed traditions of a divine revelation somewhere on Sinai, but it will no doubt be useful to avoid preconceived notions as to the contents of such a revelation. This is so since its present main ingredient, the covenant, does not seem to have played any significant role in the religious life of Israel before the 6th century. Nor, for that matter, is there any reason to deny that the god himself, Yahweh, had his origins outside of Palestine. However, it would be wise to recall that when we have said something about where a god came from, we have said nothing about his nature. Finally, there is no reason to dismiss Moses as a legendary figure who was associated with the introduction of the Yahwistic religion at some point in the development of the tradition, whether early or late. Noth pointed out long ago that Moses was a legendary figure, and E. Nielsen has demonstrated recently that it was only in relatively late times that Moses was understood as a *law-giver*[59]. These views accord brilliantly with the working model suggested here for the further study of Israelite religion, which also implies that its special characteristics were the results of a long historical development, rather than its point of departure.

---

[59] Nielsen 1982.

BIBLIOGRAPHY

Aberbach, M. and Smolar, L.
  1967   Aaron, Jeroboam, and the Golden Calves. *Journal of Biblical Literature 68:129–140*

Abrahamian, E.
  1975   European Feudalism and Middle Eastern Despotism. *Science & Society 39:1975–1976:129–156*

Adams, R. McC.
  1969   Conclusion. *LAPIDUS 1969A:188–196*
  1974   The Mesopotamian Social Landscape: A View from the Frontier. *MOORE 1974:1–20*

Adams, W.Y.
  1968   Invasion, Diffusion, Evolution? *Antiquity 42:194–215*

Adams, W.Y., Van Gerven D.P. and Levy, R.S.
  1978   The Retreat from Migrationism. *Annual Review of Anthropology 7:483–532*

Addinal, P.
  1981   The Wilderness in Pedersen's *Israel. Journal for the Study of the Old Testament 20:75–83*

Aharoni, Y.
  1957   Problems of the Israelite Conquest in the Light of Archaeological Discoveries. *Antiquity and Survival II:2–3:131–150*
  1959   The Province-List of Judah. *Vetus Testamentum 9:225–246*
  1967   The Land of the Bible. A Historical Geography. *London*
  1970   New Aspects of the Israelite Occupation in the North. *SANDERS 1970:254–267*
  1973   Beer-Sheba I. Excavations at Tel Beer-Sheba 1969–1971 Seasons. *Tel Aviv University. Institute of Archaeology. Publications of the Institute of Archaeology No. 2. Tel Aviv*
  1975A   Arad: The Upper Mound. *EAEHL I:82–89*
  1975B   Beersheba, Tel. *EAEHL I:160–168*
  1976A   Nothing Early and Nothing Late: Re-Writing Israel's Conquest. *The Biblical Archaeologist 39:55–76*
  1976B   Galilee, Upper. *EAEHL II:406–408*

Aharoni, Y., Fritz, V. and Kempinsky, A.
  1974   Excavations at Tel Masos (Khirbet El-Meshâsh). Preliminary Report of the First Season. 1972. *Tel Aviv 1:64–74*
  1975   Excavations at Tel Masos (Khirbet El-Meshâsh). Preliminary Report of the Second Season, 1974. *Tel Aviv 2:97–124*

Aharoni, Y. and Yadin, Y.
  1977   Megiddo. *EAEHL III:830–856*

Ahlström, G.W.
  1959   Psalm 89. Eine Liturgie aus dem Ritual des leidenden Königs. *Lund*
  1980   Is Tell ed-Duweir Ancient Lachish? *Palestine Exploration Quarterly 112:7–9*

Albrektson, B.
  1967   History and the Gods. An Essay on the Idea of Historical Events as Divine Manifestations in the Ancient Near East and in Israel. *Coniectanea Biblica Old Testament Series 1. Lund*
  1979   Gudarna och historien. *Albrektson, B.: Kapitlet om Jehu och andra uppsatser om Gamla testamentet. Stockholm*

Albright, W.F.
  1924   Researches of the School in Western Judaea. *Bulletin of the American Schools of Oriental Research 15:2–11*

1932A   The Archaeology of Palestine and the Bible. *New York*
1932B   The Excavations of Tell Beit Mirsim in Palestine I. The Pottery of the First Three Campaigns. *The Annual of the American Schools of Oriental Research XII, 1930-31. New Haven*
1934   The Vocalization of the Egyptian Syllabic Orthography. *American Oriental Series Vol. 5. New Haven*
1935   Archaeology and the Date of the Hebrew Conquest of Palestine. *Bulletin of the American Schools of Oriental Research 58:10-18*
1936   The Song of Deborah in the Light of Archaeology. *Bulletin of the American Schools of Oriental Research 62:26-31*
1937   Further Light on the History of Israel From Lachish and Megiddo. *Bulletin of the American Schools of Oriental Research 68:22-26*
1938   The Excavations of Tell Beit Mirsim II. The Bronze Age. *The Annual of the American Schools of Oriental Research XVII, 1936-37. New Haven*
1939   The Israelite Conquest of Palestine in the Light of Archaeology. *Bulletin of the American Schools of Oriental Research 74:11-23*
1942   A Case of Lèse-Majesté in Pre-Israelite Lachish with some Remarks on the Israelite Conquest. *Bulletin of the American Schools of Oriental Research 87:32-38*
1943   The Excavations of Tell Beit Mirsim III. The Iron Age. *The Annual of the American Schools of Oriental Research XXI-XXII, 1941-1943. New Haven*
1944   The Oracles of Balaam. *Journal of Biblical Literature 63:207-233*
1946   Archaeology and the Religion of Israel. *The Ayer Lectures of the Colgate-Rochester Divinity School 1941. 2.ed. Baltimore*
1949   The Archaeology of Palestine. *(repr. 1963) Harmondsworth*
1950A   The Psalm of Habakkuk. *H.H. ROWLEY: Studies in Old Testament Prophecy Presented to Th.H. Robinson. Edinburgh 1950 (repr. 1957):1-18*
1950B   A Catalogue of Early Hebrew Lyric Poems. *Hebrew Union College Annual 23:1-39*
1952   The Smaller Beth-Shan Stele of Sethos I (1309-1290 B.C.). *Bulletin of the American Schools of Oriental Research 125:24-32*
1957   From the Stone Age to Christianity. Monotheism and the Historical Process. *2.ed. New York*
1961A   The Role of the Canaanites in the History of Civilization. *WRIGHT 1961:328-362*
1961B   Abraham the Hebrew. A New Archaeological Interpretation. *Bulletin of the American Schools of Oriental Research 163:36-54*
1963   The Biblical Period From Abraham to Ezra. *New York*
1966   The Proto-Sinaitic Inscriptions and their Descipherment. *Harvard Theological Studies XXII. Cambridge, Mass.*
1968   Yahweh and the Gods of Canaan. A Historical Analysis of two Contrasting Faiths. *Jordan Lectures 1965. London*
1975   The Amarna Letters from Palestine. *CAH³ II:2:98-116*

Aldred, C.
1975   Egypt: The Amarna Period and the End of the Eighteenth Dynasty. *CAH³ II:2: 49-97*

Alt, A.
1913   Israels Gaue unter Salomo. *ALT 1953:II:76-89*
1925A   Judas Gaue unter Josia. *ALT 1953:II:276-288*
1925B   Die Landnahme der Israeliten in Palästina. *ALT 1953:I:89-125*
1927   Das System der Stammegrenzen im Buche Josua. *ALT 1953:I:193-202*
1929   Der Gott der Väter. *ALT 1953:I:1-78*
1930   Die Staatenbilding der Israeliten in Palästina. *ALT 1953:II:1-65*
1936   Josua. *ALT 1953:I:176-192*
1939   Erwägungen über die Landnahme der Israeliten in Palästina. *ALT 1953:I:126-175*
1941   Herren und Herrensitze Palästinas im Anfang des zweiten Jahrtausends v. Chr. *ALT 1953:III:57-71*

1950   Jesaja 8,23–9,6. Befreiungsnacht und Krönungstag. *ALT 1953:II:206–225*
1951   Das Königtum in den Reichen Israel und Juda. *ALT 1953:II:116–134*
1953   Kleine Schriften zur Geschichte des Volkes Israel I–III. *München 1953–1959*
1956   Bemerkungen zu der Verwaltungs- und Rechtsurkunden von Ugarit und Ala-
        lach. *Die Welt des Orients 2:7–18*
1957   Bemerkungen zu den Verwaltungs- und Rechtsurkunden von Ugarit und Ala-
        lach. *Die Welt des Orients 2:234–243.*
1958   Bemerkungen zu den Verwaltungs- und Rechtsurkunden von Ugarit und Ala-
        lach. *Die Welt des Orients 2:338–342.*
1964   Bemerkungen zu den Verwaltungs- und Rechtsurkunden von Ugarit und Ala-
        lach. *Die Welt des Orients 3:3–18*

Amiran, R.
1970   Ancient Pottery of the Holy Land from its Beginnings in the Neolithic Period to
        the End of the Iron Age. *Rutgers University Press*

Ammar, H.
1970   The Social Organization of the Community. *A.M. LUTFIYYA and C.W. CHUR-
        CHILL: Readings in Arab Middle Eastern Societies and Cultures. The Hague 1970:109–
        134*

Andersen, F.I.
1969   Israelite Kinship Terminology and Social Structure. *The Bible Translator 20:29–39*

Antoun, R.T.
1972A   Arab Village. A Social Structural Study of a Transjordanian Peasant Commu-
        nity. *Bloomington*
1972B   Pertinent Variables in the Environment of Middle Eastern Village Politics. A.
        Comparative Analysis. *ANTOUN and HARIK 1972:118–162*

Antoun, R.T. and Harik, I.
1972   Rural Politics and Social Change in the Middle East. *Studies in Development No. 5.
        Bloomington*

Archi, A.
1979   The Epigraphic Evidence from Ebla and the Old Testament. *Biblica 60:556–566*

Artzi, P.
1964   »Vox Populi« in the El-Amarna Tablets. *Revue Assyriologique 58:159–166*

Asad, T.
1970   The Kababish Arabs. Power, Authority and Consent in a Nomadic Tribe. *New
        York*
1972   Political Inequality in the Kababish Tribe. *I. CUNNISON and W. JAMES: Essays
        in Sudan Ethnography Presented to Sir Edward Evans-Pritchard. London 1972:126–148*
1973   The Beduin as a Military Force: Notes on some Aspects of Power Relations Be-
        tween Nomads and Sedentaries in Historical Perspective. *NELSON 1973:61–73*
1979   Equality in nomadic social systems? Notes towards the dissolution of an anthro-
        pological category. *Pastoral Production and Society:419–428*

Ashkenazi, T.
1938   Tribus semi-nomades de la Palestine du Nord. *Paris*

Assman, J.
1973   Aton. *Lexikon der Ägyptologie I:526–540*

Aswad, B.
1971★   Property Control and Social Strategies: Settlers on a Middle Eastern Plain. *An-
        thropological Papers, Museum of Anthropology University of Michigan No. 44. Ann Arbor*

Bacon, E.E.
1954   Types of Pastoral Nomadism in Central and Southwest Asia. *Southwestern Journal
        of Anthropology 10:44–68*

Balland, D. and Kieffer, C.M.
1979   Nomadism et sécheresse en Afghanistan: l'exemple des nomades Paštun du Dašt-e Nawor. *Pastoral Production and Society:75–90*

Barnes, J.A.
1954   Politics in a Changing Society. A Political History of the Fort Jameson Ngoni. *Manchester*
1955   Seven Types of Segmentation. *The Rhodes-Livingstone Journal 17:1–22*
1971   Three Styles in the Study of Kinship. *London*

Barr, J.
1961   The Semantics of Biblical Language. *Oxford*

Barth, F.
1953   Principles of Social Organization in Southern Kurdistan. *Universitetets etnografiske Museum Bulletin no. 7. Oslo*
1954   Farther's Brother's Daughter Marriage in Kurdistan. *Southwestern Journal of Anthropology 10:164–171*
1959   Political Leadership Among Swat Pathans. *London School of Economics. Monographs on Social Anthropology No. 19. London*
1962   Nomadism in the Mountain and Plateau Areas of South West Asia. *The Problems of the Arid Zone. Proceedings of the Paris Symposium. Arid Zone Research 18. UNESCO. Paris 1962:341–355*
1964A   Nomads of South Persia. The Basseri Tribe of the Khamseh Confederacy. *Oslo*
1964B   Capital, Investment and the Social Structure of a Pastoral Nomad Group in South Persia. *R. FIRTH and B.S. YAMAY: Capital, Saving and Credit in Peasant Societies. London 1964:69–81*
1969   (ed.) Ethnic Groups and Boundaries. The Social Organization of Culture Difference. *Oslo*
1973A   A General Perspective of Nomads-Sedentary Relations in the Middle East. *NELSON 1973:11–21*
1973B   Descent and marriage reconsidered. *J. GOODY: The Character of Kinship. Cambridge 1973:3–19*
1978   (ed.) Scale and Social Organization. *Oslo*

Bates, D.G.
1971   The Role of the State in Peasant-Nomad Mutualism. *SALZMAN 1971A:109–131*
1972   Differential Access to Pasture in a Nomadic Society. The Yörük of Southeastern Turkey. *IRONS and DYSON-HUDSON 1972:48-59.*
1973   Nomads and Farmers. A Study of the Yörük of Southeastern Turkey. *Anthropological Papers, Museum of Anthropology, University of Michigan No. 52. Ann Arbor*
1980   The Yörük Settlement in Southeast Turkey. *SALZMAN 1980:124–139*

Baxter, P.T.W.
1960   The Kiga. *RICHARDS 1960A:278–310*

Beck, L.
1980   Herd Owners and Hired Shepherds: The Qashqa'i of Iran. *Ethnology 19:327–351*

Bell, B.
1971   The Dark Ages in Ancient History I. The First Dark Age in Egypt. *American Journal of Archaeology 75:1–26*

Ben-Thor, A.
1975   The First Season of Excavations at Tell-Yarmuth, 1970. *Qedem 1:54–87*
1976   Jarmut, Tell. *EAEHL II:544–545*
1979   Tell Qiri. A Look at Village Life. *The Biblical Archaeologist 42:105–113*

Bentzen, Aa.
1939   Fortolkning til de gammeltestamentlige salmer. *København*

440 BIBLIOGRAPHY

Bernhardt, K.-H.
1971   Verwaltungspraxis in spätbronzezeitlichen Palästina. *KLENGEL 1971:133-147*

Beyerlin, W.
1963   Geschichte und Heilsgeschichtliche Traditionsbildung im Alten Testament. Ein Beitrag zur Traditionsgeschichte von Richter VI-VIII. *Vetus Testamentum 13:1-25*

Bimson, J.J.
1978   Redating Exodus and Conquest. *Journal for the Study of the Old Testament Supplement Series 5. Sheffield*

Binder, L.
1976   The Study of the Middle East. Research and Scholarship in the Humanities and the Social Sciences. *New York*

Binford, L.R.
1972   An Archaeological Perspective. *New York*

Biran, A.
1977   Tel Dan, 1977. *Israel Exploration Journal 27:242-246*
1978   Sippor, Tel. *EAEHL IV:1111-1113*
1980   Tell Dan. Five Years After. *The Biblical Archaeologist 43:168-182*

Black, J.
1972   Tyranny as a strategy for survial in an »egalitarian« society: Luri facts versus an anthropological mystique. *Man N.S. 7:614-634*

Black-Michaud, J.
1976   The Economics of Oppression: Ecology and Stratification in an iranian Tribal Society. *Non-publ. Thesis. School of Oriental and African Studies, University of London*

Boecker, H.J.
1976   Recht und Gesetz im Alten Testament und im Alten Orient. *Neukirchener Studien-bücher, Bd. 10. Neukirchen*

Bohannan, L.
1958   Political Aspects of Tiv Social Organization. *MIDDLETON and TAIT 1958:33-66*

Bonte, P.
1979   Segmentarité et pouvoir chez les éleveurs nomades sahariens. Éléments d'une problématique. *Pastoral Production and Society 1979:171-199*

Boraas, R.S. and Geraty, L.T.
1979   The Long Life of Tell Hesbân, Jordan. *Archaeology 32:10-20*

Bottéro, J.
1954   Le problème des Ḫabiru à la 4e rencontre assyriologique internationale. *Cahiers de la Société asiatique 12. Paris*

Bourdillon, M.F.C.
1977   Oracles and Politics in Ancient Israel. *Man N.S. 12:124-140*

Bradburd, D.A.
1981   Never give a shepherd an even break: Class and labor among the Komachi. *American Ethnologist 7:603-620*

Brandfon, F.R.
1981   Norman Gottwald on the Tribes of Yahweh. *Journal for the Study of the Old Testament 21:101-110*

Breasted, J.H.
1906   Ancient Records of Egypt. Vol. III: The Nineteenth Dynasty. *Reissue New York 1962*

Brentjes, B.
1960   Das Kamel im Alten Orient. *Klio 38:23-52*
1979   Zur Rolle der nacheiszeitlichen Umweltenwicklung in Irak. *Das Altertum 25:197-204*

Brice, W.C.
1978   (ed.) The Environmental History of the Near and Middle East Since the Last Ice Age. *London*

Bright, J.
1951   The Date of the Prose Sermons of Jeremiah. *Journal of Biblical Literature 70:15-35*
1960   A History of Israel. *London*
1981   A History of Israel. *3.ed. Philadelphia*

Buccellati, G.
1966   The Amorites of the Ur III Period. *Pubblicazioni del seminario di Semitistica: Ricerche I. Napoli*
1967   Cities and Nations of Ancient Syria. An Essay on Political Institutions with Special Reference to the Israelite Kingdoms. *Studi Semitici 26. Rom*
1977   *'apirū* and *Munnabtūtu* - The Stateless of the First Cosmopolitan Age. *Journal of Near Eastern Studies 36:145-147*

Budde, K.
1897   Das Buch der Richter. *Kurzer Hand-Commentar zum Alten Testament VII. Freiburg i.B.*

Bujra, A.S.
1971   The Politics of Stratification. A Study of Political Change in a South Arabian Town. *Oxford*

Bulliet, R.W.
1975   The Camel and the Wheel. *Cambridge, Mass.*
1980   Sedentarization of Nomads in the Seventh Century: The Arabs in Basra and Kūfa. *SALZMAN 1980:35-47*

Burney, C.F.
1918   The Book of Judges With Introduction and Notes. *Repr. New York 1970*
1921   Israel's Settlement in Canaan. The Biblical Tradition and its Historical Background. *The Sweich Lectures 1917. 3.ed. London*

Burnham, P.
1979   Spatial mobility and political centralization in pastoral societies. *Pastoral Production and Society 1979:349-360*

Butzer, K.W.
1957   Late Glacial and Postglacial Climatic Variation in the Near East. *Erdkunde 11: 21-35*
1968   Quarternary Stratigraphy and Climate in the Near East. *Bonner Geographische Abhandlungen Hft. 24. Bonn*
1970   Physical Conditions in Eastern Europe, Western Asia and Egypt Before the Period of Agricultural and Urban Settlement. *CAH³ I:1:35-69*
1971   Environment and Archaeology. An Ecological Approach to Pre-history. *2.ed. Chicago*
1975   Patterns of Environmental Change in the Near East During Late Pleistocene and Early Holocene. Times. *F. WENDORF and A.E. MARKS: Problems in Prehistory. North Africa and the Levant. Dallas 1975:389-410*
1976   Early Hydraulic Civilization in Egypt: A Study in Cultural Ecology. *Chicago*
1978   The Late Prehistoric Environmental History of the Near East. *BRICE 1978:5-12*

Bächli, O.
1973   Von der Liste zur Beschreibung. Beobachtungen und Erwägungen zu Jos. 13-19. *Zeitschrift des Deutschen Palästina-Vereins 89:1-14*

1977   Amphiktyonie im Alten Testament. Forschungsgeschichtliche Studie zur Hypothese von Martin Noth. *Theologische Zeitschrift Sonderband VI. Basel*

Böhl, F.

1911   Kanaanäer und Hebräer. Untersuchungen zur Vorgeschichte des Volkstums und der Religion Israels auf dem Boden Kanaans. *Beiträge zur Wissenschaft vom Alten Testament 9. Leipzig*

Callaway, J.A.

1965   The 1964 'Ai (Et-Tell) Excavations. *Bulletin of the American Schools of Oriental Research 178:13-40*

1968   New Evidence on the Conquest of 'Ai. *Journal of Biblical Literature 87:312-320*

1969   The 1966 'Ai (Et-Tell) Excavations. *Bulletin of the American Schools of Oriental Research 196:2-16*

1970   The 1968-1969 'Ai (Et-Tell) Excavations. *Bulletin of the American Schools of Oriental Research 198:7-31*

1975   Ai. *EAEHL I:36-52*

1976   Excavating Ai (Et-Tell):1964-1972. *The Biblical Archaeologist 39:18-30*

Campbell, E.F.

1968   The Shechem Area Survey. *Bulletin of the American Schools of Oriental Research 190: 19-41*

1979   Response to J. Maxwell Miller. *The Biblical Archaeologist 42:46-47*

Campbell, E.F. and Ross, J.F.

1963   The Excavation of Shechem and the Biblical Tradition. *The Biblical Archeaologist Reader II:275-300*

Campbell, E.F., Ross, J.F. and Toombs, L.E.

1971   the Eight Campaign at Balâṭah (Shechem). *Bulletin of the American Schools of Oriental Research 204:2-17*

Carlson, R.A.

1964   David the Chosen King. A Traditio-Historical Approach to the Second Book of Samuel. *Stockholm*

Carneiro, R.L.

1970   A Theory of the Origin of the State. *Science 169:1970:733-738*

1974   A Reappraisal of the Roles of Technology and Organization in The Origin of Civilization. *American Antiquity 39:179-186*

1978   Political Expansion as an Expression of the Principle of Competitive Exclusion. *COHEN and SERVICE 1978:205-223*

Caskel, W.

1962   Der arabische Stamm vor dem Islam und seine gesellschaftliche und juristische Organisation. *Atti del convegne internationale sul Tema dalla tribù allo stato (Roma, 13-16 aprile 1961). Accademia Nazionale dei Lincei. Anno CCCLIX - 1962. Quaderno n. 54: 139-151*

Causse, A.

1937   Du groupe ethnique à la communauté religieuse. La problème sociologique de la religion d'Israeël. *Paris*

Chalmeta, P.

1980   The Islamic City: Markets. *SERJEANT 1980A:104-113*

Chamberlayne, J.H.

1963   Kinship Relationships Among the Early Hebrews. *Numen 10:153-167*

Childe, V.G.

1958   New Light on the Most Ancient East. *London*

Childs, B.S.
1967   Deuteronomic Formulae of the Exodus Traditions. *Vetus Testamentum Supplements* 16:30–39
1970   A Traditio-Historical Study of the Reed Sea Tradition. *Vetus Testamentum 20:406–418*
1974   The Book of Exodus. A Critical, Theological Commentary. *Old Testament Library*. Philadelphia

Chiva, I.
1963   Traditional Economy and Customary Law in Corsica. Outline of a Plan of Analysis. *J. PITT-RIVERS: Mediterranean Countrymen. Essays in the Social Anthropology of the Mediterranean. Recherches Méditerranéennes. Études I. Paris 1963:97–112*

Christensen, D.L.
1980   Review of GOTTWALD 1979A. *Journal for the Study of the Old Testament 18:113–120*

Clements, R.E.
1967   Abraham and David. Genesis XV and its Meaning for Israelite Tradition. *Studies in Biblical Theology Second Series 5. London*
1977   Review of RENDTORFF 1977A. *Journal for the Study of the Old Testament 3:46–56*

Coats, G.W.
1967   The Traditio-Historical Character of the Reed Sea Motif. *Vetus Testamentum 17: 253–265*
1977   The Yahwist as Theologian? A Critical Reflection. *Journal for the Study of the Old Testament 3:28–32*

Cohen, Ab.
1965   Arab Border-Villages in Israel. A Study of Continuity and Change in Social Organization. *Manchester*

Cohen, Am.
1973   Palestine in the 18th Century. Patterns of Government and Administration. *Jerusalem*

Cohen, E.
1977   Recent Anthropological Studies on Middle Eastern Communities and Ethnic Groups. *Annual Review of Anthropology 6:315–347*

Cohen, R.
1978A   Introduction. *COHEN and SERVICE 1978:1–19*
1978B   State Origins: A Reappraisal. *H.J.M. CLAESSEN and P. SKALNÍK: The Early State. Studies in the Social Sciences 32. The Hague 1978:31–75*
1978C   Ethnicity: Problems and Focus in Anthropology. *Annual Review of Anthropology 7: 379–403*

Cohen, R. and Middleton, J.
1967   (eds.) Comparative Political Systems. Studies in the Politics of Pre-Industrial Societies. *New York*

Cohen, R. and Service, E.R.
1978   (eds.) Origins of the State. The Anthropology of Political Evolution. *Philadelphia*

Cole, D.P.
1973   The Enmeshment of Nomads in Sa'udi Arabian Society: The Case of Āl Murrah. *NELSON 1973:113–128*
1975   Nomads of the Nomads. The Āl Murrah Bedouin of the Empty Quarter. *Works of Man. Studies in Cultural Ecology. Chicago*

Coote, R.B.
1976   The Application of Oral Theory to Biblical Hebrew Literatur. *Semeia 5:51–64*

Craigie, P.C.

1972   Some Further Notes on the Song of Deborah. *Vetus Testamentum 22:349-353*

Cresswell, R.

1976   Lineage Endogamy among Maronite Mountaineers. *PERISTANY 1976:101-114*

Cross, F.M.

1973   Canaanite Myth and Hebrew Epic. Essays in the History of the Religion of Israel. *Cambridge, Mass.*

1979   (ed.) Symposia Celebrating the Seventy-Fifth Anniversary of the Founding of the American Schools of Oriental Research (1900-1975). *Cambridge, Mass.*

Cross, F.M. and Freedman, D.N.

1948   The Blessing of Moses. *Journal of Biblical Literature 67:191-210*
1955   The Song of Miriam. *Journal of Near Eastern Studies 14:237-250*

Cross, F.M., Lemke, W.E. and Miller, P.D.

1976   (eds.) Magnalia Dei. The Mighty Acts of God. *Essays on the Bible and Archaeology in the Memory of G.E. Wright. New York*

Cross, F.M. and Wright G.E.

1956   The Boundary and Province Lists of the Kingdom of Judah. *Journal of Biblical Literature 75:202-226*

Crossland, R.A. and Birchall, A.

1974   Bronze Age Migrations in the Aegean. Archaeological and Linguistical Problems in Greek Prehistory. *Proceedings of the First International Colloquium on Aegean Prehistory, Sheffield. Park Ridge*

Crown, A.D.

1972   Toward a reconstruction of the Climate of Palestine 8000B.C.-0 B.C. *Journal of Near Eastern Studies 31:312-330*

Crüsemann, F.

1978   Der Widerstand gegen das Königtum. Die antiköniglichen Texte des Alten Testamentes und der Kampf um den frühen israelitischen Staat. *Wissenschaftliche Monographien zum Alten und Neuen Testament 49. Neukirchen*

Cuisenier, J.

1975   Économie et parenté: leurs affinités de structure dans le domaine turc et dans le domaine arabe. *Le Monde d'Outre-Mer Passé et présent 1e ser. Études LX. Paris - Le Haye*

1976   The domestic cycle in the traditional family organization in Tunesia. *PERISTIANY 1976:137-155*

Culley, R.C.

1963   An Approach to the Problem of Oral Tradition. *Vetus Testamentum 13:113-125*
1972   Oral Tradition and Historicity. *WEVERS and REDFORD 1972:102-116*
1976A   Oral Tradition and the OT: Some recent Discussion. *Semeia 5:1-33*
1976B   Studies in the Structure of Hebrew Narrative. *Semeia Supplements. Philadelphia - Missoula*

Cunnison, I.

1966   Baggara Arabs. Power and the Lineage in a Sudanese Nomad Tribe. *Oxford*

Dahl, G. and Hjort, A.

1976   Having Herds. Pastoral Herd Growth and Household Economy. *Stockholm Studies in Social Anthropology 2. Stockholm*

Dahood, M.

1968   Psalms II 51-100. Introduction, Translation, and Notes. *The Anchor Bible 17. New York*

Dalman, G.
1928   Arbeit und Sitte in Palästina I–VII. *Gütersloh 1928–1942*

Davies, G.H.
1963   Judges VIII 22–23. *Vetus Testamentum 13:151–157*

Davies, G.I.
1982   Tell Ed-Duweir=Ancient Lachish: A Response to G.W. Ahlström. *Palestine Exploration Quarterly 114:25–28*

Delekat, K.
1967   Tendenz und Theologie des David-Salomo-Erzählung. *F. MAAS: Das Ferne und Nahe Wort. Beiheft zur Zeitschrift für die alttestamentlichen Wissenschaft 105. Berlin 1967:26–36*

Demsky, A.
1977   A Proto-Canaanite Abecedary Dating from the Period of the Judges and its Implications for the History of the Alphabet. *Tel Aviv 4:14–27*

Dever, W.G.
1970   The »Middle Bronze I« Period in Syria and Palestine. *SANDERS 1970:132–163*
1976A   The beginning of the Middle Bronze Age in Syria-Palestine. *CROSS, LEMKE and MILLER 1976:3–38*
1976B   Gezer. *EAEHL II:428–443*
1977   The Patriarchal Traditions § 1. Palestine in the Second Millennium B.C.E.: The Archaeological Picture. *HAYES and MILLER 1977:70–120*
1980   New Vistas on the EB IV (»MB I«) Horizon in Syria-Palestine. *Bulletin of the American Schools of Oriental Research 237:35–64*

Dever, W.G., Lance, D.H. and Wright, G.E.
1970   Gezer I: Preliminary Report of the 1964–66 Seasons. *Annual of the Hebrew Union College Biblical and Archaeological School in Jerusalem. Jerusalem*

Dever, W.G., Lance, D.H., Bullard, R.G., Cole, D.P. and Seger, J.D.
1974   Gezer II: Preliminary Report of the 1967–70 Seasons in Fields I and II. *Annual of the Hebrew Union College Biblical and Archaeological School in Jerusalem. Jerusalem*

Diakonoff, I.M.
1969   Agrarian Conditions in Middle Assyria. *I.M. DIAKONOFF: Ancient Mesopotamia. Socio-Economic History. A. Collection of Studies by Soviet Scholars. Moskva 1969:204–234*

Diebner, B. and Schult, H.
1975★   Argumenta e Silentio. Das grosse Schweigen als Folge der Frühdatierung der »alten Pentateuchquellen«. *Dielheimer Blätter zum Alten Testament Beiheft 1 (Sefer Rendtorff)*

Dietrich, M. and Loretz, O.
1966   Die soziale Struktur von Alalaḫ und Ugarit I. Die Berufsbezeichnungen mit der hurritischen Ending -ḫuli. *Die Welt des Orients III:188–205*
1969A   Die Soziale Struktur von Alalaḫ und Ugarit II: Die sozialen Gruppen ḫupše-namê, ḫaniahhe-ekú, eḫele-sᶻubu und Marjanne nach texten aus Alalaḫ IV. *Die Welt des Orients 5:57–93*
1969B   Die soziale Struktur von Alalaḫ und Ugarit V: Die Weingärten des Gebietes von Alalaḫ im 15. Jahrhundert. *Ugarit-Forschungen 1:37–64*
1970   Die soziale Struktur von Alalaḫ und Ugarit IV: Die É=bîtu – Listen aus Alalaḫ IV als Quelle für die Erforschung der gesellschaftlichen Schichtung von Alalaḫ in 15. Jr. v. Chr. *Zeitschrift für Assyriologie 60:88–123*

Dietrich, W.
1972   Prophetie und Geschichte. Eine redaktionsgeschichtliche Untersuchung zum

deuteronomistischen geschichtswerk. *Forschungen zur Religion und Literatur des Alten und Neuen Testaments 108. Göttingen*
1979   Israel und Kanaan. Vom Ringen zweier Gesellschaftssysteme. *Stuttgarter Bibelstudien 94. Stuttgart*

Digard, J.-P.
1979   De la nécessité et des inconvénients pour un Baxtiyâri, d'être baxtiyâri. Communauté, territoire et inégalité chez des pasteurs nomades d'Iran. *Pastoral Production and Society 1979:127–139*

Dole, G.E.
1968   Tribe as the Autonomous Unit. *HELM 1968:83–100*

Donner, H.
1977   The Separate States of Israel and Judah. *HAYES and MILLER 1977:381–434*

Dostal, W.
1958   Zur Frage der Entwicklung des Beduinentum. *Archiv für Völkerkunde 13:1–14*
1959   The Evolution of Bedouin Life. *F. GABRIELI: L'Antica Società Beduina. Studi Semitici 2. Roma 1958: 11–34*
1967   Die Beduinen in Südarabien. Eine ethnologische Studie zur Entwicklung der Kamelhirtenkultur in Arabien. *Wiener Beiträge zur Kulturgeschichte und Linguistik 16. Wien*
1974   Sozio-ökonomische Aspekte der Stammedemokratie. *Sociologus 24:1–15*

Doughty, C.M.
1888   Travels in Arabia Deserta I–II. *Repr. London 1928*

Driver, G.R.
1956   Mythical Monsters in the Old Testament. *Studi orientalistici in onore di G. Levi Della Vida I. Pubblicazione dell'Istituto per l'Oriente. Roma 1956:234–249*

Durkheim, E.
1919   les règles de la méthode sociologique. *7.ed. Paris*
1922   De la division du travail social. *4.ed. Paris*

Dus, J.
1971   Mose oder Josua? Zum Problem des Stifters der israelitischen Religion. *Archiv Orientalni 39:16–45*

Dyson, R.H.
1953   Archaeology and the Domestication of Animals in the Old World. *American Anthropologist 55:661–673*

Dyson-Hudson, N.
1972   The Study and Nomads. *IRON and DYSON-HUDSON 1972:2–29.*

Dyson-Hudson, N. and R.
1980   Nomadic Pastoralism. *Annual Review of Anthropology 9:15–61*

Eberhard, W.
1953   Nomads and Farmers in Southeastern Turkey. Problems of Settlement. *Oriens 6: 32–49*

Ehmann, D.
1975   Baḫtiyâren – Persische Bergnomaden im Wandel der Zeit. *Beihefte zum Tübinger Atlas des Vorderen Orients Reihe B nr. 15. Wiesbaden*

Eissfeldt, O.
1922   Hexateuch-Synopse. Die Erzählung der fünf Bücher Mose und des Buches Josua mit dem Anfange des Richterbuches. *Leipzig (repr. Darmstadt 1962)*
1940   Lade und Stierbild. *O. EISSFELDT: Kleine Schriften 2, Tübingen 1964:282–305*
1953   Psalm 80. *O. EISSFELDT: Kleine Schriften 3, Tübingen 1966:221–232*

1964 Psalm 80 und Psalm 89. *O. EISSFELDT: Kleine Schriften 4, Tübingen 1968:132–136*
1965 The Old Testament. An Introduction. *Oxford*

Elliger, K.
1930 Die Grenze zwischen Ephraim und Manasse. *Zeitschrift des Deutschen Palästina-Vereins 53:265–309*
1937 Thappuah. *Palästinajahrbuch 33:7–21*
1938 Neues über die grenze zwischen Ephraim und Manasse. *Journal of the Palestine Oriental Society 18:7–16*
1955 Das Gesetz Leviticus 18. *K. ELLIGER: Kleine Schriften zum Alten Testament. Theologische Bücherei 32. München 1966: 232–259*
1971 Jesaja II. *Biblischer Kommentar. Altes Testament XI Hft. 2. Neukirchen*

Engel, H.
1979 Die Siegesstele des Merenptah. Kritischer Überblick über die verschiedenen Versuche historischer Auswertung des Schlussabschnitts. *Biblica 60:373–399*

English, P.W.
1966 City and Village in Iran. Settlement and Economy in the Kirman Basin. *Madison*
1973 Geographical Perspectives on the Middle East: The Passing of the Ecological Trilogy. *M.W. MIKESELL: Geographers Abroad. Essays on the Problems and Prospects of Research in Foreign Areas. University of Chicago Department of Geography Research Papers No. 152. Chicago 1973:134–164*

Engnell, I.
1945 Gamla Testamentet. En traditionshistorisk inledning I. *Stockholm*
1970 Critical Essays on the Old Testament. Ed. by J.T. Willis. *London*

Eusebius
Das Onomasticon der Biblischen Ortsnamen. Herausgegeben von E. KLOSTERMANN. *Leipzig 1904 (repr. Hildesheim 1966)*

Evans, J.D.
1974 The Archaeological Evidence and Its Interpretation: Some suggested Approaches to the Problems of the Aegean Bronze Age. *CROSSLAND and BIRCHALL 1974:17–26*

Evans-Pritchard, E.E.
1940A The Nuer. A Description of the Modes of Livelihood and Political Institutions of a Nilotic People. *Oxford (repr. 1971)*
1940B The Nuer of the Southern Sudan. *FORTES and EVANS-PRITCHARD 1940: 272–296*
1949 The Sanusi of Cyrenaica. *Oxford*

Fazel, G.R.
1973 The Encapsulation of Nomadic Societies in Iran. *NELSON 1973:129–142*

Feilberg, C.G.
1944 La tente noire. Contribution ethnographique à l'histoire culturelle des nomades. *Nationalmuseets skrifter. Etnografisk Række II. København*

Ferdinand, K.
1969A Ost-Afghanischer Nomadismus – Ein Beitrag zur Anpassungsfähigkeit der Nomaden. *Nomadismus als Entwicklingsproblem 1969:107–130*
1969B Nomadismus in Afghanistan. With an Appendix on Milk Production. *Földes 1969:127–160*

Fernea, R.A.
1970 Sheykh and Effendi. Changing Patterns of Authority Among the El Shabana of Southern Iraq. *Harvard Middle Eastern Studies 14. Cambridge, Mass.*
1972 Gaps in the Ethnographic Literature of the Middle Eastern Village: A Classificatory Exploitation. *ANTOUN and HARIK 1972:75–102*

1975   Anthropology of the Middle East and North Africa: A Critical Assessment. *Annual Review of Anthropology 4:183–206*

Feucht, C.
1964   Untersuchungen zum Heiligkeitsgesetz. *Theologische Arbeiten XX. Berlin*

Finley, M.I.
1977   The World of Odysseus. *2.ed. London*

Flanagan, J.W.
1981   Chiefs in Israel. *Journal for the Study of the Old Testament 20:47–73*

Flannery, K.V.
1972   The Cultural Evolution of Civilizations. *Annual Review of Ecology and Systematics 3: 399–426*

Fohrer, G.
1955   Ezechiel. *Handbuch zum Alten Testament I 13. Tübingen*
1964   Überlieferung und Geschichte des Exodus. Eine Analyse von Ex 1–15. *Beiheft zur Zeitschrift für die alttestamentliche Wissenschaft 91. Berlin*
1966   Altes Testament. »Amphiktyonie« und »Bund«? *G. FOHRER: Studien zur alttestamentlichen Theologie und Geschichte (1949–1966). Bieheft zur Zeitschrift für die alttestamentliche Wissenschaft 115. Berlin 1969:84–119*
1969   Einleitung in das Alte Testament. *11. Aufl. Heidelberg*
1977   Geschichte Israels. Von den Anfängen bis zur Gegenwart. *Heidelberg*

Fortes, M.
1940   The Political System of the Tallensi of the Northern Territories of the Gold Coast. *FORTES and EVANS-PRITCHARD 1940:239–271*
1953   The Structure of Unilineal Descent Groups. *The American Anthropologist 55:17–41*

Fortes, M. and Evans-Pritchard, E.E.
1940   African Political Systems. *London (repr. 1967)*

Fox, R.
1967   Kinship and Marriage. An Anthropological Perspective. *Harmondsworth*

Franken, H.J.
1969   Excavations at Tell Deir 'Alla: A Stratigraphical and Analytical Study of the Early Iron Age Pottery. *Documenta et Monumenta Orientis Antiqui 16. Leiden*
1975   Palestine in the Time of the Nineteenth Dynasty (B): Archaeological Evidence. *CAH³ II:2:331–337*
1976   The Problem of Identification in Biblical Archaeology. *Palestine Exploration Quarterly 108:3–11*

Frankena, R.
1965   The Vassal-Treaties of Esarhaddon and the dating of Deuteronomy. *Oudtestamentiedsje Studien 14:122–154*

Freedman, D.N.
1978   The Real Story of the Ebla Tablets: Ebla and the Cities of the Plain. *The Biblical Archaeologist 41:143–164*

Frick, F.S.
1971   The Rechabites reconsidered. *Journal of Biblical Literature 90:279–287*
1977   The City in Ancient Israel. *Society of Biblical Literature Dissertation Series No. 36. Missoula*
1979   Religion and Sociopolitical Structure in early Israel: An Ethno-Archaeological Approach. *Society of Biblical Literature Seminar Papers 1979:233–253*

Fried, M.H.
1966   Some Political Aspects of Clanship in a Modern Chinese City. *M.J. SWARTZ, V.W. TURNER and A. TUDEN: Political Anthropology. Chicago 1966:285–300*

1967   The Evolution of Political Society. An Essay in Political Anthropology. *New York*
1968   On the Concepts of »Tribe« and »Tribal Society«. *HELM 1968:3-20*
1975   The Notion of Tribe. *Menlo Park*
1978   The State, the Chicken, and the Egg; or, What Came First? *COHEN and SER-VICE 1978:35-47*

Friis, H.
1975   Eksilet og den israelitiske historieopfattelse. *Dansk teologisk Tidsskrift 38:1-16 (Geman translation: Das Exil und die Geschichte. Dielheimer Blätter zum Alten Testament 18 (1984) 63-84)*

Fritz, V.
1969   Die sogenannte Liste der besiegten Könige in Josua 12. *Zeitschrift des Deutschen Pa-lästina-Vereins 85:136-161*
1970   Israel in der Wüste. traditionsgeschichtliche Untersuchung der Wüstenüberliefe-rung des Jahwisten. *Marburger Theologische Studien 7. Marburg*
1973   Das Ende der spätbronzezeitlichen Stadt Hazor Stratum XIII und die biblische Überlieferung in Josua 11 und Richter 4. *Ugarit-Forschungen 5:123-139*
1975   Erwägungen zur Siedlungsgeschichte des Negeb in der Eisen I – Zeit (1200-1000 v. Chr.) im Lichte der Ausgrabungen auf der *Ḥirbet el-Mšāš. Zeitschrift des Deutschen Palästina-Vereins 91:30-45*
1980   Die kulturhistorische Bedeutung des früheisenzeitlichen Siedlung auf der *Ḥirbet el-Mšāš* und das Problem der Landnahme. *Zeitschrift des Deutschen Palästina-Vereins 96:121-135*

Földes, L.
1969   (ed.) Viehwirtschaft und Hirtenkultur. Etnographische Studien. *Budapest*

Garbini, G.
1978   Sull'alfabetario di 'Izbet Ṣarṭah. *Oriens Antiquus 17:287-295*

Gardiner, A.
1960   The Ḳadesh Inscription of Ramesses II. *Oxford*

Garsiel, M. and Finkelstein, I.
1978   The Westward Expansion of the House of Joseph in the Light of the 'Izbet Ṣarṭah Excavations. *Tel Aviv 5:192-198*

Gerleman, G.
1965   Ruth. Das Hohelied. *Biblischer Kommentar Altes Testament XVIII. Neukirchen*

Gerstensberger, E.
1965   Wesen und Herkunft des »apodiktischen Rechts«. *Wissenschaftliche Monographien zum Alten und Neuen Testament 20. Neukirchen*

Gerstenblith, P.
1980   A Reassessment of the Beginning of the Middle Bronze Age in Syria-Palestine. *Bulletin of the American Schools of Oriental Research 237:65-84*

Geus, C.H.J. de
1965   De Richteren van Israël. *Nederlands theologisch Tijdschrift 20:81-100*
1971   The Amorites in the Archaeology of Palestine. *Ugarit-Forschung 3:41-60*
1975   The Importance of Archaeological Research into the Palestinian Agricultural Terraces, with an Excursus on the Hebrew Word gbî. *Palestine Exploration Quarterly 107:65-74*
1976   The Tribes of Israel. An Investigation into Some of the Presuppositions of Martin Noth's Amphictyony Hypothesis. *Studia Semitica Neerlandica 18. Assen*
1983   Agrarian Communities in Biblical Times: 12th to 10th Centuries B.C.E. *Recueils de la Société Jean Bodin Pour l'histoire Comparatives des Institutions XLI. Les communautés rurales II partie: Antiquité Paris:207-237*

Gilbert, A.S.
   1975   Modern Nomads and Prehistoric Pastoralists. The Limits of Analogy. *Journal of
             the Ancient Near Eastern Society of the Columbia University 7:53–71*

Giveon, R.
   1971   Les Bédouins Shosou des documents égyptiens. *Documenta et monumenta Orientis
             Antiqui 18. Leiden*

Glatzer, B.
   1977   Nomaden von Gharjistān. Aspekte der wirtschaftlichen, sozialen und politischen
             Organisation nomadischer Durrānī Paschtunen in Nordwestafghanistan. *Beiträge
             zur Südasienforschung Bd. 22. Wiesbaden*

Glock, A.E.
   1978   Taanach. *EAEHL IV:1138–1147*

Gluckman, M.
   1965   Poletics, Law and Ritual in Tribal Society. *Chicago*

Goetze, A.
   1975A   The Struggle for the Domination of Syria (1400–1300 B.C.). *CAH³ II:2:1–20*
   1975B   The Hittites and Syria (1300–1200 B.C.). *CAH³ II:2:252–273*

Goldberg, H.
   1967   FBD Marriage and Demography among Tripolitanian Jews. *Southwestern Journal
             of Anthropology 23:176–191*

Goody, J.
   1959   The Mother's Brother and the Sister's Son in West Africa. *Journal of the Royal An-
             thropological Institute 89:61–88*

Gordon, C.H.
   1958   Abraham and the Merchants of Ura. *Journal of Near Eastern Studies 17:28–31*
   1963   Abraham of Ur. *D. WINTON THOMAS and W.D. MCHARDY: Hebrew and
             Semitic Studies Presented to G.R. Driver. Oxford 1963:77–84*

Gottwald, N.K.
   1959   A Light to the Nations. An Introductions to the Old Testament. *New York*
   1974   Were the early Israelites Pastoral Nomads? *J.J. JACKSON and M. KESSLER:
             Rhetorical Criticism. Essays in Honor of James Muilenburg. Pittsburg Theological Mono-
             graph Series I:223–255*
   1975   Domain Assumptions and Societal Models in the Study of Pre-Monarchic Israel.
             Vetus Testamentum Supplementum 28:89–100
   1976   Early Israel and »The Asiatic Mode of Production in Canaan«. *Society of Biblical
             Literature 1976 Seminar Papers:145–154*
   1978   The Hypothesis of the revolutionary Origins of Ancient israel: A Response to
             Hauser and Thompson. *Journal for the Study of the Old Testament 7:37–52*
   1979A   The tribes of Yahweh. A Sociology of the Religion of Liberated Israel 1250–1050
             B.C.E. *New York*
   1979B   Sociological Method in the Study of Ancient Israel. *M.J. BUSS: Encounter With the
             Text. Form and History in the Hebrew Bible. Semeia Supplements. Philadelphia og Missoula
             1979:69–81*

Granott, A.
   1952   The Land System in Palestine. History and Structure. *London*

Gray, J.
   1964   I & II Kings. A Commentary. *Old Testament Library. London*
   1967   Joshua, Judges, and Ruth. *The Century Bible New Ed. London*

Gressmann, H.
   1913   Mose und seine Zeit. Ein Kommentar zu den Mose-Sagen. *Forschungen zur Reli-
             gion und Literatur des Alten und Neuen Testaments Neue Folge 1 (18). Göttingen*

Grether, O.
1939   Die Bezeichnung »Richter« für die charismatischen Helden der vorstaatlichen
        Zeit. *Zeitschrift für die alttestamentliche Wissenschaft 57:110-121*

Grønbech, V.
1909   Vor Folkeæt i Oldtiden I–IV. *København 1909-1912*
1961   Hellas. Kultur og Religion I–IV. 2. udg. *København*

Grønbæk, J.H.
1971   Die Geschichte vom Aufstieg Davids (1. Sam 15-2. Sam 5). Tradition und Kom-
        position. *Acta Theologica Danica 10. København*
1975   Om forholdet mellem historie og eskatologi hos de klassiske profeter. *N. HYL-
        DAHL and E. NIELSEN: Hilsen til Noack. København 1975:81-93*

Grönhaug, R.
1978   Scale as a Variable in Analysis. Fields in Social Organization in Herat, Northwest
        Afghanistan. *BARTH 1978:78-121*

Grötzbach, E.
1973   Kulturgeographische Wandel in Nordost-Afghanistan seit dem 19. Jahrhundert.
        Afghanische Studien Band 4. Meisenheim am Glan

Gubser, P.
1973   Politics and Change in Al-Karak, Jordan. A Study of a small Arab Town and its
        District. *Middle Eastern Monographs 11. London*

Gulick, J.
1955   Social Structure and Cultural Change in a lebenese Village. *Viking Fund Publica-
        tions in Anthropology No. 21. New York*
1967   Tripoli. A Modern Arab City. *Cambridge, Mass.*
1969   Village and City. Cultural Continuities in Twentieth Century Middle Eastern
        Cultures. *LAPIDUS 1969B:122-158*
1976   The Middle East: An Anthropological Perspective. *Goodyear Regional Anthropology
        Series. Pacific Palisades*

Gulick, J. and M.E.
1974   Varieties of Domestic Social Organization in the Iranian City of Isfahan. *LA-
        RUFFA 1974:441-469*

Gunkel, H.
1917   Genesis übersetzt und erklärt. *Göttinger Handkommentar zum Alten Testament I 1. 4.
        Ausg. Göttingen*
1929   Die Psalmen übersetzt und erklärt. *Göttinger Handkommentar zum Alten Testament II
        2. 4. Ausg. Repr. Göttingen 1968*
1933   Einleitung in die Psalmen. Die Gattungen der religiösen Lyrik Israels. Zu ende
        geführt von H. Begrich. *Göttinger Handkommentar zum Alten Testament II Ergänzungs-
        band. Repr. Göttingen 1966*

Gunn, D.M.
1974A   Narrative Patterns and Oral Tradition in Judges and Samuel. *Vetus Testamentum
        24:286-317*
1974B   The »Battle Report«: Oral or Scribal Convention? *Journal of Biblical Literature 93:
        513-518*
1976A   On Oral Tradition: A Response to John Van Seters. *Semeia 5:155-161*
1976B   Traditional Composition in the »Succession Narrative«. *Vetus Testamentum 26:
        214-229*

Gunneweg, A.H.J.
1972   Geschichte Israels bis Bar Kochba. *Theologische Wissenschaft Bd. 2. Stuttgart*

Guthe, H.
1904   Geschichte des Volkes Israel. *Grundriss der theologischen Wissenschaften II 3. 2. Aufl.
        Tübingen und Leipzig*

Haag, H.
1967 Gideon-Jerubbaal-Abimelek. *Zeitschrift für die alttestamentliche Wissenschaft 79:305–314*

Hahn, E.
1896 Die Haustiere und ihre Beziehungen zur Wirtschaft der Menschen. Eine geographische Studie. *Leipzig*

Halbe, J.
1980 Die Reihe der Inzestverbote Lev 18,7–18. Entstehung und Gestaltstufen. *Zeitschrift für die alttestamentliche Wissenschaft 92:60–88*

Hammershaimb, E.
1960 On the Ethics of the Old Testament Prophets. *E. HAMMERSHAIMB: Old Testament Prophecy from Isaiah to Malachi. Det lærde Selskabs skrifter. Teologiske Skrifter 4. København 1966:63–90*
1967 Amos. *3. udg. København*

Harden, D.
1971 The Phoenicians. *Harmondsworth*

Harris, R.
1975 Ancient Sippar. A Demographic Study of an Old-Babylonian City (1894–1595 B.C.). *Uitgaven van het Nederlandsch Historisch-archaeologisch Instituut te Istanbul 36. Istanbul*

Ḥasan, Y.F.
1967 The Arabs and the Sudan. From the Seventh to the Early Sixteenth Century. *Edinburgh*

Hastrup, K. and Ovesen, J.
1980 Etnografisk grundbog. Metoder, teorier, resultater. *København*

Hauser, A.J.
1975 The »Minor Judges« – A Re-evaluation. *Journal of Biblical Literature 94:190–200*
1978A Israel's Conquest of Palestine: A Peasants' Rebellion? *Journal for the Study of the Old Testament 7:2–19*
1978B Response to Thompson and Mendenhall. *Journal for the Study of the Old Testament 7:35–36*
1978C The Revolutionary Origins of Ancient Israel: A Response to Gottwald. *Journal for the Study of the Old Testament 8:46–49*

Hawkes, C.F.C.
1954 Archaeological Theory and Method: Some Suggestions From the Old World. *American Anthropologist 56:155–168*

Hayes, J. and Miller, J.M.
1977 (eds.) Israelite and Judaean History. *Old Testament Library London*

Hayes, W.C.
1970 Chronology I. Egypt – To the End of the Twentieth Dynasty. *CAH³ I:1:173–193*

Heine-Geldern, R. von
1964 One Hundred Years of Ethnological Theory in the German – Speaking Countries. Some Milestones. *Current Anthropology 5:407–418*

Helck, W.
1968A Geschichte des Alten Ägypten. *Handbuch der Orientalistik I:iii. Leiden*
1968B Die Bedrohung Palästinas durch einwandernde Gruppen am Ende der 18. und am Anfang der 19. Dynastie. *Vetus Testamentum 18:472–480*
1971 Die Beziehungen Ägyptens zu Vorderasien im 3. und 2. Jahrtausend v.Chr. *Ägyptologische Abhandlungen Bd. 5. 2. verb. Aufl. Wiesbaden*

1979   Die Beziehungen Agyptens und Vorderasiens zur Ägäis bis ins 7. Jahrhundert v. Chr. *Erträge der Forschung Bd. 120. Darmstadt*

Helm, J.

1968   (ed.) Essays on the Problem of Tribe. *Proceedings of the 1967 Annual Spring Meeting of the American Ethnological Society. Seattle*

Heltzer, M.

1969A   Problems of the Social History of Syria in the Late Bronze Age. M. *LIVERANI: La Siria nel Tardo Bronzo: Orientis Antiqui Collectio IX. Roma 1969:31–46*
1969B   Vojsko ugarita i ego organizacija. *Vestnik Drevnii Historii 1969:3:21–38*
1971   Soziale Aspekte des Heerwesens in Ugarit. *KLENGEL 1971:125–131*
1976   The Rural Community in Ancient Ugarit. Wiesbaden
1977   The Metal Trade of Ugarit and the Problem of Transportation of Commercial Goods. *Iraq 39:203–211*
1981   The Suteans. With an Contribution by S. Arbeli. *Istituto Universitario Orientale. Seminario di Studi Asiatici. Series Minor XIII. Naples*

Henninger, J.

1968   Über Lebensraum und Lebensformen der Frühsemiten. *Arbeitsgemeinschaft für Forschung des Landes Nordrhein-Westfalen, Geisteswissenschaften, Hft. 115. Köln*

Herrmann, S.

1962   Das Werden Israels. *Theologische Literaturzeitung 87:561–574*
1965   Die prophetischen Heilserwartungen im Alten testament. Ursprungt und Gestaltwandel. *Beiträge zur Wissenschaft vom Alten und Neuen Testament 85. Stuttgart*
1969   Autonome Entwicklungen in den Königsreichen Israel und Juda. *Vetus Testamentum Supplementum 17:139–158*
1973   Geschichte Israels in alttestamentlicher Zeit. *München*

Hertsberg, H.W.

1965   Die Samuelbücher. *Das Alte Testament Deutsch 10. 3. Aufl. Göttingen*

Herzog, R.

1963   Sesshaftwerden von Nomaden. Geschichte, gegenwärtiger Stand eines wirtschaftlichen wie sozialen Prozesses und Möglichkeiten der sinnvollen technischen Unterstützung. *Forschungsberichte des Landes Nordrhein-Westfalen Nr. 1238. Köln*

Hilal, I.M.

1970   Fahter's Brother's Daughter Marriage in Arab Communities: A Problem for Sociological Explanation. *Middle East Forum 46:73–84*

Hoebel, E.A.

1972   Anthropology. The Study of Man. *4.ed. New York*

Hoffmann, H.-D.

1980   Reform und Reformen. Untersuchungen zu einem Grundthema der deuteronomistischen Geschictschreibung. *Abhandlungen zur Theologie des Alten und Neuen Testaments 66. Zürich*

Hoffmeister, B.

1961   Wesen- und Erscheinungsformen des Transhumance. *Erdkunde 15:121–135*

Hole, F.

1973   Questions of theory in the explanation of culture change in Prehistory. *RENFREW 1973A:19–34*

Holstein, J.A.

1975   Max Weber and Biblical Scholarship. *Hebrew Union College Annual 46:159–179*

Honigmann, J.J.

1976   The Development of Anthropological Ideas. *Homewood*

Hopkins, N.S.
1974   Traditional Tunis and its transformations. *LARUFFA 1974:427–436*

Horn, S.H.
1976   Hesbon. *EAEHL II:510–514*

Hornung, E.
1964   Untersuchungen zur Chronologie und Geschichte des Neuen Reiches. *Ägyptologische Abhandlingen 11. Wiesbaden*

Huffmon, H.B.
1965   Amorite Personal Names in the Mari Texts. A Structural and Lexical Study. *Baltimore*

Huntington, H.G.
1972   The Rate of Return From the Basseri's Livestock Investment. *MAN N.S. 7:476–479*

Hymes, D.
1968   Linguistic Problems in Defining the Concept of »Tribe«. *HELM 1968:23–48*

Hütteroth, W.-D.
1959   Bergnomaden und Yaylabauern im mittlerem kurdischen Taurus. *Marburger geographische Schriften heft 11. Marburg*
1961   Beobachtungen zur Sozialstruktur kurdischer Stämme in östlichen Taurus. *Zeitschrift für Ethnologie 86:23–42*
1970   Schwankungen von Siedlungsdichte und Siedlungsgrenze in Palästina und Transjordanien seit dem 16. Jahrhundert. *Deutscher geographentag Kiel 1969. Tagungsbericht und wissenschaftliche Abhandlungen. Verhandlung des Deutschen Geographentages Band 37:463–475. Wiesbaden*
1973   Zum Kenntnissstand über Verbreitung und Typen von Bergnomadismus und Halbnomadismus in den Gebirgs- und Plateaulandschaften Südwestasiens. *C. RATHJENS, C. TOLL and H. UHLIG: Vergleichende Kulturgeographie der Hochgebirge des südliche Asien. Erdwissenschaftliche Forschung V. Wiesbaden 1973:146–156*
1974   The Influence of Social Structure on Land Division and Settlement in Inner Anatolia. *P. BENEDICT, E. TÜMERTEKIN and F. MANSUR: Turkey. Geographic and Social Perspectives. Social, Economic and Political Studies of the Middle East 9. Leiden 1974:19–47*
1975   The Patterns of Settlement in Palestine in the Sixteenth Century. Geographical Research on Turkish *Defter-i Mūfaṣṣal. MA'OZ 1975:3–10*

Hütteroth, W.-D. and Abdulfattah, K.
1977   Historical Geography of Palestine, Trandjordan and Southern Syria in the Late 16th Century. *Erlanger geographischer Arbeiten Sonderband 5. Erlangen*

Ibn Khaldun
1958   The Muqaddimah. An Introduction to History. Translated by F. Rosenthal. I–III. *London*

Ibrahim, M., Sauer, J.A. and Yassine, K.
1976   The East Jordan Valley Survey, 1975. *Bulletin of the American Schools of Oriental Research 222:41–66*

Irons, W.
1971   Variation in Political Stratification Among the Yomut Turkmen. *SALZMAN 1971A:143–156.*
1972   Variations in Economic Organization. A Comparison of the Pastoral Yomut and the Basseri. *IRONS and DYSON-HUDSON 1972:88–104*
1974   Nomadism as a political adaption: the case of the Yomut Turkmen. *Amrican Ethnologist 1:635–658*
1975   The Yomut Turkmen: A Study of Social Organization Among a Central Asian

Turkic-Speaking Population. *Anthropological Papers. Museum of Anthropology, University of Michigan No. 58. Ann Arbor*
1979 Political Stratification among pastoral nomads. *Pastoral Production and Society 1979:361-374*

Irons, W. and Dyson-Hudson, N.
1972 Perspectives on Nomadism. *International Studies in Sociology and Social Anthropology 13. Leiden*

Ishida, T.
1977 The Royal Dynasties in Ancient Israel. A Study of the Formation and development of Royal-Dynastic Ideology. *Beiheft zur Zeitschrift für die alttestamentliche Wissenschaft 142. Berlin*

Jaroš, K.
1974 Die Stellung des Elohisten zur kanaanäischen Religion. *Orbis Biblicus et Orientalis 4. Freiburg und Göttingen*

Jenni, E.
1958 Historisch-topographische Untersuchungen zur Grenze zwischen Ephraim und Manasse. *Zeitschrift des Deutschen Palästina-Vereins 74:35-40*

Jentsch, C.
1973 Das Nomadentum in Afghanistan. Eine geographische Untersuchung. Zu Lebens- und Wirtschaftsformen im asiatischen Trockengebiet. *Afghanische Studien Bd. 9. Meisenheim am Glan*

Jeppesen, K.
1978 New Aspects of Micah Research. *Journal for the Study of the Old Testament 8:3-32*
1979 How the Book of Micah Losts its Integrity: Outline of the History of the Criticism of the Book of Micah with Emphasis on the 19th Century. *Studia Theologica 33:101-131*

Jettmar, K.
1969 Organisation des Nomadismus und Möglichkeiten der politischen Integration. *Nomadismus als Entwicklungsproblem 1969:79-91*

Jirku, A.
1917 Die älteste Geschichte Israels in Rahmen lehrhafter Darstellungen. *Leipzig*

Johnson, D.L.
1969 The nature of Nomadism. A Comparative Study of Pastoral Migrations in Southwestern Asia and Northern Africa. *The University of Chicago. Department of Geography Research Paper No. 118. Chicago*

Kaiser, O.
1958 Traditionsgeschichtliche Untersuchung von Genesis 15. *Zeitschrift für die alttestamentliche Wissenschaft 70:107-126*
1963 Der Prophet Jesaja Kapitel 1-12. *Das Alte Testament Deutsch 17. 2. Aufl. Göttingen*
1969 Einleitung in das Alte Testament. Eine Einführung in ihre Ergebnisse und Probleme. *Gütersloh*

Kallai-Kleinman, Z.
1958 The Town Lists of Judah, Simeon and Dan. *Vetus Testamentum 8:134-160*

Kamp, K.A. and Yoffee, N.
1980 Ethnicity in Ancient Western Asia During the Early Second Millennium B.C.: Archaeological Assessment and Ethnoarchaeological Prospectives. *Bulletin of the American Schools of Oriental Research 237:85-104*

Kelso, J.L.
    1968   The Excavations of Bethel (1934–1960). *The Annual of the American Schools of Oriental Research XXXIX. Cambridge, Mass.*
    1975   Bethel. *EAEHL I:190–193*

Kempinsky, A.
    1977   Masos, Tel (Khirbet el-meshash). *EAEHL III:816–819*

Kempinsky, A. and Fritz, V.
    1977   Excavations at Tel Masos (Khirbet el-Meshâsh), Preliminary Report of the Third Season, 1975. *Tel Aviv 4:136–158*

Kenyon, K.M.
    1957   Digging up Jericho. *London*
    1965   Archaeology in the Holy Land. *2.ed. London*
    1966   Amorites and Canaanites. *The Schweich Lectures 1963. London*
    1971   Syria and Palestine c. 2160–1780 B.C.: The Archaeological Sites. *CAH³ I:2:567–594*
    1976   Jericho. *EAEHL II:550–564*
    1979   Archaeology in the Holy Land. *4.ed. London*

Keyser, J.H.B.
    1974   The Middle Eastern Case: Is There a Marriage Rule? *Ethnology 13:293–309*

Khuri, F.I.
    1970   Parallel Cousin Marriage Reconsidered: A Middle Eastern Practice that Nullifies the Effects of Marriage on the Intensity of Family Relationships. *Man N.S. 5: 597–618*
    1976   A Profile of family associations in two suburbs of Beirut. *PERISTIANY 1976: 81–99*

Kiesow, K.
    1979   Exodustexte im Jesajabuch. Literarkritische und motivgeschichtliche Analysen. *Orbis Biblicus et Orientalis 24. Freiburg und Göttingen*

Kilian, R.
    1963   Literarkritische und formgeschichtliche Untersuchung des Heiligkeitsgesetzt. *Bonner Biblische Beiträge 19. Bonn*

Kimbrough, S.T.
    1978   Israelite Religion in Sociological Perspective. The Work on Antonin Causse. *Studies in Oriental Religions 4. Wiesbaden*

King, T.F.
    1978   Don't that beat the Band? Nonegalitarian Political Organization in Prehistoric Central California. *REDMAN 1978B:225–248*

Kirk, G.S.
    1962   The Songs of Homer. *Cambridge*
    1976   Homer and the Oral Tradition. *Cambridge*

Kittel, R.
    1925   Geschichte des Volkes Israel II. *7. Aufl. Stuttgart*
    1932   Geschichte des Volkes Israel I. *7. Aufl. Stuttgart*

Klengel, H.
    1958A   Benjaminiten und Hanäer zur Zeit der Könige von Mari. *Diss. Berlin*
    1958B   Benjaminiten und Hanäer. *Wissenschaftliche Zeitschrift Berlin 8:211–226*
    1959   Halbnomaden am mittleren Euphrat. *Das Altertum 5:195–205*
    1962   Zu einigen Problemen des altvorderasiatischen Nomadentums. *Archiv Orientalni 30:585–596*

1964   Aziru von Amurru und seine Rolle in der Geschichte der Amarnazeit. *Mittei-*
        lungen des Institut für Orientforschung 10:57–83
1966   Sesshafte und Nomaden in der alten Geschichte Mesopotamiens. *Saeculum 17:*
        205–222
1969   Geschichte Syriens im 2. Jahrtausend v.u.Z. Teil 2. Mittel- und Südsyrien. *Deut-*
        sche Akademie der Wissenschaften zu Berlin Institut für Orientforschung. Veröffentlichung
        Nr. 70. Berlin
1971   (ed.) Beiträge zur sozialen Struktur des Alten Vorderasien. *Schriften zur Geschichte*
        und Kultur des Alten Orients 1. Berlin
1972   Zwischen Telt und Palast. Die Begegnung von Nomaden und Sesshaften im alten
        Vorderasien. *Leipzig und Wien*
1974   »Hungerjahre« in Hatti. *Altorientalische Forschungen I:165–174*
1977   Nomaden und Handel. *Iraq 39:163–169*
1979   Handel und Händler im alten Orient. *Wien*

Koch, K.
1972   (ed.) Um das Prinzip der Vergeltung in Religion und Recht des Alten Testament.
        Wege der Forschung 125. Darmstadt

Kochavi, M.
1972★   Judaea, Samaria and Golan (hb.). *Jerusalem*
1974   Khirbet Rabûd=Debir. *Tel Aviv 1:2–33*
1977   An Ostracon of the Period of the Judges from 'Izbet Ṣarṭah. *Tel Aviv 4:1–13*
1978   Rabud, Khirbet. *EAEHL IV:995*

Kraus, H.-J.
1966   Die Psalmen I–II. *Biblischer Kommentar Altes Testament XV. 3. Aufl. Neukirchen*
1969   Geschichte des historisch-kritischen Erforschung des Alten Testaments. *2. Aufl.*
        Neukirchen

Kuhn, T.
1962   The Structure of Scientific Revolution. *Chicago*

Kupper, J.-R.
1957   Les nomades en Mésopotamie au temps des rois de Mari. *Bibliothèque de la Faculté*
        de Philosophie et Lettres de l'Université de Liege Fasc. 142. Paris
1959   Le rôle des nomades dans l'histoire de la Mésopotamie. *Journal of the Social and*
        Economic History of the Orient 2:113–127
1973   Northern Mesopotamia and Syria. *CAH³ II:1:1–41*

Kuschke, A.
1965   Historisch-topographische Beiträge zum Buche Josua. *H. GRAF REVENT-*
        LOW: Gottes Wort und Gottes Land. H.-W. Hertsberg zum 70. Geburtstag. Göttingen
        1965:90–109

Kutsch, E.
1963   Salbung als Rechtsakt im Alten Testament und im Alten Orient. *Beiheft zur Zeit-*
        schrift für die alttestamentliche Wissenschaft 87. Berlin

Kühlewein, J.
1973   Geschichte in den Psalmen. *Calwer Theologische Monographien A:2. Stuttgart*

Lactacz, J.
1979   Homer. Tradition und Neuerung. *Wege der Forschung 463. Darmstadt*

Lamb, H.H.
1977   Climate, Present, Past and Future. Vol. 2. Climatic history and the future. *London*

Lamon, R.S. and Shipton, G.M.
1939   Megiddo I. Seasons of 1925–34. Strata I–V. *The University of Chicago. Oriental Insti-*
        tute Publications XLII. Chicago

Lancaster, W.
1981   The Rwala Bedouin Today. *Cambridge*

Lapidus, I.M.
1969A   Muslim Cities and Islamic Societies. *LAPIDUS 1969B:47–79*
1969B   Middle Eastern Cities. A Symposium on Ancient, Islamic, and Contemporary Middle Eastern Urbanism. *Berkeley*

Lapp, P.W.
1964   The 1963 Excavation at Ta'annek. *Bulletin of the American Schools of Oriental Research 1973:4–44*
1967   The 1966 Excavations at Tell Ta'annek. *Bulletin of the American Schools of Oriental Research 185:2–39*
1969   The 1968 Excavations at Tell Ta'annek. *Bulletin of the American Schools of Oriental Research 195:2–49*
1975   The Tale of the *Tell*. Archaeological Studies edited by N.L. Lapp. *Pittsburgh Theological Monograph Series 5. Pittsburgh*

LaRuffa, A.L.
1974   (etc. eds.) City and Peasant: A Study in Sociocultural Dynamics. *Annals of the New York Academy of Sciences Vol. 220:6:345–568*

Lauha, A.
1945   Die Geschichtsmotive in den alttestamentlichen Psalmen. *Annales Academiae Scientiarum Fennicae V LVI, 1. Helsinki*
1963   Das Schilfmeermotiv im Alten Testament. *Vetus Testamentum Suuplements 9:32–46*

Lauring, P.
1976   A History of the Kingdom of Denmark. *2.ed. København*

Lawrence, T.E.
1935   Seven Pillars of Wisdom, a Triumph. *London*

Leach, E.
1973   Concluding Address. *RENFREW 1973A:761–771*

Lefébure, C.
1979A   Introduction: the specificity of nomadic pastoral societies. *Pastoral Production and Society 1979:1–14*
1979B   Accès aus ressources collectives et structure sociale: l'estivage chez les Ayt Atta (Maroc). *Pastoral Production and Society 1979:115–126*

Lehming, S.
1958   Zur Überlieferung von Gn 34. *Zeitschrift für die alttestamentliche Wissenschaft 70: 228–250*

Lemche, N.P.
1972   Israel i Dommertiden. En oversigt over diskussionen om Martin Noths »Das System der zwölf Stämme Israels«. *Tekst og Tolkning 4. København*
1975   »The Hebrew Slave«. Comments on the Slave Law Ex. xxi 2–11. *Vetus Testamentum 25:129–144*
1976   The Manumission of Slaves – the Fallow Year – the Sabbatical Year – the Jobel Year. *Vetus Testamentum 26:38–59*
1977   The Greek »Amphictyony« – Could it be a Prototype for the Israelite Society in the Period of the Judges? *Journal for the Study of the Old Testament 4:48–59*
1979A   »Hebrew« as a National Name for Israel. *Studia Theologica 33:1–23*
1979B   *Andurārum* and *Mîšarum:* Comments on the Problem of Social Edicts and their Application in the Ancient Near East. *Journal of Near Eastern Studies 38:11–22*
1980   »Hebræerne« – Nyt lys over *ḫabiru* – hebræerproblemet. *Dansk teologisk Tidsskrift 43:153–190*

1982   Det revolutionære Israel. En præsentation af en moderne forskningsretning. *Dansk teologisk Tidsskrift 45:16–39*

1984   'Israel in the Period of the Judges' – The Tribal League in Recent Research. *Studia Theologica 38:1–28*

Lewis, I.M.

1961   A Pastoral Democracy. A Study of Pastoralism and Politics Among the Northern Somali of the Horn of Africa. *London*

1968   Introduction. *I.M. LEWIS (ed.): History and Social Anthropology. London 1968:ix-xxviii*

1976   Social Anthropology in Perspective. The relevance of Social Anthropology. *Harmondsworth*

Lewis, L.S.

1968   Typology and Process in Political Evolution. *HELM 1968:101–110*

Liddell Hart, B.

1976   The Sword and the Pen. Edited by A. Liddell Hart. *New York*

Lienhardt, G.

1958   The Western Dinka. *MIDDLETON and TAIT 1958:97–135*

Lindars, B.

1965   Gideon and Kingship. *Journal of Theological Studies New Series 16:315–326*

Liverani, M.

1962   Storia di Ugarit nell'età degli Archivi Politici. *Studi Semitici 6. Roma*

1963   Introduzione alle storia dell'Asia Anteriore antica. *Sussidi Didattici 2. Roma*

1965A   Implicazioni sociali nella politica di Abdi-Ashirta di Amurru. *Rivista degli Studi Orientali 40:267–277 < Translated in LIVERANI 1979>*

1965B   Il fuoruscitismo in Siria nella Tarda età del Bronzo. *Rivista Storica Italiana 77: 315–336*

1967   Contraste e confluenze di concezioni politiche nell'età di El-Amarna. *Revue Assyriologique 61:1–18*

1968   Variazioni climatiche e fluttuazioni demographiche nella storia Siriana. *Oriens Antiquus 7:77–89*

1970   Per una considerazione storica del problema Amorreo. *Oriens Antiquus 9:5–27*

1971A   Le lettere del Faraone a Rib-Adda. *Oriens Antiquus 10:253–268 < Translated in LIVERANI 1979>*

1971B   Sydyke Misor. *Studi in onore di Edoardo Volterra, VI. Pubblicazioni della Facolà di giurisprudenza dell'Università di Roma. Milano 1971:55–74*

1971C   Partire sul carro, per il deserto. *Annali dell'Istituto Universitario Orientale di Napoli N.S. 22:403–415*

1972   Elementi irrazionali nel commercio amarniano. *Oriens Antiquus 11:297–317 < Translated in LIVERANI 1979>*

1973A   La royaté syrienne de l'âge du bronze rêcent. *P. GARELLI: Le palais et la royaté (archéologie et civilisation). XIX rencontre assyriologique internationale. Paris 1973:329–356*

1973B   Memorandum on the Approach to Historiographic Texts. *Orientalia N.S. 43: 178–194*

1973C   The Amorites. *D.J. WISEMAN: Peoples of Old Testament Times. Oxford 1973:100–133*

1973D   Storiografia politica hittita – I: Šunaššura, ovvero: Della reciprocità. *Oriens Antiquus 12:267–297*

1974   Rib-Adda, giusto sofferente. *Altorientalische Forschungen I:175–205*

1975   Communautés de village et palais royal dans la Syrie du IIème Millénaire. *Journal for the Economic and Social History of the Orient 18:146–164*

1976   Anmeldelse: R. de Vaux, Histoire ancienne d'Israël I–II. *Oriens Antiquus 15:145–159*

1977 Storiografia politica hittita – II: Telipinu, ovvero: Della Solidarietà. *Oriens Antiquus 16:105–131*

1979 Three Amarna Essays. *Monographs on the ancient near east 1:5. Malibu*

1980 Le »Origini« d'Israele progetto irrealizzabile di ricerca etnogenetica. *Rivista Biblica Italiana 28:9–31*

Long, B.O.

1976A Recent Field Studies in Oral Literature and the Question of *Sitz im Leben. Semeia 5:35–49*

1976B Recent Field Studies in Oral Literature and their Bearing on OT Criticism. *Vetus Testamentum 26:187–198*

Lord, A.B.

1960 The Singer of Tales. *Harvard Studies in Comparative Literature 24. Cambridge, Mass.*

1976 Formulaic and Non-Narrative Theme in South Slavic Oral Epic and the OT. *Semeia 5:93–105*

Loretz, O.

1977 Die hebräischen Termini *ḤPŠJ* »Freigelassen, Freigelassener« und *ḤPŠH* »Freilassung«. *Ugarit-Forschungen 9:163–167*

Lowie, R.H.

1937 The History of Ethnological Theory. *London*

Luke, J.T.

1965 Pastoralism and Politics in the Mari Period. A Re-Examination of the Character and Political Significance of the Major West Semitic Tribal Groups on the Middle Euphrates ca. 1828–1758 B.C. *Diss. University of Michigan, Ann Arbor*

Lutfiyya, A.M.

1966 Baytîn. A Jordanian Village. A Study of Social Institutions and Social Change in a Folk Community. *Studies in Social Anthropology Vol. 1. The Hague*

McCarthy, D.J.

1963 Treaty and Covenant. A Study in Form on the Ancient Oriental Documents and in the Old Testament. *Analecta Biblica 21. Roma*

1966 Der Gottesbund im Alten Testament. Ein Bericht über die Forschung der letzten Jahren. *Stuttgarter Bibelstudien 13. Stuttgart*

McKay, J.

1973 Religion in Judah under the Assyrians 732–608 B.C. *Studies in Biblical Theology Second Series 26. London*

Magnarella, P.J.

1974 Tradition and Change in a Turkish Town. *New York.*

Malbran-Labat, F.

1980 Éléments pour une recherche sur le nomadisme en Mésopotamie au premier millénaire av. J.-C. I: »L'image du nomade«. *Journal Asiatique 268:11–33*

Ma'oz, M.

1975 (ed.) Studies on Palestine During the Ottoman Period. *Jerusalem*

Marfoe, L.

1979 The Integrative Transformation. Patterns of Sociopolitical Organization in Southern Syria. *Bulletin of the American Schools of Oriental Research 234:1–42*

Marti, K.

1904 Das Dodekapropheton. *Kurzer Hand-Commentar zum Alten Testament XIII. Tübingen*

Marx, E.

1967 Bedouin of the Negev. *Manchester*

1973   The Organization of Nomadic Groups in the Middle East. *M. MILSON: Society and Political Structure in the Arab World. New York 1973:305–336*

1977A   The Tribe as a Unit of Subsistence: Nomadic Pastoralism in the Middle East. *American Anthropologist 79:343–363*

1977B   Communal and Individual Pilgrimage: The Region of Saints' Tombs in South Sinai. *R.P. WERBNER: Regional Cults. Association of Social Anthropologists Monograph No. 16. London 1977:29–51*

1978   The Ecology and Politics of Nomadic Pastoralists in the Middle East. *WEISS-LEDER 1978:41–74*

1980   Wage Labor and Tribal Economy of the Bedoiun in South Sinai. *SALZMAN 1980:111–123*

Masry, A.H.

1973   Prehistory in Northeastern Arabia: The Problem of Interregional Interaction. *Chicago*

Matthews, V.H.

1978   Pastoral Nomadism in the Mari Kingdom (ca. 1830–1760 B.C.). *American Schools of Oriental Research Dissertation Series No. 3. Cambridge, Mass.*

Matthiae, P.

1980A   Ebla. *The Biblical Archaeologist 43:133–134*

1980B   Ebla. An Empire Rediscovered. *London*

Mayes, A.D.H.

1969   The Historical Context of the Battle Against Sisera. *Vetus Testamentum 19:353–360*

1973   Israel in the Pre-Monarchy Period. *Vetus Testamentum 23:151–170*

1974   Israel in the Period of the Judges. *Studies in Biblical Theology Second Series 29. London*

1977   The Period of the Judges and the Rise of the Monarchy. *HAYES and MILLER 1977:285–331*

Meeker, M.E.

1979   Literature and Violence in North Arabia. *Cambridge Studies in Cultural Systems 3. Cambridge*

1980   The Twilight of a South Asian Heroic Age: A Rereading of Barth's Study of Swat. *Man N.S. 15:682–701*

Mendenhall, G.E.

1954A   Ancient Oriental and Biblical Law. *The Biblical Archaeologist Reader III:3–24*

1954B   Covenant Forms in Israelite Tradition. *The Biblical Archaeologist Reader III:24–53*

1958   The Census Lists of Numbers 1 and 26. *Journal of Biblical Literature 77:52–66*

1961   Biblical History in Transition. *WRIGHT 1961:32–53*

1962   The Hebrew Conquest of Palestine. *The Biblical Archaeologist Reader III:100–120*

1969   Review: WEIPPERT 1967. *Biblica 50:432–436*

1973   The Tenth Generation. The Origins of the Biblical Tradition. *Baltimore*

1975   The Monarchy. *Interpretation 29:155–170*

1976A   »Change and Decay in All Around I See«: Conquest, Covenant, and *the Tenth Generation. The Biblical Archaeologist 39:152–157*

1976B   Migration Theories vs. Cultural Change as an Explanation for Early Israel. *Society of Biblical Literature 1976 Seminar Papers:135–143*

1976C   Social Organization in Early Israel. *CROSS, LEMKE and MILLER 1976:132–151*

1978   Between Theology and Archaeology. *Journal for the Study of the Old Testament 7:28–34*

Merendino, R.P.

1969   Das deuteronomische Gesetz. Eine literarkritische, gattungs- und überlieferungsgeschichtliche Untersuchung zu Dt 12–26. *Bonner Biblische Beiträge 31. Bonn*

462   BIBLIOGRAPHY

Mettinger, T.N.D.
1971   Solomonic State officials. A Study of the Civil Government Officials of the
          Israelite Monarchy. *Coniectanea Biblica Old Testament Series 5. Lund*
1976   King and Messiah. The Civil and Sacral Legitimation of the Israelite Kings.
          Coniectanea Biblica Old Testament Series 8. Lund

Meyer, E.
1906   Die Israeliten und ihre Nachbarstämme. Alttestamentliche Untersuchungen mit
          Beiträgen von B. Luther. *Halle (repr. Darmstadt 1967)*
1913   Geschichte des Altertums I,2. *3. Ausg. Stuttgart (8. Aufl. Darmstadt 1965)*
1931   Geschichte des Altertums II. *2. Ausg. Stuttgart (4. Aufl. Darmstadt 1965)*

Middleton, J.
1958   The Political System of the Lugbara of the Nile-Congo Divide. *MIDDLETON
          and TAIT 1958:203-229*

Middleton, J. and Tait, D.
1958   Tribes Without Rulers. Studies in African Segmentary Systems. *London*

Miller, J.M.
1977A   The Israelite Occupation of Canaan. *HAYES and MILLER 1977:213-284*
1977B   Archaeology and the Israelite Conquest of Canaan: Some Methodological Ob-
          servations. *Palestine Exploration Quarterly 109:87-93*
1977C   The Partriarchs and Extra-Biblical Sources: A Response. *Journal for the Study of the
          Old Testament 2:62-66*
1979   W.F. Albright and Historical Reconstruction. *The Biblical Archaeologist 42:37-47*

Moore, C.B.
1974   (ed.) Reconstructing Complex Societies. An Archaeological Colloquium. *Bulletin
          of the American Schools of Oriental Research. Supplement Studies 20. Cambridge, Mass.*

Moore, C.F.
1895   A Critical and Exegetical Commentary on Judges. *The International Critical Com-
          mentary. 2.ed. (5. repr. 1918). Edingburgh*

Morgan, L.H.
1877   Ancient Society. Edited by L.A. White. *Cambridge, Mass. 1964*

Morsey, K.
1976   T.E. Lawrence und der arabische Aufstand 1916/18. *Studien zur Militärgeschichte,
          Militärwissenschaft und Konfliktforschung Bd. 7. Osnabrück*

Mowinckel, S.
1914   Zur Komposition des Buches Jeremia. *Videnskapsselskapets Skrifter. II. Hist.-Filos.
          Klasse, 1913 no. 5. Kristiania*
1922   Psalmenstudien II. Das Thronbesteigungsfest Jahwäs und der Ursprung der
          Eschatologie. *(Repr. Amsterdam 1966)*
1946   Zur Frage nach dokumentarischen Quellen in Josua 13-19. *Avhandlinger utgitt av
          Det Norske Videnskabs-Akademi i Oslo II. Hist.-Filos. Klasse. 1946 No. 1. Oslo*
1951   Offersang og Sangoffer. Salmediktningen i Bibelen. *Oslo*
1953   Der achtundsechzigste Psalm. *Avhandlinger utgitt av Det Norske Videnskabs-Akademi
          i Oslo II. Hist.-Filos. Klasse 1953 No. 1. Oslo*
1964   Tetrateuch-Pentateuch-Hexateuch. Die Berichte über die Landnahme in den
          drei altsraelitischen Geschictswerken. *Beihefte zur Zeitschrift für die alttestamentliche
          Wissenschaft 90. Berlin*
1967   Israels opphav og eldste historie. *Oslo*

Muhly, J.D.
1980   The Bronze Age Setting. *WERTIME and MUHLY 1980:25-67*

Muntigh, L.M.
1974   Amorite Married and Family Life According to the Mari Texts. *Journal of the Northwest Semitic Languages 3:50–70*

Munton, R.J.C.
1973   Systems analysis: a comment. *RENFREW 1973A:685–690*

Murdock, G.P.
1949   Social Structure. *Repr. 1965. New York*

Murphy, R.E. and Kasdan, L.
1959   The Structure of Parallel Cousin Marriage. *American Anthropologist 61:17–29*
1967   Agnation and Endogamy: Some Further Considerations. *Southwestern Journal of Anthropology 23:1–14*

Musil, A.
1907   Arabia Petraea I–III. *Wien 1907–1908*
1927   Arabia Deserta. A Topographical Itenerary. *American Geographical Society. Oriental Exploitations and Studies No. 2. Repr. 1978. New York*
1928   The Manners and Customs of the Rwala Bedouins. *American Geographical Society. Oriental Explorations and Studies No. 6. Repr. 1978. New York*

Mühlmann, W.E.
1938   Staatsbildung und Amphiktyonie in Polynesien. Eine Studie zur Ethnologie und politischen Soziologie. *Stuttgart*

Müller, H.P.
1969   Ursprünge und Strukturen alttestamentlicher Eschatologie. *Beiheft zur Zeitschrift für die alttestamentliche Wissenschaft 109. Berlin*

Na'aman, N.
1980   The Inheritance of the Sons of Simeon. *Zeitschrift des Deutschen Palästina-Vereins 96· 136–152*

Nadel, S.F.
1967   Nupe State and Community. *COHEN and MIDDLETON 1967:293–337*

Naroll, R.
1964   On Ethnic Unit Classification. *Current Anthropology 5:283–291*

Naveh, J.
1978   Some Considerations on the Ostracon From 'Izbet Ṣarṭah. *Israel Exploration Journal 28:31–35*

Nelson, C.
1973   (ed.) The Desert and the Sown. Nomads in the Wider Society. *Institute of International Studies. University of California. Berkeley*

Nicholson, E.W.
1970   Preaching to the Exiles. A Study of the Prose Tradition in the Book of Jeremiah. *Oxford*

Nicolaisen, J.
1963A   Primitive kulturer. Nogle hovedtræk af etnologiens historie. *København*
1963B   Ecology and Culture of the Pastoral Tuareg. With Particular Reference to the Tuareg of Ahaggar and Ayr. *Nationalmuseets Skrifter. Etnografisk Række, IX. København*
1965   Kulturvidenskab. *Berlingske Leksikonbibliotek 29. København*
1976   The Penan of Sarawak. Further Notes on the Neo-Evolutionary Concept of Hunters. *Folk 18:205–236*

Nielsen, E.

1954   Oral Tradition. A Modern Problem in Old Testament Introduction. *Studies in Biblical Theology 11*. London
1959   Shechem. A Traditio-Historical Investigation. *2.ed.* København
1965   De ti Bud. En traditionshistorisk skitse. *København*
1970   Deuterozakarja. Nye bidrag til belysning af Zak. 9–14. *Tekst og Tolkning 1*. København
1972   Johannes Pedersen's Contribution to the Research and Understanding of the Old Testament. *Annual of the Swedish Theological Institute 8:1970–1971:4–20*
1982   Moses and the Law. *Vetus Testamentum 32:87–98*

Nieuwenhuijze, C.A.O. van

1971   Sociology of the Middle East. A Stocktaking and Interpretation. *Social, Economic and Political Studies of the Middle East Vol. 1.* Leiden

Norin, S.I.L.

1977   Er spaltete das Meer. Die Auszugsüberlieferung in Psalmen und Kult des alten Israel. *Coniectanea Biblica Old Testament Series 9.* Lund

Noth, M.

1927   Das Krongut der israelitischen Könige und seine Verwaltung. *NOTH 1971A:I: 159–1982*
1928   Die israelitischen Personennahmen im Rahmen der gemeinsemitischen Namengebung. *Beiträge zur Wissenschaft vom Alten und Neuen Testament III:10. Stuttgart (repr. Hildesheim 1966)*
1930   Das System der zwölf Stämme Israel. *Beiträge zur Wissenschaft vom Alten und Neuen Testament IV:1. Stuttgart (repr. Darmstadt 1966)*
1935   Studien zu den historisch-geographischen Dokumenten des Josuabuches. *NOTH 1971A:I:229–280*
1938   Grundsätzliches zur geschichtlichen Deutung archäologischer Befunde auf dem Boden Palästinas. *NOTH 1971A:I:3–16*
1941   Das Land Gilead als Siedlungsgebiet israelitischer Sippen. *NOTH 1971A:I:347–390*
1943   Überlieferungsgeschichtliche Studien I. *Schriften der königsberger gelehrten Gesellschaft Geist. Wiss. Kl. 18. Repr. Darmstadt 1963*
1944   Israelitischer Stämme zwischen Ammon und Moab. *NOTH 1971A:I:391–433*
1946   Die Nachbarn der israelitischen Stämme im Ostjordanland. *NOTH 1971A:I: 435–475*
1948   Überlieferungsgeschichte des Pentateuch. *Stuttgart (repr. Darmstadt 1966)*
1950A   Geschichte Israels. *(5. Aufl. 1963) Göttingen*
1950B   Das Amt des »Richters Israels«. *M. NOTH: Gesammelte Studien zum Alten Testament II. Theologische Bücherei 39. München 1969:71–85*
1950C   Überlieferungsgeschichtliches zur zweiten Hälfte des Josuabuches. *H. JUNKER and J. BOTTERWECK: Alttestamentliche Studien F. Nötscher gewidmet. Bonner Biblische Beiträge 1. Bonn 1950:152–167*
1953A   Das Buch Josua. *Handbuch zum Alten Testament I 7. 2. Aufl. Tübingen*
1953B   Mari und Israel. Eine Personennamenstudie. *NOTH 1971A:II:213–233*
1953C   Jabes-Gilead. Ein Beitrag zur Methode alttestamentlicher Topographie. *NOTH 1971A:I:476–488*
1953D   Die Katastrophe von Jerusalem im Jahre 587 v. Chr. und ihre bedeutung für Israel. *M. NOTH: Gesammelte Studien zum Alten Testament. Theologische Bücherei 6. 2. Aufl. München 1960:346–371*
1957   Hat die Bibel doch Recht? *NOTH 1971A:I:17–33*
1959   Gilead und Gad. *NOTH 1971:I:489–543*
1960   Der Beitrag der Archäologie zur Geschichte Israels. *NOTH 1971A:I:34–51*
1962A   Der Hintergrund von Ri 17–18. *NOTH 1971A:I:133–147*
1962B   Die Welt des Alten Testament. Einführung in die Grenzgebiete der alttestament-

lichen Wissenschaft. 4. neubearb. Aufl. *Sammlung Töpelmann Zweite Reihe: Theologische Hilfsbücher, Band 3. Berlin*

1965   Das zweite Buch Mose. Exodus. *Das Alte Testament Deutsch 5. 3. Aufl. Göttingen*

1966A   Das dritte Buch Mose. Leviticus. *Das Alte Testament Deutsch 6. 2. Aufl. Göttingen*

1966B   Das vierte Buch Mose. Numeri. *Das Alte Testament Deutsch 7. Göttingen*

1968   Könige 1. *Biblischer Kommentar Altes Testament IX/I. Neukirchen*

1971A   Aufsätze zur biblischen Landes- und Altertumskunde I–II. Herausgegeben von H.W. Wolff. *Neukirchen*

1971B   Die Topographie Palästinas und Syriens im Licht ägyptischer Quellen. *NOTH 1971A:II:1–132*

Nowack, W.

1902   Richter, Ruth u. Bücher Samuelis. *Handkommentar zum Alten Testament I 4. Göttingen*

1903   Die Kleinen Propheten. *Handkommentar zum Alten Testament III 4. 2. Aufl. Göttingen*

Nyberg, H.S.

1938   Studien zum Religionskampf im Alten Testament. *Archiv für Religionswissenschaft 35:329–387*

Nyström, S.

1946   Beduinentum und Jahwismus. Eine soziologisch- religionsgeschichtliche Untersuchung zum Alten Testament. *Lund*

Nützel, W.

1975A   Das Mesopotamien der Frühkulturen in Abhängigkeit der nacheiszeitlichen Klimaschwankungen und Meeresspiegeländerungen. *Mitteilungen des Deutschen Orient-Gesellschaft 107:27–38*

1975B   The Formation of the Arabian Gulf From 14000. *Sumer 31:101–109*

1976A   Kann die Naturwissenschaft der mesopotamischen Archäologie neue Impulse geben? *Zeitschrift für Assyriologie 66:120–134*

1976B   The Climate Changes of Mesopotamia and Bordering Areas 14000 to 2000 B.C. *Sumer 32:11–24*

1980A   Die ökologischen Vorzüge küstennaher Besiedlungsstätten Mesopotamien. *Mitteilungen des Deutschen Orient-Gesellschaft 112:103–114*

1980B   Lag Ur einst am Meer? *Mitteilungen des Deutschen Orient-Gesellschaft 112:95–102*

Oakley, S.

1972   The Story of Denmark. *London (in U.S.A.: A Short History of Denmark)*

Oberling, P.

1974   The Qahqā'i Nomads of Fars. *Near and Middle East Monographs VI. The Hague*

Oelsner, J.

1971   Zur sozialen lage in Ugarit. *KLENGEL 1971:117–123*

Olrik, A.

1903   Danmarks Heltedigtning 1–2. En Oldtidsstudie. *København 1903–1910*

1909 ★ Epische Gesetze der Volksdichtung. *Zeitschrift für deutsche Altertum 51:1–12*

1919   The Heroic Legends of Denmark. Ed. by L.M. Hollander. *Repr. 1976. New York*

1921   Nogle Grundsætninger for Sagnforskning. Udg. af. H. Ellekilde. *Danmarks Folkeminder Nr. 23. København*

Oppenheim, A.L.

1969   Mesopotamia – Land of Many Cities. *LAPIDUS 1969B:3–18*

Oppenheim, M. Freiherr von

1939   Die Beduinen I–IV. Unter mittarbeitung von E. Bräunlich und W. Caskel. *Leipzig og Wiesbaden 1939–1968*

Oren, E.D.

1978   Esh-Shari'a (Tel Sera'). *EAEHL IV:1059–1068*

Otto, E.

1975   Das Mazzotfest in Gilgal. *Beiträge zur Wissenschaft vom Alten und Neuen Testament VI:7 (107)*. *Stuttgart*

1977   Stehen wir vor einem Umbruch in der Pentateuchkritik? *Verkündung und Forschung 22:1977/2:82–98*

1978   Survey-archäologische Ergebnisse zur geschichte der früheisenzeitlichen Siedlung Janoah (Josh. 16,6.7). *Zeitschrift des Deutschen Palästina-Vereins 94:108–118*

1979   Jacob in Sichem. Überlieferungsgeschichtliche, archäologische und territorialgeschichtliche Studien zur Entstehungsgeschichte Israels. *Beiträge zur Wissenschaft vom Alten und Neuen Testament 110. Stuttgart*

1981   Sozialgeschichte Israels. Probleme und Perspektiven. Ein Diskussionspapier. *Biblische Notizen 15:87–92*

Ottosson, M.

1969   Gilead. Tradition and History. *Coniectanea Biblica Old Testament Series 3. Lund*

1980   Temples and Cult Places in Palestine. *Uppsala Studies in Ancient Mediterranean and Near Eastern Civilizations 12. Uppsala*

Otzen, B.

1964   Studien über Deuterosacharja. *Acta Theologica Danica Vol. VI. København*

1977   Israeliterne i Palæstina. Det gamle Israels historie, religion og litteratur. *København*

Owen, D.I.

1981   An Akkadian Letter From Ugarit at Tel Aphek. *Tel Aviv 8:1–17*

Parry, M.

1953   Serbocroatian Heroic Songs 1. *Cambridge, Mass. og Beograd*

1971   The Making of Homeric Verse. The Collected Papers of Milman Parry. ed. by A. Parry. *Oxford*

Pastner, C. McC.

1978   Kinship Terminology and Feudal Versus Tribal Orientations in Baluch Social Organization: A Comparative View. *WEISSLEDER 1978:261–274*

1979   Cousin Marriage Among the Zikri Baluch of Central Pakistan. *Ethnology 8:31–47*

Pastner, S.

1978   Conservatism and Change in a Desert Feudalism: The Case of Southern Baluchistan. *WEISSLEDER 1978:247–260*

Pastner S. and C. McC.

1972   Agriculture, Kinship and Politics in Southern Baluchistan. *Man N.S. 7:128–136*

Patai, R.

1955   Cousin-Right in Middle Eastern Marriage. *Southwestern Journal of Anthropology 11:371–390*

1959   Sex and Family in the Bible and the Middle East. *New York*

1962   Golden River to Golden Road. Society, Culture, and Change in the Middle East. *Philadelphia*

1965   The Structure of Endogamous Unilineal Descent Groups. *Southwestern Journal of Anthropology 21:325–350*

Pedersen, J.

1931   Die Auffassung vom Alten Testament. *Zeitschrift für die alttestamentliche Wissenschaft 49:161–181*

1934   Passahfest und Passahlegende. *Zeitschrift für die alttestamentliche Wissenschaft 52: 161–175*

1958   Israel I–II. Sjæleliv og Samfundsliv. *3.ed. København*

1960   Israel III–IV. Hellighed og Guddommelighed. *2.ed. København*

Pehrson, R.N.
  1966   The Social Organization of the Mari Baluch. Compiled and Analyzed from his Notes by F. Barth. *Chicago*

Peristiany, J.G.
  1976   Mediterranean Family Structures. *Cambridge*

Perlitt, L.
  1965   Vatke und Wellhausen. Geschichtsphilosophische Voraussetzungen und historiographische Motive für die Darstellung der Religion und Geschichte Israels durch Wilhelm Vatke und Julius Wellhausen. *Beiheft zur Zeitschrift für die alttestamentliche Wissenschaft 94. Berlin*
  1969   Bundestheologie im Alten Testament. *Wissenschaftliche Monographien zum Alten und Neuen Testament 36. Neukirchen*

Peters, E.L.
  1960   The Proliferation of Segments in the Lineage of the Bedouin of Cyrenaica. *SWEET 1970:I:363–398*
  1963   Aspects of Rank and Status Among Muslims in a Lebanese Village. *SWEET 1970:II:76–123*
  1965   Aspects of the Family Among the Bedouin of Cyrenaica. *M.F. NIMKOFF: Comparative Family Systems. Boston 1965:121–146*
  1967   Some Structural Aspects of the Feud Among the Camel-Herding Bedouin of Cyrenaica. *Africa 37:261–282*
  1968   The Tied and the Free. An Account of a Type of Patron-Client Relationship Among the Bedouin Pastoralists of Cyrenaica. *J.G. PERISTIANY: Contributions to Mediterranean Sociology. Publications of the Social Sciences Centre Athens IV. Paris 1968:167–188*
  1976   Aspects of Affinity in a Lebanese Maronite Village. *PERISTIANY 1976:27–79*

Petersen, D.L.
  1979   Max Weber and the Sociological Study of Ancient Israel. *Sociological Inquiry 49/2–3:117–149*

Planhol, X. de
  1958   De la plaine pamphylienne aux lacs pisidiens. Nomadisme et vie paysanne. *Bibliothèque archéologique et historique de l'Institut francais d'archéologie d'Istanbul III. Paris*
  1965   Les nomades, la steppe et la fôret en Anatolie. *Geographische Zeitschrift 53:101–116*
  1969   L'evolution du nomadisme en Anatolie et en Iran. *FÖLDES 1969:69–93*
  1972   Regional Diversification and Social Structure in North Africa and the Islamic Middle East. A Geographical Approach. *ANTOUN and HARIK 1972:103–117*
  1979   Saturation et sécurité: sur l'organisation des sociétés de pasteurs nomades. *Pastoral Production and Society 1979:29–42*

Posener, G.
  1940   Princes et pays d'Asie et de Nubie. Textes hiératiques sur des figurines d'envoûtement du Moyen Empire. *Brussel*

Prag, K.
  1974   The Intermediate Early Bronze – Middle Bronze Age: An Interpretation of the Evidence from Transjordan, Syria and Lebanon. *Levant 6:69–116*

Preiser, W.
  1972   Vergeltung und Sühne im altisraelitischen Strafrecht. *KOCH 1972:236–277*

Pritchard, J.B.
  1962   Gibeon, Where the Sun Stood Stil. The Discovery of the Biblical City. *Princeton*

Pury, A. de
  1969   Genèse XXXIV et l'histoire. *Revue Biblique 76:5–49*

Rabast, K.

1948★ Das apodiktische Recht in Deuteronomium und im Heiligkeitsgesetz

Rad, G. von

1938 Das formgeschichtliche Problem des Hexateuch. *VON RAD 1958:9–86*

1944 Der Anfang der Geschichtschreibung im Alten Israel. *VON RAD 1958:148–188*

1951 Der Heilige Krieg im alten Israel. *Zürich (4. Aufl. Göttingen 1965)*

1957 Theologie des Alten Testaments 1. Die Theologie der geschichtlichen Überliefe-rungen Israels. *5. Aufl. München 1966*

1958 Gesammelte Studien zum Alten Testament. *Theologische Bücherei 8. 3. Aufl. 1965. München*

1964 Das fünfte Buch Mose. Deuteronomium. *Das alte Testament Deutsch 8. Göttingen*

Radcliffe-Brown, A.R.

1950 Introduction. *A.R. RADCLIFFE-BROWN and D. FORDE: African Systems of Kin-ship and Marriage. London 1950:1–85*

Rainey, A.F.

1962 The Social Stratification of Ugarit. *Diss. Brandeis University. Ann Arbor*

Rathjens, C.

1969 Geographische Grundlagen und Verbreitung des Nomadismus. *Nomadismus als Entwicklungsproblem 1969:19–28*

Redfield, R.

1956 Peasant Society and Culture. An Anthropological Approach to Civilization. *Chicago*

Redford, D.B.

1970 A Study of the Biblical Story of Joseph (genesis 37–50). *Vetus Testamentum Supplementum 20. Leiden*

Redman, C.L.

1978A The Rise of Civilization. From Early Farmers to Urban Society in the Ancient Near East. *San Francisco*

1978B (etc. eds.) Social Archaeology: Beyond Subsistence and Dating. *New York*

Rendtorff, R.

1969 Traditio-Historical Method and the Documentary Hypothesis. *Proceedings of the Fifth World Congress of Jewish Studies Jerusalem 1969, Vol. I:5–11*

1977A Das Überlieferungsgeschichtliche Problem des Pentateuch. *Beiheft zur Zeitschrift für die alttestamentlichen Wissenschaft 147. Berlin*

1977B The 'Yahwist' as Theologian? The Dilemma of Pentateuchal Criticism. *Journal for the Study of the Old Testament 3:2–9*

1977C Pentateuchal Studies on the Move. *Journal for the Study of the Old Testament 3:43–45*

Renesse, E. and Sponeck, H.G. Graf

1969 Nomadismus in Afghanistan als sozioökonomisches Problem. Versuch einer Konferenzanalyse. *Nomadismus als Entwicklungsproblem 1969:161–171*

Renfrew, C.

1973A (ed.) The Explanation of Culture Change. Models in Prehistory. *London*

1973B Social Archaeology. An Inaugural Lecture. *Southhampton*

1974 Beyong a Subsistence Economy: The Evolution of Social Organization in Pre-historic Europe. *MOORE 1974:69–95*

Renger, J.

1973A *mārat ilim*. Exogamie bei den semitischen Nomaden des 2. Jahrtausends. *Archiv für Orientforschung 24:103–107*

1973B Who Are all Those People? *Orientalia N.S. 42:259–273*

Reventlow, H. Graf
1961   Das Heiligkeitzgesetz formgeschichtlich untersucht. *Wissenschaftliche Monographien zum Alten und Neuen Testament 6. Neukirchen*

Reviv, H.
1966   The Government of Shechem in the El-Amarna Period and in the Days of Abimelech. *Israel Exploration Journal 16:252–257*

Richard, S.
1980   Toward a Consensus of Opinion on the End of the Early Bronze Age in Palestine-Transjordan. *Bulletin of the American Schools of Oriental Research 237:5–34*

Richards, A.I.
1960A   (ed.) East African Chiefs. A Study of Political Development in some Uganda and Tanganyika Tribes. *London*
1960B   The Alur. *RICHARDS 1960A:311–325*
1960C   Social Mechanisms for the Transfer of Political Rights in Some African Tribes. *Journal of the Royal Anthropological Institute 90:175–190*

Richter, W.
1963   Traditionsgeschichtliche Untersuchung zum Richterbuch. *Bonner Biblische Beiträge 18. Bonn*
1965   Zu den »Richtern Israels«. *Zeitschrift für die alttestamentliche Wissenschaft 77:40–72*

Robertson, D.A.
1972   Linguistic Evidence in Dating Early Hebrew Poetry. *Society of Biblical Literature Dissertation Series 3. Missoula*

Robinson, Th.H. and Horst, F.
1964   Die zwölf kleinen Propheten. *Handbuch zum Alten Testament I 14. 3. Aufl. Tübingen*

Rogerson, J.W.
1978   Anthropology and the Old Testament. *Growing Points in Theology. Oxford*

Rohland, E.
1979   Die Bedeutung der Erwählungstraditionen Israels für die Eschatologie des alttestamentlichen Propheten. *P.H.A. NEUMANN: Das Prophetenverständnis in der deutschsprachigen Forschung seit Heinrich Ewald. Wege der Forschung 307. Darmstadt*

Ron, Z.
1966   Agricultural Terraces in the Judaean Mountains. *Israel Exploration Journal 16:33–49. 111–122*

Rose, M.
1975   Der Ausschliesslichkeitsanspruch Jahwes. Deuteronomistische Schultheologie und die Volksfrömmigkeit in der späten Königszeit. *Beiträge zur Wissenschaft vom Alten und Neuen Testament 106. Stuttgart*
1981   Deuteronomist und Jahwist. Untersuchungen zu den Berührungspunkten beider Literaturwerke. *Abhandlungen zur Theologie des Alten und Neuen Testaments 67. Zürich*

Rosenfeld, H.
1965   The Social Composition of the Military in the Process of State Formation in the Arabian Desert. *Journal of the Royal Anthropological Institute 95:174–194*
1972   An Overview and Critique of the Literature on Rural Politics and Social Change. *ANTOUN and HARIK 1972:45–74*
1976   Social and Economic Factors in Explanation of the Encreased Rate of Patrilineal Endogamy in the Arab Village in Israel. *PERISTIANY 1976:115–136*

Rosenthal, F.
1958   Cf. *IBN KHALDUN 1958*

Rost, L.
1926   Die Überlieferung von der Thronnachfolge Davids. *ROST 1965B:119–253*
1965A   Das kleine geschichtliche Credo. *ROST 1965B:11–25*
1965B   Das kleine Credo und andere Studien zum Alten Testament. *Heidelberg*

Rowton, M.B.
1959   The Background of the Treaty between Ramesses II and Ḫattusilis III. *Journal of Cuneiform Studies 13:1–11*
1960   Comparative Chronology at the Time of Dynasty XIX. *Journal of Near Eastern Studies 19:15–22*
1965   The Topological Factor in the *Ḫapiru* Problem. *Assyriological Studies 16:375–387*
1967   The Woodlands of Ancient Western Asia. *Journal of Near Eastern Studies 26:261–277*
1973A   Urbanism and Nomadism in Western Asia. *Orientalia N.S. 42:247–258*
1973B   Urban Autonomy in a Nomadic Environment. *Journal of Near Eastern Studies 32:201–215*
1974   Enclosed Nomadism. *Journal of the Economic and Social History of the Orient 17:1–30*
1976A   Dimorphic Structure and Topology. *Oriens Antiquus 15:17–31*
1976B   Dimorphic Structure and the Problem of the *ʿapirû* – *ʿIbrîm. Journal of Near Eastern Studies 35:13–20*
1976C   Dimorphic Structure and the Tribal Elite. *Al-Bahit. Festschrift J. Henninger. Studi Instituti Anthropos Vol. 30:219–257*
1977   Dimorphic Structure and the Parasocial Element. *Journal of Near Eastern Studies 36:181–198*
1980   Pastoralism and the Periphery in Evolutionary Perspective. *Colloques internationaux de C.N.R.S. no 580 – L'archéologie de l'Iraq: Paris 1980:291–301*

Rudolph, W.
1938   Der »Elohist« von Exodus bis Josua. *Beihefte zur Zeitschrift für die alttestamentliche Wissenschaft 68. Berlin*
1958   Jeremia. *Handbuch zum Alten Testament I 12. 2. Aufl. Tübingen*
1962   Das Buch Ruth. Das Hohe Lied. Die Klagelieder. *Kommentar zum Alten Testament XVII 1–3. Gütersloh*
1971   Joel-Amos-Obadja-Jona. *Kommentar zum Alten Testament XIII 2 Gütersloh*

Rösel, H.
1980   Jephtah und das Problem der Richter. *Biblica 61:251–255*
1981   Die »Richter Israels«. Rückblick und neuer Ansatz. *Biblische Zeitschrift NF 25: 1981:180–203*

Sahlins, M.D.
1961   The Segmentary Lineage. An Organization of Predatory Expansion. *COHEN and MIDDLETON 1967:89–119*
1968   Tribesmen. *Foundations of Modern Anthropology Series. Englewood Cliffs*

Salzman, P.C.
1967   Political Organization among Nomadic Peoples. *Proceedings of the American Philosophical Society, Vol. 111, no. 2. April 1967:115–131*
1971A   (ed.) Comparative Studies of Nomadism and Pastoralism. *Special Issue Anthropological Quarterly 44*
1971B   National Integration of the tribes in Modern Iran. *The Middle East Journal 25: 325–336*
1971C   Adaption and Political Organization in Iranian Baluchistan. *Ethnology 10:433–444*
1972   Multi-Resource Nomadism in Iranian Baluchistan. *IRONS and DYSON-HUDSON 1972:60–68*
1974   Tribal Chiefs as Middlemen: The Political Encapsulation in the Middle East. *Anthropological Quarterly 47:203–210*

1978A   Ideology and Change in Middle Eastern tribal Societies. *Man N.S.13:618–637*
1978B   The Proto-State in Iranian Baluchistan. *COHEN and SERVICE 1978:125–140*
1978C   Does Complementary Opposition Exist? *American Anthropologist 80:53–70*
1978D   The Study of 'Complex Society' in the Middle East: A Review Essay. *International Journal of Middle Eastern Studies 9:539–557*
1979   Inequality and Oppression in Nomadic Society. *Pastoral Production and Society 1979:429–446*
1980   (ed.) When Nomads Settle. Processes of Sedentarization as Adaption and Response. *New York*

Sanders, J.A.
1970   (ed.) Near Eastern Archaeology in the Twentieth Century. Essays in Honor of Nelson Glueck. *New York*

Sanders, W.T. and Webster, D.
1978   Unilinealism, Multilinealism, and the Evolution of Complex Societies. *REDMAN 1978B:249–302*

Sasson, J.
1981   On Choosing Models for recreating Israelite Pre-Monarchic History. *Journal for the Study of the Old Testament 21:13–24*

Schmid, H.H.
1976   Der sogenannte Jahwist. Beobachtungen und Fragen zur Penteteuchforschung. *Zürich*
1977   In Search of New Approaches in Pentateuchal Research. *Journal for the Study of the Old Testament 3:33–42*

Schmidt, W.H.
1965   Die deuteronomistische Redaktion des Amosbuches. Zu den theologischen Unterschied zwischen dem Prophetenwort und seinem Sammler. *Zeitschrift für die alttestamentliche Wissenschaft 77:168–192*
1979   Einführung in das Alte Testament. *Berlin*
1981   Ein Theologe in salomonischer Zeit? Plädoyer für den Jahwisten. *Biblische Zeitschrift NF 25:82–102*

Schmitt, H.C.
1972   Elisa. Traditionsgeschichtliche Untersuchungen zur vorklassischen nordisraelitischen Prophetie. *Gütersloh*
1980   Die nichtpriesterliche Josephgeschichte. Ein Beitrag zur neuesten Pentateuchkritik. *Beiheft zur Zeitschrift für die alttestamentliche Wissenschaft 154. Berlin*

Scholz, F.
1972   Formen regionaler Mobilität bei den Brahui-Stämmen als Ausdruck sozial- und wirtschaftsgeographischer Wandlungen in Belutschistan (West-Pakistan). *Deutscher Geographentag Erlangen-Nürnberg 1971. Tagungsbericht und wissenschaftliche Abhandlungen. Verhandlungen der Deutschen Geographentages Bd. 38. Wiesbaden 1972: 355–370*
1974   Belutschistan (Pakistan). Eine sozialgeographische Studie des Wandels im einem Nomadenland seit Beginn der Kolonialzeit. *Göttinger Geographische Abhandlungen Hft. 63. Göttingen*

Schwertner, S.
1966   »Das verheissene Land«. Bedeutung und Verständnis des Landes nach den frühen Zeugnissen des Alten Testament. *Diss. Heidelberg*

Seale, M.S.
1962   Deborah's Ode and the Ancient Arabian Qasida. *Journal of Biblical Literature 81: 343–347*
1974   The Desert Bible. Nomadic Tribal Culture and Old Testament Interpretation. *London*

Seebass, H.

1978   Erwägungen zum altisraelitischen System der zwölf Stämme. *Zeitschrift für die alt-testamentliche Wissenschaft 90:196-220*

1980   League of Tribes or Amphictyony? A Review of O. Bächli, Amphiktyonie im Alten Testament, 1977. *Journal for the Study of the Old Testament 16:61-66*

Seger, J.D.

1972   Shechem Field XIII, 1969. *Bulletin of the American Schools of Oriental Research 205: 20-35*

Seitz, G.

1971   Redaktionsgeschichtliche Studien zum Deuteronomium. *Beiträge zur Wissenschaft vom Alten und Neuen Testament 93. Stuttgart*

Sellin, E.

1922   Das Zwölfprophetenbuch. *Kommentar zum Alten Testament XII. Leipzig*

1924   Geschichte des israelitisch-jüdischen Volkes I. *Leipzig*

Serjeant, R.B.

1980A   (ed.) The Islamic City. *UNESCO. Paris*

1980B   Social Stratification in Arabia. *SERJEANT 1980A:126-147*

Service, E.R.

1971   Primitive Social Organization. An Evolutionary Perspective. *2.ed. New York*

1975   The Origins of the State and Civilization: The Process of Cultural Evolution. *New York*

1978   Classical and Modern Theories of the Origins of Government. *COHEN and SERVICE 1978:21-33*

1979   The Hunters. *Foundations of Modern Anthropology Series 2.ed. Englewood Cliffs*

Seters, J. van

1972A   Confessional Reformulation in the Exilic Period. *Vetus Testementum 22:448-459*

1972B   The Conquest of Sihon's Kingdom: A Literary Examination. *Journal of Biblical Literature 91:182-197*

1975   Abraham in History and Tradition. *New Haven*

1976   Oral Patterns or Literary Conventions in Biblical Narrative. *Semeia 5:139-154*

1977   The Yahwist as Theologian? A Response. *Journal for the Study of the Old Testament 3:15-19*

1979   Recent Studies on the Pentateuch: A Crisis in Method. *Journal of the American Oriental Society 99:663-673*

1980   The Religion of the Patriarchs in Genesis. *Biblica 61:220-233*

1981   Histories and Historians of the Ancient Near East: The Israelites. *Orientalia N.S. 50:137-185*

Sethe, K.

1926   Die Ächtung feindlicher Fürsten, Völker und Dinge auf altägyptischen Tonge-fässcherben des Mittleren Reiches. *Abhandlungen des Preussischen Akademie der Wissenschaften Phil.hist. Klasse 1926:6. Berlin*

Sharon, M.

1975   The Political Role of the Bedouins in Palestine in the Sixteenth and Seventeenth Centuries. *MA'OZ 1975:11-30*

Shiloh, Y.

1970   The Four-Room House. Its Situation and Function in the Israelite City. *Israel Exploration Journal 20:180-190*

1973   The Four-Room House – The Israelite Type-House? *Eretz-Israel 11:277-285 (hb.)*

Sigrist, C.

1967   Reguliertes Anarchie. Untersuchungen zum Fehlen und zur Entstehung politischer Herrschaft in segmentären Gesellschaften Afrikas. *Olten und Freibug im Breisgau*

Simons, J.
1937   Handbook for the Study of Egyptian Topographical Lists relating to Western Asia. *Leiden*
1942   Caesurae in the History of Megiddo. *Oudtestamentische Studien 1:17–54*
1959   The Geographical and Topographical Texts of the Old Testament. *Studia Francisci Scholten Memoriae Dicata Vol. II. Leiden*

Skafte Jensen, M.
1980   The Homeric Question and the Oral-Formulaic Theory. *Opuscula Graecolatina Vol. 20. København*

Smend, R.
1966   Jahwekrieg und Stämmebund. Erwägungen zur ältesten Geschichte Israels. *Forschungen zur Religion und Literatur des Alten Testaments 84. 2. Aufl. Göttingen*
1967   Gehörte Juda zum vorstaatlichen Israel? *IV World Congress of Jewish Studies 1. Jerusalem 1967:57–62*
1971A   Zur Frage der altisraelitischen Amphiktyonie. *Evangelische Theologie 31:623–630*
1971B   Das Gesetz und die Völker. Ein Beitrag zur deuteronomistischen Redaktionsgeschichte. *H.W. WOLFF: Probleme biblischer Theologie (Festschrift G. von Rad). München 1971:494–509*
1978   Die Entstehung des Alten Testaments. *Theologische Wissenschaft 1. Stuttgart*

Smith, M.G.
1956   On Segmentary Lineage Systems. *Journal of the Royal Anthropological Institute 86: 39–80*

Snodgrass, A.M.
1971   The Dark Age of Greece. An Archaeological Survey of the Eleventh to the Eight Centuries B.C. *Edinburgh*
1980   Iron and Early Metallurgy in the Mediterranean. *WERTIME and MUHLY 1980:335–374*

Soggin, J.A.
1962   Archaeological Discoveries and the Israelite Conquest of Palestine in the Thirteenth and Twelfth Centuries. *J.A. SOGGIN: Old Testament and Oriental Studies. Biblica et Orientalia 29. Roma 1975:11–30*
1967   Das Königtum in Israel. Ursprünge, Spannungen, Entwicklung. *Beiheft zur Zeitschrift für die alttestamentliche Wissenschaft 104. Berlin*
1970   Le livre de Josué. *Commentaire de l'Ancien Testament Va. Neuchâtel*
1971   Il regno di 'Abimelek ('Giudici', 9) e le istituzioni della città-stato siro-palestinese nei secoli XV–XI avanti Cristo. *Studi in onore di E. Volterra VI. Pubblicazioni della facoltà di giurisprudenza dell'Università di Roma t.45. Milano 1971:161–189*
1976   Introduction to the Old Testament From its Origins to the Closing of the Alexandrine Canon. *Old Testament Library. Philadelphia*

Southall, A.
1970A   Alur Society. A Study in Processes and Types of Domination. *Repr. Nairobi*
1970B   The Illusion of Tribe. *Journal of Asian and African Studies 5:28–50*
1976   Nure and Dinka are people: Ecology, ethnicity and logical possibility. *Man N.S. 11:463–491*

Speiser, E.A.
1963   Background and Function of the Biblical Naśi'. *E.A. SPEISER: Oriental and Biblical Studies. Collected Writings of E.A. Speiser edited by. J.J. Finkelstein and M. Greenberg. Philadelphia 1967:113–122*

Spiegelberg, W.
1896   Der Siegeshymnus des Merenptah auf der Flinders Petrie-Stele. *Zeitschrift für ägyptische Sprache und Altertumskunde 34:1–25*

Spooner, B.
  1972   The Status of Nomadism as a Cultural Phenomenon in the Middle East. *IRONS and DYSON-HUDSON 1972:122-131*

Stade, B.
  1887   Geschichte des Volkes Israel I. *Berlin*

Stamm, J.J. and Andrews, M.E.
  1967   The Ten Commandmens in recent Research. *Studies in Biblical Theology Second Series 2. London*

Stech-Wheeler, T., Muhly, J.D. and Maxwell-Hyslop, K.R.
  1981   Iron at Taanach and Early Iron Metallurgy in the Eastern Mediterranean. *American Journal of Archaeology 85:245-268*

Stein L.
  1967   Die Šammar-Ǧerba. Beduinen im Übergang vom Nomadismus zur Sesshaftigkeit. *Veröffentlichung des Museums für Völkerkunde zu Leipzig Hft. 17. Berlin*

Steingrimsson, S.Ö.
  1979   Vom Zeichen zur Geschichte. Eine Literar- und formkritische Untersuchung von Ex 6,28-11,10. *Coniectanea Biblica Old Testament Series 14. Lund*

Steuernagel, C.
  1901   Die Einwanderung der israelitischen Stämme in Kanaan. Historisch-kritische Untersuchungen. *Berlin*

Stevens, J.H.
  1978   Post-Pluvial Changes in the Soils of the Arabian Peninsula. *BRICE 1978:263-274*

Stief, C.
  1969   Den russiske nihilisme. *Festskrift udgivet i anledning af Universitetets Årsfest november 1969. København*

Stirling, P.
  1965   Turkish Village. *London*

Stolz, F.
  1972   Jahves und Israels Kriege. Kriegstheorien und Kriegserfahrungen im Glauben des alten Israels. *Abhandlungen zur Theologie des Alten und Neuen Testamentes 60. Zürich*

Stoebe, H.J.
  1973   Das erste Buch Samuelis. *Kommentar zum Alten Testament VIII 1. Gütersloh*

Strange, J.
  1966   The Inheritance of Dan. *Studia Theologica 20:120-139*
  1980   Caphtor/Keftiu. A new investigation. *Acta Theologica Danica 14. Leiden*
  N.P.   The Transition from the bronze Age to the Iron Age in the Eastern Mediterranean and the Emergence of the Israelite State (to appear in Scandinavian Journal of the Old Testament vol. 1 (1986))

Sturdy, J.
  1980   The Authorship of the »Prose Sermons« of Jeremiah. *J.A. EMERTON: Prophecy. Essays Presented to G. Fohrer. Beiheft zur Zeitschrift für die alttestamentliche Wissenschaft 150. Berlin 1980:143-150*

Stöber, G.
  1978   Die Afshār Nomadismus im Raume Kermān (Zentraliran). *Marburger geographische Schriften Hft. 76. Marburg/Lahn*

Sweet, L.E.
1960   Tell Toqaan. A Syrian Village. *Anthropological Papers No. 14. University of Michigan. Ann Arbor*
1965A   Camel Pastoralism in North Arabia and the Minimal Camping Unit. *A. LEEDS and A.F. VAYDA: Man, Culture, and Animals. The Role of Animals in Human Ecological Adjustments. Washington D.C. 1965:129–152*
1965B   Camel Raiding of North Arabian Bedoiun: A Mechanism of Ecological Adaption. *SWEET 1970:I:265–289*
1970   Peoples and Cultures of the Middle East I–II. An Anthropological Reader. *New York*

Swiddler, N.
1972   The Development of the Kalat Khanate. *IRONS and DYSON-HUDSON 1972: 115–121*
1973   The Political Context of Brahui Sedentarization. *Ethnology 12:299–314*

Swiddler, W.W.
1972   Some Demographic Factors Regulating the Formation of Flocks and Camps Among the Brahui of Baluchistan. *IRONS and DYSON-HUDSON 1972:69–75*

Swift, J.
1977   Sahelian Pastoralists: Underdevelopment, Desertification, and Famine. *Annual Review of Anthropology 6:457–478*

Syme, R.
1949   The Roman Revolution. *Oxford (Repr. 1960)*

Tait, D.
1958   The Territorial Pattern and Lineage System of Komkomba. *MIDDLETON and TAIT 1958:167–202*

Talmon, S.
1965   The Town Lists of Simeon. *Israel Exploration Journal 15:235–241*

Tapper, R.L.
1979A   Individuated grazing rights and social organization among the Shasevan nomads of Azerbaijan. *Pastoral Production and Society 1979:95–114*
1979B   Pasture and Politics. Economics, conflict and ritual among the Shahsevan nomads of northwestern Iran. *London*

Tengström, S.
1976   Die Hexateucherzählung. Eine literaturgeschichtliche Studie. *Coniectanea Biblica Old Testament Series 7. Uppsala*

Thiel, W.
1973   Die deuteronomistische Redaktion von Jeremia 1–25. *Wissenschaftliche Monographien zum Alten und Neuen Testament 41. Neukirchen*
1976   Verwandtschaftsgruppe und Stamm in der halbnomadischen Frühgeschichte Israels. *Altorientalische Forschungen 4:151–165*
1980A   Die soziale Entwicklung Israels in vorstaatlicher Zeit. *Berlin*
1980B   Die Anfänge von Landwirtschaft und Bodenrecht in der Frühzeit Alt-Israels. *Altorientalische Forschungen 7:127–141*
1981   Die deuteronomistische Redaktion von Jeremia 26–45. *Wissenschaftliche Monographien zum Alten und Neuen Testament 52. Neukirchen*

Thompson, L.L.
1981   The Jordan Crossing: ṣidqot Yahweh and World Building. *Journal of Biblical Literature 100:343–358*

Thompson, S.
1946   The Folktale. Stories Men Tell From Egyptian Myth to Uncle Remus. *New York*

Thompson, T.L.
1974   The Historicity of the Patriarchal Narratives. The Quest for the Historical Abraham. *Beiheft zur Zeitschrift für die alttestamentliche Wissenschaft 133. Berlin*
1975   The Settlement of Sinai and the Negev in the Bronze Age. *Tübinger Atlas des Vorderen Orients. Beiheft B 8. Wiesbaden*
1978A   Historical Notes on »Israel's Conquest of Palestine: A Peasants' Rebellion«? *Journal for the Study of the Old Testament 7:20–27*
1978B   A New Attempt to Date the Patriachal Narratives. *Journal of the American Oriental Society 98:76–84*
1978C   The Background of the Patriarchs: A Reply to William Dever and Malcolm Clark. *Journal for the Study of the Old Testament 9:2–43*
1979   The Settlement of Palestine in the bronze Age. *Beihefte zum Tübinger Atlas des Vorderen Orients. Reihe B 34. Wiesbaden*

Toombs, L.E.
1976   The Stratification of Tell Balâṭah (Shechem). *Bulletin of the American Schools of Oriental Research 223:57–59*
1979   Shechem: Problems of the Early Israelite Era. *CROSS 1979:69–84*

Trigger, B.
1978   Time and Traditions. Essays in Archaeological Interpretation. *Edinburgh*

Tritsch, F.J.
1974   The »Sackers of Cities« and the »Movement of Populations«. *CROSSLAND and BIRCHALL 1974:233–238*

Tufnell, O.
1953   Lachish III. The Iron Age. *London*
1958   Lachish IV. The Bronze Age. *London*

Täubler E.
1958   Biblische Studien. Die Epoche der Richter. *Herausgegeben von H.-J. Zobel. Tübingen*

Ussishkin, D.
1977   Lachish. *EAEHL III:735–753*
1978   Excavations at Tel Lachish – 1973–1977. Preliminary Report. *Tel Aviv 5:1–97*

Vajda, L.
1968   Untersuchungen zur Geschichte der Hirtenkulturen. *Veröffentlichungen des Osteuropa-Institutes München Band 31. München*

Vansina, J.
1965   Oral Tradition. A Study in Historical Methodology. *London*

Vaux, R. de
1961   Les institutions de l'Ancien Testament I. Le nomadisme et ses survivances. Institutions familiales. Institutions civiles. *2.ed. Paris*
1964   Le roi d'Israël, vassal de Yahvé. *R. DE VAUX: Bible et Orient. Paris 1967:287–301*
1968   Le problème des Ḫapiru après quinze années. *Journal of Near Eastern Studies 27: 221–228*
1970A   The Settlement of the Israelites in Southern Palestine and the Origins of the Tribe of Judah. *H.T. FRANK and W.L. REED: Translating and Understanding the Old Testament. Essays in Honor of H.G. May. Nashville 1970:108–134*
1970B   On Right and Wrong Uses of Archaeology. *SANDERS 1970:64–80*
1971A   La thèse de l'»amphictyonie israélite«. *Harvard Theological Review 64:415–436*
1971B   Histoire ancienne d'Israël I. Des origines à l'installation en Canaan. *Paris*

Volk, O.H.
1969   Ökologische Grundlagen des Nomadismus. *Nomadismus als Entwicklungsproblem 1969:57–66*

Vollmer, J.
1971   Geschichtliche Rückblicke und Motive in der Prophetie des Amos, Hosea und
        Jesaja. *Beiheft zur Zeitschrift für die alttestamentliche Wissenschaft 119. Berlin*

Volz, P. and Rudolph, W.
1933   Der Elohist als Erzähler – Ein Irrweg der Pentateuchkritik? *Beihefte zur Zeitschrift
        für die alttestamentliche Wissenschaft 63. Giessen*

Vorländer, H.
1975   Mein Gott. Die Vorstellungen vom persönlichen Gott im Alten Orient und im
        Alten Testament. *Alter Orient und Altes Testament 23. Neukirchen*
1978   Die Entstehungszeit des jehowistischen Geschichtswerkes. *Europäische Hochschul-
        schriften Reihe XXIII: Theologie Bd. 109 Frankfurt a.M.*

Vuilleunier, P. and Keller, A.-A.
1971   Michée, Nahoum, Habacuc, Sophonie. *Commentaire de l'Ancien Testament XIB.
        Neuchâtel*

Wagner, N.E.
1967   Pentateuchal Criticism: No Clear Future. *Canadian Journal of Theology 13:225–232*
1972   Abraham and David? *J.W. WEVERS and D.B. REDFORD: Studies in the Ancient
        Palestinian World Presented to F.V. Winnett. Toronto Semitic Texts and Studies 2. Toronto
        1972:117–140*
1977   A Response to Professor Rendtorff. *Journal for the Study of the Old Testament 3:20–27*

Wainwright, G.A.
1960   Merneptah's Aid to the Hittites. *Journal of Egyptian Archaeology 46:24–28*

Waldbaum, J.C.
1978   From Bronze to Iron. The Transition from the Bronze Age to the Iron Age in the
        Eastern Mediterranean. *Studies in Mediterranean Archaeology vol LIV. Göteborg*
1980   The First Archaeological Appearance of Iron and the transition to the Iron Age.
        WERTIME and MUHLY 1980:69–98

Walz, R.
1951   Zum Problem des Zeitpunktes der Domestikation der altweltlichen Cameliden.
        Zeitschrift der Deutschen Morgenländischen Gesellschaft 101:29–51
1954   Neue Untersuchungen zum Domestikationsproblem der altweltlichen Cameli-
        den. *Zeitschrift der Deutschen Morgenländischen Gesellschaft 104:45–87*

Warner, S.M.
1976   The Period of the Judges Within the Structure of Early Israel. *Hebrew Union Col-
        lege Annual 47:57–79*
1977   The Patriarchs and Extra-Biblical Sources. *Journal for the Study of the Old Testament
        2:50–61*
1978   The Dating of the Period of the Judges. *Vetus Testamentum 28:455–463*
1979   Primitive Saga Men. *Vetus Testamentum 29:325–335*

Watson, W.G.E.
1970   David Ousts the City Ruler of Jebus. *Vetus Testamentum 20:501–502*

Weber, M.
1921   Gesammelte Aufsätze zur Religionssoziologie III. Das antike Judentum. *Tü-
        bingen*
1976   The Agrarian Sociology of Ancient Civilizations. *Foundations of History Library.
        London*

Wehr, H.
1966   A Dictionary of Modern Written Arabic. Ed. by J.M. Cowan. 2. *Printing. Wies-
        baden*

478 BIBLIOGRAPHY

Weidner, E.F.
1957   Die Feldzüge und Bauten Tiglathpilesers I. *Archiv für Orientforschung 18:342–360*

Weimar, P.
1977   Untersuchungen zur Redaktionsgeschichte des Pentateuch. *Beiheft zur Zeitschrift für die alttestamentliche Wissenschaft 146. Berlin*

Weinfeld, M.
1972   Deuteronomy and the Deuteronomic School. *Oxford*

Weippert, H.
1973   Die Prosareden des Jeremiabuches. *Beiheft zur Zeitschrift für die alttestamentliche Wissenschaft 132. Berlin*

Weippert, H. and M.
1976   Jericho in der Eisenzeit. *Zeitschrift des Deutschen Palästina-Vereins 92:105–148*

Weippert, M.
1961   Gott und Stier. Bemerkungen zu eine Terrakotte aus *Jāfa. Zeitschrift des Deutschen Palästina-Vereins 77:93–117*
1967   Die Landnahme der israelitischen Stämme in der neueren wissenschaftliche Diskussion. *Forschungen zur Religion und Literatur des Alten und Neuen Testaments 92. Göttingen*
1972   »Heilige Krieg« in Israel und Assyrien. Kritische Anmerkungen zu Gerhard von Rads Konzept des »Heiligen Kriegs in alten Israel«. *Zeitschrift für die alttestamentliche Wissenschaft 84:460–493*
1974   Semitische Nomaden des zweiten Jahrtausends. Über die š',šw der ägyptischen Quellen. *Biblica 55:265–280. 427–433*
1979   The Israelite »Conquest« and the Evidence from Transjordan. *CROSS 1979:15–34*

Weiser, A.
1950   Die Psalmen. *Das Alte Testament Deutsch 14/15. Göttingen*
1958   Samuels »Philistersieg«. Die Überlieferungen in 1. Samuel 7. *A. WEISER: Samuel. Seine geschichtliche Aufgabe und religiöse Bedeutung. Forschungen zur Religion und Literatur des Alten und Neuen Testamentes 81. Göttingen 1962:5–24*
1959   Das Deboralied. Eine Gattungs- und traditionsgeschichtliche Studie. *Zeitschrift für die alttestamentliche Wissenschaft 71:67–97*
1966   Einleitung in das Alte Testament. *6. Aufl. Göttingen*

Weissleder, W.
1978   (ed.) The Nomadic Alternative. Modes and Models of Interaction in the African-Asian Deserts and Steppes. *The Hague*

Wellhausen, J.
1878   Prolegomena to the History of Ancient Israel. Preface by Prof. W. Robertson Smith. *Repr. 1965. New York*
1894   Israelitische und jüdische Geschichte. *9. Aufl. 1958. Berlin*
1963   Die Composition des Hexateuchs und der historischen Bücher des Alten Testaments. *4. Aufl. Berlin*

Welten, P.
1973   Geschichte und Geschichtsdarstellung in den Chronikbüchern. *Wissenschaftliche Monographien zum Alten und Neuen Testament 42. Neukirchen*

Wertime, T.A. and Muhly, J.D.
1980   (eds.) The Coming of the Age of Iron. *New York og London*

Westermann, C.
1976   Die Verheissung an die Väter. Studien zur Vätergeschichte. *Forschungen zur Religion und Literatur des Alten und Neuen Testaments 116. Göttingen*
1981   Genesis. 2. Genesis 12–36. *Biblischer Kommentar Altes Testament I/2. Neukirchen*

Weullersse, J.
1946   Paysans de Syrie et du Proche-Orient. *Le paysan et la terre. Paris*

Whybray, R.N.
1968   The Succession Narrative. A Study of II Sam. 9–20 and I Kings 1 and 2. *Studies in Biblical Theology Second Series 9. London*
1977   Response to Professor Rendtorff. *Journal for the Study of the Old Testament 3:11–14*

Wildberger, H.
1972   Jesaja, I. Jesaja 1–12. *Biblischer Kommentar Altes Testament X 1. Neukirchen*

Willi, T.
1977   Die Freiheit Israels. Philologische Notizen zu den Wurzeln *ḥpš*, *'zb* und *drr. H. DONNER, R. HANHART and R. SMEND: Beiträge zur alttestamentlichen Theologie (Festschrift W. Zimmerli). Göttingen 1977:531–546*

Wilson, R.R.
1977   Genealogy and History in the Biblical World. *Yale Near Eastern Researches, 7. New Haven*

Winnett, F.V.
1965   Reexamining the Foundations. *Journal of Biblical Literature 84:1–19*

Wirth, E.
1969   Der Nomadismus in der modernen Welt des Orients. Wege und Möglichkeiten einer wirtschaftlichen Integration. *Nomadismus als Entwicklungsproblem 1969:93–106*
1973   Die Beziehungen der orientalisch-islamischen Stadt zum umgebenden Lande. Ein Beitrag zur Theorie des Rentenkapitalismus. *E. MEYNEN: Geographie heute. Einheit und Vielfalt. Ernst Plewe gewidmet. geographische Zeitschrift. Beihefte. Erkundliches Wissen Heft 33. Wiesbaden 1973:323–333*

Wiseman, D.J.
1975   Assyria and Babylonia c. 1200–1000 B.C. *CAH³ II:2:443–481*

Wittfogel, K.
1957   Oriental despotism. A Comparative Study of Total Power. *Repr. New Haven og London 1978*

Wittig, S.
1976   Theories of Formulaic Narrative. *Semeia 5:65–91*

Wolf, E.R.
1966A   Peasants. *Foundations of Modern Anthropology Series. Englewood Cliffs*
1966B   Peasant Wars of the Twentieth Century. *New York*

Wolff, H.W.
1965   Dodekapropheton I. Hosea. *Biblischer Kommentar Altes testament XIV 1. Neukirchen*
1975   Dodekapropheten 2. Joel und Amos. *Biblischer Kommentar Altes Testament XIV 2. 2. Aufl. Neukirchen*

Wright, G.E.
1950   The Discoveries at Megiddo, 1935–1939. *The Biblical Archaeologist Reader II:225–240*
1957   Biblical Archaeology. *London*
1961   (ed.) The Bible and the Ancient Near East. Essays in honor of W.F. Albright. *New York and London*
1965   Shechem. The Biography of a Biblical City. *London*
1967   The Provences of Solomon (1 Kings 4:7–19). *Eretz-Israel 8:58★–68★*
1978   A Characteristic North Israelite House. *R. MOOREY and P. PARR: Arcaeology in the Levant. Essays for Kathleen Kenyon. Warminster 1978:149–154*

Wright, H.T.

1978   Toward an Explanation of the Origin of the State. *COHEN and SERVICE 1978:* *49–67*

Würtwein, E., Galling, K. and Plöger, O.

1969   Die fünf Megilloth. *Handbuch zum Alten Testament I 18. Tübingen*

Würtwein, E.

1974   Die Erzählung von der Thronnachfolge Davids – theologische oder politische Geschichtsschreibung? *Theologische Studien 115. Zürich*

Wüst, F.R.

1954   Amphiktyonie, Eidgenossenschaft, Symmachie. *Historia III:129–153*

Wüst, M.

1975   Untersuchungen zu den siedlungsgeographischen texten des Alten Testaments. 1. Ostjordanland. *Beihefte zum Tübinger Atlas des Vorderen Orients Reihe B 9. Wiesbaden*

Yadin, Y.

1972   Hazor. The Head of all Those Kingsdoms. Joshua 11:10. *The Schweich Lectures 1970. London*

1979   The Transition from a Semi-Nomadic to a Sedentary Society in the Twelth Century B.C.E. *CROSS 1979:57–68*

Yadin, Y., Aharoni, Y., Amiran, R., Dothan, T., Dunayevski, Y. and Parrot, J.

1958   Hazor I–IV. *Jerusalem 1958–1961*

Ürpmann, H.-P.

1979   Probleme der Neolithisierung des Mittelmeerraums. *Beihefte zum Tübinger Atlas des Vorderen Orients Reihe B 28. Wiesbaden*

Zarins, J.

1978   The Camel in Ancient Arabia: a Further Note. *Antiquity 52:44–46*

Zimmerli, W.

1932   Geschichte und Tradition von Beerseba im Alten Testament. *Diss. Göttingen*

1969   Ezechiel. *Biblischer Kommentar Altes Testament XIII 1–2. Neukirchen*

Zuber, B.

1976   Vier Studien zu den Ursprungen Israels. Die Sinaifrage und Probleme der Volks- und Traditionsbildung. *Orbis Biblicus et Orientalis 9. Freiburg og Göttingen*

Anonymous

1969   Nomadismus als Entwicklungsproblem. *Bochumer Schriften zur Entwicklungsfor- schung und Entwicklungspolitik 5. Bielefeld*

1979   Pastoral Production and Society. Proceedings of the international meeting on nomadic pastoralism Paris 1–3 Déc. 1979. *Cambridge and Paris*

★ *indecates works which have been unavailable to me at the moment of writing.*

INDICES

AUTHOR INDEX

SCRIPTURE REFERENCES